Plutarch, Hubert Ashton Holden

Life of Pericles

With Introduction, Critical and Explanatory Notes and Indices

Plutarch, Hubert Ashton Holden

Life of Pericles
With Introduction, Critical and Explanatory Notes and Indices

ISBN/EAN: 9783337417956

Printed in Europe, USA, Canada, Australia, Japan

Cover: Foto ©Thomas Meinert / pixelio.de

More available books at **www.hansebooks.com**

Classical Series

PLUTARCH'S

LIFE OF PERICLES

HOLDEN

ΠΛΟΥΤΑΡΧΟΥ ΠΕΡΙΚΛΗΣ

PLUTARCH'S
LIFE OF PERICLES

*WITH INTRODUCTION
CRITICAL AND EXPLANATORY NOTES
AND INDICES*

BY

HUBERT ASHTON HOLDEN M.A.

LL.D. CAMBRIDGE, HON. D. LITT. DUBLIN
FORMERLY FELLOW OF TRINITY COLLEGE CAMBRIDGE

London
MACMILLAN AND CO.
AND NEW YORK
1894

All rights reserved

Printed and Stereotyped by
R. & R. CLARK *Edinburgh* 1894

PREFACE

THE present edition of Plutarch's *Life of Pericles* for the use of English-speaking students was begun two years ago and has been prepared on the same lines as that of his *Life of Themistocles* (Third Edition 1892), and I venture to express a hope that it may meet with as favourable a reception as its predecessor, in spite of its shortcomings of which I am myself fully conscious.

The text is based on two of the best MSS, but a few conjectural emendations have been admitted where necessary, chiefly those of Cobet contributed to the sixth volume of the New Series of the *Mnemosyne*. Those of Theodor Bergk, which were copied from the margin of a copy of the *Lives* belonging to that eminent scholar and published by Dr. Rudolf Peppmüller as an Appendix to a Gymnasial-Programm (Halle 1887) containing his own critical notes on Theognis and other Greek poets, reached me too late for the insertion of the whole in the main body of the work. Those which do not appear in their proper place will be found among the *Addenda et Corrigenda*.

The chronological Table, in drawing up which I have consulted Busolt's *Griechische Geschichte* with much advantage, has cost me a considerable amount of time and pains. The same may be said of the *Index Graecitatis*, which was compiled for my own use and guidance and which is now printed unabridged in the hope and belief that it will be found of service to the few who have a love of Greek for its own sake, if not to the ordinary student.

The most completely annotated edition, hitherto without a rival, is that of C. Sintenis with a Latin commentary published sixty years ago at Leipzig, when classical studies were more in vogue than at the present day. The best subsequent editions—that of Fr. Blass and Fuhr's revision of that of Sintenis in the Haupt-Sauppe series, both with notes and introductions in German, together with the modest and unpretending edition of Alfred Jacob with notes in French which did not reach me until my own was in type—are in a greater or less degree founded upon this.

I have endeavoured to bring my book up to date by consulting, along with the above-mentioned editions, the most recent works and scattered suggestions bearing in any way on the Periclean age, but the literature is so vast that I cannot pretend to have touched it otherwise than *primoribus labris*.

I must once again gratefully acknowledge my obligation to the now well-known acuteness and accuracy of Messrs. R. & R. Clark's Reader.

ATHENAEUM CLUB, LONDON, S.W.
October 10, 1894.

CONTENTS

INTRODUCTION   PAGE
   I *Life of Plutarch* . .   ix
   II *The Parallel Lives* . . .   xxiv
   III *The Life of Pericles*   xxx

CHRONOLOGICAL TABLE OF THE PRINCIPAL EVENTS
   IN THE LIFE OF PERICLES . . .   xlvii

ADDENDA ET CORRIGENDA . .   lxi

MANUSCRIPTS AND EDITIONS . .   2

THE GREEK TEXT WITH CRITICAL NOTES . .   3–70

COMMENTARY   73–209

INDEX I AUTHORITIES QUOTED .   212

INDEX II MATTERS . .   213–227

INDEX III GRAMMAR . . .   228

INDEX IV GREEK   231–303

INTRODUCTION

I *Life of Plutarch*

NOTHING is known of the personal history of Plutarch but what may be gathered from various notices scattered through his own writings.[1] He was born between A.D. 46 and A.D. 51 at Chaeronea in northwest Boeotia, a town small and insignificant, but rich in historical memories. It was one of the five cities in the famous plain, called by his favourite hero Epaminondas 'the dancing-plot of Ares,'[2] at the time when the two great battles[3] which were

---

[1] Eunapius *Vit. Soph.* prooem. ὁ θεσπέσιος Πλούταρχος τόν τε ἑαυτοῦ βίον ἀναγράφει τοῖς βιβλίοις ἐνδιεσπαρμένως καὶ τὸν τοῦ διδασκάλου ('Αμμωνίου) . . . τὸ ἴδιον καὶ τὸ τοῦ διδασκάλου καθ' ἕκαστον τῶν βιβλίων κατέσπειρεν, ὥστε, εἴ τις ὀξυδορκοίη περὶ ταῦτα καὶ ἀνιχνεύοι κατὰ τὸ προσπῖπτον καὶ φαινόμενον καὶ σωφρόνως τὸ κατὰ μέρος ἀναλέγοιτο, δύνασθαι τὰ πλεῖστα τῶν βεβιωμένων αὐτοῖς εἰδέναι. Cp. M. Octave Gréard *De la morale de Plutarque* ed. 3 Paris 1880:—Nul écrivain, grec ou latin, n'a fait pour lui ce qu'il avait fait pour tant d'autres; le Biographe de l'antiquité n'a pas de biographie.

[2] *Marc.* c. 21, 2 "Άρεως ὀρχήστραν. Cp. R. Volkmann *Leben, Schriften und Philosophie des Plutarch von Chaeronea* Berlin 1873 p. 16.

[3] That in B.C. 338 when Philip of Macedon defeated the united forces of the Athenians and Boeotians—a day fatal to the liberties of Greece (Strabo x 2, 37); and that in B.C. 86 when Sulla defeated the army of Mithridates (*Sull.* c. 19).

named after it were as yet not fought. Here his family had been settled for many years, and was of good standing and local repute. He speaks incidentally of his great-grandfather (πρόπαππος) Nicarchus recording an incident of the struggle between Antony and Octavius,[4] and makes constant mention of Lamprias, his grandfather, as taking part in the 'Table talk' (συμποσιακὰ προβλήματα), which occupies so considerable a portion of his miscellaneous writings;[5] and of his father, who also was a man of cultivation and could occasionally take part in the discourses on various topics recorded by his son. He had two brothers, Lamprias[6] and Timon.[7] He married, it is not known at what period of his life, Timoxena, daughter of Alexion, by whom he had four sons and one daughter. The eldest and fourth sons died young.[8] To the two survivors, Autobulus and Plutarchus, he dedicated his Treatise 'Concerning the procreation of the soul as discoursed in the *Timaeus* of Plato' (περὶ τῆς ἐν Τιμαίῳ ψυχογονίας). The only daughter, named

---

[4] *Anton.* c. 68, 3.

[5] *e.g.* I 5, 5 ἦν δὲ Λαμπρίας, ὁ ἡμέτερος πάππος, ἐν τῷ πίνειν εὑρετικώτατος αὐτὸς αὑτοῦ καὶ λογιώτατος. Cp. IV 5 where he takes part in a discourse on the reasons why the Jews abstain from pork; also I 2, 2, V 2, 6, and *Ant.* c. 28, 2 where he repeats a story told him by the physician Philotas of Amphissa, in illustration of the luxuriousness of Antony's life at Alexandria.

[6] *Symp.* I 2, 5; II 2, 1; VIII 6, 5; IX 5, 1.

[7] *Symp.* I 2; II 5. Plutarch gives a touching record of his fraternal affection *Mor.* 487 E:—ἐμοὶ μὲν γὰρ ὅτι πολλῶν ἀξίων χάριτος παρὰ τῆς τύχης γεγονότων, ἡ Τίμωνος εὔνοια τἀδελφοῦ πρὸς ἅπαντα τἆλλα καὶ γέγονε καὶ ἔστιν, οὐδεὶς ἀγνοεῖ τῶν ὁπωσοῦν ἐντετυχηκότων ἡμῖν, ἥκιστα δ' οἱ συνήθεις ὑμεῖς. Volkmann seeks to identify this brother with the Timon mentioned in a letter of Pliny (I 5, 5).

[8] *Mor.* 609 D.

Timoxena after her mother, died when she was but two years old during her father's temporary absence. It was on this occasion that the affectionate and sensible letter of consolation (παραμυθητικὸς πρὸς τὴν ἰδίαν γυναῖκα)[9] was addressed by Plutarch to his wife, 'showing him' as has been said 'in a very tender and attractive light as a husband and father, and affording us glimpses of a family life, the existence of which we are too apt to forget when taking account of the moral condition of the ancient heathen world.'[10]

Plutarch commenced his studies, when he was about 16 years old, at Athens, under the direction of Ammonius,[11] the syncretist philosopher, with a fellow-student named Themistocles, a descendant of the hero of Salamis.[12] He speaks of his having been at Alexandria,[13] among other places, but it was his visit to Italy and Rome which exercised the greatest influence on his after-life. He makes a general reference to it in his *Life of Demosthenes*,[14] where—after pleading the necessity that an author,

[9] *Mor.* 608 A–612 B.
[10] Archbp. Trench *Five Lectures on Plutarch* p. 32, who compares two striking passages, *Erotic.* c. 24 and *Praec. coniug.* c. 31. Cp. Volkmann *l.c.* p. 29.
[11] Ammonius is spoken of as his καθηγητής *Mor.* 70 F, a more honourable term than διδάσκαλος. It appears from *Mor.* 720 D that he was three times chief magistrate (στρατηγός) at Athens. When Nero was travelling in Greece A.D. 66, he acted as his ἐξηγητής over the temple buildings at Delphi.
[12] *Them.* c. 32, 4. Cp. *Mor.* 626 E.
[13] *Mor.* 678 C ἐν ταῖς ὑποδοχαῖς ἃς ἐποιεῖτο τῶν φίλων ἕκαστος ἑστιῶν ἡμᾶς ἥκοντας ἀπὸ τῆς Ἀλεξανδρείας.
[14] c. 2, 1 ἡμεῖς δὲ μικρὰν μὲν οἰκοῦντες πόλιν, καὶ ἵνα μὴ μικροτέρα γένηται φιλοχωροῦντες, ἐν δὲ Ῥώμῃ καὶ ταῖς περὶ τὴν Ἰταλίαν διατριβαῖς οὐ σχολῆς οὔσης γυμνάζεσθαι περὶ τὴν Ῥωμαϊκὴν διάλεκτον ὑπὸ χρειῶν πολιτικῶν καὶ τῶν διὰ φιλοσοφίαν πλησιαζόντων ὀψέ ποτε καὶ πόρρω τῆς ἡλικίας ἠρξάμεθα Ῥωμαϊκοῖς γράμμασιν ἐντυγχάνειν.

who has undertaken to compile a history of some foreign country from materials scattered in different places, should be a resident in some historically famous, cultivated and populous town, where he can have unlimited use of books of all kinds, and where he can also pick up trustworthy information on such particulars as rest on popular tradition—he says of himself:—'As to myself, I live in a small town and am fond of staying in it, that it may not be the smaller for the absence of a single inhabitant. But when I was in Rome and during my stay in different parts of Italy, I found my time so taken up with the public commissions with which I was charged and with the number of those who flocked to me for instruction, that I had not the leisure to study the Latin language. Consequently, it was not until late and at an advanced period of my life that I began to read works written in Latin.' Plutarch then proceeds to explain that it was not from words that he learned to discover things, but rather words from familiar things. He professes himself unable to appreciate the beauty, fluency and precision of the Latin language, because to do so would require more pains and practice than he had time for. The fact of his being but an indifferent Latin scholar is pretty evident from the absurd mistakes he makes in the construction, meaning and derivation of words.[15] As to his χρεῖαι πολιτικαί, it is probable that during his stay at Rome he was representative of his native town.[16]

---

[15] Several instances will be found in my Introduction to *Life of Nicias* p. xxi note 15. See also Sickinger *De linguae latinae apud Plutarchum reliquiis*, Freib. Diss. 1883.

[16] Gréard *l.c.* p. 32:—Tout le temps, qu'il demeura en Italie, il fut, en quelque sorte, le *chargé d'affaires* de sa ville natale.

One limit for the date of his visit is given in the Treatise 'On the skill of animals,'[17] where in recording an instance of wonderful sagacity in a dog, which he had himself witnessed in the theatre of Marcellus at Rome, Plutarch expressly mentions the presence of the old Emperor Vespasian (παρῆν γὰρ ὁ γέρων Οὐεσπασιανὸς ἐν τῷ Μαρκέλλου θεάτρῳ). This must have been before the year A.D. 79, in which Vespasian died. Again he relates casually in his *De curiositate*,[18] how on one occasion, when he was lecturing, Arulenus Rusticus, who was put to death A.D. 94 by the Emperor Domitian, was amongst his audience. A passage in the *Symposiaca*[19] seems to show that Plutarch paid more than one visit to Rome, Σύλλας ὁ Καρχηδόνιος εἰς Ῥώμην ἀφικομένῳ μοι διὰ χρόνου τὸ ὑποδεκτικόν, ὡς Ῥωμαῖοι καλοῦσι, καταγγείλας δεῖπνον ἄλλους τε τῶν ἑταίρων παρέλαβεν οὐ πολλοὺς κτλ. At that time he was accompanied by his compatriot Philinus. Now we know from the *Life of Poplicola*[20] that Plutarch was again in Greece and at Athens before A.D. 82, the year when the Capitol, which had been burnt down at the death of Vespasian, was restored by Domitian, for he saw there the columns of Pentelican marble destined for that building, which, he continues, when he saw them subsequently at Rome, had been again cut and polished, and lost thereby some of their original symmetry, being too slender. Plutarch therefore must have been at Rome after A.D. 82.

[17] c. 19, *Mor.* 974 A.   [18] c. 15, *Mor.* 522 F.
[19] VIII 7, 1, *Mor.* 727 C.
[20] c. 15, 3 οἱ δὲ κίονες ἐκ τοῦ Πεντελῆσιν ἐτμήθησαν λίθου κάλλιστα τῷ πάχει πρὸς τὸ μῆκος ἔχοντες· εἴδομεν γὰρ αὐτοὺς Ἀθήνησιν. ἐν δὲ Ῥώμῃ πληγέντες αὖθις καὶ ἀναξυσθέντες οὐ τοσοῦτον ἔσχον γλαφυρίας, ὅσον ἀπώλεσαν συμμετρίας <καὶ> τοῦ καλοῦ διάκενοι καὶ λαγαροὶ φανέντες.

We find many other notices also of his presence at Rome scattered throughout his writings, as when he refers to various innovations,[21] or speaks of buildings and localities, which he has seen, such as the sacred island of the Tiber,[22] the temple of Vica Pota,[23] the bronze statue of Titus Quintus Flamininus, opposite the Circus, with the Greek inscription on it,[24] or the market of monstrosities,[25] and the ἀποφράδες πύλαι.[26] In the *Life of Numa* he states that he had himself heard many Romans narrate how in obedience to an oracle bidding the Romans set up in their own city a statue of the wisest and the bravest of the Greeks, they had erected in the Forum two bronze statues, one of Alcibiades, the other of Pythagoras.[27]

At Rome Plutarch became acquainted with many eminent men — philosophers, poets, grammarians, historians, musicians, physicians — and also renewed his acquaintance with several whom he had known before in Greece, as with Favorinus of Arles,[28] the renowned rhetorician and eclectic philosopher, to whom he dedicated his Treatise 'On the principle of cold' (περὶ τοῦ πρώτου ψυχροῦ), and with Gaius

---

[21] *Marcell.* c. 3, 4.
[22] *Poplic.* c. 8, 3.
[23] *Poplic.* c. 10, 4 ἱερὸν Οὔλκας πότας ὀνομαζόμενον.
[24] *Flamin.* c. 1, 1.
[25] *Mor.* 520 C περὶ τῶν τεράτων ἀγορὰν ἀναστρέφονται, τοὺς ἀκνήμους καὶ τοὺς γαλεάγκωνας καὶ τοὺς τριοφθάλμους καὶ τοὺς στρουθοκεφάλους καταμανθάνοντες.
[26] *Mor.* 518 B.
[27] c. 8, 10 αὐτοὶ δ' ἀκηκόαμεν πολλῶν ἐν Ῥώμῃ διεξιόντων ὅτι χρησμοῦ ποτε Ῥωμαίοις γενομένου τὸν φρονιμώτατον καὶ τὸν ἀνδρειότατον Ἑλλήνων ἱδρύσασθαι παρ' αὐτοῖς, ἔστησαν ἐπὶ τῆς ἀγορᾶς εἰκόνας χαλκᾶς δύο, τὴν μὲν Ἀλκιβιάδου τὴν δὲ Πυθαγόρου.
[28] Cp. Aul. Gell. *Noct. Att.* II 22, 27; XII 1, 24. A list of his works is given by J. L. Marks *Diss. de Favorini Arelatensis vita, studiis, scriptis*, Traiecti ad Rhenum, Kemink & Son, 1853.

Sossius Senecio, one of Pliny's correspondents,[29] who became an intimate friend and to whom he dedicates three of his Parallel Lives.[30] It was at his suggestion also that he compiled his 'Records of Table-talk' (συμποσιακά) held at entertainments in which he was himself the central figure among a circle of scholars or gentlemen devoted to literature and philosophy at Rome and elsewhere.[31] Now we know from the Fasti that Sossius was four times consul under Trajan, viz. *consul suffectus* in A.D. 98 and *consul ordinarius* in A.D. 99, 102, 107. It is not quite clear, however, whether Plutarch made his acquaintance first at Rome or in Greece, where it is plain, from references in the *Symposiaca*, that Sossius must have stayed some considerable time.[32]

Another man of consular rank, a scholar and archaeologist,[33] was also a friend of Plutarch's, viz. Mestrius Florus. In his company he travelled through Gallia Cisalpina, where the family of Mestrius was well known, and visited the battlefield of Bedriacum,[34]

---

[29] *Ep.* I 13.
[30] Those of *Theseus—Romulus; Demosthenes—Cicero; Dion—Brutus*: also the Treatise *de profectibus in virtute*.
[31] *Prooem.* § 4 ᾠήθης τε δεῖν ἡμᾶς τῶν σποράδην πολλάκις ἔν τε Ῥώμῃ μεθ' ὑμῶν καὶ παρ' ἡμῖν ἐν τῇ Ἑλλάδι, παρούσης ἅμα τραπέζης καὶ κύλικος, φιλολογηθέντων συναγαγεῖν τὰ ἐπιτήδεια.
[32] From II 1, 1 it is plain that Plutarch was once at Patrae with him; and in V 1, 1 he speaks of their being in each other's company at Athens. Again we are told in IV 3, 1 that Sossius came from Chaeronea to be present at the marriage feast of Plutarch's son Autobulus.
[33] φιλαρχαῖος *Symp.* VII 4, 1: cp. VIII 2, 2, Suet. *Vesp.* c. 22.
[34] *Oth.* c. 14, 1 ἐμοὶ δὲ ὕστερον ὁδεύοντι διὰ τοῦ πεδίου Μέστριος Φλῶρος, ἀνὴρ ὑπατικὸς τῶν τότε μὴ κατὰ γνώμην ἀλλ' ἀνάγκῃ μετὰ τοῦ Ὄθωνος γενομένων, νεὼν ὄντα παλαιὸν ἐπιδείξας διηγεῖτο μετὰ τὴν μάχην ἐπελθὼν ἰδεῖν νεκρῶν σωρὸν τηλικοῦτον, ὥστε τοὺς ἐπιπολῆς ('on the top') ἅπτεσθαι τῶν ἀετῶν (i.e. 'the pediments').

Brixellum,[35] Ravenna where he saw the marble statue of Gaius Marius.[36]

Fundanus, another friend, who, with Sextius Sulla of Carthage, is the interlocutor in the dialogue about 'the cure of anger' (ἀοργησία)—a very noble and humane character, and the counterpart of Plutarch himself in his domestic life[37]—is probably to be identified with Minucius Fundanus, a distinguished friend of Pliny the younger.[38] A common friend of Sextius Sulla, Fundanus and Plutarch was Paccius, to whom the Treatise 'Of tranquillity of mind' (περὶ εὐθυμίας)[39] is dedicated, a distinguished forensic speaker.

Plutarch's occupation during his residence at Rome was akin to that of the ancient *grammaticus*, whom we should describe as lecturer or private tutor,[40] ready to give advice to any one consulting him on questions of practical morality, as a sort of physician of the soul, able to make a diagnosis of a diseased moral condition, one of 'the domestic chaplains of heathendom,' as Bishop Lightfoot calls them, ready to help all who sought his assistance as their moral director and adviser. He had cultivated,

---

[35] *Oth.* c. 18, 1 εἶδον δὲ ἐν Βριξίλλῳ γενόμενος καὶ μνῆμα μέτριον καὶ τὴν ἐπιγραφὴν οὕτως ἔχουσαν, εἰ μεταφρασθείη, 'Δηλώσει (δαίμοσι, *dis manibus* Lobeck) Μάρκου Ὄθωνος.'

[36] *Mar.* c. 2, 1 τῆς δ' ὄψεως τῆς Μαρίου λιθίνην εἰκόνα κειμένην ἐν Ῥαβέννῃ τῆς Γαλατίας ἐθεώμεθα πάνυ τῷ λεγομένῳ περὶ τὸ ἦθος στρυφνότητι καὶ πικρίᾳ πρέπουσαν.

[37] Volkmann *l.c.* p. 41.

[38] See his three Epistles I 9, IV 15 and VI 6. There is also a fourth letter (V 6) concerning the death of his young daughter in which Pliny speaks of his being *eruditus et sapiens, ut qui se ab ineunte aetate altioribus studiis artibusque dederit.*

[39] *Mor.* 464 F.

[40] *Dem.* c. 2, 1 where he speaks of his being prevented from learning much of the Latin language ὑπὸ τῶν διὰ φιλοσοφίαν πλησιαζόντων. See note 14.

in a greater or less degree, the three branches of study recognized by the ancients, viz. philosophy, rhetoric and mathematics.[41] But his attention was mainly given to moral and religious speculations, in all of which he took the most profound interest; the one aim and end of his life and writings being the illumination of the intellect by the force of morals. Thus Poetry, in his judgment, was mischievous, if it had not a direct moral tendency; his rhetorical precepts and his rules of historical criticism are alike based upon morals. Does he find himself in presence of some physical phenomenon,[42] or confronted by a question of erudition, the solution is to be found only by recurring to moral principles. Even his rules for the preservation of health are for the most part observations of moral hygiene. If he attacks the Stoics and Epicureans, it is to vindicate Providence and the moral government of the world against their tenets. Politics, moreover, are in his view nothing but the most perfect exercise of moral philosophy applied to the amelioration of society.[43]

Thus we see why, from the first, his miscellaneous essays on all sorts of topics were comprised under the common title of *Moral Works*. His *Parallel Lives* are but the complement of his Moral Essays; his leading purpose in writing them was not, as will be seen hereafter, historical but ethical: history is only a school of manners for him; what he looks for in

---

[41] *Symp.* ix 14, 3, 3 ἁπάσας τὰς διὰ λόγου περαινομένας ἐπιστήμας καὶ τέχνας οἱ παλαιοὶ καταμαθόντες ἐν τρισὶ γένεσιν οὔσας τῷ φιλοσόφῳ καὶ τῷ ῥητορικῷ καὶ τῷ μαθηματικῷ κτλ.

[42] *Nic.* c. 23.

[43] *Mor.* 775 F περὶ τοῦ ὅτι μάλιστα τοῖς ἡγεμόσι δεῖ τὸν φιλόσοφον διαλέγεσθαι, 779 D πρὸς ἡγεμόνα ἀπαίδευτον.

regarded the Roman empire as a special creation of Providence [57] for helping men to lasting peace and undisturbed possession of their property after a long and dreary period of warfare.

From the noise and bustle of Rome—a fitter residence for him because of the opportunities it afforded of intercourse with great men and the ampler supply of books—he returned to the modest and quiet place of his birth, where he spent the remaining years of his tranquil life, 'being loth' as he says 'to make the small town yet smaller by the absence of even one inhabitant.' [58] He made a point of undertaking its humblest offices at first [59]—entertaining as he did the strong conviction that the exercise of public functions was the duty and the proper education of Man. Subsequently he became its ἄρχων ἐπώνυμος for more than one year, [60] and was also nominated by his fellow-townsmen to the office of Boeotarch. He was likewise chosen to officiate as priest of Apollo at Delphi [61]—a still higher testimony to the worth of his character, and he was an important personage at many of the Pythian games. [62] But his public duties did not hinder him from making frequent excursions

---

[57] *Rom.* c. 8, 7 οὐκ ἂν ἐνταῦθα προῦβη δυνάμεως (τὰ Ῥωμαίων πράγματα), μὴ θείαν τινα ἀρχὴν λαβόντα καὶ μηδὲν μέγα μηδὲ παράδοξον ἔχουσαν. Cp. *Pomp.* c. 75, 3, *Mor.* 316 c–326 c (*de fortuna Romanorum*).

[58] *Dem.* c. 2, 2 ἡμεῖς μικρὰν οἰκοῦντες πόλιν καί, ἵνα μὴ μικροτέρα γένηται, φιλοχωροῦντες. See above note 14.

[59] *Mor.* 811 A (*Praec. ger. reip.* cc. 15, 17).

[60] *Mor.* 643 A (*Symp.* II 10, 1, 1), 694 A (VI 8, 1, 2).

[61] *Mor.* 700 F (*Symp.* VII 2, 2, 1) where he speaks of Euthydemus as his colleague in the priesthood (συνιερεύς). Hertzberg (*Gesch. Griechenl. unter d. Herrschaft d. Römer*, Th. II p. 166) thinks that he held the office at Chaeronea.

[62] *Mor.* 792 F.

from Chaeronea; for it is clear from allusions in his *Lives* that he was familiar with all the principal localities, not to say the nooks and corners of Greece; he delights to relate his personal reminiscences and all he has seen of the memorials and records of her past splendour.[63]

In the retirement of a happy domestic life Plutarch enjoyed abundant leisure for the pursuit of his favourite literary and moral studies. But, unlike other philosophers, he did not allow these to absorb his whole attention, to the neglect of other important claims on his time. His useful virtues were actively employed for the good of others. Besides taking his full share in the civil and religious duties of his station, he disbursed the stores of his learning liberally, diffusing knowledge in an age which stood greatly in need of education. His profound sympathy with the young made the task of their spiritual direction a pleasant one: his lecture-room was open to those who, longing to order their lives according to some higher rule in a corrupt age, sought special help in private and familiar intercourse. He gave lectures on philosophical and other subjects, expounding at one time some writing of Plato, at another answering offhand the various questions (προβλήματα) put to him, or warning his hearers against the manifold corrupt practices and principles of the time. Many of these lectures were afterwards enlarged by him and published as separate Treatises,[64]

---

[63] See especially *Phoc.* c. 18, 5; c. 22, 1, *Arist.* c. 1, 2; cc. 19, 21; c. 27, 1, *Per.* c. 13, 2 ff., *Nic.* c. 3, 3, *Dem.* c. 7, 3; c. 31, 1, *Them.* c. 22, 1, *Alex.* c. 69, 4, *Ages.* c. 19, 5; c. 35, 1, *Sol.* c. 25, 1, *Lyc.* c. 18, 1.

[64] To this category belong the treatises *de audiendis poetis*, and *de audiendo*; also the ὑγιεινὰ παραγγέλματα, *de sanitate praecepta*.

and it is plain that they were no mere showy declamations, like those of ordinary sophists, but 'earnest efforts, as of a spiritual physician, to heal the hurts of men's souls.'[65]

Plutarch must have been an extensive reader, and had access to a select library, which contained a good many treasures, but at Chaeronea he felt the want of a large library of reference,[66] so necessary to a literary man. His wont at Rome, where he commanded an ample store of books, had been to make extracts from the more eminent writers in Biography, History or Philosophy for his pupils or audience, which he afterwards employed in the composition of his miscellaneous works; most of which were originally written or added to on some particular occasion, some festive event in the circle of his acquaintance or at the particular request of some friend.[67] His first series of biographies also was written at the instance of others, as appears from a passage in his Introduction to the *Life of Timoleon*, which shows us at the same time incidentally how much Plutarch valued them as a means of improving and elevating his own character.

As to the chronological order of his works we are left very much in the dark. Most of them must have been written in his riper years, after the reign of Domitian. For the date of his *Biographies*, there is an important passage in that of *Sulla* c. 21, 4, where, after describing the battle of Orchomenus

[65] Trench *l.c.* p. 107.
[66] *Dem.* c. 2, *Mor.* 384 D (*de EI ap. Delph.* c. 1).
[67] 'He was as indefatigable a gleaner of literary and ethical curiosities as Southey himself: and could we have his Commonplace Book, it might be far more valuable and interesting than the very unequal collection of Photius.' *Edinburgh Review*, Jan. 1869 p. 73.

(B.C. 85), he says that many relics of the dead were found in the neighbouring marshes—σχεδὸν ἐτῶν διακοσίων ἀπὸ τῆς μάχης ἐκείνης διαγεγονότων. From which it follows that Plutarch must have composed this *Life* at least not much before A.D. 115, consequently at the close of Trajan's reign. He does not appear to have lived long after A.D. 120. For he speaks in the *Life of Solon* c. 32, 2 of the Olympieion at Athens as unfinished (ἀτελές), which we know that Hadrian completed some time between A.D. 125 and A.D. 130.

There is sufficient evidence that Plutarch's works were much read and used soon after his death. Aelius Aristides,[68] the celebrated rhetorician of the 2d century, and Polyaenus, author of the στρατηγήματα, borrowed largely from him. He is quoted by Aulus Gellius and Galen [69] and referred to by Tatian the Christian apologist in his λόγος πρὸς Ἕλληνας. In the 3d century we find Athenaeus constantly quoting or making tacit reference to him, also Porphyrius the neo-Platonist, and Eunapius.[70] Stobaeus made extracts of all kinds from his works, including some that are lost. Macrobius in his *Saturnalia* has made constant use of his 'Table talk.' In the 6th century he was carefully read by Sopater the younger of Apamea, the eighth and twelfth books of whose ἐκλογαὶ διάφοροι contained extracts from his writings, among others from the lost *Lives* of Crates, Daiphantus, Pindar, Epaminondas: also from his philosophical treatise περὶ φύσεως καὶ πόνων, and from another περὶ ὀργῆς, a fragment of which is

[68] v. Sintenis ad Plut. *Per. Excurs.* 3 p. 302 ff. ed. Lips. 1835.
[69] *de dogmate Platonis et Hippocratis*.
[70] See above note 46.

found in the *Florilegium* of Stobaeus. It is remarkable that Sopater made extracts from the spurious works also, such as that 'On rivers' and 'The apophthegms of Kings and Generals.' Ecclesiastical writers, as Clement of Alexandria and even Basil, were not ashamed to adorn themselves with his feathers — an easy proceeding which proved too tempting for compilers like Zonaras and Michael Psellus not to imitate.

II *The Parallel Lives of Plutarch*

The collection known as *The Parallel Lives*, which is a complement to the other half of Plutarch's writings entitled *The Morals*—the one exhibiting to us from ideal points of view what the ancients had aimed at and accomplished in the world of action, the other, what in like manner it had aimed at and accomplished in the world of thought—is not what its author left behind him, either in form or arrangement. The *Lives* were originally put forth in a series of Books ($\beta\iota\beta\lambda\iota\alpha$), each containing the biography of a pair ($\sigma\upsilon\zeta\upsilon\gamma\iota\alpha$)—one Greek and one Roman hero—and followed by a comparison ($\sigma\upsilon\gamma\kappa\rho\iota\sigma\iota\varsigma$).[71] Some of these $\beta\iota\beta\lambda\iota\alpha$ have been lost, as that containing the *Lives* of Epaminondas—Scipio (?), which appears to have been the first he wrote, also that containing the *Lives* of Metellus and some parallel Greek.

The 46 extant *Lives* are contained in 22 $\beta\iota\beta\lambda\iota\alpha$ —

---

[71] The σύγκρισις is wanting in the *Lives* of Phocion—Cato minor; Themistocles—Camillus; Pyrrhus—Marius; Alexander—Caesar.

those of Agis–Cleomenes—Gracchi, a double pair, being reckoned as one. They are of special value to us for the knowledge of Greek and Roman Antiquity, in fact, for many periods the only extant source of information, and they are still regarded as the legacy of a highly-cultivated man, a thorough-going advocate of truth and morality. 'It is a mistake to suppose' says F. A. Paley 'that Plutarch was content with writing merely amusing or popular biographies: the *Lives* are works of great learning and research, and they must for this very reason, as well as from their considerable length, have taken many years in their compilation.' His original idea in writing them was simply to set a distinguished Greek—warrior, statesman, orator or legislator—side by side with some noted Roman, celebrated for the same qualities. In his age, when, though Rome held the supremacy, Greece was looked up to as the source of wisdom and art, such a comparison between the greatest men of both nations had a special propriety and significance and was more than a mere literary exercise. It was a patriotic theme, to show the superiority of this or that race; and Plutarch, in some sense, belonged to both.

We have the interesting testimony of the Biographer himself that the *Lives* were not written by him on the same model. Those of the First Series, which were composed in deference to the wishes of some of his friends, partake more of an historical than an ethical character. To this Series belong the following pairs, which, as may be gathered from internal evidence, appeared in the following order [72] approximately:—

---

[72] See C. T. Michaelis *de ordine vitarum parallelarum Plutarchi* p. 20 ff., where the evidence is stated very clearly. The

1. Epaminondas—Scipio (?) (not extant)
2. Sertorius—Eumenes
3. Cimon—Lucullus
4. Lysander—Sulla
5. Demosthenes—Cicero
6. Agis-Cleomenes—Gracchi
7. Pelopidas—Marcellus
8. Phocion—Cato minor
9. Aristides—Cato maior

(It will be observed that No. 2 is the only pair in which the Roman takes precedence of the Greek; the others are in chronological sequence.)

The Second Series—which was not written at the suggestion of friends but for his own satisfaction and improvement (as he himself records in the Proem to the *Life of Timoleon*), and partook of a more distinctly ethical character [73]—comprised the following:

10. Pericles—Fabius Maximus [74]
11. Nicias—Crassus
12. Dion—Brutus [75]
13. Timoleon—Aemilius Paulus
14. Philopoemen—Titus Flamininus
15. Themistocles—Camillus
16. Alexander—Caesar
17. Agesilaus—Pompeius
18. Pyrrhus—Marius
19. Solon—Poplicola

Life of Epaminondas is quoted in *Agesilaus* c. 28, 4; that of Scipio ma. in *Pyrrhus* c. 8, and that of Scipio mi. in *Ti. Gracch.* c. 21, 4 and *C. Gracch.* c. 10, 2. We have no authority, except the spurious catalogue of Lamprias, for coupling the *Life* of Scipio with that of Epaminondas.

[73] *Nic.* c. 1, 5 τὴν πρὸς κατανόησιν ἤθους καὶ τρόπου ἱστορίαν.

[74] *Per.* c. 2, 4 ἔδοξεν οὖν καὶ ἡμῖν ἐνδιατρῖψαι τῇ περὶ τοὺς βίους ἀναγραφῇ· καὶ τοῦτο τὸ βιβλίον δέκατον συντετάχαμεν τὸν Περικλέους βίον καὶ τὸν Φαβίου Μαξίμου.

[75] *Dion* c. 2, 4 ἐν τούτῳ, δωδεκάτῳ τῶν παραλλήλων ὄντι βίων.

The lost *Life of Metellus*, which was promised in that of Marius (c. 29, 8), was probably written before those of Solon—Poplicola. After exhausting the great characters of Grecian and Roman history whose example was worthy of imitation, in 'his gallery of portraits,' it occurred to Plutarch that he might teach virtue in a different way by painting its opposite.[76] Hence he composed a Third Series of *Parallel Lives*: but it comprises only two, viz. those of Demetrius—Antonius and Alcibiades—Coriolanus.

It was not until after the completion of the above three Series that the Biographer seems to have turned his attention to prehistoric times and 'like a geographer delineating unknown countries' (to use his own expressive simile[77]) to have commenced yet a Fourth Series of *Lives*, of which the only ones extant are those of Theseus—Romulus and Lycurgus —Numa, usually placed first of all. But the order in which the Lives are arranged in the MSS is purely arbitrary. The four extant *Lives* of Artoxerxes, Aratus, Galba and Otho, together with the lost *Lives* of Heracles, Aristomenes, Hesiod, Pindar, Daïphantus, Crates and others, were detached narratives and do not come under the same category. Those of Galba and Otho indeed are placed in most of the MSS and in editions prior to that of Stephanus (Henri Estienne) among the *Morals*.

We are not left to conjecture what Plutarch's aim and purpose were in the composition of the Second Series of *Lives*, which, as has been already stated, was a continuation of those written at the instance of others. In the Introduction to the *Life of Alexander* he expressly says :—'I am not a writer of

---

[76] *Demetr.* c. 1, 1.
[77] *Thes.* c. 1, 1.

histories but of biographies. My readers therefore must excuse me if I do not describe in minute detail, but only briefly touch upon, the noblest and most famous events. For it is not the most conspicuous actions that of necessity exhibit a man's virtues or failings, but it often happens that some trifling incident, a word or a jest, gives a clearer insight into character, than battles with their slaughters of tens of thousands, and the greatest arrays of armies and sieges of cities. Accordingly, as painters produce a likeness by a representation of the countenance only and features, whereby the character is revealed, and pay least attention to the other parts of the body, so I must be allowed to study rather the indications of a man's character, and by means of these to portray the life of each, leaving to others the description of the grand events and struggles in which they were engaged.'

So again in the Proem to the *Life of Nicias*, while he takes the historian Timaeus to task for aspiring to emulate Thucydides by giving a full narrative of the events of the Sicilian campaign, and ridicules his feeble and senseless attempts at imitating such a great and unapproachable model, he professes his own immunity from such an error. He will not do more than make a cursory reference to the chief events so ably recorded by that historian and by Philistus, and, for the rest, endeavour to collect materials for his Biography from various other sources—the scattered remarks of writers not commonly known, ancient records and decrees—selecting such as would throw most light upon the character and disposition of his hero.

Herein lies the broad difference between Plutarch and such writers as Herodotus and Thucydides.

Their interest is for the doings and destinies of political communities, while they are comparatively indifferent to those of individuals—a fact easily accounted for from the circumstances of the age in which they lived, when the state was all in all and the individual entirely merged in it. But a change in this respect had set in as early as the following century, when it became the fashion to connect great events and achievements with the names of individuals; so that, while Marathon and Salamis were always described as victories of the Athenian people and not of Miltiades only and Themistocles, Timotheus is frequently spoken of as the conqueror of Corcyra, Chabrias of Naxos, and Iphicrates of the Lacedaemonians.[78] In Theopompus, for example, the historian of King Philip, we find greater prominence given to the characteristics of individuals and their actions more carefully described in detail: while in Plutarch—by whose time the Greeks as a nation were politically effaced, and all interest in their country extinct, when there was 'Greece but living Greece no more'—the whole becomes absorbed in the individual, history in biography; personal character and the actions and motives of individuals are the objects of his interest and study. More or less of historical background he was obliged by the necessity of the case to give to his portraits, but always in subordination to the portrait itself: he is, in short, an historian only by accident, really and essentially

---

[78] Demosth. *Aristocr.* § 198 τῶν ἔργων τῶν τότε οὐδενός, ὦ ἄνδρες Ἀθηναῖοι, ἀπεστέρησαν ἑαυτούς, οὐδ' ἔστιν οὐδεὶς ὅστις ἂν εἴποι τὴν ἐν Σαλαμῖνι ναυμαχίαν Θεμιστοκλέους ἀλλ' Ἀθηναίων, οὐδὲ τὴν Μαραθῶνι μάχην Μιλτιάδου, ἀλλὰ τῆς πόλεως. νῦν δὲ πολλοὶ τοῦτο λέγουσιν, ὡς Κέρκυραν εἷλε Τιμόθεος καὶ τὴν μόραν κατέκοψεν Ἰφικράτης καὶ τὴν περὶ Νάξον ἐνίκα ναυμαχίαν Χαβρίας. Cp. Aesch. c. *Ctesiph.* § 186 f.

a philosopher and moralist: and his *Biographies* take their tone from the spirit which animated the writer in his philosophical works, a proof of which is furnished by the Proem to the *Life of Pericles*, which is to the moral treatises what the example is to the rule.

III *Plutarch's Life of Pericles*

The comparative silence even of earlier antiquity on the important and interesting epoch between the Persian and Peloponnesian wars, which covered the greater part of the life of Pericles, is, indeed, remarkable. The brief sketch by Thucydides [79] of the historical development of Athens μετὰ τὰ Μηδικά does not fill up the gap, nor was it filled up by later historians. In the absence, then, of other sources of information Plutarch's *Life of Pericles* remains a precious monument, for most of the writings which he had before him or might have consulted have been lost. He has drawn upon a wide range of authorities of very unequal value, and it is to be regretted that the Biographer to whom Pericles was only a remote historical figure, did not proceed with the necessary caution and criticism in the choice of his aids to judgment or in his weighing of evidence. But he has furnished us with details not to be found elsewhere, and the anecdotes, even the scandalous gossip, which he reports, give us a glimpse of the world in which Pericles moved. They contain the necessary elements for a picture of political society such as it was in the fifth century B.C.

[79] I 89–118.

Of the eighteen writers whom Plutarch quotes, one half were actual contemporaries or nearly so of Pericles; these were Thucydides the historian, the two memoir-writers Ion of Chios and Stesimbrotus of Thasos, and the six comic poets Telecleides, Cratinus, Hermippus, Plato, Eupolis, Aristophanes. The other half were posterior to Pericles and therefore must be considered as only secondary or tertiary sources, viz. Ephorus the chronicler of Cyme (Asia Minor), Idomeneus of Lampsacus, and Duris of Samos, with the philosophers Plato, Aristotle, Theophrastus, Aeschines the Socratic, Heracleides Ponticus, and Critolaus. Theopompus is not named by Plutarch, though, as will be seen hereafter, he borrowed largely from him.

But, to proceed with details, Plutarch makes use of Thucydides for the general characteristics of Pericles (cc. 9, 15, 16) where he expressly quotes him as the foundation of his narrative, although not as his only or even his principal source; for his expedition to the Peloponnesus (c. 19, 2); for the Sacred War (c. 21); for that against Euboea and the Peloponnesians until the conclusion of the Thirty Years' truce (cc. 22-23); again, for the Samian War (cc. 25-28, he quotes him c. 28); and finally for the origin and commencement of the Peloponnesian War (c. 29, c. 31, 1; cc. 33-35). Ephorus, who was the author of a general history of the Hellenes and Barbarians from B.C. 1090 to B.C. 340 [80] in thirty Books—the XIth, XIIth and XIIIth of which extended from the siege of Paros (B.C. 489) to the beginning of the Peloponnesian War (B.C. 431)—is twice quoted by name as a supplementary authority

---

[80] Polyb. v 33, 2 τὸν πρῶτον καὶ μόνον ἐπιβεβλημένον τὰ καθόλου γράφειν. See my Introd. to Life of Themistocles p. xl.

to Thucydides.[81] He is also responsible for the story of the bribery of the Spartan king Pleistoanax and of the circumstances connected with it,[82] as well as for some details of the Samian War (cc. 27, 28); but he is especially Plutarch's principal authority for what he considers to have been the cause of the Peloponnesian War.[83]

It is less easy to determine what belongs to Philochorus, one of the composers of the Ἀτθίδες, though Blass seems to find no difficulty in ascribing to him the account of the abasement of the court of Areopagus (c. 7, 6),[84] and of the elimination of those who were not genuine-born Athenians (c. 37, 3 f.); but the former notice at any rate is more probably taken from an older authority, the newly-discovered work of Aristotle on the Constitution of Athens. The description of Pericles' activity in building (cc. 12-13) appears to be mostly original, although it is possible that Plutarch availed himself to some extent of Philochorus' work. As to special biographical details, there is little enough in any of the above-mentioned sources; for these, we must look to four other writers:—Theopompus, Ion, Stesimbrotus and Idomeneus.

Theopompus of Chios, who is Plutarch's principal authority for the *Life of Cimon*, was a violent political partisan and showed great rancour in assail-

---

[81] c. 27, 1 and c. 28, 1, where, speaking of the cruelty towards the Samians with which Duris had charged Pericles, he adds that neither Thucydides nor Ephorus nor Aristotle had made any mention of it.

[82] This appears from the Schol. to Arist. *Nub.* 855.

[83] This is ascertained from Diodorus XII cc. 38-41, who bases his history of this period chiefly upon that of Ephorus.

[84] See Müll. *FHG.* 1 407, *fr.* 141ᵇ ὅτε Ἐφιάλτης μόνα κατέλιπε τῇ ἐξ᾽Α. π. τὰ ὑπὲρ τοῦ σώματος, compared with Plut. *Per.* c. 9, 4.

ing Greek democracies and their failings. He lived for a long time in exile on account of his father's laconism. The Xth Book of his voluminous work τὰ Φιλιππικά contained an episode on the inner history of Athens and its δημαγωγοί from the Median war downwards, in which their chief characteristics were portrayed.[85] Though he is nowhere mentioned in the present Biography, we have the evidence of Athenaeus[86] that the passage about Cimon (c. 9, 2) comes from him.[87] He is the accepted authority also for c. 7, 1–4; for part of c. 11, 3[88]; for c. 16, 2–4; and, in its main outlines, for c. 10, 1–3.[89]

Ion, the genial lyric, elegiac and tragic poet of Chios (B.C. 493–422), came to Athens when young and spent a great part of his life in that city, where he lived on terms of intimacy with Cimon. He is quoted by name in two passages only, c. 5, 3 and c. 28, 5. But there can be little doubt that his prose work Ἐπιδημίαι—which is a record of his experiences during his visits to other cities and in particular his interviews with celebrated men—furnished the Biographer with other interesting or characteristic traits of Pericles. The anecdote about Thucydides, the leader of the opposition, and the Spartan king

---

[85] On the different opinions concerning the merits of his style, see my *Introduction* to Plutarch's *Life of Timoleon* pp. xx f.

[86] XII p. 533 A.

[87] Busolt *Gr. Gesch.* II p. 450 Anm. 1, p. 456 Anm. 1 sees traces of some high-sounding Theopompic expressions and rhetorical turns, such as πολυτελῆ καὶ ἀκόλαστον l. 9, σώφρονος καὶ αὐτουργοῦ l. 10, καταδημαγωγούμενος l. 22, συνδεκάσας l. 27, κατεστασίασε l. 31, and ἀδέκαστον καὶ ἄθικτον in the corresponding passage of the *Life of Cimon* c. 10.

[88] Busolt *l. c.* p. 536 Anm. 1.

[89] Busolt *l. c.* p. 492 Anm. 1.

Archidamus in reference to him, is very probably taken from Ion.[90]

Stesimbrotus of Thasos, an Homeric scholar, lived at Athens at the same time as Ion.[91] Plutarch, who speaks in disparaging terms of him in his *Life of Themistocles* also (c. 24, 3), quotes him four times (c. 8, 6 ; c. 13, 11 ; c. 26, 1 ; c. 36, 3); but, as his contemporary pamphlet[92] was for the most part a sort of *chronique scandaleuse* or a medley of anecdotes of the private life of Themistocles, Thucydides and Pericles, we shall not go far wrong in assuming that the account of Elpinice's mediation between Cimon and Pericles[93] (c. 10, 4 ff.) and that of the attitude of Pericles to Cimon's sons (c. 29, 2 f.) are founded on the same work[94]; as also the other very similar anecdote about Elpinice (c. 28, 4 f.); and the details of his private life in cc. 5, 7 and 36.[95]

Idomeneus of Lampsacus (B.C. 310–270), a friend and pupil of Epicurus,[96] is also, like Stesimbrotus, a wholly untrustworthy writer and the author of reckless calumnies. Plutarch himself did not reckon

---

[90] c. 8, 4. It is repeated in *Praec. ger. reip.* c. 5 (*Mor.* p. 802 c). See Busolt *Gr. Gesch.* II p. 513 Anm. 1.

[91] Plut. *Cim.* c. 4, 4 Στησίμβροτος ὁ Θάσιος περὶ τὸν αὐτὸν ὁμοῦ τι χρόνον τῷ Κίμωνι γεγονώς. So Athenae. p. 589 D says of him κατὰ τοὺς αὐτοὺς αὐτῷ (sc. τῷ Περικλεῖ) χρόνους γενόμενος καὶ ἑωρακὼς αὐτόν. See my *Introd.* to *Life of Themistocles* p. xlv.

[92] In c. 13, 12 it is referred to as τῶν πράξεων καὶ τῶν βίων ἡλικιῶτις ἱστορία. Its title as given by Athenaeus *l. c.* was περὶ Θεμιστοκλέους καὶ Θουκυδίδου καὶ Περικλέους.

[93] Busolt *l. c.* p. 492 Anm. 1 ; p. 536 Anm. 1. Fr. Jacobs assigns it to Aeschines Socraticus on the strength of the passage in Athenaeus.

[94] Cp. *Cim.* c. 16, 1.

[95] See Busolt *l. c.* p. 446 Anm. 3. Cp. *Mor.* p. 800 B, p. 812 D.

[96] Diog. Laert. X 10, 22 ; Strabo *Geogr.* XIII 1, 19.

him amongst οἱ δοκιμώτατοι συγγραφεῖς,[97] and might have neglected him altogether, if only for the comparatively late period at which he lived. He quotes him in two passages only, c. 10, 5 and c. 35, 4, where the reference is probably to his work περὶ δημαγωγῶν.[98]

For the Samian War, besides Ephorus and Thucydides Plutarch used Duris (c. 28) who was born about B.C. 342, when Athenian allottees (κληροῦχοι) were in possession of his native island. He was the author of a work entitled Ὧροι Σαμίων. 'Annals of Samos.' Duris is the authority for the story of the branding of the prisoners of war on both sides (c. 26, 2); and it was he who tried to make out that Aspasia was the chief cause of the Samian War.[99] Aristotle's Ἀθηναίων πολιτεία also was laid under contribution for the Samian War (c. 26, 3; c. 28, 1). The same work is given as an authority for the introduction of salaries to the dicasts (c. 9, 3) and for the murder of Ephialtes (c. 10, 7). The notice of Pythocleides as one of the teachers of Pericles appears to have been taken indirectly not from this but from some other of Aristotle's writings.

To these sources are to be added a number of other writers, in whom merely incidental mention is made of Pericles, or who handled a part only of the period in which he lived, such as Herodotus and

---

[97] See *Dem.* c. 23, 3, where he is coupled with Duris of Samos.

[98] See my n. to *Dem.* c. 15, 3.

[99] The severe judgment which Plutarch himself (c. 28, 3) passes upon him is wholly confirmed by what we learn from other sources. Dionysius of Halicarnassus (*de comp. verb.* p. 61 ed. G. H. Schäfer) classes him with Phylarchus, Demetrius of Calacte, Hieronymus, Hegesias Magnes and other such uncritical writers, who have left behind them τοιαύτας συντάξεις οἵας οὐδεὶς ὑπομένει μέχρι κορωνίδος διελθεῖν.

Plato; from the former of whom comes the notice of the mother of Pericles (c. 3, 2); the latter is quoted c. 7, 6; c. 8, 1; c. 15, 4; c. 24, 4, as an indirect source of historical information. The last of the quotations, which is from the dialogue *Menexenus*—the only work of which the title is given by the Biographer—concerns Aspasia. Theophrastus, the pupil and successor of Aristotle, is quoted c. 23, 1; c. 35, 4 and c. 38, 2 [100]; Heracleides of Heraclea (Pontus), hence named ὁ Ποντικός, a pupil of Plato, of Speusippus and Aristotle, c. 27, 3; c. 35, 4; and Critolaus, another member of the Peripatetic School and one of the Athenian commission to Rome B.C. 155, which was so important for the introduction of Greek culture, c. 7, 4. Heracleides is made use of to correct Ephorus.

The decree of Pericles for a grand Hellenic congress at Athens is doubtless taken from the συναγωγή ψηφισμάτων of Craterus, son of the famous Macedonian [101] general of that name, which is unnamed in this *Life*, but is referred to in that of *Aristides* (c. 26) and *Cimon* (c. 13). The section about Pericles and Aspasia (c. 24) was borrowed from various sources. Aeschines the Socratic, in his dialogue *Aspasia*, a somewhat doubtful authority, supplied some information, whether direct or indirect. Lastly, in c. 35, 1, 2 an anecdote, whether true or false, is recorded on the authority of the σχολαὶ τῶν φιλοσόφων.

The quotations from the poets of the old Attic Comedy [102] cannot be considered as historical sources,

---

[100] The two first quotations may possibly have been taken from his work Πολιτικὰ τὰ πρὸς καιρούς.

[101] See note to c. 17 l. 5.

[102] See notes to c. 33, 6 l. 3; c. 3, 4 l. 30; c. 4, 2 l. 16; also that to c. 7, 6 l. 53. Meineke thinks that the lines of

except in so far as they reflect the opinion of the anti-Periclean party, to which the writers mostly belonged.[103] The hateful insinuations of dark immorality against him may safely be disregarded as the mere suggestions of spite or prurience, or failure to comprehend the real nature of a remarkable man.

What the Biographer worked up out of such materials, selected from a wide range of authorities, bears unmistakeable impress in itself of its origin. The unevenness and want of homogeneousness in his narrative are much greater than in the *Life of Themistocles*, especially in the conception and delineation of Pericles' character, which has no simplicity about it, but wavers hesitatingly between contradictory statements, unlike anything in the *Life of Alcibiades* or of *Cimon* or of *Nicias*.

Teleclides quoted c. 16, 2 were written soon after the expulsion of Thucydides, son of Melesias, and that they are taken from the same play as those quoted c. 3, 4, viz. the Ἡσίοδοι, in which we learn from Athenaeus x p. 436 F, that Pericles was satirised for his passion for Chrysilla, a lady of Corinth.

[103] It is, as Blass says, an open question whether Plutarch, who had no special knowledge of this branch of literature, setting Aristophanes aside, quoted directly from the poets themselves or from some grammarians who had made a special study of them. It so happens, moreover, that in one of these passages viz. that which concerns Aspasia, there is such a suspicious resemblance between it and an ancient scholion to Plato's *Menexenus*, that we cannot resist the conviction that Plutarch drew from this source at second hand, when he quoted from that dialogue. And it was probably from another such scholion that something still more important proceeds. What Plutarch says of Anaxagoras (c. 4, 4) agrees word for word with a scholion to Plato's *Alcibiades* I (p. 118 C), and, since in the same passage of Plato Pythocleides and Damon are both mentioned as Pericles' teachers in music, we may fairly suppose that Plutarch's remarks on them are taken from a lost scholion on the passage. The same conclusion applies to his remark on Zeno (c. 4, 3), who is also mentioned by Plato *l. c.* p. 119 A. Blass carries his suggestion still farther, and suspects that the

The unique greatness of the man and his mighty personality has found in all antiquity only one impartial and clear-sighted judge. The sublime picture, which Thucydides has drawn of him, stands in bold relief against the distortions of party spirit, jealousy and frivolity, with which his detractors have endeavoured to blur it. He has touched indeed on the two last years only of his life and work, and it would have been foreign to the general scope of his history to enter into details of his public administration, yet, in spite of his conservative prejudices, in the general brief review of his entire policy which he gives in the celebrated sixty-fifth chapter of his second book, the historian bears the most honourable testimony to him, as the highest example of a great and noble statesman. Now Plutarch knows Thucydides and appreciates him, but he has not the courage to oppose his single testimony to the general obloquy and depreciation. It would seem, indeed, as if Pericles were too imposing a figure for his Biographer. Plutarch cannot overlook his superiority nor refuse him his admiration, but it is an admiration without sympathy. Nothing could be more fair or natural than that he should discover weak points in him, and that he should let us see them. But he never allows him to act upon high political

passage about branding (c. 26, 3) is not taken direct from Duris, but from a scholion to the lines of Aristophanes, which contained some learned remarks about the σάμαινα. So again, what is said of the different interpretations of Pericles' surname 'Ολύμπιος (c. 8, 2) is quite after the manner of the Scholiasts, and here likewise we come unexpectedly upon passages from the Comic poets. This borrowing of quotations was a common habit of the writers of that period, and few have the candour to acknowledge their sources. In spite of this habit, Plutarch's book-learning is comparatively very extensive and it must be remembered that he disclaims all pretensions to learned research.

grounds, and does not hesitate to attribute to him mean ideas and to pre-suppose personal aims and selfish motives. His democratic measures, forsooth, were due to nothing but his love of popular favour and greed of distinction. Plutarch extols, it is true, his incorruptibility and recognises an unfailing unselfishness at the bottom of the marvellous ascendency which he retained so long over the Athenian public. He rejects, it is true, the scandalous imputation of Idomeneus of Lampsacus on the subject of the assassination of Ephialtes and the declamations of Duris of Samos on his cruelty. He cannot conceive it possible that a man of noble and lofty spirit like Pericles should be capable of murdering a friend out of mere political jealousy. But, when he comes to consider the causes of the Peloponnesian War, the minuteness with which he dwells on that which he admits to be the most objectionable of all,[104] because, forsooth, it has most witnesses in its favour as compared with his curtness in the statement of opposite opinions, and the mode in which he assigns personal motives without any attempt at refutation, furnish evidence of his own belief in its reality. He has not Thucydides' critical sureness of judgment and clear insight into the circumstances, and he treats with all seriousness even the despicable imputation, put by the great comic poet into the mouth of the valiant Dicaeopolis, as an historical fact.

Plutarch seems, in short, to believe that Pericles was really the principal, if not sole, cause of the Peloponnesian War, and that it was brought about by him from selfish fear or to gratify mere personal bias and aversion; he finds no difficulty in believing that his overthrow of the council of Areopagus was because

[104] c. 31, 2.

he had been baffled in his endeavour to gain admission to it [105]; that it was merely to gratify the personal caprice of Aspasia, that he undertook a war, which, if it did not jeopardize the naval supremacy of Athens, at any rate caused numerous citizens to assume mourning, although, according to his last words, as reported by the Biographer himself, it was Pericles' boast that he had never willingly done any such thing; and, lastly, that he sent Cimon's son wilfully with an insufficient force to help Corcyra, in order that, if he failed as he must do, the poor man might be compromised and suspected as a secret friend of the Spartans. Besides, Plutarch proceeds on the assumption that there could be but one motive for the war, where a concurrence of many motives was not only possible but, as it happened, very probable. For the war itself was an inevitable necessity at some time or other in the strained relations between Athens and Sparta: the materials were laid for a conflagration, ready to burst out at any time. As far as Pericles was concerned, nothing more can be truly said against him than that it was mainly due to his policy that the war broke out at that particular time; but the truth is, the war, so far from serving his private ends, on the contrary proved disadvantageous to him, inasmuch as it weakened his position and caused his extraordinary influence to wane. It was not the grand idea of raising Athens to the position of a state which might command admiration for all time—not the consideration of what must be new modelled and re-shaped, what abolished, to the fulfilment of this noble purpose—not the wish that the general body of citizens might share in the internal prosperity and external grandeur of the state, and that

[105] c. 9. 3.

the ennobling influences of poetry and art might
be extended to all alike,—no sentiments of this
kind, forsooth, dictated the policy of Pericles, but
all was shrewd reckoning how he might make
himself the biggest man in the state and continue
such.

But there are reasons why Plutarch's judgment
cannot be accepted without mistrust and must be
submitted to a careful test. 'Tis not the wish to
round off his narrative or to produce some striking
effects that leads him astray, but his fondness for
the personal and anecdotic. He does not succeed
in comprehending really great characters but loses
himself in miniature painting, and often finds in
the ordinary gossip of the day special characteristic
traits for the picture he is about to give. In order
to find such material, he had to turn away from the
great writers to inferior scribblers of every description, who treat Pericles as if he were the incarnation
of uncompromising radicalism, of a tyrannical lust
of power and of shameless frivolity. But it is in
the nature of things that every detail of ancient
life, which relates strictly to persons as such, must
be uncertain: only the few, who were admitted into
close relations with eminent men, could possibly become acquainted with incidents of their private life
and with their daily utterances. What ample scope
then is there here for intentional and unintentional
misrepresentation! Hence the importance of a
careful investigation of the sources from which the
Biographer drew, of analysing each statement of his
into its elements and assigning each to its proper
author.

The Biography before us, however, must not be
considered as an historical work; Plutarch cannot

and will not be so judged. He is essentially, indeed,
a moralist, as he more than once professes,[106] a por-
trayer of character and not an historian and, if his
work be regarded in this its proper light, its
blemishes, indeed, will not disappear altogether, but
they will be considerably lessened. On the other
hand, there are many lively and beautiful passages,
where the writer warms with his theme and com-
municates his own animation to the reader. The
chief of these is certainly that about the splendid
Periclean buildings at Athens,[107] which is the pearl
of the whole biography and distinguished by the
life-like character and energy of its description.
His account also of the last days [108] of Pericles
and the picture of a character so dignified and affecting appeal not less to our sympathy than the
reflexions, full of noble sentiment and right feeling,
which are combined therewith. In such passages
as these, Plutarch has shown that he can soar
occasionally to the height of a great subject.

The Biography—setting aside the brief Proem
to the pair of Lives, *Pericles—Fabius Maximus* (cc. 1,
2) and the Epilogue (c. 39)—falls naturally into the
three following distinct divisions :—

A. c. **3**—c. **6**. The personal relations of Pericles.
His lineage, external appearance (c. 3), his education
(c. 4), his prominent characteristic qualities as
founded thereon, his gravity, earnestness and composure (c. 5, 1), which some of his contemporaries
misrepresented as due to excessive pride and assump-

---

[106] *Alex.* c. 1, *Cim.* c. 2, *Nic.* c. 1.
[107] cc. 12, 13.   [108] cc. 38–39.

tion of superiority. He owed much to the teaching of Anaxagoras in natural science; especially his freedom from vulgar superstition (c. 6, 1).

The story of the incident of the unicorn ram shortly before B.C. 445 (§§ 2 ff.) and of the different explanations of the portent by Anaxagoras and Lampon, is irrelevant to the subject as the biographer himself confesses. These trifling events in the private life of Pericles were doubtless to be found in the work of Stesimbrotus.

B. c. **7**—c. **16**. The home policy of Pericles from B.C. 469 to B.C. 429.

His shyness and reserve and the dread of ostracism, because of his high birth, kept him back from taking part in politics when a young man, but he distinguished himself in military campaigns by his personal courage and adventure. His first appearance as a statesman, and the corresponding change effected in his daily mode of living and habits (c. 7); his most efficient instrument of power was his eloquence ἡ τοῦ λόγου δύναμις (c. 8), which, however, he reserved for great occasions. The manner in which he transformed himself from a leader of the popular party (προστάτης τοῦ δήμου or δημαγωγός)—a rôle which circumstances forced upon him contrary to his natural bias in his struggle with Cimon B.C. 467–449 (cc. 9, 10) and afterwards with Thucydides B.C. 449–445 (cc. 11–14)—to an aristocratic and kingly director of the state after a complete triumph over his opponents (cc. 15, 16).

There is an episode in c. 13, 9 ff., only loosely connected with the main subject, concerning the relation between Phidias and Pericles and the scandalous gossip of the day

CHRONOLOGY

OF

EVENTS IN THE LIFE-TIME OF PERICLES

N.B.—The numerals in heavy type refer to the Text

B.C.

493/192   Ol. 71, 4. *Themistocles.*
            Birth of PERICLES.
            Birth of Ion of Chios, not later than this year (c. **5**, 3).

492/191   Ol. 72, 1. *Diognetus.*
            First Persian armament under Mardonius almost totally destroyed off Mt. Athos.

491/190   Ol. 72, 2. *Hybrilides.*
            Feud between Athens and Aegina, the latter of which sided with the Persians (c. **29**, 4).

490/489   Ol. 72, 3. *Phaenippus.*
            First Persian War.
            Defeat of the second armament under Datis and Artaphernes on the plain of MARATHON by Athenians and Plataeans alone.
            Naxos (c. **11**, 5) becomes a dependency of Persia.

B.C.	
	Disastrous undertaking of Miltiades, father of Cimon, against Paros; his impeachment by Xanthippus (c. 3, 1), son of Ariphron and father of Pericles; his condemnation and death.
489/488	Ol. 72, 4. *Aristides.*
488/487	Ol. 73, 1. *Anchises.* Law of Ostracism enforced for the first time in the person of Hipparchus, son of Charmus (Plut. *Nic.* c. 11, 6, Aristot. 'Αθ. πολ. c. 22, 4).
487/486	Ol. 73, 2. *Telesinus.* Revolt of Egypt from Persia. Ostracism of Megacles, brother of Agariste (c. 3, 1). The nine archons—hitherto chosen by open voting (αἱρετοί)—appointed by lot (κληρωτοί) from the selected candidates proposed by the tribes (c. 9, 3, Aristot. 'Αθ. πολ. c. 22, 5).
485/484	Ol. 73, 4. *Philocrates.* Xerxes succeeds Darius as king of Persia (—466/5). Naval empire of the Aeginetans. Ostracism of Xanthippus, son of Ariphron (c. 3, 1, Aristot. 'Αθ. πολ. c. 22, 6).
484/483	Ol. 74, 1. *Leostratus.* Egypt recovered by the Persians. Ostracism of ARISTIDES, son of Lysimachus, Aristot. *l. c.* Birth of Herodotus.
483/482	Ol. 74, 2. *Nicodemus.* Athens under the guidance of THEMISTOCLES, Aristot. *l. c.*
482/481	Ol. 74, 3. *Themistocles.*
481/480	Ol. 74, 4. *Hypsichides.* Congress of patriot states at the Isthmus. Recall of Aristides and other ostracised citizens διὰ

B.C.	
	τὴν Ξέρξου στρατείαν, Aristot. 'Αθ. πολ. c. 22, 8, Audoc. or. 1 § 109.
480/479	Ol. 75, 1. *Calliades.* Second Persian Invasion. Removal of Athenian families to Aegina, Salamis and Troezen. Battles of THERMOPYLAE, ARTEMISIUM, and SALAMIS under the leadership of Sparta. *Birth of Euripides.* *Birth of Antiphon.* Anaxagoras visits Athens acc. to Diog. Laert. II 7.
479/478	Ol. 75, 2. *Xanthippus.* Mardonius occupies Athens. Battles of PLATAEA and MYCALE (Lydia); Pausanias and Aristides in command at the former, Xanthippus (c. **3**, 1) at the latter. <small>The victory of Mycale is the first step towards the assumption of the offensive by the Hellenes and towards the liberation of the islands and towns on the coast of the Aegean sea (*Peter*).</small> Siege and capture of Sestos by the Hellenic fleet under the command of Xanthippus—the last event recorded by Herodotus, the first by Thucydides.
478/477	Ol. 75, 3. *Timosthenes.* Return of Athenian families. Athens rebuilt after the Persian occupation and, in spite of Sparta's opposition, surrounded with a stronger wall (μείζων περίβολος πανταχῇ Thuc. I c. 89, 3; c. 93, 2).
477/476	Ol. 75, 4. *Adeimantus.* <small>The whole of the Peiraeus peninsula with the harbour and two smaller bays Zea and Munychia enclosed by a wall. The Hellenic confederate fleet with Pausanias, the Spartan regent, as ἀρχηγός, and Aristides, as commander of the Athenian squadron, proceeds ἐλευθεροῦν τὰς Ἑλληνίδας πόλεις ὅσαι βαρβαρικαῖς φυλακαῖς διέμενον ἔτι φρουρούμεναι (Diod. XI 44, 1). It despoils the Persians of a great part of Cyprus, the chief source of the Persian naval power (Thuc. I c. 94), and captures Byzantium with large store of treasure (*ib.* c. 128, 5).</small>

B.C.	
	Treason of Pausanias and transfer of the naval hegemony from Sparta to Athens by the allies (Herod. VIII 3, Thuc. I 95, 4). Supremacy of the Council of the Areopagus revived (Aristot. Ἀθ. πολ. c. 23, 1 ; c. 41, 2 ; *Pol.* VIII (V) p. 1304^a, 20).
476/475	Ol. 76, 1. *Phaedon*. Creation of the Delian league. Athens acclaimed president. Capture of Eion at the mouth of the Strymon by the island-states, its first achievement. Recovery of the Thracian coast from the Persians, who were now expelled from Europe after forty years' occupation of it (Thuc. I 98). Themistocles choregus at the representation of the *Phoenissae* of Phrynichus—a glorification of the victory at Salamis.
475/474	Ol. 76, 2. *Dromoclcides*.
474/473	Ol. 76, 3. *Acestorides*.
473/472	Ol. 76, 4. *Menon*. Rhodes added to the Athenian empire. The *Persae* of Aeschylus exhibited.
472/471	Ol. 77, 1. *Chares*.
471/470	Ol. 77, 2. *Praxiergus*. Elidis συνοικισμός. Ostracism and banishment of THEMISTOCLES. *Birth of Thucydides*.
470/469	Ol. 77, 3. *Demotion*.
469/468	Ol. 77, 4. *Apsephion*. Pericles begins to take part in public affairs—forty years before his death (c. **16**, 2, 3 ; c. **7**, 2). The island of Scyros conquered and colonised. The bones of Theseus, the founder and champion of democracy, removed thence to Athens (Plut. *Thes.* c. 36, 1).

B.C.	
	Carystus (Euboea) compelled to join the Delian league. The whole island remains henceforth quietly in the Athenian alliance until 415 B.C.
468/467	Ol. 78, 1. *Theagenides.* Decay of the Delian league and development of the Athenian empire. Revolt of Naxos, the most important island of the Cyclades, from the Delian league (c. **11**, 5, Thuc. I 98, 3 ; 137, 2). *Death of Aristides. Birth of Socrates.* Destruction of the Persian fleet and subsequently of their camp at the mouth of the EURYMEDON (Pamphylia) by Cimon, c. **9**, 4 *note.* Sophocles gains his first tragic victory, *act.* 28.
467/466	Ol. 78, 2. *Lysistratus.* Pericles choregus at the representation of Aeschylus' *Seven against Thebes.*
466/465	Ol. 78, 3. *Lysanias.* Capture of Naxos, Thuc. I 98, 3; Arist. *Vesp.* 355. The Naxians reduced to the condition of subjects and 500 Athenian cleruchs established in the island, c. **11**, 2. Flight of Themistocles from Greece to Asia. Attempted colonisation of Amphipolis (Macedonia) by Athenians. Their demand of a share in the neighbouring mines leads to the revolt and siege of Thasos. Death of Xerxes and accession of Artaxerxes I. (—425 B.C.).
465/464	Ol. 78, 4. *Lysitheus.* Destruction of 10,000 Athenian colonists to Amphipolis at Drabescus (Thrace), Thuc. I 100, 3.
464/463	Ol. 79, 1. *Archidemides.* Capitulation of Thasos in the absence of Spartan aid, Thuc. I 101, 3. Charge of treason against Cimon on his return from Thasos (c. **10**, 5) ; Pericles appointed state prosecutor.

	Disastrous earthquake at Sparta. Insurrection of the Messenian Helots (—455/454 B.C.) and their occupation of Ithome. Appeal to Athens for aid by the Spartans (c. **9**, 4 note; *Cim.* c. 9, 4; Thuc. 1 102, 1: Arist. *Lys.* 1137 ff.). Cimon commanded the 4000 hoplites who were sent to their assistance, but they are soon mistrusted and ignominiously dismissed by the Spartans.
463/462	Ol. 79, 2. *Tlepolemus.*
462/461	Ol. 79, 3. *Conon.* Democratic judicial and political reforms of Pericles and Ephialtes (c. **7**, 6). Secret assassination of Ephialtes (c. **10**, 7). Introduction of pay to dicasts, c. **9**, 3. Probable date of the arrival of Anaxagoras at Athens (c. **4**), Busolt *Gr. Gesch.* II 306 Anm. 3.
461/460	Ol. 79, 4. *Euippus.* The Athenians, sensitive to the affront put upon them by their dismissal by the Spartans before Ithome, banish Cimon (Plut. *Cim.* c. 17, 2), who was chiefly accountable for the despatch of the expedition, renounce their alliance with Sparta and conclude a counter alliance with her enemy Argos, the third state in Greece. Thessaly and Megara join them. The Athenians build the long walls from Megara to the sea-port of Nisaea (Saronic gulf), so as to give the town still greater strategic importance.
460/459	Ol. 80, 1. *Phrasicleides.* Athenian expedition in support of the satrap Inaros, king of Libya, in his revolt against the Persian king Artaxerxes (c. **20**, 4). First year of the war between Egypt and Persia (—455/454 B.C.)
459/458	Ol. 80, 2. *Philocles.*

CHRONOLOGY OF EVENTS liii

B.C.	
	Definite rupture between Athens and Sparta. Sixth year of the Messenian war. Second year of the Egyptian war. Defeat of the Athenians at Halieis (Argolis) by a combined force of Corinthians and Epidaurians (Thuc. I 105, 1). The repulse was compensated by a victory over the enemy's fleet in the following winter at Cecryphaleia (Saronic gulf). Pleistoanax king of Sparta (c. **22**, 2). *Birth of Lysias, the orator.*
458/457	Ol. 80, 3. *Bion*. Third year of the Egyptian war. Annihilation of the Aeginetan naval power by the Athenians. War between Corinth and Megara. Victory of the Athenians under Myronides (c. **16**, 2) over the Corinthians in the Megarid during the absence of the main body of soldiers in Egypt and Aegina, Thuc. I 105, 3 ff. The *Oresteia* of Aeschylus exhibited.
457/456	Ol. 80, 4. *Mnesitheides*. Archonship thrown open to the third class (ζευγῖται, Aristot. 'Αθ. πολ. c. 26, 2), of whom Mnesitheides was the first to be chosen. Spartan victory at TANAGRA (Boeotia), c. **10**, 2. Recall of Cimon from exile (c. **10**) and compromise between him and Pericles by which the internal affairs of the city are left to the one and the conduct of foreign expeditions to the other, c. **10**, 4.
456/455	Ol. 81, 1. *Callias*. The Athenians under Myronides (c. **16**, 2), son of Callias, win a decisive victory over the Boeotians at OENOPHYTA (c. **10**, 2 *note*). Thebes alone of the Boeotian cities preserves her independence, but not without a political change; the rest become subject allies on the same footing as the πόλεις of the Delian league.

B.C.	
	Completion of the long walls from Athens to Peiraeus and Phalerum, c. **13**, 5, Thuc. I 108, 3.
Success of Leocrates (c. **16**, 2) and surrender of Aegina after a long blockade. The Aeginetans henceforth included among the tributaries to the Athenian treasury, c. **29**, 4, Thuc. I 108, 4.
Naval expedition under Tolmides round the Peloponnesus, c. **19**, 3 ; c. **18**, 2 *note*.
Death of Aeschylus, aet. 69.
455/454	Ol. 81, 2. *Sosistratus.*
End of the Messenian war by the capture of Ithome, and transportation of the Messenian refugees by Tolmides to Naupactus, which henceforward becomes an important Athenian naval station.
Annihilation of the Athenian armament sent to help Inaros in Egypt, Thuc. I 109, 110.
Initiation of a grand scheme of Hellenic convention by Pericles defeated by the secret opposition of Sparta (c. **17**).
[Plutarch gives no precise date. Grote places it after the Thirty Years' truce; O. Müller before 457 B.C.; Oncken at 448 B.C.; A. Schmidt at 460 B.C.]
454/453	Ol. 81, 3. *Ariston.*
Operations of Pericles in the Crissaean gulf and its outlet westward (c. **19**, 2); Achaia joins the Athenian alliance, Thuc. I 111, 2–3.
453/452	Ol. 81, 4. *Lysicrates.*
Diodorus places the mission of 1000 cleruchs to the Thracian Chersonese in this year; but see Busolt *Gr. Gesch.* II 536 Anm. 2.
452/451	Ol. 82, 1. *Chaerephanes.*
The transference of the common fund of the Delian league from Delos—the great religious centre of the Ionian race—to Athens (c. **12**, 1) seals the conversion of the Athenian headship into an empire.
451/450	Ol. 82, 2. *Antidotus.*

	Ion of Chios (c. **5**, 3), tragic poet, begins to exhibit, Schol. ad Arist. *Pac.* 835.
450/449	Ol. 82, 3. *Euthynus.*
	Five years' truce between Athens and Sparta, c. **10**, 2 *n*, Thuc. I 112, 1.
	Defection of Argos from the Athenian alliance.
	Anaxagoras withdraws from Athens.
	Pericles divorces his wife, c. **24**, 5.
449/448	Ol. 82, 4. *Pedieus.*
	Resumption of the war against Persia by the Athenians under Cimon.
	Death of Cimon (c. **10**, 7) at Citium, and subsequent Athenian double victory over the Persians both by sea and land at Salamis (Cyprus).
	Cessation of hostilities between Persia and Hellas. Pericles checks the eagerness of the Athenians to harass the Persian sea-board, or to embark again in an Egyptian war (c. **20**, 3).
	Thucydides, son of Melesias, becomes leader of the anti-Periclean party, c. **11**, 1.
448/447	Ol. 83, 1. *Philiscus.*
	Pericles conducts a body of κληροῦχοι to the Thracian Chersonese, and Tolmides a similar body to Andros, Naxos and Euboea (c. **11**, 5).
	Renewal of hostilities between Athens and Sparta owing to the Phocian attack on Delphi. Pericles places the oracle once more in the hands of the Phocians, c. **21**, 2 *n*, Thuc. I 112, 5.
	The *Archilochi* of Cratinus.
447/446	Ol. 83, 2. *Timarchides.*
	Commencement of the great Periclean buildings (cc. **12**, **13**).
	Defeat of Athenians by Boeotians at CORONEIA and death of Tolmides, c. **18**, 3 *n*, Thuc. I 113.
446/445	Ol. 83, 3. *Callimachus.*
	Foundation of the colony of Brea (Thrace), c. **11**, 5 *n*.

B.C.	
	The unfortunate expedition of Tolmides, which Pericles did his best to avert by his warnings—leading as it did to the overthrow of Athenian influence in Boeotia, won by the battle of Oenophyta—raises still higher the prestige of Pericles as a statesman and commander, while it removes his only competitor in military distinction (c. **18**, 2, 3).
Pericles proceeds to Euboea to repress the revolt there, but recrosses in haste to Attica on the news of the revolt of Megara and of the simultaneous invasion of Attica by the Peloponnesians under the command of the Spartan king Pleistoanax, c. **22**, 1, Thuc. I 114, 2. Cleandridas, his adviser, bribed to withdraw (c. **22**, 2).
Pericles attaches himself to Aspasia, as his second wife, c. **24**, 1.
Birth of the comic poet EUPOLIS (c. **3**, 4 ; c. **24**, 6).
445/444	Ol. 83, 4. *Lysimachides.*
Recovery of Euboea by Pericles, and re-establishment of Athenian control over the whole island ; an Athenian colony settled at Hestiaea, c. **23**, 2, Thuc. I 114, 3.
Ostracism of Thucydides, son of Melesias (c. **14**, 2).
Conclusion of truce between Athens and Sparta by mutual arrangement for thirty years (c. **24**, 1 *note*, c. **29**, 4) leaves Pericles free to develop his schemes for promoting the internal welfare of Athens and making it the centre of the intellectual and artistic life of Hellas.
Pericles now obtains the sole direction of affairs, holding office as Strategus continuously from this year to B.C. 430, c. **15**, c. **16**, 3.
A gift of corn from Egypt is the occasion of a revision of the Athenian burgher-roll, c. **37**, 3.
[Some think that Inaros was the donor, and the date 460/459.]
444/443	Ol. 84. 1. *Praxiteles.*
The Pontic expedition of Pericles (c. **20**, 1).
Completion of the Odeion (c. **13**, 5).
The Ὀρῆτται of Cratinus (c. **13**, 6).

B.C.	
443/442	Ol. 84, 2. *Lysanias.* The Athenians send a national Greek colony to Thurii under the conduct of Lampon (c. **11**, 5). Herodotus *aet.* 41 one of the colonists; also Lysias either now or later. The poet Sophocles chairman of the Board of Hellenotamiae. The quota-list of tribute (Kirchhoff *C.I.* I 237) paid to Athens this year is the last which was drawn up on the principle of keeping the total amount at the Aristidean level of 460 talents. The assessment of B.C. 442 for the most part did away with abatements to individual states and so produced a large total: at the opening of the Peloponnesian war it is said to average 600 talents (Thuc. II 13, 3). In B.C. 440 an additional payment (ἐπιφορά) is required of certain Ionian and Hellespontine states, evidently to meet the increasing scale of expenditure (Hicks *Gr. Hist. Inscr.* no. 30, pp. 39, 40). The assessment of B.C. 425 largely increased the previous payments.
442/441	Ol. 84, 3. *Diphilus.* Diodorus (XII c. 26) notes that the world was now in the enjoyment of universal peace. The Persians were under treaty with Athens in respect to the Hellenic cities in Asia; the truce for thirty years was subsisting between Athens and Sparta; western Hellas was equally at rest by the pacification of Syracuse and Agrigentum, of Sicily and Carthage. Italy, Gaul and Spain were quiet.
441/440	Ol. 84, 4. *Timocles.* Birth of Pericles, son of Pericles and Aspasia.
440/439	Ol. 85, 1. *Morychides.* Feud between Miletus and Samos, one of the three great privileged autonomous island allies of Athens. The Samian fleet defeated by an armament under the command of the ten generals (including Pericles as αὐτοκράτωρ and the poet Sophocles, c. **8**, 5) and the city after a contest of nine months' duration disarmed and dismantled, cc. **24 28**, Thuc. I 116, 117. Pericles delivers the funeral oration over those who had fallen in the Samian war, c. **8**, 6; c. **28**, 3. The *Antigone* of Sophocles. A decree to limit the freedom of comedy: Schol.

B.C.	
	ad Aristoph. *Ach.* 67 ψήφισμα τοῦ μὴ κωμῳδεῖν γραφὲν ἐπὶ Μορυχίδου· ἴσχυσε δὲ (ἐκεῖνόν τε τὸν ἐνιαυτὸν καὶ δύο τοὺς ἑξῆς) ἐπὶ Γλαυκίνου τε καὶ Θεοδώρου, μεθ' οὓς ἐπ' Εὐθυμένους κατελύθη.
439/438	Ol. 85, 2. *Glaucines.* The *Alcestis* of Euripides.
438/437	Ol. 85, 3. *Theodorus.* Completion and dedication of the PARTHENON, c. **13**, 4. Condemnation of Phidias *act.* 50 (Müller *FHG.* v p. 18. According to the Schol. to Arist. *Pax* this was in B.C. 438).
437/436	Ol. 85, 4. *Euthymenes.* Building of the PROPYLAEA commenced, c. **13**, 7. Successful settlement of an Athenian colony under Hagnon at Amphipolis (Macedonia). Repeal of the decree restricting comedy.
436/435	Ol. 86, 1. *Lysimachus.* *Birth of Isocrates.* The Zeus at Olympia completed by Phidias.
435/434	Ol. 86, 2. *Antiochides.* Outbreak of the war between Corinth and Corcyra on account of Epidamnus, Thuc. I 24–55. Defeat of the Corinthians by the Corcyraeans in a sea-fight off Actium. Surrender of Epidamnus to Corcyra.
434/433	Ol. 86, 3. *Chares.* Further hostilities of Corcyra and naval preparations of Corinth during this and the next year.
433/432	Ol. 86, 4. *Apseudes.* Completion of the PROPYLAEA, c. **13**, 7. Successful appeal of the Corcyraeans to Athens for aid against Corinth, c. **29**, 1. The Athenians make a defensive alliance with them

B.C.

and Pericles despatches ten ships under Lacedaemonius, son of Cimon.
Colony to the Propontis (Diod. Sic. XII 34, 5).

432/431 Ol. 87, 1. *Pythodorus.*
Indecisive naval engagement off Sybota (Thesprotis) between the Corinthians and Corcyraeans, in which the Athenians also take part.
Revolt of Potidaea, a colony of Corinth, from the Athenian alliance, c. 29, 4, Thuc. I cc. 56–66.
Congress at Sparta in which war is resolved on.
Pericles advises the Athenians to resist the Spartan demands, and carries the decree against the Megarians (c. 29, 4 ; c. 30, 3) excluding them from all harbours under the jurisdiction of Athens.
He is elected generalissimo over all his nine colleagues.
Prosecution of Aspasia for ἀσέβεια by the comic poet Hermippus, c. 32, 1.
Prosecution and imprisonment of Phidias for ἀσέβεια, c. 31, 2–5.
Anaxagoras also prosecuted (c. 32, 1); he withdraws (c. 32, 2) to Lampsacus, where he died about four years afterwards.
First year of the Peloponnesian war, Thuc. II 1–47. Aristot. Ἀθ. πολ. c. 27, 2 μετὰ δὲ τὴν ἐν Σαλαμῖνι ναυμαχίαν ἑνὸς δεῖν πεντηκόστῳ ἔτει ἐπὶ Πυθοδώρου ἄρχοντος ὁ πρὸς Πελοποννησίους ἐνέστη πόλεμος ἐν ᾧ κατακλησθεὶς ὁ δῆμος ἐν τῷ ἄστει καὶ συνεθισθεὶς ἐν ταῖς στρατείαις μισθοφορεῖν τὰ μὲν ἑκὼν τὰ δὲ ἄκων προῃρεῖτο τὴν πολιτείαν διοικεῖν αὐτός.

431/430 Ol. 87, 2. *Euthydemus.*
Attempt of the Thebans on Plataea.
Commencement of the fifteenth year of the Thirty Years' truce.
First invasion of Attica eighty days after by the Peloponnesians under Archidamus, c. 33, 3. After ravaging Oenoe, Eleusis, the Thriasian plain and Acharnae they return by Oropus.
Solar eclipse August 3rd (Thuc. II 28), c. 35, 1.
A body of cleruchs sent to Aegina to take the place

B.C.	
	of the expelled population. It thus becomes a strong outpost on the side of the Peloponnesus. The exiles are settled by the Lacedaemonians at Thyrea, c. **34**, 1.
Invasion of Megara by Pericles.
Attack on Pericles by Hermippus in his Μοῖραι, c. **33**, 6–7.
Pericles speaks the ἐπιτάφιος of those who had fallen in the first year of the war.
Euripidis *Medea*.
430/429	Ol. 87, 3. *Apollodorus*.
Second invasion of Attica by the Peloponnesians, who penetrate as far as Laureium and lay waste the whole country during forty days.
Outbreak of the plague at Athens, c. **34**, 3.
Naval expedition round Peloponnesus under the command of Pericles, c. **35**, 1 *note*.
On his return, Hagnon takes the fleet to Potidaea, c. **29**, 4, but the mortality among the troops and crews compels him to return after forty days' absence.
Pericles, becoming unpopular, is fined and suspended from the office of strategus, which he had held for fifteen years continuously (c. **35**, 4), in the last prytany of Euthydemus, the first of Apollodorus (Wilamowitz-Möllendorf, *Arist. u. Ath.* I p. 248). His reinstatement follows soon after for this year, c. **35**, 4.
429/428	Ol. 87, 4. *Epameinon*.
Capitulation of Potidaea on conditions after a siege of two years, which had cost the Athenians 2000 talents, Thuc. II 70, 2.
Phormion, in command of the Athenian fleet, gains two victories over the Peloponnesians in the Corinthian gulf.
Death of Pericles, September 1, c. **38**, 3, 4 (Thuc. II 65, 6, Athenaeus V 217 E).
Cleon acquires influence in public affairs (—422), c. **33**, 7; c. **35**, 4.
Birth of Plato (May).

ADDENDA ET CORRIGENDA

p. 4 CH. I § 3 l. 20 *add* :—θεωρῇ μόνον <ὁ νοῦς> ci Bergk § 5 l. 36 [ἐστιν] ci Bergk

p. 6 CH. III § 1 l. 7 *add* :—καὶ βεβαίως νόμους ἔθετο ci R Peppmüller

p. 7 § 2 l. 16 aut Ἀττικοί aut ποιηταί secludendum putat Bergk

p. 8 CH. IV § 2 l. 19 *add* :—ὥς φασ' ὁ Χείρων ci Bergk

p. 9 CH. V § 1 l. 3 *add* :—[μετεωρολογίας καί] ut glossema vocabuli μεταρσιολεσχίας ci Bergk || l. 7 συστάσει ἀθρύπτῳ . . . πραΰτητι . . . καταστολῇ . . . ἐκταραττομένῃ . . . πλάσματι . . . ἀθορύβῳ ci Bergk

p. 18 CH. X § 1 l. 7 *add*:—for εἰς λόχον Bergk ci μεθεὶς χόλον

p. 20 CH. X § 7 l. 68 *add* :—ἐπειδὴ δὲ Κίμων ἐτελεύτησε . . . οἱ [δ'] ἀριστοκρατικοί ci Bergk

p. 23 CH. XII § 2 l. 21 *add* :—ἀναγκαίοις ci Bergk ; l. 23 λίθους πολυτελεῖς [καὶ] ἀγάλμασι καὶ ναοῖς χιλιοταλάντοις ci Bergk

p. 30 CH. XV § 4 l. 35 *add* :—δεομένης ci Bergk

p. 41 CH. XXIII § 2 l. 21 *add* :—Bergk would read μόνους and transpose it after διαφέροντας

p. 47 CH. XXVII § 1 l. 5 *add* :—Bergk doubts about the change into αὖθις proposed by Sauppe || l. 8 Bergk transposes τὴν πόλιν after περιετείχιζε l. 5 || § 4 ll. 30 ff. Bergk transposes χαλκῆν ἀσπίδα . . . τῶν ἄνωθεν after κομίζεσθαι l. 34

p. 48 CH. XXVIII § 3 l. 19 *add*:—Bergk ci κοσμεῖν τὴν διήγησιν ἐπὶ τὸ πλέον or ἐπὶ βλάβῃ τῆς ἀληθείας

p. 52 CH. XXX § 1 l. 7 *add*:—Bergk also ci ἕνα and proposes ingeniously to read σὺ δ' αἴ κα μὴ καθελεῖν λῇς ἀλλά κτλ

p. 56 CH. XXXII § 3 l. 24 *add* :—Bergk proposes κατά but doubtfully

p. 57 l. 29 Bergk transposes τὸ δικαστήριον to l. 27 after φοβηθείς

P. 61 CH. XXXIV § 3 l. 33 *add* :—Bergk retains εἰς ἰατρόν and in l. 35 prefers πεισθέντες with Cobet to the vulgate ἀναπεισθέντες

P. 63 CH. XXXVI § 1 l. 2 *add* :— <κακὰ> καθάπερ ei Bergk

P. 66 CH. XXXVII § 2 l. 15 *add* :—Bergk would read περὶ τὸν οἶκον or τοῦ οἴκου ‖ § 5 l. 35 <ὅμως> ἡ παροῦσα δυστυχία ei Bergk

P. 67 CH. XXXVIII § 1 l. 6 καὶ σχολαίως ei Bergk

P. 108 CH. VIII § 6 l. 50 *add* :—ep. Lysias ἐπιτάφιος § 79 f. τοίγαρτοι ἀγήρατοι μὲν αὐτῶν αἱ μνῆμαι, ζηλωταὶ δ' ὑπὸ πάντων ἀνθρώπων αἱ τιμαί· οἳ πενθοῦνται μὲν διὰ τὴν φύσιν ὡς θνητοί, ὑμνοῦνται δ' ὡς ἀθάνατοι διὰ τὴν ἀρετήν.

P. 184 CH. XXXI § 2 l. 23 *add* :—J. A. Heikel *Beiträge z. Erkl. von Plutarchs Biogr. d. Per.* p. 17 raises a difficulty in reconciling this narrative with the law which enacted εἰ μὲν τἀληθῆ μηνύσειέ τις, εἶναι τὴν ἄδειαν, εἰ δὲ τὰ ψευδῆ, τεθνάναι acc. to Andocides *Myst.* § 20. Menon prayed for ἄδεια, because as a σύνεργος of Phidias he was involved in his guilt; but the charge of κλοπή, we are told, was unproved, and therefore according to this law he should have forfeited his life. Consequently the other charge also must have been laid by him, on which Phidias was found, presumably, guilty, unless we are to assume that he was really convicted of another distinct charge of ἀσέβεια.

P. 185 CH. XXXI § 4 l. 34 *add at end of note* :—M. Salomon Reinach in a notice of Furtwängler's *Meisterwerke der Griechischen Plastik*, communicated to the *Revue critique d'histoire et de littérature* 5 Février 1894, says : 'Sur le bouclier même de Parthénos, Phidias est figuré sous les traits d'un homme mûr, presque âgé. Si M. F. nie qu'il y ait là un portrait de Phidias, malgré Plutarque, il ne donne aucune bonne raison de son scepticisme.'

On Plutarch's portrait of Pericles on the shield of the Parthenos, see Michaelis *Parthenon* p. 268 and Plate XV; also Overbeck *Gesch. d. Plast.* I 255. The famous (ep. *CIA.* I 102, 403) portrait-bust of Pericles by Cresilas, which justified his surname 'the Olympian,' was put up, Furtwängler suggests, in B.C. 439 to commemorate his success at Samos. The bust of Pericles in the British Museum is now generally taken to be a copy of this.

ὅσον χρόνον προύστη τῆς πόλεως, ἐγένετο μεγίστη . . . αἴτιον δ' ἦν ὅτι ἐκεῖνος μὲν δυνατὸς ὢν τῷ τε ἀξιώματι καὶ τῇ γνώμῃ χρημάτων τε διαφανῶς ἀδωρότατος γενόμενος κατεῖχε τὸ πλῆθος ἐλευθέρως, καὶ οὐκ ἤγετο μᾶλλον ὑπ' αὐτοῦ ἢ αὐτὸς ἦγε, διὰ τὸ μὴ κτώμενος ἐξ οὐ προσηκόντων τὴν δύναμιν πρὸς ἡδονήν τι λέγειν ἀλλ' ἔχων ἐπ' ἀξιώσει καὶ πρὸς ὀργήν τι ἀντειπεῖν

THUCYDIDES

ΠΛΟΥΤΑΡΧΟΥ

ΒΙΩΝ ΠΑΡΑΛΛΗΛΩΝ

ΒΙΒΛΙΟΝ ΔΕΚΑΤΟΝ

—

ΠΕΡΙΚΛΗΣ

The larger Numerals in heavy type in the margin represent the pages of the Paris Edition a. 1624 (= Frankfurt a. 1599) by which references are sometimes made.

For fuller information concerning the MSS and Editions of Plutarch's *Lives*, the reader may consult my edition of the *Life of Timoleon* (Cambridge 1889). The *Codex Seitenstettensis* (**S**)—the oldest and most important MS containing the *Life of Pericles*—is preserved in the Benedictine Monastery of Seitenstetten in Austria. It is a parchment MS of the XIth century, and may be regarded as the best representative of the group to which F^a—the XVth century Paris MS, **1676** in the National Library—belongs, and probably a transcript of it. Neither of these MSS, however, is of such value in this *Life* as in some of the others: indeed, some of the readings in the two Paris MSS **1672** (**B**) and **1673** (**C**)— the former ascribed by Wyttenbach to the 14th century, by Bähr to the 16th, the latter of the 13th century—are to be preferred. Fuhr's revised text of Sintenis and that of Blass are based on **S**.

St = H. Stephanus (Estienne) 13 voll. 8vo Geneva 1572.
Br = A. Bryan, 5 voll. 4to London 1723-9.
Rk = J. J. Reiske, 12 voll. 8vo Paris 1774-82.
Ko = Adamant Koraës (Coray) Paris 1809-1814.
Bk = Immanuel Bekker, 5 voll. Tauchnitz, Leipzig 1855-7.
Si^1 = the *Life of Pericles*, with Latin Commentary, by C. Sintenis, Leipzig 1835.
Si^2 = Sintenis's critical ed. 4 voll. Koehler, Leipzig 1839-46.
Si^3 = Sintenis's ed. in Teubner's *Bibliotheca*, Leipzig 1877.
Si^4 = Sintenis's ed. of the *Life* with German notes, Weidmann, Leipzig 1851.
Do = Döhner, Bibliothèque Didot, 2 vols. Paris 1846-7.
Bl^1 = the *Life of Pericles* by Fr. Blass, with German notes, Teubner, Leipzig 1872 ; Bl^2 = 2nd ed. of same 1883.
Fu = K. Fuhr's revised ed. of Si^4, Weidmann, Berlin 1880.
Jb = A. Jacob's *Vie de Périclès*, Hachette, Paris 1893.
x = *lectiones anonymi* printed at the end of the Frankfurt ed. 1599, being chiefly conjectures of Xylander.
Hu = the Editor.
ci = conjectures *or* is conjectured by.
cl = *collato* or *collatis*, 'comparing.'
codd = the MSS.
corr = corrected by.
del = omitted by.
v = vulgo or vulgate, the common reading.

ΠΛΟΥΤΑΡΧΟΥ

ΒΙΩΝ ΠΑΡΑΛΛΗΛΩΝ

ΒΙΒΛΙΟΝ ΔΕΚΑΤΟΝ

ΠΡΟΟΙΜΙΟΝ

1 Ξένους τινὰς ἐν Ῥώμῃ πλουσίους κυνῶν τέκνα καὶ πιθήκων ἐν τοῖς κόλποις περιφέροντας καὶ ἀγαπῶντας ἰδὼν ὁ Καῖσαρ, ὡς ἔοικεν, ἠρώτησεν, εἰ παιδία παρ' αὐτοῖς οὐ τίκτουσιν αἱ γυναῖκες, ἡγεμονικῶς σφόδρα νουθετήσας τοὺς τὸ φύσει φιλητικὸν ἐν ἡμῖν καὶ φιλόστοργον εἰς θηρία καταναλίσκοντας ἀνθρώποις ὀφειλόμενον. ἆρ' οὖν, ἐπεὶ φιλομαθές τι κέκτηται καὶ φιλο- 2 θέαμον ἡμῶν ἡ ψυχὴ φύσει, λόγον ἔχει ψέγειν τοὺς καταχρωμένους τούτῳ πρὸς τὰ μηδεμιᾶς

CH. 1 § 1 l. 1 Si² after x ci but does not adopt κυνῶν τε καὶ πιθήκων ἔκγονα: Blass ci κυνῶν τ' ἔκ < γο >να καὶ πιθήκων but see comm ‖ 6 ἡγεμονικῶς vulgo: Cobet ci κηδεμονικῶς, *benigne et leniter*: γελοίως ci Bergk

ἄξια σπουδῆς ἀκούσματα καὶ θεάματα, τῶν δὲ καλῶν καὶ ὠφελίμων παραμελοῦντας; τῇ μὲν γὰρ αἰσθήσει κατὰ πάθος <τὸ> τῆς πληγῆς ἀντιλαμβανομένῃ τῶν προστυγχανόντων ἴσως ἀνάγκη πᾶν τὸ φαινόμενον, ἄν τε χρήσιμον ἄν 3 τ' ἄχρηστον ᾖ, θεωρεῖν, τῷ νῷ δ' ἕκαστος, εἰ βούλοιτο χρῆσθαι, καὶ τρέπειν ἑαυτὸν ἀεὶ καὶ μεταβάλλειν ῥᾷστα πρὸς τὸ δοκοῦν πέφυκεν, ὥστε χρὴ διώκειν τὸ βέλτιστον, ἵνα μὴ θεωρῇ μόνον, ἀλλὰ καὶ τρέφηται τῷ θεωρεῖν. ὡς γὰρ ὀφθαλμῷ χρόα πρόσφορος, ἧς τὸ ἀνθηρὸν ἅμα καὶ τερπνὸν ἀναζωπυρεῖ καὶ τρέφει τὴν ὄψιν, οὕτω τὴν διάνοιαν ἐπάγειν δεῖ θεάμασιν ἃ τῷ χαίρειν πρὸς τὸ οἰκεῖον αὐτὴν ἀγαθὸν ἐκκαλεῖ· 4 ταῦτα δ' ἔστιν ἐν τοῖς ἀπ' ἀρετῆς ἔργοις, ἃ καὶ ζῆλόν τινα καὶ προθυμίαν ἀγωγὸν εἰς μίμησιν ἐμποιεῖ τοῖς ἱστορήσασιν. ἐπεὶ τῶν γ' ἄλλων οὐκ εὐθὺς ἀκολουθεῖ τῷ θαυμάσαι τὸ πραχθὲν ὁρμὴ πρὸς τὸ πρᾶξαι· πολλάκις δὲ καὶ τοὐναντίον χαίροντες τῷ ἔργῳ τοῦ δημιουργοῦ καταφρονοῦμεν, ὡς ἐπὶ τῶν μύρων καὶ τῶν ἁλουργῶν, τούτοις μὲν ἡδόμεθα, τοὺς δὲ βαφεῖς καὶ μυρεψοὺς ἀνελευθέρους ἡγούμεθα καὶ βαναύσους. 5 διὸ καλῶς μὲν Ἀντισθένης ἀκούσας ὅτι σπουδαῖός ἐστιν αὐλητὴς Ἰσμηνίας "Ἀλλ' ἄνθρωπος" ἔφη "μοχθηρός· οὐ γὰρ ἂν οὕτω σπουδαῖος

§ 2 l. 14 τῆς πληγῆς A S Fᵃ (Rk who however wrongly makes it depend upon ἀντιλαμβανομένῃ, Si Do Bk Fu): < τὸ > τῆς πληγῆς ci Blass: τὴν πληγήν v. Ko would omit altogether
§ 3 l. 24 τῷ χαρίεντι, *venustate, amoenitate sua* ci Rk
§ 4 l. 28 τοῖς ἱστορήσασιν, *iis qui ciusmodi spectacula noscitarunt*, ci Amyot (Rk Ko Si Do Bk Fu Bl): τοῖς ἱστορήμασιν v

ἦν αὐλητής·" ὁ δὲ Φίλιππος πρὸς τὸν υἱὸν ἐπιτερπῶς ἔν τινι πότῳ ψήλαντα καὶ τεχνικῶς εἶπεν "Οὐκ αἰσχύνῃ καλῶς οὕτω ψάλλων;" ἀρκεῖ γὰρ ἂν βασιλεὺς ἀκροᾶσθαι ψαλλόντων σχολάζῃ, καὶ πολὺ νέμει ταῖς Μούσαις ἑτέρων ἀγωνιζομένων τὰ τοιαῦτα θεατὴς γιγνόμενος.

II Ἡ δ' αὐτουργία τῶν ταπεινῶν τῆς εἰς τὰ καλὰ ῥᾳθυμίας μάρτυρα τὸν ἐν τοῖς ἀχρήστοις πόνον παρέχεται καθ' αὑτῆς· καὶ οὐδεὶς εὐφυὴς νέος ἢ τὸν ἐν Πίσῃ θεασάμενος Δία γενέσθαι Φειδίας ἐπεθύμησεν ἢ τὴν Ἥραν τὴν ἐν Ἄργει Πολύκλειτος, οὐδ' Ἀνακρέων ἢ Φιλητᾶς ἢ Ἀρχίλοχος ἡσθεὶς αὐτῶν τοῖς ποιήμασιν. οὐ γὰρ ἀναγκαῖον, εἰ τέρπει τὸ ἔργον ὡς χαρίεν, ἄξιον σπουδῆς εἶναι τὸν εἰργασμένον. ὅθεν οὐδ' ὠφελεῖ τὰ τοιαῦτα τοὺς θεωμένους, πρὸς ἃ μιμητικὸς οὐ γίνεται ζῆλος οὐδὲ ἀνάδοσις κινοῦσα προθυμίαν καὶ ὁρμὴν ἐπὶ τὴν ἐξομοίωσιν. ἀλλ' ἥ γε ἀρετὴ ταῖς πράξεσιν εὐθὺς οὕτω διατίθησιν, ὥστε ἅμα θαυμάζεσθαι τὰ ἔργα καὶ ζηλοῦσθαι τοὺς εἰργασμένους. τῶν μὲν γὰρ ἐκ τῆς τύχης ἀγαθῶν τὰς κτήσεις καὶ ἀπολαύσεις, τῶν δ' ἀπ' ἀρετῆς τὰς πράξεις ἀγαπῶμεν, καὶ τὰ μὲν ἡμῖν παρ' ἑτέρων, τὰ δὲ μᾶλλον ἑτέροις παρ' ἡμῶν ὑπάρχειν βουλόμεθα. τὸ γὰρ καλὸν ἐφ' αὑτὸ πρακτικῶς κινεῖ καὶ πρακτικὴν εὐθὺς ὁρμὴν

CH. II § 1 l. 6 Φιλητᾶς ci Bryan (Si Do Bk Fu): Φιλήμων Ko Bl v: Cobet ci Ἱππῶναξ, a name found elsewhere in conjunction with that of Archilochus

§ 2 l. 12 ὁρμὴν ci Rk (Fu Bl): ἀφορμήν, *repugnantium, aversationem* in the language of the Stoics, St Ko Si Do Bk vulgo

ἐντίθησιν, ἠθοποιοῦν οὐ τῇ μιμήσει τὸν θεατήν, ἀλλὰ τῇ ἱστορίᾳ τοῦ ἔργου τὴν προαίρεσιν 4 παρεχόμενον. Ἔδοξεν οὖν καὶ ἡμῖν ἐνδιατρῖψαι τῇ περὶ τοὺς βίους ἀναγραφῇ· καὶ τοῦτο τὸ βιβλίον δέκατον συντετάχαμεν τὸν Περικλέους βίον καὶ τὸν Φαβίου Μαξίμου τοῦ διαπολεμήσαντος πρὸς Ἀννίβαν περιέχον, ἀνδρῶν κατά τε τὰς ἄλλας ἀρετὰς ὁμοίων μάλιστα δὲ πραότητι καὶ δικαιοσύνῃ καὶ τῷ δύνασθαι φέρειν δήμων καὶ συναρχόντων ἀγνωμοσύνας ὠφελιμωτάτων ταῖς πατρίσι γενομένων. εἰ δ' ὀρθῶς στοχαζόμεθα τοῦ δέοντος, ἔξεστι κρίνειν ἐκ τῶν γραφομένων.

ΠΕΡΙΚΛΕΟΥΣ ΒΙΟΣ

III Περικλῆς γὰρ ἦν τῶν μὲν φυλῶν Ἀκαμαντίδης, τῶν δὲ δήμων Χολαργεύς, οἴκου δὲ καὶ γένους τοῦ πρώτου κατ' ἀμφοτέρους. Ξάνθιππος γὰρ ὁ νικήσας ἐν Μυκάλῃ τοὺς βασιλέως στρατηγοὺς ἔγημεν Ἀγαρίστην Κλεισθένους ἔγγονον, ὃς ἐξήλασε Πεισιστρατίδας καὶ κατέλυσε τὴν τυραννίδα γενναίως καὶ νόμους ἔθετο καὶ πολιτείαν ἄριστα κεκραμένην πρὸς ὁμόνοιαν καὶ 2 σωτηρίαν κατέστησεν. αὕτη κατὰ τοὺς ὕπνους

§ 4 l. 29 πραότητι καὶ δικαιοσύνῃ B F[a] S corr[2] (Ko Blass): πραότητα καὶ δικαιοσύνην S Rk Si Do Fu v : διὰ πραότητα καὶ δικαιοσύνην ci Bergk ‖ 32–33 εἰ δ' ὀρθῶς . . . γραφομένων om S, bracketed by Fuhr as an addition of late MSS ‖ 32 τοῦ δέοντος v : τοῦ πρέποντος St (Fuhr)
CH. III § 1 l. 6 ἔγγονος and ἔκγονος are both found in inscriptions of the vth and ivth cent. : the former fell into disuse in the iiird cent., to reappear in the iind cent. A.D. Meisterhans[2] p. 83

ἔδοξε τεκεῖν λέοντα καὶ μεθ' ἡμέρας ὀλίγας
ἔτεκε Περικλέα, τὰ μὲν ἄλλα τὴν ἰδέαν τοῦ
σώματος ἄμεμπτον, προμήκη δὲ τῇ κεφαλῇ καὶ
ἀσύμμετρον. ὅθεν αἱ μὲν εἰκόνες αὐτοῦ *His personal*
σχεδὸν ἅπασαι κράνεσι περιέχονται, *appearance ridiculed*
μὴ βουλομένων, ὡς ἔοικε, τῶν τεχνιτῶν *by the comic poets of the*
ἐξονειδίζειν. οἱ δ' Ἀττικοὶ ποιηταὶ *day.*
cχινοκέφαλοΝ αὐτὸν ἐκάλουν· τὴν γὰρ σκίλλαν
ἔστιν ὅτε καὶ σχῖνον ὀνομάζουσι. τῶν δὲ 3
κωμικῶν ὁ μὲν Κρατῖνός φησιν ἐν Χείρωσι

Cτάcιc Δὲ καὶ πρεcΒυγενὴc Κρόνοc ἀλλήλοιcι μιγέντε
Μέγιcτον τίκτετον τύραννον,
ὅν Δὴ κεφαληγερέταν θεοὶ καλέουcιν·

καὶ πάλιν ἐν Νεμέσει

μόλ', ὦ Ζεῦ ξένιε καὶ καράνιε.

Τηλεκλείδης δὲ ποτὲ μὲν ὑπὸ τῶν πραγμάτων 4
ἠπορημένον καθῆσθαί φησιν αὐτὸν ἐν τῇ πόλει
καρηΒαροῦντα, ποτὲ Δὲ

Μόνον ἐκ κεφαλῆς ἑνδεκακλίνου θόρυΒον πολὺν
ἐξανατέλλειν·

ὁ δ' Εὔπολις ἐν τοῖς Δήμοις πυνθανόμενος περὶ
ἑκάστου τῶν ἀναβεβηκότων ἐξ ᾅδου δημαγωγῶν,
ὡς ὁ Περικλῆς ὠνομάσθη τελευταῖος·

ὅ τι περ κεφάλαιον τῶν κάτωθεν ἤγαγες.

§ 2 l. 12 τῇ κεφαλῇ B F^a S M^c (Fu Bl): τὴν κεφαλήν St Ko Si Do Bk vulgo: τὴν κεφαλὴν . . . ἔχοντα ci Bergk
§ 3 l. 20 Κρόνος x (Ko Si Bk Fu Bl): Χρόνος v ‖ 24 καράνιε Kock *CGF* i 49: κάριε S v: καραιέ F^a (Do Fuhr Blass¹): Καραῖε Meineke after Unger: καράϊε Blass²: μακροκάρηνε Xylander: μακάριε St Bk Ko v
§ 4 l. 28 μόνον, ποτὲ δ' ἐκ κεφαλῆς ci Bergk

IV Διδάσκαλον δ' αὐτοῦ τῶν μουσικῶν οἱ πλεῖστοι Δάμωνα γενέσθαι λέγουσιν, οὗ φασι δεῖν τοὔνομα βραχύνοντας τὴν προτέραν συλλαβὴν ἐκφέρειν· Ἀριστοτέλης δὲ παρὰ Πυθοκλείδῃ μουσικὴν διαπονηθῆναι τὸν ἄνδρα φησίν. ὁ δὲ Δάμων ἔοικεν ἄκρος ὢν σοφιστὴς καταδύεσθαι μὲν εἰς τὸ τῆς μουσικῆς ὄνομα πρὸς τοὺς πολλοὺς ἐπικρυπτόμενος τὴν δεινότητα, τῷ δὲ Περικλεῖ συνῆν καθάπερ ἀθλητῇ τῶν πολιτικῶν ἀλείπτης 2 καὶ διδάσκαλος. οὐ μὴν ἔλαθεν ὁ Δάμων τῇ λύρᾳ παρακαλύμματι χρώμενος, ἀλλ' ὡς μεγαλοπράγμων καὶ φιλοτύραννος ἐξωστρακίσθη καὶ παρέσχε τοῖς κωμικοῖς διατριβήν. ὁ γοῦν Πλάτων καὶ πυνθανόμενον αὐτοῦ τινα πεποίηκεν οὕτω·

ΠΡΩΤΟΝ ΜΕΝ ΟΥΝ ΜΟΙ ΛΕΞΟΝ, ἈΝΤΙΒΟΛΩ· ΣΥ ΓΆΡ,
ΩΣ ΦΑΣΙ, ΧΕΙΡΩΝ ἘΞΕΘΡΕΨΑΣ ΠΕΡΙΚΛΕΑ.

3 διήκουσε δὲ Περικλῆς καὶ Ζήνωνος τοῦ Ἐλεάτου, πραγματευομένου μὲν < καὶ αὐτοῦ > περὶ φύσιν, ὡς Παρμενίδης, ἐλεγκτικὴν δέ τινα καὶ δι' ἀντιλογίας κατακλείουσαν εἰς ἀπορίαν ἐξασκήσαντος ἕξιν, ὥς που καὶ Τίμων ὁ Φλειάσιος εἴρηκε διὰ τούτων·

CH. IV § 2 l. 19 ὥς φασι, Χείρων ci Cobet (Bl²): ὥς φασιν, ὁ Χείρων Vulcobius Si Do Bk Fu Bl¹ : ὥς φασιν, ὦ Χείρων St Ko v
§ 3 l. 21 πραγματευομένου μὲν < καὶ αὐτοῦ > περὶ φύσιν, ci Hu cl c. 21, 2: πραγματευομένου < μέν > Rk Ko Bl: πραγματευομένου v ‖ 24 ὥς που καὶ B F^a S (Ko Bk Fu Bl): ὥσπερ καί Si Do v ‖ Φλειάσιος Bl², as the more correct form ; but, as Φλιάσιος is found in inscriptions of the imperial age, Plut. may well have spelt it so

ἀμφοτερογλώccoy τε μέγα cθένοc ογκ ἀλαπαδνόν
Ζήνωνοc, πάντων ἐπιλήπτοροc.

Ὁ δὲ πλεῖστα Περικλεῖ συγγενόμενος καὶ μάλιστα 4
περιθεὶς ὄγκον αὐτῷ καὶ φρόνημα δημαγωγίας
ἐμβριθέστερον ὅλως τε μετεωρίσας καὶ συνεξάρας
τὸ ἀξίωμα τοῦ ἤθους Ἀναξαγόρας ἦν ὁ Κλαζομένιος, ὃν οἱ τότ' ἄνθρωποι Νοῦν προσηγόρευον,
εἴτε τὴν σύνεσιν αὐτοῦ μεγάλην εἰς φυσιολογίαν
καὶ περιττὴν διαφανεῖσαν θαυμάσαντες, εἴθ' ὅτι
τοῖς ὅλοις πρῶτος οὐ τύχην οὐδ' ἀνάγκην
διακοσμήσεως ἀρχήν, ἀλλὰ νοῦν ἐπέστησε καθαρὸν καὶ ἄκρατον ἐν μεμιγμένοις πᾶσι τοῖς ἄλλοις,
ἀποκρίνοντα τὰς ὁμοιομερείας. V τοῦτον ὑπερ- 1
φυῶς τὸν ἄνδρα θαυμάσας ὁ Περικλῆς καὶ τῆς
λεγομένης μετεωρολογίας καὶ μεταρσιολεσχίας
ὑποπιμπλάμενος, οὐ μόνον, ὡς ἔοικε, τὸ φρόνημα σοβαρὸν καὶ τὸν λόγον ὑψηλὸν εἶχε καὶ
καθαρὸν ὀχλικῆς καὶ πανούργου βωμολοχίας,
ἀλλὰ καὶ προσώπου σύστασις ἄθρυπτος εἰς
γέλωτα καὶ πραότης πορείας καὶ καταστολὴ
περιβολῆς πρὸς οὐδὲν ἐκταραττομένη πάθος ἐν
τῷ λέγειν καὶ πλάσμα φωνῆς ἀθόρυβον καὶ ὅσα
τοιαῦτα πάντας θαυμαστῶς ἐξέπληττε.
λοιδορούμενος γοῦν ποτε καὶ κακῶς ἀκούων ὑπό 2
τινος τῶν βδελυρῶν καὶ ἀκολάστων
ὅλην ἡμέραν ὑπέμεινε σιωπῇ κατ' Anecdote concerning Pericles.
ἀγοράν, ἅμα τι τῶν ἐπειγόντων κατα-
πραττόμενος· ἑσπέρας δ' ἀπῄει κοσμίως

§ 4 l. 37 ἐν μεμιγμένοις ci Rk (Ko Si Do Bk Fu Bl): ἐμμεμιγ-
μένοις codd : συμμεμιγμένοις π. τ. ἄ. ἐναποκρίνοντα ci Bergk

οἴκαδε παρακολουθοῦντος τοῦ ἀνθρώπου καὶ πάσῃ χρωμένου βλασφημίᾳ πρὸς αὐτόν. ὡς δ' ἔμελλεν εἰσιέναι σκότους ὄντος ἤδη, προσέταξέ τινι τῶν οἰκετῶν φῶς λαβόντι παραπέμψαι καὶ καταστῆσαι πρὸς τὴν οἰκίαν τὸν ἄνθρωπον.

The poet Ion finds fault with his brusque and disdainful manner, which he contrasts with the tact and condescension of Cimon.

Ὁ δὲ ποιητὴς Ἴων μοθωνικήν φησι τὴν ὁμιλίαν καὶ ὑπότυφον εἶναι τοῦ Περικλέους, καὶ ταῖς μεγαλαυχίαις αὐτοῦ πολλὴν ὑπεροψίαν ἀναμεμῖχθαι καὶ περιφρόνησιν τῶν ἄλλων· ἐπαινεῖ δὲ τὸ Κίμωνος ἐμμελὲς καὶ ὑγρὸν καὶ μεμουσωμένον ἐν ταῖς συμπεριφοραῖς. ἀλλ' Ἴωνα μέν, ὥσπερ τραγικὴν διδασκαλίαν, ἀξιοῦντα τὴν ἀρετὴν ἔχειν τι πάντως καὶ σατυρικὸν μέρος ἐῶμεν· τοὺς δὲ τοῦ Περι-

Zeno's rebuke of such fault-finders.

κλέους τὴν σεμνότητα δοξοκοπίαν τε καὶ τῦφον ἀποκαλοῦντας ὁ Ζήνων παρεκάλει καὶ αὐτούς τι τοιοῦτο δοξοκοπεῖν, ὡς τῆς προσποιήσεως αὐτῆς τῶν καλῶν ὑποποιούσης τινὰ λεληθότως ζῆλον καὶ συνήθειαν.

VI Οὐ μόνον δὲ ταῦτα τῆς Ἀναξαγόρου συνουσίας ἀπέλαυσε Περικλῆς, ἀλλὰ

Freedom from superstition another advantage Pericles gained from his intercourse with Anaxagoras.

καὶ δεισιδαιμονίας δοκεῖ γενέσθαι καθυπέρτερος, ὅσην τὸ πρὸς τὰ μετέωρα θάμβος ἐνεργάζεται τοῖς αὐτῶν τε τούτων τὰς αἰτίας ἀγνοοῦσι καὶ περὶ τὰ

CH. V § 3 l. 28 συμπεριφοραῖς ci Madvig (Cobet Fu Bl): περιφοραῖς Ko Si Do Bk v
CH. VI § 1 l. 2 συνουσίας Si Bk Fu Bl v: συνηθείας S ‖ 4 ὅσην τό Ko Fu Bl: ὅση codd Bk: ὅσην Si Do: ἥν Cobet Bergk ‖ 5 ἐνεργάζεται, *in hominum animis excitat* S Fᵃ (Ko Si Bk Fu Bl): ἐργάζεται St Do v

θεῖα δαιμονῶσι καὶ ταραττομένοις δι' ἀπειρίαν αὐτῶν, ἣν ὁ φυσικὸς λόγος ἀπαλλάττων ἀντὶ τῆς φοβερᾶς καὶ φλεγμαινούσης δεισιδαιμονίας τὴν ἀσφαλῆ μετ' ἐλπίδων ἀγαθῶν εὐσέβειαν ἐνεργάζεται. Λέγεται δέ ποτε κριοῦ μονόκερω κεφαλὴν ἐξ ἀγροῦ τῷ Περικλεῖ κομισθῆναι, καὶ Λάμπωνα μὲν τὸν μάντιν, ὡς εἶδε τὸ κέρας ἰσχυρὸν καὶ στερεὸν ἐκ μέσου τοῦ μετώπου πεφυκός, εἰπεῖν ὅτι δυεῖν οὐσῶν ἐν τῇ πόλει δυναστειῶν, τῆς Θουκυδίδου καὶ Περικλέους, εἰς ἕνα περιστήσεται τὸ κράτος παρ' ᾧ γένοιτο τὸ σημεῖον· τὸν δ' Ἀναξαγόραν τοῦ κρανίου διακόπεντος ἐπιδεῖξαι τὸν ἐγκέφαλον οὐ πεπληρωκότα τὴν βάσιν, ἀλλ' ὀξὺν ὥσπερ ᾠὸν ἐκ τοῦ παντὸς ἀγγείου συνωλισθηκότα κατὰ τὸν τόπον ἐκεῖνον, ὅθεν ἡ ῥίζα τοῦ κέρατος εἶχε τὴν ἀρχήν. καὶ τότε μὲν θαυμασθῆναι τὸν Ἀναξαγόραν ὑπὸ τῶν παρόντων, ὀλίγῳ δ' ὕστερον τὸν Λάμπωνα, τοῦ μὲν Θουκυδίδου καταλυθέντος, τῶν δὲ τοῦ δήμου πραγμάτων ὁμαλῶς ἁπάντων ὑπὸ τῷ Περικλεῖ γενομένων. ἐκώλυε δ' οὐδέν, οἶμαι, καὶ τὸν φυσικὸν ἐπιτυγχάνειν καὶ τὸν μάντιν, τοῦ μὲν τὴν αἰτίαν, τοῦ δὲ τὸ τέλος καλῶς ἐκλαμβάνοντος· ὑπέκειτο γὰρ τῷ μέν, ἐκ τίνων γέγονε καὶ πῶς πέφυκε θεωρῆσαι, τῷ δέ, πρὸς τί γέγονε καὶ τί σημαίνει προειπεῖν. οἱ δὲ τῆς αἰτίας τὴν εὕρεσιν ἀναίρεσιν εἶναι τοῦ σημείου λέγοντες οὐκ

§ 3 l. 31 γέγονε ci Rk (Ko Si Do Bk Fu Bl): γεγονέναι St v
§ 4 l. 31 τοῦ σημείου λέγοντες, a transposition due to Sintenis to avoid the hiatus (Fu Bl): λέγοντες τοῦ σημείου v

ἐπινοοῦσιν ἄμα τοῖς θείοις καὶ τὰ τεχνητὰ τῶν
συμβόλων ἀθετοῦντες, ψόφους τε δίσκων καὶ
φῶτα πυρσῶν καὶ γνωμόνων ἀποσκιασμούς· ὧν
ἕκαστον αἰτίᾳ τινὶ καὶ κατασκευῇ σημεῖον εἶναί
τινος πεποίηται.   Ταῦτα μὲν οὖν ἴσως ἑτέρας
ἐστὶ πραγματείας.   VII ὁ δὲ Περικλῆς νέος

Pericles' introduction to public life.
μὲν ὢν σφόδρα τὸν δῆμον εὐλαβεῖτο·
καὶ γὰρ ἐδόκει Πεισιστράτῳ τῷ τυ-
ράννῳ τὸ εἶδος ἐμφερὴς εἶναι, τήν τε
φωνὴν ἡδεῖαν οὖσαν αὐτοῦ καὶ τὴν γλῶτταν
εὔτροχον ἐν τῷ διαλέγεσθαι καὶ ταχεῖαν οἱ
σφόδρα γέροντες <γνόντες> ἐξεπλήττοντο πρὸς
τὴν ὁμοιότητα· πλούτου δὲ καὶ γένους προσόντος
αὐτῷ λαμπροῦ καὶ φίλων, οἳ πλεῖστον ἠδύναντο,
φοβούμενος ἐξοστρακισθῆναι, τῶν μὲν πολιτικῶν
οὐδὲν ἔπραττεν, ἐν δὲ ταῖς στρατείαις ἀνὴρ
ἀγαθὸς ἦν καὶ φιλοκίνδυνος.   ἐπεὶ δ' Ἀριστείδης
μὲν ἀποτεθνήκει καὶ Θεμιστοκλῆς ἐξεπεπτώκει,
Κίμωνα δ' αἱ στρατεῖαι τὰ πολλὰ τῆς Ἑλλάδος
ἔξω κατεῖχον, οὕτω δὴ φέρων ὁ Περικλῆς

He espouses the popular party, contrary to his natural bias, as a measure of safety.
τῷ δήμῳ προσένειμεν ἑαυτόν, ἀντὶ τῶν
πλουσίων καὶ ὀλίγων τὰ τῶν πολλῶν
καὶ πενήτων ἑλόμενος παρὰ τὴν αὑτοῦ
φύσιν ἥκιστα δημοτικὴν οὖσαν.   ἀλλ',
ὡς ἔοικε, δεδιὼς μὲν ὑποψίᾳ περιπεσεῖν τυραννίδος, ὁρῶν δ' ἀριστοκρατικὸν τὸν Κίμωνα καὶ
διαφερόντως ὑπὸ τῶν καλῶν κἀγαθῶν ἀνδρῶν
ἀγαπώμενον, ὑπῆλθε τοὺς πολλοὺς ἀσφάλειαν

    CH. VII § 1 l. 7 the construction is awkward without γνόντες,
the omission of which is easily accounted for by lipography
|| 9 ἠδύναντο Si Bk Bl v; ἐδύναντο S (Fuhr)

μὲν ἑαυτῷ, δύναμιν δὲ κατ' ἐκείνου παρασκευαζόμενος. εὐθὺς δὲ καὶ τοῖς περὶ τὴν
δίαιταν ἑτέραν τάξιν ἐπέθηκεν. ὁδόν
τε γὰρ ἐν ἄστει μίαν ἑωρᾶτο τὴν ἐπ'
ἀγορὰν καὶ τὸ βουλευτήριον πορευόμενος, κλήσεις
τε δείπνων καὶ τὴν τοιαύτην ἅπασαν φιλοφροσύνην καὶ συνήθειαν ἐξέλιπεν, ὡς ἐν οἷς
ἐπολιτεύσατο χρόνοις μακροῖς γενομένοις πρὸς
μηδένα τῶν φίλων ἐπὶ δεῖπνον ἐλθεῖν, πλὴν
Εὐρυπτολέμου τοῦ ἀνεψιοῦ γαμοῦντος ἄχρι τῶν
σπονδῶν παραγενόμενος εὐθὺς ἐξανέστη. δειναὶ
γὰρ αἱ φιλοφροσύναι παντὸς ὄγκου περιγενέσθαι,
καὶ δυσφύλακτον ἐν συνηθείᾳ τὸ πρὸς δόξαν
σεμνόν ἐστι· τῆς ἀληθινῆς δ' ἀρετῆς κάλλιστα
φαίνεται τὰ μάλιστα φαινόμενα, καὶ τῶν ἀγαθῶν
ἀνδρῶν οὐδὲν οὕτω θαυμάσιον τοῖς ἐκτὸς ὡς ὁ
καθ' ἡμέραν βίος τοῖς συνοῦσιν. ὁ δὲ
καὶ τῷ δήμῳ, τὸ συνεχὲς φεύγων καὶ
τὸν κόρον, οἷον ἐκ διαλειμμάτων ἐπλησίαζεν, οὐκ ἐπὶ παντὶ πράγματι λέγων
οὐδ' ἀεὶ παριὼν εἰς τὸ πλῆθος, ἀλλ'
ἑαυτὸν ὥσπερ τὴν Σαλαμινίαν τριήρη
(φησὶ Κριτόλαος) πρὸς τὰς μεγάλας
χρείας ἐπιδιδούς, τἆλλα δὲ φίλους καὶ
ῥήτορας ἑτέρους καθιεὶς ἔπραττεν. ὧν ἕνα φασὶ

§ 4 l. 26 ἐπέθηκεν C (Ko Si Do Bk Fu Bl): ὑπέθηκεν St v
§ 5 l. 37 σεμνόν ἐστι· τῆς ἀληθινῆς δ' ci Br (Ko Si Do Bk Fu Bl): σεμνόν· ἐπὶ τῆς ἀ. δ' St v ‖ 38 μάλιστα vulgo: ἥκιστα ci Cobet: ἐλάχιστα ci Bergk ‖ 41 τῷ δήμῳ ci HSauppe (Fu Bl): τοῦ δήμου Si Bk v ‖ 47 φίλους καὶ ῥήτορας ἑτέρους ci Xylander Geel (Ko Si Bk Fu Bl): φίλους καὶ ἑταίρους ῥήτορας (*i.e.* 'as speakers') Holzapfel with codd, Bergk

γενέσθαι τὸν Ἐφιάλτην, ὃς κατέλυσε τὸ κράτος τῆς ἐξ Ἀρείου πάγου βουλῆς, πολλήν, κατὰ τὸν Πλάτωνα, καὶ ἄκρατον τοῖς πολίταις ἐλευθερίαν οἰνοχοῶν· ὑφ᾽ ἧς, ὥσπερ ἵππον, ἐξυβρίσαντα τὸν δῆμον οἱ κωμῳδοποιοὶ λέγουσι πειθαρχεῖν οὐκέτι τολμᾶν ἀλλὰ δάκνειν τὴν Εὔβοιαν καὶ ταῖς νήσοις ἐπιπηδᾶν.

VIII. Τῇ μέντοι περὶ τὸν βίον κατασκευῇ καὶ τῷ μεγέθει τοῦ φρονήματος ἁρμόζοντα λόγον, ὥσπερ ὄργανον, ἐξαρτυόμενος παρενέτεινε πολλαχοῦ τὸν Ἀναξαγόραν, οἷον βαφὴν τῇ ῥητορικῇ τὴν φυσιολογίαν ὑποχεόμενος. τὸ γὰρ ὑψηλόνουν τοῦτο καὶ πάντῃ τελεσιουργόν, ὡς ὁ θεῖος Πλάτων φησί, πρὸς τῷ εὐφυὴς εἶναι κτησάμενος ἐκ φυσιολογίας, καὶ τὸ πρόσφορον ἑλκύσας ἐπὶ τὴν τῶν λόγων τέχνην

His style, as a speaker, influenced by the teaching of Anaxagoras.

2 πολὺ πάντων διήνεγκε. διὸ καὶ τὴν ἐπίκλησιν αὐτῷ γενέσθαι λέγουσι· καίτοι τινὲς ἀπὸ τῶν οἷς ἐκόσμησε τὴν πόλιν, οἱ δ᾽ ἀπὸ τῆς ἐν τῇ πολιτείᾳ καὶ ταῖς στρατηγίαις δυνάμεως Ὀλύμπιον αὐτὸν οἴονται προσαγορευθῆναι· καὶ συνδραμεῖν οὐδὲν ἀπέοικεν ἀπὸ πολλῶν προσόντων τῷ ἀνδρὶ τὴν

Origin of the name 'The Olympian' given to Pericles.

3 δόξαν. αἱ μέντοι κωμῳδίαι τῶν τότε διδασκάλων, σπουδῇ τε πολλὰς καὶ μετὰ γέλωτος ἀφεικότων φωνὰς εἰς αὐτόν, ἐπὶ τῷ λόγῳ μάλιστα τὴν προσωνυμίαν γενέσθαι δηλοῦσι, βροντᾶν μὲν αὐτὸν καὶ ἀστράπτειν, ὅτε δημηγοροίη, δεινὸν δὲ

CH. VIII § 1 l. 3 παρενέτεινε Bodl 3 (Ko Si Do Bk Fu Bl): παρέτεινε v: παρενεῖρε, *inscrebat orationibus suis* ci Cobet ‖ 5 βαφήν ci Bryan (Ko Si Do Bk Fu Bl): βαφῇ St v

κεραγνὸν ἐν γλώccη φέρειν λεγόντων. διαμνημονεύεται δέ τις καὶ Θουκυδίδου
τοῦ Μελησίου λόγος εἰς τὴν δεινότητα
τοῦ Περικλέους μετὰ παιδιᾶς εἰρημένος.
ἦν μὲν γὰρ ὁ Θουκυδίδης τῶν καλῶν καὶ
ἀγαθῶν ἀνδρῶν καὶ πλεῖστον ἀντεπολιτεύσατο τῷ
Περικλεῖ χρόνον· Ἀρχιδάμου δὲ τοῦ Λακεδαιμονίων βασιλέως πυνθανομένου, πότερον αὐτὸς ἢ
Περικλῆς παλαίει βέλτιον "Ὅταν" εἶπεν "ἐγὼ
καταβάλω παλαίων, ἐκεῖνος ἀντιλέγων ὡς οὐ
πέπτωκε νικᾷ καὶ μεταπείθει τοὺς ὁρῶντας."

Οὐ μὴν ἀλλὰ καὶ οὕτως ὁ Περικλῆς
περὶ τὸν λόγον εὐλαβὴς ἦν, ὥστ' ἀεὶ πρὸς τὸ
βῆμα βαδίζων ηὔχετο τοῖς θεοῖς μηδὲ ῥῆμα μηδὲν
ἐκπεσεῖν ἄκοντος αὐτοῦ πρὸς τὴν προκειμένην
χρείαν ἀνάρμοστον. ἔγγραφον μὲν οὖν
οὐδὲν ἀπολέλοιπε πλὴν τῶν ψηφισμά-
των· ἀπομνημονεύεται δ' ὀλίγα παντά-
πασιν· οἷον τὸ τὴν Αἴγιναν ὡς λήμην
τοῦ Πειραιῶς ἀφελεῖν κελεῦσαι, καὶ τὸ
τὸν πόλεμον ἤδη φάναι καθορᾶν ἀπὸ
Πελοποννήσου προσφερόμενον. καί
ποτε τοῦ Σοφοκλέους, ὅτε συστρατηγῶν ἐξέ-
πλευσε μετ' αὐτοῦ, παῖδα καλὸν ἐπαινέσαντος
"Οὐ μόνον" ἔφη "τὰς χεῖρας, ὦ Σοφόκλεις, δεῖ
καθαρὰς ἔχειν τὸν στρατηγόν, ἀλλὰ καὶ τὰς
ὄψεις." ὁ δὲ Στησίμβροτός φησιν ὅτι τοὺς ἐν
Σάμῳ τεθνηκότας ἐγκωμιάζων ἐπὶ τοῦ βήματος

§ 4 l. 33 οὕτως ci Holzapfel *Philologus* Bd. 51 Heft 2 p. 276:
αὐτός St Si Bk Fu Bl v

ἀθανάτους ἔλεγε γεγονέναι καθάπερ τοὺς θεούς· οὐδὲ γὰρ ἐκείνους αὐτοὺς ὁρῶμεν, ἀλλὰ ταῖς τιμαῖς, ἃς ἔχουσι, καὶ τοῖς ἀγαθοῖς, ἃ παρέχουσιν, ἀθανάτους εἶναι τεκμαιρόμεθα· ταῦτ' οὖν ὑπάρχειν καὶ τοῖς ὑπὲρ τῆς πατρίδος ἀποθανοῦσιν.

IX. Ἐπεὶ δὲ Θουκυδίδης μὲν ἀριστοκρατικήν τινα τὴν τοῦ Περικλέους ὑπογράφει πολιτείαν, λόγῳ μὲν οὖσαν δημοκρατίαν, ἔργῳ δ' ὑπὸ τοῦ πρώτου ἀνδρὸς ἀρχήν, ἄλλοι δὲ πολλοὶ πρῶτον ὑπ' ἐκείνου φασὶ τὸν δῆμον ἐπὶ κληρουχίας καὶ θεωρικὰ καὶ μισθῶν διανομὰς προαχθῆναι κακῶς ἐθισθέντα καὶ γενόμενον πολυτελῆ καὶ ἀκόλαστον ὑπὸ τῶν τότε πολιτευμάτων ἀντὶ σώφρονος καὶ αὐτουργοῦ, θεωρείσθω διὰ τῶν πραγμάτων αὐτῶν ἡ αἰτία τῆς μεταβολῆς. ἐν ἀρχῇ μὲν γάρ, ὥσπερ εἴρηται, πρὸς τὴν Κίμωνος δόξαν ἀντιταττόμενος ὑπεποιεῖτο τὸν δῆμον· ἐλαττούμενος δὲ πλούτῳ καὶ χρήμασιν, ἀφ' ὧν ἐκεῖνος ἀνελάμβανε τοὺς πένητας, δεῖπνόν τε καθ' ἡμέραν τῷ δεομένῳ παρέχων Ἀθηναίων, καὶ τοὺς πρεσβυτέρους ἀμφιεννύων, τῶν τε χωρίων τοὺς φραγμοὺς ἀφαιρῶν, ὅπως ὀπωρίζωσιν οἱ βουλόμενοι, τούτοις ὁ Περικλῆς καταδημαγωγούμενος τρέπεται πρὸς τὴν τῶν δημοσίων διανομήν, συμβουλεύσαν-

§ 6 l. 51 οὐδὲ γάρ S F^a (HSauppe Fu Bl): οὐ γάρ Si Bk v ‖ 52 ἃ παρέχουσι ci Br (Ko Si Do Bk Fu Bl): ἄπερ ἔχουσι codd ‖ 53 ταῦτ' ci Koraës (HSauppe Fu Bl): ταῦτ' St Si Bk v

τος αὐτῷ Δαμωνίδου τοῦ Ὄαθεν, ὡς *noted of laconism*. Ἀριστοτέλης ἱστόρηκε. καὶ ταχὺ θεωρικοῖς καὶ δικαστικοῖς λήμμασιν ἄλλαις τε μισθοφοραῖς καὶ χορηγίαις συνδεκάσας τὸ πλῆθος ἐχρῆτο κατὰ τῆς ἐξ Ἀρείου πάγου βουλῆς, ἧς αὐτὸς οὐ μετεῖχε διὰ τὸ μήτ' ἄρχων μήτε βασιλεὺς μήτε πολέμαρχος μήτε θεσμοθέτης λαχεῖν. αὗται γὰρ αἱ ἀρχαὶ κληρωταί τε ἦσαν ἐκ παλαιοῦ καὶ δι' αὐτῶν οἱ δοκιμασθέντες ἀνέβαινον εἰς Ἄρειον πάγον. διὸ καὶ μᾶλλον ἰσχύσας ὁ Περικλῆς ἐν τῷ δήμῳ κατεστασίασε τὴν βουλήν, ὥστε τὴν μὲν ἀφαιρεθῆναι τὰς πλείστας κρίσεις δι' Ἐφιάλτου, Κίμωνα δ' ὡς φιλολάκωνα καὶ μισόδημον ἐξοστρακισθῆναι, πλούτῳ μὲν καὶ γένει μηδενὸς ἀπολειπόμενον, νίκας δὲ καλλίστας νενικηκότα τοὺς βαρβάρους καὶ χρημάτων πολλῶν καὶ λαφύρων ἐμπεπληκότα τὴν πόλιν, ὡς ἐν τοῖς περὶ ἐκείνου γέγραπται. τοσοῦτον ἦν τὸ κράτος ἐν τῷ δήμῳ τοῦ Περικλέους.

X Ὁ μὲν οὖν ἐξοστρακισμὸς ὡρισμένην εἶχε νόμῳ δεκαετίαν τοῖς φεύγουσιν· ἐν δὲ τῷ διὰ μέσου στρατῷ μεγάλῳ Λακεδαιμονίων ἐμβαλόντων εἰς τὴν Ταναγρικὴν καὶ τῶν Ἀθηναίων εὐθὺς ὁρμησάντων ἐπ' αὐτοὺς ὁ μὲν Κίμων ἐλθὼν ἐκ τῆς φυγῆς

The usual term of ostracism was ten years. But, when the Athenian army was in Boeotia, Cimon

CH. IX § 2 l. 24 Δαμωνίδου τοῦ Ὄαθεν Si³ ci Steph. Byz. v Οα (HSauppe Fu Bl): Δημωνίδου τοῦ Οἰήθεν Ko Si¹ Do Bk v: < Δάμωνος > Δαμωνίδου τοῦ Ὄαθεν ci Cobet (Busolt and others)
§ 3 l. 29 μήτε βασιλεὺς μήτε πολέμαρχος μήτε θεσμοθέτης Η Sauppe (Bl): μήτε θ. μήτε βασιλεὺς μήτε πολ. Ko Si Do Bk Fu v
CH. X § 1 l. 3 στρατῷ μεγάλῳ Λακεδ. ci Si (Fu Bl): Λακεδ. στρατῷ μεγάλῳ Ko Si³ Do Bk v

ΠΛΟΥΤΑΡΧΟΥ   X 1

begged permission of the generals to take his place among the soldiers of his tribe, and, when repulsed, adjured those

2 *of his followers who were most suspected of laconism to exert themselves for his vindication as well as their own. They responded to the appeal and fell on the battlefield of Tanagra to the number of 100.*

3 πόλεμον.

This act of patriotism made the Athenians sorry for Cimon; they cancelled the decree of ostracism on the motion of Pericles
4 *himself*

Elpinice is reported to have negoti-

ἔθετο μετὰ τῶν φυλετῶν εἰς λόχον
τὰ ὅπλα καὶ δι' ἔργων ἀπολύεσθαι τὸν
λακωνισμὸν ἐβούλετο συγκινδυνεύσας
τοῖς πολίταις, οἱ δὲ φίλοι τοῦ Περικλέους 10
συστάντες ἀπήλασαν αὐτὸν ὡς φυγάδα.
διὸ καὶ δοκεῖ Περικλῆς ἐρρωμενέστατα
τὴν μάχην ἐκείνην ἀγωνίσασθαι καὶ
γενέσθαι πάντων ἐπιφανέστατος ἀφειδήσας τοῦ σώματος. ἔπεσον δὲ καὶ τοῦ 15
Κίμωνος οἱ φίλοι πάντες ὁμαλῶς, οὓς
Περικλῆς συνεπῃτιᾶτο τοῦ λακωνισμοῦ·
καὶ μετάνοια δεινὴ τοὺς Ἀθηναίους καὶ
πόθος ἔσχε τοῦ Κίμωνος, ἡττημένους
μὲν ἐπὶ τῶν ὅρων τῆς Ἀττικῆς, προσ- 20
δοκῶντας δὲ βαρὺν εἰς ἔτους ὥραν

αἰσθόμενος οὖν ὁ Περικλῆς οὐκ
ὤκνησε χαρίσασθαι τοῖς πολλοῖς, ἀλλὰ
τὸ ψήφισμα γράψας αὐτὸς ἐκάλει τὸν
ἄνδρα, κἀκεῖνος κατελθὼν εἰρήνην 25
ἐποίησε ταῖς πόλεσιν. οἰκείως γὰρ
εἶχον οἱ Λακεδαιμόνιοι πρὸς αὐτὸν
ὥσπερ ἀπήχθοντο τῷ Περικλεῖ καὶ
τοῖς ἄλλοις δημαγωγοῖς. ἔνιοι δέ
φασιν οὐ πρότερον γραφῆναι τῷ Κίμωνι τὴν 30
κάθοδον ὑπὸ τοῦ Περικλέους ἢ συνθήκας αὐτοῖς ἀπορρήτους γενέσθαι δι'

§ 2 l. 12 ἐρρωμενέστατα τήν ci Cobet (Bl² Si³ Fu): ἐρρωμενεστάτην <τήν> ci Ko: ἐρρωμενεστάτην Si¹ Bk Bl¹ v || 17 συνεπῃτίατο, una olim insimulaverat Cobet *V L.* p. 391 (Fu Bl²): συνεπῃτιᾶτο, una insimulabat Si Bk Bl¹ vulgo: συνεπῃτιάσατο ci Bergk

§ 3 l. 25 κατελθών ci Si (Do Fu Bl): ἀπελθών, *profectus Spartam puta* Reiske Bk vulgo: ἐπανελθών ci Ko

ΠΕΡΙΚΛΗΣ

Ἐλπινίκης, τῆς Κίμωνος ἀδελφῆς, ὥστε Κίμωνα μὲν ἐκπλεῦσαι λαβόντα ναῦς διακοσίας καὶ τῶν ἔξω στρατηγεῖν καταστρεφόμενον τὴν βασιλέως χώραν, Περικλεῖ δὲ τὴν ἐν ἄστει δύναμιν ὑπάρχειν. Ἐδόκει δὲ καὶ πρότερον ἡ Ἐλπινίκη τῷ Κίμωνι τὸν Περικλέα πραότερον παρασχεῖν, ὅτε τὴν θανατικὴν δίκην ἔφευγεν. ἦν μὲν γὰρ εἷς τῶν κατηγόρων ὁ Περικλῆς ὑπὸ τοῦ δήμου προβεβλημένος· ἐλθούσης δὲ πρὸς αὐτὸν τῆς Ἐλπινίκης καὶ δεομένης μειδιάσας εἶπεν "Ὦ Ἐλπινίκη, γραῦς εἶ, γραῦς [εἶ], ὡς πράγματα τηλικαῦτα διαπράσσεσθαι." οὐ μὴν ἀλλὰ καὶ πρὸς τὸν λόγον ἅπαξ ἀνέστη, τὴν προβολὴν ἀφοσιούμενος, καὶ τῶν κατηγόρων ἐλάχιστα τὸν Κίμωνα λυπήσας ἀπεχώρησε.

Πῶς ἂν οὖν τις Ἰδομενεῖ πιστεύσειε κατηγοροῦντι τοῦ Περικλέους, ὡς τὸν δημαγωγὸν Ἐφιάλτην, φίλον γενόμενον καὶ κοινωνὸν ὄντα τῆς ἐν τῇ πολιτείᾳ προαιρέσεως, δολοφονήσαντος διὰ ζηλοτυπίαν καὶ φθόνον τῆς δόξης; ταῦτα γὰρ οὐκ οἶδ᾽ <ὁπ>όθεν συναγαγὼν ὥσπερ χολὴν τἀνδρὶ προσ-

§ 5 l. 45 the second εἶ is probably, as Reiske suggests, interpolated, though retained by edd. By its omission we avoid a harsh hiatus. Cp. Cim. c. 14, 4 ‖ 46 διαπράσσεσθαι ci Blass el Cim. c. 14, 4 (AJacob) : πράσσειν ci Vulcobius (Ko Si Do Bk Fu) : δράσειν vulgo

§ 6 l. 56 ὁπόθεν ci Blass : ὅθεν Si Bk Fu v ‖ 57 προσβέβληκε ci Reiske i.e. quasi προσεμέμηκε vomito in os cius reiecit (Si Do Bk Fu Bl) : προβέβληκε vulgo : προσβέβλυκε ci Ko

ΠΛΟΥΤΑΡΧΟΥ X 6

of credit. Whatever his failings may have been, Pericles was incapable of such an act of inhumanity.

βέβληκε, πάντῃ μὲν ἴσως οὐκ ἀνεπιλήπτῳ, φρόνημα δ' εὐγενὲς ἔχοντι καὶ ψυχὴν φιλότιμον, οἷς οὐδὲν ἐμφύεται πάθος ὠμὸν οὕτω καὶ θηριῶδες. Ἐφιάλτην μὲν οὖν φοβερὸν ὄντα τοῖς ὀλιγαρχικοῖς καὶ περὶ τὰς εὐθύνας καὶ

The truth is, Ephialtes was secretly made away with by a conspiracy of the oligarchical party, who were afraid of him.

διώξεις τῶν τὸν δῆμον ἀδικούντων ἀπαραίτητον ἐπιβουλεύσαντες οἱ ἐχθροὶ δι' Ἀριστοδίκου τοῦ Ταναγρικοῦ κρυφαίως ἀνεῖλον, ὡς Ἀριστοτέλης εἴρηκεν. Ἐτελεύτησε δὲ Κίμων ἐν Κύπρῳ στρατηγῶν.

XI Οἱ δ' ἀριστοκρατικοὶ μέγιστον μὲν ἤδη τὸν Περικλέα καὶ πρόσθεν ὁρῶντες

After the death of Cimon, the oligarchical party at Athens adopt Thucydides for their leader in his place.

γεγονότα τῶν πολιτῶν, βουλόμενοι δ' ὅμως εἶναί τινα τὸν πρὸς αὐτὸν ἀντιτασσόμενον ἐν τῇ πόλει καὶ τὴν δύναμιν ἀμβλύνοντα, ὥστε μὴ κομιδῇ μοναρχίαν εἶναι, Θουκυδίδην τὸν Ἀλωπεκῆθεν, ἄνδρα σώφρονα καὶ κηδεστὴν Κίμωνος,

2 ἀντέστησαν ἐναντιωσόμενον, ὃς ἧττον μὲν ὢν πολεμικὸς τοῦ Κίμωνος, ἀγοραῖος δὲ καὶ πολιτικὸς μᾶλλον, οἰκουρῶν ἐν ἄστει καὶ περὶ τὸ βῆμα τῷ Περικλεῖ συμπλεκόμενος ταχὺ τὴν πολιτείαν εἰς ἀντίπαλον κατέστησεν. οὐ γὰρ

He organises them into a compact

εἴασε τοὺς καλοὺς κἀγαθοὺς καλουμένους ἄνδρας ἐνδιεσπάρθαι καὶ συμμεμῖχθαι

1. 60 ἧς οὐδὲν ἐκφύεται ci Reiske
CH. XI § 1 l. 4 τὸν πρὸς αὐτόν : τινα αὐτῶν, *aliquem ex suo numero* ci Bryan : τινα τῶν πρὸς αὐτῶν, 'quelqu'un de leur part' Amyot

πρὸς τὸν δῆμον, ὡς πρότερον, ὑπὸ
πλήθους ἠμαυρωμένους τὸ ἀξίωμα,
χωρὶς δὲ διακρίνας καὶ συναγαγὼν εἰς
ταὐτὸ τὴν πάντων δύναμιν ἐμβριθῆ
γενομένην ὥσπερ ἐπὶ ζυγοῦ ῥοπὴν
ἐποίησεν. ἦν μὲν γὰρ ἐξ ἀρχῆς διπλόη
τις ὕπουλος, ὥσπερ ἐν σιδήρῳ, διαφορὰν
ὑποσημαίνουσα δημοτικῆς καὶ ἀριστοκρατικῆς προαιρέσεως, ἡ δ' ἐκείνων
ἅμιλλα καὶ φιλοτιμία τῶν ἀνδρῶν
βαθυτάτην τομὴν τεμοῦσα τῆς πόλεως
τὸ μὲν δῆμον, τὸ δ' ὀλίγους ἐποίησε
καλεῖσθαι. διὸ καὶ τότε μάλιστα τῷ
δήμῳ τὰς ἡνίας ἀνεὶς ὁ Περικλῆς ἐπολιτεύετο
πρὸς χάριν, ἀεὶ μέν τινα θέαν πανη-
γυρικὴν ἢ ἑστίασιν ἢ πομπὴν εἶναι
μηχανώμενος ἐν ἄστει καὶ διαπαιδαγωγῶν οὐκ ἀμούσοις ἡδοναῖς τὴν πόλιν, ἑξήκοντα
δὲ τριήρεις καθ' ἕκαστον ἐνιαυτὸν ἐκπέμπων, ἐν
αἷς πολλοὶ τῶν πολιτῶν ἔπλεον ὀκτὼ μῆνας
ἔμμισθοι, μελετῶντες ἅμα καὶ μανθάνοντες τὴν
ναυτικὴν ἐμπειρίαν. πρὸς δὲ τούτοις
χιλίους μὲν ἔστειλεν εἰς Χερρόνησον
κληρούχους, εἰς δὲ Νάξον πεντακο-
σίους, εἰς δὲ Ἄνδρον ἡμίσεις τούτων,
εἰς δὲ Θρᾴκην χιλίους Βισάλταις
συνοικήσοντας· ἄλλους δ' εἰς Ἰταλίαν
⟨ἀν⟩οικιζομένης Συβάριος, ἣν Θουρίους

§ 2 l. 13 τἀντίπαλον ci Reiske
§ 3 l. 21 διπλόη ci Ruhnken (Ko Si Bk Fu Bl): διαπλοκή vulgo
§ 5 l. 10 τοὺς ἡμίσεις Fu after Cobet ‖ 43 ἀνοικιζομένης,

προσηγόρευσαν. καὶ ταῦτ' ἔπραττεν ἀποκουφίζων μὲν ἀργοῦ καὶ διὰ σχολὴν πολυπράγμονος ὄχλου τὴν πόλιν, ἐπανορθούμενος δὲ τὰς ἀπορίας τοῦ δήμου, φόβον δὲ καὶ φρουρὰν τοῦ μὴ νεωτερίζειν τι παρακατοικίζων τοῖς συμμάχοις.

XII Ὁ δὲ πλείστην μὲν ἡδονὴν ταῖς Ἀθήναις καὶ κόσμον ἤνεγκε, μεγίστην δὲ τοῖς ἄλλοις ἔκπληξιν ἀνθρώποις, μόνον δὲ τῇ Ἑλλάδι μαρτυρεῖ μὴ ψεύδεσθαι τὴν λεγομένην δύναμιν αὐτῆς ἐκείνην καὶ τὸν παλαιὸν ὄλβον, ἡ τῶν ἀναθημάτων κατασκευή, τοῦτο μάλιστα τῶν πολιτευμάτων τοῦ Περικλέους ἐβάσκαινον οἱ ἐχθροὶ καὶ διέβαλλον ἐν ταῖς ἐκκλησίαις, βοῶντες ὡς "Ὁ μὲν δῆμος ἀδοξεῖ καὶ κακῶς ἀκούει τὰ κοινὰ τῶν Ἑλλήνων χρήματα πρὸς αὐτὸν ἐκ Δήλου μεταγαγών, ἡ δ' ἔνεστιν αὐτῷ πρὸς τοὺς ἐγκαλοῦντας εὐπρεπεστάτη τῶν προφάσεων, δείσαντα τοὺς βαρβάρους ἐκεῖθεν ἀνελέσθαι καὶ φυλάττειν ἐν ὀχυρῷ τὰ κοινά, ταύτην ἀνῄρηκε Περικλῆς· καὶ δοκεῖ δεινὴν ὕβριν ἡ Ἑλλὰς ὑβρίζεσθαι καὶ τυραννεῖσθαι περιφανῶς,

'being re-settled,' Bl with HSauppe Cobet and Eberhard obs. polyb. p. 40: οἰκιζομένης Ko Si Bk Fu v || Συβάριος Cobet: Συβάρεως v || 48 τι del Cobet as 'ex sequente π vitio natum'
CH. XII § 1 l. 7 τοῦτο anon (Ko Si Bk Fu Bl): τούτῳ Do v
§ 2 l. 13 ἔνεστιν v: ἔστιν ci Cobet, for 'ἐνεῖναι homini esse dicuntur ea omnia quae ad indolem aut naturam plerumque animi, nonnumquam et corporis, pertinent' (Bergk). But see expl n

ὁρῶσα τοῖς εἰσφερομένοις ὑπ' αὐτῆς ἀναγκαίως πρὸς τὸν πόλεμον ἡμᾶς τὴν πόλιν καταχρυσοῦντας καὶ καλλωπίζοντας ὥσπερ ἀλαζόνα γυναῖκα, περιαπτομένην λίθους πολυτελεῖς καὶ ἀγάλματα καὶ ναοὺς χιλιοταλάντους." Ἐδίδασκεν οὖν ὁ Περικλῆς τὸν δῆμον ὅτι "Χρημάτων μὲν οὐκ ὀφείλουσι τοῖς συμμάχοις λόγον, προπολεμοῦντες αὐτῶν καὶ τοὺς βαρβάρους ἀνείργοντες, οὐχ ἵππον, οὐ ναῦν, οὐχ ὁπλίτην, ἀλλὰ χρήματα μόνον τελούντων· ἃ τῶν διδόντων οὐκ ἔστιν, ἀλλὰ τῶν λαμβανόντων, ἂν παρέχωσιν ἀνθ' οὗ λαμβάνουσι· δεῖ δὲ τῆς πόλεως κατεσκευασμένης ἱκανῶς τοῖς ἀναγκαίοις πρὸς τὸν πόλεμον εἰς ταῦτα τὴν εὐπορίαν τρέπειν αὐτῆς, ἀφ' ὧν δόξα μὲν γενομένων ἀίδιος, εὐπορία δὲ γινομένων ἑτοίμη παρέσται, παντοδαπῆς ἐργασίας φανείσης καὶ ποικίλων χρειῶν, αἳ πᾶσαν μὲν τέχνην ἐγείρουσαι, πᾶσαν δὲ χεῖρα κινοῦσαι, σχεδὸν ὅλην ποιοῦσιν ἔμμισθον τὴν πόλιν ἐξ αὐτῆς ἅμα κοσμουμένην καὶ τρεφομένην." τοῖς μὲν γὰρ ἡλικίαν ἔχουσι καὶ ῥώμην αἱ στρατεῖαι τὰς ἀπὸ τῶν κοινῶν εὐπορίας παρεῖχον, τὸν δ' ἀσύντακτον καὶ

§ 2 l. 21 ἀναγκαίοις ci Bergk
§ 3 l. 33 δεῖν δέ ci Cobet, who adds, 'fert in talibus Graecae compositionis ratio, ut ubi ὅτι non repetitur ad indirectam orationem transitus fiat' (Bergk)
§ 4 l. 35 ἐξουσίαν ci Bergk || 36 γενομένων ... γινομένων anon (Ko Si Do Bk Fu Bl): γινομένων ... γενομένων v

diffusion of activity and industry with an order and system admirably conceived and carried out in the execution of his great works.

βάναυσον ὄχλον οὔτ' ἄμοιρον εἶναι λημμάτων βουλόμενος οὔτε λαμβάνειν ἀργὸν καὶ σχολάζοντα, μεγάλας κατασκευασμάτων ἐπιβολὰς καὶ πολυτέχνους ὑποθέσεις ἔργων διατριβὴν ἐχόντων ἐνέβαλε φέρων εἰς τὸν δῆμον, ἵνα μηδὲν ἧττον τῶν πλεόντων καὶ φρουρούντων καὶ στρατευομένων τὸ οἰκουροῦν ἔχῃ πρόφασιν ἀπὸ τῶν δημοσίων ὠφελεῖσθαι καὶ μεταλαμβάνειν. ὅπου γὰρ ὕλη μὲν ἦν λίθος χαλκὸς ἐλέφας χρυσὸς ἔβενος κυπάρισσος, αἱ δὲ ταύτην ἐκπονοῦσαι καὶ κατεργαζόμεναι τέχναι τέκτονες πλάσται χαλκοτύποι λιθουργοὶ βαφεῖς, χρυσοῦ μαλακτῆρες < καὶ > ἐλέφαντος, ζωγράφοι ποικιλταὶ τορευταί, πομποὶ δὲ τούτων καὶ κομιστῆρες ἔμποροι καὶ ναῦται καὶ κυβερνῆται κατὰ θάλατταν, οἱ δὲ κατὰ γῆν ἁμαξοπηγοὶ καὶ ζευγοτρόφοι καὶ ἡνίοχοι καὶ καλωστρόφοι καὶ λινουργοὶ καὶ σκυτοτόμοι καὶ ὁδοποιοὶ καὶ μεταλλεῖς,—ἑκάστη δὲ τέχνη, καθάπερ στρατηγὸς ἴδιον στράτευμα, τὸν θητικὸν ὄχλον καὶ ἰδιώτην συντεταγμένον εἶχεν, ὄργανον καὶ σῶμα τῆς ὑπηρεσίας γινόμενον—εἰς πᾶσαν, ὡς ἔπος εἰπεῖν, ἡλικίαν καὶ φύσιν αἱ χρεῖαι διένεμον καὶ διέσπειρον τὴν εὐπορίαν.

XIII Ἀναβαινόντων δὲ τῶν ἔργων ὑπερηφάνων

§ 6 l. 58 βαφεῖς, χρυσοῦ μαλακτῆρες, ἐλέφαντος Ko Bl vulgo: βαφεῖς χρυσοῦ, μαλακτῆρες ἐλέφαντος ci Wyttenbach (Do Fuhr): βαφεῖς, χρυσοῦ μαλακτῆρες < καὶ > ἐλέφαντος ci Rk (Si⁴ Bk Holzapfel): . . . χρυσοῦ, μαλακτῆρες ἐλέφαντος ci AJacob
§ 7 l. 64 λινουργοί Xylander (Ko Si Do Fu Bl): λιθουργοί v

μὲν μεγέθει, μορφῇ δ' ἀμιμήτων καὶ χάριτι, τῶν δημιουργῶν ἁμιλλωμένων ὑπερβάλλεσθαι τὴν δημιουργίαν τῇ καλλιτεχνίᾳ, μάλιστα θαυμάσιον ἦν τὸ τάχος. ὧν γὰρ ἕκαστον ᾤοντο πολλαῖς διαδοχαῖς καὶ ἡλικίαις μόλις ἐπὶ τέλος ἀφίξεσθαι, ταῦτα πάντα μιᾷ ἀκμῇ πολιτείας ἐλάμβανε τὴν συντέλειαν. καίτοι ποτέ φασιν Ἀγαθάρχου τοῦ ζωγράφου 2 μέγα φρονοῦντος ἐπὶ τῷ ταχὺ καὶ ῥᾳδίως τὰ ζῷα ποιεῖν ἀκούσαντα τὸν Ζεῦξιν εἰπεῖν " Ἐγὼ δὲ πολλῷ χρόνῳ." ἡ γὰρ ἐν τῷ ποιεῖν εὐχέρεια καὶ ταχύτης οὐκ ἐντίθησι βάρος ἔργῳ μόνιμον οὐδὲ κάλλους ἀκρίβειαν· ὁ δ' εἰς τὴν γένεσιν τῷ πόνῳ προδανεισθεὶς χρόνος ἐν τῇ σωτηρίᾳ τοῦ γενομένου τὴν ἰσχὺν ἀποδίδωσιν. ὅθεν καὶ 3 μᾶλλον θαυμάζεται τὰ Περικλέους ἔργα πρὸς πολὺν χρόνον ἐν ὀλίγῳ γενόμενα. κάλλει μὲν γὰρ ἕκαστον εὐθὺς ἦν τότε ἀρχαῖον, ἀκμῇ δὲ μέχρι νῦν πρόσφατόν ἐστι καὶ νεουργόν· οὕτως ἐπανθεῖ καινότης ἀεί τις ἄθικτον ὑπὸ τοῦ χρόνου διατηροῦσα τὴν ὄψιν, ὥσπερ ἀειθαλὲς πνεῦμα

CH. XIII § 1 l. 4 ὑπερβάλλεσθαι ci Schäfer (Si Do Bk Fu Bl): ὑπερβαλέσθαι Ko vulgo ‖ τῆς δημιουργίας ci Blass: τὴν δημιουργίαν Ko Si Do Bk Fu A Jacob vulgo

§ 2 l. 10 ποτέ Xylander (Si Do Bk Fu Bl): τότε v ‖ 13 πολλῷ χρόνῳ ci Wyttenbach cl *Mor.* 970 (Do Fu Bl): ἐν πολλῷ χρόνῳ Ko Si Bk Co Bergk ‖ 16 Madvig would read προσδανεισθείς, on the ground that προδανεισθείς would require the gen. τοῦ πόνου: but προ- is here the equivalent of πρότερον, meaning 'before the work is completed' ‖ 17 τὴν ἰσχύν v: τὸν τόκον ci Cobet. See comm

§ 3 l. 18 εἰς π. χρόνον ci Cobet ‖ 22 καινότης τις ἄθικτον Si

καὶ ψυχὴν ἀγήρω καταμεμιγμένην τῶν ἔργων

4 Illustrious artists and architects employed, under the supervision of PHIDIAS. Parthenon. Telesterion at Eleusis.

ἐχόντων. πάντα δὲ διεῖπε καὶ πάντων ἐπίσκοπος ἦν αὐτῷ Φειδίας, καίτοι μεγάλους ἀρχιτέκτονας ἐχόντων καὶ τεχνίτας τῶν ἔργων. τὸν μὲν γὰρ ἑκατόμπεδον Παρθενῶνα Καλλικράτης εἰργάζετο καὶ Ἰκτῖνος, τὸ δ' ἐν Ἐλευσῖνι τελεστήριον ἤρξατο μὲν Κόροιβος οἰκοδομεῖν καὶ τοὺς ἐπ' ἐδάφους κίονας ἔθηκεν οὗτος καὶ τοῖς ἐπιστυλίοις ἐπέζευξεν· ἀποθανόντος δὲ τούτου Μεταγένης ὁ Ξυπέτιος τὸ διάζωμα
5 καὶ τοὺς ἄνω κίονας ἐπέστησε τὸ δ' ὀπαῖον ἐπὶ τοῦ ἀνακτόρου Ξενοκλῆς ὁ Χολαργεὺς ἐκορύφωσε· τὸ δὲ Μακρὸν τεῖχος, περὶ οὗ

The (Third) Long Wall.

Σωκράτης ἀκοῦσαί φησιν αὐτὸς εἰσηγουμένου γνώμην Περικλέους, ἠργολάβησε Καλλικράτης. κωμῳδεῖ δὲ τὸ ἔργον Κρατῖνος ὡς βραδέως περαινόμενον·

πάλαι γὰρ αὐτό (φησί)
λόγοισι προάγει Περικλέης, ἔργοισι δ' οὐδὲ κινεῖ.

τὸ δ' Ὠιδεῖον, τῇ μὲν ἐντὸς διαθέσει πολύεδρον καὶ πολύστυλον, τῇ δ' ἐρέψει περικλινὲς

The Odeion.

καὶ κάταντες ἐκ μιᾶς κορυφῆς πεποιημένον, εἰκόνα λέγουσι γενέσθαι καὶ μίμημα τῆς βασιλέως σκηνῆς, ἐπιστατοῦντος καὶ τούτῳ
6 Περικλέους. διὸ καὶ πάλιν Κρατῖνος ἐν Θρᾴτταις παίζει πρὸς αὐτόν·

§ 4 l. 34 Ξυπέτιος Si Bk Fu Bl v: Ξυπεταών (vel -αιών vel -εών) ci Cobet ‖ διάζωσμα S (Fuhr AJacob)
§ 5 l. 43 λόγοισι ci St (Si Bk Fu Bl): λόγαις v ‖ προάγει ci Reiske (Si Bk Fu Bl): προσάγει v ‖ οὐδ' ἄκαιναν ci Bergk

ὁ σχινοκέφαλος Ζεὺς ὅδε
προσέρχεται τῳδεῖον ἐπὶ τοῦ κρανίου
ἔχων, ἐπειδὴ τοὔστρακον παροίχεται.

φιλοτιμούμενος δ' ὁ Περικλῆς τότε πρῶτον
ἐψηφίσατο μουσικῆς ἀγῶνα τοῖς Παναθηναίοις
ἄγεσθαι, καὶ διέταξεν αὐτὸς ἀθλοθέτης αἱρεθεὶς
καθότι χρὴ τοὺς ἀγωνιζομένους αὐλεῖν ἢ ᾄδειν
ἢ κιθαρίζειν. ἐθεῶντο δὲ καὶ τότε καὶ τὸν 7
ἄλλον χρόνον ἐν Ὠιδείῳ τοὺς μουσικοὺς
ἀγῶνας. τὰ δὲ Προπύλαια τῆς ἀκρο-
πόλεως ἐξειργάσθη μὲν ἐν πενταετίᾳ
Μνησικλέους ἀρχιτεκτονοῦντος· τύχη
δὲ θαυμαστὴ συμβᾶσα περὶ τὴν
οἰκοδομίαν ἐμήνυσε τὴν θεὸν οὐκ ἀποστατοῦσαν,
ἀλλὰ συνεφαπτομένην τοῦ ἔργου καὶ συνεπιτελοῦσαν. ὁ γὰρ ἐνεργότατος καὶ προθυμότατος 8
τῶν τεχνιτῶν ἀποσφαλεὶς ἐξ ὕψους ἔπεσε καὶ
διέκειτο μοχθηρῶς, ὑπὸ τῶν ἰατρῶν ἀπεγνωσμένος. ἀθυμοῦντος δὲ τοῦ Περικλέους ἡ θεὸς
ὄναρ φανεῖσα συνέταξε θεραπείαν, ᾗ χρώμενος ὁ
Περικλῆς ταχὺ καὶ ῥᾳδίως ἰάσατο τὸν ἄνθρωπον.
ἐπὶ τούτῳ δὲ καὶ τὸ χαλκοῦν ἄγαλμα τῆς Ὑγιείας
Ἀθηνᾶς ἀνέστησεν ἐκ ἀκροπόλει παρὰ τὸν
βωμόν, ὃς καὶ πρότερον ἦν, ὥς λέγουσιν.

Ὁ δὲ Φειδίας εἰργάζετο μὲν τῆς θεοῦ 9

The Propylaea. Strange incident which occurred during its erection.

§ 6 l. 51 the old reading was ὁ σχινοκέφαλος Ζεὺς ὅδε προσ-
έρχεται | Περικλέης: Meineke substituted ὁδί for ὅδε and added
the art. before Περικλέης. Cobet divides the verse differently
and omits Περικλέης as 'fatue et insulse additum post ὁ σχιν.
Ζεὺς ὅδε.' Similarly in c. 24, 6, the insertion of Ἀσπασίαν is
probably due to a copyist

τὸ χρυσοῦν ἕδος καὶ τούτου δημιουργὸς ἐν τῇ στήλῃ <κατα >γέγραπται, πάντα δ' ἦν σχεδὸν ἐπ' αὐτῷ καὶ πᾶσιν, ὡς εἰρήκαμεν, ἐπεστάτει τοῖς τεχνίταις διὰ φιλίαν Περικλέους. καὶ τοῦτο τῷ μὲν φθόνον, τῷ δὲ βλασφημίαν ἤνεγκεν, ὡς ἐλευθέρας τῷ Περικλεῖ γυναῖκας εἰς τὰ ἔργα φοιτώσας ὑποδεχομένου τοῦ Φειδίου. δεξάμενοι δὲ τὸν λόγον οἱ κωμικοὶ πολλὴν ἀσέλγειαν αὐτοῦ κατεσκέδασαν, εἴς τε τὴν Μενίππου γυναῖκα διαβάλλοντες, ἀνδρὸς φίλου καὶ ὑποστρατηγοῦντος, εἴς τε τὰς Πυριλάμπους ὀρνιθοτροφίας, ὃς ἑταῖρος ὢν Περικλέους αἰτίαν εἶχε ταῶνας ὑφιέναι ταῖς γυναιξίν, αἷς ὁ Περικλῆς ἐπλησίαζε.

Καὶ τί ἄν τις ἀνθρώπους σατυρικοὺς τοῖς βίοις καὶ τὰς κατὰ τῶν κρειττόνων βλασφημίας ὥσπερ δαίμονι κακῷ τῷ φθόνῳ τῶν πολλῶν ἀποθύοντας ἑκάστοτε θαυμάσειεν, ὅπου καὶ Στησίμβροτος ὁ Θάσιος δεινὸν ἀσέβημα καὶ μυθῶδες ἐξενεγκεῖν ἐτόλμησεν εἰς τὴν γυναῖκα τοῦ υἱοῦ κατὰ τοῦ Περικλέους; οὕτως ἔοικε πάντῃ χαλεπὸν εἶναι καὶ δυσθήρατον ἱστορίᾳ τἀληθές, ὅταν οἱ μὲν ὕστερον γεγονότες τὸν χρόνον ἔχωσιν ἐπιπροσθοῦντα τῇ γνώσει τῶν

§ 9 l. 77 γέγραπται Si Bl : ἀναγέγραπται ci Cobet Bergk : εἶναι γέγραπται Ko Do Bk with codd : καταγέγραπται ci Fuhr

§ 10 l. 87 συστρατηγοῦντος ci Cobet, who says that ὑποστρατηγοῦντος must be faulty because 'neque res neque nomen Atheniensibus in usu erat' (Bergk) ‖ 90 πιαίνειν (πιᾶναι), deinde ἐφιέναι, tum ὑποτεῖναι ci Bergk

πραγμάτων, ἡ δὲ τῶν πράξεων καὶ τῶν βίων ἡλικιῶτις ἱστορία τὰ μὲν φθόνοις καὶ δυσμενείαις, τὰ δὲ χαριζομένη καὶ κολακεύουσα λυμαίνηται καὶ διαστρέφῃ τὴν ἀλήθειαν.

XIV Τῶν δὲ περὶ τὸν Θουκυδίδην ῥητόρων καταβοώντων τοῦ Περικλέους ὡς σπαθῶντος τὰ χρήματα καὶ τὰς προσόδους ἀπολλύντος, ἠρώτησεν ἐν ἐκκλησίᾳ τὸν δῆμον, εἰ πολλὰ δοκεῖ δεδαπανῆσθαι· φησάντων δὲ πάμπολλα, "Μὴ τοίνυν" εἶπεν "ὑμῖν, ἀλλ' ἐμοὶ δεδαπανήσθω, καὶ τῶν ἀναθημάτων ἰδίαν ἐμαυτοῦ ποιήσομαι τὴν ἐπιγραφήν." εἰπόντος οὖν ταῦτα τοῦ Περικλέους, εἴτε τὴν μεγαλοφροσύνην αὐτοῦ θαυμάσαντες εἴτε πρὸς τὴν δόξαν ἀντιφιλοτιμούμενοι τῶν ἔργων, ἀνέκραγον κελεύοντες ἐκ τῶν δημοσίων ἀναλίσκειν καὶ χορηγεῖν μηδενὸς φειδόμενον. τέλος δὲ πρὸς τὸν Θουκυδίδην εἰς ἀγῶνα περὶ τοῦ ὀστράκου καταστὰς καὶ διακινδυνεύσας ἐκεῖνον μὲν ἐξέβαλε, κατέλυσε δὲ τὴν ἀντιτεταγμένην ἑταιρείαν.

XV Ὡς οὖν, παντάπασι λυθείσης τῆς διαφορᾶς καὶ τῆς πόλεως οἷον ὁμαλῆς καὶ μιᾶς γενομένης κομιδῇ, περιήνεγκεν εἰς ἑαυτὸν τὰς Ἀθήνας καὶ τὰ τῶν Ἀθηναίων ἐξηρτημένα πράγματα, φόρους καὶ στρατεύματα καὶ τριήρεις καὶ νήσους καὶ θάλασσαν καὶ πολλὴν μὲν δι' Ἑλλήνων, πολλὴν δὲ καὶ διὰ βαρβάρων ἥκουσαν ἰσχὺν καὶ ἡγεμονίαν ὑπηκόοις ἔθνεσι καὶ φιλίαις βασιλέων καὶ συμμαχίαις πεφραγμένην δυναστῶν,

2 οὐκέθ' ὁ αὐτὸς ἦν οὐδ' ὁμοίως χειροήθης τῷ δήμῳ καὶ ῥᾴδιος ὑπείκειν καὶ συνενδιδόναι ταῖς ἐπιθυμίαις ὥσπερ πνοαῖς τῶν πολλῶν, ἀλλ' ἐκ τῆς ἀνειμένης ἐκείνης καὶ ὑποθρυπτομένης ἔνια δημαγωγίας ὥσπερ ἀνθηρᾶς καὶ μαλακῆς ἁρμονίας ἀριστοκρατικὴν καὶ βασιλικὴν ἐντεινάμενος πολιτείαν, καὶ χρώμενος αὐτῇ πρὸς τὸ βέλτιστον 3 ὀρθῇ καὶ ἀνεγκλίτῳ, τὰ μὲν πολλὰ βουλόμενον ἦγε πείθων καὶ διδάσκων τὸν δῆμον, ἦν δ' ὅτε καὶ μάλα δυσχεραίνοντα κατατείνων καὶ προσβιβάζων ἐχειροῦτο τῷ συμφέροντι, μιμούμενος ἀτεχνῶς ἰατρὸν ποικίλῳ νοσήματι καὶ μακρῷ κατὰ καιρὸν μὲν ἡδονὰς ἀβλαβεῖς, κατὰ καιρὸν δὲ δηγμοὺς καὶ φάρμακα προσφέροντα 4 σωτήρια. παντοδαπῶν γάρ, ὡς εἰκός, παθῶν ἐν ὄχλῳ τοσαύτην τὸ μέγεθος ἀρχὴν ἔχοντι φυομένων, μόνος ἐμμελῶς ἕκαστα διαχειρίσασθαι πεφυκώς, μάλιστα δ' ἐλπίσι καὶ φόβοις ὥσπερ οἴαξι προσστέλλων τὸ θρασυνόμενον αὐτῶν καὶ τὸ δύσθυμον ἀνιεὶς καὶ παραμυθούμενος, ἔδειξε τὴν ῥητορικὴν κατὰ Πλάτωνα ψυχαγωγίαν οὖσαν καὶ μέγιστον ἔργον αὐτῆς τὴν περὶ τὰ ἤθη καὶ πάθη μέθοδον, ὥσπερ τινὰς τόνους καὶ φθόγγους ψυχῆς μάλ' ἐμμελοῦς ἁφῆς 5 καὶ κρούσεως δεομένους. αἰτία δ' οὐχ ἡ τοῦ λόγου ψιλῶς δύναμις, ἀλλ', ὡς Θουκυδίδης φησίν, ἡ περὶ τὸν βίον δόξα καὶ πίστις τοῦ ἀνδρός, ἀδωροτάτου περιφανῶς γενομένου καὶ χρημάτων

CH. XV § 3 l. 20 προσβιβάζων ci Schäfer (Si Do Bk Fu Bl): προσβιάζων Ko v || 23 ἡδονὰς ἀβλαβεῖς, voluptates noxia vacantes ci Rk (Si Do Bk Fu Bl): εὐλαβεῖς, cum cautione coniunctas v

κρείττονος· ὃς καὶ τὴν πόλιν ἐκ μεγάλης μεγίστην καὶ πλουσιωτάτην ποιήσας καὶ γενόμενος δυνάμει πολλῶν βασιλέων καὶ τυράννων ὑπέρτερος, ὧν ἔνιοι καί τι τοῖς υἱέσι διέθεντο, ἐκεῖνος μιᾷ δραχμῇ μείζονα τὴν οὐσίαν οὐκ ἐποίησεν ἧς ὁ πατὴρ αὐτῷ κατέλιπε.

XVI Καίτοι τὴν δύναμιν αὐτοῦ σαφῶς μὲν ὁ Θουκυδίδης διηγεῖται, κακοήθως δὲ παρεμφαίνουσιν οἱ κωμικοί, Πεισιστρατίδας μὲν νέους τοὺς περὶ αὐτὸν ἑταίρους καλοῦντες, αὐτὸν δ᾽ ἀπομόσαι μὴ τυραννήσειν κελεύοντες, ὡς ἀσυμμέτρου πρὸς δημοκρατίαν καὶ βαρυτέρας περὶ αὐτὸν οὔσης ὑπεροχῆς. ὁ δὲ

His immense and long-continued ascendency attested by enemies as well as friends—by the contemporary comic poets, as well as by the contemporary historian, Thucydides. His re-election to the office of Strategus for fifteen years after the peace of 445 B.C. the strong- 2

§ 5 l. 10 <ἐκ πλουσίας> πλουσιωτάτην ci HSauppe ‖ 12 ὧν ἔνιοι καὶ ἐπὶ τοῖς υἱέσι διέθεντο ἐκείνῳ ci L. Holzapfel; the MSS have ὧν ἔνιοι καὶ ἐπὶ τοῖς υἱέσι διέθεντο, ἐκεῖνος, which Jacob retains, substituting τι for ἐπί: Fuhr and Blass accept Madvig's emendation καὶ ἐπίτροπον τοῖς υἱέσι διέθεντο ἐκεῖνον, the objection to which, as pointed out by Bernardakis (*Symb. cr.* p. 6), is that ἐπίτροπον καθιστάναι, not διατίθεσθαι, is the proper Greek for 'appointing' a guardian, and that the statement is historically improbable. Bernardakis's own translation *patrimonium ne una quidem drachma amplius effecit ex iis pecuniis, quarum partem* (= ὧν) *nonnulli etiam filiis reliquerant* is scarcely more satisfactory. HSauppe (*die Quellen* p. 34) conjectures ὧν ἔνιοι καὶ ἐπὶ τοῖς υἱέσι διέθεντο τοῖς ἐκείνου, μιᾷ δραχμῇ κτλ but, as A. Schmidt (*Perikl.* II 237) remarks, the statement which follows that Per. had not increased his paternal estate by a single drachma would then be strangely out of keeping, for the property of Paralus who died before his father, and had no descendants or collateral heirs, would naturally have reverted to Pericles. Schmidt's own translation 'some of whom bequeathed their power to their sons' is considered unsatisfactory, as it involves the assumption of an improbable fact

CH. XVI § 1 l. 8 τῆς περὶ αὐτόν ?

est proof of the confidence reposed in him by the people.

Τηλεκλείδης παραδεδωκέναι φησὶν
αὐτῷ τοὺς Ἀθηναίους

πόλεών τε φόρους αὐτάς τε πόλεις, τὰς μὲν δεῖν,
τὰς δ' ἀναλύειν,
λάϊνα τείχη, τὰ μὲν οἰκοδομεῖν τὰ δὲ τἄμπαλιν αὖ
καταβάλλειν,
σπονδὰς δύναμιν κράτος εἰρήνην πλοῦτόν τ' εὐδαιμονίαν τε.

καὶ ταῦτα καιρὸς οὐκ ἦν οὐδ' ἀκμὴ καὶ χάρις ἀνθούσης ἐφ' ὥραν πολιτείας, ἀλλὰ τεσσαράκοντα μὲν ἔτη πρωτεύων ἐν Ἐφιάλταις καὶ Λεωκράταις καὶ Μυρωνίδαις καὶ Κίμωσι καὶ Τολμίδαις καὶ Θουκυδίδαις, μετὰ δὲ τὴν Θουκυδίδου κατάλυσιν καὶ τὸν ὀστρακισμὸν οὐκ ἐλάττω τῶν πεντεκαίδεκα ἐτῶν διηνεκῆ καὶ μίαν οὖσαν ἐν ταῖς

His incorruptibility and disinterestedness as a statesman not inconsistent with the careful administration of his private property, by which he gave offence to some members of his household, although he was liberal enough in the relief of the needy.

ἐνιαυσίοις στρατηγίαις ἀρχὴν καὶ δυναστείαν κτησάμενος, ἐφύλαξεν ἑαυτὸν ἀνάλωτον ὑπὸ χρημάτων, καίπερ οὐ παντάπασιν ἀργῶς ἔχων πρὸς χρηματισμόν, ἀλλὰ τὸν πατρῷον καὶ δίκαιον πλοῦτον, ὡς μήτ' ἀμελούμενος ἐκφύγοι μήτε πολλὰ πράγματα καὶ διατριβὰς ἀσχολουμένῳ παρέχοι, συνέταξεν εἰς οἰκονομίαν, ἣν ᾤετο ῥᾴστην καὶ ἀκριβεστάτην εἶναι. τοὺς γὰρ ἐπετείους καρποὺς ἅπαντας ἀθρόους ἐπίπρασκεν, εἶτα τῶν ἀναγκαίων ἕκα-

§ 2 l. 13 τὰ δὲ τἄμπαλιν αὖ Bl² after Koek 1 220 : τὰ δέ γ' αὐτὰ πάλιν Bl¹ : εἶτ' αὐτὰ πάλιν ci Si¹ : τὰ δ' ἔπειτα πάλιν ci Fu Bergk : τὰ δὲ ταῦτα πάλιν Bk : vulgo τὰ δὲ αὐτὰ πάλιν ‖ 16 ἐφ' ὥραν ci Reiske : ἐφ' ὥρᾳ Si Do Fu Bl AJacob v: see n. to c. 28, 2
§ 3 l. 21 διηνεκῆ ci Pflugk (Si Do Bk Fu Bl) : διήνεγκε Ko v

στον εξ αγοράς ωνούμενος διώκει τον βίον και τα περί την δίαιταν. όθεν ούχ ηδύς ην ενηλίκοις παισίν ουδέ γυναιξί δαψιλής χορηγός, αλλ' εμέμφοντο την εφήμερον ταύτην και συνηγμένην εις το ακριβέστατον δαπάνην, ουδενός οίον εν οικία μεγάλη και πράγμασιν αφθόνοις περιρρέοντος, αλλά παντός μεν αναλώματος, παντός δε λήμματος δι' αριθμού και μέτρου βαδίζοντος. ο δε πάσαν αυτού την τοιαύτην συνέχων ακρίβειαν εις ην οικέτης, Ευάγγελος, ως έτερος ουδείς ευ πεφυκώς η κατεσκευασμένος υπό του Περικλέους προς οικονομίαν. απάδοντα μεν ουν ταύτα της Αναξαγόρου σοφίας, είγε και την οικίαν εκείνος εξέλιπε και την χώραν αφήκεν αργήν και μηλόβοτον υπ' ενθουσιασμού και μεγαλοφροσύνης· ου ταυτόν δ' εστίν, οίμαι, θεωρητικού φιλοσόφου και πολιτικού βίος, αλλ' ο μεν ανόργανον και απροσδεή της εκτός ύλης επί τοις καλοίς κινεί την διάνοιαν, τω δ' εις ανθρωπείας χρείας αναμιγνύντι την αρετήν έστιν ου γένοιτ' αν ου των αναγκαίων μόνον, αλλά και των καλών ο πλούτος, ώσπερ ην και Περικλεί βοηθούντι πολλοίς των πενήτων.

(Herein he was unlike his master Anaxagoras, who fell into abject poverty from the neglect of his estate.

§ 5 l. 45 απάδοντα ci Valckenaer *Diatr.* p. 223 (Si Fu Bl): απάδει ci Bryan (Bk): απεναντία Koraës (Si¹): άπαντα libri || 48 ανήκεν ci Bryan (Fuhr, Cobet who collects a number of instances to show that ανιέναι was the proper technical expression, Isocr. *Plut.* § 31, Lycurg. *Leocr.* § 144, Dion. Hal. *A. R.* II 16, Diod. Sic. I 36, Diog. Laert. VI 87 to which add Plut. *Lys.* c. 15, 2) Bergk: αφήκεν vulgo Wyttenbach Si Bk Bl; cp. Herod. VIII 70 απέντες την εωυτών αφύλακτον, Soph. *Ant.* 887 άφετέ (νυν) μόνην έρημον, *Oed. C.* 1279

Καὶ μέντοι γε τὸν Ἀναξαγόραν αὐτὸν λέγουσιν ἀσχολουμένου Περικλέους ἀμελούμενον κεῖσθαι συγκεκαλυμμένον ἤδη γηραιὸν ἀποκαρτεροῦντα· προσπεσόντος δὲ τῷ Περικλεῖ τοῦ πράγματος ἐκπλαγέντα θεῖν εὐθὺς ἐπὶ τὸν ἄνδρα καὶ δεῖσθαι πᾶσαν δέησιν, ὀλοφυρόμενον οὐκ ἐκεῖνον, ἀλλ' ἑαυτόν, εἰ τοιοῦτον ἀπολεῖ τῆς πολιτείας σύμβουλον. ἐκκαλυψάμενον οὖν τὸν Ἀναξαγόραν εἰπεῖν πρὸς αὐτὸν "Ὦ Περίκλεις, καὶ οἱ τοῦ λύχνου χρείαν ἔχοντες ἔλαιον ἐπιχέουσιν."

XVII Ἀρχομένων δὲ Λακεδαιμονίων ἄχθεσθαι τῇ αὐξήσει τῶν Ἀθηναίων, ἐπαίρων ὁ Περικλῆς τὸν δῆμον ἔτι μᾶλλον μέγα φρονεῖν καὶ μεγάλων αὐτὸν ἀξιοῦν πραγμάτων γράφει ψήφισμα, πάντας Ἕλληνας τοὺς ὁπήποτε κατοικοῦντας Εὐρώπης ἢ τῆς Ἀσίας παρακαλεῖν, καὶ μικρὰν πόλιν καὶ μεγάλην, εἰς σύλλογον πέμπειν Ἀθήναζε τοὺς βουλευσομένους περὶ τῶν Ἑλληνικῶν ἱερῶν ἃ κατέπρησαν οἱ βάρβαροι, καὶ τῶν θυσιῶν ἃς ὀφείλουσιν ὑπὲρ τῆς Ἑλλάδος εὐξάμενοι τοῖς θεοῖς ὅτε πρὸς τοὺς βαρβάρους ἐμάχοντο, καὶ τῆς θαλάττης ὅπως πλέωσι πάντες ἀδεῶς καὶ τὴν εἰρήνην ἄγωσιν. 2 ἐπὶ ταῦτα δ' ἄνδρες εἴκοσι τῶν ὑπὲρ πεντήκοντα

CH. XVII § 1 l. 7 Cobet adds τῆς before Εὐρώπης, but cp. *Pomp.* c. 45, 5 τὸν μὲν πρῶτον ἐκ Λιβύης, τὸν δὲ δεύτερον ἐξ Εὐρώπης, τοῦτον δὲ τὸν τελευταῖον ἀπὸ τῆς Ἀσίας with *Arist.* c. 9, 3 κρεῖττον δὲ λείπεσθαι (ἔργον) τὸ λαβεῖν ἐν τῇ Εὐρώπῃ τὴν Ἀσίαν

ἔτη γεγονότων ἐπέμφθησαν, ὧν πέντε μὲν Ἴωνας καὶ Δωριεῖς τοὺς ἐν Ἀσίᾳ καὶ νησιώτας ἄχρι Λέσβου καὶ Ῥόδου παρεκάλουν, πέντε δὲ τοὺς ἐν Ἑλλησπόντῳ καὶ Θρᾴκῃ μέχρι Βυζαντίου τόπους ἐπῄεσαν, καὶ πέντε ἐπὶ τούτοις εἰς Βοιωτίαν καὶ Φωκίδα καὶ Πελοπόννησον, ἐκ δὲ ταύτης διὰ Λοκρῶν ἐπὶ τὴν πρόσοικον ἤπειρον ἕως Ἀκαρνανίας καὶ Ἀμβρακίας ἀπεστάλησαν· οἱ δὲ λοιποὶ δι' Εὐβοίας ἐπ' Οἰταίους καὶ τὸν Μαλιέα κόλπον καὶ Φθιώτας Ἀχαιοὺς καὶ Θεσσαλοὺς ἐπορεύοντο, συμπείθοντες ἰέναι καὶ μετέχειν τῶν βουλευμάτων ἐπ' εἰρήνῃ καὶ κοινοπραγίᾳ τῆς Ἑλλάδος. ἐπράχθη δὲ οὐδὲν οὐδὲ συνῆλθον αἱ πόλεις, Λακεδαιμονίων ὑπεναντιωθέντων, ὡς λέγεται, καὶ τὸ πρῶτον ἐν Πελοποννήσῳ τῆς πείρας ἐλεγχθείσης. τοῦτο μὲν οὖν παρεθέμην ἐνδεικνύμενος αὐτοῦ τὸ φρόνημα καὶ τὴν μεγαλοφροσύνην.

XVIII Ἐν δὲ ταῖς στρατηγίαις εὐδοκίμει μάλιστα διὰ τὴν ἀσφάλειαν, οὔτε μάχης ἐχούσης πολλὴν ἀδηλότητα καὶ κίνδυνον ἑκουσίως ἁπτόμενος, οὔτε τοὺς ἐκ τοῦ παραβαλέσθαι χρησαμένους τύχῃ λαμπρᾷ καὶ θαυμασθέντας ὡς μεγάλους ζηλῶν καὶ μιμούμενος στρατηγούς, ἀεί τε λέγων πρὸς τοὺς πολίτας, ὡς ὅσον ἐπ' αὐτῷ μενοῦσιν ἀθάνατοι πάντα τὸν χρόνον. ὁρῶν δὲ Τολμίδην τὸν Τολμαίου διὰ τὰς πρό-

Estimate of Pericles, as general. Caution a prominent feature in his military character.

CH. XVIII § 1 l. 5 παραβαλέσθαι ci Si (Fu Bl): παραβάλλεσθαι Bk vulgo

τερον εὐτυχίας καὶ διὰ τὸ τιμᾶσθαι διαφερόντως ἐκ τῶν πολεμικῶν σὺν οὐδενὶ
καιρῷ παρασκευαζόμενον εἰς Βοιωτίαν
ἐμβαλεῖν καὶ πεπεικότα τῶν ἐν ἡλικίᾳ
τοὺς ἀρίστους καὶ φιλοτιμοτάτους
ἐθελοντὶ στρατεύεσθαι, χιλίους γενομένους ἄνευ τῆς ἄλλης δυνάμεως, κατ-
έχειν ἐπειρᾶτο καὶ παρακαλεῖν ἐν τῷ
δήμῳ, τὸ μνημονευόμενον εἰπών, ὡς,
εἰ μὴ πείθοιτο Περικλεῖ, τόν γε σοφώτατον οὐχ ἁμαρτήσεται σύμβουλον
3 ἀναμείνας χρόνον. τότε μὲν οὖν μετρίως εὐδοκίμησε τοῦτ᾽ εἰπών· ὀλίγαις δ᾽ ὕστερον ἡμέραις,
ὡς ἀνηγγέλθη τεθνεὼς μὲν αὐτὸς Τολμίδης περὶ
Κορώνειαν ἡττηθεὶς μάχῃ, τεθνεῶτες δὲ πολλοὶ
κἀγαθοὶ τῶν πολιτῶν, μεγάλην τοῦτο τῷ Περικλεῖ μετ᾽ εὐνοίας δόξαν ἤνεγκεν, ὡς ἀνδρὶ
φρονίμῳ καὶ φιλοπολίτῃ.

XIX Τῶν δὲ στρατηγιῶν ἠγαπήθη μὲν ἡ περὶ
Χερρόνησον αὐτοῦ μάλιστα, σωτήριος
γενομένη τοῖς αὐτόθι κατοικοῦσι τῶν
Ἑλλήνων· οὐ γὰρ μόνον ἐποίκους
Ἀθηναίων χιλίους κομίσας ἔρρωσεν
εὐανδρίᾳ τὰς πόλεις, ἀλλὰ καὶ τὸν
αὐχένα διαζώσας ἐρύμασι καὶ προ-
βλήμασιν ἐκ θαλάττης εἰς θάλατταν
ἀπετείχισε τὰς καταδρομὰς Θρᾳκῶν τῶν

§ 2 l. 16 ἐθελοντί vulgo : ἐθελοντάς ci Cobet, who also would read συστρατεύονται on the ground that such is the more proper expression for 'lecti iuvenes sua uoluntate militantes' ‖ 18 παραστέλλειν ci Bergk

CH. XIX § 1 l. 9 Θρᾳκῶν τῶν ci Hn : τῶν Θρᾳκῶν v

ΧΧ 1 ΠΕΡΙΚΛΗΣ 37

περικεχυμένων τῇ Χερρονήσῳ, καὶ πόλεμον 2
ἐνδελεχῆ καὶ βαρὺν ἐξέκλεισεν, ᾧ συνείχετο
πάντα τὸν χρόνον ἡ χώρα, βαρβαρικαῖς ἀναμεμιγμένη
γειτνιάσεσι καὶ γέμουσα λῃστηρίων
ὁμόρων καὶ συνοίκων· ἐθαυμάσθη δὲ καὶ διεβοήθη
πρὸς τοὺς ἐκτὸς ἀνθρώπους περιπλεύσας Πελοπόννησον,
ἐκ Πηγῶν τῆς Μεγαρικῆς ἀναχθεὶς
ἑκατὸν τριήρεσιν. οὐ γὰρ μόνον ἐπόρθησε τῆς 3
παραλίας πολλήν, ὡς Τολμίδης πρότερον, ἀλλὰ
καὶ πόρρω θαλάττης προελθὼν τοῖς ἀπὸ τῶν
νεῶν ὁπλίταις τοὺς μὲν ἄλλους εἰς τὰ τείχη
συνέστειλε δείσαντας αὐτοῦ τὴν ἔφοδον, ἐν δὲ
Νεμέᾳ Σικυωνίους ὑποστάντας καὶ συνάψαντας
μάχην κατὰ κράτος τρεψάμενος ἔστησε τρόπαιον.
ἐκ δ᾽ Ἀχαΐας φίλης οὔσης στρατιώτας ἀναλαβὼν 4
εἰς τὰς τριήρεις ἐπὶ τὴν ἀντιπέρας ἤπειρον
ἐκομίσθη τῷ στόλῳ, καὶ παραπλεύσας τὸν
Ἀχελῷον Ἀκαρνανίαν κατέδραμε καὶ κατέκλεισεν
Οἰνιάδας εἰς τὸ τεῖχος καὶ τεμὼν τὴν
γῆν καὶ κακώσας ἀπῆρεν ἐπ᾽ οἴκου, φοβερὸς μὲν
φανεὶς τοῖς πολεμίοις, ἀσφαλὴς δὲ καὶ δραστήριος
τοῖς πολίταις. οὐδὲν γὰρ οὐδ᾽ ἀπὸ τύχης πρόσκρουσμα
συνέβη περὶ τοὺς στρατευομένους.

ΧΧ Εἰς δὲ τὸν Πόντον εἰσπλεύσας στόλῳ
μεγάλῳ καὶ κεκοσμημένῳ λαμπρῶς ταῖς His expedition to the
μὲν Ἑλληνίσι πόλεσιν ὧν ἐδέοντο Pontus,
διεπράξατο καὶ προσηνέχθη φιλαν- where he appeared

§ 2 l. 15 ἀνθρώπους <μάλιστα> ci Bergk ‖ εἰς Πελοπόννησον ci A Jacob
§ 3 l. 18 πολλήν ci Emperius (Si Fu Bl) : πόλιν v
§ 4 l. 28 Οἰνιάδας ci Si (Do Bk Fu Bl) : Οἰνεάδας Ko v

θρώπως, τοῖς δὲ περιοικοῦσι βαρβάροις ἔθνεσι καὶ βασιλεῦσιν αὐτῶν καὶ δυνάσταις ἐπεδείξατο μὲν τῆς δυνάμεως τὸ μέγεθος καὶ τὴν ἄδειαν καὶ τὸ θάρσος, ᾗ βούλοιντο πλεόντων καὶ πᾶσαν ὑφ' αὑτοῖς πεποιημένων τὴν θάλασσαν, Σινωπεῦσι δὲ τρισκαίδεκα ναῦς ἀπέλιπε μετὰ Λαμάχου καὶ στρατιώτας ἐπὶ Τιμησίλεων τύραννον. ἐκπεσόντος δὲ τούτου καὶ τῶν ἑταίρων ἐψηφίσατο πλεῖν εἰς Σινώπην Ἀθηναίων ἐθελοντὰς ἑξακοσίους καὶ συγκατοικεῖν Σινωπεῦσι, νειμαμένους οἰκίας καὶ χώραν ἣν πρότερον οἱ τύραννοι κατεῖχον. τἆλλα δ' οὐ συνεχώρει ταῖς ὁρμαῖς τῶν πολιτῶν, οὐδὲ συνεξέπιπτεν ὑπὸ ῥώμης καὶ τύχης τοσαύτης ἐπαιρομένων Αἰγύπτου τε πάλιν ἀντιλαμβάνεσθαι καὶ κινεῖν τῆς βασιλέως ἀρχῆς τὰ πρὸς θαλάσσῃ. πολλοὺς δὲ καὶ Σικελίας ὁ δύσερως ἐκεῖνος ἤδη καὶ δύσποτμος ἔρως εἶχεν, ὃν ὕστερον ἐξέκαυσαν οἱ περὶ τὸν Ἀλκιβιάδην ῥήτορες. ἦν δὲ καὶ Τυρρηνία καὶ Καρχηδὼν ἐνίοις ὄνειρος, οὐκ ἀπ' ἐλπίδος διὰ τὸ μέγεθος τῆς ὑποκειμένης ἡγεμονίας καὶ τὴν εὔροιαν τῶν πραγμάτων·

XXI ἀλλ' ὁ Περικλῆς κατεῖχε τὴν ἐκδρομὴν ταύτην καὶ περιέκοπτε τὴν πολυπραγμοσύνην καὶ τὰ πλεῖστα τῆς δυνάμεως ἔτρεπεν εἰς φυλακὴν καὶ βεβαιότητα τῶν ὑπαρχόντων, μέγα ἔργον ἡγούμενος ἀνείργειν Λακεδαιμονίους καὶ ὅλως ὑπεναντιούμενος ἐκείνοις, ὡς ἄλλοις τε πολλοῖς ἔδειξε καὶ μάλιστα τοῖς περὶ τὸν ἱερὸν πραχθεῖσι πόλεμον. ἐπεὶ γὰρ οἱ Λακεδαιμόνιοι στρατεύσαντες εἰς Δελφοὺς Φωκέων ἐχόντων τὸ ἱερὸν Δελφοῖς ἀπέδωκαν, εὐθὺς ἐκείνων ἀπαλλαγέντων ὁ Περικλῆς ἐπιστρατεύσας πάλιν εἰσήγαγε τοὺς Φωκέας. καὶ τῶν Λακεδαιμονίων ἣν ἔδωκαν αὐτοῖς Δελφοὶ προμαντείαν εἰς τὸ μέτωπον ἐγκολαψάντων τοῦ χαλκοῦ λύκου, λαβὼν καὶ αὐτὸς προμαντείαν τοῖς Ἀθηναίοις εἰς τὸν αὐτὸν λύκον κατὰ τὴν δεξιὰν πλευρὰν ἐνεχάραξεν.

XXII Ὅτι δ' ὀρθῶς ἐν τῇ Ἑλλάδι τὴν δύναμιν τῶν Ἀθηναίων συνεῖχεν, ἐμαρτύρησεν αὐτῷ τὰ γενόμενα. πρῶτον μὲν γὰρ Εὐβοεῖς ἀπέστησαν, ἐφ' οὓς διέβη μετὰ δυνάμεως. εἶτ' εὐθὺς ἀπηγγέλλοντο Μεγαρεῖς ἐκπεπολεμωμένοι καὶ στρατιὰ Πελοποννησίων ἐπὶ τοῖς ὅροις τῆς Ἀττικῆς οὖσα, Πλειστώνακτος ἡγουμένου, βασιλέως Λακεδαιμονίων. πάλιν οὖν ὁ Περικλῆς κατὰ τάχος ἐκ τῆς Εὐβοίας ἀνεκομίζετο πρὸς τὸν ἐν τῇ Ἀττικῇ πόλεμον· καὶ συνάψαι μὲν εἰς χεῖρας οὐκ ἐθάρσησε πολλοῖς καὶ ἀγαθοῖς ὁπλίταις προκαλουμένοις· ὁρῶν δὲ τὸν Πλειστώνακτα νέον ὄντα κομιδῇ, χρώμενον δὲ μάλιστα Κλεανδρίδῃ τῶν συμβούλων, ὃν οἱ ἔφοροι φύλακα καὶ πάρεδρον αὐτῷ διὰ τὴν ἡλικίαν συνέπεμψαν, ἐπειρᾶτο τούτου κρύφα· καὶ ταχὺ διαφθείρας χρήμασιν αὐτὸν ἔπεισεν ἐκ τῆς Ἀττικῆς ἀπαγαγεῖν τοὺς Πελοποννησίους. ὡς δ᾽ ἀπεχώρησεν ἡ στρατιὰ καὶ διελύθη κατὰ πόλεις, βαρέως φέροντες οἱ Λακεδαιμόνιοι τὸν μὲν βασιλέα χρήμασιν ἐζημίωσαν, ὧν τὸ πλῆθος οὐκ ἔχων ἐκτῖσαι μετέστησεν ἑαυτὸν ἐκ Λακεδαίμονος, τοῦ δὲ Κλεανδρίδου φεύγοντος θάνατον κατέγνωσαν. οὗτος δ᾽ ἦν πατὴρ Γυλίππου τοῦ περὶ Σικελίαν Ἀθηναίους καταπολεμήσαντος. ἔοικε δ᾽ ὥσπερ συγγενικὸν αὐτῷ προστρίψασθαι νόσημα τὴν φιλαργυρίαν ἡ φύσις, ὑφ᾽ ἧς καὶ αὐτὸς αἰσχρῶς ἐπὶ καλοῖς ἔργοις ἁλοὺς ἐξέπεσε τῆς Σπάρτης.

Ταῦτα μὲν οὖν ἐν τοῖς περὶ Λυσάνδρου δεδηλώκαμεν. XXIII τοῦ δὲ Περικλέους ἐν τῷ τῆς στρατηγίας ἀπολογισμῷ δέκα ταλάντων ἀνάλωμα γράψαντος ἀνηλωμένων εἰς τὸ δέον, ὁ δῆμος ἀπεδέξατο μὴ πολυπραγμονήσας μηδ᾽ ἐλέγξας τὸ ἀπόρρητον. ἔνιοι δ᾽ ἱστορήκασιν, ὧν ἐστι καὶ Θεόφραστος ὁ φιλόσοφος, ὅτι καθ᾽ ἕκαστον ἐνιαυτὸν εἰς τὴν Σπάρτην ἐφοίτα δέκα τάλαντα παρὰ τοῦ Περικλέους, οἷς τοὺς

§ 2 l. 18 συνεξέπεμψαν ci Fuhr
§ 3 l. 32 καὶ οὗτος vel αὐτοῖς ci Bergk ‖ καλοῖς ci Si¹ (Bk Fu Bl): κακοῖς Ko Do Bergk vulgo

ἐν τέλει πάντας θεραπεύων παρῃτεῖτο τὸν πόλεμον, οὐ τὴν εἰρήνην ὠνούμενος ἀλλὰ τὸν χρόνον, ἐν ᾧ παρασκευασάμενος καθ' ἡσυχίαν ἔμελλε πολεμήσειν βέλτιον. αὖθις οὖν ἐπὶ τοὺς ἀφεστῶτας τραπόμενος καὶ διαβὰς εἰς Εὔβοιαν πεντήκοντα ναυσὶ καὶ πεντακισχιλίοις ὁπλίταις κατεστρέψατο τὰς πόλεις. καὶ Χαλκιδέων μὲν τοὺς ἱπποβότας λεγομένους πλούτῳ καὶ δόξῃ διαφέροντας ἐξέβαλεν, Ἑστιεῖς δὲ πάντας ἀναστήσας ἐκ τῆς χώρας Ἀθηναίους κατῴκισε, μόνοις τούτοις ἀπαραιτήτως χρησάμενος, ὅτι ναῦν Ἀττικὴν αἰχμάλωτον λαβόντες ἀπέκτειναν τοὺς ἄνδρας. XXIV Ἐκ τούτου γενομένων σπονδῶν Ἀθηναίοις καὶ Λακεδαιμονίοις εἰς ἔτη τριάκοντα ψηφίζεται τὸν εἰς Σάμον πλοῦν, αἰτίαν ποιησάμενος κατ' αὐτῶν, ὅτι τὸν πρὸς Μιλησίους κελευόμενοι διαλύσασθαι πόλεμον οὐχ ὑπήκουον.

Ἐπεὶ δ' Ἀσπασίᾳ χαριζόμενος δοκεῖ πρᾶξαι τὰ πρὸς Σαμίους, ἐνταῦθα ἂν εἴη καιρὸς διαπορῆσαι μάλιστα περὶ τῆς ἀνθρώπου, τίνα τέχνην ἢ δύναμιν τοσαύτην ἔχουσα τῶν τε πολιτικῶν

CH. XXIII § 2 l. 13 αὖθις ci HSauppe (Fu Bl): εὐθύς Ko Si Do Bk v | 17 καὶ Χαλκιδέων μέν ci Bryan (Ko Si Do Bk Bl): καὶ Χαλκιδέων δέ vulgo : καὶ ... Χαλκιδέων δέ ci Fuhr, who proposes to fill up the supposed gap by supplying the words καὶ τοὺς μὲν ἄλλους ὁμολογίᾳ κατεστήσατο from Thuc. 1 114 καὶ τὴν μὲν ἄλλην ὁμολογίᾳ κατεστήσαντο. But the opposition clearly lies between τοὺς ἱπποβότας and πάντας || 20 Ἀθηναίοις κατῴκισε, μόνοις τούτοις ci Reiske (Ko Si³ Bk Fu Bl): Ἀθηναίοις μόνους κατῴκισε τούτοις Do vulgo

Aspasia, and the extraordinary influence she acquired over Pericles.

τοὺς πρωτεύοντας ἐχειρώσατο καὶ τοῖς φιλοσόφοις οὐ φαῦλον οὐδ' ὀλίγον ὑπὲρ αὐτῆς παρέσχε λόγον. ὅτι μὲν γὰρ ἦν Μιλησία γένος, Ἀξιόχου θυγάτηρ, ὁμολογεῖται· φασὶ δ' αὐτὴν Θαργηλίαν τινὰ τῶν παλαιῶν Ἰάδων ζηλώσασαν ἐπιθέσθαι τοῖς δυνατωτάτοις ἀνδράσι. καὶ γὰρ ἡ Θαργηλία τό τ' εἶδος εὐπρεπὴς γενομένη καὶ χάριν ἔχουσα μετὰ δεινότητος πλείστοις μὲν Ἑλλήνων συνῴκησεν ἀνδράσι, πάντας δὲ προσεποίησε βασιλεῖ τοὺς πλησιάσαντας αὐτῇ, καὶ ταῖς πόλεσι μηδισμοῦ δι' ἐκείνων ὑπέσπειρεν ἀρχὰς δυνατωτάτων ὄντων καὶ μεγίστων. τὴν δ' Ἀσπασίαν οἱ μὲν ὡς σοφήν τινα καὶ πολιτικὴν ὑπὸ τοῦ Περικλέους σπουδασθῆναι λέγουσι· καὶ γὰρ Σωκράτης ἔστιν ὅτε μετὰ τῶν γνωρίμων ἐφοίτα, καὶ τὰς γυναῖκας ἀκροασομένας οἱ συνήθεις ἦγον ὡς αὐτήν, καίπερ οὐ κοσμίου προεστῶσαν ἐργασίας οὐδὲ σεμνῆς, ἀλλὰ παιδίσκας ἑταιρούσας τρέφουσαν· Αἰσχίνης δέ φησι καὶ Λυσικλέα τὸν προβατοκάπηλον ἐξ ἀγεννοῦς καὶ ταπεινοῦ τὴν φύσιν Ἀθηναίων γενέσθαι πρῶτον, Ἀσπασίᾳ συνόντα μετὰ τὴν Περικλέους τελευτήν. ἐν δὲ τῷ Μενεξένῳ τῷ Πλάτωνος, εἰ καὶ μετὰ παιδιᾶς τὰ πρῶτα γέγραπται, τοσοῦτόν γ' ἱστορίας ἔνεστιν, ὅτι δόξαν εἶχε τὸ γύναιον ἐπὶ ῥητορικῇ πολλοῖς Ἀθηναίων ὁμιλεῖν. φαίνεται μέντοι μᾶλλον ἐρωτική τις ἡ τοῦ Περικλέους ἀγάπησις

CH. XXIV § 3 l. 28 ἦγον Bl v: συνῆγον S Fu | 29 ὡς S Vulcob. εἰ Reiske Ko (Fu Bl): εἰς St Si v
§ 4 l. 32 ἀγεννοῦς S

γενομένη πρὸς Ἀσπασίαν. ἦν μὲν γὰρ αὐτῷ γυνὴ προσήκουσα μὲν κατὰ γένος, συνῳκηκυῖα δ' Ἱππονίκῳ πρότερον, ἐξ οὗ Καλλίαν ἔτεκε τὸν πλούσιον· ἔτεκε δὲ καὶ παρὰ τῷ Περικλεῖ Ξάνθιππον καὶ Πάραλον. εἶτα τῆς συμβιώσεως οὐκ οὔσης αὐτοῖς ἀρεστῆς, ἐκείνην μὲν ἑτέρῳ βουλομένην συνεξέδωκεν, αὐτὸς δὲ τὴν Ἀσπασίαν λαβὼν ἔστερξε διαφερόντως. καὶ γὰρ ἐξιών, ὥς φασι, καὶ εἰσιὼν ἀπ' ἀγορᾶς ἠσπάζετο καθ' ἡμέραν αὐτὴν μετὰ τοῦ καταφιλεῖν. ἐν δὲ ταῖς κωμῳδίαις Ὀμφάλη τε νέα καὶ Δηάνειρα καὶ πάλιν Ἥρα προσαγορεύεται. Κρατῖνος δ' ἄντικρυς παλλακὴν αὐτὴν εἴρηκεν ἐν τούτοις·

Ἥραν τέ οἱ Ἀσπασίαν τίκτει
Καταπυγοσύνη παλλακὴν κυνώπιδα.

Δοκεῖ δὲ καὶ τὸν νόθον ἐκ ταύτης τεκνῶσαι, περὶ οὗ πεποίηκεν Εὔπολις ἐν Δήμοις αὐτὸν μὲν οὕτως ἐρωτῶντα

ὁ νόθος δέ μοι ζῇ;

τὸν δὲ Μυρωνίδην ἀποκρινόμενον

καὶ πάλαι γ' ἂν ἦν ἀνήρ,
εἰ μὴ τὸ τῆς πόρνης ὑπωρρώδει κακόν.

οὕτω δὲ τὴν Ἀσπασίαν ὀνομαστὴν καὶ κλεινὴν γενέσθαι λέγουσιν, ὥστε καὶ Κῦρον τὸν πολεμήσαντα βασιλεῖ περὶ τῆς τῶν Περσῶν ἡγεμονίας

§ 6 l. 57 Καταπυγοσύνη ci Bergk (Emperius Si Do Fu Bl): καὶ καταπυγοσύνην Ku v 59 Δήμοις ci St: Δημοσίοις libri

τὴν ἀγαπωμένην ὑπ' αὐτοῦ μάλιστα τῶν παλλακίδων Ἀσπασίαν ὀνομάσαι, καλουμένην Μιλτὼ πρότερον. ἦν δὲ Φωκαῒς τὸ γένος, Ἑρμοτίμου θυγάτηρ· ἐν δὲ τῇ μάχῃ Κύρου πεσόντος ἀπαχθεῖσα πρὸς βασιλέα πλεῖστον ἴσχυσε.

Ταῦτα μὲν ἐπελθόντα τῇ μνήμῃ κατὰ τὴν γραφὴν ἀπώσασθαι καὶ παρελθεῖν ἴσως ἀπάνθρωπον ἦν. XXV τὸν δὲ πρὸς Σαμίους πόλεμον

Alleged cause of the war between Athens and Samos.

αἰτιῶνται μάλιστα τὸν Περικλέα ψηφίσασθαι διὰ Μιλησίους Ἀσπασίας δεηθείσης. αἱ γὰρ πόλεις ἐπολέμουν τὸν περὶ Πριήνης πόλεμον, καὶ κρατοῦντες οἱ Σάμιοι παύσασθαι τῶν Ἀθηναίων

First expedition under Pericles against Samos.

κελευόντων καὶ δίκας λαβεῖν καὶ δοῦναι παρ' αὐτοῖς οὐκ ἐπείθοντο. πλεύσας οὖν ὁ Περικλῆς τὴν μὲν οὖσαν ὀλιγαρχίαν ἐν Σάμῳ κατέλυσεν, τῶν δὲ πρώτων λαβὼν ὁμήρους πεντήκοντα καὶ παῖδας ἴσους εἰς Λῆμνον ἀπέστειλε. καίτοι φασὶν ἕκαστον μὲν αὐτῷ τῶν ὁμήρων διδόναι τάλαντον ὑπὲρ ἑαυτοῦ, πολλὰ δ' ἄλλα τοὺς μὴ θέλοντας ἐν τῇ πόλει γενέσθαι δημοκρατίαν. ἔτι δὲ Πισσούθνης ὁ Πέρσης ἔχων τινὰ πρὸς Σαμίους εὔνοιαν ἀπέστειλεν αὐτῷ μυρίους χρυσοῦς παραιτούμενος τὴν πόλιν. οὐ μὴν ἔλαβε τούτων οὐδὲν ὁ Περικλῆς, ἀλλὰ χρησάμενος ὥσπερ ἐγνώκει τοῖς Σαμίοις καὶ καταστήσας δημοκρατίαν ἀπέπλευσεν εἰς τὰς Ἀθήνας. οἱ δ' εὐθὺς ἀπέστησαν, ἐκκλέψαντος αὐτοῖς τοὺς ὁμήρους Πισσούθνου καὶ τἆλλα παρασκευά-

ΠΕΡΙΚΛΗΣ

σαντος πρὸς τὸν πόλεμον. αὖθις οὖν ὁ Περικλῆς ἐξέπλευσεν ἐπ' αὐτούς, οὐχ ἡσυχάζοντας οὐδὲ κατεπτηχότας, ἀλλὰ καὶ πάνυ προθύμως ἐγνωκότας ἀντιλαμβάνεσθαι τῆς θαλάττης. γενομένης δὲ καρτερᾶς ναυμαχίας περὶ νῆσον, ἣν Τραγίας καλοῦσι, λαμπρῶς ὁ Περικλῆς ἐνίκα τέσσαρσι καὶ τεσσαράκοντα ναυσὶν ἑβδομήκοντα καταναυμαχήσας, ὧν <αἱ> εἴκοσι στρατιώτιδες ἦσαν.

XXVI Ἅμα δὲ τῇ νίκῃ καὶ τῇ διώξει τοῦ λιμένος κρατήσας ἐπολιόρκει τοὺς Σαμίους ἁμῶς γέ πως ἔτι τολμῶντας ἐπεξιέναι καὶ διαμάχεσθαι πρὸ τοῦ τείχους. ἐπεὶ δὲ μείζων ἕτερος στόλος ἦλθεν ἐκ τῶν Ἀθηνῶν καὶ παντελῶς κατεκλείσθησαν οἱ Σάμιοι, λαβὼν ὁ Περικλῆς ἑξήκοντα τριήρεις ἔπλευσεν εἰς τὸν ἔξω πόντον, ὡς μὲν οἱ πλεῖστοι λέγουσι, Φοινισσῶν νεῶν ἐπικούρων τοῖς Σαμίοις προσφερομένων ἀπαντῆσαι καὶ διαγωνίσασθαι πορρωτάτω βουλόμενος, ὡς δὲ Στησίμβροτος, ἐπὶ Κύπρον στελλόμενος· ὅπερ οὐ δοκεῖ πιθανὸν εἶναι. ὁποτέρῳ δ' οὖν ἐχρήσατο τῶν λογισμῶν, ἁμαρτεῖν ἔδοξε. πλεύσαντος γὰρ αὐτοῦ Μέλισσος ὁ Ἰθαγένους, ἀνὴρ φιλόσοφος στρατηγῶν τότε τῆς Σάμου, καταφρονήσας τῆς ὀλιγότητος τῶν νεῶν ἢ τῆς ἀπειρίας τῶν στρατηγῶν ἔπεισε τοὺς πολίτας ἐπιθέσθαι

CH. XXVI § 2 l. 15 ἀποπλεύσαντος ci Cobet (Bergk)

τοῖς Ἀθηναίοις. καὶ γενομένης μάχης νικήσαντες
οἱ Σάμιοι καὶ πολλοὺς μὲν αὐτῶν
ἄνδρας ἑλόντες, πολλὰς δὲ ναῦς διαφθείραντες, ἐχρῶντο τῇ θαλάσσῃ
καὶ παρετίθεντο τῶν ἀναγκαίων πρὸς
τὸν πόλεμον ὅσα μὴ πρότερον εἶχον.
ὑπὸ δὲ τοῦ Μελίσσου καὶ Περικλέα
φησὶν αὐτὸν Ἀριστοτέλης ἡττηθῆναι
ναυμαχοῦντα πρότερον. οἱ δὲ Σάμιοι
τοὺς αἰχμαλώτους τῶν Ἀθηναίων ἀνθυβρίζοντες ἔστιζον εἰς τὸ μέτωπον
γλαῦκας· καὶ γὰρ ἐκείνους οἱ Ἀθηναῖοι
σάμαιναν· ἡ δὲ σάμαινα ναῦς ἐστιν ὑόπρῳρος
μὲν τὸ σίμωμα, κοιλοτέρα δὲ καὶ γαστροειδής,
ὥστε καὶ ποντοπορεῖν καὶ ταχυναυτεῖν. οὕτω
δ' ὠνομάσθη διὰ τὸ πρῶτον ἐν Σάμῳ φανῆναι,
Πολυκράτους τοῦ τυράννου κατασκευάσαντος.
πρὸς ταῦτα τὰ στίγματα λέγουσι καὶ τὸ
Ἀριστοφάνειον ᾐνίχθαι—

Σαμίων ὁ δῆμός ἐστιν ὡς πολυγράμματος.

XXVII Πυθόμενος δ' οὖν ὁ Περικλῆς τὴν ἐπὶ
στρατοπέδου συμφορὰν ἐβοήθει κατὰ
τάχος. καὶ τοῦ Μελίσσου πρὸς αὐτὸν
ἀντιταξαμένου κρατήσας καὶ τρεψά-

§ 3 l. 32 ὑόπρῳρος ci Koraës (Si Do Bk Fu Bl): ὑπόπρῳρος vulgo ‖ 34 ποντοπορεῖν Bl vulgo: φορτοφορεῖν ci Koraës (Si Do Bk Fu) ‖ 36 Ko Si Do Bk omit τοῦ: cp. c. 20, 1 ‖ 39 Cobet divides the line between two interlocutors:—A. Σαμίων ὁ δῆμός ἐστιν. B. ὡς πολυγράμματος: Fritzsche and Kock punctuate ἐστίν· ὡς πολυγράμματος cl Ar. Av. 281

μενος τοὺς πολεμίους εὐθὺς περιετείχιζε, δαπάνῃ καὶ χρόνῳ μᾶλλον ἢ τραύμασι καὶ κινδύνοις τῶν πολιτῶν περιγενέσθαι καὶ συνελεῖν τὴν πόλιν βουλόμενος. ἐπεὶ δὲ δυσχεραίνοντας τῇ τριβῇ τοὺς Ἀθηναίους καὶ μάχεσθαι προθυμουμένους ἔργον ἦν κατασχεῖν, ὀκτὼ μέρη διελὼν τὸ πᾶν πλῆθος ἀπεκλήρου, καὶ τῷ λαβόντι τὸν λευκὸν κύαμον εὐωχεῖσθαι καὶ σχολάζειν παρεῖχε τῶν ἄλλων τρυχομένων. διὸ καί φασι τοὺς ἐν εὐπαθείαις τισὶ γινομένους λευκὴν ἡμέραν ἐκείνην ἀπὸ τοῦ λευκοῦ κυάμου προσαγορεύειν. Ἔφορος δὲ καὶ μηχαναῖς χρήσασθαι τὸν Περικλέα, τὴν καινότητα θαυμασταῖς, Ἀρτέμωνος τοῦ μηχανικοῦ παρόντος, ὃν χωλὸν ὄντα καὶ φορείῳ πρὸς τὰ κατεπείγοντα τῶν ἔργων προσκομιζόμενον ὀνομασθῆναι Περιφόρητον. τοῦτο μὲν οὖν Ἡρακλείδης ὁ Ποντικὸς ἐλέγχει τοῖς Ἀνακρέοντος ποιήμασιν, ἐν οἷς ὁ Περιφόρητος Ἀρτέμων ὀνομάζεται πολλαῖς ἔμπροσθεν ἡλικίαις τοῦ περὶ Σάμον πολέμου καὶ τῶν πραγμάτων ἐκείνων. τὸν δ᾽ Ἀρτέμωνά φησι τρυφερόν τινα τῷ βίῳ καὶ πρὸς τοὺς φόβους μαλακὸν ὄντα καὶ καταπλῆγα τὰ πολλὰ μὲν οἴκοι καθέζεσθαι, χαλκῆν

ἀσπίδα τῆς κεφαλῆς αὐτοῦ δυεῖν οἰκετῶν
ὑπερεχόντων, ὥστε μηδὲν ἐμπεσεῖν τῶν ἄνωθεν·
εἰ δὲ βιασθείη προελθεῖν, ἐν κλινιδίῳ κρεμαστῷ
παρὰ τὴν γῆν αὐτὴν παραφερόμενον κομίζεσθαι,
καὶ διὰ τοῦτο κληθῆναι Περιφόρητον.

XXVIII Ἐνάτῳ δὲ μηνὶ τῶν Σαμίων παραστάντων ὁ Περικλῆς τὰ τείχη καθεῖλε
καὶ τὰς ναῦς παρέλαβε καὶ χρήμασι
πολλοῖς ἐζημίωσεν· ὧν τὰ μὲν εὐθὺς εἰσήνεγκαν
οἱ Σάμιοι, τὰ δ᾽ ἐν χρόνῳ ῥητῷ ταξάμενοι
κατοίσειν ὁμήρους ἔδωκαν. Δοῦρις δ᾽ ὁ
Σάμιος τούτοις ἐπιτραγῳδεῖ πολλὴν
ὠμότητα τῶν Ἀθηναίων καὶ τοῦ Περικλέους κατηγορῶν, ἣν οὔτε Θουκυδίδης
ἱστόρηκεν οὔτ᾽ Ἔφορος οὔτ᾽ Ἀριστοτέλης, ἀλλ᾽ οὐδ᾽ ἀληθεύειν ἔοικεν, ὡς
ἄρα τοὺς τριηράρχους καὶ τοὺς ἐπιβάτας
τῶν Σαμίων εἰς τὴν Μιλησίων ἀγορὰν
καταγαγὼν καὶ σανίσι προσδήσας ἐφ᾽
ἡμέρας δέκα κακῶς ἤδη διακειμένους
προσέταξεν ἀνελεῖν, ξύλοις τὰς κεφαλὰς συγκόψαντας, εἶτα προβαλεῖν ἀκήδευτα τὰ σώματα.
Δοῦρις μὲν οὖν οὐδ᾽ ὅπου μηδὲν αὐτῷ πρόσεστιν
ἴδιον πάθος εἰωθὼς κρατεῖν τὴν διήγησιν
ἐπὶ τῆς ἀληθείας, μᾶλλον ἔοικεν ἐνταῦθα

CH. XXVIII § 1 l. 4 εἰσήνεγκαν S Fᵃ (Fu Bl²): ἤνεγκαν Bl¹
v ‖ 5 ἐν χρόνῳ ῥητῷ vulgo: χρόνῳ ῥητῷ S ‖ 6 κατοίσειν v:
Cobet ci καταθήσειν (Arist. *Nub.* 245) on the ground that
καταφέρειν is not used in the sense here required
§ 2 l. 11 ἀληθέσιν (sic) S ‖ 14 καταγαγών S Fᵃ (Fu Bl²):
ἀγαγών Bl¹ v ‖ 15 ἡμέρας ci Reiske (Si Bk Fu Bl); cp. c. 16,
2: ἡμέραις vulgo

ΧΧVIII 5   ΠΕΡΙΚΛΗΣ   49

δεινῶσαι τὰς τῆς πατρίδος συμφορὰς ἐπὶ διαβολῇ τῶν Ἀθηναίων. Ὁ δὲ Περικλῆς καταστρεψάμενος τὴν Σάμον ὡς ἐπανῆλθεν εἰς τὰς Ἀθήνας, ταφάς τε τῶν ἀποθανόντων κατὰ τὸν πόλεμον ἐνδόξους ἐποίησε καὶ τὸν λόγον εἰπών, ὥσπερ ἔθος ἐστίν, ἐπὶ τῶν σημάτων ἐθαυμαστώθη. καταβαίνοντα δ' αὐτὸν ἀπὸ τοῦ βήματος αἱ μὲν ἄλλαι γυναῖκες ἐδεξιοῦντο καὶ στεφάνοις ἀνέδουν καὶ ταινίαις ὥσπερ ἀθλητὴν νικηφόρον, ἡ δ' Ἐλπινίκη προσελθοῦσα πλησίον "Ταῦτ'" ἔφη "θαυμαστά, Περίκλεις, καὶ ἄξια στεφάνων, ὃς ἡμῖν πολλοὺς καὶ ἀγαθοὺς ἀπώλεσας πολίτας οὐ Φοίνιξι πολεμῶν οὐδὲ Μήδοις, ὥσπερ οὑμὸς ἀδελφὸς Κίμων, ἀλλὰ σύμμαχον καὶ συγγενῆ πόλιν καταστρεφόμενος." ταῦτα 5 τῆς Ἐλπινίκης λεγούσης ὁ Περικλῆς μειδιάσας ἀτρέμα λέγεται τὸ τοῦ Ἀρχιλόχου πρὸς αὐτὴν εἰπεῖν

ΟΥΚ ἂν ΜΥΡΟΙϹΙ ΓΡΑΥϹ ΕΟΥϹ' ΗΛΕΙΦΕΟ.

Θαυμαστὸν δέ τι καὶ μέγα φρονῆσαι καταπολεμήσαντα τοὺς Σαμίους φησὶν αὐτὸν ὁ Ἴων ὡς τοῦ μὲν Ἀγαμέμνονος ἔτεσι δέκα βάρβαρον πόλιν, αὐτοῦ δὲ μησὶν ἐννέα

Public funeral at the close of the campaign. The funeral oration pronounced by Pericles who is the object of a general 4 ovation.

Scene with Elpinice.

Ion says that in the pride of his heart at his success

§ 3 l. 28 ἐθαυμαστώθη Bl A Jacob v : ἐθαυμάσθη S ci Cobet (Fu)
§ 4 l. 32 ταῦτ', ἔφη, <σοῦ τὰ> θαυμαστά ci Reiske   33 ἄξια : ἄξιος ci Fuhr ‖ 41 σὺ κἂν μύροισι ci Reiske, which he thus explains: *tam es expudoratae et perfrictae frontis, ut, quamvis sis anus, tamen nil te pudeat unguentis uti*. In ista oris tui foeditate et in isto aetatis marcore, tamen affectas mores prostibulorum: Bergk also ci σὺ κἂν in *Poet. lyr. ed.* 4

E

Pericles compared himself with Agamemnon. His pride was justified, for he delivered Athens from a real danger.

τοὺς πρώτους καὶ δυνατωτάτους Ἰώνων ἑλόντος. καὶ οὐκ ἦν ἄδικος ἡ ἀξίωσις, ἀλλ' ὄντως πολλὴν ἀδηλότητα καὶ μέγαν ἔσχε κίνδυνον ὁ πόλεμος, εἴπερ, ὡς Θουκυδίδης φησί, παρ' ἐλάχιστον ἦλθε Σαμίων ἡ πόλις ἀφελέσθαι τῆς θαλάττης τὸ κράτος Ἀθηναίους.

XXIX Μετὰ ταῦτα κυμαίνοντος ἤδη τοῦ Πελοποννησιακοῦ πολέμου Κερκυραίοις πολεμουμένοις ὑπὸ Κορινθίων ἔπεισε τὸν δῆμον ἀποστεῖλαι βοήθειαν καὶ προσλαβεῖν ἐρρωμένην ναυτικῇ δυνάμει νῆσον, ὡς ὅσον οὐδέπω Πελοποννησίων ἐκπεπολεμωμένων πρὸς αὐτούς. ψηφισαμένου δὲ τοῦ δήμου τὴν βοήθειαν ἀπέστειλε δέκα ναῦς μόνας ἔχοντα Λακεδαιμόνιον, τὸν Κίμωνος υἱόν, οἷον ἐφυβρίζων· πολλὴ γὰρ ἦν εὔνοια καὶ φιλία τῷ Κίμωνος οἴκῳ πρὸς Λακεδαιμονίους. ὡς ἂν οὖν, εἰ μηδὲν ἔργον μέγα μηδ' ἐκπρεπὲς ἐν τῇ στρατηγίᾳ τοῦ Λακεδαιμονίου γένοιτο, προσδιαβληθείη μᾶλλον εἰς τὸν λακωνισμόν, ὀλίγας αὐτῷ ναῦς ἔδωκε καὶ μὴ βουλόμενον ἐξέπεμψε. καὶ ὅλως διετέλει κολούων ὡς μηδὲ τοῖς ὀνόμασι γνησίους ἀλλ' ὀθνείους καὶ ξένους, ὅτι τῶν Κίμωνος υἱῶν τῷ μὲν ἦν Λακεδαιμόνιος ὄνομα, τῷ δὲ Θεσσαλός, τῷ δὲ Ἠλεῖος. ἐδόκουν δὲ πάντες ἐκ γυναικὸς

CH. XXIX § 3 l. 18 κολούων x (Ko Si Do Fu Bl): κωλύων St vulgo. See expl. note ‖ γνησίων ... ὀθνείων ... ξένων [ὅτι] τῶν Κίμωνος υἱῶν, τῷ μὲν <γὰρ> ἦν κτλ ci Bergk

ΠΕΡΙΚΛΗΣ

Ἀρκαδικῆς γεγονέναι. Περικλῆς ἀκούων διὰ τὰς δέκα ταύτας τριήρεις, ὡς μικρὰν μὲν βοήθειαν τοῖς δεηθεῖσι, μεγάλην δὲ πρόφασιν τοῖς ἐγκαλοῦσι παρεσχηκώς, ἑτέρας αὖθις ἔστειλε πλείονας εἰς τὴν Κέρκυραν, αἳ μετὰ τὴν μάχην ἀφίκοντο. χαλεπαίνουσι δὲ τοῖς Κορινθίοις καὶ κατηγοροῦσι τῶν Ἀθηναίων ἐν Λακεδαίμονι προσεγένοντο Μεγαρεῖς, αἰτιώμενοι πάσης μὲν ἀγορᾶς, πάντων δὲ λιμένων, ὧν Ἀθηναῖοι κρατοῦσιν, εἴργεσθαι καὶ ἀπελαύνεσθαι παρὰ τὰ κοινὰ δίκαια καὶ τοὺς γεγενημένους ὅρκους τοῖς Ἕλλησιν. Αἰγινῆται δὲ κακοῦσθαι δοκοῦντες καὶ βίαια πάσχειν ἐποτνιῶντο κρύφα πρὸς τοὺς Λακεδαιμονίους, φανερῶς ἐγκαλεῖν τοῖς Ἀθηναίοις οὐ θαρροῦντες.

Ἐν δὲ τούτῳ καὶ Ποτείδαια, πόλις ὑπήκοος Ἀθηναίων ἄποικος δὲ Κορινθίων, ἀποστᾶσα καὶ πολιορκουμένη μᾶλλον ἐπετάχυνε τὸν πόλεμον. οὐ μὴν ἀλλὰ πρεσβειῶν τε πεμπομένων Ἀθήναζε καὶ τοῦ βασιλέως τῶν Λακεδαιμονίων Ἀρχιδάμου τὰ πολλὰ τῶν ἐγκλημάτων εἰς διαλύσεις ἄγοντος καὶ τοὺς συμμάχους πραΰνοντος, οὐκ ἂν δοκεῖ συμπεσεῖν ὑπό γε τῶν ἄλλων αἰτιῶν ὁ πόλεμος

§ 4 l. 32 πάντων Bl vulgo: ἁπάντων S (Fu AJacob) | 36 βίαν S Fᵃ || 39 Ποτείδαια Blass² AJacob: Ποτίδαια Fu vulgo
§ 5 l. 42 πρεσβειῶν τε Bl v: καὶ πρεσβειῶν Fuhr with S Fᵃ || 47 δοκεῖ corr x (Si Fu Bl): ἐδόκει S Fᵃ v

τοῖς Ἀθηναίοις, εἰ τὸ ψήφισμα καθελεῖν τὸ Μεγαρικὸν ἐπείσθησαν καὶ 50
διαλλαγῆναι πρὸς αὐτούς. διὸ καὶ
μάλιστα πρὸς τοῦτο Περικλῆς ἐναντιωθεὶς καὶ παροξύνας τὸν δῆμον ἐμμεῖναι τῇ πρὸς τοὺς Μεγαρεῖς φιλονικίᾳ μόνος
ἔσχε τοῦ πολέμου τὴν αἰτίαν. 55

XXX Λέγουσι δέ, πρεσβείας Ἀθήναζε περὶ
τούτων ἐκ Λακεδαίμονος ἀφιγμένης καὶ
τοῦ Περικλέους νόμον τινὰ προβαλλομένου κωλύοντα καθελεῖν τὸ πινάκιον
ἐν ᾧ τὸ ψήφισμα γεγραμμένον ἐτύγ- 5
χανεν, εἰπεῖν Πολυάλκη τῶν πρέσβεων
τινά "Σὺ δὲ μὴ καθέλῃς, ἀλλὰ στρέψον
εἴσω τὸ πινάκιον· οὐ γὰρ ἔστι νόμος
ὁ τοῦτο κωλύων." κομψοῦ δὲ τοῦ
λόγου φανέντος οὐδέν τι μᾶλλον ὁ 10
2 Περικλῆς ἐνέδωκεν. ὑπῆν μὲν οὖν τις, ὡς ἔοικεν,
αὐτῷ καὶ ἰδίᾳ πρὸς τοὺς Μεγαρεῖς ἀπέχθεια·
κοινὴν δὲ καὶ φανερὰν ποιησάμενος αἰτίαν κατ᾽
αὐτῶν ἀποτέμνεσθαι τὴν ἱερὰν ὀργάδα γράφει
ψήφισμα κήρυκα πεμφθῆναι πρὸς αὐτοὺς καὶ 15
πρὸς Λακεδαιμονίους τὸν αὐτὸν κατηγοροῦντα

1. 54 τοὺς Μεγαρεῖς B C S Fᵃ (Fu Bl²) : Μεγαρεῖς v ‖ φιλονικίᾳ
Fu Bl² : φιλονεικίᾳ Bl¹ v

CH. XXX § 1 l. 1 πρεσβείας ἀφιγμένης ci Br (Ko Si Do Bk Fu
Bl): πρέσβεων ἀφιγμένων ci St : πρέσβεις ἀφιγμένους v | 7 Cobet
ci ἕνα for τινά, as in Latin *unus e legatis* would be said, not
legatorum aliquis

§ 2 l. 16 κατεροῦντα ci Cobet 'quod in ea re solemne et
legitimum verbum est et saepe a scribis corrumpi solitum,'
pronouncing κατηγοροῦντα wrong because the future participle
is required. Koraës also notes ἄμεινον ἂν εἶπε "κατηγορήσοντα"

XXX 4   ΠΕΡΙΚΛΗΣ   53

τῶν Μεγαρέων. τοῦτο μὲν οὖν τὸ ψήφισμα 3
Περικλέους ἐστίν, εὐγνώμονος καὶ φιλ- They are
ανθρώπου δικαιολογίας ἐχόμενον· ἐπεὶ suspected of
being the
authors of
δ' ὁ πεμφθεὶς κῆρυξ Ἀνθεμόκριτος αἰτίᾳ the death of
τῶν Μεγαρέων ἀποθανεῖν ἔδοξε, γράφει the Athenian herald
ψήφισμα κατ' αὐτῶν Χαρῖνος ἄσπονδον sent to re-
monstrate
μὲν εἶναι καὶ ἀκήρυκτον ἔχθραν, ὃς with them,
which leads
δ' ἂν ἐπιβῇ τῆς Ἀττικῆς Μεγαρέων to a second
decree, on
θανάτῳ ζημιοῦσθαι, τοὺς δὲ στρατη- the motion
of Charinus,
γούς, ὅταν ὀμνύωσι τὸν πάτριον ὅρκον, of truceless
enmity
ἐπομνύειν ὅτι καὶ δὶς ἀνὰ πᾶν ἔτος εἰς against
them; but
τὴν Μεγαρικὴν ἐμβαλοῦσι· ταφῆναι the Megarians deny
δ' Ἀνθεμόκριτον παρὰ τὰς Θριασίας their guilt
and lay the
πύλας, αἳ νῦν Δίπυλον ὀνομάζονται. blame of the
war on Peri-
Μεγαρεῖς δὲ τὸν Ἀνθεμοκρίτου φόνον cles and   4
Aspasia,
ἀπαρνούμενοι τὰς αἰτίας εἰς Ἀσπα- quoting to
that effect
σίαν καὶ Περικλέα τρέπουσι, χρώμενοι the well-
known lines
τοῖς περιβοήτοις καὶ δημώδεσι τούτοις of Aristophanes.
ἐκ τῶν Ἀχαρνέων στιχιδίοις·

πόρνην δὲ Σιμαίθαν ἰόντες Μέγαράδε
νεανίαι κλέπτουσι μεθυσοκότταβοι·
κᾆθ' οἱ Μεγαρῆς ὀδύναις πεφυσιγγωμένοι
ἀντεξέκλεψαν Ἀσπασίας πόρνα δύο.

§ 3 l. 18 Sintenis¹ p. 208 rightly places a comma after ἐστίν,
for if ἐστίν be taken with ἐχόμενον we should expect τὸ Περικλέους: Holzapfel suggests ἐχομένου, on the ground that, if
ἐχόμενον be taken as attributive to ψήφισμα, the order of words
should have been τοῦτο μὲν οὖν τὸ ψήφισμα εὐγνώμονος . . . δικαιολογίας ἐχόμενον Περικλέους ἐστίν   28 εἰσβαλοῦσιν S Fᵃ   29 Θριασίας ci Rk (Si Do Bk Fu Bl): Θριασίους St Ko v : Θριασίου S Fᵃ
§ 4 l. 38 μεγαρῆς S : Μεγαρεῖς v   39 πόρνας B C Fᵃ S,
Athenae. XIII c. 25 and the Ravenna MS (Si Do Bk): πόρνα St
Ko Fu Bl v

169 XXXI Τὴν μὲν οὖν ἀρχὴν ὅπως ἔσχεν οὐ ῥᾴδιον γνῶναι· τοῦ δὲ μὴ λυθῆναι τὸ ψήφισμα πάντες ὡσαύτως τὴν αἰτίαν ἐπιφέρουσι τῷ Περικλεῖ. πλὴν οἱ μὲν ἐκ φρονήματος μεγάλου μετὰ γνώμης κατὰ τὸ βέλτιστον ἀπισχυρίσασθαί φασιν αὐτόν, πεῖραν ἐνδόσεως τὸ πρόσταγμα καὶ τὴν συγχώρησιν ἐξομολόγησιν ἀσθενείας ἡγούμενον· οἱ δὲ μᾶλλον αὐθαδείᾳ τινὶ καὶ φιλονικίᾳ πρὸς ἔνδειξιν ἰσχύος περιφρονῆσαι 2 Λακεδαιμονίων. ἡ δὲ χειρίστη μὲν αἰτία πασῶν, ἔχουσα δὲ πλείστους μάρτυρας, οὕτω πως λέγεται. Φειδίας ὁ πλάστης ἐργολάβος μὲν ἦν τοῦ ἀγάλματος, ὥσπερ εἴρηται· φίλος δὲ τῷ Περικλεῖ γενόμενος καὶ μέγιστον παρ' αὐτῷ δυνηθεὶς τοὺς μὲν δι' αὐτὸν ἔσχεν ἐχθροὺς φθονούμενος, οἱ δέ, τοῦ δήμου ποιούμενοι πεῖραν ἐν ἐκείνῳ ποῖός τις ἔσοιτο τῷ Περικλεῖ κριτής, Μένωνά τινα τῶν Φειδίου συνεργῶν πείσαντες ἱκέτην ἐν ἀγορᾷ καθίζουσιν αἰτούμενον ἄδειαν ἐπὶ μηνύσει καὶ κατηγορίᾳ 3 τοῦ Φειδίου. προσδεξαμένου δὲ τοῦ δήμου τὸν ἄνθρωπον ἐν ἐκκλησίᾳ καὶ γενομένης διώξεως,

CH. XXXI § 1 l. 7 πρόσταγμα vulgo : πρᾶγμα S Fª. There is the same confusion between these words in *Demosth*. c. 3, 2 where N has incorrectly πρᾶγμα for the vulgate πρόσταγμα ‖ 11 ἔνδειξιν ἰσχύος C (Ko Si Do Fu Bl²) : ἔνδοξον ἰσχύν vulgo Bl¹

§ 2 l. 18 πολλοὺς μέν ci Bergk ‖ αὐτόν vulgo : αὑτόν S ‖ 20 τις vulgo : τέ (sic) S Fª ‖ τῷ Περικλεῖ S Fª (Si Fu Bl²) : Περικλεῖ St Ko Do Bk Bl¹ v

κλοπαὶ μὲν οὐκ ἠλέγχοντο· τὸ γὰρ χρυσίον
οὕτως εὐθὺς ἐξ ἀρχῆς τῷ ἀγάλματι προσειργάσατο καὶ περιέθηκεν ὁ Φειδίας γνώμῃ τοῦ
Περικλέους, ὥστε πᾶν δυνατὸν εἶναι περιελοῦσιν
ἀποδεῖξαι τὸν σταθμόν, ὃ καὶ τότε τοὺς κατη-
γόρους ἐκέλευσε ποιεῖν ὁ Περικλῆς· ἡ δὲ δόξα 4
τῶν ἔργων ἐπίεζε φθόνῳ τὸν Φειδίαν, καὶ
μάλισθ' ὅτι τὴν πρὸς Ἀμαζόνας μάχην ἐν τῇ
ἀσπίδι ποιῶν αὐτοῦ τινα μορφὴν ἐνετύπωσε
πρεσβύτου φαλακροῦ πέτρον ἐπηρμένου δι'
ἀμφοτέρων τῶν χειρῶν, καὶ τοῦ Περικλέους
εἰκόνα παγκάλην ἐνέθηκε μαχομένου πρὸς
Ἀμαζόνα. τὸ δὲ σχῆμα τῆς χειρός, ἀνατεινούσης δόρυ πρὸ τῆς ὄψεως τοῦ Περικλέους,
πεποιημένον εὐμηχάνως οἷον ἐπικρύπτειν βούλεται τὴν ὁμοιότητα παραφαινομένην ἑκατέρωθεν.

Ὁ μὲν οὖν Φειδίας εἰς τὸ δεσμω- Imprison- 5
τήριον ἀπαχθεὶς ἐτελεύτησε νοσήσας, ὡς death of
δέ φασιν ἔνιοι, φαρμάκοις, ἐπὶ διαβολῇ Phidias.
τοῦ Περικλέους τῶν ἐχθρῶν παρασκευασάντων.
τῷ δὲ μηνυτῇ Μένωνι γράψαντος Γλύκωνος
ἀτέλειαν ὁ δῆμος ἔδωκε καὶ προσέταξε τοῖς
στρατηγοῖς ἐπιμελεῖσθαι τῆς ἀσφαλείας τοῦ
ἀνθρώπου.

XXXII Περὶ δὲ τοῦτον τὸν χρόνον Ἀσπασία

§ 3 l. 25 ἐν ἐκκλησίᾳ καὶ γενομένης διώξεως ci HSauppe : καὶ
γενομένης ἐν ἐκκλησίᾳ διώξεως v 26 ἠλέγχοντο ci Orelli Schäfer
(Si Do Bk Fu Bl) : ἐλέγοντο St v   29 πᾶν Si Bk Bl AJacob v :
πάνυ S Fᵃ (St Ko Fu)
§ 4 l. 34 αὐτοῦ v ; αὐτοῦ S 36 καὶ τοῦ Περικλέους δ' ci Bl²
§ 5 l. 46 Λύκωνος or Γλαύκωνος ci Bergk
CH. XXXII § 1 l. 1 <καὶ> Ἀσπασία ci Reiske

δίκην ἔφευγεν ἀσεβείας, Ἑρμίππου τοῦ κωμῳδο-
ποιοῦ διώκοντος καὶ προσκατηγοροῦντος, ὡς Περικλεῖ γυναῖκας ἐλευθέρας
εἰς τὸ αὐτὸ φοιτώσας ὑποδέχοιτο. Καὶ ψήφισμα Διοπείθης
ἔγραψεν εἰσαγγέλλεσθαι τοὺς τὰ θεῖα
μὴ νομίζοντας ἢ λόγους περὶ τῶν μεταρσίων
διδάσκοντας, ἀπερειδόμενος εἰς Περικλέα δι᾽ Ἀναξαγόρου τὴν ὑπόνοιαν.
δεχομένου δὲ τοῦ δήμου καὶ προσιεμένου
τὰς διαβολὰς οὕτως ἤδη ψήφισμα
κυροῦται, Δρακοντίδου γράψαντος, ὅπως
οἱ λόγοι τῶν χρημάτων ὑπὸ Περικλέους
εἰς τοὺς πρυτάνεις ἀποτεθεῖεν, οἱ δὲ
δικασταὶ τὴν ψῆφον ἀπὸ τοῦ βωμοῦ
φέροντες ἐν τῇ πόλει κρίνοιεν. Ἅγνων
δὲ τοῦτο μὲν ἀφεῖλε τοῦ ψηφίσματος,
κρίνεσθαι δὲ τὴν δίκην ἔγραψεν ἐν
δικασταῖς χιλίοις καὶ πεντακοσίοις,
εἴτε κλοπῆς καὶ δώρων εἴτ᾽ ἀδικίου
βούλοιτό τις ὀνομάζειν τὴν δίωξιν.
Ἀσπασίαν μὲν οὖν ἐξῃτήσατο πολλὰ πάνυ
παρὰ τὴν δίκην, ὡς Αἰσχίνης φησίν,
ἀφεὶς ὑπὲρ αὐτῆς δάκρυα καὶ δεηθεὶς τῶν δικαστῶν· Ἀναξαγόραν δὲ
φοβηθεὶς ἐξέκλεψε καὶ προὔπεμψεν

§ 1 l. 2 κωμωδιοποιοῦ S ‖ 10 εὔνοιαν ci Bergk
§ 2 l. 15 τούς om S Fᵃ ‖ 21 ἀδικίου ci Reiske (Si Do Bk Fu Bl): ἀδικίας S (St Ko) v
§ 3 l. 27 ἐξέκλεψε καὶ προὔπεμψεν ci Emperius (Fu Bl): ἐξέπεμψε καὶ προὔπεμψεν St Ko Do v : ἐξέπεμψε [καὶ προὔπεμψεν] Si³ Bk AJacob with B C S Fᵃ : φοβηθεὶς ὑπεξέπεμψεν ci Cobet

ἐκ τῆς πόλεως. Ὡς δὲ διὰ Φειδίου προσέπταισε τῷ δήμῳ, φοβηθεὶς τὸ
30 δικαστήριον μέλλοντα τὸν πόλεμον καὶ ὑποτυφόμενον ἐξέκαυσεν, ἐλπίζων διασκεδάσειν τὰ ἐγκλήματα καὶ ταπεινώσειν τὸν φθόνον, ἐν πράγμασι μεγάλοις καὶ κινδύνοις τῆς πόλεως
35 ἐκείνῳ μόνῳ διὰ τὸ ἀξίωμα καὶ τὴν δύναμιν ἀναθείσης ἑαυτήν.

Αἱ μὲν οὖν αἰτίαι, δι' ἃς οὐκ εἴασεν ἐνδοῦναι Λακεδαιμονίοις τὸν δῆμον, αὗται λέγονται, τὸ δ' ἀληθὲς ἄδηλον. XXXIII οἱ δὲ Λακεδαιμόνιοι γιγνώσκοντες ὡς ἐκείνου καταλυθέντος εἰς πάντα μαλακωτέροις χρήσονται τοῖς Ἀθηναίοις ἐκέλευον
5 αὐτοὺς τὸ ἄγος ἐλαύνειν τὸ Κυλώνειον, ᾧ τὸ μητρόθεν γένος τοῦ Περικλέους ἔνοχον ἦν, ὡς Θουκυδίδης ἱστόρηκεν. ἡ δὲ πεῖρα περιέστη τοῖς πέμψασιν εἰς τοὐναντίον· ἀντὶ γὰρ ὑποψίας καὶ
10 διαβολῆς ὁ Περικλῆς ἔτι μείζονα πίστιν ἔσχε καὶ τιμὴν παρὰ τοῖς πολίταις, ὡς μάλιστα μισούντων καὶ φοβουμένων ἐκεῖνον τῶν πολεμίων. διὸ καὶ πρὶν ἐμβαλεῖν εἰς τὴν Ἀττικὴν τὸν Ἀρχίδαμον ἔχοντα τοὺς Πελοποννησίους προεῖπε τοῖς Ἀθηναίοις,

l. 36 ἀνατιθείσης ci Ko
CH. XXXIII § 1 l. 5 τὸ Κυλώνειον added in B S F^a (Fu Bl² AJacob); om St Ko Si Do v 7 ἱστόρηκεν B C S F^a (Ko Fu Bl²); εἴρηκεν St Si Do Bl¹ v 8 τοῖς ἀπελάσασιν ci Bergk

ἂν ἄρα τἆλλα δῃῶν ὁ Ἀρχίδαμος
ἀπέχηται τῶν ἐκείνου διὰ τὴν ξενίαν
τὴν οὖσαν αὐτοῖς ἢ διαβολῆς τοῖς
ἐχθροῖς ἐνδιδοὺς ἀφορμάς, ὅτι τῇ πόλει
καὶ τὴν χώραν καὶ τὰς ἐπαύλεις
3 ἐπιδίδωσιν. ἐμβάλλουσιν οὖν εἰς τὴν Ἀττικὴν
στρατῷ μεγάλῳ Λακεδαιμόνιοι μετὰ
τῶν συμμάχων, Ἀρχιδάμου τοῦ βασιλέως ἡγουμένου. καὶ δῃοῦντες τὴν
χώραν προῆλθον εἰς Ἀχαρνὰς καὶ
κατεστρατοπέδευσαν, ὡς τῶν Ἀθηναίων
οὐκ ἀνεξομένων ἀλλ' ὑπ' ὀργῆς καὶ
φρονήματος διαμαχουμένων πρὸς αὐ-
4 τούς. τῷ δὲ Περικλεῖ δεινὸν ἐφαίνετο
πρὸς τοὺς ἑξακισμυρίους Πελοποννησίων καὶ Βοιωτῶν ὁπλίτας (τοσοῦτοι γὰρ
ἦσαν οἱ τὸ πρῶτον ἐμβαλόντες) ὑπὲρ
αὐτῆς τῆς πόλεως μάχην συνάψαι·
τοὺς δὲ βουλομένους μάχεσθαι καὶ
δυσπαθοῦντας πρὸς τὰ γιγνόμενα κατεπράϋνε λέγων, ὡς δένδρα μὲν τμηθέντα καὶ κοπέντα φύεται ταχέως, ἀνδρῶν δὲ διαφθαρέντων
αὖθις τυχεῖν οὐ ῥᾴδιόν ἐστι. Τὸν δὲ δῆμον
5 εἰς ἐκκλησίαν οὐ συνῆγε, δεδιὼς βιασθῆναι παρὰ
γνώμην, ἀλλ' ὥσπερ νεὼς κυβερνήτης ἀνέμου
κατιόντος ἐν πελάγει θέμενος εὖ πάντα καὶ
κατατείνας τὰ ὅπλα χρῆται τῇ τέχνῃ, δάκρυα

§ 2 l. 18 διὰ ξενίαν S ‖ 19 ἢ om S
§ 4 l. 31 ἑξακισμυρίοις v (St Ko Si Bk Fu Bl AJacob): ἑξακισ-
χιλίοις S (Cobet Bergk)

καὶ δεήσεις ἐπιβατῶν ναυτιώντων καὶ φοβουμένων ἐάσας, οὕτως ἐκεῖνος τό τε ἄστυ συγκλείσας καὶ καταλαβὼν πάντα φυλακαῖς πρὸς
ἀσφάλειαν ἐχρῆτο τοῖς αὐτοῦ λογισμοῖς, βραχέα
φροντίζων τῶν καταβοώντων καὶ δυσχεραινόντων.
καίτοι πολλοὶ μὲν αὐτῷ τῶν φίλων δεόμενοι προσ- 6
έκειντο, πολλοὶ δὲ τῶν ἐχθρῶν ἀπειλοῦντες καὶ
κατηγοροῦντες, χόροι δ' ᾖδον ᾄσματα καὶ σκώμματα πρὸς αἰσχύνην, ἐφυβρίζοντες αὐτοῦ τὴν
στρατηγίαν ὡς ἄνανδρον καὶ προϊεμένην τὰ
πράγματα τοῖς πολεμίοις. ἐπεφύετο δὲ καὶ 7
Κλέων ἤδη διὰ τῆς πρὸς ἐκεῖνον ὀργῆς τῶν
πολιτῶν πορευόμενος ἐπὶ τὴν δημαγωγίαν, ὡς
τἀνάπαιστα ταῦτα δηλοῖ ποιήσαντος Ἑρμίππου·

Βασιλεῦ cατύρων, τί ποτ' οὐκ ἐθέλεις
Δόρυ Βαστάζειν, ἀλλὰ λόγους μὲν
περὶ τοῦ πολέμου Δεινοὺς παρέχῃ,
ψυχὴν Δὲ Τέλητος ὕπεστιν;
κἀγχειριδίου Δ' ἀκόνῃ σκληρᾷ
παραθηγομένης βρύχεις κοπίδος,
Δηχθεὶς αἴθωνι Κλέωνι.

§ 6 l. 49 αὑτῷ ci Bl: αὑτοῦ St Fu v ‖ 51 χόροι δ' ci Fu (Bl): χόροι B F^a S: πολλοὶ δ' St vulgo

§ 7 l. 57 δηλοῖ ποιήσαντος Ἑρμίππου ci Sabinius (Si^3 Fu Bl): δηλοποιεῖ τὰ Ἑρμ. Ko Si^1: δηλοποιήσαντος St v ‖ 60 παρέχῃ St Do Si Bl v: παρέχεις S (Vulc. Fu AJacob) ‖ 61 ψυχὴ δὲ Τέλητος ὕπεστιν ci Emperius (Do Fu Bl): ψυχὴν δὲ Τέλητος ὑπέστης codd (Si Bk) i.e. Teletis unimum et virtutem pollicitus es, as interpreted by Meineke ad l. 62 ἀκόνῃ σκληρᾷ ci Muretus (Ko Si Do Bk Fu): ἀκόνη σκληρά codd (St Bl) 63 παραθηγομένης ci Dacier (Ko Si Do Fu Bl^1 AJacob): παραθηγομένου Bk: παραθηγομένην B F^a S: παραθηγομένη St Bl^2 v ‖ βρύχεις x (Si Bk Fu AJacob): βρύκει ci Bl^2: βραχεῖ S F^a: βρύχει codd St Bl^1: βρύκεις ci Meineke (H. Jacobi ind. dict. com. s.v.) κοπίδος ci Koraës (Si Fu Bl^1 AJacob): κοπίδας codd Si^4 Bl^2 64 δηχθείς v: δηχθεῖσ' ci Blass

XXXIV Πλὴν ὑπ᾽ οὐδενὸς ἐκινήθη τῶν τοιούτων ὁ Περικλῆς, ἀλλὰ πράως καὶ σιωπῇ τὴν ἀδοξίαν καὶ τὴν ἀπέχθειαν ὑφιστάμενος καὶ νεῶν ἑκατὸν ἐπὶ τὴν Πελοπόννησον στόλον ἐκπέμπων αὐτὸς οὐ συνεξέπλευσεν, ἀλλ᾽ ἔμεινεν οἰκουρῶν καὶ διὰ χειρὸς ἔχων τὴν πόλιν, ἕως ἀπηλλάγησαν οἱ Πελοποννήσιοι. θεραπεύων δὲ τοὺς πολλοὺς ὅμως ἀσχάλλοντας ἐπὶ τῷ πολέμῳ διανομαῖς τε χρημάτων ἀνελάμβανε καὶ κληρουχίας ἔγραφεν· Αἰγινήτας γὰρ ἐξελάσας ἅπαντας διένειμε τὴν νῆσον Ἀθηναίων τοῖς λαχοῦσιν. ἦν δέ τις παρηγορία καὶ ἀφ᾽ ὧν ἔπασχον οἱ πολέμιοι. καὶ γὰρ οἱ περιπλέοντες τὴν Πελοπόννησον χώραν τε πολλὴν κώμας τε καὶ πόλεις μικρὰς διεπόρθησαν, καὶ κατὰ γῆν αὐτὸς ἐμβαλὼν εἰς τὴν Μεγαρικὴν ἔφθειρε πᾶσαν. ᾗ καὶ δῆλον ὅτι πολλὰ μὲν δρῶντες κατὰ γῆν κακὰ τοὺς Ἀθηναίους, πολλὰ δὲ πάσχοντες ὑπ᾽ ἐκείνων ἐκ θαλάττης, οὐκ ἂν εἰς μῆκος τοσοῦτον πολέμου προύβησαν, ἀλλὰ ταχέως ἀπεῖπον, ὥσπερ ἐξ ἀρχῆς ὁ Περικλῆς προηγόρευσεν, εἰ μή τι δαιμόνιον ὑπηναν-

CH. XXXIV § 1 l. 7 'τὴν ὅλην πόλιν in quibusdam scriptum est' St ‖ 12 ἔγραφεν B C Fᵃ S (Co Si³ Fu Bl² AJacob Bergk): ἀνέγραφεν St Ko Si¹ Do Bk Bl¹ v

§ 2 l. 18 οὐ μικράς S ‖ 20 δῆλον ὅτι St Bl v : δῆλον ἦν ὅτι C (Vulcob. Ko Si Do Bk Fu AJacob) ‖ κατὰ γῆν κακά B Fᵃ S (Fu Bl² AJacob): κακά St Ko Do Bl¹ v

τιώθη τοῖς ἀνθρωπίνοις λογισμοῖς.
νῦν δὲ πρῶτον μὲν ἡ λοιμώδης ἐνέπεσε
φθορὰ καὶ κατενεμήθη τὴν ἀκμάζουσαν
ἡλικίαν καὶ δύναμιν· ὑφ' ἧς καὶ τὰ
σώματα κακούμενοι καὶ τὰς ψυχὰς
παντάπασιν ἠγριώθησαν πρὸς τὸν
Περικλέα, καὶ καθάπερ ἰατρὸν ἢ
πατέρα τῇ νόσῳ παραφρονήσαντες
ἀδικεῖν ἐπεχείρησαν [ἀνα]πεισθέντες
ὑπὸ τῶν ἐχθρῶν, ὡς τὴν μὲν νόσον ἡ τοῦ
χωριτικοῦ πλήθους εἰς τὸ ἄστυ συμφόρησις
ἀπεργάζεται, θέρους ὥρᾳ πολλῶν ὁμοῦ χύδην ἐν
οἰκήμασι μικροῖς καὶ σκηνώμασι πνιγηροῖς
ἠναγκασμένων διαιτᾶσθαι δίαιταν οἰκουρὸν καὶ
ἀργὴν ἀντὶ καθαρᾶς καὶ ἀναπεπταμένης τῆς
πρότερον, τούτου δ' αἴτιος ὁ τῷ πολέμῳ τὸν ἀπὸ
τῆς χώρας ὄχλον εἰς τὰ τείχη καταχεάμενος καὶ
πρὸς οὐδὲν ἀνθρώποις τοσούτοις χρώμενος, ἀλλ'
ἐῶν ὥσπερ βοσκήματα καθειργμένους ἀναπίμπλασθαι φθορᾶς ἀπ' ἀλλήλων, καὶ μηδεμίαν
μεταβολὴν μηδ' ἀναψυχὴν ἐκπορίζων.

XXXV Ταῦτα βουλόμενος ἰᾶσθαι καί τι
παραλυπεῖν τοὺς πολεμίους ἑκατὸν
καὶ πεντήκοντα ναῦς ἐπλήρου, καὶ

§ 3 l. 33 καὶ καθάπερ ἰατρόν ci Rk (Ko Si Bk Fu Bl AJacob).
Constructio est καὶ ἐπεχείρησαν ἀδικεῖν (αὐτὸν) καθάπερ ἀδι-
κοῦσιν οἱ νοσοῦντες παραφρονήσαντες τὸν ἰατρόν, et conabantur
cum vexare, ut faciunt aegri, mentis de statu a vi morbi deiecti,
in medicum insurgentes. καὶ καθάπερ πρὸς (εἰς F^a) ἰατρόν St v,
which might be retained by transposing the καί before ἀδικεῖν
‖ 37 χωρικοῦ S F^a (Fuhr) ‖ 38 ἀπεργάζεται B F^a S (Fu Bl²
AJacob): ἐργάζεται St Ko Si Do Bk Bl¹ v
§ 4 l. 40 ἀναγκαζομένων S F^a (Fu): ἠναγκασμένων St Si Bl v

πολλοὺς καὶ ἀγαθοὺς ὁπλίτας καὶ ἱππέας
ἀναβιβασάμενος ἔμελλεν ἀνάγεσθαι,
μεγάλην ἐλπίδα τοῖς πολίταις καὶ φόβον οὐκ ἐλάττονα τοῖς πολεμίοις ἀπὸ
τοσαύτης ἰσχύος παρασχών. ἤδη δὲ
πεπληρωμένων τῶν νεῶν καὶ τοῦ Περικλέους ἀναβεβηκότος ἐπὶ τὴν ἑαυτοῦ
τριήρη τὸν μὲν ἥλιον ἐκλιπεῖν συνέβη
καὶ γενέσθαι σκότος, ἐκπλαγῆναι δὲ
πάντας ὡς πρὸς μέγα σημεῖον. ὁρῶν
οὖν ὁ Περικλῆς περίφοβον τὸν κυβερνήτην καὶ διηπορημένον ἀνέσχε τὴν
χλαμύδα πρὸ τῶν ὄψεων αὐτοῦ καὶ
παρακαλύψας ἠρώτησε, μή τι δεινὸν ἢ
δεινοῦ τινος οἴεται σημεῖον· ὡς δ' οὐκ
ἔφη "Τί οὖν" εἶπεν "ἐκεῖνο τούτου
διαφέρει, πλὴν ὅτι μεῖζόν τι τῆς χλαμύδος ἐστὶ
τὸ πεποιηκὸς τὴν ἐπισκότησιν;" ταῦτα μὲν οὖν
ἐν ταῖς σχολαῖς λέγεται τῶν φιλοσόφων. ἐκπλεύσας δ' οὖν ὁ Περικλῆς οὔτ' ἄλλο τι δοκεῖ
τῆς παρασκευῆς ἄξιον δρᾶσαι, πολιορκήσας τε
τὴν ἱερὰν Ἐπίδαυρον ἐλπίδα παρασχοῦσαν ὡς
ἁλωσομένην ἀπέτυχε διὰ τὴν νόσον. ἐπιγενομένη γὰρ οὐκ αὐτοὺς μόνον, ἀλλὰ καὶ τοὺς
ὁπωσοῦν τῇ στρατιᾷ συμμίξαντας προσδιέφθειρεν.
ἐκ τούτου χαλεπῶς διακειμένους τοὺς Ἀθηναίους
πρὸς αὐτὸν ἐπειρᾶτο παρηγορεῖν καὶ ἀναθαρρύ-

CH. XXXV § 2 l. 16 τῶν ὄψεων B Fᵃ S (Fu Bl² AJacob): τῆς ὄψεως St Si Bl¹ v
§ 3 l. 25 ἱεράν: Cobet ci Λιμηράν, but see explanatory note

ΠΕΡΙΚΛΗΣ

νειν. οὐ μὴν παρέλυσε τῆς ὀργῆς οὐδὲ μετέπεισε 4
πρότερον ἢ τὰς ψήφους λαβόντας ἐπ'
αὐτὸν εἰς τὰς χεῖρας καὶ γενομένους
κυρίους ἀφελέσθαι τὴν στρατηγίαν καὶ
35 ζημιῶσαι χρήμασιν, ὧν ἀριθμὸν οἱ τὸν
ἐλάχιστον πεντεκαίδεκα τάλαντα, πεντήκοντα δ' οἱ τὸν πλεῖστον γράφουσιν.
ἐπεγράφη δὲ τῇ δίκῃ κατήγορος, ὡς
μὲν Ἰδομενεὺς λέγει, Κλέων, ὡς δὲ
40 Θεόφραστος, Σιμμίας· ὁ δὲ Ποντικὸς
Ἡρακλείδης Λακρατείδαν εἴρηκε.

Pericles deposed from his office of strategus by a vote of the ecclesia, and sentenced to a heavy fine for supposed embezzlement. His old opponent Cleon is said to have been among the leaders of the prosecution.

XXXVI Τὰ μὲν οὖν δημόσια ταχέως ἔμελλε
παύσεσθαι, καθάπερ κέντρον εἰς τοῦτο
ἅμα πληγῇ τὸν θυμὸν ἀφεικότων τῶν
πολλῶν· τὰ δ' οἰκεῖα μοχθηρῶς εἶχεν
5 αὐτῷ, κατά τε τὸν λοιμὸν οὐκ ὀλίγους
ἀποβαλόντι τῶν ἐπιτηδείων καὶ στάσει
διατεταραγμένα πόρρωθεν. ὁ γὰρ
πρεσβύτερος αὐτοῦ τῶν γνησίων υἱῶν
Ξάνθιππος φύσει τε δαπανηρὸς ὢν καὶ
10 γυναικὶ νέᾳ καὶ πολυτελεῖ συνοικῶν,
Τισάνδρου θυγατρὶ τοῦ Ἐπιλύκου,
χαλεπῶς ἔφερε τὴν τοῦ πατρὸς ἀκρί-

His private misfortunes rendered the bitterness of his fall more acute. The elder of his two sons, Xanthippus, who had been on bad terms with his father for some time, avenged himself by spreading scandalous stories about him.

§ 1 l. 31 παρέλυσε τῆς ὀργῆς ci Bl cl Thuc. II 65 (Fu AJacob) : παρέλυσε τὴν ὀργήν A C : ἔλυσε τ. ὀργήν St v ‖ 40 Σιμμίας vulgo : Σιμίας (ex σιμός) ci Cobet   41 Λακρατείδαν ci Cobet cl Arist. Ach. 220 : Λακρατίδαν v

CII. XXXVI § 1 l. 2 παύσεσθαι B F^a S ci Rk (Fu Bl^2 AJacob) : παύεσθαι Si Bk Bl^1 v ‖ εἰς τοῦτο ci Bl AJacob : εἰς τοῦτον Si Bk Fu v ‖ 3 ἅμα ⟨τῇ⟩ πληγῇ ci Ko   5 κατά τε Bl v : κατά S (Fu) 7 διατεταραγμένα ci HSauppe (Fu Bl AJacob) : διατεταραγμένῳ ci Rk (Ko Si Bk) : διατεταραγμένων St v ‖ 8 πρεσβύτερος ci Bl (Fu A Jacob) : πρεσβύτατος v ‖ 9 δαπανηρός S A C (St Si Bl) : πονηρός v

βειαν γλίσχρως καὶ κατὰ μικρὸν αὐτῷ χορηγοῦντος. πέμψας οὖν πρός τινα τῶν φίλων
ἔλαβεν ἀργύριον ὡς τοῦ Περικλέους κελεύσαντος.
ἐκείνου δ' ὕστερον ἀπαιτοῦντος, ὁ μὲν Περικλῆς
καὶ δίκην αὐτῷ προσέλαχε, τὸ δὲ μειράκιον ὁ
Ξάνθιππος ἐπὶ τούτῳ χαλεπῶς διατεθεὶς ἐλοιδόρει τὸν πατέρα, πρῶτον μὲν ἐκφέρων ἐπὶ
γέλωτι τὰς οἴκοι διατριβὰς αὐτοῦ καὶ τοὺς
λόγους, οὓς ἐποιεῖτο μετὰ τῶν σοφιστῶν. πεντάθλου γάρ τινος ἀκοντίῳ πατάξαντος Ἐπίτιμον
τὸν Φαρσάλιον ἀκουσίως καὶ κτείναντος ἡμέραν
ὅλην ἀναλῶσαι μετὰ Πρωταγόρου διαποροῦντα,
πότερον τὸ ἀκόντιον ἢ τὸν βαλόντα μᾶλλον ἢ
τοὺς ἀγωνοθέτας κατὰ τὸν ὀρθότατον λόγον
αἰτίους χρὴ τοῦ πάθους ἡγεῖσθαι. πρὸς δὲ
τούτοις καὶ τὴν περὶ τῆς γυναικὸς διαβολὴν ὑπὸ
τοῦ Ξανθίππου φησὶν ὁ Στησίμβροτος εἰς
τοὺς πολλοὺς διασπαρῆναι, καὶ ὅλως ἀνήκεστον
ἄχρι τῆς τελευτῆς τῷ νεανίσκῳ πρὸς τὸν πατέρα
παραμεῖναι τὴν διαφοράν· ἀπέθανε γὰρ ὁ
Ξάνθιππος ἐν τῷ λοιμῷ νοσήσας. ἀπέβαλε δὲ καὶ τὴν ἀδελφὴν ὁ Περικλῆς
τότε καὶ τῶν κηδεστῶν καὶ φίλων τοὺς
πλείστους καὶ χρησιμωτάτους πρὸς
τὴν πολιτείαν. οὐ μὴν ἀπεῖπεν οὐδὲ
προὔδωκε τὸ φρόνημα καὶ τὸ μέγεθος

1. 13 γλίσχρα vulgo : γλίσχρως C (Ko Cobet)
§ 2 l. 17 [ὁ Ξάνθιππος] ci Cobet ‖ 21 ἐποιεῖτο B F^a S ci
HSauppe Cobet (Fu Bl AJacob) : ἐποίει Si Bk v. Cp. c. 38 l. 17
§ 3 l. 23 κτείναντος F^a S (Ko Fu) : κατακτείναντος St Si Bk
Bl AJacob v ‖ 25 τὸν βαλόντα μᾶλλον B F^a S (Fu Bl² AJacob) :
τὸν βαλόντα St Ko Si Bk Bl¹ v

τῆς ψυχῆς ὑπὸ τῶν συμφορῶν, ἀλλ' οὐδὲ
κλαίων οὔτε κηδεύων οὔτε πρὸς τάφῳ
τινὸς ὤφθη τῶν ἀναγκαίων, πρίν γε δὴ
καὶ τὸν περίλοιπον αὐτοῦ τῶν γνησίων
υἱῶν ἀποβαλεῖν Πάραλον. ἐπὶ τούτῳ δὲ
καμφθεὶς ἐπειρᾶτο μὲν ἐγκαρτερεῖν τῷ ἤθει καὶ
διαφυλάττειν τὸ μεγαλόψυχον, ἐπιφέρων δὲ τῷ
νεκρῷ στέφανον ἡττήθη τοῦ πάθους πρὸς τὴν
ὄψιν, ὥστε κλαυθμόν τε ῥῆξαι καὶ πλῆθος ἐκχέαι
δακρύων, οὐδέποτε τοιοῦτον οὐδὲν ἐν τῷ λοιπῷ
βίῳ πεποιηκώς.

XXXVII Τῆς δὲ πόλεως πειρωμένης τῶν ἄλλων
στρατηγῶν εἰς τὸν πόλεμον καὶ ῥητόρων,
ὡς δ' οὐδεὶς βάρος ἔχων ἰσόρροπον οὐδ'
ἀξίωμα πρὸς τοσαύτην ἐχέγγυον ἡγεμονίαν ἐφαίνετο, ποθούσης ἐκεῖνον καὶ
καλούσης ἐπὶ τὸ βῆμα καὶ τὸ στρατήγιον, ἀθυμῶν καὶ κείμενος οἴκοι διὰ
τὸ πένθος ὑπ' Ἀλκιβιάδου καὶ τῶν
ἄλλων ἐπείσθη φίλων προελθεῖν.
ἀπολογησαμένου δὲ τοῦ δήμου τὴν
ἀγνωμοσύνην τὴν πρὸς αὐτὸν ὑποδεξάμενος αὖθις τὰ πράγματα καὶ στρατηγὸς
αἱρεθεὶς ᾐτήσατο λυθῆναι τὸν περὶ τῶν νόθων

§ 1 l. 40 οὔτε κηδεύων οὔτε ei Bl² Jb: οὐδὲ κηδεύων οὐδὲ Fu v
|| 12 γνησίων υἱῶν B Fª S (Fu Bl² Jb): γνησίων Si Bk Bl¹ v
CH. XXXVII § 1 l. 3 ὡς δ' οὐδεὶς ... ποθούσης ei Bekker (Si³
Bl Jb): ὡς οὐδεὶς ... ποθούσης δ' St Si² v: οὐδείς S (Fu) |
5 ποθούσης S | 7 κείμενος v: καθήμενος ei Cobet
§ 2 l. 11 τὴν πρὸς αὐτόν S (St Ko Fu Bl²) v: πρὸς αὐτόν A C
Fª (Si Do Bk Bl¹) || 13 the old reading εἰσηγήσατο retained by
St has been discarded by modern edd

F

νόμον, ὃν αὐτὸς εἰσενηνόχει πρότερον, ὡς μὴ
παντάπασιν ἐρημίᾳ διαδοχῆς [τὸν οἶκον] ἐκλίποι
τοὔνομα καὶ τὸ γένος. εἶχε δ' οὕτω τὰ περὶ
τὸν νόμον. ἀκμάζων ὁ Περικλῆς ἐν τῇ
πολιτείᾳ πρὸ πάνυ πολλῶν χρόνων καὶ
παῖδας ἔχων, ὥσπερ εἴρηται, γνησίους
νόμον ἔγραψε, μόνους Ἀθηναίους εἶναι
τοὺς ἐκ δυεῖν Ἀθηναίων γεγονότας.
ἐπεὶ δὲ τοῦ βασιλέως τῶν Λιγυπτίων
δωρεὰν τῷ δήμῳ πέμψαντος τετρα-
κισμυρίους πυρῶν μεδίμνους ἔδει διανέμεσθαι τοὺς πολίτας, πολλαὶ μὲν
ἀνεφύοντο δίκαι τοῖς νόθοις ἐκ τοῦ
γράμματος ἐκείνου τέως διαλανθάνουσι καὶ
παρορωμένοις, πολλοὶ δὲ καὶ συκοφαντήμασι
περιέπιπτον. ἐπράθησαν δ' οὖν ἁλόντες ὀλίγῳ
πεντακισχιλίων ἐλάττους, οἱ δὲ μείναντες ἐν τῇ
πολιτείᾳ καὶ κριθέντες Ἀθηναῖοι μύριοι καὶ
τετρακισχίλιοι καὶ τεσσαράκοντα τὸ πλῆθος
ἐξητάσθησαν. ὄντος οὖν δεινοῦ τοῦ κατὰ
τοσούτων ἰσχύσαντα τὸν νόμον ὑπὲρ αὐτοῦ πάλιν
ἰδίᾳ λυθῆναι τοῦ γράψαντος, ἡ παροῦσα δυστυχία

---

l. 15 Bl² and Jb follow Madvig in bracketing τὸν οἶκον so that ἐκλίποι may be intransitive 'should fail,' 'become extinct.' Cp. *Lyc.* c. 31, 4 οὗ τελευτήσαντος ἀτέκνου τὸ γένος ἐξέλιπεν, *Rom.* c. 18, 1 τοὔνομα τῆς Ταρπηίας ἐξέλιπε

§ 3 l. 27 διαλανθάνουσι καὶ παρορωμένοις ci HSauppe (Fu Bl Jb) : διαλανθάνουσαι καὶ παρορώμεναι v

§ 4 l. 29 δ' οὖν B Fª S (Bl² Jb) : οὖν Si Bk Bl¹ Fu v

§ 5 l. 33 τοῦ κ. τ. ἰσχύσαντα τὸν νόμον ἐπ' αὐτοῦ πάλιν ἰδίᾳ λυθῆναι ci Rk (Bl) : τὸν κ. τ. ἰσχύσαντα νόμον B C Fª S corr (τὸν νόμον v) Ko Si Do Bk Fu ‖ 34 ὑπ' αὐτοῦ St Si Fu v : ἐπ' αὐτοῦ Bl Jb : ὑπὲρ αὐτοῦ ci Holzapfel ‖ 35 λυθῆναι B C Fª S (Ko Si Do Bk Fu Bl Jb) : διαλυθῆναι St v

ΠΕΡΙΚΛΗΣ

τῷ Περικλεῖ περὶ τὸν οἶκον ὡς δίκην τινὰ δεδωκότι τῆς ὑπεροψίας καὶ τῆς μεγαλαυχίας ἐκείνης ἐπέκλασε τοὺς Ἀθηναίους, καὶ δόξαντες αὐτὸν νεμεσητά τε παθεῖν ἀνθρωπίνων τε δεῖσθαι συνεχώρησαν ἀπογράψασθαι τὸν νόθον εἰς τοὺς φράτερας, ὄνομα θέμενον τὸ αὐτοῦ. καὶ τοῦτον μὲν ὕστερον ἐν Ἀργινούσαις καταναυμαχήσαντα Πελοποννησίους ἀπέκτεινεν ὁ δῆμος μετὰ τῶν συστρατήγων.

XXXVIII Τότε δὲ τοῦ Περικλέους ἔοικεν ὁ λοιμὸς λαβέσθαι λαβὴν οὐκ ὀξεῖαν, ὥσπερ ἄλλων, οὐδὲ σύντονον, ἀλλὰ βληχρᾷ τινι νόσῳ καὶ μῆκος ἐν ποικίλαις ἐχούσῃ μεταβολαῖς διαχρωμένην τὸ σῶμα σχολαίως καὶ ὑπερείπουσαν τὸ φρόνημα τῆς ψυχῆς. ὁ γοῦν Θεόφραστος ἐν τοῖς Ἠθικοῖς διαπορήσας, εἰ πρὸς τὰς τύχας τρέπεται τὰ ἤθη καὶ κινούμενα τοῖς τῶν σωμάτων πάθεσιν ἐξίσταται τῆς ἀρετῆς, ἱστόρηκεν, ὅτι νοσῶν ὁ Περικλῆς ἐπισκοπουμένῳ τινὶ τῶν φίλων δείξειε περίαπτον ὑπὸ τῶν γυναικῶν τῷ τραχήλῳ περιηρτημένον, ὡς σφόδρα κακῶς ἔχων, ὁπότε καὶ ταύτην ὑπομένοι τὴν ἀβελτερίαν. ἤδη δὲ πρὸς τῷ τελευτᾶν ὄντος αὐτοῦ παρακαθήμενοι

Death of Pericles from the plague.

1. 36 τινά vulgo: ἱκανήν ci Cobet || 39 ἀνεμέσητα, non digna cuiusquam insectatione ci Rk || ἀνθρωπίνων B Fᵃ S ci Bryan (BF Jb): ἀνθρωπίνως St Si Bk Fu Bl¹ || 41 φράτερας ci Cobet el Arist. Av. 1669: φράτορας v || 12 ἀργικνούσαις S
cп. XXXVIII § 1 l. 1 τότε δὲ καί ci Rk |. 3 ἀλλ' ἀβληχρᾷ S
§ 3 l. 15 παρακαθήμενοι, assidentes C ci Cobet el Charit. p. 139 ὤφθη Καλλιρρόη μὲν ἐπὶ χρυσηλάτου κλίνης ἀνακειμένη ... Χαιρέας δὲ αὐτῇ παρακαθήμενος ubi vulgatur περικαθήμενος: 'παρά scilicet et περί propter compendii similitudinem ubique temere

τῶν πολιτῶν οἱ βέλτιστοι καὶ τῶν φίλων οἱ
περιόντες λόγον ἐποιοῦντο τῆς ἀρετῆς καὶ τῆς
δυνάμεως, ὅση γένοιτο, καὶ τὰς πράξεις ἀνεμετροῦντο καὶ τῶν τροπαίων τὸ πλῆθος· ἐννέα γὰρ
ἦν ἃ στρατηγῶν καὶ νικῶν ἔστησεν ὑπὲρ τῆς
4 πόλεως. ταῦτα ὡς οὐκέτι συνιέντος, ἀλλὰ
καθῃρημένου τὴν αἴσθησιν αὐτοῦ διελέγοντο
πρὸς ἀλλήλους· ὁ δὲ πᾶσιν ἐτύγχανε τὸν νοῦν
προσεσχηκὼς καὶ φθεγξάμενος εἰς μέσον ἔφη
θαυμάζειν, ὅτι ταῦτα μὲν ἐπαινοῦσιν αὐτοῦ καὶ

His greatest boast.
μνημονεύουσιν, ἃ καὶ πρὸς τύχην ἐστὶ
κοινὰ καὶ γέγονεν ἤδη πολλοῖς στρατηγοῖς, τὸ δὲ κάλλιστον καὶ μέγιστον οὐ λέγουσιν.
" Οὐδεὶς γὰρ " ἔφη " δι' ἐμὲ τῶν ὄντων Ἀθηναίων
μέλαν ἱμάτιον περιεβάλετο."

XXXIX Θαυμαστὸς οὖν ὁ ἀνὴρ οὐ μόνον τῆς

Epilogue containing a panegyric of Pericles.
ἐπιεικείας καὶ πραότητος, ἣν ἐν πράγμασι πολλοῖς καὶ μεγάλαις ἀπεχθείαις
διετήρησεν, ἀλλὰ καὶ τοῦ φρονήματος,
εἰ τῶν αὑτοῦ καλῶν ἡγεῖτο βέλτιστον εἶναι τὸ
μήτε φθόνῳ μήτε θυμῷ χαρίσασθαι μηδὲν ἀπὸ
τηλικαύτης δυνάμεως, μηδὲ χρήσασθαί τινι τῶν
2 ἐχθρῶν ὡς ἀνηκέστῳ. καί μοι δοκεῖ τὴν
μειρακιώδη καὶ σοβαρὰν ἐκείνην προσωνυμίαν
ἓν τοῦτο ποιεῖν ἀνεπίφθονον καὶ πρέπουσαν,
οὕτως εὐμενὲς ἦθος καὶ βίον ἐν ἐξουσίᾳ καθα-

confundi solent' (Fu Jb): περικαθήμενοι St Bl v ‖ 17 λόγους
ἐποιοῦντο <περί> ci Cobet (Jb but substituting λόγον)
§ 4 l. 26 προστυχῇ ἐστί ci Bergk ‖ 29 Cobet ci τῶν πολιτῶν for
τῶν ὄντων and del 'Αθηναίων: 'gloriatur Pericles civium neminem
se accusante damnatum esse necatum' : ἐτῶν τοσούτων ci Bergk
CH. XXXIX § 1 l. 5 εἰπὼν ὡς τῶν αὑτοῦ καλῶν ἡγοῖτο S Fa

ρὸν καὶ ἀμίαντον Ὀλύμπιον προσαγορεύεσθαι, καθάπερ τὸ τῶν θεῶν γένος ἀξιοῦμεν αἴτιον μὲν ἀγαθῶν, ἀναίτιον δὲ κακῶν πεφυκὸς ἄρχειν καὶ βασιλεύειν τῶν ὄντων, οὐχ ὥσπερ οἱ ποιηταὶ συνταράττοντες ἡμᾶς ἀμαθεστάταις δόξαις ἁλίσκονται τοῖς αὑτῶν μυθεύμασι, τὸν μὲν τόπον, ἐν ᾧ τοὺς θεοὺς κατοικεῖν λέγουσιν, ἀσφαλὲς ἕδος καὶ ἀσάλευτον καλοῦντες, οὐ πνεύμασιν, οὐ νέφεσι χρώμενον, ἀλλ' αἴθρᾳ μαλακῇ καὶ φωτὶ καθαρωτάτῳ τὸν ἅπαντα χρόνον ὁμαλῶς περιλαμπόμενον, ὡς τοιαύτης τινὸς τῷ μακαρίῳ καὶ ἀθανάτῳ διαγωγῆς μάλιστα πρεπούσης, αὐτοὺς δὲ τοὺς θεοὺς ταραχῆς καὶ δυσμενείας καὶ ὀργῆς ἄλλων τε μεστοὺς παθῶν ἀποφαίνοντες οὐδ' ἀνθρώποις νοῦν ἔχουσι προσηκόντων. Ἀλλὰ ταῦτα μὲν ἴσως ἑτέρας δόξει πραγματείας εἶναι. τοῦ δὲ Περικλέους ταχεῖαν αἴσθησιν καὶ σαφῆ πόθον Ἀθηναίοις ἐνειργάζετο τὰ πράγματα. καὶ γὰρ οἱ ζῶντος βαρυνόμενοι τὴν δύναμιν ὡς ἀμαυροῦσαν αὐτούς, εὐθὺς ἐκ ποδῶν γενομένου πειρώμενοι ῥητόρων καὶ δημαγωγῶν ἑτέρων ἀνωμολογοῦντο μετριώτερον ἐν ὄγκῳ καὶ σεμνότερον ἐν

His great merits were not fully recognised until after his death, which caused unfeigned regret.

§ 2 l. 12 [Ὀλύμπιον προσαγορεύεσθαι] ci Reiske
§ 3 l. 17 μυθεύμασιν (μηθεύμασι B F^a) S (Si¹ Fu Bl² Jb): ποιήμασι St Si³ Bk Bl¹ v ‖ 19 οὐ πνεύμασιν οὐ νέφεσιν St Si Fu v: οὔτε π. οὔτε ν. ci Bl² (Jb): οὔτε π. οὐ ν. B F^a S ‖ 20 αἴθραι B F^a S (Bl Fu Jb): αἰθρίᾳ St Si v ‖ 21 καθαρωτάτῳ B F¹ S (Fu Bl² Jb): καθαρῷ St Si Bk v ‖ 22 τοιαύτης τινός B F^a S (Fu Bl²): τοιαύτης Si Bk Bl¹ v ‖ 26 προσηκόντων v: προσόντων ci Cobet cl c. 7, 1 ; c. 8, 2

5 πραότητι μὴ φῦναι τρόπον· ἡ δ' ἐπίφθονος
ἰσχὺς ἐκείνη, μοναρχία λεγομένη καὶ τυραννὶς
πρότερον, ἐφάνη τότε σωτήριον ἔρυμα τῆς πολιτείας γενομένη· τοσαύτη φθορὰ καὶ πλῆθος
ἐπέκειτο κακίας τοῖς πράγμασιν, ἣν ἐκεῖνος 40
ἀσθενῆ καὶ ταπεινὴν ποιῶν ἀπέκρυπτε καὶ
κατεκώλυεν ἀνήκεστον ἐν ἐξουσίᾳ γενέσθαι.

§ 5 l. 42 ἐν ἐξουσίᾳ B C F^a S (Fu Bl^2 Jb): ἐξουσίᾳ St Ko Si
Do Bk Bl^1 v: καὶ ἐξαίσιον ci Bergk

EXPLICIT TEXTUS

COMMENTARY ON

PLUTARCH'S

LIFE OF PERICLES

ABBREVIATIONS

G. *Gr.* = W. W. Goodwin's *Greek Grammar.* Macmillan, 1883.

G. *MT.*² = W. W. Goodwin's *Syntax of the Moods and Tenses of the Greek Verb,* rewritten and enlarged. Macmillan, 1889.

HA. *Gr.* = J. Hadley's *Greek Grammar,* revised and in part rewritten by F. de F. Allen. Macmillan, 1884.

NOTES ON
PLUTARCH'S
LIFE OF PERICLES

CHAPTERS I and II form the Proem to the Tenth Book of the *Parallel Lives*—containing those of Pericles-Fabius Maximus—which stood at the head of the *Second Series*. The *Lives* in this series were written, as the Biographer himself tells us in c. 2, 3 (cp. *Life of Timoleon* c. 1, 1), with a more distinctly ethical purpose than those of his *First Series*, which were undertaken at the suggestion and for the gratification of some of his personal friends. See my *Introduction* to *Life of Themistocles* p. xxviii ed. 3.

CHAPTER I

Page of Text

§ 1 l. 2. τέκνα is applied to the inferior animals also in *Mor.* 3
562 B ἄρκτων μὲν γὰρ ἔτι νήπια καὶ λύκων τέκνα καὶ πιθήκων εὐθὺς ἐμφαίνει τὸ συγγενὲς ἦθος, and in Xen. *Cyr.* IV i 17 αἱ σύες φεύγουσι σὺν τοῖς τέκνοις: so that ἔκγονα, the conjectural emendation of Sintenis, adopted by Blass, is superfluous as well as a less suitable word for pointing the contrast.

κόλποις: cp. *Cam.* c. 21, 1 ὡς εἶδε τὰς παρθένους φερούσας ἐν τοῖς κόλποις τὰ τῶν θεῶν ἱερά. ὁ κόλπος was the name given to the fold formed by the tunic (χιτών) when its superfluous length was pulled through the girdle round the waist and allowed to hang over it in a kind of bag.—See Lady Evans *Chapters on Greek Dress* p. 19.

3. ἀγαπῶντας, 'fondling.' Cp. the Homeric use of φιλεῖν, 'to treat kindly,' 'to manifest affection for,' *Il.* VI 15, *Od.* V 135.

4. Καῖσαρ: probably Caesar Augustus (ὁ σεβαστός), with whose other utterances recorded by his biographer Suetonius (cc. 32, 42) the severe rebuke here administered was in keeping.　　ὡς ἔοικεν, *ut fertur*, 'as it seems,' *i.e.* appears from the testimony of men, frequently so used by Plut., as c. 5, 1 ; c. 30, 2, *Them.* c. 3, 2, *Arist.* c. 3, 4 ; c. 5, 6, *Agis* c. 21, 1, *Tib. Gr.* c. 8, 4 ; c. 10, 3, *Mor.* p. 162 c.

εἰ . . . οὐ: indirect questions keep generally the tense and negative of the direct. So *Sol.* c. 29, 5 ἠρώτησεν εἰ τοσούτων ἐναντίον οὐκ αἰσχύνεται τηλικαῦτα ψευδόμενος, *Arat.* c. 49, 2 ἐρωτῶν τοὺς πολλοὺς εἰ νόμους κατὰ τῶν πολλῶν οὐκ ἔχουσιν. But *Pelop.* c. 29, 7 τοὺς Θηβαίους ἐρωτῶν εἰ μηδὲν αὐτοῖς καλὸν πέπρακται ὃ μή κτλ., *Caes.* c. 56, 2 ἐβόα εἰ μηδὲν αἰδοῦνται λαβόντες αὐτὸν ἐγχειρίσαι τοῖς παιδαρίοις, *Cat. mi.* c. 22, 5 εἰ δ' ἄλλῃ πῃ μὴ καλῶς πέπρακται τὰ περὶ τὸν γάμον ἐπισκεπτέον.

6. ἡγεμονικῶς σφόδρα, 'in a very imperious fashion.' Plut. uses ἡγεμών for 'chief magistrate' or 'emperor,' *Cic.* c. 2, 1, *Galb.* c. 16, 3.　　τὸ φύσει φιλητικόν, 'the natural propensity to love.' Cp. *Sol.* c. 7, 2 ἐχούσης τι τῆς ψυχῆς ἀγαπητικὸν ἐν ἑαυτῇ καὶ πεφυκυίας, ὥσπερ αἰσθάνεσθαι καὶ διανοεῖσθαι καὶ μνημονεύειν, οὕτω καὶ φιλεῖν.

8. καταναλίσκοντας εἰς, 'lavishing,' 'wasting on.' Cp. c. 23, 1, *Mor.* 351 A τὸ ἔνατον μέρος τοῦ βίου καταναλίσκουσαν εἰς ἕνα λόγον, Xen. *Cyr.* VI ii 30.　　ὀφειλόμενον, 'whereas it (*sc.* τὸ φύσει φιλητικόν) is due to mankind.'

§ 2 l. 9. ἆρα in interrogationibus simplicibus non raro ita usurpatur, ut interrogatio vim habeat enunciati modeste vel dubitanter affirmantis ; H. Bonitz *Ind. Arist.* 90ᵇ.

10. λόγον ἔχει, 'is it agreeable to reason,' 'rational ?'
Cp. *Num.* c. 4, 3 καί που λόγον ἔχει τὸν θεόν, οὐ φίλιππον οὐδὲ φίλορνιν ἀλλὰ φιλάνθρωπον ὄντα, τοῖς διαφερόντως ἀγαθοῖς ἐθελεῖν συνεῖναι, c. 19, 2 ἄλλως δὲ καὶ λόγον εἶχε τὸν Μάρτιον Ἄρει καθιερωμένον ὑπὸ τοῦ Ῥωμύλου πρῶτον ὀνομάζεσθαι, *Caes.* c. 1, 2 ἐνίων λεγόντων ὡς οὐκ ἔχοι λόγον ἀποκτιννύναι παῖδα τηλικοῦτον.

11. τοὺς καταχρωμένους τούτῳ, *sc.* τῷ φιλομαθεῖ καὶ φιλοθεάμονι: cp. *Luc.* c. 39, 1 εἰς ταῦτα τῷ πλούτῳ ῥύδην καταχρώμενος, *Arat.* c. 6, 5 μειράκιον εἰς ἡδονὰς καὶ πότους μεθημερινοὺς τὰ τῆς ψυχῆς ἐφόδια καταχρώμενον.　　πρὸς τὰ μηδεμιᾶς ἄξια σπουδῆς, 'for objects not deserving any serious attention.' Cp. *Nic.* c. 7, 3 ἔργον ἄξιον σπουδῆς, *Crass.* c. 28, 2 ὄχλον σύμμικτον οὐκ ἀξίων σπουδῆς ἀνθρώπων. Observe that μηδεμιᾶς is the normal usage, the expression being general and indefinite ; so *Cat. mi.* c. 46, 5 εἰς τὰ μηδενὸς ἄξια φροντίδας κατατιθέμενον.

13. τῇ ... αἰσθήσει is not, as Sintenis takes it, dependent on 4 ἀνάγκη but, as τῷ νῷ l. 17, an instrumental dat. dependent on θεωρεῖν. Translate: 'For whereas with sense, apprehending, as it does, by a merely passive impression the objects that fall in its way, we cannot help observing every sensible object, be it of use or not; with his intellect, on the other hand, if he chooses to exercise it, a man has the natural faculty of turning himself from time to time and shifting with the greatest ease to what he pleases' (or 'according as he pleases').

§ 3 l. 19. τὸ δοκοῦν is opposed to τῶν προστυγχανόντων.

Sintenis compares *Demetr.* c. 1, 1 ἡ αἴσθησις οὐδέν τι μᾶλλον ἐπὶ λευκῶν ἢ μελαίνων διαγνώσει γέγονεν, οὐδὲ γλυκέων ἢ πικρῶν, οὐδὲ μαλακῶν καὶ εἰκόντων ἢ σκληρῶν καὶ ἀντιτύπων, ἀλλ' ἔργον αὐτῆς ἑκάστοις ἐντυγχάνουσαν ὑπὸ πάντων τε κινεῖσθαι καὶ κινουμένην πρὸς τὸ φρονοῦν ἀναφέρειν ὡς πέπονθεν.

20. ὥστε, *quasi ita*. ἵνα ... τρέφηται τῷ θεωρεῖν, 'in order that he may receive nourishment from contemplation.'

22. πρόσφορος sc. ἐστί, 'is suitable to.' τὸ ἀνθηρόν, 'freshness,' 'brightness.' Cp. *Mor.* 51 E οἱ γραφεῖς ἀνθηρὰ χρώματα καὶ βάμματα μιγνύουσιν, 395 B ἐθαύμαζε τοῦ χαλκοῦ τὸ ἀνθηρὸν ὡς προσεοικὸς βαφῇ κυάνου στίλβοντος, Lucian *Nigr.* c. 13 τῶν χρωμάτων τὸ ἀνθηρὸν ἐπισκώπτοντες.

23. τρέφει, 'sustains,' 'strengthens.'

24. τῷ χαίρειν sc. αὐτοῖς, 'because of the delight it (sc. ἡ διάνοια) takes in them.'

25. πρὸς τὸ οἰκεῖον ἀγαθόν, 'to its proper good' *i.e.* to virtue and wisdom. Cp. *Mor.* 789 F τὴν φρόνησιν ἧς τὸ οἰκεῖον ἀγαθὸν καὶ τέλειον ἐν γήρᾳ μόλις ἡ φύσις ἀποδίδωσι.

ἐκκαλεῖ, *provocat*. In this sense the middle only is found in Attic prose.

§ 4 l. 26. ταῦτα sc. τὰ θεάματα. τοῖς ἀπ' ἀρετῆς, 'that spring from moral worth.' Cp. c. 2, 3 τῶν ἀπ' ἀρετῆς (ἀγαθῶν).

27. ζῆλον, 'emulation.' ἀγωγὸν εἰς μίμησιν: cp. *Mor.* 381 F τῇ ψυχῇ ὄρεξιν ἐμποιῶν ἀγωγὸν ἐπὶ τὴν ἀλήθειαν.

28. τοῖς ἱστορήσασιν, 'in those who are cognisant of them.' Cp. c. 2, 3. τῶν ἄλλων sc. ἔργων, a genitive at the head of the sentence in loose relation to and unconnected with the construction of what follows. Cp. Xen. *Oecon.* c. 3, 11. The construing order is ὁρμὴ πρὸς τὸ πρᾶξαι οὐκ εὐθὺς ἀκολουθεῖ τῷ θαυμάσαι τὸ πραχθέν.

32. ὡς ἐπὶ τῶν ... ἀλουργῶν (ἀλουργός), 'as in the case of purple dyes.' Cp. Aesch. *Agam.* 946 ἐμβαίνονθ' ἁλουργέσιν.

33. μέν.—δέ, 'although,—yet.' μυρεψούς, 'perfumers,'

lit. 'those who prepare unguents by boiling (ἔψοντες).' Cp. Arist. *Lys.* 946 κάκισθ' ἀπόλοιθ' ὁ πρῶτος ἐψήσας μύρον.

34. **ἡγούμεθα βαναύσους**, 'we regard them as sordid,' 'ignoble.' Cp. Athenae. XIII 612 D Σωκράτους τὴν χρῆσιν τῶν μύρων ἀποδοκιμάσαντος, Σόλωνος δὲ τοῦ νομοθέτου οὐδ' ἐπιτρέποντος ἀνδρὶ τοιαύτης (sc. τῆς μυρεψικῆς) προίστασθαι τέχνης. The βαναυσικαὶ τέχναι, 'mechanical and sedentary arts' (properly such as required the fire to work by; Etym. Magn. βάναυσος: κυρίως πᾶς τεχνίτης διὰ πυρὸς ἐργαζόμενος· βαῦνος γὰρ ἡ κάμινος εἴρηται· καταβέβηκε δὲ ἡ λέξις εἰς πάντα χειροτέχνην), as Socrates tells us in Xen. *Oecon.* c. 4, 2 εἰκότως ἀδοξοῦνται πρὸς τῶν πόλεων· καταλυμαίνονται γὰρ τὰ σώματα τῶν τε ἐργαζομένων καὶ τῶν ἐπιμελομένων ἀναγκάζουσαι καθῆσθαι καὶ σκιατραφεῖσθαι, ἔνιαι δὲ καὶ πρὸς πῦρ ἡμερεύειν. τῶν δὲ σωμάτων θηλυνομένων καὶ αἱ ψυχαὶ πολὺ ἀρρωστότεραι γίγνονται. καὶ ἀσχολίας δὲ μάλιστα ἔχουσι καὶ φίλων καὶ πόλεως συνεπιμελεῖσθαι, Aristot. *Eth. Eud.* 1, 4, 2. In ecclesiastical writers (Chrysostom, Clemens Alexandrinus) they came to signify the arts that minister to luxury and mere comfort.

§ 5 l. 35. **καλῶς** (*i.q.* ὀρθῶς) goes with ἔφη. **Ἀντισθένης**: Antisthenes of Athens (fl. B.C. 366), the well-known pupil of Socrates, and founder of the Cynic school of philosophy.

36. **Ἰσμηνίας** was a famous piper or player on the oboe, a native of Thisbe in Boeotia, where the αὐλός was the national instrument (*Demetr.* c. 1, 6, *Pelop.* c. 19, 1, *Mor.* p. 334 B, p. 632 D, Ps.-Plut. *Mor.* p. 174 F, Lucian *adv. ind.* c. 5, Aelian *VH.* IV 15, Max. Tyr. *Diss.* c. 23, 2). It fell into disuse at Athens, because it distorted the face and did not allow the accompaniment of the voice, about the time of the Peloponnesian war, Aristot. *Pol.* p. 1341b, 2 ff. Plato excluded it from his ideal state (*Rep.* IV 399 D). The lines of an anonymous poet quoted by Athenaeus (VIII 337 E)

ἀνδρὶ μὲν αὐλητῆρι θεοὶ νόον οὐκ ἐνέφυσαν
ἀλλ' ἅμα τῷ φυσῆν χὠ νόος ἐκπέτεται,

show in how little estimation it came to be held. Cp. *Alc.* c. 2. **ἀλλά** at the beginning of an answer introduces an objection.

37. **μοχθηρός**, 'good for nothing.' **γάρ**, 'or else': εἰ μὴ ἄνθρωπος ἦν μοχθηρός is implied.

39. **ἐπιτερπῶς**, 'charmingly.' *Num.* c. 13, 5 ἡ δὲ ἄλλη τῆς ὀρχήσεως ποδῶν ἔργον ἐστί· κινοῦνται γὰρ ἐπιτερπῶς ἑλιγμούς τινας ἐν ῥυθμῷ τάχος ἔχοντι ... ἀποδιδόντες.
ἔν τινι πότῳ, 'at a drinking-bout'; cp. *Timol.* c. 15, 4 παρὰ πότον τινα, Plat. *Prot.* c. 32 ἀλλήλοις συνεῖναι ἐν τῷ πότῳ. Distinguish πότος, *potatio*, 'drinking,' from ποτόν, 'drink.'
τεχνικῶς, 'with professional skill.'

40. **οὐκ αἰσχύνῃ**, *nonne pudet te?*

41. **ἀρκεῖ γάρ**: the sentiment is Plutarch's own and not, as Stephanus takes it, that of Philip. **ἂν βασιλεὺς ἀκροᾶσθαι**

σχολάζῃ. 'if a king find time to listen.' For the construction, cp. *Timol.* c. 15, 4 ταῦτα ποιεῖν ἐσχόλαζεν, *Mor.* 136 D πῶς ἐσχόλασεν ἀνὴρ ἀποθανεῖν ἐν τοσούτοις πράγμασι;

42. **πολὺ νέμει κτλ.**, 'does them great honour, by being present at such performances.' Cp. *Pelop.* c. 30, 4 πλεῖστον νέμων ἐκείνῳ.

43. **τὰ τοιαῦτα** for τοὺς τοιούτους ἀγῶνας, the neut. adj. replacing the kindred noun, HA. *Gr.* § 716 b. The article is used, because a definite class is designated, as c. 7, 4. **θεατής** is a general term for 'spectator' or 'hearer.' Cp. c. 2, 3; c. 13, 5, *Mor.* p. 241 A τῆς λέξεως καὶ προφορᾶς τῶν ἀγωνιζομένων εἶναι θεατήν.

CHAPTER II

§ 1 l. 1. **αὐτουργία τῶν ταπεινῶν**, 'personal labour on mean and servile occupations.' **τὰ καλά**, in moral sense, things worthy of a philosopher's attention. Construe ἡ δ' αὐτ. τῶν ταπ. παρέχεται καθ' αὑτῆς τὸν ἐν τοῖς ά. πόνον μάρτυρα τῆς εἰς τὰ καλὰ ῥ.

2. **τὸν ἐν τοῖς ἀχρήστοις πόνον**, 'the pains it bestows on things of no use.' The more finished therefore and artistic the work, the worse for the artist who misspends his time over it to the neglect of τὰ καλά.

3. **καὶ οὐδείς** ... **Πολύκλειτος**: this sentiment, so foreign to our notions, is not peculiar to Plutarch, but finds an exponent in Lucian also, *Somn.* c. 14 εἰ δὲ καὶ Φειδίας ἢ Πολύκλειτος γένοιο καὶ θαυμαστὰ πολλὰ ἐξεργάσαιο, τὴν μὲν τέχνην ἅπαντες ἐπαινέσονται, οὐκ ἔστι δὲ ὅστις τῶν ἰδόντων, εἰ νοῦν ἔχοι, εὔξαιτ' ἂν σοι ὅμοιος γενέσθαι· οἷος γὰρ ἂν ᾖς, βάναυσος καὶ χειρῶναξ καὶ ἀποχειροβίωτος νομισθήσῃ. We are told that Socrates once practised the art of sculpture, but abandoned it as incompatible with the higher moral pursuits. **εὐφυής**: c. 8, 1.

4. **τὸν ἐν Πίσῃ** ... **Δία**, the colossal ivory and gold statue of Zeus, in the prodomus of his great temple in the Altis or Sacred Grove of Olympia—the greatest work of the most distinguished sculptor of antiquity (c. 13, 4). The god was represented seated on a throne, which was itself a marvel of decoration and architecture. A detailed description of it is given by Pausanias v 11. Pisa is here identified with Olympia. Its inhabitants had originally the presidency of the Olympic games, but they were deprived of it by the Eleans in B.C. 572, when their city was destroyed (Pausan. VI 22, 4).

6. **Polycleitus** of Sicyon and Argos (B.C. 452–412), whose *chef-d'œuvre* was his ivory and gold statue of Hera in her temple between Argos and Mycenae, intended to rival that of

Zeus by Phidias, which, in the judgment of Strabo (*Geogr.* VIII c. 6, 10), it equalled in beauty, though in costliness and size (πολυτελείᾳ καὶ μεγέθει) it was inferior.

Anacreon of Teos (Ionia) c. 530 B.C., the poet who sang of love and wine; **Philetas** of Cos (Athenae. XII c. 77), the distinguished poet, a contemporary of Philip and Alexander of Macedon acc. to Suidas, of Ptolemy, son of Lagus, acc. to others. Only a few fragments remain of his poetry, which was chiefly erotic and formed a model for the Roman elegy, especially in the hands of Propertius; see his *El.* III 26, 31; IV 1, 1; 3, 52; V 6, 3.

7. **Archilochus** of Paros, who belonged to the first half of the seventh century B.C., the oldest writer of satiric iambic poetry, was in ill repute on account of the unmeasured licence of his language. The three are coupled together, because their poetry, with all its art, had no good moral tendency. Plutarch is of course speaking relatively of these pursuits as compared with those of wisdom and virtue.

§ 2 l. 8. ἀναγκαῖον, 'it is a necessary consequence.'

9. ἄξιον σπουδῆς, c. 1, 2.   οὐδέ, *ne—quidem*, 'not either,' 'also not.'

10. τὰ τοιαῦτα, c. 1, 4.   πρός, 'in respect to.'

11. ἀνάδοσις, *impulsus intimo expectore suscitatus*, 'transport.'

For a like use of the word, cp. Clem. Alex. *Strom.* II c. 20 § 115 ed. Klotz ὥσπερ αἱ ἀναθυμιάσεις αἵ τε γῆθεν αἵ τε ἀπὸ τελμάτων εἰς ὀμίχλας συνίστανται καὶ νεφελώδεις συστροφάς, οὕτως αἱ τῶν σαρκικῶν ἐπιθυμιῶν ἀναδόσεις καχεξίαν προστρίβονται τῇ ψυχῇ, § 116 ἐπισπωμένης τῆς ψυχῆς τὰς ἐκ τῆς ἐπιθυμίας ἀναδόσεις. The word means sometimes 'conversion of food into tissue,' as Galen 243 D, but the meaning, 'digestion of knowledge,' assigned to it here by Liddell-Scott, is clearly out of place. They appear to have been misled by Wyttenbach, who from an oversight renders it in his Index '*lectionis quasi concoctio.*'

13. ταῖς πράξεσιν, 'by its actions,' the actions in which it shows itself. Observe that stress is to be laid on εὐθύς, as in c. 1 l. 29.   οὕτω διατίθησιν ὥστε, 'puts (one) in such a frame of mind that.' Cp. *Ti. Gr.* c. 16, 2, *Arat.* c. 46, 2 παραλαβὼν αὐτὸν οὕτως διέθηκεν ὥστε πολλῆς εὐνοίας πρὸς αὐτὸν μεστὸν ἀποστεῖλαι.

§ 3 l. 15. τῶν μὲν γὰρ κτλ., 'we love the possession and enjoyment of the goods of fortune, but of those which are the results of virtue we fall in love with the acts which produce them and we like others to benefit at our hands by them.'

19. τὸ γὰρ καλὸν . . . παρεχόμενον, 'car la vertu a ceste force qu'elle incite la volunté de l'homme qui la considere, à la vouloir incontinent exercer, et engendre en son cueur une envie de la mettre en execution, formant les mœurs de

celuy qui la contemple, non point par l'imitation ains par la seule intelligence et cognoisance de l'acte vertueux, qui tout soudain luy apporte un instinct et un propos deliberé de faire semblable' (*Amyot*).

21. **ἠθοποιοῦν**: like poetry, which by its imitative re- 6 presentation of men's actions exercises a formative influence on the character. History also ἠθοποιεῖ, but it does more than that. Observe that μιμήσει is contrasted with ἱστορίᾳ τοῦ ἔργου, προαίρεσιν with ἠθοποιοῦν. Cp. *Them.* c. 2, 2, *Mor.* 450 F τοῦτο (τὸ παθητικὸν) καὶ τὰς τῶν θηρίων ἠθοποιεῖ πρὸς τὰ πάθη φύσεις, 799 Β τὸ εὐθὺς ἐπιχειρεῖν ἠθοποιεῖν καὶ μεθαρμόττειν τοῦ δήμου τὴν φύσιν οὐ ῥᾴδιον οὐδ' ἀσφαλές, 814 Α πολλὰ γάρ ἐστιν ἄλλα διεξιόντα τοῖς νῦν ἠθοποιεῖν καὶ σωφρονίζειν.

§ 4 l. 23. **οὖν**: because familiarity with the lives of great and good men has such potency in forming the character.

24. **ἐνδιατρίψαι**, 'to continue,' 'go on with,' lit. 'to linger on in.' **τῇ περὶ τοὺς βίους ἀναγραφῇ** is for τῇ τῶν βίων ἀ.' Cp. c. 8, 1; c. 15, 5; c. 16, 1; c. 37, 5, and see my n. to *Them.* c. 3, 3.

25. **δέκατον**, 'as the tenth,' predicate. So Plut. tells us that the *Lives* of *Demosthenes Cicero* formed his 5th βιβλίον, those of *Dion Brutus*, the 12th. See my *Introd.* to *Life of Themistocles* pp. xxvii ff. **συντετάχαμεν**, 'we have composed.' Cp. *Mor.* 1131 F περὶ τῆς ἀρχαίας μουσικῆς συντάξαι ἐσπούδασαν. Hence σύνταγμα (*Num.* c. 22, 3, *Dem.* c. 2, 2) and σύνταξις (c. 2, 1), 'a composition,' especially 'an historical work.'

27. **τοῦ διαπολεμήσαντος πρὸς Ἀ.**, 'who kept up the struggle, carried on the campaign against Hannibal.' This was Q. Fabius Maximus Verrucosus, surnamed Cunctator (B.C. 275–203), the hero of the second Punic war.

28. **τε . . . μάλιστα δέ**, an adversative for a copulative connexion (rare). So Plat. *Rep.* III 394 ἔν τε τῇ τῶν ἐπῶν ποιήσει πολλαχοῦ δὲ καὶ ἄλλοθι, Xen. *Anab.* V V 8 ἐπαινέσοντάς τι ὑμᾶς, ἔπειτα δὲ καὶ ξυνησθησομένους, VII viii 11, [Dem.] *de Halonneso* c. 39 ἅ τ' ἐπιστέλλει πρὸς ὑμᾶς, ἔτι δὲ καὶ ἃ πράττει.

30. **φέρειν . . . ἀγνωμοσύνας**, 'to put up with the unjust humours and caprices.' ἀγνωμοσύνη may mean either 'want of feeling' or 'want of judgment': it recurs c. 37, 1. The plural of abstract nouns used distributively is very common in Plutarch and late Greek writers, also in Xenophon; for instances from the latter author, see my n. to *Oecon.* c. 1, 21.

συναρχόντων: Plutarch is thinking of M. Minucius Rufus, the impetuous *magister equitum* to Fabius.

32. **εἰ δ' ὀρθῶς στοχαζόμεθα τοῦ δέοντος**, 'whether I take a right aim at that which I have to aim at' *i.e.* whether I am

correct in my judgment. Cp. *Alex.* c. 31 στοχάζεσθαι τοῦ μέλλοντος ὀρθῶς, *Cor.* c. 18, 2, *Fab. Max.* c. 10, *Arist.* c. 8, 1.

CHAPTER III

§ 1 l. 1. **γάρ**, 'namely,' referring to κρίνειν ἐκ τῶν γραφομένων, and introductory to the narrative. **τῶν μὲν φυλῶν Ἀκαμαντίδης, τῶν δὲ δήμων Χολαργεύς**, 'of the tribe Acamantis and the township Cholargus': φυλῶν, δήμων are the usual partitive genitives; cp. *Them.* c. 1, 1 Νεοκλέους Φρεαρρίου τῶν δήμων, *Cim.* c. 4, 2 Ἁλιμούσιος γέγονε τῶν δήμων, Plat. *Euthyphr.* c. 1 p. 2 B ἔστι δὲ τῶν δήμων Πιτθεύς, Dem. *or.* 39, 30 γέγονας τῶν δήμων Θορίκιος. Cp. Aristot. Ἀθην. πολ. c. 21, 4 καὶ δημότας ἐποίησεν (ὁ Κλεισθένης) ἀλλήλων τοὺς οἰκοῦντας ἐν ἑκάστῳ τῶν δήμων, ἵνα μὴ πατρόθεν προσαγορεύοντες ἐξελέγχωσιν τοὺς νεοπολίτας, ἀλλὰ τῶν δήμων ἀναγορεύωσιν· ὅθεν καὶ καλοῦσιν Ἀθηναῖοι σφᾶς αὐτοὺς τῶν δήμων, c. 55, 3 ἐπερωτῶσιν δ', ὅταν δοκιμάζωσιν, "τίς σοι πατὴρ καὶ πόθεν τῶν δήμων;" It was Cleisthenes who ruled that every Athenian should be described by his demonym.

2. **οἴκου**, the predicate genitive of origin, H.A. *Gr.* § 732.

3. **κατ' ἀμφοτέρους** sc. τοὺς γονεῖς. Cp. Herod. III 31, 3 ἦν οἱ ἀπ' ἀμφοτέρων ἀδελφεή, VII 97 Ξέρξεω ἀπ' ἀμφοτέρων ἀδελφεός.

4. **ἐν Μυκάλῃ**: c. 37, 5. The battle at the foot of Mount Mycale (Lydia) opposite Samos, in which the Persians were defeated, was on the same day as that of Plataea (Her. IX c. 114), September B.C. 479, the year in which Xanthippus was archon (Diod. XI 27). Aristotle (Ἀθ. πολ. c. 22, 6) mentions his ostracism, which must have fallen in B.C. 485/4. Like Aristides, he returned at the time of the second Persian war; and in B.C. 480 left Athens with the other inhabitants on the approach of Xerxes: Plut. *Them.* c. 10, 5 tells the story of his dog not bearing to be left behind on the occasion. **βασιλέως**: the article is generally omitted when the Persian King is meant. Cp. c. 10, 4, *Them.* c. 7, 1 with my n. *ad l.*

6. **ἔγγονον**: Agariste was niece (not 'granddaughter') of Cleisthenes, the Alcmaeonid reformer, being the daughter of his brother Hippocrates. Plutarch confuses this Cleisthenes with his grandfather the tyrant of Sicyon, who was great-grandfather of Agariste, the mother of Pericles. The following stemma will explain this and other family connexions mentioned in the course of this Biography—

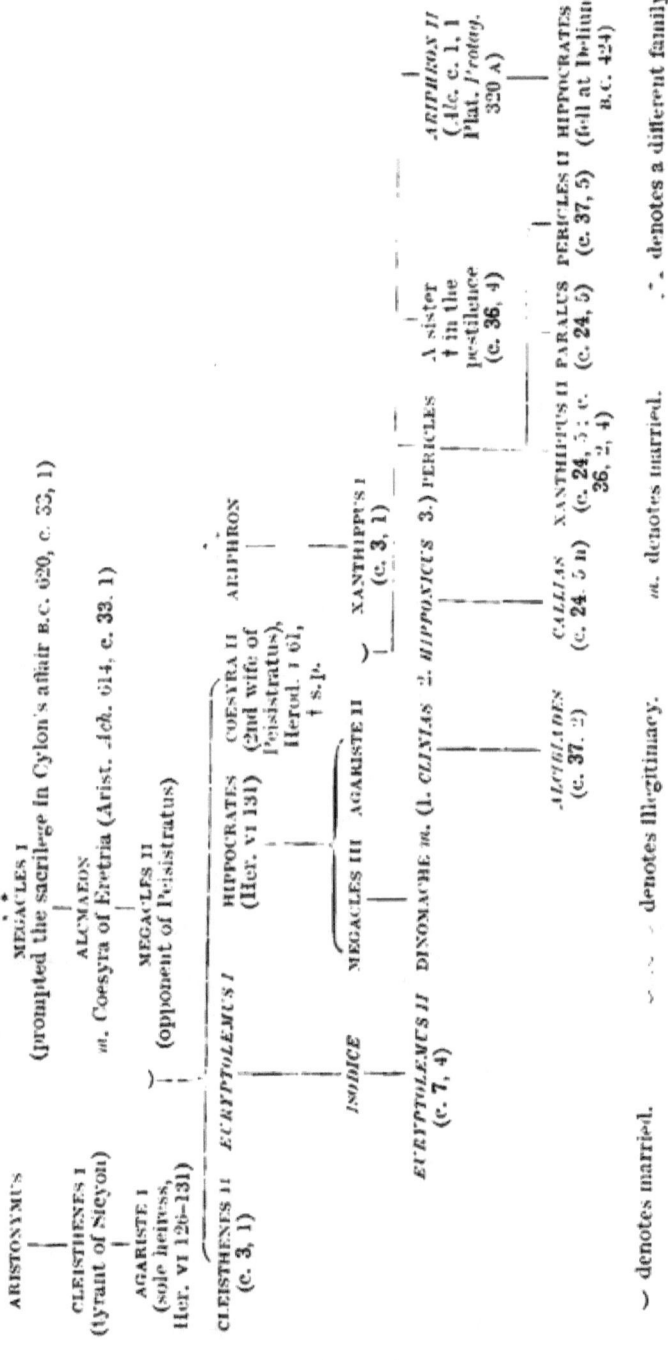

6. **ἐξήλασε Πεισιστρατίδας**: this he did as head of the Alcmaeonidae, Ol. 67, 3 = B.C. 511, through the agency of Cleomenes and the Spartans, and with the countenance of the Delphic oracle (Herod. v 62 ff.) Cp. Aristot. 'Αθ. πολ. cc. 19 f. The omission of the article with patronymic forms is not uncommon. **κατέλυσε**, 'put an end to,' 'broke up,' the technical term for 'overthrowing' an established government (more rarely a single person in authority as c. 16, 3). Cp. Aristot. *Pol.* p. 1272ᵈ, 9 καταλῦσαι τὴν βασιλείαν, p. 1301ᵇ, 21 τὴν ἐφορείαν and see Gr. Ind. to *Graech.* p. 227ᵃ.

7. **ἔθετο**, not ἔθηκε, because the laws were binding on the legislator himself also. Usually θέσθαι νόμους is said of a republican legislature who pass laws for themselves; θεῖναι of the supreme legislator who imposes them upon others; hence Aristotle ('Αθην. πολ. c. 22) applies it to Cleisthenes.

8. **ἄριστα κεκραμένην κτλ.**, 'admirably tempered and suited to promote unanimity among the people.'

This mixture of a mild democracy with aristocratic elements was regarded more favourably by late writers than by contemporaries. Isocrates indeed (or. 16, 27) highly extols it: ἐκείνην τὴν δημοκρατίαν ἐξ ἧς οἱ πολῖται πρὸς μὲν ἀνδρίαν οὕτως ἐπαιδεύθησαν, ὥστε τοὺς βαρβάρους τοὺς ἐπὶ πᾶσαν ἐλθόντας τὴν Ἑλλάδα μόνοι νικᾶν μαχόμενοι, περὶ δὲ δικαιοσύνης τοσαύτην δόξαν ἔλαβον, ὥσθ' ἑκόντας αὐτοῖς τοὺς Ἕλληνας ἐγχειρίσαι τὴν ἀρχὴν τῆς θαλάττης, τὴν δὲ πόλιν τηλικαύτην ἐποίησαν καὶ τῇ δυνάμει καὶ ταῖς ἄλλαις κατασκευαῖς, ὥστε τοὺς φάσκοντας αὐτὴν ἄστυ τῆς Ἑλλάδος εἶναι . . . δοκεῖν ἀληθῆ λέγειν.

§ 2 l. 9. **κατὰ τοὺς ὕπνους**: the plural is not uncommon, especially with prepositions. See the instances quoted in my n. to *Them.* c. 28, 3.

10. **ἔδοξε τεκεῖν**, 'fancied that she had given birth to.' Cp. *Pyrrh.* c. 11, 2 ἔδοξε κατὰ τοὺς ὕπνους ὑπ' 'Αλεξάνδρου καλεῖσθαι, *Arist.* c. 11, 6 ἔδοξε κατὰ τοὺς ὕπνους ἐπερωτώμενον αὐτὸν εἰπεῖν, *Them.* c. 26, 2 ὄναρ ἔδοξεν ἰδεῖν δράκοντα . . . προσανέρποντα τῷ τραχήλῳ, where other instances are cited in my note *ad l.* The story is borrowed from Herod. VI 131 ἔγκυος ἐοῦσα εἶδε (sc. Agariste) ὄψιν ἐν τῷ ὕπνῳ, ἐδόκεε δὲ λέοντα τεκεῖν, καὶ μετ' ὀλίγας ἡμέρας τίκτει Περικλέα Ξανθίππῳ. Cp. the parody of an oracle (Herod. v 92, 3) about Cypselus, the future tyrant of Corinth, Arist. *Eq.* 1037,

ἔστι γυνή, τέξει δὲ λέονθ' ἱεραῖς ἐν 'Αθήναις,
ὃς περὶ τοῦ δήμου πολλοῖς κώνωψι μαχεῖται
ὥστε περὶ σκύμνοισι βεβηκώς.

11. **τὰ ἄλλα**, adv. acc.; **τὴν ἰδέαν**, 'in form, aspect,' acc. of respect after ἄμεμπτον.

Cp. *Flamin.* c. 1, 1 ἰδέαν μὲν ὁποῖος ἦν πάρεστι θεάσασθαι τοῖς βουλομένοις ἀπὸ τῆς ἐν Ῥώμῃ χαλκῆς εἰκόνος, *Aler.* c. 4, 1 τὴν μὲν οὖν ἰδέαν τοῦ σώμάτος οἱ Λυσίππειοι μάλιστα τῶν ἀνδριάντων ἐμφαίνουσιν, Demetr. c. 2, 2 ἰδέᾳ καὶ κάλλει προσώπου θαυμαστὸς καὶ περιττός, Diod. Sic. III 8 (Aethiopes) ταῖς μὲν χρόαις εἰσὶ μέλανες, ταῖς δὲ ἰδέαις σιμοί, τοῖς δὲ τριχώμασιν οὖλοι.

12. προμήκη ... καὶ ἀσύμμετρον, 'longish and out of proportion' to the rest of his person; cp. Aristot. περὶ ζῴων πορ. c. 8 p. 708ᵃ 15 ὅσα κατὰ τὸ μῆκος ἀσύμμετρά ἐστι πρὸς τὴν ἄλλην τοῦ σώματος φύσιν. For τῇ κεφαλῇ, the dat. of respect, cp. c. 27, 4 τρυφερόν τινα τῷ βίῳ, Them. c. 2, 1 μαλακὸν τῇ ψυχῇ, Alcib.-Coriol. c. 2, 1 ἁπλοῦς τις τῷ τρόπῳ. This use of the dative is much affected by Polybius.

13. ὅθεν, 'for which reason,' c. 2, 2; c. 13, 3.

14. κράνεσι περιέχονται, 'are covered with helmets.' Hence the joke of Cratinus in his 'Thracian women' fr. 71 (c. 13, 6) where he speaks of him as τῳδεῖον ἐπὶ τοῦ κρανίου ἔχων, 'having (the dome of) the Music-Hall on the top of his skull.'

15. Plut. frequently uses μή with participles, especially those of βούλεσθαι, δύνασθαι and τολμᾶν, which do not represent a condition and where οὐ is the proper negative in classical Greek; cp. c. 23, 1; c. 29, 2; c. 34, 4. Stegmann quotes 341 instances from the Lives, where μή is found with causal, temporal, modal or purely attributive participles, and 211 from the Morals. On the other hand, there are 629 instances in the Lives, and 538 in the Morals, where οὐ is employed. As a rule, Plut. prefers μή where the negative is emphasised, and sometimes, as in the passage before us, to avoid a disagreeable hiatus.

ὡς ἔοικε, videlicet. The real reason was that he continued to be Strategus for so many years that the helmet seemed an indispensable part of him. See c. 37, 1, and E. Curtius (Hist. Gr. II p. 457) who quotes (ib. p. 599) Arch. Zeitung 1860 p. 40.

16. οἱ Ἀττικοὶ ποιηταί, i.e. the Attic comic poets.

17. cχινοκέφαλον, 'with a head like a squill' (σχῖνος) i.e. pointed, peaked. See the quotation from Cratinus in c. 13, 4.

18. ἔστιν ὅτε, est ubi, 'sometimes.' So c. 24, 3; c. 15, 3 ἦν ὅτε.

§ 3 l. 18. τῶν κωμικῶν, 'the comic poets,' c. 4, 2; c. 13, 10.

19. Cratinus, Telecleides (l. 25), and Eupolis (l. 30) were all poets of the old or political and personal period of comedy, who lived just before and during the Peloponnesian war, and therefore were contemporaries of Pericles. The last of the three flourished after his death. They belonged to the conservative or anti-demagogic party at Athens; their hero and idol was Cimon (see Cratin. Archilochi fr. 1 ed. Kock), after whose death, when Thucydides, son of Melesias, was at the head of the party, Cratinus was more bitter and venomous than ever in his invective against Pericles, whether ridiculing his personal appearance, as here and fr. 355 ἀνελκταῖς ὀφρύσι σεμνόν, 'high and mighty with up-drawn eye-brows,' or seeking to make the people jealous and suspicious of him by calling him Zeus and Πανδιονίδα πόλεως βασιλεὺς τῆς ἐριβώλακος (Drapetides fr. 56), or throwing contempt on his eloquence, the chief source of his power and in the poet's view an unsupportable tyranny. Cratinus attacked also the lax morals of his day in his Μαλθακοί, Πλοῦτοι, Χειρῶνες, the rich debauchees in his

Ἀρχίλοχοι, foreign cults and strange superstitions in his Θρᾷτται and Τροφώνιος, the Sophists as corrupters of the ancient discipline and regime when men lived a happy life ἀγανόφρονος ἡδυλόγου σοφίας πόθῳ περισσοκαλλεῖς, *mitis et dulce loquentis sapientiae amore supra modum pulcri.*

ἐν Χείρωσι : the Cheirons — so named from the chorus which was composed of sages, bearing in their outward appearance a certain resemblance to the instructor of Achilles—was one of Cratinus' strongest political pieces. It contained bitter attacks on Aspasia and Pericles with frequent appeals to the ancient constitution of Solon against the dangerous experiments of the great demagogue.

20. Στάcιc δὲ καὶ πρεcβγενὴc Κρόνοc κτλ. : Mein. II 147, Kock I 86. The lines are from a choral song, to be taken in connexion with the fragment quoted c. 24, 4, where also the genealogy of Aspasia is given in the style of the old theogonies. As Pericles is dubbed 'the Olympian Zeus,' so his father naturally is the old Κρόνος (*Saturnus*), the representative of all old-fashioned things, his mother 'faction,' 'party-strife,' for it was the contention between political parties which made him great, and, like Zeus, he is enthroned on the destruction of ancient order. Curtius *Hist. Gr.* II pp. 454–5. ΜΙΓΕΝΤΕ, 'embracing.'

22. κεφαληγερέταν, a parody on the Homeric epithet νηφεληγερέτην, 'cloud-compeller'; the word has no meaning in itself, but it is suggestive of the peculiar shape of Pericles' head, and of his being a Zeus upon earth. θεοὶ καλέουcιν, as in Hom. *Il.* i 403, *Od.* XII 61, Hesiod *Theog.* 187.

23. ἐν Νεμέσει : Mein. II 85, Kock I 49. The *Nemesis* was one of the most scurrilous attacks of Cratinus on Pericles and Aspasia, the former under the name of Zeus, the latter under that of Nemesis.

The allegorical tradition according to the author of the Κύπρια (ap. Athenae. VIII c. 10) about Nemesis, the virgin divinity of Rhamnus (Attica), was identical with that of Leda, as mother of that Helen who was the cause of so many woes to Greece. Cp. Isocr. Ἑλένης ἐγκώμιον c. 59 κύκνος γενόμενος (Ζεὺς) εἰς τοὺς Νεμέσεως κόλπους κατέφυγε, Hyginus *Astron.* 8 (p. 44, 5 Bunte), Apollodorus 3, 10, 7. The poet accepts and mixes up the dual tradition according as it suited his fancy. Phidias set the example in the group on the base of his statue of Nemesis, in which he represented Leda bringing Helen to Nemesis (Pausanias I c. 33, 7-8).

24. μόλ', ὦ Ζεῦ ξένιε καὶ καράνιε, an iambic trimeter with the first foot wanting. The point of the former epithet 'protector of strangers' is not clear. It may refer to his proposed abrogation of his own law affecting illegitimate (νόθοι) children (c. 37, 2) in favour of Pericles his son by Aspasia (Mein. *Fr. Com. Gr.* V p. XXXVI); the latter has reference to his personal peculiarity (l. 12) with a play perhaps on κεραύνιε.

Blass retains the MS. reading καρδίᾳ, a name of the god familiar to a Boeotian but not to an Athenian audience.

§ 4 l. 25. **Τηλεκλείδης**: *Fr. inc.* 43 (Mein. II 373, Kock I 220). This passage must be taken in connexion with that quoted c. 16, 1.

26. **ἠπορημένον**, 'reduced to his wits' end'; cp. Eur. *Iph. A.* 537 ὡς ἠπύρημαι πρὸς θεῶν τὰ νῦν τάδε. **αὐτόν** sc. Pericles.
ἐν τῇ πόλει *i.q.* ἐν τῇ ἀκροπόλει, a meaning often found in official documents and inscriptions. See Thuc. II 15, 6, and cp. c. 32, 2, Aristot. Ἀθην. πολ. c. 21, 3, Xen. *de red.* c. 5, 12, *Anab.* VII 1, 27, Antiph. *or.* 6 § 39, but in Aristophanes, *Eq.* 267, *Av.* 832, *Nub.* 69, always ἐν πόλει without the article.

27. **καρηβαροῦντα**, 'top-heavy,' *i.e.* sinking with the weight of the cares of state, also because of the abnormal size of his head. Aristophanes has another form καρηβαριᾶν. Bergk (*Rel. Com. att. ant.* p. 330) suggests that the anapaestic tetrameter ran as follows:—

ποτὲ μέν γ' ἀπορῶν . . . . . καρηβαριῶν τε κάθηται,
ποτὲ δ' ἐκ κεφαλῆς ἐνδεκακλίνου θόρυβον πολὺν ἐξανατέλλει.

28. **κεφαλῆς ἐνδεκακλίνου**, not, as Liddell-Scott, 'a head as long as eleven couches,' nor, as Denis (*La Comédie grecque* I p. 170 note 1), 'tête longue comme onze lits ou plutôt d'une longueur telle qu'il eut fallu onze lits pour la porter,' nor, as F. H. Bothe (*Poet. com. gr. fr.* Didot p. 128), 'tam grandis ut undecim stratis indigeat (Pericles), in quibus accumbat'; but 'large enough to hold ten couches,' 'roomy.' Cp. Xen. *Oec.* c. 8, 13 καὶ ὅσα λέγω, ἔφη, πάντα οὐκ ἐν πολλῷ τινι μείζονι χώρᾳ ἔκειτο ἢ ἐν δεκακλίνῳ στέγῃ συμμέτρῳ, *Symp.* c. 2, 18 οἶκος ἑπτάκλινος, Athenae. II c. 29 ὅτι καὶ τρίκλινοι οἶκοι καὶ τετράκλινοι καὶ ἑπτάκλινοι καὶ ἐννεάκλινοι . . . ἦσαν παρὰ τοῖς παλαιοῖς.

Ἀντιφάνης (Mein. III 117, Kock II 129),

συναγαγὼν
τρεῖς ὄντας εἰς τρίκλινον ὑμᾶς.

Φρύνιχος (Mein. II 607, Kock I 387),

ἑπτάκλινος οἶκος ἦν καλός,
εἶτ' ἐννεάκλινος.

Cp. also Plut. *Mor.* 679 B οὐκ ὀρθῶς οἱ πλούσιοι νεανιεύονται κατασκευάζοντες οἴκους τριακοντακλίνους καὶ μείζους, Diod. Sic. XXXI (Excerpt. Phot. p. 516 Wessel. (de carcere Albano)) ἔστι δὲ ὁ κάρκαρος ὄρυγμα κατάγειον βαθύ, τὸ μὲν μέγεθος ἔχον οἴκου μάλιστά πως ἐννεακλίνου.

In a notice of Ussing's *Om Grækernes og Romernes Huse*, contributed to the *Revue Critique et Littéraire* 14 July 1877, C. Graux quotes three passages of Aristotle, which he thinks may throw doubt on the traditional interpretation. Speaking of a fabulous animal, called sometimes βόλινθος, sometimes βόνασος by the ancients, Aristotle says, *Hist. Anim.* 1 45 = p. 630ᵃ, 22 τὸ δὲ δέρμα αὐτοῦ κατέχει εἰς ἑπτάκλινον ἀποταθέν, and *de mirab. ausc.* c. 1 = p. 830ᵃ, 16 ὅταν δὲ ἐκδαρῇ τὸ δέρμα κατέχειν τόπον ὀκτάκλινον, and then in the same book c. 127 = p. 842ᵃ, 22 in speaking of the space covered by a certain fire burning, ὁ δὲ καιόμενος τόπος ἐστὶν οὐ πολύς, ὡς ἔοικεν, ἀλλ' ὅσον μάλιστα πεντακλίνου τὸ μέγεθος. Comparing these three texts with Pollux 1 79 λέγεται δὲ καὶ οἶκος τρίκλινος, πεντάκλινος καὶ δεκάκλινος, καὶ ἁπλῶς πρὸς τὸ μέτρον τοῦ μεγέθους ὁ τῶν κλινῶν ἀριθμός, Graux is inclined to agree with Beckmann that κλίνη had come to be used by the Greeks for a certain superficial measure, which he reckons at 10 square cubits (4 × 2½). This is probably its meaning in Diodor. Sic. xx c. 91 where in describing a siege-engine (ἑλέπολις) used by Demetrius before Rhodes, the writer says ἐκ δὲ τῶν γωνιῶν ὑπῆρχον <κίονες> ἴσοι τῷ μήκει οὕτω συννενευκότες εἰς ἀλλήλους ὥστε, τοῦ παντὸς κατασκευάσματος ὄντος ἐννεαστέγου, τὴν μὲν πρώτην στέγην ὑπάρχειν κλινῶν μγ΄, τὴν δ' ἀνωτάτω θ΄.

28. θόρυβον πολὺν ἐξανατέλλειν, 'causes a loud noise of war to arise.'

30. ὁ δ' Εὔπολις ἐν τοῖς Δήμοις: Mein. II 458, Kock I 280.

The Δῆμοι of Eupolis was a political piece, so called because the chorus was composed of representatives of the Attic demes. It turned on the internal politics or rather on the moral condition of Athens, just as his Πόλεις, in which the chorus was composed of representatives of towns of the Athenian confederation, criticised the conduct of the Athenians towards their allied or subject city-states. In the former play, the dramatist introduced deceased legislators on the stage—Solon, Miltiades, Aristides, Pericles (*Aristid.* III 433 B)—conferring on state affairs. The quotation in c. 24, 6 is taken from the same play. It must have been brought out before Ol. 91, 1 = B.C. 416/7, because Nicias is supposed to be alive and still at Athens at the time of its representation. Cp. c. 24, 6.

πυνθανόμενος, 'asking questions' *i.e.* representing his characters as putting questions. Cp. Thuc. I 5, 2 οἱ παλαιοὶ τῶν ποιητῶν τὰς πύστεις τῶν καταπλεόντων πανταχοῦ ὁμοίως ἐρωτῶντες εἰ λῃσταί εἰσιν for ἐρωτῶντας ποιοῦντες. See c. 4, 2.

31. τῶν . . . δημαγωγῶν, 'popular leaders,' in good sense; c. 10, 3; *Them.* c. 2, 2.

33. ὅ τι περ κεφάλαιον . . . ἤγαγες, 'him you brought from below, who is the very (*i.e.* right and real) head of those in the nether world.' Cp. Lucian *Philops.* c. 6 ὅτι περ τὸ κεφάλαιον αὐτὸ ἐξ ἑκάστης προαιρέσεως ('school'), αἰδεσίμους ἅπαντας καὶ μονονουχὶ φοβεροὺς τὴν πρόσοψιν, where, as in other passages, the writer deviates from Attic usage in adding the article, as is pointed out by Cobet *Var. L.* p. 312. The proper expressions were ὅτι περ ὄφελος (Arist. *Eccl.* 56), ὅτι <περ> ἦν αὐτῶν ἄνθος (Thuc. IV 133, 4 acc. to Cobet's correction of the vulgate), ὅτι περ ἐσθλόν (not ὅτι or ὅπερ). Plutarch, of course, presupposes an allusion to the peculiar shape of the head of

the statesman. τῶν κάτωθεν ἤγαγες is for τῶν κάτω κάτωθεν ἤγαγες—a very common form of attraction, when the verb of the clause implies movement. Cp. c. 27, 4 : c. 31, 4 ; *Timol.* c. 16, 5 τὸν ἀπὸ τῆς πέτρας κατῆγον. The person addressed must be the old general Myronides, not, as Hermann (*Opusc.* v 292) thinks, Ἑρμῆς ψυχόπομπος.

CHAPTER IV

§ 1 l. 1 **τῶν μουσικῶν**, *artis musicae*. 8

Cp. Xen. *Cyr.* I vi 38 ἐν τοῖς μουσικοῖς τὰ νέα καὶ ἀνθηρὰ εὐδοκιμεῖ. The ancient Greeks attached so much importance to music, at least playing on the cithara and learning lyric poetry by heart, as to make it an essential part of public education (παιδεία ἐλευθέριος, Aristot. *Pol.* p. 1338ᵃ, 13), not only as being a noble and worthy occupation πρὸς τὸ καλῶς σχολάζειν, but as exercising a valuable influence in the formation and development of mind and character. Plato *Rep.* IV 424 c quotes an utterance of Damon's with approbation : —εἶδος καινὸν μουσικῆς μεταβάλλειν εὐλαβητέον ὡς ἐν ὅλῳ κινδυνεύοντα· οὐδαμοῦ γὰρ κινοῦνται μουσικῆς τρόποι ἄνευ πολιτικῶν νόμων τῶν μεγίστων.

2. **Δάμωνα** : according to the Scholiast on Plato *Alc.* I p. 118 c, Damon was the pupil of Lamprocles, Lamprocles of Agathocles, Agathocles himself of Pythocleides. Pericles in his youth, according to Plato *ib.*, was at first a pupil of the last mentioned teacher and not until later of Damon. The same writer (*Laches* 180 D) extols Damon as ἀνδρῶν χαριέστατον οὐ μόνον τὴν μουσικήν, ἀλλὰ καὶ τἆλλα ὁπόσα βούλει ἄξιον συνδιατρίβειν νεανίσκοις. He makes mention of him again *Rep.* III p. 400 B, IV p. 424 c. Isocrates also (*or.* 15, 235), as well as the comic poet Plato (l. 16), represents him as Pericles' master : Περικλῆς δ᾽ δυοῖν ἐγένετο μαθητής, Ἀναξαγόρου τε καὶ Δάμωνος τοῦ κατ᾽ ἐκεῖνον τὸν χρόνον φρονιμωτάτου δόξαντος εἶναι τῶν πολιτῶν. Cp. *Arist.* c. 1, 7 Δάμων ὁ Περικλέους διδάσκαλος, ὅτι τὸ φρονεῖν ἐδόκει τις εἶναι περιττός, ἐξωστρακίσθη.

3. **βραχύνοντας** : the name therefore comes from the root δαμ- 'tame,' and is not a dialectic form of Δήμων.

4. **ἐκφέρειν**, 'to pronounce.'

Cp. *Mor.* 738 B ἔλεγε πρώτην φύσει φωνὴν τῶν ἐνάρθρων ἐκφέρεσθαι διὰ τῆς τοῦ ἄλφα δυνάμεως, 747 E, 1010 A, 1011 C, Athenae. III p. 94 F οἱ δὲ διὰ τοῦ ῡ στοιχείου ἐκφέροντες (σταγόνα) κατ᾽ ἀναλογίαν λέγουσιν ἀπὸ τοῦ ὑός, Apollonius *lex. Hom.* p. 1 ἃ ψιλῶς καὶ δασέως ἐκφερόμενον δηλοῖ σχετλιασμόν.

5. **παρά**, *apud*, 'in the school of.' Cp. Arist. *Ran.* 910 παρὰ Φρυνίχῳ τραφέντες. **Πυθοκλείδης** of Ceos, according to the Schol. on Plato *Alcib.* I p. 118 c, μουσικὸς ἦν, τῆς σεμνῆς μουσικῆς διδάσκαλος καὶ Πυθαγόρειος.

6. **διαπονηθῆναι**, 'worked at.' Cp. Plat. *legg.* 846 D δύο τέχνας ἀκριβῶς διαπονεῖσθαι σχεδὸν οὐδεμία φύσις ἱκανὴ τῶν ἀνθρωπίνων, *Phaedr.* 273 E. **τὸν ἄνδρα** is instead of personal or demonstrative pronoun. Cp. *Them.* c. 12, 2 with my n. *ad l.*

7. **ἄκρος**, *summus in arte sua.* Cp. *Num.* c. 13, 3 ἵνα τῶν ἄκρων δημιουργῶν, *Dem.* c. 6, 2 τῶν ἄκρων γενέσθαι δολιχοδρόμων, *Pelop.* c. 23, 3 πάντων ἄκροι τεχνῖται καὶ σοφισταὶ τῶν πολεμικῶν ὄντες.

The source of this statement is Plato *Protag.* 316 D, where Protagoras explains that, though he was the first to dub himself Sophist, sophistic existed long before his time, only the early professors were afraid to declare themselves Sophists, and practised the art under various disguises, as poets, musicians, gymnasts : μουσικὴν δὲ Ἀγαθοκλῆς τε ὁ ὑμέτερος πρόσχημα ἐποιήσατο, μέγας ὢν σοφιστής, καὶ Πυθοκλείδης καὶ ἄλλοι πολλοί· οὗτοι πάντες φοβηθέντες τὸν φθόνον ταῖς τέχναις ταύταις παραπετάσμασιν ἐχρήσαντο.

καταδύεσθαι εἰς, 'took refuge in,' 'sheltered himself behind.' Cp. *Mor.* 1072 F ὑπὸ Καρνεάδου πιεζόμενον εἰς ταύτας καταδύεσθαι τὰς εὑρησιλογίας.

9. **ἐπικρυπτόμενος**, 'by way of concealing,' imperf. participle which is used more often than the present in a conative sense. See on *Them.* c. 2, 6, *Dem.* c. 6, 2. Δεινότης is used of conspicuous 'cleverness' in anything, especially of 'oratorical skill' and 'political insight.' Cp. *Cim.* c. 3, 4 ; *Dem.* c. 8, 2.

11. **ἀθλητῇ** with **τῶν πολιτικῶν**. The function of the ἀλείπτης was to anoint with oil the body of an ἀθλητής before and after the exercises of the palaestra, and was thus a subordinate branch of that of the γυμναστής or παιδοτρίβης. From meaning 'a trainer in gymnastic exercises' it came to mean 'a trainer' or 'teacher' generally. (See my n. to *Them.* c. 1, 2.) The word is especially applicable here, because Damon was not himself a practical statesman but only helped Pericles to become one, just as the ἀλείπτης did not himself enter the lists, but only helped others to win prizes.

§ 2 l. 13. **παρακαλύμματι**, 'as a veil,' *i.e.* 'excuse, pretext.'

For this figurative meaning of παρακάλυμμα, cp. *Poplic.* c. 3, 4 τῇ ἀβελτερίᾳ προσποιήματι καὶ παρακαλύμματι . . . χρησάμενος ἀσφαλείας ἕνεκα πρὸς τοὺς τυράννους, *Mor.* c. 29, 4 τοῦτο προσέθηκε τὸ σοφὸν ὥσπερ παρακάλυμμα τῆς αἰσχύνης, *Ages.* c. 37, 6 ἀτόπου καὶ ἀλλοκότου πράγματος παρακαλύμματι τῷ συμφέροντι τῆς πατρίδος χρησάμενος, *Galb.* c. 20, 1 εἰδὼς φυγῆς ὑποκόρισμα καὶ παρακάλυμμα αὐτῷ τὴν ἀρχὴν διδομένην, *Mor.* 27 E ἐχρήσατο τῆς ἀπορίας παρακαλύμματι κοιμωμένῳ ποιήσας ὅμοιον ἑαυτόν, Lucian *de merc. cond.* c. 5.

15. **παρέσχε . . . διατριβήν**, 'furnished a subject of merriment.' Cp. *Timol.* c. 11, 1 διατριβὴν τοῖς Ῥηγίνοις παρεῖχον, *Arat.* c. 31, 2 διατριβὴν καὶ γέλωτα πολὺν παρασχόντες, *Alcib.* c. 13, 3 τοῖς κωμικοῖς ὁμοῦ τι πᾶσι διατριβὴν ἀεὶ

σκωπτόμενος ἐν τοῖς θεάτροις παρεῖχε.   γοῦν, 'at all events,' confirms a general assertion by giving a particular instance of the truth of it; c. 5, 2; c. 38, 2.

16. Plato, the comic dramatist, flourished B.C. 428-B.C. 389. His *Cleophon* gained the third prize, when Aristophanes was first with the *Ranae*. Cobet (*obs. cr. in Plat. rel.* p. 188) thinks that the quotation here given is from his Σοφισταί.

καί, 'even' or perhaps 'amongst other gibes.'   πεποίηκεν, *finxit*; c. 24, 6.

18. λέξον: the question is put in a following verse.

19. Χείρων, *ta alter Chiron*, predicate. Cheiron, the wisest and justest of all the centaurs, the instructor of Jason, Asclepius and Achilles, is here taken as the type of a teacher of great men.

Such instances of apposition are common especially in proverbial expressions, as Arist. *Lys.* 928 Ἡρακλῆς ξενίζεται, Cratinus Δραπετίδες fr. 52 ὁ δ' ὄνος ὕεται sc. *qui madmodum asinus ob cutis duritiem pluvia nihil offenditur*, Χείρωνες fr. 229 ὄνοι δ' ἀπωτέρω κάθηνται τῆς λύρας. Theopompus fr. 40 τέττιξ κιλαδεῖ, *garrit ut cicada*, Theognis 1364 παῖς πέτρῃ προσέκυρσας, Herondas VI 14 κύων ὑλακτέω ταύταις, Plat. *Hipp. mai.* 292 D οὐδέν σοι μᾶλλον γεγωνεῖν δύναμαι ἢ εἰ μοι παρεκάθησο λίθος.

§ 3 l. 20. διήκουσε, 'was a hearer, disciple, of.' *Them.* c. 2, 3. Zenon of Elea or Velia (Magna Graecia) lived in the middle of the 5th century. He was the favourite pupil of Parmenides, and inventor of dialectic. Plato (*Phaedr.* 261 D) refers to his paradoxes on the subjects of the 'One and Many,' 'Rest and Motion' etc.: τὸν Ἐλεατικὸν Παλαμήδην (Zenon) λέγοντα ἴσμεν τέχνῃ, ὥστε φαίνεσθαι τοῖς ἀκούουσι τὰ αὐτὰ ὅμοια καὶ ἀνόμοια, καὶ ἕν καὶ πολλά, μένοντά τε αὖ καὶ φερόμενα. The dialogue Sophista was written to overthrow this antilogic method, in order to make way for a rational logic. See W. H. Thompson *ad l.c.*

21. πραγματευομένου περὶ φύσιν, 'when he was discoursing of natural philosophy.' "Πραγματεύεσθαι περί τι vel περί τινος is dicitur ab Aristotele, qui in investiganda et cognoscenda aliqua re via ac ratione procedit; itaque coniunctum legitur cum verbis διαλέγεσθαι, ζητεῖν, θεωρεῖν" H. Bonitz, *Ind. Arist. s. v.*

23. ἀπορίαν, 'puzzle.'

24. ἕξιν, 'skill as the result of practice in discussion.' See Bonitz *Index Aristot.* p. 261ᵃ.

Timon of Phleius (N.E. Peloponnesus) lived about B.C. 280. He was a pupil of Pyrrhon, the Sceptic, and a famous σιλλογράφος or writer of satiric compositions (σίλλοι) in hexameter verse on the dogmatic systems of philosophers of his own and earlier ages.

9 26. ἀμφοτερογλώccογ, 'of two-edged tongue,' who could argue equally for and against the same thesis.   cθένοc ογκ ἀλαπαδνόν, a reminiscence of the Homeric line (*Il.* VII 257) ἤ συσὶ κάπροισιν τῶν τε σθένος οὐκ ἀλαπαδνόν.

27. πάντων ἐπιλήπτοροc, 'assailant, censurer, of things or men in general.'

§ 4 l. 28. ὁ πλεῖcτα Π. cυγγενόμενοc, 'the man who had most intercourse with Pericles.' Cp. [Dem.] *or.* LXI 45 for the statement. The verb συγγίγνεσθαι is generally used of the disciple holding converse with the master, rarely, as here, of the master with the disciple. So *Arat.* c. 13, 1 ὥστε καὶ Ἀπελλῆν ἐκεῖνον ἤδη θαυμαζόμενον συγγενέσθαι τοῖς ἀνδράσιν ἐπὶ ταλάντῳ. Cp. συνῆν l. 10.

29. ὄγκον, 'weight,' 'air of importance.' Cp. *Nic.* c. 5, 2 ὁ μάλιστα... συμπεριθεὶς ὄγκον αὐτῷ καὶ δόξαν, *Mar.* c. 28, 1 πρὸς χάριν ἐνδιδοὺς τοῖς πολλοῖς παρὰ τὸν ὄγκον καὶ τὸ κοινὸν ἀξίωμα τῆς ἀρχῆς, *Mor.* 813 D ταῖς μικροτέραις ἀρχαῖς ἀξίωμα προστιθέναι καὶ ὄγκον, *Demetr.* c. 41, 4 ὡς ἐπὶ σκηνῆς τὸ βάρος ὑποκρίνοιντο καὶ τὸν ὄγκον τοῦ ἀνδρός.   φρόνημα δημαγωγίας ἐμβριθέστερον, 'jene Kraft, jenen festen und standhaften Muth das Volk zu leiten' (*Kaltwasser*), but it may mean 'a gravity of sentiment too great for an ordinary leader of the people.'

The adjective ἐμβριθής, lit. 'weighty,' 'ponderous,' has various shades of metaphorical meaning in Plutarch, which are to be determined by the context, as 'solid' (sometimes 'stolid'), 'grave,' 'earnest,' 'staid,' 'firm,' 'imperturbable.' *Arat.* c. 4, 1 φρόνημα διέφαινεν οὐ μικρὸν οὐδὲ ἀργόν, ἐμβριθὲς δὲ καὶ παρ' ἡλικίαν ἀσφαλεστέρᾳ γνώμῃ κεκραμένον, *Demetr.* c. 5, 4 πάθος οὐ μειρακίου παθῶν ἐν ἀρχῇ πράξεως ἀνατραπέντος ἀλλ' ἐμβριθοῦς στρατηγοῦ κεχρημένου πραγμάτων μεταβολαῖς, *Cor.* c. 4, 1 τὰ δ' ἐμβριθῆ καὶ βέβαια φρονήματα αὔξουσιν αἱ τιμαί, *Marc.* c. 28, 3 πολλὴν πεῖραν παρεσχήκει τοῦ ... ἐμβριθὴς γεγονέναι καὶ φρόνιμος, *Alcr.* c. 4, 5 ἡ φιλοτιμία παρ' ἡλικίαν ἐμβριθὲς εἶχε τὸ φρόνημα καὶ μεγαλόψυχον, *Ti. Gr.* c. 10, 1 νεανίαν ἐμβριθῆ τὸ ἦθος καὶ κόσμιον, *Brut.* c. 1, 1 τὴν φύσιν ἐμβριθῆ ('unexcitable,' 'phlegmatic') καὶ πραεῖαν οὖσαν ἐπεγείρας ταῖς πρακτικαῖς ὁρμαῖς, but in c. 6, 4 τὸ ἐμβριθὲς αὐτοῦ καὶ μὴ ῥᾳδίως μηδὲ παντὸς ὑπήκοον τοῦ δεομένου πρὸς χάριν it means 'firmness of purpose,' 'resolute character,' *Dion* c. 2, 3 Δίων καὶ Βροῦτος ἄνδρες ἐμβριθεῖς καὶ πρὸς οὐδὲν ἀκροσφαλεῖς οὐδ' εὐάλωτοι πάθος, *Dem.-Cic.* c. 2, 3 ἀγαπᾶν ἀγεννὲς καὶ λιχνεύειν τὴν ἀπὸ τοῦ λόγου δόξαν, ὅθεν ἐμβριθέστερος ταύτῃ καὶ μεγαλοπρεπέστερος ὁ Δημοσθένης (τοῦ Κικέρωνος), *Dion* c. 11, 1 νέαν ψυχὴν κατασχεῖν ἐμβριθεστέροις λογισμοῖς.

30. (ὁ) cυνεξάραc, 'who helped to call forth,' or 'to elevate, ennoble.'

31. Anaxagoras of Clazomenae (Ionia) was born about 500 B.C. He appears to have visited Athens about 480 B.C. Plutarch is more just to the great philosopher than Cicero, who (*Brut.* c. 11, 44) merely says that 'ab Anaxagora physico

eruditus exercitationem mentis a reconditis abstrusisque rebus ad causas forensis popularisque facile traduxerat (Pericles).'

32. **οἱ τότ' ἄνθρωποι.** It was rather those of a later age who gave him the surname of Νοῦς. Of the two reasons assigned by Plutarch the latter is without doubt the true one.

34. **περιττήν,** 'uncommon.' Cp. *Arist.* e. 1, 5 τὸ φρονεῖν ἐδόκει τις εἶναι περιττός, *Mor.* 255 F τὸ φρονεῖν ἐδόκει περιττή τις εἶναι, p. 295 A περιττῷ τινι καὶ οὐκ ἰδιώτῃ προσέοικεν, *Demetr.* c. 2, 2 quoted c. 3 l. 11. **θαυμάσαντες** = ὅτι ἐθαύμασαν.

Plato (*Phaedr.* 279 A) maintains that it was to his frequent converse with Anaxagoras that the great master of rhetoric owed his immense superiority. For, as he makes Socrates say, no really great art can attain perfection without endless discussion and high speculative discourse upon nature. It is by that door that the loftiness of thought (τὸ ὑψηλόνουν), the all-sided completeness (τὸ πάντῃ τελεσιουργόν) which characterize such arts would seem to enter, and those qualities Pericles acquired and added to them his great natural endowments (πρὸς τῷ εὐφυὴς εἶναι). 'It was from such converse' he continues 'that he stored his mind with lofty speculations (μετεωρολογίας ἐνεπλήσθη) and was able to penetrate to the essential nature of the Intelligent (νοῦς) and Unintelligent principle (ἄνοια) in nature—the theme on which he chiefly loved to descant ; and from that source he borrowed, for the behoof of his own art, all that could be made available for it (τὸ πρόσφορον αὐτῇ).

35. **τοῖς ὅλοις πρῶτος ... νοῦν ἐπέστησε,** 'he was the first to dethrone Chance and Necessity, and set up pure Intelligence in their room as the principle of law and order over the Universe.' His celebrated βιβλίον commenced with the words ὁμοῦ πάντα χρήματα· εἶτα νόος ἐλθὼν αὐτὰ διεκόσμησε.

37. **ἐν μεμιγμένοις κτλ.,** 'discriminating original simple substances where everything else is a medley.' μεμιγμένοις is predicative.

Cp. Aristot. *de anima* c. 1, 2 ἀρχήν γε τὸν νοῦν τίθεται μάλιστα πάντων· μόνον γοῦν φησιν αὐτὸν τῶν ὄντων ἁπλοῦν εἶναι καὶ ἀμιγῆ τε καὶ καθαρόν. Anaxagoras held that in everything there is a part of everything (ἐν παντὶ παντὸς μοῖρα ἔνεστι); νοῦς is the only thing that remains pure and unmixed. Cp. *Mor.* p. 876 c 'Ἀναξαγόρας ὁ Κλαζομένιος ἀρχὰς τῶν ὄντων τὰς ὁμοιομερείας ἀπεφήνατο, and again ἀπὸ τοῦ ὁμοια τὰ μέρη εἶναι ἐν τῇ τροφῇ τοῖς γεννωμένοις ὁμοιομερείας αὐτὰς ἐκάλεσε καὶ ἀρχὰς τῶν ὄντων ἀπεφήνατο, καὶ τὰς μὲν ὕλην, τὸ δὲ ποιοῦν αἴτιον, τὸν νοῦν, τὸν πάντα διαταξάμενον. Aristotle does not use the substantive but only the adjective τὰ ὁμοιομερῆ (στοιχεῖα), though the substantive may be traced back to Epicurus (Munro on Lucretius I 834). It means 'the element possessing similarity of parts with the thing in being.'

CHAPTER V

§ 1 l. 2. **τῆς λεγομένης μετεωρολογίας ... ὑποπιμπλάμενος,** an adaptation from Plato's *Phaedr.* 270 A, quoted c. 8, 1 below. For μεταρσιολεσχία, 'talk about τὰ μετάρσια,' *supera ac caelestia*

(Cic. *Ac. pr.* II 41) the Ionic-poetic equivalent of τὰ μετέωρα 'celestial phaenomena,' the corresponding word in Plato, by whom it is paraded with a sort of defiance, is ἀδολεσχία, 'garrulity,' 'twaddle'—the vulgar term of reproach for philosophic διάλεξις. Cp. *Nic.* c. 23, 3 οὐ γὰρ ἠνείχοντο τοὺς φυσικοὺς καὶ μετεωρολέσχας τότε καλουμένους ὡς εἰς αἰτίας ἀλόγους καὶ δυνάμεις ἀπρονοήτοις καὶ κατηναγκασμένα πάθη διατρίβοντας τὸ θεῖον, Arist. *Nub.* 333 μετεωροφένακες, 360 μετεωροσοφισταί, Eur. *fr.* 913 ed. Nauck[2]:—

τίς τάδε λεύσσων θεὸν οὐχὶ νοεῖ
μετεωρολόγων δ᾽ ἑκὰς ἔρριψεν
σκολιὰς ἀπάτας, ὧν ἀτηρὰ
γλῶσσ᾽ εἰκοβολεῖ περὶ τῶν ἀφανῶν
οὐδὲν γνώμης μετέχουσα;

4. ὡς ἔοικε, c. 1, 1.

5. σοβαρόν not here in its ordinary sense 'swaggering,' 'haughty,' 'over-bearing,' but 'dignified.' Cp. c. 39, 2.

6. καθαρὸν ... βωμολοχίας, 'free from, unsullied by, vulgar and unscrupulous buffoonery'; ὀχλικῆς may also mean 'that truckles to the mob.' Cp. *Lyc.-Num.* c. 2, 3 τῆς διαιρέσεως τῶν πολιτευμάτων ὀχλικὴ ἀκράτως ἡ τοῦ Νομᾶ καὶ θεραπευτικὴ τοῦ πλήθους. βωμολοχίας: cp. *Arist.* c. 2, 2 φύσιν ψεῦδος καὶ βωμολοχίαν καὶ ἀπατὴν οὐδ᾽ ἐν παιδιᾶς τινὶ τρόπῳ προσιεμένην. It is the very word which is applied by Plutarch (*Demetr.* c. 11, 2) to Cleon: τὴν τοῦ παλαιοῦ Κλέωνος ἀπομιμεῖσθαι δοκῶν βωμολοχίαν.

For the gen. after καθαρός, cp. *Cic.* c. 29, 7 γάμου οὐ πράξεως αἰσχρᾶς μόνον ἀλλὰ καὶ φήμης καθαρόν, *Coriol.* c. 24, 1 καθαρὸς δεισιδαιμονίας, *Timol.* c. 37, 4 καθαρὰν συνοίκων κακῶν, *Cat. mi.* c. 18, 2 ταμιεῖον καθαρὸν συκοφαντῶν, *Philop.* c. 3, 1 ἦθος φιλονικίας καθαρόν.

7. προσώπου σύστασις κτλ. 'composure, gravity, of countenance never relaxing into a smile.' Cp. *Demetr.* c. 17, 4 συνεστῶτι τῷ προσώπῳ, Eur. *Hipp.* 983 ξύστασις φρενῶν, *Alc.* 797 τοῦ συνεστῶτος φρενῶν. ἄθρυπτος εἰς γέλωτα: in this respect he resembled Anaxagoras his master and Euripides, both of whom are said to have been ἀγέλαστοι. Cp. Aelian *V. H.* VIII 13 Ἀναξαγόραν ... φασὶ μὴ γελῶντά ποτε ὀφθῆναι μήτε μειδιῶντα τὴν ἀρχήν, Aul. Gell. *N. A.* XV 20, Cic. *Acad.* II c. 23, 72.

8. πραότης πορείας = the κίνησις βραδεῖα which Aristotle ascribes to the μεγαλόψυχος *Eth. Nic.* c. 4, 8 p. 1125[a], 12. Demosthenes (*adv. Pantaen.* § 52), on the other hand, mentions ταχέως βαδίζειν as one of the marks of an ἐπίφθονος ἀνήρ, together with a loud voice (μέγα φθέγγεσθαι). Cp. or. 1 *contr. Steph.* § 77 τῆς μὲν ὄψεως τῇ φύσει καὶ τῷ ταχέως βαδίζειν καὶ τῷ λαλεῖν μέγα, οὐ τῶν εὐτυχῶς πεφυκότων ἐμαυτὸν κρίνω.

καταστολὴ περιβολῆς, not, as Liddell-Scott, 'moderation in dress,' from the meaning of καταστέλλειν, 'to repress,' but rather, as Kaltwasser, 'den anständigen Umwurf des Mantels' i.e. 'graceful, careful, adjustment of mantle.'

The ἱμάτιον or 'mantle' was a large square cloth, first thrown over the left shoulder, and then round the back to the right side and above or below the right arm and again brought over the left shoulder or arm so as to keep the right hand within the folds. This was called ἐπὶ δεξία (or ἐπιδέξια, 'dexterously')(awkwardly) ἀναβάλλεσθαι, and according to a man's skill or awkwardness in doing it, he was pronounced genteel or clownish and un-Greek (Athenae. 1 21, Theophr. Char. c. 26 (29), Plato Theaet. 175 E, Arist. Av. 1565). See Dem. de f. leg. § 281 ἔφη τὸν Σόλωνα ἀνακεῖσθαι τῆς τότε τῶν δημηγορούντων σωφροσύνης παράδειγμα, εἴσω τὴν χεῖρα ἔχοντα ἀναβεβλημένον, 'he (i.e. Aeschines Tim. § 25) said that the sobriety of the popular speakers of former days was illustrated by the statue of Solon with his robe drawn round him and his hand within the folds.' So Phocion, says Plut. Phoc. c. 4, 2, was never seen ἐκτὸς ἔχων τὴν χεῖρα τῆς περιβολῆς, ὅτε τύχοι περιβεβλημένος. The first popular orator who broke through the custom and loosened his mantle so as to free his right hand, in order that he might gesticulate, was Cleon. See Nic. c. 8, 3 τὸν ἐπὶ τοῦ βήματος κόσμον ἀνελὼν καὶ πρῶτος ἐν τῷ δημηγορεῖν ἀνακραγὼν καὶ περισπάσας τὸ ἱμάτιον καὶ τὸν μηρὸν πατάξας καὶ δρόμῳ μετὰ τοῦ λέγειν ἅμα χρησάμενος and cp. my note to Tib. Gr. c. 2, 2.

9. πρὸς οὐδὲν ἐκταραττομένη, 'not discomposed at anything.' Cp. c. 6, 1; c. 33, 4; c. 35, 1. So Lucian Somn. c. 16 ἐκταραχθεὶς πρὸς τὸν τῶν πληγῶν φόβον.

10. πλάσμα, not, as Liddell-Scott, 'affectation.' but, as Kaltwasser, 'modulation.' Cp. Brut. c. 34, 4 μετὰ πλάσματος φωνῆς ἔπη περαίνων οἷς τὸν Νέστορα χρώμενον "Ὅμηρος πεποίηκε, and see Wyttenb. on Mor. 41 B, 711 c. Demosthenes imitated Pericles in this respect: see Dem. c. 9, 3 with my note ad l. καὶ ὅσα τοιαῦτα sc. ἐστί, 'and the like.'

§ 2 l. 12. γοῦν as in c. 4, 2, c. 38, 2. κακῶς ἀκούων (c. 12, 1, c. 29, 3) serves for the passive of κακῶς λέγειν, hence it is joined with ὑπό: cp. c. 31, 2, Arist. Eq. 820 ταυτί μ' ἀκούειν ὑπὸ τούτου, Nub. 528 ὑπ' ἀνδρῶν ἄριστ' ἠκουσάτην. The participles are to be taken closely with ὑπέμεινε.

13. βδελυρῶν: the word is without an English equivalent: it implies 'buffoonery' as well as 'blackguardism.'

14. σιωπῇ: c. 34, 1. κατ' ἀγοράν: local designations, which are equivalent to Proper Names, are frequently anarthrous, especially after prep. as ἐκ πόλεως, ἐξ ἀγροῦ (c. 6, 2), ἐν ἄστει (c. 7, 4), ἐν ἀκροπόλει (c. 13, 8), ἐν ἐκκλησίᾳ (c. 14, 1), εἰς θέατρον, ἐπ' ἀγοράν (c. 7, 4), etc. In inscriptions after the 4th cent. the article is more generally found, Meisterhans[2] p. 187, 21.

15. ἅμα τι τῶν ἐπειγόντων καταπραττόμενος, 'while he was engaged in the despatch of some urgent business.' Cp. Caes.

c. 17, 5 τὴν κατὰ πρόσωπον ἔντευξιν ὑπὲρ τῶν ἐπειγόντων τοῦ καιροῦ διὰ πλῆθος ἀσχολιῶν μὴ περιμένοντος, Sertor. c. 3, 2 τὰ μὲν ἰδὼν τὰ δ' ἀκοῇ πυθόμενος τῶν ἐπειγόντων.

10   17. τοῦ ἀνθρώπου, 'the fellow' (c. 24, 1), with a connotation of contempt or pity, as in l. 21; c. 13, 8. See *Them.* c. 16, 2.

18. πάσῃ ... βλασφημίᾳ, 'every (possible) kind of abuse.'

§ 3 l. 19. εἰσιέναι sc. εἰς τὴν οἰκίαν. Cp. c. 24, 6; *Dem.* c. 7, 1.   σκότους: c. 35, 1.

20. φῶς λαβόντι, 'with a torch'—a necessary precaution, since the streets of ancient towns were not provided with lamps. In Sparta however it was the custom to walk at night δίχα λαμπάδος, οὐ γὰρ ἔξεστι πρὸς φῶς βαδίζειν ὅπως ἐθίζωνται σκότους καὶ νυκτὸς εὐθαρσῶς καὶ ἀδεῶς ὁδεύειν, *Lyc.* c. 12, 7.

παραπέμψαι, 'to escort him all the way'; προπέμψαι would mean 'to accompany only part of the way.' So l. 17 παρακολουθοῦντος means 'following him the whole way.'

22. Ion the aristocrat of Chios (B.C. 484-424) was one of the five Athenian tragic poets of the canon and a composer of other kinds of poetry besides; he was also a writer both on historical and philosophical subjects. The passage before us is taken probably from the Ὑπομνήματα (ἱστορικά), mentioned by the Scholiast on Arist. *Pac.* v. 836, or, as they are also called, Ἐπιδημίαι (Müller *FHG.* II 44ᵃ). Ion was a friend of Cimon and therefore not partial to Pericles (*Cim.* c. 9, 1).

μοθωνικήν, *vernilem,* 'forward,' 'assuming,' lit. 'such as is peculiar to μόθακες (*Cleom.* c. 8, 1) or μόθωνες, *vernae,* young Helots, who being brought up together with young Spartans obtained freedom without civic rights. Slaves so favoured would be likely to presume too much upon their position (Müller *Hist. Dor.* II 44).

23. ὁμιλίαν, 'ordinary social intercourse.'   ὑπότυφον, 'somewhat arrogant,' 'pretentious.'   εἶναι = ἦν (not ἐγένετο) of direct speech. Cp. *Them.* c. 3, 3.

24. μεγαλαυχίαις: c. 2, 3.

25. ὑπεροψίαν, 'superciliousness,' c. 37, 5.

27. τὸ ... ἐμμελές, 'ease,' 'tact,' 'civility.' The word is properly applied to sound and signifies that it is capable of being used in the same melody with other sounds. Its opposite is πλημμελές.   (τὸ) ὑγρόν, 'good humour,' 'complaisance.'

Ὑγρός in its secondary sense = *mollis,* 'yielding,' 'lithe,' 'elastic,' as in Eur. *Ion* 806 ἂν ὑγρὸν ἀμπταίην αἰθέρα, Milton's 'buxom air,' *fragm.* 941 ed. Nauck² αἰθέρα καὶ γῆν πέριξ ἔχονθ' ὑγραῖς ἐν ἀγκάλαις, Xen. *de re*

cp. c. 10 τὸ ὑγρὸν τοῦ χαλίνου καὶ τὸ σκληρόν, c. 12 τὰ σκέλη ὑγρὰ (*agilia*) μετεωρίζει ὁ ἵππος, *cyn.* c. 4, 1 τραχήλους (τῶν κυνῶν) χρὴ εἶναι) μακρούς, ὑγρούς, Arist. *Vesp.* 1213 ὑγρὸν χύτλασον σεαυτὸν *i.e.* 'in an easy position.' Hence figuratively of persons 'facile,' 'easily moved': *Mor.* c. 28, 1 ὑγρός τις εἶναι βουλόμενος καὶ δημοτικός, ἥκιστα τοιοῦτος πιφυκώς, *Sull.* c. 30, 5 πρὸς οἶκτον ὑγρός, *Mor.* 51 Β ὑγρὸς ὢν καὶ πιθανὸς μεταβάλλεσθαι, 558 C ὑγρός ἐστι λίαν καὶ ῥᾴθυμος, 97 Β ψυχὴν πολύτροπον καὶ ὑγράν.

28. (τὸ) ... μεμονσωμένον ἐν ταῖς συμπεριφοραῖς, 'his polished and graceful address in society.'

For the former word, cp. *Mor.* 1121 F πολυγράμματος ὢν καὶ μεμονσωμένος, Ar. *Lys.* 1127 οὐ μεμούσωμαι κακῶς (where the Scholiast explains by πεπαίδευμαι): for the latter, which is generally taken here to mean 'familiar intercourse' (though it also may mean 'accommodation to circumstances'), cp. *Mor.* 141 D ἐν οἷς ἅπτεται μάλιστα (ἡ γυνὴ) τοῦ ἀνδρός, ὁμιλίᾳ τε καὶ ἤθει καὶ συμπεριφορᾷ, 981 Β ἆρ᾽ οὖν ἄξιόν ἐστι ταύταις ταῖς κοινωνίαις καὶ συμπεριφοραῖς παραβάλλειν φιλίας ἀλωπέκων καὶ ὀφέων διὰ τὸ κοινὸν αὐτοῖς πολέμιον εἶναι τὸν ἀετόν; Polyb. v 37, 2 κατὰ τὴν ἑξῆς συμπεριφορὰν ἐγένετό τις αὐτοῖς ὁλοσχερὴς εὔνοια, XXXII 9, 6 ὥστε ... τοῖς πορρωτέρω γνωρίμων γενέσθαι τὴν αἵρεσιν καὶ συμπεριφορὰν αὐτῶν (*sc.* Scipionis et Polybii), where the writer has just been speaking of their φιλίαν καὶ συνήθειαν, *ib.* 6 τῆς συμπεριφορᾶς ἐπὶ πολὺ προκοπτούσης.

§ 4 l. 29. ἀλλ' "Ιωνα μέν κτλ. This must refer to some remark of Ion's elsewhere, that as a Satyr-drama is a necessary complement of an Attic tetralogy, so every character, however virtuous, cannot be without its weak side. τραγικὴν διδασκαλίαν, 'a complete tragic drama,' 'tetralogy,' lit. 'the preparation or rehearsing of the chorus under the author's training'; *Them.* c. 5, 3.

30. πάντως, *profecto, omnino*.

31. σατυρικόν, not 'satirical' but 'fit for a Satyr,' 'Satyr-like,' hence 'vulgar,' 'low'; cp. c. 13, 7, *Cat. mi.* c. 7, 1 Πλάτων τὸν Σωκράτη φησὶν ἔξωθεν σατυρικὸν καὶ ὑβριστὴν τοῖς ἐντυγχάνουσι φαινόμενον, *Galb.* c. 16 σατυρικοὶ τοῖς βίοις ἄνθρωποι. The Σατυρικὸν δρᾶμα was so called because the chorus was composed of persons in the garb of Satyrs. The only specimen remaining is the *Cyclops* of Euripides.

ἐῶμεν, *omittamus*, c. 33, 3.

32. δοξοκοπίαν, 'thirst for popularity.' The best commentary on the import of σεμνός, 'high and mighty,' is furnished by Euripides *Hipp*. 91 ff. :—

A. οἶσθ᾽ οὖν βροτοῖσιν ὃς καθέστηκεν νόμος,
  μισεῖν τὸ σεμνὸν καὶ τὸ μὴ πᾶσιν φίλον;

B. ὀρθῶς γε· τίς δ᾽ οὐ σεμνὸς ἀχθεινὸς βροτῶν;

cp. Arist. *Nub.* 48, *Vesp.* 1174 etc.

33. ἀποκαλοῦντας, 'calling by a disparaging name.' The student will find a history of this word in my n. to *Ti. Gr.* c. 21, 3.

34. καὶ αὑτούς τι τοιοῦτο δοξοκοπεῖν, 'to play the charlatan also themselves in some such fashion,' 'to go and affect the like sort of notoriety.'

35. ὡς conveys Plutarch's explanation of Zeno's meaning, 'with the idea that'; cp. c. 33, 3. αὑτῆς, 'of itself,' 'alone.' τῶν καλῶν, c. 2, 1. ὑποποιούσης, 'producing gradually.' In the only other passage of Plut. (*Mor*. 671 c) where the act. is used, it means *subicere*, 'to put under.'

36. λεληθότως, 'imperceptibly,' used for λανθανούσης, probably to avoid the awkward concurrence of two participles.

CHAPTER VI

§ 1 l. 3. δεισιδαιμονίας ... καθυπέρτερος, 'is generally thought to have risen above superstition.' So *Arist.* c. 11, 2 καθυπερτέρους τῶν πολεμίων. Cf. Thuc. II 60, 5 χρημάτων κρείσσων, Xen. *Cyr.* IV ii 45 γαστρὸς κρείττους.

Plutarch begins his treatise περὶ δεισιδαιμονίας, 'fear of supernatural beings' (*Mor.* p. 164 E) by saying that 'The stream of ignorance and uneducated opinion divides at its source into two channels; in hard natures it produces atheism, in the softer superstition (τὸ μὲν ὥσπερ ἐν χωρίοις σκληροῖς τοῖς ἀντιτύποις ἤθεσι τὴν ἀθεότητα, τὸ δ' ὥσπερ ἐν ὑγροῖς τοῖς ἁπαλοῖς τὴν δεισιδαιμονίαν πεποίηκεν), and again (p. 165 B) he says τὴν δεισιδαιμονίαν μηνύει καὶ τοὔνομα δόξαν ἐμπαθῆ καὶ δέους ποιητικὴν ὑπόληψιν οὖσαν ἐκταπεινοῦντος καὶ συντρίβοντος τὸν ἄνθρωπον, οἰόμενον μὲν εἶναι θεούς, εἶναι δὲ λυπηροὺς καὶ βλαβερούς. Theophrastus *Char.* XVI (XXVIII) defines the word as δειλία πρὸς τοὺς θεούς. In classical Greek it sometimes means 'due reverence of the god,' 'religion,' but it must always have had potentially a bad sense, and in post-classical Greek it came to have a depreciatory sense ordinarily. Philo (*Quod Deus imm.* § 35 I p. 297 M) defines it, in the manner of Aristotle, as the 'excess' of which impiety (ἀσέβεια) is the corresponding 'defect' and piety (εὐσέβεια c. 6, 1) the 'mean.' Cp. *Alex.* c. 75, 2, *Acts Ap.* c. XVII 22 with Field's note *ad l.*

4. ὅσην, *quantam*. πρὸς τὰ μετέωρα, c. 5, 1.

5. ἐνεργάζεται, c. 39, 4. αὐτῶν τούτων *sc.* τῶν μετεώρων.

6. (τοῖς) περὶ τὰ θεῖα δαιμονῶσι, 'in those who are mad about the gods' (c. 32, 1), *i.e.* whose dread of them amounts to madness.

For the poetical word δαιμονᾶν=ὑπὸ δαίμονος κατέχεσθαι (Hesychius), *furore corripi*, 'to be possessed,' cp. *Mor.* 169 D τετύφωνται καὶ δαιμονῶσιν οἱ θεοῖς ταῦτα δρᾶσθαι νομίζοντες, Marc. c. 20, 6 μηδενὸς δὲ τολμῶντος ἅψασθαι μηδ' ἀπαντῆσαι διὰ δεισιδαιμονίαν ἐπὶ τὰς πύλας ἐξέδραμεν, οὔτε φωνῆς τινὸς οὔτε κινήσεως πρεπούσης δαιμονῶντι καὶ παραφρονοῦντι φεισάμενος. Menander *Hautontim.* fr. 1 πρὸς τῆς Ἀθηνᾶς δαίμονας γεγονὼς ἔτη | τοσαῦθ'; ὁμοῦ γάρ ἐστιν ἑξήκοντά σοι, Xen. *Mem.* I i 9.

8. αὐτῶν sc. τῶν θείων. ἥν sc. ἀπειρίαν, ignorance of **11** celestial phaenomena. ὁ φυσικὸς λόγος, 'the knowledge of natural causes,' 'natural philosophy.' Cp. *Mor.* 44 B ὁ γὰρ φιλόσοφος λόγος τὸ μὲν ἐξ ἀπειρίας καὶ ἀγνοίας θαῦμα καὶ θάμβος ἐξαιρεῖ γνώσει καὶ ἱστορίᾳ τῆς περὶ ἕκαστον αἰτίας.
ἀπαλλάττων, *amoveus.* Cp. *Cor.* c. 32, 1 ἀπαλλάξας τὸν πόλεμον, *Flamin.* c. 5, 6 τὰς φρουρὰς ἀπαλλάττειν, *Eumen.* c. 11, 3 τὸν ἅλων αὐτῶν . . . ἀπαλλάξαι βουλόμενος.
9. φοβερᾶς, 'timid,' as in Thuc. IV 128, Xen. *Oec.* c. 7, 25; *Cyr.* III iii 19. φλεγμαινούσης, 'feverish,' 'morbid')(ἀσφαλῆ.
10. ἀσφαλῆ, 'which rests on a solid foundation.' μετ' ἐλπίδων ἀγαθῶν, 'supported by a rational hope,' see Gr. Ind. s. v. μετά.
§ 2 l. 12. ἐξ ἀγροῦ, 'from his country estate.' For the omission of the article, see n. to c. 5, 2. Cp. Plato *Theaet.* 143 A, *Legg.* 844 c ἐν ἄστει)(ἐν ἀγρῷ, Luc. *Ev.* c. xxiii 26 ἐρχόμενον ἀπ' ἀγροῦ, c. xv 25 ἦν ὁ υἱὸς ἐν ἀγρῷ.
13. Lampon of Athens, a celebrated soothsayer and interpreter of oracles, was appointed by Pericles (*Mor.* 812 D, Diodor. XII 10) founder of the colony of Thurii (Magna Graecia). He was the frequent butt of the contemporary comic poets for his hypocrisy, orthodoxy and greed. See my *Onomast. Arist.* p. 878 ed. 3.
11. ἰσχυρὸν καὶ στερεόν, predicates to πεφυκός.
15. ἐκ μέσου τοῦ μετώπου: G. *Gr.* § 142, 4 note 1.
16. δυεῖν. un-Attic form. According to HSchmidt, Plutarch has 69 exx. of Gen. δυοῖν, 101 of G. δυεῖν, Aristotle has 90 exx. of G. δυοῖν, only 8 of G. δυεῖν. Polybius, Strabo and Dionysius Hal. never use δυοῖν but always δυεῖν. δυναστειῶν, c. 16, 3.
17. Θουκυδίδου: see c. 8, 3; c. 11, 1. εἰς ἕνα περιστήσεται . . . παρ' ᾧ γένοιτο τὸ σημεῖον, 'will fall to one person, him with whom the prodigy was found'; therefore Pericles. For σημεῖον, an unusual occurrence out of the common course of nature, portending some remarkable event in the future, cp. *Dem.* c. 19, 1, *Timol.* c. 8, 2, *Nic.* c. 13, 2, Xen. *Cyr.* I vi 1, II iv 19; and for the moods of περιστήσεται, γένοιτο, G. *MT.*² § 670 (b).
20. οὐ πεπληρωκότα τὴν βάσιν, 'that it had not filled its pan.' After certain verbs of showing, proving, etc. δεικνύναι (ἀποδεικνύναι, ἐπιδεικνύναι) and ἐλέγχειν Plut. uses οὐ or μή indifferently: cp. c. 13, 7 note. For βάσις, cp. *Pyrrh.* c. 31, 2 τῶν σφονδύλων ('the spinal processes') πρὸς τὴν βάσιν τοῦ τραχήλου συντριβέντων.

H

21. ὀξύν, 'pointed.' Cp. Aristot. *de gen. an.* III 2 p. 752ᵇ, 2 κατὰ τὸ ὀξὺ τοῦ ᾠοῦ. ἐκ τοῦ παντὸς ἀγγείον, 'from the entire cranial cavity')(a particular region (τόπος).

§ 3 l. 26. καταλυθέντος, c. 3, 1 note.

27. ὁμαλῶς ἁπάντων, 'all alike,' 'all without distinction,' c. 10, 2; c. 39, 3; *C. Gr.* c. 2, 1, *Timol.* c. 31, 4. ὑπὸ τῷ Περικλεῖ γενομένων : cp. 20, 1 ὑφ' αὑτοῖς πεποιημένων τὴν θάλασσαν.

28. ἐκώλυε δ' οὐδὲν . . . ἐπιτυγχάνειν, 'there was nothing to prevent (both) from hitting the mark,' 'there was no reason why they should not both be in the right.' For οὐδὲν κωλύει = ἐγχωρεῖ, ἐνδέχεται, cp. Xen. *Cyr.* VII v 61, VIII iv 11, *Hier.* c. 9, 5, *Oec.* c. 2, 12.

Observe that ἐπιτυγχάνειν, *proposito satisfacere*, is used absolutely, as in *Mor.* 438 γ οἱ πολλὰ βάλλοντες ἐπιτυγχάνουσι πολλάκις, *Brut.* c. 16, 1 εὐξάμενος τοῖς περὶ Βροῦτον ἐπιτυγχάνειν καὶ κατορθοῦν, Iamblich. *vit. Pythag.* § 40 ἀπεφαίνετο δὲ καὶ ταῖς πρὸς ἀλλήλους ὁμιλίαις οὕτως ἂν χρωμένους ἐπιτυγχάνειν.

τὸν φυσικόν, *i.e.* τὸν πραγματευόμενον τὴν φυσικὴν φιλοσοφίαν, as often in Aristotle.

30. ἐκλαμβάνοντος, 'taking in a certain sense,' judging from appearances, interpreting: as in Aristot. *Rhet.* III 15, 10, 1416ᵇ, 11 ἐκλαμβάνοντι τοὺς νόμους ἐπὶ τὸ χεῖρον, *Top.* II 6, p. 112ᵃ, 33 διχῶς ἔστιν ἐκλαβεῖν, *Anal. Pr.* 13, p. 32ᵇ, 26.

31. ὑπέκειτο τῷ μὲν . . . θεωρῆσαι, 'the object in view (or 'the business') of the one (Anaxagoras) was to speculate on.'
γέγονε sc. a phaenomenon in general.

32. πρὸς τί, 'to what end,' 'for what purpose.' So Arist. *Eq.* 206 ὁ δράκων δὲ πρὸς τί; *Pac.* 45 ὁ κάνθαρος δὲ πρὸς τί;

§ 4 l. 34. οὐκ ἐπινοοῦσιν . . . ἀθετοῦντες, 'do not take into consideration that in doing away with supernatural phaenomena they do away at the same time with such as are of man's creation.' There is a *petitio principii* in Plutarch's reasoning, which consists in pretending that facts interpreted as prophetic signs have different causes and a different object to their natural ones (*A. Jacob*).

36. For ἀθετεῖν, cp. *Mor.* 663 Β εἰ ὅλως τὸ μικτὸν ἀθετεῖς καὶ ποικίλον, *Cor.* c. 38, 4 τοῖς ὑπ' εὐνοίας καὶ φιλίας πρὸς τὸν θεὸν ἄγαν ἐμπαθῶς ἔχουσι καὶ μηδὲν ἀθετεῖν μηδ' ἀναίρεσθαι τῶν τοιούτων δυναμένοις μέγα πρὸς πίστιν ἐστὶ τὸ θαυμάσιον καὶ μὴ καθ' ἡμᾶς τῆς τοῦ θεοῦ δυνάμεως, *Mor.* 420 Β ἀθετουμένη (φωνὴ σεμνὴ) πολλὰ τῶν ἐνδεχομένων δειχθῆναι δὲ μὴ δυναμένων ἀναιρεῖ. It means properly 'to do away with θετόν τι, something established.' It occurs several times in the N.T. in the sense in which it is used here (*Gal.* ii 21, *Mark* vi 26, *Luke* x 16, *Joh.* xii 48, 1 *Thess.* iv 8, *Jude* 8) and frequently in Polybius.

ψόφους τε δίσκων, 'namely, clanking of (metal) quoits.'

That such quoits sometimes served the purpose of our bells or gongs, is evident from the following passage of Sextus Empiricus *adv. astrologos* § 27 ed. Fabric. 1840·41 νύκτωρ μὲν γὰρ ὁ Χαλδαῖος ἐφ' ὑψηλῆς τινος ἀκρωρείας ἐκαθέζετο ἀστεροσκοπῶν, ἕτερος δὲ παρήδρευε τῇ ὠδινούσῃ μέχρις ἀποτέξοιτο. ἀποτεκούσης δὲ εὐθὺς δίσκῳ διεσήμαινε τῷ ἐπὶ τῆς ἀκρωρείας. ὁ δὲ ἀκούσας καὶ αὐτὸς παρεσημειοῦτο τὸ ἀνίσχον ζῴδιον ὡς ὡροσκοποῦν: so § 68 δίσκῳ σημαίνει, § 69 τῷ δίσκῳ διασημαίνειν . . . τὸν τοῦ δίσκου ψόφον. This explains Cic. *de orat.* II 5 *Hoc ipso tempore, cum omnia gymnasia philosophi teneant, tamen eorum auditores discum audire quam philosophum malunt; qui simul ut increpuit, in media oratione de maximis rebus et gravissimis disputantem philosophum omnes unctionis causa relinquunt.*

37. γνωμόνων ἀποσκιασμούς, 'the shadows thrown by the indexes on gnomons or sun-dials,' as measures of time. Herod. II 109 πόλον καὶ γνώμονα καὶ τὰ δώδεκα μέρεα τῆς ἡμέρης παρὰ Βαβυλωνίων ἔμαθον οἱ Ἕλληνες. Cp. I 140, 5. Anaximander, the Ionic philosopher, was the first to introduce the use of the sun-dial at Sparta. See *Dict. of Ant.* I 972^b, II 443^a ed. 3.

38. αἰτίᾳ τινὶ . . . σημεῖον εἶναί τινος πεποίηται, 'has been made, with a particular cause and contrivance, to serve as the sign of something else.'

39. ταῦτα μὲν οὖν ἴσως ἑτέρας ἐστὶ πραγματείας, 'the above reflexions are proper, I opine, to a different kind of work from the present.' μὲν οὖν is common in returning to a subject after a digression, see c. 10, 7; c. 18, 3; c. 28, 3. The μέν is correlative to δέ of c. 7; the οὖν is continuative.

For πραγματεία, cp. c. 39, 4; *Sull.* c. 30, 5 ἑτέρα τις ἂν διορίσειε πραγματεία, Dion. Hal. I c. 74, ἡ λεχθήσεται δὲ καὶ διὰ τῆσδε τῆς πραγματείας αὐτὰ τἀναγκαιότατα, Diod. Sic. I c. 1 καλλίστην ἐμπειρίαν διὰ τῆς πραγματείας ταύτης περιποιοῦσι τοῖς ἀναγιγνώσκουσιν, c. 20, 2. Polybius frequently uses the word of his own history (I i 4, iii 1, iv 1; III i 1, III 32) and of any historical work (II lvi 3, v xxxiii 8, VIII xi 1); in Aristotle it bears the sense of 'a philosophical discussion.'

CHAPTER VII

§ 1 l. 2. σφόδρα τὸν δῆμον εὐλαβεῖτο, 'was excessively shy of facing the people,' *i.e.* of coming forward as a speaker in the ecclesia. The augments in ηὐ- are not found in Greek inscriptions of the age of Plutarch. They disappeared from the Attic dialect as early as the end of the fourth century B.C. They are, however, found here and there in MSS.

3. καὶ γάρ, *etenim*, 'for in fact'; c. 39, 4.

Πεισιστράτῳ: Wenn die äussere Erscheinung des Strategen Perikles an Peisistratos erinnerte, so war auch das von ihm bekleidete Amt eine Art von Erneuerung der Stellung, die Peisistratos gehabt hatte (*Holm*). The date of the first tyranny of Pisistratus was B.C. 560, that of the third, B.C. 541–527. He died about thirty-four years before the birth of Pericles.

1. ἐμφερής, a poetical and Ionic word, rare in good Attic

prose; cp. Xen. *Cyr.* V v 31. τὴν φωνὴν ἡδεῖαν : cp. *Cic.* c. 4, 3 ἤ τε φωνὴ λαμβάνουσα πλάσιν ἡδεῖα πρὸς ἀκοὴν ἐτέθραπτο.

6. **εὔτροχον**: cp. Eur. *Bacch.* 268 σὺ δ' εὔτροχον μὲν γλῶσσαν ὡς φρονῶν ἔχεις, *Hippol.* fr. 439 ed. Nauck² νῦν δ' εὐτρόχοισι στόμασι τἀληθέστατα κλέπτουσιν (Porson's correction of the vulgate εὑρόοισιν).

7. **πρός,** *propter,* as c. 35, 1 ; c. 6, 1 ; *Thes.* c. 19, 3 πρὸς τὴν ὄψιν ἐξεπλάγη τοῦ Θήσεως. Cp. the story told by Valer. Max. VIII 9, 2 :—*fertur quidam cum admodum senex primae contioni Periclis adulescentuli interesset, idemque iuvenis Pisistratum iam decrepitum contionantem audisset, non temperasse sibi quominus exclamaret, caveri illum civem oportere, quod Pisistrati orationi simillima eius esset oratio.* Concerning the oratory of Pisistratus Cicero *Brut.* c. 7, 27 says :—*opinio est Pisistratum . . . multum, ut temporibus illis, valuisse dicendo.*

8. **πρόσοντος,** *i.q.* ὑπάρχοντος, agrees with the nearest subject. Cp. c. 8, 2 ; c. 28, 3, *Mar.* c. 16, 2 ἡγεῖτο πολλὰ ἐπιψεύδεσθαι τῶν οὐ προσόντων τὴν καινότητα, Arist. *Eq.* 217 τὰ δ' ἄλλα σοὶ πρόσεστι δημαγωγικά.

10. **φοβούμενος ἐξοστρακισθῆναι**: cp. § 2 l. 14.

For the infinitive after verbs of fearing, denoting the direct object of fear, cp. Xen. *Cyr.* VIII vii 15 φοβήσεται ἀδικεῖν, Plato *Gorg.* 457 c φοβοῦμαι διελέγχειν σε, Soph. *Aiac.* 254 πεφόβημαι ξυναλγεῖν and see G. *MT.*² § 373. So δεδιὼς περιπεσεῖν c. 7, 2 ; δεδιὼς βιασθῆναι c. 33, 5.

§ 2 l. 13. **ἀποτεθνήκει**: so *Mor.* 518 F πόσοι βόες τοῦ γείτονος ἀποτεθνήκασι, but in Attic prose the perf. and plup. are almost uniformly in the simple verb only : Veitch *Gr. Verbs* p. 281. The suppression of the syllabic augment in the pluperfect is unknown to Attic prose. **ἐξεπεπτώκει** sc. τῆς πόλεως.

14. **Κίμωνα**: Aristotle ('Αθ. πολ. c. 26) says that the Moderates or Conservative party were without a prominent leader at this time (B.C. 464), because Cimon was νεώτερος καὶ πρὸς τὴν πόλιν ὀψὲ προελθών. This statement, however, is wide of the mark, for Cimon had been στρατηγός already in B.C. 476. Herod. VII 107 ; Thuc. I 98, 1 ; Plut. *Cim.* c. 7, 1 ; Diod. XI 60. **τὰ πολλά**, c. 27, 1.

15. **οὕτω δή,** *tum demum,* 'it was in these circumstances that' etc. *Them.* c. 24, 3. **φέρων ... προσένειμεν ἑαυτόν,** 'he took and attached himself to the popular party,' c. 11, 2. On the use of φέρων to imply hasty and unhesitating decision and action, see G. *MT.*² § 837 and cp. *Lucull.* c. 7, 3 πάντες ὁμαλῶς ἐκείνῳ φέροντες ἐνεχείρισαν τὸν Μιθριδατικὸν πόλεμον, *Them.* c. 24, 2 where other instances are given in my n. *ad l.* Observe that προσένειμεν is an ingressive aorist, 'he *became* an adherent of.'

For προσινέμειν ἑαυτόν τινι, partibus alicuius se adiungere, cp. Pomp. c. 21, 4 τῷ δήμῳ προσένεμε μᾶλλον ἑαυτὸν ἢ τῇ βουλῇ, Pelop. c. 26, 1 αὐτὸς ἑαυτὸν προσένειμε τοῖς Θετταλοῖς, Cat. mi. c. 3, 4 Μαξίμῳ Φαβίῳ προσένειμεν ἑαυτόν, Mar. c. 41, 3 τούτῳ προσνέμειν ἑαυτὸν ἔγω μετὰ τῆς δυνάμεως, Sertor. c. 4, 4, Eumen. c. 3, 1 τῇ μὲν γνώμῃ τούτοις προσένειμεν ἑαυτόν, Sull. c. 4, 2 where other instances are given from post-classical authors in my note ad l.

16. ἀντὶ τῶν πλουσίων, 'instead of (that of) the wealthy classes.' A common brachylogy in comparisons. Cp. Brut. c. 4, 1 τὴν Πομπηίου νομίζων ὑπόθεσιν βελτίονα πρὸς τὸν πόλεμον εἶναι τοῦ Καίσαρος (where recent edd. foist in τῆς against the MSS.).

18. παρά, 'contrary to,' c. 29, 1; c. 33, 5.

§ 3 l. 20. περιπεσεῖν, 'to encounter.' Cp. c. 37, 3, Demosth. c. 6, 3 θορύβοις περιέπιπτε. For the infin. after a verb of fearing, see n. to l. 10.

21. ἀριστοκρατικόν sc. ὄντα: G. MT.² §§ 904, 911.

22. τῶν καλῶν κἀγαθῶν ἀνδρῶν, bonorum, optimatium. Cp. c. 8, 4; c. 11, 2 in both which passages also ἄνδρες is added contrary to general usage, Them. c. 3, 2.

23. ὑπῆλθε τοὺς πολλούς, 'he insinuated himself into the good graces of the populace.'

Cp. Lucull. c. 6, 3 ταύτην ὑπελθὼν δώροις, Cat. mi. c. 50, 2 οὐδ᾿ ὑπῆλθεν ὁμιλίᾳ φιλανθρώπῳ τὸν δῆμον, Pyrrh. c. 4, 4 δεινὸς ὢν ὑπελθεῖν ἐπ᾿ ὠφελείᾳ τοὺς κρείττονας. So ὑπεποιεῖτο c. 9, 2. Observe that in classical prose the form ὑπέρχεσθαι (not ὑπιέναι) is used, when the verb=θωπεύειν. See Cobet Var. Lect. p. 34.

24. παρασκευαζόμενος, 'by way of providing,' c. 10, 5; c. 13 11, 5. For the use of μέν and δέ, where there is only a formal opposition, cp. Them. c. 12, 1; c. 15, 1.

§ 4 l. 25. τοῖς περὶ τὴν δίαιταν, 'his manner of life.'

Arist. Vesp. 1103 τοὺς τρόπους καὶ τὴν δίαιταν σφηξὶν ἐμφερεστάτους. Eupolis Κόλακες (Mein. II 484, Kock I 301) δίαιταν ἥν ἔχουσ᾿ οἱ κόλακες. Alexis Ταραντ. (Mein. IV 483, Kock II 378) δεσμωτηρίον λέγεις δίαιταν. Menand. (Mein. IV 234, Kock III 162) τὸ σῶμ᾿ ὑγιαίνει τινα δίαιταν προσφέρων. Cp. Mor. 800 B Περικλῆς καὶ περὶ τὸ σῶμα καὶ τὴν δίαιταν ἐξήλλαξεν ἑαυτὸν ἠρέμα βαδίζειν καὶ πρᾴως διαλέγεσθαι καὶ τὸ πρόσωπον ἀεὶ συνεστηκὸς ἐπιδεικνύναι καὶ τὴν χεῖρα συνέχειν ἐντὸς τῆς περιβολῆς καὶ μίαν ὁδὸν πορεύεσθαι τὴν ἐπὶ τὸ βῆμα καὶ τὸ βουλευτήριον.

l. 27. ἐν ἄστει . . . ἐπ᾿ ἀγοράν: see n. to c. 5, 2.

ἑωρᾶτο . . . πορευόμενος: G. MT.² § 884.

28. κλήσεις δείπνων, 'invitations to dinners.' The objective genitive is rarely found as an equivalent to εἰς or ἐπί with the accusative. There are several instances of it after νόστος, see Prof. Jebb on Soph. Phil. 43.

Alex. c. 53, 1 τὰς κλήσεις τὰ πολλὰ διωθούμενος, Cat. mi. c. 14, 4 δεῖπνα καὶ κλήσεις, Mor. 197 E πρὸ ἐνιαυτοῦ τὰς κλήσεις ποιοῦνται τῶν γυναικῶν, 150 C σοφῶν ἀνδρῶν ὑποδοχὴ καὶ κλῆσις, 667 A, 707 B ἐπὶ τῷ ξένῳ ποιεῖσθαι τὴν κλῆσιν, 708 B τὰ πρὸς τοὺς ἡγεμόνας οὐκ ἔχει κλῆσιν, Xen. Symp. c. 1, 7 ἐπαινοῦντες τὴν κλῆσιν οὐχ ὑπισχνοῦντο συνδειπνήσειν.

29. τὴν τοιαύτην, the article is added because it refers to a class; c. 1, 5.   φιλοφροσύνην, 'familiarity.'

30. συνήθειαν, 'familiar intercourse.' See the passages quoted in Gr. Ind. to my ed. of *Demosth.* p. 140ª.   ἐξέλιπεν, 'he left off, discontinued.' Cp. *Lys.* c. 23, 6 αὐτὸς τὸ βοηθεῖν ἐξέλιπε.   ὡς, when used as consecutive for ὥστε, always take the infinitive—generally with μή, as *Lyc.* c. 28, 3, *Marc.* c. 13, 2, *Them.* c. 26, 1, *Cam.* c. 35, 4, *Timol.* c. 10, 2, *Pelop.* c. 29, 3, *Arist.* c. 9, 2, *Cat. ma.* c. 20, 2.

31. ἐπολιτεύσατο : see *Them.* c. 2, 5 n.   μακροῖς : c. 16, 2.

32. ἐπὶ δεῖπνον : cp. Arist. *Vesp.* 1005 ἄγων ἐπὶ δεῖπνον, εἰς ξυμπόσιον, *Pac.* 1192 ἐπὶ δεῖπνον ἦλθ᾽ εἰς τοὺς γάμους, 1208 εἴσιτ᾽ ἐπὶ δεῖπνον, *Eccl.* 652 χωρεῖν ἐπὶ δεῖπνον.   πλήν, conjunction, 'except that.'

33. Εὐρυπτολέμου: Euryptolemus was the son of Megacles (*Cim.* c. 4, 9) and the maternal great-uncle of Pericles. See pedigree c. 3, 1.   γαμοῦντος i.q. ἑστιῶντος γάμους, 'giving a wedding-feast.'   ἄχρι τῶν σπονδῶν, 'till the libations' i.e. the end of the meal (δεῖπνον) which was concluded by drink-offerings to the good genius, after which the πότος, συμπόσιον or κῶμος commenced.

34. ἐξανέστη, 'rose from his seat and left.' Cp. Plat. *Rep.* I c. 1 ἐξαναστησόμεθα μετὰ τὸ δεῖπνον, [Isocrat.] πρὸς Δημών. c. 32 ἐξανίστασο πρὸ μέθης.

§ 5 l. 34. δειναί ... περιγενέσθαι, 'are potent to overcome any kind of assumption of superiority.'   On φιλοφροσύναι, 'entertainments,' 'festive gatherings,' see *Demosth.* c. 16, 2 with my n. *ad l.*

36. δυσφύλακτον, 'hard to preserve,' 'maintain,' on the principle that familiarity breeds contempt (*non bene conveniunt nec in una sede morantur | maiestas et amor*). In the only other passage, where Plutarch uses the word (*Mor.* 49 B), it bears a different meaning, viz. 'hard to avoid.'   τὸ πρὸς δόξαν σεμνόν, 'an exterior of gravity, assumed only for show,' as opp. to ἡ ἀληθινὴ ἀρετή, 'genuine worth,' which appears all the more beautiful, the more open it is to observation. An indirect reflexion on the demeanour of Pericles, to which point is given by the opposition ὁ δὲ καί.

38. τῶν ἀγαθῶν ἀνδρῶν, 'in' or 'belonging to noble men,' a sort of partitive gen. after οὐδέν.

39. τοῖς ἐκτός, 'the outside world,' 'strangers.' Cp. *Them.* c. 26, 3, *Demosth.* c. 8, 1 with my notes *ad ll.* Busolt *Gr. Gesch.* I 446 Anm. 3 thinks the sentiment is taken direct from Stesimbrotus, but it is quite in keeping with Plutarch's own views; cp. Volkmann *Leben und Schriften des Plut.* p. 64.

41. **καὶ τῷ δήμῳ**: not his friends only.   **τὸ συνεχὲς φεύγων καὶ τὸν κόρον**. 'to avoid the natural satiety which they might feel from constantly seeing him.' The participle present is used as in § 3 l. 24.

42. **οἷον ἐκ διαλειμμάτων ἐπλησίαζεν**, 'presented himself as it were at intervals (lit. 'after pauses') only.'

44. **παριὼν εἰς τὸ πλῆθος** = τὸν δῆμον: cp. *Them.* c. 4, 1 with my n. *ad l.*

45. **ἑαυτὸν ... ἐπιδιδοὺς**: cp. c. 33, 2, *Thes.* c. 32, 1 ἐπιδόντος ἑαυτὸν ἐκουσίως σφαγιάσασθαι, *Pelop.* c. 26, 1 αὐτὸς ἑαυτὸν ἐπέδωκε τοῖς Θεσσαλοῖς, c. 31, 3, *Mor.* 794 B, *Dem.-Cic.* c. 4, 2 ἑαυτὸν ἐπέδωκεν εἰς τὴν αὐτὴν πολιτείαν, *Pomp.* c. 6, 4, *C. Gr.* c. 9, 1 ἐπιδοὺς εἰς ταῦτα τῇ βουλῇ τὴν ἑαυτοῦ δημαρχίαν.   **ὥσπερ τὴν Σαλαμινίαν τριήρη**: *Them.* c. 7, 4. Cp. *Mor.* 811 C ἕτεροι δὲ σεμνότερον οἴονται καὶ μεγαλοπρεπέστερον εἶναι τὸ τοῦ Περικλέους· ὃν καὶ Κριτόλαός ἐστιν ὁ Περιπατητικός, αἰῶν. ὥσπερ ἡ Σαλαμινία ναῦς Ἀθήνησι καὶ ἡ Πάραλος οὐκ ἐπὶ πᾶν ἔργον ἀλλ᾽ ἐπὶ τὰς ἀναγκαίας καὶ μεγάλας κατεσπῶντο πράξεις, οὕτως ἑαυτῷ πρὸς τὰ κυριώτατα καὶ μέγιστα χρῆσθαι.

46. **Κριτόλαος**: the historian, author of the Ἠπειρωτικὰ and Φαινόμενα, passages from which are quoted *Paroll.* c. 6, c. 9 and by Aul. Gell. *N. A.* XI 9. He is identified by some with the Peripatetic philosopher of Phaselis (Lydia) who went on the celebrated embassy to Rome B.C. 155, with Carneades the Academic and Diogenes the Stoic. See Müller *FHG.* VII p. 372, Voss *de Hist. Gr.* II p. 422 ed. Westermann.

48. **ῥήτορας**, 'speakers,' the official expression (*CIA.* I 31) for those who made a regular profession of speaking in the ἐκκλησία, as an avenue to office and honours; so c. 37, 1, Arist. *Ach.* 38, *Eq.* 60. Cp. *Mor.* 812 C τῷ πολιτικῷ προσήκει παραχωρεῖν μὲν ἑτέροις ἄρχειν, κινεῖν δὲ μὴ πάντα τὰ τῆς πόλεως τοῖς αὐτοῦ λόγοις καὶ ψηφίσμασιν ἢ πράξεσιν, ἀλλ᾽ ἔχοντα πιστοὺς καὶ ἀγαθοὺς ἄνδρας ἕκαστον ἑκάστῃ χρείᾳ κατὰ τὸ οἰκεῖον προσαρμόττειν, and then, after quoting the example of Pericles, Plutarch continues: οὐ γὰρ μόνον, τῆς δυνάμεως εἰς πολλοὺς διαιρεῖσθαι δοκούσης, ἧττον ἐνοχλεῖ τὸν φθόνον τὸ μέγεθος, ἀλλὰ καὶ τὰ τῶν χρειῶν ἐπιτελεῖται μᾶλλον.

καθιείς, *subornans.*   **ἔπραττεν** is substituted for πράττων to avoid the concurrence of two participles.

§ 6 l. 49. **Ἐφιάλτην**: the anti-democratic Atthis which Ephorus had before him, appears to have been unfavourable to the reformer Ephialtes, as we infer from the passage in Diodorus XI 77, 6:—οὐ μὴν ἀθῷός γε διέφυγε τηλικούτοις ἀνομήμασιν ἐπιβαλόμενος. On the other hand in *Cim.* c. 10 his incorruptibility is put on a level with Cimon's, and in c. 13 Callisthenes is quoted as an authority for his activity as στρατηγός. To the same effect are the sayings of Ephialtes in

Aelian *V. H.* XI 9 and XIII 39. There is no mention of him at all in Thucydides. **κατέλυσε**: c. 3, n 1.

Cp. Aristot. Ἀθην. πολ. c. 25, 2 (Ephialtes) τῆς βουλῆς ἐπὶ Κόνωνος ἄρχοντος ἅπαντα περιείλετο τὰ ἐπίθετα δι' ὧν ἦν ἡ τῆς πολιτείας φυλακή καὶ τὰ μὲν τοῖς πεντακοσίοις τὰ δὲ τῷ δήμῳ καὶ τοῖς δικαστηρίοις ἀπέδωκεν, c. 27, 1 τῶν Ἀρεοπαγιτῶν ἔνια παρείλετο, *Pol.* XII (IX) 3 p. 1274ᵃ τὴν μὲν ἐν Ἀρείῳ πάγῳ βουλὴν Ἐφιάλτης ἐκόλουσε καὶ Περικλῆς, Philochorus *fr.* 141ᵇ ap. Müller *FHG.* I 407 Ἐφ. μόνα κατέλιπε τῇ ἐξ Ἀρείου πάγου βουλῇ τὰ ὑπὲρ τοῦ σώματος, Plut. *Cim.* c. 10, 7 Κίμων πρὸς Ἐφιάλτην ὕστερον καταλύοντα τὴν ἐξ Ἀρείου πάγου βουλὴν διηνέχθη, c. 15, 2 (during the absence of Cimon on foreign service) οἱ πολλοὶ συγχέαντες τὸν καθεστῶτα τῆς πολιτείας κόσμον τά τε πάτρια νόμιμα, οἷς ἐχρῶντο πρότερον, Ἐφιάλτου προεστῶτος ἀφείλοντο τῆς ἐξ Ἀρείου πάγου βουλῆς τὰς κρίσεις πλὴν ὀλίγων ἁπάσας, καὶ τῶν δικαστηρίων κυρίους ἑαυτοὺς ποιήσαντες εἰς ἄκρατον δημοκρατίαν ἐνέβαλον τὴν πόλιν, *Mor.* 805 D βουλήν τινες ἐπαχθῆ καὶ ὀλιγαρχικὴν κολούσαντες, ὥσπερ Ἐφιάλτης Ἀθήνησι, . . . δύναμιν ἅμα καὶ δόξαν ἔσχον, *ib.* 812 D ὡς Περικλῆς δὲ Ἐφιάλτου τὴν ἐξ Ἀρείου πάγου βουλὴν ἐταπείνωσε, Pausan. I 29, 15 Ἐφιάλτης ὅς τὰ νόμιμα τὰ ἐν Ἀρείῳ πάγῳ μάλιστα ἐλυμήνατο.

50. **κατὰ τὸν Πλάτωνα**, 'as Plato says,' c. 15, 4. See *Rep.* VIII 562 C D, where, speaking generally of democratical states, he says ὅταν δημοκρατουμένη πόλις ἐλευθερίας διψήσασα κακῶν οἰνοχόων προστατούντων τύχῃ καὶ πορρωτέρω τοῦ δέοντος ἀκράτου αὐτῆς μεθυσθῇ, τοὺς ἄρχοντας δή, ἂν μὴ πολλὴν παρέχωσι τὴν ἐλευθερίαν, κολάζει.

52. **ἐξυβρίσαντα**, ingressive aor. part., 'becoming riotous, unruly.' Cp. Thuc. I 84, 2 εὐπραγίαις οὐκ ἐξυβρίζομεν.

53. **οἱ κωμῳδοποιοί**: Bergk *Rel. com. Att.* 330 f. considers that the lines are a part of the passage from Teleclides, quoted in c. 3, 3 and c. 16, 1. See Meineke *FCG.* IV 676 (CCCVI), Kock *CAF.* III 406 (41). **ΠΕΙΘΑΡΧΕῖΝ ΟΥΚΕΤΙ ΤΟΛΜΩ͂Ν**, 'has no longer the patience to obey the rein.' Cp. Eupolis Πόλεις fr. 232 Kock, where (speaking of Chios) he says πειθαρχεῖ καλῶς, ἄπληκτος ὥσπερ ἵππος. The second verse as it stands does not scan. Meineke's ἀλλὰ δακνάζει or Bergk's ἀλλὰ δάκνει γάρ would remove that difficulty. The overbearing conduct of Athens to the members of the confederation—Euboea, which was her granary, and the Aegean Islands which contributed so much to her commerce and wealth—is here pointed at.

CHAPTER VIII

§ 1 l. 1. **τῇ περὶ τὸν βίον κατασκευῇ** is for τῇ τοῦ βίου κ. as in c. 2, 3; c. 15, 5.

2. **τῷ μεγέθει . . . ἁρμόζοντα λόγον . . . ἐξαρτυόμενος**, 'by way of fitting himself with a style of speaking as with an instrument, in accord with (a proper vehicle for) his sublime sentiments.' L'éloquence de Périclès est comparée à un instrument de musique dont Anaxagore ou plutôt l'enseignement donné par ce philosophe est une des cordes (*A. Jacob*). There

is a similar expression in *Cic.* c. 4, 3, which has escaped the notice of commentators, αὖθις, ὥσπερ ὄργανον, ἐξηρτύετο (ὁ Κικέρων) τὸν ῥητορικὸν λόγον.

3. **παρενέτεινε**, not, as Liddell-Scott, 'strung him,' 'roused his energies,' but, as Koraës, παρενέπλεκε τοῖς ἑαυτοῦ λόγοις τὰς φιλοσόφου Ἀναξαγόρου γνώμας, or, if ὄργανον be taken to mean a musical instrument, 'strung besides' *i.e.* availed himself of him 'as an accessory chord.'

5. **οἷον βαφὴν ... ὑποχεόμενος**, 'insensibly (ὑπό) colouring, as it were, his rhetoric with (the dye of) natural science.' Kaltwasser and others understand by βαφήν the 'temper' produced by dipping red-hot iron in water, so that in their view the meaning is, 'giving his speech more strength and expression by tempering it with physical science.'

7. **Πλάτων**: *Phaedr.* 270 A πᾶσαι ὅσαι μεγάλαι τῶν τεχνῶν προσδέονται ἀδολεσχίας καὶ μετεωρολογίας φύσεως πέρι· τὸ γὰρ ὑψηλόνουν τοῦτο καὶ πάντῃ τελεσιουργὸν ('creating an ideal perfect work') ἔοικεν ἐντεῦθέν ποθεν εἰσιέναι. ὁ καὶ Περικλῆς πρὸς τῷ εὐφυὴς εἶναι ἐκτήσατο· προσπεσὼν γὰρ οἶμαι τοιούτῳ ὄντι Ἀναξαγόρᾳ, μετεωρολογίας ἐμπλησθεὶς καὶ ἐπὶ φύσιν νοῦ τε καὶ ἀνοίας ἀφικόμενος—ἐντεῦθεν εἵλκυσεν ἐπὶ τὴν τῶν λόγων τέχνην τὸ πρόσφορον αὐτῇ, *i.e.* 'all the higher arts require over and above (their immediate discipline) a subtle and speculative acquaintance with physical science; it being, I imagine, by some such door as this that there enters that elevation of thought and creation of all-round perfect or ideal works. And it was this quality which Pericles added to that of great natural gifts, for he fell into the hands, if I am not mistaken, of Anaxagoras, by whom he was imbued with the higher philosophy, and attained the knowledge of mind and matter (the rational and irrational principles) and drafted from those researches what was applicable to his art (that of speaking).' Cp. c. 5, 1, Cic. *Orat.* c. 4, 15 with Sandys' note, *de orat.* III c. 34, 138, *Brut.* c. 11, 44 quoted in note to c. 4, 4, Themistius *Orat.* XXVI p. 396 ed. Dind. (τὴν πόλιν) Περικλέα ἐπαινοῦσαν μόνον καὶ Ἀσπασίαν, ὡς ῥήτορας τελεσιουργοὺς τε καὶ ὑψηλόνους, ὅτι ἐκ τῆς Ἀναξαγόρου ἀδολεσχίας ταῦτα προσειλκύσαντο εἰς τὴν τέχνην.

9. **τὸ πρόσφορον** *sc.* ταύτῃ τῇ τέχνῃ.

10. **διήνεγκε**, *praestitit.* Cp. Blass *Att. Beredsamkeit* I² pp. 34 ff.

§ 2 l. 10. **τὴν ἐπίκλησιν**, 'his (well-known) surname' (Ὀλύμπιος).

12. **ἀπὸ τῶν οἷς**: the relative clause here takes the place of a noun—a construction which is rarer in Plutarch than in some other writers. For ἀπό, cp. c. 27, 2. **ἐκόσμησε**: see c. 13.

13. **ἀπὸ τῆς ἐν τῇ πολιτείᾳ ... δυνάμεως**; cp. *Mor.* 118 E Περικλέα τὸν Ὀλύμπιον προσαγορευθέντα διὰ τὴν περὶ τὸν λόγον καὶ τὴν σύνεσιν ὑπερβεβλημένην δύναμιν.

15. **συνδραμεῖν**, *conflatum esse.* **οὐδὲν ἀπέοικεν**, 'it is by no means improbable.' The verb ἀπέοικε is not found in good Attic prose, only in late writers.

16. προσόντων: see n. to c. 7, 1.   τῷ ἀνδρί: c. 1, 1; c. 10, 6.

§ 3 l. 17. διδασκάλων for κωμῳδοδιδασκάλων: c. 5, 3.

18. σπουδῇ, *serio*.

19. εἰς αὑτόν: c. 13, 6, 7.   ἐπί, 'because of.'

20. ΒΡΟΝΤΑΝ κτλ.: Arist. *Acharn.* 530:—

ἐντεῦθεν ὀργῇ Περικλέης οὑλύμπιος
ἤστραπτεν ἐβρόντα ξυνεκύκα τὴν Ἑλλάδα.

The quotation which follows (δεινὸν . . . φέρειν) is of unknown authorship. Plutarch might have quoted also the well-known lines from the Δῆμοι (c. 3, 4) of Eupolis (Mein. ii 458-9, Kock i 281)—

κράτιστος οὗτος ἐγένετ' ἀνθρώπων λέγειν·
ὁπότε παρέλθοι δ', ὥσπερ ἀγαθοὶ δρομῆς,
ἐκ δέκα ποδῶν ᾕρει λέγων τοὺς ῥήτορας.[1]
ταχὺν λέγεις μέν, πρὸς δέ γ' αὐτοῦ τῷ τάχει
Πειθώ τις ἐπεκάθιζεν ἐπὶ τοῖς χείλεσιν·
οὕτως ἐκήλει[2] καὶ μόνος τῶν ῥητόρων
τὸ κέντρον ἐγκατέλειπε τοῖς ἀκροωμένοις.

21. ὅτε δημηγορίη, optative of indefinite recurrence.

24. δεινότητα: c. 4, 2 note.

25. μετὰ παιδιᾶς, 'in jest,' 'playfully,' l. 18; Thuc. 6, 28, 1; Plat. *Phil.* p. 19 D.

§ 4 l. 26. τῶν καλῶν καὶ ἀγαθῶν ἀνδρῶν: see n. to c. 7, 2.

28. Archidamus II, King of Sparta (B.C. 469–427), commanded the first two expeditions into Attica in the Peloponnesian war, the first ten years of which are sometimes called after him 'the Archidamian war.' Thucydides, who on the death of Cimon (B.C. 449) became the leader of the aristocratical party against Pericles, naturally went to Sparta when in exile. The meaning of the apophthegm is that he himself had the better case of the two and the stronger argument, but that Pericles' dialectic skill and adroitness made it appear otherwise to the audience. The story derives point from an allusion in Arist. *Ach.* 708 to the skill of Thucydides as a wrestler,—ἐκεῖνος ἡνίκ' ἦν Θουκυδίδης, κατεπάλαισεν ἂν Εὐάθλους δέκα. The story is probably taken from Ion. Cp. *Praec. ger. reip.* § 5 (*Mor.* 802 c). Busolt *Gr. Gesch.* II 513 note.

31. For καταβάλω, 'throw,' a technical term, cp. *Pomp.* c. 18, 1 Νέμεσίς τις ὥσπερ ἀθλητὴν εὐδρομοῦντα πρὸς τέρμασι τοῦ βίου κατέβαλε, Arist. *Vesp.* 1384 τῇ πυγμῇ θενὼν ὁ πρεσβύτερος

---

[1] Pericles si in contionem prodiret, ut egregius cursor quamquam decem pedum intervallo post suos adversarios cursum iniit tamen eos consequitur et praevertit, sic reliquos Oratores dicendi copia vicit ac post se reliquit (*Wyttenbach*).

[2] *I.e.* ita demulcebat omnes, ut Suadam quandam eius labris insidere dicerent (*Kock*).

κατέβαλε τὸν νεώτερον. Plat. *Hipp. mi.* 374 ἃ αἴσχιον ἐν πάλῃ τὸ πίπτειν ἢ τὸ καταβάλλειν, *Euthyd.* 277 D ὅτι δὴ ἐπὶ τὸ τρίτον καταβαλὼν ὥσπερ πάλαισμα ὥρμα τὸν νεανίσκον, *Xub.* 1229 τὸν ἀκατάβλητον (i.e. ἀήττητον) λόγον. **ἀντιλέγων ὡς οὐ πέπτωκε**: this pleonastic use of οὐ is found in two other passages only of Plutarch, *Dion* c. 36, 2 αὐτὸς αὐτὸν οὐ δύναται ... ἐξελέσθαι τῆς γραφῆς, ὡς οὐ φιλοτυραννότατος γένοιτο, *Mor.* 326 Α ἀμφισβήτησίς ἐστι πρὸς τὴν τύχην, ὡς οὐχὶ τῆς σωτηρίας αἰτία κατέστη.

32. **μεταπείθει**, 'makes them change their opinion,' c. 35, 4, Arist. *Ach.* 626 τὸν δῆμον μεταπείθει περὶ τῶν σπονδῶν.

33. **οὐ μὴν ἀλλά**, 'not but that,' 'the truth, however, is that,' c. 10, 5. An elliptical expression which implies: Certainly Pericles himself had no such exalted idea of his own power, but still ...

35. **ηὔχετο**: *Mor.* 803 F καὶ Περικλῆς ἐκεῖνος ηὔχετο πρὸ τοῦ δημηγορεῖν μηδὲ ῥῆμα μηδὲν ἀλλότριον τῶν πραγμάτων ἐπελθεῖν αὐτῷ, Aelian *Var. Hist.* IV 10 ὁσάκις ἔμελλεν (ὁ Περικλῆς) ἐς τὴν ἐκκλησίαν παριέναι, ηὔχετο μηδὲν αὐτῷ ῥῆμα ἐπιπολάσαι τοιοῦτον, ὅπερ οὖν ἔμελλεν ἐκτραχύνειν τὸν δῆμον, πρόσαντες αὐτῷ γενόμενον καὶ ἀβούλητον δόξαν, Quintil. *Or. Inst.* XII 9 *nec immerito Pericles solebat optare, ne quod sibi verbum in mentem veniret quo populus offenderetur.* Cp. the story told of him in *Mor.* 813 D, that, whenever he assumed his general's cloak (ἀναλαμβάνων τὴν χλαμύδα), he used to remind himself: — πρόσεχε, Περίκλεις· ἐλευθέρων ἄρχεις, Ἑλλήνων ἄρχεις, πολιτῶν Ἀθηναίων. **μηδὲ ῥῆμα μηδὲν ἐκπεσεῖν**, 'that not even a single word might escape his lips.' For ἐκπεσεῖν, *excidere ex ore*, cp. Aristot. *Eth. Nic.* III 1, 17 p. 1111ᵃ 8, if the common reading be correct; see, however, Prof. Bywater *Contrib. to the textual cr. etc.* p. 31.

§ 5 l. 37. **ἔγγραφον οὐδέν**: Arist. c. 26, 2; Polyb. III 21, 4; 26, 4.

38. **ἀπολέλοιπε**, 'has left behind him' (unclassical): Diog. L. 8, 58, 7, 54. **πλὴν τῶν ψηφισμάτων**: Plutarch mentions several of his ψηφίσματα, c. 10, 3; c. 17, 1; c. 20, 2; c. 25, 1; c. 29, 1, 8; c. 30, 3; c. 34, 2; others are tacitly implied in c. 11, 5. These were all probably taken by him from the ψηφισμάτων συναγωγή or copies made by the antiquarian Craterus (*Arist. l.c.*) after the originals preserved in the hand-writing of their respective authors (αὐτόγραφα, Posid. ap. Athenae. V 214 D) in the Μητρῷον at Athens, whence they were surreptitiously removed by Apellicon, whose library being carried off to Rome by Sulla at the capture of Athens (Plut. *Sull.* c. 26), they were irrecoverably lost. See Cobet *Mnemos.* N.S. I pp. 97 ff. Nothing is now extant which is ascribed to Pericles; but we know

from allusions in Cicero (*Brut.* c. 7, 27 ; *de orat.* 11 c. 22, 93) that there existed in antiquity certain speeches purporting to be his, but which Quint. *Inst. or.* III i 14 pronounces spurious.

39. ἀπομνημονεύεται δ' ὀλίγα παντάπασιν, 'and (only) a very few sayings of his are recorded,' preserved in the hearer's recollection. Cp. § 3 διαμνημονεύεται, *Them.* c. 18, 1 ; c. 11, 2.

40. οἷον τὸ τὴν Αἴγιναν κτλ. See note to c. 28, 3 and to *Demosth.* c. 1, 2 where the same saying is quoted without the author's name.

41. τὸ τὸν πόλεμον κτλ. : the occasion was when he advised the Athenians to form an alliance with Corcyra (c. 29, 1).

43. προσφερόμενον, *ingruentem*, 'coming upon them,' cp. c. 26, 1, Herod. VII 9, 3 σοὶ μέλλει τις ἀντιώσεσθαι πόλεμον προσφέρων.

44. συστρατηγῶν : Sophocles was one of the ten generals in command of the expedition led by Pericles against Samos (Strabo XIV c. 1, 18, Athenae. XIII c. 81). The anecdote is familiar from Cic. *de off.* I 40, 144 : *bene Pericles cum haberet collegam in praetura Sophoclem iique de communi officio convenissent et casu formosus puer praeteriret dixissetque Sophocles 'O puerum pulchrum, Pericle!' 'At enim praetorem, Sophocle, decet non solum manus sed etiam oculos abstinentes habere.'* Cp. Valer. Max. IV 3 ext. 1. This remark of Pericles was found by Plutarch in Theopompus.

46. τὰς χεῖρας ... καθαρὰς ἔχειν for τὰς χεῖρας καθαρὸς εἶναι. Cp. *Arist.* c. 24, 4 καλὸν καὶ στρατηγικὸν ἀληθῶς ἡ περὶ τὰς χεῖρας ἐγκράτεια.

§ 6 l. 49. ἐγκωμιάζων : c. 28, 3.

51. οὐδὲ γάρ, *neque enim*, the negative of καὶ γάρ c. 7, 1. The sentiment of Pericles is expressed objectively as being a truism in an independent rather than a dependent clause (οὐδὲ γὰρ ὁρᾶν) like that which follows.

53. ταῦτ' οὖν ὑπάρχειν, 'that the same advantages therefore belong' (*i.e.* immortality). The argument is :—Those who have fallen in battle receive high honour and have done great service to the state ; this much and no more we know about the gods ; if then we conclude therefrom that the gods are immortal, we must draw the same conclusion with respect to those who have sacrificed their lives for their fatherland.

CHAPTER IX

§ 1 l. 1. Θουκυδίδης : II 65, 9.   2. ὑπογράφει, *adumbrat*.

4. ὑπὸ ... ἀνδρὸς ἀρχήν : for the gen. of the agent with ὑπό

after the verbal ἀρχή = τὸ ἄρχεσθαι, cp. Xen. *Hier.* c. 7, 5 αἱ ὑπουργίαι αἱ ὑπὸ φοβουμένων, Plat. *Rep.* 387 D ″Ηρας δεσμοὺς ὑπὸ υἱέος καὶ Ἡφαίστου ῥίψεις ὑπὸ πατρός, and Thuc. VIII 64, 4 φυγὴ ἔξω ἦν ὑπὸ τῶν Ἀθηναίων παρὰ τοῖς Πελοποννησίοις, i.e. 'a body of those who were banished by the Athenians.'

5. **ἄλλοι πολλοί**, 'many others': πολλοὶ ἄλλοι is also used, but not πολλοὶ καὶ ἄλλοι, as is sometimes assumed. See my note to *Demosth.* c. 14, 4. Plut. is probably referring to Plat. *Gorg.* 515 E, where he speaks of the bad moral effect produced by such employment of the public money:—ἀκούω Περικλέα πεποιηκέναι Ἀθηναίους ἀργοὺς καὶ δειλοὺς καὶ λάλους καὶ φιλαργύρους, εἰς μισθοφορίαν πρῶτον καταστήσαντα.

6. **κληρουχίας**: the allotment of the land of an expelled Greek population to Athenian citizens, who retained their legal status but were not, like ἄποικοι or colonists parted from their mother city-state, independent, was a prominent feature of the democratic programme at Athens. It served the double purpose of providing many individuals with the means of subsistence and of securing and strengthening the state, as we read in c. 11, 5. The first allottees (κληροῦχοι) were those sent to occupy the land of the Hippobotae near Chaleis (Euboea) B.C. 510. The number sent out between B.C. 460 and 440 was 9950, exclusive of those sent to Lemnos, Amphipolis, Imbros and Aegina at the same time. Gilbert *Gr. St.*² 1 p. 504, note 3. The system was the most hated feature of the Athenian empire, and when Athens strove to reconstitute her allied confederacy a second time in B.C. 377, she agreed to discontinue it, but on the conquest of Samos B.C. 365 it was renewed in that island and remained in force until the defeat of the Athenians in the Lamian war, when the Samian exiles were restored by Perdiccas according to the convention.

7. **θεωρικά** sc. χρήματα, i.q. τὸ θεωρικόν, 'show-money' or fund expended by the state on public festivals, which included sacrifices, processions and other entertainments, here used in its restricted sense of largess to the poorer citizens in the form of payment of the sum charged by the lessee of the theatre for their admission to dramatic performances, at the rate of two obols for each of the ordinary seats (Dem. *de cor.* § 28). Cp. Gilbert *Gr. St.*² 1 384. The payment of the θεωρικόν out of the treasury is attributed to Cleophon by Aristot. Ἀθ. πολ. c. 28, 3. Gilbert *l. c.* p. 273. Such an application of the surplus public revenue—which, by the old law, should have been carried to the military fund—was not unknown at an earlier period (*Them.* c. 4, 1), but it was reserved for Pericles to apply it as an engine for winning popular favour. **μισθῶν διανομάς**, 'the distribution of fees,' including the salaries of the dicasts (l. 26), which came afterwards to be regarded as one means of earning a living, and the pay and provision-money of citizens when on military or naval service. The μισθὸς ἐκκλησιαστικός or payment for attendance at the public assembly was introduced at a later period by Agyrrhius; see Aristot. Ἀθην. πολ. c. 41, 3 with Sandys' note *ad l.*

9. **πολυτελῆ**, 'expensive' (c. 36, 1) in chiastic opposition to **αὐτουργοῦ**, 'maintaining themselves by their own labour.'

Cp. Thuc. I. 141, 5, Eur. *Orest.* 920 αὐτουργός, οἵπερ καὶ μόνοι σώζουσι γῆν. Xen. *Oec.* v 4 opposes the αὐτουργούς as a class to τοὺς τῇ ἐπιμελείᾳ γεωργοῦντας, those whose farming consists in supervision. Plutarch leaves his readers to form their own judgment on the merits of the case from the actual circumstances.

12. **τῆς μεταβολῆς**, 'the change (for the worse), deterioration of the people.'

§ 2 l. 13. **ὥσπερ εἴρηται**, c. 7, 3.

14. **ὑπεποιεῖτο**, 'was for winning over,' 'curried favour with.'

The word is used once by *Dem. de f. l.* § 76 ἵνα μὴ δι' ὑμῶν αὐτοὺς οἱ Φωκεῖς ὑποποιήσωνται and twice by Aristot. *Pol.* v (viii) 4, p. 1303ᵇ, 24 τὸν ἐρώμενον αὐτοῦ ὑπεποιήσατο, 'Αθ. πολ. c. 6, 3 ἐξὸν αὐτῷ τοὺς ἑτέρους ὑποποιησάμενον τυραννεῖν τῆς πόλεως. Cp. ὑπῆλθε c. 7, 3.

16. **ἀνελάμβανε**, *sibi conciliare studebat*. For **ἀπό**, see Gr. Ind. *s.v.*

Cp. c. 34, 1, *Nic.* c. 3, 2 χορηγίαις ἀνελάμβανε τὸν δῆμον, *Tib. Gr.* c. 16, 1, *Mar.* c. 28, 1 τῆς ἕκτης ὑπατείας ὠρέγετο θεραπείαις τὸν δῆμον ἀναλαμβάνων, *Cic.* c. 36, 2 τοὺς χαρίεντας ἀνελάμβανεν ἐστιάσεσιν, *Ant.* c. 57, 1, *Philop.* c. 15, 3, Arist. *Eq.* 682 τὴν βουλὴν ὅλην ὀβολοῦ κοριάννοις ἀναλαβών, Aristot. *Rhet.* i 1, 10 πρὸ ἔργου ἐστὶν ἀναλαβεῖν τὸν ἀκροατήν.

17. **δεῖπνον ... τῷ δεομένῳ παρέχων Ἀθηναίων**: this is probably an exaggerated account. Aristot. 'Αθ. πολ. c. 27, 3 (quoted by Plut. *Cim.* c. 10, 2) limits this act of generosity to the Laciadae, his δημόται or *curiales* (Cic. *de off.* ii 64 after Theophrastus): ὁ γὰρ Κίμων, ἅτε τυραννικὴν ἔχων οὐσίαν ... τῶν δημοτῶν ἔτρεφε πολλούς· ἐξῆν γὰρ τῷ βουλομένῳ Λακιαδῶν καθ' ἑκάστην τὴν ἡμέραν ἐλθόντι παρ' αὐτὸν ἔχειν τὰ μέτρια, ἔτι δὲ τὰ χωρία πάντα ἄφρακτα ἦν, ὅπως ἐξῇ τῷ βουλομένῳ τῆς ὀπώρας ἀπολαύειν. Plutarch also says (*Cim.* c. 10, 1) that the latter privilege was accorded by Cimon καὶ τοῖς ξένοις καὶ τῶν πολιτῶν τοῖς δεομένοις and that he kept open house for the whole of the poorer population of Athens (τῶν πενήτων τῷ βουλομένῳ) and again (§ 6) τὴν οἰκίαν τοῖς πολίταις πρυτανεῖον ἀπέδειξε κοινόν. His authority was, probably, Theopompus *Philippica* Bk x (ap. Athenae. xii c. 41, Müller *FHG.* I 293 fr. 94), from whom Nepos also (*Cim.* c. 4, 1) and Heracleides Ponticus περὶ πολιτειῶν p. 5 borrow:—Κίμων ὁ Ἀθηναῖος ἐν τοῖς ἀγροῖς καὶ τοῖς κήποις οὐδένα τοῦ καρποῦ καθίστα φύλακα, ὅπως οἱ βουλόμενοι τῶν πολιτῶν εἰσιόντες ὀπωρίζωνται καὶ λαμβάνωσιν, εἴ τινος δέοιντο τῶν ἐν τοῖς χωρίοις. ἔπειτα τὴν οἰκίαν παρεῖχε κοινὴν ἅπασιν ὡς δεῖπνον ἀεὶ εὐτελὲς παρασκευάζεσθαι πολλοῖς ἀνθρώποις καὶ τοὺς ἀπόρους τῶν Ἀθηναίων εἰσιόντας δειπνεῖν. The expression, however, τῶν χωρίων τοὺς φραγμοὺς ἀφαιρῶν—common to Plutarch's two *Lives*—is not found in Theopompus, and appears to be taken from some other source. The whole subject has been discussed in *Mnemosyne* N.S. ix 58.

18. **τοὺς πρεσβυτέρους ἀμφιεννύων**: cp. Theopomp. *l. c.* —ποιεῖν δὲ καὶ τοῦτο πολλάκις (φασὶν αὐτόν), ὁπότε τῶν πολιτῶν τινα ἴδοι κακῶς ἠμφιεσμένον, κελεύειν αὐτῷ μεταμφιέννυσθαι τῶν νεανίσκων τινὰ τῶν συνακολουθούντων αὐτῷ.

22. **καταδημαγωγούμενος**, 'out-demagogued,' 'outdone in popular arts,' § 4 l. 33. Cp. *Thes.* c. 35, 3 ἐπιχειρῶν βιάζεσθαι κατεδημαγωγεῖτο καὶ κατεστασιάζετο, and the similar verb

καταστρατηγεῖσθαι, 'to be out-generalled,' 'outwitted,' *Timol.* c. 10, 8, *Nic.* c. 20, 1.

23. **τῶν δημοσίων**, 'the state revenues,' c. 12, 5; c. 14, 2.

24. **Δαμωνίδου τοῦ "Οαθεν**, 'Damonides of (the deme) Oa,' 17 which was in the Πανδιονὶς φυλή. It is conjectured by Busolt and others that probably Damon the musician (c. 4, 1) was his adviser and that we should read accordingly in this passage Δάμωνος Δαμωνίδου. But see Aristot. Ἀθην. πολ. c. 27, 4 πρὸς δὴ ταύτην (sc. τὴν Κίμωνος) χορηγίαν ἐπιλειπόμενος ὁ Περικλῆς τῇ οὐσίᾳ, συμβουλεύσαντος αὐτῷ Δαμωνίδου τοῦ Οἰῆθεν (ὃς ἐδόκει τῶν πολλῶν εἰσηγητὴς εἶναι τῷ Περικλεῖ· διὸ καὶ ὠστράκισαν αὐτὸν ὕστερον), ἐπεὶ τοῖς ἰδίοις ἡττᾶτο, διδόναι τοῖς πολλοῖς τὰ αὑτῶν, κατεσκεύασε μισθοφορὰν τοῖς δικασταῖς ἀφ' ὧν αἰτιῶνταί τινες χείρους γενέσθαι, κληρουμένων ἐπιμελῶς ἀεὶ μᾶλλον τῶν τυχόντων ἢ τῶν ἐπιεικῶν ἀνθρώπων. How is the discrepancy to be reconciled? Prof. Gomperz and Mr. Kenyon (followed by Dr. Sandys) suggest that Plutarch *more suo* confused two persons, the musician Damon, son of Damonides, of Ὄα, and the politician Damonides of Οἴη (in the phyle Οἰνηίς) and transferred to the former some of the attributes of the latter.

Ὄαθεν: the proper demonymic was Ὀαεύς or Ὀαιεύς (*CIG.* 318). Cp. Ἀγρυλῆθεν, Ἀλωπεκῆθεν (c. 11, 1), Ἀφιδνῆθεν, Ἑσταιόθεν, Κεφαλῆθεν, Κολωνῆθεν, Φλυῆθεν. Sometimes also ἐκ with the gen. of the deme is substituted.

§ 3 l. 25. **θεωρικοῖς καὶ δικαστικοῖς λήμμασιν**: the payment for service on juries (μισθὸς δικαστικός) was introduced by Pericles, either shortly before or at the time when Cimon's influence after his restoration in B.C. 458 was strengthened. At first it was only two obols a day, but subsequently B.C. 425/4 it was increased by Cleon (Schol. to Arist. *Vesp.* 88) to three (τριώβολον) Arist. *Eq.* 51, 255, *Vesp.* 300, with Schol. *ad l.* Aristot. Ἀθ. πολ. c. 62, 2. Cp. Aristot. *l. c.* c. 27, 3 ἐποίησε δὲ καὶ μισθοφόρα τὰ δικαστήρια Περικλῆς πρῶτος, ἀντιδημαγωγῶν πρὸς τὴν Κίμωνος εὐπορίαν, *Pol.* II 9, 3 p. 1274ᵃ, 8 τὰ δὲ δικαστήρια μισθοφόρα κατέστησε Περικλῆς.

27. **χορηγίαις**, 'largesses.' See *Them.* c. 5, 1 with my note *ad l.* **συνδεκάσας**, 'bribing wholesale.' Cp. Aesch. *Tim.* § 86 ἐάν τις συνδεκάζῃ τὴν ἐκκλησίαν καὶ τἆλλα δικαστήρια, [Xenoph.] *Ath. resp.* c. 3, 7 ed. Kirchhoff διασκευάσασθαι ῥᾴδιον ἔσται πρὸς ὀλίγους δικαστὰς καὶ συνδεκάσαι, Dem. *or.* 46 § 26 ἐάν τις . . . συνδεκάζῃ τὴν ἡλιαίαν. **ἐχρῆτο**, sc. τῷ πλήθει.

28. The Areopagus was the oldest council of Athens. As reconstituted by Solon, besides being a criminal tribunal having the cognisance of all cases of homicide (Dem. *c. Aristocr.* 66 ff.), it was invested with the general supervision of the state; watched over the conduct of magistrates in office, controlled the proceedings of the ἐκκλησία and possessed a censorial power over private citizens. The nine archons, provided they had passed their

εὔθυναι and had discharged their duties blamelessly, became life-members of it (l. 29); so that it was a close corporation of Eupatrids and the only depositary of real political power, as long as it elected the magistrates from whom it was itself to be recruited. But the degradation of the office of archon by the substitution of lot for election changed its character, and instead of being a council of the *élite* of the aristocracy, it was becoming little more than a glorified vestry. It was not likely that the growing democracy, conscious of its strength in its own assembly, would always submit to the supervision of a body composed of second-class magistrates selected by the hazard of the lot, whose prestige and considerable powers were generally directed to the retarding of its growth and development. The attack, which was at last formally made upon the ancient council, was headed by Ephialtes, the leader of the democratical party at this time, and delivered in the archonship of Conon B.C. 462. Kenyon 'Aθην. πολ. ed. 1 p. xxxviii. Pericles' advent to power is to be dated a year or two later. As to Themistocles' share in the attack, see on *Them*. c. 10, 3, Busolt in Müller's *Handb.* IV 1, 1 p. 167 note 4, Sandys on 'Aθ. πολ. c. 25, 3.

29. **ἄρχων** *i.e.* the president of the college of the nine archons or θεσμοθέται, who in later times bore the title of ἐπώνυμος, not because he was ἐπώνυμος τοῦ ἐνιαυτοῦ, but because for reasons arising from his official position his name stood at the head of several official lists as ἐπώνυμος τῶν ἡλικιῶν, τῶν λήξεων. Gilbert *Gr. St.*² 1 279 note 4.

Aristotle 'Aθην. πολ. c. 3, 2 gives a different order of precedence in the original institution from that usually accepted : μέγισται δὲ καὶ πρῶται τῶν ἀρχῶν ἦσαν βασ< ιλεὺς καὶ > πολέμαρχος καὶ ἄρχων, τούτων δὲ πρώτη μὲν ἡ τοῦ βασιλέως, αὕτη γὰρ ἐξ ἀρχῆς ἦν, δευτέρα δ' ἐπικατέστη < ἡ πολε >μαρχία.... τελευταία δ' ἡ < τοῦ ἄρχον >τος, and § 3 νεωστὶ γέγονεν ἡ ἀρχὴ μεγάλη τοῖς ἐπιθέτοις αὐξηθεῖσα. After the death of Codrus, a change was introduced into the Athenian constitution in virtue of which the Polemarch or 'commander-in-chief' and the Archon or 'chief civil magistrate' were associated with the titular King for life, as a check upon his autocracy. When kingly rule was abolished and the decennial system established, the ἄρχων was promoted to the titular headship of the state, the second position being reserved for the βασιλεύς, who retained the religious functions only of the king like the Roman *rex sacrificulus*, the third for the polemarch, who became a purely civil officer, and amongst other duties exercised a general superintendence over resident aliens (μέτοικοι). The six remaining archons came into existence only after the change from the decennial into the annual system B.C. 682, Aristot. *l. c.* c. 3, 4 θεσμοθέται δὲ πολλοῖς ὕστερον ἔτεσιν ᾑρέθησαν, ἤδη κατ' ἐνιαυτὸν αἱρ< ουμένων > τὰς ἀρχάς, ὅπως ἀναγράψαντες τὰ θέσμια φυλάττωσι πρὸς τὴν τῶν < παρανομού >ντων κρίσιν · διὸ καὶ μόνη τῶν ἀρχῶν οὐκ ἐγένετο πλείων [ἢ] ἐνιαύσιος.

διὰ τὸ μὴ ... λαχεῖν, 'because he had not been appointed by lot.'

The statement of the reason why Per. was not a Member of the Council of Areopagus is doubtless Plutarch's own, not borrowed. Aristotle and Theopompus would not have considered such an addition necessary for their readers. H. Sauppe *die Quellen Pl.* p. 18.

31. **κληρωταί**, in contra-distinction to χειροτονηταί, αἱρεταί. Kenyon ('Aθην. πολ. pp. 59 ff. ed. 1) remarks that 'we have the following stages in the history of the method of selection to this office : (1) prior to Dracon, the archons were nominated by the Areopagus ; (2) under the Draconian constitution, they were elected by the ecclesia ; (3) under the Solonian constitution, so far as it was not disturbed by internal troubles and

revolutions, they were chosen by lot from forty candidates selected by the four tribes; (4) under the constitution of Cleisthenes they were elected by the people in the ecclesia directly; (5) after B.C. 487 they were appointed by lot from one hundred candidates selected by the ten tribes; (6) at some later period the process of the lot was adopted also in the preliminary selection by the tribes.' The nine tribes, from whom the nine archons were chosen, were selected by lot; the tenth was compensated by having the election of the secretary (γραμματεύς) to the θεσμοθέται. This we learn from Aristotle *l. c. c.* 55, 1 < τὸν > δὶ κληροῦσιν θεσμοθέτας μὲν ἐξ καὶ γραμματέα τούτοις, ὅτι δ' ἄρχοντα καὶ βασιλέα καὶ πολέμαρχον, κατὰ μέρος ἐξ ἑκάστης < τῆς > φυλῆς.

32. **δι' αὐτῶν,** 'through them' *sc.* τῶν ἀρχῶν.   **οἱ δοκιμασθέντες**: the δοκιμασία properly preceded the entrance on office: Plutarch seems here to identify it with the εὔθυνα which the archons underwent on resigning their office.   **ἀνέβαινον,** 'went up,' 'were promoted.' (p. Aristot. Ἀθ. πολ. c. 60, 3 οὐκ ἔστι τῷ ἄρχοντι ἀναβῆναι πρότερον εἰς <Ἄρε>ιον πάγον πρὶν ἂν ἅπαν (τὸ ἔλαιον) παραδῷ τοῖς ταμίαις, [Dem.] *c. Neaer.* § 80 ἐγένετο τὰ ἱερὰ ταῦτα καὶ ἀνέβησαν εἰς Ἄρειον πάγον οἱ ἐννέα ἄρχοντες ταῖς καθηκούσαις ἡμέραις, Hyperid. *fr.* 141 ed. Bl. τοὺς Ἀρεοπαγίτας φησὶν ἀριστήσαντά τινα κωλῦσαι ἀνιέναι εἰς Ἄρειον πάγον.

§ 4 l. 33. **διό** refers to ἧς αὐτὸς οὐ μετεῖχε διὰ τὸ ... λαχεῖν.
μᾶλλον is to be taken with **κατεστασίασε,** 'he overpowered in party strife'—a word which savours of Theopompus, like καταδημαγωγούμενος (l. 22): see *Them.* c. 5, 4 with my note *ad l.*
ἰσχύσας, 'now that he had become powerful,' c. 7, 5.

34. **τὴν μέν,** 'the Areopagus on the one hand.'

35. **δι' Ἐφιάλτου**: c. 10, 6, *Mor.* 812 D quoted c. 7 § 6 l. 49.

36. **φιλολάκωνα,** c. 7, 3, *Cim.* c. 16. Cimon was always the staunch friend of Sparta. He wished to see the two great city-states of Greece drawing together in harmony, at peace at home and united in making war on Persia. The termination of his Lacedaemonian policy in the jealous and insulting dismissal of their Athenian auxiliaries by the Spartans at the siege of Ithome and the breach which followed between the two city-states was a serious blow to his popularity.

37. **ἐξοστρακισθῆναι,** *ostracismo ciectum esse.* This happened B.C. 459.

38. **γένει**: his father was the great Miltiades, his mother Hegesipyle, a Thracian princess.   **νίκας,** especially that on the river Eurymedon (Pamphylia) in B.C. 468/7, when he defeated the Persians by land and sea; *Cim.* cc. 12, 13 (after Callisthenes), Thuc. I c. 100, 1.

41. **ἐν τοῖς περὶ ἐκείνου,** 'in the (records) concerning him.' Cp. c. 22, 3; *Them.* c. 25, 1 ἐν τοῖς περὶ βασιλείας.

CHAPTER X

§ 1 l. 2. **νόμῳ** with ὡρισμένην, from which it is separated to avoid the hiatus in νόμῳ εἶχε. **τοῖς φεύγουσιν**, 'the exiles' (c. 22, 3). The proper technical term for those who underwent a temporary removal by ostracism would be τοῖς μεθεστῶσιν, *Them.* c. 11, 1, *Arist.* c. 8, 1 ; φεύγειν is generally applied to persons banished for life or a long period. **ἐν τῷ διὰ μέσου** sc. χρόνῳ, 'in the interval' between his removal and the expiration of the period fixed by law for its duration. The invasion took place B.C. 457.

6. **ἐλθών** for ἐπανελθών, *reversus*, as often; cp. *Pomp.* c. 47, 1 τότε δὲ Καῖσαρ ἐλθὼν ἀπὸ στρατείας ἥψατο πολιτεύματος, Dion. Hal. *A. R.* VIII 57, 3 εἰ μὲν εὖ πράξας ὁ Μάρκιος εἰς Οὐολούσκους ἔλθοι. **ἐκ τῆς φυγῆς**, from the place where he was living in exile.

7. **ἔθετο ... εἰς λόχον τὰ ὅπλα**, 'took up his arms to join a company.' The λόχος, which was a division of the τάξις, appears to have been formed of soldiers of one or more demes, according to the importance of the contingents furnished by them. Cp. *Cim.* c. 17, 5 οἱ δὲ λαβόντες αὐτοῦ τὴν πανοπλίαν εἰς τὸν λόχον ἔθεντο. For the meaning of the phrase θέσθαι τὰ ὅπλα, see my n. to Thuc. VII 3, 1. **τῶν φυλετῶν**, 'his fellow-tribesmen,' members of the phylê Oeneis. Cp. *Cim.* c. 17, 3 Κίμων μετὰ τῶν ὅπλων ἧκεν εἰς τὴν αὐτοῦ φυλὴν τὴν Οἰνηΐδα πρόθυμος ὢν ἀμύνεσθαι τὴν αἰτίαν πρὸς τοὺς πολίτας. The Athenian hoplites were divided into ten τάξεις according to their respective φυλαί and those who fell in battle were buried κατὰ φυλάς (Thuc. II 34, 3).

8. **δι' ἔργων**, as opp. to λόγων, is explained by συγκινδυνεύσας. **ἀπολύεσθαι τὸν λακωνισμόν**, 'to clear himself of the aspersion of laconism.'

Cp. *Cim.* c. 17, 4 δεηθεὶς τῶν ἑταίρων ὅσοι μάλιστα τὴν τοῦ λακωνίζειν αἰτίαν ἔσχον ἐρρωμένως ἀγωνίσασθαι πρὸς τοὺς πολεμίους καὶ δι' ἔργων ἀπολύσασθαι τὴν αἰτίαν πρὸς τοὺς πολίτας, *Arist.* c. 13, 3 ἀπολύσασθαι τὰς αἰτίας, *Lys.* c. 28, 6 σπουδάζοντες ἀπολύσασθαι τοῖς πολίταις τὴν αἰτίαν τοῦ λακωνίζειν, Thuc. v 75, 3 τήν ... ἐπιφερομένην αἰτίαν ... ἐπὶ ἔργῳ τούτῳ ἀπελύσαντο, VIII 87, 1 βουλόμενος ... ἀπολύεσθαι πρὸς αὐτοὺς τὰς διαβολάς, Dem. *de Cor.* § 4 ἀπολύσασθαι τὰ κατηγορημένα.

10. **οἱ φίλοι τοῦ Περικλέους**: according to Plutarch *Cim.* c. 17, 4, it was the Council of 500 who forbade him, being led by his enemies to suspect him of wishing συνταράξαι τὴν φάλαγγα καὶ τῇ πόλει Λακεδαιμονίους ἐπαγαγεῖν. Plut. must have found this statement in his authority for that *Life*; but it is less probable, because there was hardly time for a resolution of the senate to be passed. That there was ground for suspicion,

because of an oligarchic conspiracy to overthrow the democratic constitution, appears from Thuc. I 107, 3, ἄνδρες τῶν Ἀθηναίων ἐπῆγον αὐτοὺς κρύφα, ἐλπίσαντες δῆμόν τε καταλύσειν καὶ τὰ μακρὰ τείχη οἰκοδομούμενα. It was a knowledge of this which impelled Pericles and his friends to oppose Cimon's wish to take part in the battle since he suspected him of being concerned in the conspiracy.

11. συστάντες, 'combining,' 'leagued.' *Demosth.* c. 17, 3.

§ 2 l. 12. διὸ καὶ δοκεῖ, 'this is considered to be the reason why'; *i.e.* he redoubled his exertions during the battle in order to be on a level with Cimon in personal courage and to prove that his adversary's presence was superfluous. There is not a word about this in the *Life of Cimon*.

15. τοῦ σώματος, 'his life.' *Mor.* 137 e ἀφειδεῖν καὶ ἀμελεῖν τοῦ σώματος.

16. πάντες ὁμαλῶς, 'all alike'; c. 6, 2; c. 39, 3, *Sol.* c. 16, 3 οὐ τὰ μὲν τὰ δ᾽ οὐχί, πάντα δ᾽ ὁμαλῶς ἐπιτρέψαντες. Cp. *Cim.* c. 17, 5 οἱ δὲ (ἑταῖροι) μετ᾽ ἀλλήλων συστάντες ἐκθύμως ἑκατὸν ὄντες ἔπεσον, πολὺν αὐτῶν πόθον καὶ μεταμέλειαν ἐφ᾽ οἷς ᾐτιάθησαν ἀδίκως ἀπολιπόντες τοῖς Ἀθηναίοις. The victory rested with the Spartans in this battle, which was fought in the valley of Asopus, below Tanagra (Boeotia). It was the first occasion on which Sparta and Athens measured themselves in open conflict.

19. ἔσχε, 'seized on,' often thus used with substantives denoting emotion or passion: see note to c. 20, 3.

ἡττημένους μὲν ... προσδοκῶντας δέ, the simultaneous concurrence of two things is more often indicated by τε—καί. See *Them.* c. 12, 1.

21. εἰς ἔτους ὥραν, 'for the (next) summer,' lit. 'fine time of the year' or season for military operations. Cp. *Tim.* c. 22, 5 ὡς ἔτους ὥρᾳ διαβησομένους, *Mar.* c. 11, 3, *Dion* c. 16, 3, Thuc. II 52, 2.

As to the expectation of a Spartan invasion of Attica, cp. *Cim.* c. 17, 5 οὐδὲ τῷ πρὸς Κίμωνα θυμῷ πολὺν χρόνον ἐνέμειναν, τὰ μὲν, ὡς εἰκός, ὧν ἔπαθον εὖ μεμνημένοι, τὰ δὲ τοῦ καιροῦ συλλαμβανομένου· νενικημένοι γὰρ ἐν Τανάγρᾳ μάχῃ μεγάλῃ καὶ προσδοκῶντες εἰς ὥραν ἔτους στρατιὰν Πελοποννησίων ἐπ᾽ αὐτοὺς ἐκάλουν ἐκ τῆς φυγῆς τὸν Κίμωνα καὶ κατῆλθε τὸ ψήφισμα γράψαντος αὐτῷ Περικλέους. οὕτω τότε πολιτικαὶ μὲν ἦσαν αἱ διαφοραί, μέτριοι δὲ οἱ θυμοί καὶ πρὸς τὸ κοινὸν εὐανάκλητοι συμφέρον, ἡ δὲ φιλοτιμία πάντων ἐπικρατοῦσα τῶν παθῶν τοῖς τῆς πατρίδος ὑπεχώρει καιροῖς. In reality the Spartans gained nothing by their victory beyond the power of making their way home through the passes of Geraneia; and two months later B.C. 456/5, the battle of Oenophyta ended in a decisive victory for the Athenians under Myronides. The Boeotians became the subject allies of the Athenians who set up democracies everywhere, and in B.C. 450/49 a five years' truce was concluded between the rival states (Thuc. I 112, 1).

§ 3 l. 24. τὸ ψήφισμα γράψας, 'proposing (lit. 'drafting') the bill for his recall,' for ratification by the ἐκκλησία. τὸν ἄνδρα, *i.e.* τὸν Κίμωνα, c. 4, 1 ; c. 15, 5.

25. κατελθών, *reversus ab exilio.* This was in Ol. 81, 2 = B.C. 455/4. Cp. *Cim.* c. 18, 1 εὐθὺς μὲν οὖν ὁ Κίμων κατελθὼν ἔλυσε τὸν πόλεμον καὶ διήλλαξε τὰς πόλεις. Hostilities were suspended for four months only : a new truce was concluded in B.C. 451.

26. οἰκείως εἶχον . . . πρὸς αὐτόν, 'were kindly disposed towards him.' Cp. c. 16, 3 with note *ad l.*

28. ἀπήχθοντο, imperf. from ἀπέχθεσθαι, a late form of ἀπεχθάνεσθαι. Cp. *Marc.* c. 22, 4 'Ἀφροδίτη μάλιστα θεῶν ἀπέχθεται βίᾳ καὶ πολέμοις, Dionys. Hal. *A. R.* VIII c. 29, 2 τοῖς ἄλλοις Ῥωμαίοις ἀπέχθομαί τ' ὡς δύναμαι μάλιστα καὶ οὐδέποτε μισῶν αὐτοὺς παύσομαι.

29. δημαγωγοῖς, 'democratic statesmen.'

§ 4 l. 29. ἔνιοι : doubtless Stesimbrotus of Chios, a contemporary writer, is meant, to whom the anecdote told in § 5 is assigned in *Cim.* c. 14, 4.

30. οὐ πρότερον γραφῆναι . . . τὴν κάθοδον . . . ἤ, 'that the bill for his restoration was not drafted before that . . .'

Note that the negative is not drawn to φασί but goes with γραφῆναι. This is usually the case where οὐ is closely connected with another thought, as here. Cp. *Num.* c. 14, 2 φασὶ τοὺς Πυθαγορικοὺς οὐκ ἐᾶν, *Lyc.* c. 20, 2 ἃ ἔφην οὐκ ἀμοιρεῖν χάριτος, *Arist.* c. 10, 8 οὐ κατὰ καιρὸν ἔφη παίζειν αὐτούς, c. 15, 4 ὁ δὲ οὐ καλῶς ἔφη ἔχειν ταῦτα ἀποκρύψασθαι, *Flam.* c. 19, 2 εἴ τί φησι τῶν εἰρημένων μὴ ἀληθὲς εἶναι, *Mar.* c. 11, 5, *Nic.* c. 18, 4 φησὶν ἐν μηδενὶ λόγῳ ποιεῖσθαι, *Alex.* c. 65, 2 ; c. 69, 1, *Caes.* c. 47, 2, *Pomp.* c. 8, 4 ; c. 67, 2, *Ag.* c. 15, 2 οὐκ ἐθέλειν μάχεσθαί φησι, *Brut.* c. 12, 3, *Artax.* c. 4, 1. Stegmann p. 5 says that there are 69 instances of οὐ φάναι and 39 of φάναι οὐ with the infin. in the *Lives.*

33. ὥστε introduces the terms of the compact (συνθήκας).

34. λαβόντα, 'with.' G. *MT.*² § 844.

35. τῶν ἔξω, 'those on foreign service.' καταστρεφόμενον, 'with a design to reduce'; c. 7, 3.

36. βασιλέως, c. 3, 1.

38. ὑπάρχειν, 'should be ceded.'

§ 5 l. 40. παρασχεῖν, *fecisse, reddidisse,* as *Them.* c. 7, 2.

τὴν θανατικὴν δίκην ἔφευγεν, 'was indicted on the (well-known) capital charge,' a classical expression. The converse of φεύγειν (c. 32, 1) in this sense is διώκειν 'to prosecute' (l. 64); αἱρεῖν is 'to convict,' 'get a conviction'; ἁλῶναι, 'to be convicted and condemned'; ἀποφεύγειν, 'to be acquitted' (*Cim.* c. 15, 1, Arist. *Vesp.* 579, *Nub.* 167).

The charge brought against Cimon was that he had failed in his duty after the subjugation of Thasos, when he might have acquired a portion of

Macedonia for Athens, had he not been bribed by Alexander, king of the country, to forego the opportunity, *Cim.* c. 14, 2 ἐκεῖθεν (from Thasos) ῥᾳδίως ἐπιβῆναι Μακεδονίας καὶ πολλὴν ἀποτεμέσθαι παρασχόν, ὡς ἐδόκει, μὴ θελήσας αἰτίαν ἔσχε δώροις ὑπὸ τοῦ βασιλέως Ἀλεξάνδρου συμπεπεῖσθαι καὶ δίκην ἔφυγε τῶν ἐχθρῶν συστάντων ἐπ' αὐτόν.

41. ἦν εἷς τῶν κατηγόρων προβεβλημένος, 'he had been chosen one of the (ten) state prosecutors' (συνήγοροι, Schoemann *de Com. Ath.* pp. 111–113). Cp. Aristot. 'Aθ. πολ. c. 27, 1 Περικλέους πρῶτον εὐδοκιμήσαντος, ὅτε κατηγόρησε τὰς εὐθύνας Κίμωνος στρατηγοῦντος νέος ὤν. This was in the spring of B.C. 461. The subject of εὔθυνα στρατηγῶν has been handled by Wilamowitz-Möllendorff in his recent publication *Aristoteles und Athen* II pp. 213–51. See n. on c. 32, 2.

For προβάλλειν (or προβάλλεσθαι) 'to nominate, propose, as a candidate for election,' cp. *Demosth.* c. 14, 3 τῶν Ἀθηναίων ἐπί τινα προβαλλομένων αὐτὸν κατηγορίαν, *Timol.* c. 3, 1. Here it means 'to choose after nomination.' The number of advocates in cases of charges of high treason (εἰσαγγελία) was limited to ten. Thus we find ten κατήγοροι chosen by the people to bring Demosthenes and others to trial for receiving bribes from Harpalus (Dinarch. c. *Dem.* § 51), and the στρατηγοί were empowered to choose from the council συνηγόρους μέχρι δέκα, to assist in the prosecution of Antiphon and others for προδοσία ([Plut.] *vit. decem or.* 833, 25).

45. γραῦς εἶ, γραῦς, ὥς . . . διαπράσσεσθαι, 'you are full old to undertake such weighty matters.' G. *MT.*² § 588.

Cp. Plato *Prot.* 314 B νέοι ὥστε τοσοῦτον πρᾶγμα διελέσθαι, 'full young to explain so great a matter,' Xen. *Mem.* III 13, 3 ψυχρῶν (ἐστι τὸ ὕδωρ) ὥστε λούσασθαι, *Cyr.* IV V 15 ὀλίγοι ἐσμὲν ὥστε ἐγκρατεῖς εἶναι αὐτῶν, Eur. *Andr.* 80 γέρων ὥστε σ' ὠφελεῖν παρών, Antiph. *or.* 5, 79 γέρων ἐκεῖνος ὥστ' ἐμοὶ βοηθεῖν, Thuc. I 50, οἱ δείσαντες μὴ αἱ σφέτεραι δέκα νῆες ὀλίγαι ἀμύνειν ὦσι, where Shilleto rightly observes that the expression is not precisely our 'too few to aid,' which would be ἐλάσσονες ἢ ὥστε ἀμύνειν. The latter expresses disbelief, the former (merely) misgiving. 'He is a young man for the office' is not the same as 'he is too young a man for the office.'

46. οὐ μὴν ἀλλά, 'however'; an elliptical expression (c. 8, 4) generally at the beginning of a sentence, especially in passing on to a new thought, the verb belonging to οὐ μήν being understood from the preceding sentence or implied in the general connexion. This is inferred from the passages where there is no ellipsis of the verb, as c. 25, 2, *C. Gr.* c. 12, 1 βοηθήσειν ἐπαγγελλόμενος, οὐ μὴν ἐβοήθησεν, ἀλλὰ παρῆλθε, *Ag.* c. 18, 1 μένειν ἐδεῖτο . . . οὐ μὴν ἔπεισεν, ἀλλὰ κτλ. For other exx., see *Rom.* c. 27, 2, *Lys.* c. 31, 1, *Num.* c. 3, 7, *Sol.* c. 15, 1, *Fab.* c. 22, 3, *Cam.* c. 37, 1, *Tim.* c. 34, 4, *Pelop.* c. 1, 2, *Flam.* c. 1, 1, *Sall.* c. 14, 2, etc.

47. ἅπαξ ἀνέστη, 'rose (but) once to speak.' τὴν προβολὴν ἀφοσιούμενος, 'by way of formally satisfying his appointment,' 'to acquit himself of his commission,' as a public κατήγορος, lit. 'to do the least possible consistently with keeping ὅσιος.' See more on this verb in my n. on *Timol.* c. 39, 2.

Cp. *Cim.* c. 14, 4 μνησθεὶς δὲ τῆς κρίσεως ἐκείνης ὁ Στησίμβροτός φησι τὴν Ἐλπινίκην ὑπὲρ τοῦ Κίμωνος δεομένην ἐλθεῖν ἐπὶ τὰς θύρας τοῦ Περικλέους (οὗτος γὰρ ἦν τῶν κατηγόρων ὁ σφοδρότατος), τὸν δὲ μειδιάσαντα "Γραῦς εἶ" φάναι "γραῦς, ὦ Ἐλπινίκη, ὡς τηλικαῦτα διαπράττεσθαι πράγματα·" πλὴν ἔν γε τῇ δίκῃ πραότατόν (φησι) γενέσθαι τῷ Κίμωνι καὶ πρὸς τὴν κατηγορίαν ἅπαξ ἀναστῆναι μόνον, ὥσπερ ἀφοσιούμενον.

49. **ἐλάχιστα ... λυπήσας**, 'after doing him the least harm of any of his accusers.' Yet Cimon was fined fifty talents and narrowly escaped a capital sentence, having only a majority of three votes in his favour.

§ 6 l. 50. **οὖν**: if he behaved so mildly to a political adversary. **Ἰδομενεῖ**: c. 35, 4. See *Introduction*.

53. **κοινωνὸν ὄντα τῆς ἐν τῇ πολιτείᾳ προαιρέσεως**, 'when he was a partner in the position he had deliberately taken up in public life,' in other words, 'a member of his political party.' Cp. c. 11, 3; Dem. *de f. l.* § 27 τὴν προαίρεσιν αὐτοῦ τῆς πολιτείας ἀναμνησθέντες.

56. **οὐκ οἶδ' ὁπόθεν**, parenthetical, *nescio unde*, '(raking up) from some unknown source or other'; ταῦτα is object to προσβέβληκε, cp. *Mor.* 859 A τηλικοῦτο δὲ Ἑλληνίδι πόλει προσβαλεῖν ὄνειδος.

57. **τἀνδρί**, c. 10, 3.

58. **οὐκ ἀνεπιλήπτῳ**, 'not irreproachable.'

60. **οἷς**, sc. φρονήματι εὐγενεῖ καὶ ψυχῇ φιλοτίμῳ.

§ 7 l. 62. μὲν οὖν, c. 6, 4.   **φοβερόν**, c. 19, 4.

63. **τὰς εὐθύνας** κτλ. There was at Athens a γραφὴ ἀδικίου or ἐάν τις τὸν τῶν Ἀθηναίων ἀδικῇ, in cases of embezzlement of money, or any action detrimental to the public welfare. See c. 32 l. 21 with note *ad l.* Cp. Aristot. Ἀθ. π. c. 25, 1 γενόμενος τοῦ δήμου προστάτης Ἐφιάλτης ὁ Σοφωνίδου ... ἐπέθετο τῇ βουλῇ (τῶν Ἀρεοπαγιτῶν) ἀγῶνας ἐπιφέρων περὶ τῶν διῳκημένων.

66. **δι' Ἀριστοδίκου**: according to Antiphon *or.* 5 § 68, delivered c. B.C. 420, οὐδέπω νῦν εὕρηνται οἱ ἀποκτείναντες, and so Diodorus XI 77, 6 τῆς νυκτὸς ἀναιρεθεὶς ἄδηλον ἔσχε τὴν τοῦ βίου τελευτήν. Whoever his assassin was, he must have been a tool in the hands of the conservative party, who, deprived of the constitutional means which the Areopagus had secured to it, began to open a countermine upon the democracy by means of secret intrigues and shunned no way of furthering its design.

67. **Ἀριστοτέλης**: in Ἀθην. πολ. c. 25, 4 ἀνῃρέθη δὲ καὶ ὁ Ἐφιάλτης δολοφονηθεὶς μετ' οὐ πολὺν χρόνον δι' Ἀριστοδίκου τοῦ Ταναγραίου.

68. **ἐτελεύτησε**, Ol. 82, 4 = B.C. 449/8, aet. 51, at the siege of

Citium, a town on the south coast of Cyprus, birth-place of the Stoic philosopher Zeno, then governed by a Phoenician prince. According to most authorities, including Theopompus (Nepos *Cim*. c. 3) and Ephorus (Diodor. XII 4, 6) he fell sick and died. Other authorities attribute his death to a wound which he received πρὸς τοὺς βαρβάρους ἀγωνιζόμενος (*Cim*. c. 19, 1).

Cimon's death marks an epoch in the history of Athens. He was the last of the great generals who thought it the mission of Hellas to be at war with Persia. With him closed the generation of the heroes of Marathon. For the next fifty years Greece is occupied with the duel between Athens and Sparta (*E. Abbott*).

CHAPTER XI

§ 1 l. 1. ἤδη ... καὶ πρόσθεν, *i.e.* before their leader Cimon's death. Join μέγιστον τῶν πολιτῶν.

4. ὅμως: although they could not expect to meet with any one who would be wholly a match for Pericles, 'nevertheless' ... τὸν ἀντιτασσόμενον: G. *MT.*² § 825.

6. ὥστε μὴ κομιδῇ μοναρχίαν εἶναι, 'so that it (τὴν δύναμιν) might not be a downright monarchy,' or 'there might be absolutely no monarchy, none at all,' according as κομιδῇ is taken with μοναρχίαν or εἶναι. Cp. c. 39, 5.

7. On Thucydides, son of Melesias, of Alopece (c. 9, 2), a deme in the phylê Antiochis, see c. 8, 4.

8. κηδεστήν, *i.q.* γαμβρόν, *affinem*, 'a connexion by marriage' (κῆδος), probably 'son-in-law,' according to Schol. Aristid. III p. 116 ed. Dind., as in Antipho *or*. 6, 12: though the word might also mean 'brother-in-law' or 'father-in-law.'

9. ἐναντιωσόμενον: G. *MT.*² § 840.

§ 2 l. 10. ἀγοραῖος, (not in its usual contemptuous connotation but) 'versed in forensic business,' as *Mor*. 532 A δίκην ἔχοντες πολλάκις οὐκ ἴσμεν εἰπεῖν τὸν ὠφέλιμον καὶ ἀγοραῖον.

11. πολιτικός, *civitati utilis*. The word has several other meanings: —I (1) 'relating to citizens' generally; (2) *civilis, civis decens*, 'befitting a citizen,' 'civic,' 'civil'; (3) 'consisting of citizens'; (4) 'living in a community' II *civitatis administrandae peritus*, 'statesman-like,' or, 'a statesman,' as c. 24, 1, 3 III *publicus*, 'belonging to the state or its administration' as c. 1, 1; c. 7, 1 τῶν πολιτικῶν οὐδὲν ἔπραττεν —IV 'having relation to public life,' 'political.'

οἰκουρῶν, 'staying at home' instead of going out to serve in war; c. 12, 3, c. 31, 1, Hermippus Μοῖραι fr. 45 (Mein. II 399, Kock I 236) τοὺς μὲν ἄρ' ἄλλους οἰκουρεῖν χρῆν, πέμπειν δὲ Νόθιππον ἔν' ὄντα. ἐν ἄστει: c. 5, 2 note.

12. συμπλεκόμενος, 'engaging with,' an expression originally borrowed from the ring, hence applied to any kind of combatants: Sull. c. 15, 1, Luc. c. 3, 3, Aesch. de f. l. § 153 συμπέπλεγμαι δ' ἐν τῇ πολιτείᾳ καθ' ὑπερβολὴν ἀνθρώπῳ γόητι καὶ πονηρῷ, Arist. Ach. 704 συμπλακέντα τῇ Σκυθῶν ἐρημίᾳ (i.e. Cephisodemo), Lucian Conv. c. 30 ἐβούλετο γὰρ συμπλακῆναι τοῖς Στωϊκοῖς. τὴν π. εἰς ἀντίπαλον κατέστησεν, 'brought the government to an equilibrium,' i.e. produced a balance of power between the parties who were contending for the government. Cp. Thuc. VII c. 13, 2 ἐπειδὴ εἰς ἀντίπαλα καθεστήκαμεν.

14. τοὺς καλοὺς κἀγαθοὺς καλουμένους ἄνδρας, 'the honourable and respectable citizens, as they are designated' i.e. the aristocratical party, c. 7, 2 ; c. 8, 3.

15. ἐνδιεσπάρθαι, sc. τῷ δήμῳ, 'should remain scattered up and down' among the mass of citizens (c. 7, 2) in the ecclesia. For this use of ἐν in composition see Cope on Aristot. Rhet. II 4, 12. Cp. Num. c. 17, 1 τὴν μεγάλην διαφορὰν ἀφανίσαι τοῖς ἐλάσσοσιν ἐνδιασπαρεῖσαν, Mor. 417 B, 720 F πολὺ κενὸν ἐνδιέσπαρται καὶ μέμικται τοῖς τοῦ ἀέρος ἀτόμοις, 762 A λεπταί τινες ἀπορροαί ... τῆς ἀληθείας ἔνεισι ταῖς Αἰγυπτίων ἐνδιεσπαρμέναι μυθολογίαις, 99 C ἀποτρίμματα φρονήσεως ἐνδιεσπαρμένα ταῖς χρείαις ταῖς περὶ τὸν βίον. Aristotle uses the word once fr. 209, p. 1516ᵃ 15 τῇ θαλάττῃ τὸ τραχὺ καὶ γεῶδες ἐνδιέσπαρται.

This consolidation of his party into a single compact body as a kind of côté droit was the first political move of Thucydides. The ἑταιρεῖαι, which he founded, were originally intended for mutual support in elections and lawsuits, but became subsequently mere political clubs, whose object was to overthrow the democracy. See Dict. Ant. I 759ᵇ ed. 3. Grote compares the Speech of Nicias in reference to the younger citizens and partisans of Alcibiades sitting together near the latter in the assembly— οὓς ἐγὼ ὁρῶν νῦν ἐνθάδε τῷ αὐτῷ ἀνδρὶ παρακελευστοὺς καθημένους φοβοῦμαι καὶ τοῖς πρεσβυτέροις ἀντιπαρακελεύομαι μὴ καταισχυνθῆναι εἴ τῳ τις παρακάθηται τῶνδε (Thuc. VI 13, 1). He refers also to Arist. Eccl. 298 f. about partisans sitting close together.

17. πλήθους, '(the preponderance of) numbers' of the οἱ πολλοί, among whom they were isolated.

18. συναγαγών, sc. τοὺς καλοὺς κἀγαθοὺς ἄνδρας. εἰς ταὐτό, in unum.

19. ἐμβριθῆ, 'weighty,' a word suitable to the metaphor which follows. See n. to c. 4, 4.

20. ὥσπερ ἐπὶ ζυγοῦ ῥοπὴν ἐποίησεν, 'he produced, caused a counterpoise as it were.' Cp. Mor. 21 D οὐ χεῖρόν ἐστιν ἑτέρων ἐνδόξων ἀποφάσεις ἀντιτάττοντας ὥσπερ ἐπὶ ζυγοῦ ῥέπειν πρὸς τὸ βέλτιον, Arist. c. 5, 2 γνώμῃ τῇ Μιλτιάδου προσθέμενος οὐ μικρὰν ἐποίησε ῥοπήν, Cleom. c. 13, 1, Dion c. 33, 2, Phoc. c. 14, 3.

§ 3 l. 21. **διπλόη τις**, 'a sort of flaw or seam, as it might be in a piece of iron.' Cp. *Mor.* 441 D, 802 B διπλόας ἐν σιδήρῳ μαλάσσων καὶ καταλεαίνων, 715 F τὸ ὕπουλον, ὥσπερ τινας διπλόας, ἀναπτύσσει τῆς ψυχῆς.

22. **ὕπουλος** (ὑπό, οὐλή) properly said of a wound only skinned over, 'festering under the scar,' came to mean generally 'unsound beneath,' and was applied to any kind of latent blemish.

24. **προαιρέσεως**, 'political principles'; see n. to c. 10, 6. Cp. *Aem. Paul.* c. 38, 2 σπουδαζόμενον ὑπὸ τοῦ δήμου ἐπὶ τῆς ἀριστοκρατικῆς μεῖναι προαιρέσεως.

27. **τὸ μὲν — τὸ δέ**, 'the one section — the other section,' neuter, in collective sense, to be taken with τῆς πόλεως: cp. Thuc. VII 43, 7 with my n. *ad l.*

§ 4 l. 28. **διὸ καί**, because of the increased strength of the opposite party. **τῷ δήμῳ τὰς ἡνίας ἀνείς**, 'giving rein to the people': for the metaphor, cp. c. 7, 6; c. 15, 3.

29. **ἐπολιτεύετο πρὸς χάριν κτλ.**, 'shaped his administration with a view to their gratification (*Them.* c. 3, 2) by always providing at home some public pageant or feast or procession and thus entertaining the city with elegant pleasures, and by sending out every year sixty triremes, in which many of the citizen-seamen served for eight months on full pay, being thus kept in practice, at the same time that they acquired the (proper) nautical skill.'

32. **διαπαιδαγωγῶν**, 'entertaining,' 'amusing,' a favourite word with Plut. *Anton.* c. 29, 1 ἡ δὲ Κλεοπάτρα ἀεί τινα καινὴν ἡδονὴν ἐπιφέρουσα καὶ χάριν διεπαιδαγώγει τὸν Ἀντώνιον, *Crass.* c. 22, 6 οὕτω μὲν ὁ βάρβαρος διεπαιδαγώγησε τοὺς Ῥωμαίους, *Sertor.* c. 16, 4 τοιαῦτα πλέκων παραμύθια τοῖς βαρβάροις διεπαιδαγώγει (*follebat*) τὸν καιρόν, *Pelop.* c. 10, 2 εἰς ἄκρατον πολὺν κατέβαλεν (αὐτὸν) καὶ ταῖς περὶ τῶν γυναικῶν ἐλπίσι διεπαιδαγώγει τὸν πότον, *Mor.* 614 B αἷς (διηγήσεσι) ἤν τις ἀνυπόπτως χρώμενος διαπαιδαγωγῇ τοὺς πίνοντας, 586 F τοιαύτης τὸν πότον ἐλπίδος διαπαιδαγωγησάσης. Plut. uses the verb also in the sense of 'guiding,' 'disciplining,' as *Cic.* c. 8, 3 τοῦτον τὸν τρόπον διαπαιδαγωγῶν τὴν ἕξιν ἄνοσον συνεῖχεν. In this sense Plato uses it once *Timae.* 89 D διαπαιδαγωγῶν καὶ διαπαιδαγωγούμενος ὑφ' αὑτοῦ μάλιστ' ἂν κατὰ λόγον ζῴη. HSauppe supposes that διαπαιδαγωγῶν ... ἡδοναῖς, which scans as an iambic trimeter, is a verse taken from Euripides or from some comic poet.

33. **ἀμούσοις**: cp. Plat. *Phaedr.* 240 B ἡδονήν τινα οὐκ ἄμουσον.

35. **ἔπλεον**, 'served on board as oarsmen.' **ὀκτὼ μῆνας**, during the time of the year proper for navigating.

36. **ἔμμισθοι**: ever since the institution of the naval confederacy and the beginning of great naval operations, the

Athenian burghers had received an allowance for provisions (σιτηρέσιον Dem. *or.* 4, 4) for their service as hoplites or in the fleet (cp. Plut. *Cim.* c. 10, 1 ἐφόδια τῆς στρατιᾶς, c. 9, 4 τεσσάρων μηνῶν τροφὰς εἰς τὰς ναῦς); but they did not receive pay until the time of Pericles. Cp. Aristot. 'Αθην. πολ. c. 27, 2, Thuc. VI 31, 3, VIII c. 29, 1; c. 45, 2, Xen. *Hell.* I v 5; Busolt II 569. ἅμα καί, a further object besides that of providing for them.

§ 5 l. 38. **εἰς Χερρόνησον**: the Thracian Chersonese (mod. *peninsula of the Dardanelles* or *Gallipoli*) extending in a south-westerly direction into the Aegean, between the Hellespont and the bay of Melas, was colonised by one of Cimon's ancestors, Miltiades II son of Cypselus. It was won from the Persians, who occupied it during the Persian war, by Cimon (*Cim.* c. 14, 1) B.C. 476/5, but it was continually exposed to the incursions of the neighbouring Thracians, as appears from c. 19, 1. Hence it was considered advisable to despatch a body of 1000 κληροῦχοι to it, which was done, according to Busolt *Gr. Gesch.* II 536 Anm. 2, B.C. 448/7=Ol. 83, 1, after which time the aggregate φόρος of the towns in it was reduced from 18 to 2½ talents.

39. **κληρούχους**, those who had obtained grants of land in a conquered country, where they might fix their residence or not, as they thought fit, but without in either case renouncing their Athenian franchise; see n. to c. 9, 1. Cp. Diodorus XI 88, 3, Gilbert *Handb. d. Gr. St.* I² pp. 502 ff.

Naxos, one of the largest and most fertile of all the Cyclades, was occupied by the Persians B.C. 490, but B.C. 470 after the Persian wars it became a subject ally of the Athenians. It revolted and lost its independence B.C. 467 (*Them.* c. 25, 1, Thuc. I 98, 4). According to Diodorus XI 88, 3 and Pausanias I 27, 6, Tolmides was the leader of the cleruchs, who were sent to occupy the island B.C. 448/7. As a compensation for the cession of their land, there was a corresponding reduction in the amount to be paid by the Naxians as φόρος, which was only 6⅔ talents, whereas the neighbouring island Paros paid more than 16 (*Busolt*).

40. Andros, the most northerly and one of the largest of the Cyclades, lay S.E. of Euboea. The φόρος of Andros had been reduced as early as 450/49 by one-half, from 12 to 6 talents, probably because the land had been surrendered some years before it was occupied by the allottees. It is probable that Lemnos and Imbros also were occupied by cleruchs about the same period. Busolt *l. c.* II p. 538. ἡμίσεις τούτων, i.e. 250.

41. **Βισάλταις**, a Thraco-Macedonian tribe which occupied the tract of land west of the Strymon, including the metalliferous mountains which lie between the valley of that river and Mygdonia. See Herod. VII 115; VIII 116; Thuc. II 99, 6; Strabo *Geogr.* VII 329 *fr.* 11, 331 *fr.* 36. The colony in Bisaltia is doubtless to be identified with that at Brea, B.C. 446/5, allusion to which is made in a fragment of Cratinus (Mein. II 196, Kock I 121), probably from the Θρᾷτται. The decree for the establishment of it has been in great part preserved, *C.I.* I 31, Hicks no. 29, and is the only inscription known relating to Greek colonisation. We learn from it that ten

Commissioners (γεωνόμοι) were chosen, one from each phyle, to divide the land among the colonists. Democleides, author of the decree, was appointed founder (οἰκιστὴς αὐτοκράτωρ). All the existing sacred buildings were to be preserved, but no new ones to be provided. The connexion with the mother-city was to be maintained by θεωρίαι and contributions to the two great Athenian festivals, Panathenaea and Dionysia. The decree contains also regulations for the sacrifices to be offered for the new colony, the erection of columns (στῆλαι) containing the public records, guarantees for the maintenance of the decrees concerning the colony, regulations about the time of the departure of the colonists, and the requisite supply of money. In a rider, carried by Phantocles, express provision is made for the colonists being taken exclusively from the third (ζευγῖται) and fourth (θῆτες) classes (ἐc Δὲ <B> ρέΑΝ ἐχθΗΤῶΝ καὶ ζε<Υ>ΓιΤῶΝ ἰέΝΑΙ ΤΟῪC Ἀπο<ί>ΚΟΥC). See note to l. 47 τὰς ἀπορίας τοῦ δήμου. If the numbers given by Plutarch and Diodorus are to be trusted, nearly 9000, if not 10,000, citizens must have left Athens between 460-410 B.C. This does not include those sent to Lemnos, Imbros, Amphipolis and Aegina. Gilbert *Headb. d. Gr. St.* 1² p. 504.

42. **εἰς Ἰταλίαν**: the name was applied by the Greeks to a part only of the Peninsula, south of the country which afterwards bore the name of Bruttium. See Thuc. VII 33, 4 with my n. *ad l.*

43. **ἀνοικιζομένης**: Fuhr quotes from *Timol.* c. 39, 3 τὰς μεγίστας τῶν ἀναστάτων πόλεων οἰκίσας, to show that there is no necessity to correct the MSS. reading οἰκιζομένης: but perhaps ἀνοικίσας may be the correct reading in that passage.

Sybaris was one of the two most famous and oldest Achaean settlements in Magna Graecia. Both it and its rival Crotona stood on the shores of the gulf named after the Dorian city of Tarentum. Its luxury and commercial prosperity, which it owed to its position between two seas and its carrying trade, became proverbial. About seventy years after its utter destruction by the Crotoniates (B.C. 510), the Sybarite refugees returned B.C. 452 and rebuilt their ruined city at a short distance from the ancient site. But their old enemies soon expelled them and levelled their newly-built walls to the ground. A few years later the exiles combined with a body of Athenian and other colonists under Lampon and Xenocritus in the foundation of the great Panhellenic settlement of Thurii B.C. 443 at a spot not far from the site of the ruined Sybaris, where there was a fountain named Thuria (Diod. Sic. XII 10).

44. **προσηγόρευσαν**, an unclassical form for προσεῖπον. See 22 Cobet *Var. L.* p. 39, *Nov. L.* p. 778.

45. **ἀποκουφίζων**, 'by way of easing, relieving,' cp. c. 9, 1.

46. **ἐπανορθούμενος**, 'by way of redressing'; cp. *Cleom.* c. 16, 4 ἀναίρεσιν πλούτου καὶ πενίας ἐπανόρθωσιν. Plutarch's statement is to a certain extent confirmed by the rider to the decree which was carried by Phantocles; see n. to l. 41. For ἀπορίας, cp. Dem. *de f. l.* § 146 εὐπορίας κτήματα πλοῦτον ἀντὶ τῶν ἐσχάτων ἀποριῶν.

47. **φόβον καὶ φρουρὰν... παρακατοικίζων τοῖς συμμάχοις**,

'by way of establishing settlements in the neighbourhood of the allies to over-awe and keep a watch on them.'

48. **τοῦ μὴ νεωτερίζειν**, not with φρουράν, as Stegmann p. 25 takes it, comparing Crass. c. 20, 2 φύλακα τοῦ μὴ κυκλωθῆναι τὸν ποταμὸν ἔχοντας, but an infinitive of purpose. This final use of the articular infin. is seen first and chiefly in Thucydides, only twice (I 5, 1, VIII 39, 4) without μή.

CHAPTER XII

§ 1 l. 2. **ἤνεγκε**, c. 18, 2.

3. **μόνον**, without any other evidence.

4. **μαρτυρεῖ**, c. 22, 1.   **μὴ ψεύδεσθαι**, 'was not misrepresented,' 'was not a mere romance.' The passive as in [Dem.] adv. Callipp. § 23 πάντα πρὸς ὑμᾶς ἐψευσται. For the use of μή after μαρτυρεῖ see G. $MT.^2$ § 685.

5. **ἐκείνην** with δύναμιν, used of remoteness in time, as c. 15, 2; Arist. Vesp. 235 ὃ δὴ λοιπόν γ' ἔτ' ἐστὶν . . . ἥβης ἐκείνης.

6. **ἡ τῶν ἀναθημάτων κατασκευή**, 'the construction of the sacred edifices,' here designated as 'votive offerings.' The entire temple of the Parthenon should be regarded as one vast ἀνάθημα to the national deity, rather than as a place for her worship. (Cp. c. 14, 1 ; Dem. or. c. Andr. § 76 τῶν ἀναθημάτων τῶν ἐπ' ἐκείνοις (τοῖς ἔργοις) σταθέντων τὸ κάλλος, προπύλαια ταῦτα, ὁ παρθενών, with Wayte's note ad l.

That ll. 10–24 contain an extract from a public speech is shown by ἡμᾶς l. 21 : the reply of Pericles follows l. 26–l. 42. See HSauppe p. 26.

11. **κακῶς ἀκούει**: c. 5, 2 ; c. 29, 3.   **τὰ κοινὰ . . . μεταγαγών**, 'for transferring the common treasure of the Hellenes from Delos to its own keeping.'

The removal of the confederate Treasury (ταμιεῖον Thuc. I 96, 2) from the sanctuary of the Delian Apollo and the old Ionian place of gathering to the temple of Athena on the Acropolis at Athens took place B.C. 452/1, twenty years after the institution of the league. It was effected on the proposal of the Samians in the interest of the Confederation (Theophrastus ap. Plut. Arist. c. 25, 2) because of the insecurity of Delos against an attack of the Persian fleet.   Justin Hist. III 6, 4 assigns a different reason : —ne deficientibus a fide sociis Lacedaemoniis praedae ac rapinae esset. The entire administration of the league and its funds was conducted at Athens, and in both ordinary and official language the Athenian empire (ἡ 'Αθηναίων ἀρχή Thuc. v c. 18, 7 ; c. 47, 2) was substituted for ἡ 'Αθηναίων συμμαχία (CIA. I 9), its original designation ; while the tributaries were called merely πόλεις (CIA. I 31, 37, 40 etc.); cp. Arist. Ach. 192, 506, 636, 643, Eq. 802, Vesp. 657, 707, Eupolis' Πόλεις. It is uncertain what became of the Synod. The city-states probably lost together with their autonomy their right of voting, so that their meetings became gradually less frequent and in course of time ceased to exist without any formal abolition. Busolt *Gr. Gesch.* ii p. 447. The lists of the different quotas of the φόροι, as fixed by the Hellenotamiai, date from this period. A new assessment was made every four years (Aristot. Ἀθ. πολ. c. 3, 5). The Quota-lists show that there was one in 450, 446 and 439 B.C.

12. **πρὸς αὐτόν** = 'Ἀθήναζε.

§ 2 l. 13. **ἔνεστιν αὐτῷ**, 'is possible for him,' Xen. *Cyr.* ii i 25 οὐκ ἐν ἦν πρόφασις μειονεξίας. **τοὺς ἐγκαλοῦντας**, 'his detractors,' c. 29, 3.

14. **εὐπρεπεστάτη**, 'most specious.'

15. **δείσαντα**, sc. τὸν δῆμον: translate 'the most plausible of the pretexts, viz. that it was because the people were afraid of the barbarians that . . .'

Ruhl *Jahrb. f. kl. Phil.* 97, 671 suspects Ephorus to be the author of this statement. But, according to Justin iii 6, Ephorus regarded the removal of the treasure as a precautionary measure against the robbery of the Peloponnesians. He placed it in B.C. 459 (Spring) before the battle of Halieis, when the Corinthian-Aeginetan fleet was still dangerous. It could scarcely be from fear of the Persians merely, when the war in Egypt took a bad turn and a Phoenician fleet appeared in the offing.

16. **ἐν ὀχυρῷ**: so *Flam.* c. 8, 1 ἐν βραχεῖ, Arist. *Eccl.* 320 ἐν καθαρῷ, *in loco puro*, *Th.* 292 ἐν καλῷ, *in loco opportuno*.

17. **ἀνῄρηκε**, *sustulit*, 'has made impossible' viz. by his disposal of the tribute-money for beautifying Athens. Cp. the complaints of the Lesbians at the moment of their revolt in the fourth year of the Peloponnesian war (Thuc. iii 10, 2).

20. **τοῖς εἰσφερομένοις ὑπ' αὐτῆς ἀναγκαίως**, 'with the contribution paid by her under compulsion.' See *Cim.* c. 11, 1, Thuc. i 99, 1 οἱ γὰρ Ἀθηναῖοι ἀκριβῶς ἔπρασσον (τὰς ἐκδείας) . . προσάγοντες τὰς ἀνάγκας.

21. **πρὸς τὸν πόλεμον**, 'for the war' against Persia, which was the original object of the φόρος to be contributed in lieu of ships by the smaller states.

23. **ἀλαζόνα**, 'vain.' **περιαπτομένην**, 'putting on herself to wear' as an ornament. Cp. *Galb.* c. 17, 4 ἐκέλευσε (τὴν παλλακίδα) τὸν περιδέραιον κόσμον ἀφελομένην ἐκείνη περιάψαι, Arist. *Ach.* 654 ἀφύων τιμὴν περιάψας sc. by the epithet λιπαραί. HSauppe justly surmises, p. 28, that these bold expressions may have been borrowed from one of the comic playwrights.

§ 3 l. 29. **οὐχ – οὐ – οὐχ** for οὔτε – οὔτε – οὔτε, as in *Lyc.* c. 9, 3, *Sol.* c. 7, 1, *Fab.* c. 17, 2 and twenty-one other passages of the *Lives*, twenty-six of the *Morals*. Cp. c. 39, 3.

30. **τελούντων** with αὐτῶν.

32. **ἂν παρέχωσιν ἀνθ' οὗ λαμβάνουσι**, 'should they perform that in return for what they receive,' viz. the undisturbed enjoyment of the Aegean.

§ 4 l. 36. τρέπειν, 'to apply,' c. 21, 1.   γενομένων, 'when once executed, completed'; γινομένων, 'during execution,' 'while in process of completion.'

38. ἑτοίμη, 'immediate.'

39. πᾶσαν τέχνην, 'every (possible) kind of art and craft.'

41. ποιοῦσιν ἔμμισθον, 'put in receipt of wages.'

42. ἅμα ... καί: cp. c. 11, 4.

§ 5 l. 42. τοῖς μὲν γάρ introduces a practical elucidation of the vindication put into the mouth of Pericles, viz. ὅλην ποιοῦσιν ἔμμισθον τὴν πόλιν.

44. ἀπὸ τῶν κοινῶν, by means of the pay instituted by Pericles, which amounted to four obols a day.

45. ἀσύντακτον, not belonging to the regular forces, for the Thetes, the fourth class in the Solonian division, were exempt from service as hoplites or troopers as late as B.C. 427. See Gilbert *l. c.* 1 p. 501.

47. λαμβάνειν *sc.* λήμματα.

48. κατασκευασμάτων ἐπιβολάς, 'projects of structures.' *Mor.* 226 D τῶν κ. δημιουργός, Dem. *c. Aristocr.* 207 τὰ τῆς πόλεως οἰκοδομήματα καὶ κατασκευάσματα, Paus. 1 20, 4 quoted c. 13, 5 l. 47.

49. πολυτέχνους ὑποθέσεις, 'plans, undertakings requiring many arts,' § 4.

50. διατριβὴν ἐχόντων, 'involving time to finish them.' See Gr. Ind. *s. v.* ἔχειν.

51. φέρων: see note to c. 7, 2. In this passage it expresses rather the grandeur of the projects.

52. τῶν ... φρουρούντων, 'those on garrison duty.'

53. τὸ οἰκουροῦν, c. 11, 4; c. 34, 1, Arist. *Ach.* 1060. πρόφασιν, 'title,' 'claim.'

§ 6 l. 55. ὅπου, as in c. 13, 11. So Shakspeare uses 'where' for 'whereas.' The protasis extends to γινόμενον l. 68; the conclusion is contained in εἰς πᾶσαν ... εὐπορίαν.

ὕλη ἦν, 'there was as material,' c. 16, 1. Aristot. *Pol.* 1 3, 1 p. 1256^a 8 λέγω δὲ ὕλην τὸ ὑποκείμενον, ἐξ οὗ τι ἀποτελεῖται ἔργον, οἷον ὑφάντῃ μὲν ἔρια, ἀνδριαντοποιῷ δὲ χαλκόν.

56. ταύτην, *sc.* τὴν ὕλην.

57. τέκτονες, as if τεχνῖται had preceded. See n. on τέχναι l. 65.

58. πλάσται, 'artists who moulded in soft materials (clay or

wax),' 'modellers'; the term afterwards was applied also to those who worked in metal, or statuary of any kind, stone or marble.

59. **χρυσοῦ μαλακτῆρες** is used for χρυσόχοοι, the common term, probably because μαλακτῆρες is applicable also to ἐλέφαντος. With regard to the softening of ivory in use amongst the ancients, cp. *Mor.* 499 D τὸν ἐλέφαντα τῷ ζύθει ('sour beer') μαλακὸν γινόμενον καὶ χαλῶντα κάμπτουσι καὶ διασχηματίζουσιν, ἄλλως δὲ οὐ δύνανται. The process, now lost, is said to have been invented by Democritus, Seneca *Ep.* xc 33.

60. **ποικιλταί**, 'weavers of variegated stuffs,' 'embroiderers' (Aesch. *Timarch.* § 97, LXX *Exod.* c. 28, 15) *i.e.* of the tapestries (παραπετάσματα)—an art which was especially practised in Phoenicia, Cyprus and Carthage. Fuhr takes it to mean 'enamellers'; Amyot renders the word by 'ouvriers de marquetterie.' But see O. Müller *Ancient Art etc.* § 113, 1 Engl. Tr. **τορευταί**, 'toreutic artists' *i.e.* artists in ornamental metal work, including engraved designs and embossed figures. See W. Wroth's article *Caelatura* in *Dict. of Antiqq.* 3rd ed. vol. I pp. 323–327, Müller *l. c.* § 311. **τούτων**, *sc.* λίθων, χαλκοῦ κτλ.

Plutarch, as is observed by Thiersch *Epoch* p. 102, classes a number of arts together, without making any distinction between those which we regard as liberal professions and others which we treat as mechanical. He shows from Lucian (*Somn.* § 1) that the epithet βάναυσος was applied no less to Phidias or Polycletus than to a common mason. But they seem to have been brought down to this level only in contrast with the higher dignity of political or military functions, according to the sentiment in *Per.* c. 2, 1–3; as Aeschylus thought little of his poetry in comparison with the honour of having fought at Marathon, Athenaeus xiv c. 23 (*Thirlwall*).

§ 7 l. 62. **οἱ κατὰ γῆν**, 'landsmen')(ἔμποροι κτλ. κατὰ θάλασσαν.

65. **ἑκάστη δὲ . . . γινόμενον** may be regarded as a parenthetic clause, independent of the main proposition. The meaning is:—'Each particular handicraft had its own corps of unskilled labourers enrolled, who acted as the instrument and body of the subordinate service,' *i.e.* who were in relation to their employers what the body is in relation to the soul. With στρατηγός understand ἔχει. For τέχνη in the sense of τεχνίτης, as it appears to be used here, cp. *Agesil.* c. 26, 5 δεύτερον ἐκήρυττε τοὺς χαλκεῖς, εἶτα τέκτονας ἑξῆς καὶ οἰκοδόμους καὶ τῶν ἄλλων τεχνῶν ἑκάστην.

66. On **ἰδιώτην**)(τεχνίτην, cp. Plat. *Theag.* 124 c τῶν τε δημιουργῶν καὶ ἰδιωτῶν, and see my n. to *Them.* c. 27, 3, Xen. *Hier.* c. 4, 6.

67. **συντεταγμένον**, the opposite of ἀσύντακτον l. 45.

68. ὡς ἔπος εἰπεῖν, 'so to say,' an absolute infinitive qualifying πᾶσαν, and implying that it is not to be taken literally, G. *MT.*² § 777, 1.

69. πᾶσαν φύσιν, 'every kind of capacity.'

CHAPTER XIII

§ 1 l. 1. ἀναβαινόντων depends on τὸ τάχος.   ὑπερηφάνων, 'magnificent.' *Fab.* c. 26, 2 πράξεις ὑπερήφανοι τὸ μέγεθος, *Demetr.* c. 41, 4 ἦν τις ὑφαινομένη χλαμὺς αὐτῷ... ἔργον ὑπερήφανον, Plat. *Gorg.* 511 D οὐ σεμνύνεται ὡς ὑπερήφανόν τι διαπραττομένη.

2. μεγέθει: cp. c. 3, 2 l. 12 and see G. *Gr.* § 188, 1 Note 1.

3. ἁμιλλωμένων: the participle expresses the reason why they were ὑπερήφανα μεγέθει and ἀμίμητα μορφῇ. Construe ἁμιλλωμένων ὑπερβάλλεσθαι τὴν δημιουργίαν, *certatim nitentibus ut ars sua excelleret*. Blass reads τῆς δημιουργίας, taking ὑπερβάλλεσθαι as in Herod. IX 71 ὑπερεβάλοντο ἀρετῇ Λακεδαιμόνιοι. Cp. *Lyc.* c. 9, 5 ἀπηλλαγμένοι γὰρ οἱ δημιουργοὶ τῶν ἀχρήστων ἐν τοῖς ἀναγκαίοις ἐπεδείκνυντο τὴν καλλιτεχνίαν.

5. τὸ τάχος, 'the rapidity of progress.'

7. διαδοχαῖς, 'successive generations.'   ἡλικίαις, c. 27, 3.

8. μιᾷ ἀκμῇ πολιτείας, 'in the prime of a single administration,' during the most brilliant period of one statesman's tenure of office.

9. ἐλάμβανε τὴν συντέλειαν, 'were being finished one after another' (an unclassical expression), found in Polybius VIII 35, 10 τοῦ τείχους λαμβάνοντος τὴν συντέλειαν, 36, 11 ἅμα τῷ λόγῳ τοὔργον εἰλήφει συντέλειαν, XVIII 10, 1 (27, 1) πανταχόθεν τοῦ κινδύνου συντέλειαν εἰληφότος, XXII 12, 13 ἔλαβε τὸ πρᾶγμα συντέλειαν. Cp. Plut. *Nic.* c. 7, 2 ἡ πολιορκία μῆκος ἐλάμβανε, *Flam.* c. 13, 1 τοῦ πολέμου μῆκος λαμβάνοντος, Thuc. I 91, 1 ἤδη ὕψος λαμβάνει τὸ τεῖχος, Polyb. V 31, 2 ὁ πόλεμος πέρας λαμβάνει, II 46, 7 ὁ πόλεμος ἔλαβε τὴν ἀρχήν.

§ 2 l. 10. καίτοι: generally, however, quickness of execution is not attended with excellence of workmanship; he who works for the future, must be content to spend time over his work, as Zeuxis did.   Ἀγαθάρχου: Agatharchus, the painter of Samos, known to us from the story, told by Plut. *Alcib.* c. 16, 4 and Andocides *e. Alc.* § 17, of his having been inveigled by Alcibiades to his house and kept there for more than three months in durance, that he might embellish it with his paintings.

12. **Zeuxis** of Heraclea (Magna Graecia) was the most famous painter of his time (Xen. *Mem.* I iv 3), the second half of the fifth century. His masterpiece is said to have been the picture of Helen, painted for the Heraeon at Crotona. **ζῷα**, 'figures' of all kinds, not necessarily of animals (Herod. IV 88); hence ζωγραφεῖν, 'to paint from life.' **ποιεῖν** for γράφειν.

13. **πολλῷ χρόνῳ**, in the double sense of ἐν πολλῷ χρόνῳ, *in multo tempore*, and πρὸς πολὺν χρόνον (§ 3 l. 1), *in multum tempus*, 'for a considerable time.' Cp. *Mor.* 94 F ὁ Ζεῦξις αἰτιωμένων αὐτόν τινων ὅτι ζωγραφεῖ βραδέως "Ὁμολογῶ" εἶπεν "ἐν πολλῷ χρόνῳ γράφειν, καὶ γὰρ εἰς πολύν," where Wyttenbach quotes a similar retort from Valerius Max. III 7 ext. 1. The **γάρ** explains the saying of Zeuxis. **εὐχέρεια**, 'dexterity.' Cp. [Lucian] *Amor.* c. 11 ὑμνεῖται δὲ τούτου (sc. τοῦ ἱεροῦ) τὸ τῆς Πραξιτέλους εὐχερείας ὄντως ἐπαφρόδιτον.

14. **βάρος ... μόνιμον**, 'permanence,' 'lasting solidity': ἔργῳ with ἐντίθησι.

15. **ὁ δ' εἰς τὴν γένεσιν τῷ πόνῳ προδανεισθεὶς χρόνος ... τὴν ἰσχὺν ἀποδίδωσιν**: the time expended on labour in the production of a work of art is regarded in the light of capital invested, which is repaid (as interest) by its greater durability (σωτηρία). For εἰς, see Gr. Ind. s. v.

17. **ἀποδίδωσιν**, 'yields,' 'produces in repayment.' Cp. *Mor.* 388 C ἡ φύσις λαβοῦσα πυρὸν ἐν σπέρματι ... ἐπὶ πᾶσι πυρὸν ἀνέδειξεν ἀποδοῦσα τὴν ἀρχὴν ἐν τῷ τέλει τοῦ παντός, 437 C πᾶσα γὰρ δύναμις ὃ πέφυκε σὺν καιρῷ βέλτιον ἢ χεῖρον ἀποδίδωσι, 637 A ὥσπερ ὄφλημα τῇ φύσει τὴν γένεσιν ἀποδιδόντων, 796 B ὅσα, καθάπερ τὰ φάρμακα, δάκνει παραχρῆμα ... τὸ δὲ καλὸν καὶ λυσιτελὲς ὕστερον ἀποδίδωσι. For γένεσις, 'production,' cp. Plat. *Rep.* 281 B E τῆς γενέσεως τῆς τῶν ἱματίων, *Legg.* 920 E ὀργάνων τε καὶ ἔργων ἀποτελοῦντες γένεσιν ἔμμισθον.

§ 3 l. 17. **ὅθεν**, 'for which reason,' c. 2, 2; c. 3, 2.

19. **ἐν ὀλίγῳ** sc. χρόνῳ.

20. **ἀρχαῖον**, 'antique,' the idea being that the age and beauty of a work of art were identical. **ἀκμῇ**, 'in freshness.'

21. **πρόσφατον**, 'modern': see my n. to *Them.* c. 24, 2 ed. 3. **οὕτως ἐπανθεῖ καινότης ἀεί τις**, 'there is such an everlasting bloom, as it were, of freshness on the surface.' Cp. *Mor.* 54 D αἱ τῶν φίλων χάριτες ἐπὶ καλῷ τινι τὸ εὐφραῖνον ὥσπερ ἐπανθοῦν ἔχουσιν, Lucian *Pseud.* 29 ὅσα ἄλλα καλὰ τοῖς σοῖς λόγοις ἐπανθεῖ.

K

22. ἄθικτον, 'intact.' Cp. *Pyrrh.* c. 3, 5 δάκτυλον ἀπαθῆ καὶ ἄθικτον ὑπὸ τοῦ πυρός. Elsewhere ἄθικτος takes a simple gen. as in *Num.* c. 20 πάσης κακίας ἄθικτον διαφυλάττουσα τὸν βίον, *Cim.* c. 10, 8 αὐτὸν ἄθικτον ἐν τῇ πολιτείᾳ δωροδοκίας παρέσχεν: or a dat. as *Pomp.* c. 23, 3 ταῖς τῶν πολλῶν ἐντεύξεσι καὶ συνηθείαις ἄθικτον οἰόμενος δεῖν τὸ ἀξίωμα διατηρεῖν.

23. διατηροῦσα, 'preserving': Polyb. VII 8, 7 διατηρεῖν πάντα τὰ τοῦ σώματος μέρη ἀβλαβῆ.

24. ἀγήρω: Thuc. II c. 43, 2 τὸν ἀγήρων ἔπαινον: c. 41, 4 τὸ φιλότιμον ἀγήρων μόνον.

§ 4 l. 25. διεῖπε, '*administrabat.*'

26. καίτοι with participle instead of the usual καίπερ is very rare in classical Greek, but not uncommon in Plutarch and Polybius. G. *MT.*² § 861.

29. Παρθενῶνα, 'the temple of Athena Παρθένος' (not Polias) on the south side of the Acropolis, the most magnificent relic of Periclean times. It was built of white marble of Pentelicus on the site of the old temple—called from its dimensions Ἑκατόμπεδος (νεώς)—which had been burnt by the Persians. It was divided into three chambers, the Pronaos (πρόνεως) at the East entrance, the Hecatompedos into which this opened, the western portion of which formed the Parthenon proper, where a number of articles were kept for use at festival time, and behind this the Opisthodomos, where the money-treasures were deposited. The middle chamber, the *cella* proper, where the colossal chryselephantine statue of the goddess was placed, preserved the original length and was called τὸ ἐκατόμπεδον in a narrower sense. The entire temple measured 228 feet in length from East to West, 100 in breadth and 64 in height.

30. εἰργάζετο, 'was the architect of.' According to Pausanias VIII 41, 9 and Strabo *Geogr.* IX c. 1, 12 it was the work of Ictinus alone, who was the designer also of the beautiful temple dedicated to Apollo Epicureios at Bassae (Arcadia), a complete frieze from which is now at the British Museum. Leake suggests that Callicrates may have been no more than the contractor (ἐργολάβος) for building the temple, as he was for the long wall, ll. 37–39. τὸ ἐν Ἐλευσῖνι τελεστήριον: the Attic deme Eleusis was situated on a bay of the same name opposite Salamis, about a dozen miles from Athens, with which it was connected by the Sacred Way (ἡ ἱερὰ ὁδός), which was also the principal strategic and commercial artery of Attica leading to the Peloponnesus. It was a place of especial sanctity in the eyes of the Athenians, being the chief seat of the worship of the venerable goddess Demeter, in whose honour and for the

celebration of whose mysteries the temple here mentioned was erected—a building considered as one of the greatest masterpieces of the age. The temple had no outward façade till the time of Demetrius Phalereus. The lower storey (ἔδαφος)—which was nearly a square, measuring 175 by 179 feet—contained six rows of seven Doric columns, which divided the interior space into seven parallel naves. These supported a gallery with a second colonnade (τοὺς ἄνω κίονας). The whole was surmounted by a cupola roof with a central opening (ὀπαῖον) for the admission of light. The temple was built on this large scale (ὄχλον θεάτρου δέξασθαι δυνάμενον, Strabo IX c. 1, 12) to accommodate the crowd of worshippers who flocked to it from all parts at the annual celebration of the mysteries in the autumn. According to Strabo l. c., the architect was Ictinus.

33. τοῖς ἐπιστυλίοις ἐπέζευξεν, 'connected them by means of ('joined them to') their architraves,' Herod. VII 36, 7 θέντες δὲ (τοὺς κορμοὺς) ἐπεξῆς ἐνταῦθα αὖθις ἐπεζεύγνυον i.e., arte inter se constrinxerant, as Schweighaeuser interprets.

34. Ξυπέτιος, 'of the deme Ξυπέτη,' in the Κεκροπὶς φυλή. Other forms are Ξυπεταιών (in inscriptions) and Ξυπετεών: see L. Dindorf Thesaur. vol. v p. 1689. διάζωμα, 'frieze.'

§ 5 l. 36. ἀνακτόρου, 'shrine,' a poetico-Ionic word, used especially of the temple at Eleusis. Cp. Herod. IX 65, Athenae. p. 167 F Ἐλευσῖνί τε μυστηρίων ὄντων ἔθηκεν αὐτῇ θρόνον παρὰ τὸ ἀνάκτορον, p. 213 D μὴ περιίδωμεν ... τὸ σεμνὸν ἀνάκτορον τοῖν θεοῖν κεκλεισμένον. Another name for the cella was μέγαρον. The whole building was also called μυστικὸς σηκός.
Χολαργεύς, c. 3, 1.

37. ἐκορύφωσε (not, as Liddell-Scott, 'finished' but) 'vaulted.'

τὸ Μακρὸν τεῖχος, i.e. τὸ διὰ μέσου τεῖχος (Plato Gorg. 455 E) or τὸ νότιον τ. as it was named. The space between the two long walls (σκέλη) already built—one extending between four and five miles from the western wall of Athens to the north-west edge of Piraeus (τὸ Βόρειον), another nearly due south of Athens to the eastern edge of the harbour of Phalerum (τὸ Φαληρικόν)—was broad, and, if in the hands of an enemy, the communication with Piraeus would be interrupted. Pericles, accordingly, induced the people to construct a third or intermediate wall, running parallel with the first wall to Piraeus and within a short distance (less than a furlong) from it, so that the communication between the city and its port might be kept open, if either of the outer walls happened to be surprised by an enemy. They could never separate Athens from the sea. The actual length of the north wall, according to Curtius-Kaupert, was 40 stadia, that of the Phaleric 35. See Busolt Gr. Gesch. II p. 485 Anm. 3.

38. Σωκράτης: in Plato's Gorg. 455 E Περικλέους δὲ καὶ αὐτὸς ἤκουον ὅτε συνεβούλευεν ἡμῖν περὶ τοῦ διὰ μέσου τείχους.
εἰσηγουμένον γνώμην, 'when he was introducing a motion.' See n. to Them. c. 20, 2.

39. ἠργολάβησε, 'undertook the contract for.'

41. Κρατῖνος: the passage is from an unknown play. It is quoted also *Mor.* p. 351 A ('Ισοκράτης) οἴκοι καθῆστο βιβλίον ἀναπλάττων . . . ὅσῳ χρόνῳ τὰ προπύλαια Περικλῆς ἀνέστησε καὶ τοὺς ἑκατομπέδους· καίτοι καὶ τοῦτον ὡς βραδέως ἀνύοντα τοῖς ἔργοις ἐπισκώπτων Κρατῖνος οὕτω πως λέγει περὶ τοῦ διὰ μέσου τείχους, λόγοισι γὰρ αὐτὸ προάγει Περικλέης, ἔργοισι δ' οὐδὲ κινεῖ.

43. λόγοισι . . . κινεῖ, an iambic tetrameter catalectic. The meaning is 'he has been long professing to go on with it, but in fact does not even advance it a step.' 'It does not appear' says Thirlwall 'whether the motives to which this delay was imputed were such as to call his integrity into question.'

44. The Odeum or 'Music Hall' of Pericles (so called to distinguish it from that built, about A.D. 150, by Herodes Atticus in honour of his deceased wife Regilla) lay at the southeast corner of the Acropolis, by the side of the theatre of Dionysus. It was finished between 444 and 437 B.C. and burnt B.C. 86 at the capture of Athens by Sulla, but restored on the original plan shortly afterwards. διαθέσει, 'arrangement,' 'plan.' For the dat. see n. to c. 3, 2. πολύεδρον, 'with many tiers of seats' raised one above another.

45. πολύστυλον: Theophrastus *Char.* XVIII represents the garrulous man as asking πόσοι εἰσὶ κίονες τοῦ Ὠιδείου; περικλινές κτλ., 'with a round roof sloping from a single point.' In this respect it differed from a theatre, which it resembled in its semi-circular form.

47. τῆς βασιλέως σκηνῆς: Pausan. I 20, 4 ἔστι δὲ πλησίον τοῦ τε ἱεροῦ τοῦ Διονύσου καὶ τοῦ θεάτρου κατασκεύασμα, ποιηθῆναι δὲ τῆς σκηνῆς αὐτὸ εἰς μίμησιν τῆς Ξέρξου λέγεται. Vitruvius (*de Archit.* 5, 9) records a tradition that the woodwork was made out of the masts and yard-arms of the Persian ships that fought at Salamis: *excuntibus e theatro sinistra parte Odeum, quod Themistocles, columnis lapideis dispositis, navium malis et antennis e spoliis Persicis pertexit.* Cp. c. 3, 1 with note.

48. καὶ τούτῳ, sc. τῷ Ὠιδείῳ 'this as well as the Long Wall.'

§ 6 l. 49. ἐν Θρᾴτταις: nothing is known of the subject or contents of this play, which is said to have taken its name from the chorus composed of female house-slaves at Athens. Kock *CAF.* I p. 34 after Bergk thinks that it may have had something to do with the worship of the Thracian goddess Bendis (Plat. *Rep.* I 1), who had a temple, as we know from

Xen. *Hell.* II iv 11, in the Piraeus, and that the chorus was composed of Thracian women engaged in her service.

51. cχινοκέφαλος κτλ.: see note on c. 3, 2. 27

53. ἐπειδὴ τοὖστρακον παροίχεται, 'now that the potsherd is a thing of the past,' not 'he has past by the ordeal of the potsherd,' *i.e.* ostracism, cp. c. 11, 2. The sentence fell on Thucydides in the spring of B.C. 444, and the Θρᾶτται was probably acted in the following year.

55. τοῖς Παναθηναίοις: the article is usually absent from the names of festivals when used as indications of time; the absence of the preposition is normal. The Panathenaea, the greatest of Athenian festivals, was kept in honour of Athena every fourth year with extraordinary magnificence (τὰ μεγάλα Παν.), and lasted six days. To the usual equestrian, gymnastic and other contests (*C.I.A.* II 965) Pericles added those of fluteplayers, singers and citharists, but only at the Greater festival.

56. ἀθλοθέτης αἱρεθείς: the *locus classicus* on the athlothetae and their functions is Aristot. 'Αθ. πολ. c. 60, 1 κληροῦσι δὲ καὶ ἀθλοθέτας δέκα <ἄ>νδρας, ἕνα τῆς φυλῆς ἑκάστης. οὗτοι δὲ δοκιμασθέντες ἄρχουσι τέτταρ<α ἔ>τη, καὶ διοικοῦσι τήν τε πομπὴν τῶν Παναθηναίων καὶ τὸν ἀγῶνα τῆς μουσικῆς καὶ τὸν γυμνικὸν ἀγῶνα καὶ τὴν ἱπποδρομίαν, καὶ τὸν πέπλον ποιοῦνται, καὶ τοὺς ἀμφορεῖς ποιοῦνται μετὰ τῆς βουλῆς, καὶ τὸ ἔλαιον τοῖς ἀθληταῖς ἀποδιδόασι. συλλέγεται δὲ τὸ ἔλαιον <ἀ>πὸ τῶν μορίων... οἱ δὲ ταμίαι τὸν μὲν ἄλλον χρόνον τηροῦσιν (τὸ ἔλαιον) ἐν ἀκροπόλει, τοῖς δὲ Παναθηναίοις ἀπομετροῦσι τοῖς ἀθλοθέταις, οἱ δ' ἀθλοθέται τοῖς νικῶσι τῶν ἀγωνιστῶν. ἔστι γὰρ ἆθλα... τοῖς τὸν γυμνικὸν ἀγῶνα καὶ τὴν ἱπποδρομίαν (νικῶσιν) ἔλαιον. Again in c. 62, 2 ἀθλοθέται δ' ἐν πρυτανείῳ δειπνοῦσι τὸν ἐκ<ατομβ>αιῶνα μῆνα, ὅ<τ>αν ᾖ τὰ Παναθήναια, ἀρξάμενοι ἀπὸ τῆς τετράδος ἰσταμένου. Plato *Legg.* VI 764 c, D speaks of them as μουσικῆς καὶ γυμναστικῆς ἄρχοντες: cp. VIII 835 A, XI 935 E, 955 A. It was one of the offices of little or no political importance and was filled by open vote. Cp. Pollux 8, 93, 88, *C.I.A.* I 188, 5 ff., where an account of the sums disbursed to the athlothetes in the archonship of Glaucippus, *i.e.* Ol. 92, 3, is given, Schubert *de aedil.* pp. 52–57. The ten ἀθλοθέται had the appointment to λειτουργίαι at the Panathenaea, as the Archon had at the greater Dionysia, and the Βασιλεύς at the Lenaea: see [Dem.] *adv. Boeot. de nom.* § 9. In the *Dict. of Antiq.* ed. 3, vol. I p. 44 b, they are still wrongly identified with ἀγωνοθέται (c. 36, 3), but not so in vol. II p. 327 b.

§ 7 l. 58. τὸν ἄλλον χρόνον, 'in later, after times.'

60. τὰ Προπύλαια. The Propylaea—the greatest and

most beautiful work of Pericles after the Parthenon—formed the great gateway of the Acropolis and covered the whole of its west end, which was 168 feet broad. It was constructed entirely of Pentelic marble and took five years (πενταετίαν) to build, between B.C. 437 (the year after the consecration of the Parthenon) and 433. For an account of the original plan of Mnesicles and the supposed subsequent modifications of it, see Miss Jane Harrison *l. c.* 355 ff. It was destroyed by an explosion in 1656. Cicero (*de off.* II 60) says that Demetrius Phalereus found great fault with Pericles *quod tantam pecuniam in praeclara illa Propylaea coniecerit*. His censure is not surprising if Harpocration's statement, taken from Philochorus, that it cost 2012 talents, is to be relied on. Col. Leake, however, considers it a great exaggeration.

63. περί, c. 32, 1.

64. ἐμήνυσεν ... οὐκ ἀποστατοῦσαν, 'indicated that she did not stand aloof from.' Cp. *Mor.* 613 B οὔτε τινὸς παιδιᾶς ... ἀποστατεῖν, 758 A οὐ μὴν οὐδὲ νοσοῦντος ἀνθρώπου θεὸς ἀποστατεῖ ... ἀλλ' οὐδ' ἀποθανόντος. Note that Plutarch always uses οὐ, not μή, after the verbs ἀποφαίνειν, δηλοῦν and μηνύειν.

65. συνεπιτελοῦσαν *sc.* αὐτό.

§ 8 l. 68. μοχθηρῶς, c. 36, 1. ἀπεγνωσμένος, *deploratus*, 'after he had been given up,' 'his life despaired of.' On Plutarch's use of this verb the student may consult my note on *Ti. Gr.* c. 5, 2.

70. ὄναρ, 'in a dream,' adverbially, *Them.* c. 26, 2.

συνέταξε, 'prescribed'; *Alex.* c. 8, 1 νοσοῦσιν ἐβοήθει τοῖς φίλοις καὶ συνέταττε θεραπείας τινας καὶ διαίτας.

θεραπείαν, *curationem*, 'mode of treatment,' 'cure.' Cp. Luc. *Ev.* c. 9, 11 τοὺς χρείαν ἔχοντας θεραπείας ἰάσατο. The remedy prescribed was the shoots of a plant which grows commonly on the Acropolis, and which thereafter bore the name παρθένιον from Ἀθηνᾶ Παρθένος. See *Sull.* c. 13, 2 with my note *ad l.*, also Dr. Sandys' *Easter Vacation in Greece* p. 86 note.

71. τὸν ἄνθρωπον, 'the poor fellow'; c. 5, 2 note.

72. On the base of the statue found *in situ* during the excavation of the Propylaea there is the following inscription, given in Kirchhoff *C.I.A.* I 335, Hicks no. 36 pp. 50–1 Ἀθηναῖοι τῇ Ἀθηναίᾳ τῇ Ὑγιείᾳ. Πύρρος ἐποίησεν Ἀθηναῖος. Cp. Plin. *N.H.* XXII 17, 20 § 44; XXXIV 8, 19 § 81. Pausanias I 31, 6 mentions an altar at Acharnae dedicated to Ἀθηνᾶ Ὑγίεια.

§ 9 l. 75. ὁ Φειδίας: Plut. here reverts to the subject of § 4.

εἰργάζετο, l. 30. He was also the contractor (ἐργολάβος) for the execution of it, c. 31, 2.

76. τὸ χρυσοῦν ἕδος: ἕδος meant primarily 'a seated statue,' and ultimately any temple-statue: it is never used of a mere εἰκών or 'portrait-statue.' See Miss Harrison *Myth. and Mon. of Anc. Ath.* p. 456. The celebrated chryselephantine statue of the goddess, which was 39 feet high inclusive of the pedestal, was placed within the Hekatompedos of her temple 438/437 B.C. The ivory was used in the parts where the flesh was visible, the drapery was of gold. In the statue of Zeus at Olympia, also the work of Phidias, the gold was enriched with enamelled colours.

Pausanias 1 24, 7 gives a description of the statue as follows:— τὸ δὲ ἄγαλμα τῆς Ἀθηνᾶς ὀρθόν ἐστιν ἐν χιτῶνι ποδήρει καί οἱ κατὰ τὸ στέρνον ἡ κεφαλὴ Μεδούσης ἐλέφαντός ἐστιν ἐμπεποιημένη, καὶ Νίκην ὅσον τε τεσσάρων πηχῶν, ἐν δὲ τῇ <ἑτέρᾳ> χειρὶ δόρυ ἔχει, καί οἱ πρὸς τοῖς ποσὶν ἀσπίς τε κεῖται καὶ πλησίον τοῦ δόρατος δράκων ἐστίν. εἴη δ' ἂν Ἐριχθόνιος οὗτος ὁ δράκων· ἔστι δὲ τῷ βάθρῳ τοῦ ἀγάλματος ἐπειργασμένη Πανδώρας γένεσις.

τῇ στήλῃ, 'the block' or 'slab' of marble on the Acropolis inscribed with the record of the buildings, accounts, etc.

77. κατα γέγραπται: 'has been publicly recorded.' Cp. *Sol.* c. 25, 1 κατεγράφησαν (οἱ νόμοι) εἰς ξυλίνους ἄξονας. The technical word in Attic would be ἀναγέγραπται (as Aristot. 'Αθ. πολ. c. 53, 1 εἰς στήλην χαλκῆν ἀναγράφονται, c. 54, 3 ἐν ταῖς στήλαις ἀναγράφεται), and this is Cobet's conjectural reading, but it leaves an awkward hiatus.

78. ἐπ' αὐτῷ, 'under his control.' Cp. c. 18, 1. ὡς εἰρήκαμεν, § 4.

80. τῷ μέν, *i.e.* Phidias.

82. ἐλευθέρας ... γυναῖκας, c. 31, 1. εἰς τὰ ἔργα φοιτώσας, 'whenever they paid a visit to the works,' Phidias, as chief inspector, conducted them round.

§ 10 l. 84. δεξάμενοι: c. 32, 2 δεχομένου τὰς διαβολάς. οἱ κωμικοί, c. 3, 3; c. 16, 1.

85. πολλὴν ἀσέλγειαν αὐτοῦ κατεσκέδασαν, 'poured upon him (Pericles) a shower of wanton invective.' Cp. *Thes.* c. 16, 3 οἱ τραγικοὶ πολλὴν ἀπὸ τοῦ λογείου καὶ τῆς σκηνῆς ἀδοξίαν αὐτοῦ κατεσκέδασαν ὡς βιαίου γενομένου, *Mor.* 10 c Ἀριστοφάνους πᾶσαν ὕβριν αὐτοῦ κατασκεδαννύντος, Lucian *Eunuch.* § 2 ὅλας ἁμάξας βλασφημιῶν κατεσκέδασαν ἀλλήλων, Dem. *de cor.* § 50.

86. εἰς, 'in regard to,' 'concerning.' Cp. c. 13, 2; c. 29, 2 ὡς ἂν προσδιαβληθείη μᾶλλον εἰς τὸν λακωνισμόν.

87. ὑποστρατηγοῦντος, 'who served as lieutenant under him,' *Mor.* 812 D Περικλῆς Μενίππῳ μὲν ἐχρῆτο πρὸς τὰς στρατηγίας.

90. **αἰτίαν εἶχε = ᾐτιᾶτο.** See Gr. Ind. s. v. ἔχειν. **ὑφιέναι,** *clam submittere,* stupri pretium.

91. **ἐπλησίαζε,** c. 24, 2.

§ 11 l. 92. **καὶ τί:** καί is thus prefixed to interrogatives, when an abrupt urgent question is put. **σατυρικούς,** πρὸς ἀφροδίσια καταφερεῖς, c. 5, 4.

93. **τοῖς βίοις,** e. 27, 4, c. 39, 2; *Galb.* c. 16, 2 σατυρικοὶ τοῖς βίοις ἄνθρωποι.

Plutarch gives his judgment of the ancient comedy in *Mor.* 711 F : τῶν δὲ κωμῳδιῶν ἡ μὲν ἀρχαία διὰ τὴν ἀνωμαλίαν ἀνάρμοστος ἀνθρώποις πίνουσιν· ἥ τε γὰρ ἐν ταῖς λεγομέναις παραβάσεσιν αὐτῶν σπουδὴ καὶ παρρησία λίαν ἄκρατός ἐστι καὶ σύντονος, ἥ τε πρὸς τὰ σκώμματα καὶ βωμολοχίας εὐχέρεια δεινῶς κατάκορος καὶ ἀναπεπταμένη καὶ γέμουσα ῥημάτων ἀκόσμων καὶ ἀκολάστων ὀνομάτων. ἔτι δὲ ... δεήσει γραμματικὸν ἑκάστῳ τὸ καθ' ἕκαστον ἐξηγεῖσθαι, τίς ὁ Λαισποδίας παρ' Εὐπόλιδι καὶ ὁ Κινησίας παρὰ Πλάτωνι καὶ ὁ Λάμπων παρὰ Κρατίνῳ καὶ τῶν κωμῳδουμένων ἕκαστος. Cobet suspects that Plutarch's quotations from it are not always at first hand, but taken from Craterus and others.

94. **τῶν πολλῶν,** e. 7, 2.

95. **ἀποθύοντας,** 'offering as the due and proper victim.' **ἑκάστοτε,** 'on each occasion' of their exhibiting a farce. **ὅπου,** 'when,' 'whereas,' c. 12, 6; *Nic.* c. 18, 5; c. 22, 2.

96. **Στησίμβροτος:** see *Introduction.*

97. **μυθῶδες,** *fabulosum.* **ἐξενεγκεῖν,** *edere,* 'to publish,' 'give currency to,' e. 36, 2; *Nic.* e. 5, 3, Arist. *Eccl.* 442.

98. **τοῦ υἱοῦ,** sc. Xanthippus: see e. 36, 3.

§ 12 l. 98. **οὕτως,** *usque adeo,* with χαλεπόν, § 3 l. 21.

99. **δυσθήρατον ἱστορίᾳ,** 'hard for history to come at,' or 'difficult to be tracked by historical inquiry.'

101. **ἐπιπροσθοῦντα,** *i.q.* ἐπίπροσθεν ὄντα, 'intercepting,' 'obstructing.' *Mor.* 471 C τοιαῦτα πολλὰ πλούτῳ πρόσεστιν ἄδηλα τοῖς πολλοῖς· ἐπιπροσθεῖ γὰρ ὁ τῦφος.

103. **φθόνοις,** c. 2, 3; e. 5, 3.

104. **χαριζομένη,** 'by way of showing favour,' participle co-ordinated with dative of means or manner.

CHAPTER XIV

§ 1 l. 1. **τῶν περὶ τὸν Θουκυδίδην,** 'those belonging to the party of Thucydides,' including Thuc. himself.

2. **σπαθῶντος,** 'squandering'; a cant phrase. For ὡς, ep. c. 5, 4.

Cp. *Mor.* 168 Α πάντα ἀκρίτως φέρεται καὶ σπαθᾶται (ταράττεται *v. l.*) τὰ τῶν ἀνθρώπων, Lucian *Gall.* c. 29 τἀμὰ οὗτοι σπαθῶσι τοῦ κακοδαίμονος, *Prom.* c. 19 ἡ κἀκεῖνον αἰτιασθε ὡς σπαθῶντα ἡμῶν τὸ κτῆμα; *Cataρl.* c. 20 ὅσα τάλαντα ὁ κληρονόμος σπαθήσει παραλαβών, Diphil. ap. Athenae. VII p. 292 C μειράκιον ἐρῶν τὰ πατρῷα βρύκει καὶ σπαθᾷ, Aciphron *Ep.* 3, 34 σπαθήσας τὴν οὐσίαν εἰς ἡμᾶς, Arist. *Nub.* 55 ὦ γύναι, λίαν σπαθᾷς.

4. **ἐν ἐκκλησίᾳ**. For the omission of the article see n. to c. 5, 2. Aristophanes has always ἐν τἠκκλησίᾳ, *Eq.* 76, 1310, *Pac* 667, *Lys.* 390, *Eccl.* 135, *Pl.* 330, for metrical reasons.

5. **εἰ**, 'whether.' The verb (δοκεῖ) is retained in the mood of the direct discourse. G. *MT.*² § 669, 2.

6. **φησάντων** = φήσαντος τοῦ δήμου: cp. c. 12, 3 l. 25.

7. **ἐμοὶ δεδαπανήσθω** *sc.* αὐτά, 'let it have been expended by me,' 'let the cost be put to my account.' For the dative of the agent, cp. c. 33, 7. 'The offer, if it had been accepted, could not, of course, have been made good. But it was probably only meant to signify the firm reliance which Per. placed on the liberality of his countrymen' (*Thirlwall*). The anecdote, however, is probably apocryphal. **τῶν ἀναθημάτων**: c. 12, 1.

8. **ἰδίᾳ ἐμαυτοῦ ποιήσομαι**, 'I will have stand in my own private name.' For τῶν ἀναθημάτων, see n. to c. 12, 1.

§ 2 l. 10. **πρός**, 'at,' 'in view of,' as c. 5, 2: see Gr. Ind. *s. v.*

11. **τὴν δόξαν** ... **τῶν ἔργων**: cp. c. 31, 4.

13. **χορηγεῖν**, *suppeditare*. On the various constructions of this verb, my n. to *Sull.* c. 12, 2 may be consulted. Cp. χορηγός c. 16, 5; χορηγία c. 9, 3. **τέλος**, 'finally.'

14. **ἀγῶνα περὶ τοῦ ὀστράκου**, 'a contest about the shell,' *i.e.* as to which of the two should be ostracised, as in c. 13, 6. This happened in the spring of 441 B.C.=Ol. 84, 1, simultaneously with the conclusion of the Thirty Years' truce.

On the original purpose of ostracism, cp. *Alcib.* c. 13, 4 τὸ ὄστρακον ἐπιφέρειν ἔμελλεν, ᾧ κολούοντες ἀεὶ τὸν προὔχοντα δόξῃ καὶ δυνάμει τῶν πολιτῶν ἐλαύνουσι, Aristot. *Pol.* III 8, 1 p. 1284ᵇ, 36 ὁ γὰρ ὀστρακισμὸς τὴν αὐτὴν ἔχει δύναμιν τρόπον τινὰ τῷ κολούειν τοὺς ὑπερέχοντας καὶ φυγαδεύειν, *ib.* VIII (v) 2, p. 1302ᵇ 15. But in course of time it was used as a means to prevent mischief arising from political factions (στάσεις) by getting the leader of the opposition out of the way, and leaving the majority free to follow their bent without let or hindrance. See Sandys on Aristot. Ἀθ. πολ. c. 22, 1 and the authorities quoted by him *ad l.*

16. **τὴν** ... **ἑταιρείαν**, c. 11, 2. The dissolution (κατάλυσις c. 2, 1, c. 25, 1) of the oligarchical faction followed as an immediate consequence of the disappearance of their leader, and for the next fifteen years Pericles controlled the destinies

of the imperial city. The opposition lies between ἐκεῖνον and τὴν ἑταιρείαν: hence we should have expected either ἐξέβαλε μὲν ἐκεῖνον or τὴν δ' ἀντιτεταγμένην ἑταιρείαν κατέλυσε. Cp. c. 20, 1.

CHAPTER XV

§ 1 l. 1. ὡς, *postquam*.

2. οἷον ὁμαλῆς, 'level as it were,' because of the removal of a great obstruction.

3. περιήνεγκεν εἰς ἑαυτόν: *Galb.* c. 8, 1 συλλήβδην ὁμοῦ πάντα πράγματα φέρων περιήνεγκεν εἰς ἑαυτόν. Cp. c. 6, 2 εἰς ἕνα περιστήσεται τὸ κράτος.

4. τῶν Ἀθηναίων depends on ἐξηρτημένα.

5. φόρους ... καὶ θάλασσαν: by omission of the article in copulative expressions there is a gain in emphasis.

7. πολλὴν μὲν ... πολλὴν δέ, an *epanaphora*, as l. 23; c. 16, 4.   δι' Ἑλλήνων ... ἤκουσαν, 'realised by means of Greeks.'

9. ὑπηκόοις ἔθνεσι: the maritime confederation extended as far as the shores of Thrace and the Hellespont and from thence to Ionia and Caria, some of whose rulers were tributaries of Athens. Blass compares Plato *Alcib.* 1 104 B (Περικλέα) ὃς οὐ μόνον ἐν τῇδε τῇ πόλει δύναται πράττειν ὅ τι ἂν βούληται, ἀλλ' ἐν πάσῃ τῇ Ἑλλάδι καὶ τῶν βαρβάρων ἐν πολλοῖς καὶ μεγάλοις γένεσι.

10. βασιλέων: among others, the King of Egypt, cp. c. 37, 2. δυναστῶν: c. 20, 1.   Carian dynasts appear in the Quota-Lists.

§ 2 l. 11. χειροήθης, *mansuetus*, 'tame,' 'submissive.'

Cp. *Demetr.-Ant.* c. 6, 2 οἴνῳ καὶ γαστρὶ καθάπερ τὰ ζῷα χειροήθης γενόμενος, *Mor.* 139 B ὁ γαμήλιος πράους παρέχει καὶ χειροήθεις ἀλλήλοις, Xen. *Oec.* c. 7, 10 ἐπεὶ ἤδη μοι χειροήθης ἦν (*uxor*), Dem. *Olynth.* III 31 τιθασεύουσιν ὑμᾶς χειροήθεις αὑτοῖς ποιοῦντες.

12. ῥᾴδιος ὑπείκειν, G. *MT.*[2] § 758.   συνενδιδόναι, 'to give in to,' 'to comply with.'

13. ὥσπερ πνοαῖς, 'shifting and changeable as the winds, the proverbial *aura popularis*.   ἐκ marks succession, passage from one state of things to another; cp. § 5 l. 39, c. 24, 4, Arist. *Eq.* 1321 τὸν Δῆμον καλὸν ἐξ αἰσχροῦ πεποίηκα, *Av.* 799 ἐξ οὐδενὸς μεγάλα πράττει.

14. ἀνειμένης, 'lax,' 'remiss.'   ἐκείνης, 'former,' c. 10, 2. ὑποθρυπτομένης ἔνια, 'in some points (or 'sometimes') making weak concessions.'

15. ἀνθηρᾶς, 'fresh,' 'modern.' Cp. Xen. *Cyr.* I vi 38 ἐν τοῖς μουσικοῖς τὰ νέα καὶ ἀνθηρὰ εὐδοκιμεῖ. Observe that the comparison is incomplete, instead of 'tightening as it were the strings of the instrument to a more austere and earnest tune after a modern voluptuous one.' Plutarch is fond of metaphors borrowed from music, as c. 8, 1.

16. ἐντεινάμενος is opp. to ἀνειμένης: πολιτείαν ('a statesmanship' that deserves the name) to δημαγωγίας.

17. πρὸς τὸ βέλτιστον, 'to the best interests of the commonwealth.'

18. ὀρθῇ καὶ ἀνεγκλίτῳ, 'straightforward and unswerving.'

§ 3 l. 19. πείθων, 'by moral suasion.' ἦν δ' ὅτε ἐνίοτε δέ, c. 3, 2 ; c. 24, 3.

20. καί intensive of μάλα, c. 25, 2. κατατείνων, *stringens habenas*, 'drawing the rein tight, pulling in.' Cp. c. 33, 5; *Popl.* c. 13, 3 οἱ δὲ ἵπποι πτοηθέντες ἵεντο παντὶ τάχει . . . ἔχοντες τὸν ἡνίοχον, ὡς οὐδὲν ἦν ἔργον αὐτοῦ κατατείνοντος οὐδὲ παρηγοροῦντος. For the metaphor, cp. c. 11, 4.

προσβιβάζων τῷ συμφέροντι, 'bringing to a certain feeling (prevailing upon) on the ground of expediency.' Cp. *Cat. mi.* c. 36, 2 ἰδίᾳ τοῖς ὠνουμένοις διαλεγόμενος καὶ προσβιβάζων ἕκαστον, Arist. *Eq.* 35 εὖ προσβιβᾷς με, *Ar.* 426 ὡς σὰ τὰ πάντα ταῦτα (ἐστὶ) προσβιβᾷ λέγων, Xen. *Mem.* 1 2, 17 δεικνύντας τι τοῖς μανθάνουσιν καὶ τῷ λόγῳ προσβιβάζοντας, Lucian *Anach.* c. 12 οὐ γὰρ οὕτω λέγων ἄν τις προσβιβάσειέ σε.

22. ἀτεχνῶς, *plane, omnino*; to be distinguished from ἀτέχνως, *sine arte*. ποικίλῳ, 'complicated.'

23. κατὰ καιρὸν μὲν . . . κατὰ καιρὸν δέ: l. 7.

24. δηγμούς, 'violent and painful means,' 'caustics.'

§ 4 l. 25. παθῶν, 'variable passions,' 'distempers.'

26. τὸ μέγεθος, determinant accusative with τοσαύτην.

27. διαχειρίσασθαι πεφυκώς, c. 1, 3 ; c. 39, 2.

29. προσστέλλων, *adstringens*, 'drawing tight' like a close-fitting garment for the purpose of adjusting it, opp. to ἀνιείς. Cf. Plat. *Gorg.* 511 D ἡ ἐπιστήμη προσεσταλμένη ('orderly,' 'modest') ἐστὶ καὶ κοσμία. The sentiment is borrowed from Thuc. II 65, 9 ὁπότε γοῦν αἴσθοιτό τι αὐτοὺς παρὰ καιρὸν ὕβρει θαρσοῦντας, λέγων κατέπλησσεν ἐπὶ τὸ φοβεῖσθαι καὶ δεδιότας αὖ ἀλόγως ἀντικαθίστη πάλιν ἐπὶ τὸ θαρσεῖν. τὸ θρασυνόμενον αὐτῶν for τοὺς θρασυνομένους αὐτῶν, cp. *Lyc.* c. 3, 5 ἦν δέ τι

καὶ τὸ φθονοῦν καὶ πρὸς τὴν αὔξησιν ὄντι νέῳ πειρώμενον ἐνίστασθαι. For τὸ δύσθυμον, cp. Theophr. ap. Athenae. 463 c παραμυθεῖται ὁ οἶνος τὴν τοῦ γήρως δυσθυμίαν.

30. **ἀνιείς**, 'allaying,' 'relieving.' Cf. *Cic*. c. 30, 3 πάντα πᾶσιν αὐτοῦ τὸν φόβον ἀνῆκεν.

31. **κατὰ Πλάτωνα**, c. 7, 6; Arist. *Thesm*. 134 κατ' Αἰσχύλον ἐρέσθαι βούλομαι, *Fr*. 599 ἐκφέρετε πεύκας κατ' Ἀγάθωνα φωσφόρους. The idea is expressed in the *Phaedr*. 261 A ἆρ' οὖν οὐ τὸ μὲν ὅλον ἡ ῥητορικὴ ἂν εἴη τέχνη ψυχαγωγία τις διὰ λόγων οὐ μόνον ἐν δικαστηρίοις καὶ ὅσοι ἄλλοι δημόσιοι σύλλογοι ἀλλὰ καὶ ἐν ἰδίοις, and again 271 C λόγου δύναμις τυγχάνει ψυχαγωγία οὖσα.

32. **μέγιστον ἔργον αὐτῆς** sc. ὄν.

33. **τὴν περὶ τὰ ἤθη . . . μέθοδον**, 'the knowledge of men's characters and passions,' Plato's τὰ τῆς ψυχῆς γένη καὶ τὰ τούτων παθήματα.

34. **τόνους καὶ φθόγγους** in definitive apposition to πάθη. **ἀφῆς**, 'touch,' a general term, applicable to ψυχή: **κρούσεως** is a special term denoting 'musical expression.'

§ 5 l. 36. **ψιλῶς**, *tantummodo*, 'barely,' 'merely' (unclassical). **Θουκυδίδης**: II 65, 8 αἴτιον δ' ἦν ὅτι ἐκεῖνος μὲν δυνατὸς ὢν τῷ τε ἀξιώματι καὶ τῇ γνώμῃ, χρημάτων τε διαφανῶς ἀδωρότατος γενόμενος, κατεῖχε τὸ πλῆθος ἐλευθέρως καὶ οὐκ ἤγετο μᾶλλον ὑπ' αὐτοῦ ἢ αὐτὸς ἦγε κτλ.

37. **ἡ περὶ τὸν βίον δόξα**, cp. c. 2, 3; c. 8, 1; c. 16, 1. **ἡ πίστις τοῦ ἀνδρός**, 'their confidence in the man,' objective gen.

38. **χρημάτων κρείττονος**: Thuc. II 60, 5, *Mor*. 809 F, 705 E τῶν ἡδονῶν κρείττονες. The opposite χρημάτων ἥσσων occurs in *Them*. c. 6, 1.

39. **ἐκ**, l. 13.

42. The construing order is: — **ἐκεῖνος οὐκ ἐποίησε τὴν οὐσίαν μείζονα (ταύτης) ἧς ὁ πατὴρ αὐτῷ κατέλιπε μιᾷ δραχμῇ (ἐκ τούτων τῶν χρημάτων) ὧν ἔνιοι καί τι τοῖς υἱέσι διέθεντο**, 'he did not make his fortune greater than that which his father had left him by a single drachma of the moneys, which some even disposed of in part in favour of their sons.' For διέθεντο, cp. Xen. *Cyr*. v ii 7. See critical note.

43. **μιᾷ δραχμῇ**, dat. of degree of difference. Cp. *Aem*. c. 4, 3 οὐδὲ δραχμῇ μιᾷ γεγονὼς εὐπορώτερος ἀπὸ τῆς στρατείας, *Timol.-Aem*. c. 2, 4 τηλικαύτην βασιλείαν καταστρεψάμενος οὐδὲ δραχμῇ μείζονα τὴν οὐσίαν ἐποίησεν.

CHAPTER XVI

§ 1 l. 1. καίτοι, 'and yet' (though his unselfishness stands out in such clear light) there is unequivocal testimony to the greatness of his power. **σαφῶς διηγεῖται**)(**παρεμφαίνουσιν,** which means 'intimate indirectly,' 'hint at.' Cp. *Mor.* 107 E τὰ γὰρ δίδυμα τὴν ὁμοιότητα μάλιστα παρεμφαίνει, 617 c καὶ τοῦτο παρεμφαίνει μὲν ὁ ποιητὴς δι' ὧν ἐπὶ τῆς Θέτιδός φησιν.

3. **οἱ κωμικοί**: c. 3, 3; c. 4, 2.

4. **νέους,** 'new.' Cp. c. 21, 6 'Ομφάλη νέα. For Ἡσιο-στρατίδας, see note to c. 7, 1.

6. **ἀπομόσαι μὴ τυραννήσειν,** 'to take a solemn oath that he would not make himself a despot.' For μή with the infinitive in indirect discourse after verbs of swearing, cp. Plat. *Legg.* XI 936 E τοὺς τρεῖς θεοὺς ἀπομόσας ἦ μὴν μὴ εἰδέναι, and see G. *MT.*² § 685. Plutarch uses also οὐ twice, *Num.* c. 10, 3 δεῖ δὲ ἀπομόσαι τὴν παρθένον οὐκ ἐξεπίτηδες γεγονέναι τὴν ἀπάντησιν, *Eum.* c. 12, 2 ἔπειτα ὤμνυεν οὐκ 'Αντιγόνῳ μόνον εὐνοήσειν.

7. **ὡς ... οὔσης,** c. 5, 4; c. 33, 3.

8. **βαρυτέρας,** 'too oppressive.' **περὶ αὐτόν** is for αὐτοῦ: c. 15 l. 37.

§ 2 l. 10. Τηλεκλείδης, c. 3, 4. The play from which the quotation is taken, is not known.

12. **δεῖν ... ἀναλύειν,** 'to bind ... to unbind,' *i.e.* to do with them as he pleased. These and the following infinitives depend on παραδεδωκέναι.

13. **λάϊνα τείχη** (Hom. *Il.* XII 177). On the construction of the walls, see c. 13, 5.

14. **πλοῦτον,** in reference to the state-treasures, which had been removed to the Acropolis; see c. 12, 1.

15. **ταῦτα,** 'all this' *i.e.* the possession of this unlimited power. **ἀκμή,** 'momentary *éclat*,' cp. c. 13, 1. **χάρις,** 'vogue,' 'popularity.'

16. **ἐφ' ὥραν,** 'for (during) a given season.' **τεσσα-ράκοντα ἔτη,** B.C. 469–429 = Ol. 77, 1—Ol. 87, 4. Cp. Cic. *de orat.* III 34, 138.

17. **'Εφιάλταις,** 'men of the stamp of Ephialtes,' c. 7, 6.

Λεωκράταις: proper names of the third declension form their plurals according to the first. So τοὺς 'Αριστοφάνας Plat. *Symp.* 218 B. See Krüger *Gr. Gr.* 19, 1, 2. Leocrates, son of Stroebus, was the Athenian commander in the victorious engagement with Aegina B.C. 456 (Thuc. I 105, 2). Myronides (c. 24, 6) delivered Megara from an attack of the Corinthians B.C. 457/6 and in the following year ruined the plans of the Boeotians by his victory at Oenophyta (Thuc. I 108, 2). For Tolmides, see c. 18, 2, 3.

§ 3 l. 19. Θουκυδίδου: see c. 8, 4; c. 11, 1.   κατάλυσιν, c. 3, 1; c. 7, 6.

20. τῶν πεντεκαίδεκα ἐτῶν, 'the fifteen years,' Ol. 84, 1—Ol. 87, 4, which are regarded as a definite part or fraction of the whole forty during which his authority was supreme; hence the article.

21. ἐν ταῖς ἐνιαυσίοις στρατηγίαις, 'in his annual tenure of the office of general (στρατηγός),' which might therefore be regarded as a continuous whole. It was as a member of the College of στρατηγοί that Pericles governed Athens so long.

24. ἀνάλωτον ὑπὸ χρημάτων, 'proof against bribery,' 'impregnable to money.' Cp. *Dem.* c. 11, 2 τῷ παρὰ Φιλίππου (χρυσίῳ) ἀνάλωτος ὤν, *Philip.* c. 15, 5 οὐδ' ἁλωτὸν ὑπὸ χρημάτων, Xen. *Ages.* c. 8, 8 ψυχὴν ἀνάλωτον ὑπὸ χρημάτων. καίπερ οὐ, as in c. 24, 3, is the normal usage of Plutarch; he once (*Pyrrh.* c. 18, 4) has καίπερ μηδέν abnormally.

25. ἀργῶς ἔχων πρὸς χρηματισμόν, 'being indifferent to money-making.'

Plutarch affects the phrase ἔχειν πρός τινα (τι) with modal adverb. Cp. c. 10, 3, *Thes.* c. 19, 5 πολεμικῶς ἔχων πρὸς τοὺς Ἀθηναίους, *Num.* c. 6, 3 ἀκρατῶς ἔχουσι καὶ μανικῶς πρὸς πόλεμον, *Lyc.* c. 23, 2 πρὸς εἰρήνην οἰκείως ἔχοντες, *Cim.* c. 12, 3 πρὸς τοὺς Φασηλίτας φιλικῶς ἔχοντες, *Them.* c. 2, 6 πρὸς τοὺς δημαγωγοὺς τῶν πολλῶν ὁμοίως ἐχόντων, c. 29, 4 ἀπαραιτήτως ἔχειν πρὸς αὐτόν, *Lucull.* c. 22, 4 ὑπούλως εἶχε πρὸς τὸν ἄνδρα, *Alex.* c. 47, 6.

27. δίκαιον, 'legitimate,' which belonged to him of right. ἀμελούμενος ἐκφύγοι, sc. ὁ πλοῦτος: cp. Soph. *O. T.* 111 ἐκφεύγει δὲ τἀμελούμενον.

28. ὡς μὴ πολλὰ πράγματα καὶ διατριβὰς ἀσχολουμένῳ παρέχοι, 'that it might not cause him much trouble and loss of time when he was busy.'

29. συνέταξεν, 'organised.'

30. ῥᾴστην, 'most convenient,' 'simplest.'

31. ἀκριβεστάτην, 'strictest.'

§ 4 l. 32. ἀθρόους, 'in the lump,' 'at a single sale.'

33 34. βίον, 'his general mode of living.'   τὰ περὶ τὴν δίαιταν = τὰ τῆς διαίτης, *victum cultumque;* c. 7, 4.

35. ἡδύς, *gratus;* cp. *Nic.* c. 5, 1 τοῖς φίλοις οὐ προσηνὴς οὐδ' ἡδύς ἐστιν.   ἐνηλίκοις, 'adults.' Cp. *Cat. ma.* c. 24, 5,

Lyc. c. 21, 1 ἡ παιδεία μέχρι τῶν ἐνηλίκων διέτεινεν, *Tim.* c. 13, 5 υἱῶν ἐνηλίκων θανάτους. The reference is to Xanthippus (c. 36, 1), and in γυναιξί probably to his daughters-in-law, rather than to his wife (c. 24, 5).

36. οὐδὲ δαψιλὴς χορηγός, 'and not liberal enough in his allowance for household expenses,' c. 9, 3, c. 14, 2.

37. ἐφήμερον, 'settled from day to day.' ταύτην, contemptuously. συνηγμένην, 'narrowed,' 'reduced.'

38. οὐδενὸς οἷον ἐν οἰκίᾳ μεγάλῃ ... περιρρέοντος, 'there being none of the superfluities to be expected in a great house.' Cp. Hor. *Ep.* 1 6, 45 *exilis domus est ubi non et multa supersunt.*

39. πράγμασιν, 'circumstances'; cp. *Cat. ma.* c. 21, 3 τῶν πραγμάτων ἐπιδιδόντων ποιούμενος τὰς ἑστιάσεις, *Crass.* c. 6, ὁ ὠνούμενος τιμῆς βραχείας μεγάλα πράγματα.

§ 5 l. 42. τὴν τοιαύτην : c. 2, 2 ; c. 7, 4 ; c. 31, 1.

43. ἀκρίβειαν : c. 36, 1. ὡς ἕτερος οὐδείς, 'as no one else was,' 'better than anybody else.'

44. κατεσκευασμένος, *institutus*, 'trained,' Xen. *Cyr.* VIII i 13.

45. ἀπᾴδοντα *sc.* ἦν (c. 15, 4), 'were not in accord with.' By ταῦτα is meant 'such well-ordered economy.'

47. εἴγε, *siquidem*, 'inasmuch as.' Cp. *Mor.* 831 E Ἀναξαγόρας δὲ τὴν χώραν κατέλιπε μηλόβοτον, Diog. Laert. 2, 6, 7 Ἀναξαγόρας εὐγενείᾳ καὶ πλούτῳ διαφέρων ἦν, ἀλλὰ καὶ μεγαλοφροσύνῃ, ὅς γε καὶ τὰ πατρῷα παρεχώρησε τοῖς οἰκείοις· αἰτιαθεὶς γὰρ ὑπ' αὐτῶν ὡς ἀμελῶν "Τί οὖν" ἔφη "οὐχ ὑμεῖς ἐπιμελεῖσθε;"

48. ἀφῆκεν ἀργήν, 'left uncultivated.' Cp. Xen. *Cyr.* III ii 19 βούλοιο ἄν σοι τὴν νῦν ἀργὸν οὖσαν χώραν ἐνεργὸν γενέσθαι ; *Oecon.* c. 4, 8. 10, Aristot. *Oecon.* II 1349ᵃ, 3 χώρα ἀργός, *Rhet.* III 9, 1410ᵃ, 29 ἀγρὸς ἀργός. Hence καταργεῖν, *sterilem, inutilem reddere*, as Luke *Ev.* XIII 7 ἵνα τί καὶ τὴν γῆν καταργεῖ (ἡ συκῆ);

49. ὑπό, *prae*, c. 7, 6 ; c. 33, 3.

§ 6 l. 50. ταὐτόν, neuter pred. adj., expressing the gen. notion.

51. πολιτικοῦ, 'a practical statesman,' such as Pericles was, c. 24, 1, 3. ὁ μέν. *i.e.* 'the philosopher.'

52. ἀνόργανον, 'without mechanical appliances.' τῆς ἐκτὸς ὕλης, 'external matter,' material things, c. 12, 6.

53. ἐπὶ τοῖς καλοῖς κινεῖ κτλ., 'sets his intelligence astir for good and noble objects' (c. 2, 1). τῷ ... ἀναμιγνύντι

κτλ., 'who brings his superior knowledge into touch with the common needs of mankind, the daily round of life,' applies his good qualities to the furtherance of human interests.

55. ἔστιν οὗ, 'there are cases where,' 'sometimes'; c. 15, 3 ; c. 24, 3.   τῶν ἀναγκαίων, 'one of the mere necessaries of life.'

56. τῶν καλῶν, 'one of the noble things,' *i.e.* those which enable him to perform morally beautiful actions.

34 § 7 l. 58. καὶ μέντοι introduces some additional fact that is to be noted (or, as here, a strong instance in point), and differs from καὶ δέ only in that the μέντοι is stronger than the δέ, and that the two particles are not necessarily separated by the intervention of other words. The anecdote which follows has no appearance of authenticity.

60. κεῖσθαι, *cubare*, 'was confined to his bed.'

συγκεκαλυμμένον, *capite obvoluto*, 'with his head covered,' as one at the point of death. Cp. *Demosth*. c. 29, 3, Plat. *Phaed.* 118 A, Xen. *Cyr.* VIII vii 28, Liv. VIII 9, Suet. *Caes.* c. 82.

61. ἀποκαρτεροῦντα, 'because he was starving himself to death,' *Num.* c. 21, 3 ; *Lyc.* c. 29, 5.   προσπεσόντος, 'when it had come to his ears.' Cp. *C. Gr.* c. 2, 3 τούτων αὐτῷ προσπεσόντων, *Cat. mi.* c. 59, 1, *Pelop.* c. 9, 3, *Mor.* 325 F προσπεσούσης αὐτοῖς ἀγγελίας. Dr. Blaydes applies this passage in illustration of Arist. *Eq.* 344 τι πρᾶγμα προσπεσόν σοι, but there the participle means simply 'befalling.'

63. δεῖσθαι πᾶσαν δέησιν, 'used every (possible) entreaty'; c. 9, 4 ; c. 11, 3.

64. εἰ ἀπολεῖ, 'if he is to lose.' For the use of the indicative, see G. *MT.*[2] § 670 (6) and cp. c. 18, 2.

66. ἐκκαλυψάμενον, 'uncovering his head,' 'unmuffling.'

CHAPTER XVII

§ 1 l. 1. ἄχθεσθαι, from jealousy.

2. ἐπαίρων, 'by way of inducing them.' For the infinitive, cp. c. 20, 2, *Timol.* c. 16, ὁ ἐπῆρεν αὐτοὺς τὸν Τιμολέοντα σέβεσθαι, *Philop.* c. 9, 3, Arist. *Nub.* 42 ἥτις με γῆμ' ἐπῆρε τὴν σὴν μητέρα, Herod. I 90 ἐπάρας Κροῖσον στρατεύεσθαι.

There is no mention of the proposed congress in any other writer; it was however, in any case, not a mere piece of ostentation, as Plutarch seems to make out (§ 3 ll. 33 f.), but it had a real and substantial object in view, to make Athens the principal place of all Hellas under a convenient pretext, and especially to give her the supremacy in all Greek waters. A similar object seems to have been the occasion of a decree (after B.C. 445), contained in a recently discovered inscription, by which the Hellenes were invited to bring there the firstfruits of their corn, in pursuance of a Delphic oracle of the Eleusinian Demeter (*Bloss*).

3. **μέγα φρονεῖν**, c. 28, 5.

5. **πάντας Ἕλληνας**: Fallitur Plutarchus quum scribit Periclem in concilium Athenas convocare voluisse πάντας Ἕλληνας τοὺς ὁπήποτε κατοικοῦντας < τῆς > Εὐρώπης καὶ τῆς Ἀσίας. Pericles enim solos Atheniensium socios et amicos convocat, ut et res ipsa clamat et iter legatorum qui mittuntur εἰς Βοιωτίαν καὶ Φωκίδα καὶ Πελοπόννησον, ἐκ δὲ ταύτης διὰ Λοκρῶν ἐπὶ τὴν πρόσοικον ἤπειρον ἕως Ἀκαρνανίας καὶ Ἀμβρακίας, nam facile intelligitur in eo itinere solam Achaiam legatis esse peragratam atque inde iterum traiecto freto ad Locros perventum. Nemo, opinor, existimabit Atheniensium legatos aut Elidem aut Arcadiam aut Spartam aut Corinthum adiisse et inde reduces διὰ Λοκρῶν Acarnaniam petiisse et Ambraciam. Hic ipse error argumento esse potest Plutarchum describere aliquod antiquitatis monumentum, idque nihil aliud esse quam τὸ Περικλέους ψήφισμα ἐκ τῆς τοῦ Κρατεροῦ συναγωγῆς satis mihi nunc videor ostendisse. Cobet *Mnemosyne* N.S. vol. i. p. 114.

6. **ὁπήποτε** . . . **Εὐρώπης**, 'in any part soever of Europe.' For the absence of the article, which is generally used by Plut. and inserted here by Cobet, cp. *Pomp.* c. 45, 5.

7. **παρακαλεῖν** depends on γράφει ψήφισμα, which is equivalent to a single verb.

8. **πόλιν** in definitive apposition to τοὺς κατοικοῦντας.

9. **τοὺς βουλευσομένους**, fut. part. for final rel. clause. Cp. *Fab.* c. 16, 5 τὸν ἐπισφάξοντα ἀναμένων, *Alc.* c. 25, 6 ἔπεμψε τοὺς αὑτοῦ κατηγορήσοντας.

11. **κατέπρησαν**, 'had burnt down,' an unclassical word but found several times in Plut. For the tense, cp. c. 15 l. 11; c. 21, 2, and see G. *MT.*² § 58.

12. **ὑπέρ**, 'in the name of.'

§ 2 l. 16. **ἐπὶ ταῦτα**, 'for this purpose.' **ὑπὲρ πεντήκοντα ἔτη**: this appears to have been a common limit of age for members of an embassy: cp. *CIA.* 10, 17 πρέσβεις δὲ τρεῖς πέμψαι ὑπὲρ πεντήκοντα ἔτη γεγονότας ὡς Περδίκκαν. For ὑπέρ, cp. *Alc.* c. 20, 5 καταβαλὼν ὑπὲρ ἕνδεκα μυριάδας, *Marc.* c. 28, 3, Xen. *Cyr.* I ii 4 τοῖς ὑπὲρ τὰ στρατεύσιμα ἔτη γεγονόσιν, Arist. *Eccl.* 1025 οὐ κύριος ὑπὲρ μέδιμνόν ἐστι.

18. **ἄχρι Λέσβου καὶ Ῥόδου**, the limits north and south 35 respectively.

20. **ἐν Ἑλλησπόντῳ**, 'on the coast of the Hellespont.'

21. **ἐπὶ τούτοις**, 'over and above these.'

23. **ταύτης**, sc. τῆς Πελοποννήσου. **Λοκρῶν**, i.e. Western Locris. **τὴν πρόσοικον ἤπειρον**, in opp. to the peninsula of Peloponnesus, and the eastern part of central Greece.

L.

24. ἕως, in local sense; see Gr. Ind. s. v. The usage dates from Aristotle downwards and is common in the Gr. N. T.

§ 3 l. 25. οἱ λοιποί, 'the remaining' five. Οἰταίους, 'the inhabitants of Oeta' (Thessaly). τὸν Μαλιέα κόλπον, on the coast of Thessaly, over against the northernmost point of Euboea. The Attic form is Μηλιᾶ, as in Soph. *Phil.* 4 τὸν Μηλιᾶ Ποίαντος υἱόν.

26. Φθιώτας Ἀχαιούς, in South Thessaly.

27. Θεσσαλούς, 'the (other) Thessalians,' a frequent idiom.

32. τῆς πείρας ἐλεγχθείσης, 'the overture being rejected.'

33. παρεθέμην, *memoravi*, 'I quote,' 'adduce.' Cp. *Arist.* c. 26, 2 εἰωθὼς παρατίθεσθαι τοὺς ἱστοροῦντας, *Alex.* c. 41, 2 σημεῖα μεγάλης εὐνοίας ὧν ὀλίγα παραθήσομαι, *Mor.* 940 A, Athenae. p. 556 A παρέθετο δὲ περὶ τῶν γυναικῶν ψήφισμα Ἱερώνυμος, p. 696 F παρέθετο δ' αὐτὸν (τὸν παιᾶνα) Πολέμων ὁ περιηγητής.

Ipsum verbum παρεθέμην indicio est descripta esse haec ex antiquo scriptore, cuius fidem et auctoritatem Plutarchus sequeretur, cuius testimonio uteretur, ut est verbum παραθέσθαι in auctoritatibus afferendis usitatum (*Cobet*).

ἐνδεικνύμενος αὐτοῦ τὴν μεγαλοφροσύνην: Hoc enim ante omnia Plutarchus agebat οὐ τὴν ἄχρηστον ἀθροίζων ἱστορίαν ἀλλὰ τὴν πρὸς κατανόησιν ἤθους καὶ τρόπου παραδιδούς (*Cobet*).

Plutarch must have had before him the original psephism of Pericles, which he found in the ψηφισμάτων συναγωγή of Craterus (c. 8, 5 note) — a book much consulted by him. Cobet attempts a reconstruction of it from the Biographer's words :—Ἔδοξε τῇ βουλῇ καὶ τῷ δήμῳ — Περικλῆς Ξανθίππου Χολαργεὺς εἶπεν·—πάντας Ἕλληνας παρακαλεῖν καὶ μικρὰν πόλιν καὶ μεγάλην πέμπειν Ἀθήναζε οἵτινες βουλεύσονται περί τε τῶν Ἑλληνικῶν ἱερῶν ἃ κατέπρησαν οἱ βάρβαροι κτέ . . . πέμπειν δὲ ἄνδρας εἴκοσι τῶν ὑπὲρ πεντήκοντα ἐτῶν γεγονότων ὧν πέντε μὲν Ἴωνας καὶ Δωριᾶς τοὺς ἐν Ἀσίᾳ καὶ νησιώτας ἄχρι Λέσβου καὶ Ῥόδου παρακαλοῦσι . . . πέντε δὲ τοὺς ἐν Ἑλλησπόντῳ καὶ Θρᾴκῃ μέχρι Βυζαντίου τόπους ἐπιέναι καὶ πέντε ἐπὶ τούτοις εἰς Βοιωτίαν καὶ Φωκίδα καὶ Πελοπόννησον. ἐκ δὲ ταύτης διὰ Λοκρῶν ἐπὶ τὴν πρόσοικον ἤπειρον ἕως Ἀκαρνανίας καὶ Ἀμβρακίας ἀποσταλῆναι, τοὺς δὲ λοιποὺς δι' Εὐβοίας ἐπ' Οἰταίους καὶ τὸν Μηλιᾶ κόλπον καὶ Θεσσαλοὺς πορεύεσθαι.

CHAPTER XVIII

§ 1 l. 2. τὴν ἀσφάλειαν, 'his caution.' See Gr. Ind. s. v.

3. ἐχούσης ἀδηλότητα, c. 28, 6. For οὔτε . . . τε, cp. c. 35, 3. Plutarch uses οὔτε . . . καί almost as often; see Stegmann *l. c.* § 37 p. 28.

4. ἐκ τοῦ παραβαλέσθαι, 'after engaging in rash adventures.'

8. ὅσον ἐπ' αὐτῷ sc. ἐστί, 'as far as depends on himself,' c. 13, 9, *Fab.* c. 10, 2. *Marc.* c. 18, 1, *Philop.* c. 3, 4. The common Attic expression was τὸ ἐπ' αὐτῷ or τὸ ἐπ' αὐτῷ εἶναι.

§ 2 l. 10. Τολμίδην, c. 16, 2. Tolmides had commanded a naval expedition round Peloponnesus B.C. 456. See c. 19, 3. A summary of his exploits is given by Pausanias 1 27, 5.

The expedition here referred to was undertaken to avert the danger, which threatened the interest of Athens in the north of Greece, arising from the occupation of Chaeronea and Orchomenus by the Boeotian exiles, who had been driven out of their respective cities by the ascendancy which the battle of Oenophyta had everywhere given to the Athenian or democratical party. His reputation drew a thousand volunteers, including the flower of the Athenian youth, to share his enterprise. With this force and some allied troops he entered Boeotia and first attacked Chaeronea. He succeeded in reducing it and was retiring with his little army, which he had weakened by leaving a garrison in the captured town, when in the neighbourhood of Coroneia, he was surprised by the appearance of a hostile army. . . . The Athenians were completely defeated (Thuc. 1 113). The immediate consequence of their defeat was a counter-revolution, which overthrew the Athenian influence throughout Boeotia. To recover their prisoners, the Athenians had to withdraw all their troops from the country, and their departure was everywhere followed by the return of the exiles and the predominance of the party hostile to Athens (*Thirlwall*).

διὰ . . . τὸ τιμᾶσθαι : Thuc. v 16, 1 uses nearly the same 36 expressions (διὰ τὸ εὐτυχεῖν τε καὶ τιμᾶσθαι ἐκ τοῦ πολεμεῖν) in speaking of Brasidas.

12. σὺν οὐδενὶ καιρῷ = ἀκαίρως. So σὺν οὐδενὶ λογισμῷ = ἀλογίστως *Them.* c. 23, 2, σὺν οὐδενὶ κόσμῳ - ἀκόσμως Arrian *Anab.* IV 26, 3 (for which Thuc. II 52, 1, III 108, 3 has οὐδενὶ κόσμῳ), σὺν μηδενὶ πόνῳ *Cleom.* c. 26, 1.

14. ἐμβαλεῖν : this was in the spring of B.C. 446 = Ol. 83, 3. Busolt *Gr. Gesch.* II p. 546 note 3. τῶν ἐν ἡλικίᾳ, c. 12, 5.

16. ἐθελοντί, an adverb not found elsewhere in Plutarch.

17. ἄνευ, *praeter*, 'without reckoning': cp. *Dem.* c. 17, 2 and Gr. Ind. *ibid.* p. 164 ᵃ. τῆς ἄλλης δυνάμεως, the contingent of allies mentioned by Thuc. *l. c.*

18. παρακαλεῖν, *obsecrare*. ἐν τῷ δήμῳ = ἐν τῇ ἐκκλησίᾳ, *Them.* c. 22, 1.

19. τὸ μνημονευόμενον = τὸ ἀπομνημονευόμενον, 'the saying on record,' c. 8, 5 ; cp. *Them.* c. 11, 2, *Cat. ma.* c. 15, 4.

21. οὐχ ἁμαρτήσεται . . . ἀναμείνας, 'he will not do amiss to wait for' ; ἀναμείνας = ἐὰν ἀναμείνῃ, G. *MT.*² § 472. For the use of the future indicative, see note to c. 16 l. 64.

§ 3 l. 22. μετρίως εὐδοκίμησε, 'made (only) a slight impression by this saying of his.'

24. ἀνηγγέλθη τεθνεώς : see G. *MT.*² § 904 and cp. c. 22, 1, *Dem.* c. 28, 2 ἠγγέλλοντο προσιόντες, *Cic.* c. 4, 3 ἐπεὶ ὁ' αὐτῷ Σόλλας προσηγγέλθη τεθνηκώς. Clinias, father of Alcibiades, also fell (*Alc.* c. 1, 1) in the same battle. Thuc. is silent about the death of Tolmides. περὶ Κορώνειαν, 'in the environs of Coroneia (Bocotia),' c. 27, 3, usually ἐν Κορωνείᾳ, as Thuc. I 113, 2; III 62, 4; IV 92, 6; Diod. XII 6, Plat. *Alc.* I 112. Xenophon names Lebadea (mod. *Livadia*) as the site of the battle. Pausanias I 27, 5 tells us that the Athenians were attacked on their march to Haliartus.

27. μετ' εὐνοίας δόξαν, 'repute as well as goodwill'; cp. c. 24, 2; c. 31, 1.

28. φιλοπολίτῃ, 'anxious for the welfare of his fellow-citizens,' 'patriotic.' The usual form is φιλόπολις.

CHAPTER XIX

§ 1 l. 1. ἠγαπήθη . . . μάλιστα, 'gave most satisfaction,')(ἐθαυμάσθη l. 14.

2. Χερρόνησον : c. 11, 5. The amount of the φόρος paid by the Chersonesites up to B.C. 448/7 was eighteen talents. This was reduced in B.C. 447/6 to two and a half. Such a considerable reduction was most probably synchronous with the Athenian colonisation.

3. αὐτόθι = αὐτοῦ, *ibi.*

4. ἐποίκους, colonists sent to reinforce the population of towns already existing, Thuc. II 27, 1 ; V 5, 1.

Plutarch (Theopompus) places the foundation of this as well as other cleruchies at the time of the party struggle between Pericles and Thucydides, which began immediately after the death of Cimon. Consequently the earliest possible date of the colonisation would be B.C. 447. But Diodorus (XI 88, 3) places it earlier, in the archonship of Lysicrates, B.C. 453/2 = OL. 81, 4, after Pericles' expedition to the Gulf of Corinth.

6. εὐανδρίᾳ, 'with store of goodly men.' *Mor.* 322 Α οὐκ ἂν αἱ πρῶται τῆς πόλεως ἀρχαὶ εἰς εὐανδρίαν καὶ πλῆθος ἐπέδωκαν, 824 C τῶν μεγίστων ἀγαθῶν ταῖς πόλεσιν, εἰρήνης, ἐλευθερίας, εὐετηρίας, εὐανδρίας, Xen. *Mem.* III 3, 12 οὐδ' εὐανδρία ἐν ἄλλῃ πόλει ὁμοία τῇ ἐνθάδε συνάγεται. τὸν αὐχένα διαζώσας, 'by belting the neck of land.' Cp. *Them.* c. 12, 2 διαζῶσαι τὰς νήσους, Xen. *Mem.* III 5, 25 (ἡ χώρη ἡμῶν)

μίση διέζωσται ὄρεσιν ἐρυμνοῖς, Polyb. V 69, 1 τοῦτον αὐτὸν (τὸν τόπον) ῥάχει δυσβάτῳ καὶ τραχείᾳ διεζῶσθαι.

This had been already done by the first Miltiades, who as we learn from Herodotus VI 36 ἀπετείχισε τὸν ἰσθμὸν τῆς Χερσονήσου ἐκ Καρδίης πόλιος ἐς Πακτύην, ἵνα μὴ ἔχοιεν σφέας οἱ Ἀψίνθιοι δηλέεσθαι ἐσβάλλοντες ἐς τὴν χώρην· εἰσὶ δὲ οὗτοι στάδιοι ἕξ τε καὶ τριάκοντα τοῦ ἰσθμοῦ. At a later period (B.C. 398) the Spartan Dercyllidas Χερρόνησον κεκακωμένην, ὥσπερ ἔλεγετο, ὑπὸ τῶν Θρᾳκῶν, ἐπεὶ μέτρον εὗρε τοῦ ἰσθμοῦ ἑπτὰ καὶ τριάκοντα στάδια, ... ἐτείχιζε ... καὶ ἐποίησεν ἐντὸς τοῦ τείχους ἕνδεκα μὲν πόλεις, πολλοὺς δὲ λιμένας, πολλὴν δὲ κἀγαθὴν σπόριμον, πολλὴν δὲ πεφυτευμένην, παμπληθεῖς δὲ καὶ παγκάλας νομὰς παντοδαποῖς κτήνεσι, Xen. Hell. III ii 10. But these lasted for a short time only. The fortifications of Pericles must have been destroyed soon after their erection.

9. **ἀπετείχισε**, *muro interclusit*, 'intercepted.' Cp. *Nic.* c. 26, 2 τὰς διαβάσεις τῶν ποταμῶν ἀπετείχισαν.
καταδρομάς, 'raids': cp. *Cim.* c. 1, 4 λῃστείαις καὶ καταδρομαῖς πορθοῦντα τὴν χώραν, *Pyrrh.* c. 7, 2 καταδρομαὶ τῆς Θεσσαλίας ἐγεγόνεισαν ὑπ' ἐκείνου, Thuc. VII 27, 2 etc.

§ 2 l. 11. **ἐξέκλεισεν**, 'closed the door against.' συν- 37 εἴχετο, *premebatur*.

12. **ἀναμεμιγμένῃ**, 'having had relations (good or bad) with.'

13. **λῃστηρίων**, 'bands of robbers,' Xen. *Hell.* V iv 42.

14. **συνοίκων**, 'living amongst them.' **ἐθαυμάσθη** sc. Περικλῆς: this was because of the small force with which he had gained the victory over and inflicted considerable loss on the enemy.

15. **πρὸς τοὺς ἐκτὸς ἀνθρώπους**, 'amongst foreigners.'

16. **τῆς Μεγαρικῆς**, 'in the Megarid,' a partitive genitive denoting a country with the name of a single place in it.

Ηγαί (or Παγαί) was a Megarian harbour on the Corinthian Gulf, which belonged at this time to the Athenians (Thuc. I 111, 2). The expedition, undertaken in the spring of 453 B.C., was not strictly a περίπλους Πελοποννήσου, because operations were limited to the Corinthian Gulf, and they could not have committed much devastation outside the district of Sicyon, because Achaia was friendly. Plutarch is the only writer who says the fleet was composed of 100 triremes. Diodorus (Ephorus) gives the number as 50 (c. 85 δόντες αὐτῷ τῷ Περικλεῖ τριήρεις πεντήκοντα καὶ χιλίους ὁπλίτας ἐξέπεμψαν ἐπὶ τὴν Πελοπόννησον), but he makes a mistake, confusing two expeditions (c. 88) which were really one and the same. Thucydides (*l. c.*) says only that 1000 Athenians embarked on board the triremes stationed at Pegae, without mentioning the number of the vessels.

§ 3 l. 17. **τῆς παραλίας πολλήν**: G. *Gr.* § 168 n. 1, HA. *Gr.* § 730.

18. **πρότερον**, in the latter half of the summer of B.C. 456 = Ol. 81, 1; c. 18, 2. Thuc. (I 108, 5) gives only a brief account of this expedition: καὶ Πελοπόννησον περιέπλευσαν Ἀθηναῖοι

Τολμίδου τοῦ Τολμαίου στρατηγοῦντος καὶ τὸ νεώριον τὸ Λακεδαιμονίων ἐνέπρησαν καὶ Χαλκίδα Κορινθίων πόλιν εἷλον, καὶ Σικυωνίους ἐν ἀποβάσει τῆς γῆς μάχῃ ἐκράτησαν. See Busolt *Gr. Gesch.* II p. 497 Anm. 1.

19. **πόρρω θαλάττης**, 'at some distance from the sea-board,' 'inland.' For the omission of the article, see n. to c. 24, 7.

τοῖς ἀπὸ τῶν νεῶν ὁπλίταις, 'with the troops he had on board,' the *dativus militaris*, as l. 17, c. 10, 1.

21. **συνέστειλε**, 'drove back.' Cp. *Pyrrh.* c. 25, 4 συσταλεὶς πρὸς τὸ στρατόπεδον and see my note to *Nic.* c. 26, 4.

22. **Νεμέᾳ**: Plutarch's authority doubtless meant the stream of Nemea, which forms the boundary between Sicyon and Corinth, not the place, which was too far inland for Pericles to have ventured there with so small a force. See Busolt *Gr. Gesch.* II p. 504 Anm. 3. **Σικυωνίους**, as opp. to τοὺς ἄλλους.

23. **κατὰ κράτος**, 'by main force,' with τρεψάμενος.

§ 4 l. 24. **ἐκ δ' Ἀχαΐας κτλ.** : Thuc. I 101, 2 καὶ εὐθὺς παραλαβόντες Ἀχαιοὺς καὶ διαπλεύσαντες πέραν τῆς Ἀκαρνανίας ἐς Οἰνιάδας ἐστράτευσαν καὶ ἐπολιούρκουν, οὐ μέντοι εἷλόν γε, ἀλλ' ἀπεχώρησαν ἐπ' οἴκου. **φίλης**, rare (in prose) for φιλίας. Cp. Lys. *or.* 12, 38 πόλεις πολεμίας οὔσας φίλας ἐποίησαν, Isocr. *or.* 16, 21 ὅσας πόλεις κατὰ κράτος εἷλεν ἢ λόγῳ πείσας φίλας ὑμῖν ἐποίησεν. **ἀναλαβών**: Thuc. II 25, 5 ; VII 25, 4.

25. **τὴν ἀντιπέρας ἤπειρον**: c. 17, 2 note.

26. **παραπλεύσας**, 'sailing past the mouth of.'

27. **κατέδραμε**, 'overran,' l. 9. Diod. XI 85, 2 says, πλὴν Οἰνιαδῶν ἀπάσας τὰς πόλεις προσηγάγετο, which is a more likely account, considering that we find the Athenians at a later period on friendly terms with all the Acarnanians (Thuc. II 68, 5) except the Oeniadae, who ἀεί ποτε πολέμιοι ἦσαν (c. 102, 5).

Busolt (*Gr. Gesch.* II 505) suggests that the expedition of Pericles may have had something to do with a quarrel between the Acarnanians and the Messenians who had been settled at Naupactus for the possession of Oeniadae, in the course of which Naupactus itself had been threatened. Cp. Paus. IV 25. Acarnania, moreover, must have been commercially important to the Corinthians, who could not have watched unmoved the Athenian operations on the coast. As to Oeniadae, its position on a hill near the west bank of the Achelous, surrounded by a morass, which on the north deepens into a lake (Melite) must have secured it at all times against invasion (Thuc. II 102, 2).

28. **Οἰνιάδας**: οἱ Οἰνιάδαι was the name of the people as well as of their chief town, which ranked as the second in all Acarnania and was considered one of the strongest fortresses in

Greece, partly from its situation, partly from its artificial defences. It was long the inexpugnable and only bulwark of the Spartan cause in the district. During the Macedonian and Roman war it continued to be a place of great importance. In B.C. 219 it was taken by Philip king of Macedon, and in B.C. 211 it fell into the hands of the Romans, who gave it to the Aetolians. Mure *Tour in Greece* 1 pp. 107 ff.

29. ἐπ' οἴκου, 'in the direction of home,' 'homewards.'

30. ἀσφαλής: cp. *Phoc.* c. 6, 2 ἀσφαλὴς ὁ Φωκίων καὶ δραστήριος φαινόμενος τὴν μέλλησιν ἀνεθέρμαινε τοῦ Χαβρίου. Thucydides merely says that Pericles laid siege to the place but failed to take it. Plutarch makes his narrative as much as possible favourable to Pericles. **δραστήριος**: see Gk. Ind. s.v.

31. οὐδ' ἀπὸ τύχης, *ne fortuitum quidem*. The failure to take Oeniadae is not reckoned a miscarriage.

CHAPTER XX

§ 1. The source of Plutarch's information about this expedition and its date are alike uncertain; the latter was probably B.C. 444/3. See Busolt *Gr. Gesch.* II p. 538 Anm. 4, who quotes it as the opinion of Duncker, *Des Perikles Fahrt in den Pontus*, Ber. d. Berl. Akad. 1885 p. 536.

This was probably the first appearance of an Athenian general with an imposing force beyond the Bosporus; unless we accept the tradition of the mission of Aristides to the Pontus and his death there, Plut. *Arist.* c. 26 (Busolt *Gr. Gesch.* II p. 397 Anm. 3). The commercial dealings of Athens with the trading places on the shores of the Pontus were considerable, and it was therefore of the utmost importance that they should be on good terms with the neighbouring princes, who might interfere with their communication. A timely display of force would serve to impress these potentates with a proper sense of the power which might be brought to the aid of the Hellenic colonies if required. But the Athenians had not only a strong interest in the command of the highways communicating with the Euxine, and the superintendence of the grain conveyed along them, but also in their relation with the Pontic towns especially. If these were hard pressed by the surrounding barbarians, the Athenian merchandise suffered, especially the corn-market. The Pontic Greeks might, on the other hand, look to the Athenian navy for support. And so political relations at an early time of the Athenian naval supremacy were developed between them and Athens. The rising power of the two kings Teres and Ariapeithes must have given trouble to the Hellenic towns on the west and north coast of the Pontus. It was, perhaps, in consequence of these relations to the barbarian states that the Pontic towns made their appeal to Athens.

3. ὧν ἐδέοντο: the removal of grievances of which they complained, and the settlement of disputes between them and the dynasts.

4. προσηνέχθη φιλανθρώπως, 'behaved kindly to.' Cp. *Cleom.* c. 13, 1 τραχέως προσφερομένων τοῖς ἐντυγχάνουσι. For διαπράξασθαί τινί τι, cp. *Mor.* 577 E διαπράξασθαι φυγὴν ἀντὶ θανάτου τῷ ἀνθρώπῳ, 760 Β διαπράξασθαί τινα δυναστείαν αὑτῷ, *Cic.* c. 24, 5 Κρατίππῳ διεπράξατο 'Ρωμαίῳ γενέσθαι παρὰ Καίσαρος: Herod. III c. 61, 4 uses the active in the same way.

6. βασιλεῦσι, Teres, king of the Odrysians, whose dominion reached from the Hebrus to the Danube (Thuc. II 29, 2 ; Xen. *Anab.* VII ii 22), and Ariapeithes, his son-in-law, king of the Scythians (Herod. IV 76–78). The cities on the western coast of the Pontus were tributaries of the former.

7. δυνάσταις, 'petty local princes,' c. 15, 1. ἐπεδείξατο μέν: the opposition, which should be in ἀπέλιπε, is transferred to Σινωπεῦσι. Similar transpositions of correlative particles are not uncommon. One has been already noticed c. 14, 2. Cp. c. 3, 2 ; c. 11, 1, 5 ; c. 13, 1 ; Xen. *Cyr.* VIII v 8, vi 11.

9. ᾖ βούλοιντο, 'wherever they liked,' opt. of recurrence as c. 8, 3. See G. *MT.*² § 532.

11. Σινωπεῦσι: those who were banished from Sinope (Paphlagonia), a town of great mercantile importance to Athens, situate on a peninsula on the south coast of the Pontus (Polyb. IV 56, 5 f.). It was the principal trade-centre for iron goods, finer species of wood, fish, Paphlagonian shell-fruit, and slaves. The colony was planted by the Milesians c. 785 B.C.

12. μετὰ Λαμάχου, 'under Lamachus,' *Timol.* c. 19, 1 note. But in the case of the Roman army, where there was a less spirit of comradeship between officers and men, Plutarch uses ὑπό instead of μετά, as *Cam.* c. 2, 1. Lamachus had the command of another Pontic expedition later on in B.C. 424 (Thuc. IV 75, 1). He was the general who lost his life before Syracuse, in the great Sicilian expedition B.C. 414 (Thuc. VI 101, 5).

13. Τιμησίλεων : Timesilaus probably was an officer representing the Persian power in the city, and any attempt to expel him was equivalent to an attack on the Persian king (*Abbott*).

§ 2 l. 13. ἐκπεσόντος, c. 7, 2.

14. ἐψηφίσατο, 'got a bill passed,' c. 13, 6, c. 24, 1, *Agis* c. 12, 1, Schömann *de com.* p. 124.

16. νειμαμένους, 'dividing among themselves,' 'taking possession of.'

17. οἱ τύραννοι, 'the family of the despot and their adherents.'

18. ὁρμαῖς, 'impulses.' *Agis* c. 1, 2, *Them.* c. 2, 5, *Cut. mi.* c. 1, 2, *Galb.* c. 1, 3, Aristot. Ἀθ. πολ. c. 28, 3 with Sandys' n. *ad l.*

19. οὐδὲ συνεξέπιπτεν, 'nor did he allow himself to be hurried along with them' *sc.* ταῖς ὁρμαῖς. Cp. *Cleom.* c. 37, 3, *Phoc.* c. 6, 1 συνεξέπιπτε τοῖς θρασυτάτοις παραβολώτερον, *Mor.* 547 c συνεκπίπτοντα τοῖς ἐπαίνοις. ῥώμης: cp. *Per.–Fab.* c. 1, 1 ὑπὸ κοινῆς εὐτυχίας καὶ ῥώμης πραγμάτων ἀσφαλὴς διαγενέσθαι, *Nic.* c. 18, 6 ὑπὸ τῆς ἐν τῷ παρόντι ῥώμης καὶ τύχης ἀνατεθαρρηκώς, *Pyrrh.* c. 23, 2 εὐτυχίᾳ καὶ ῥώμῃ τῶν παρόντων ἐπαιρόμενος, *Aem. Paul.* c. 9, 1 ὑπὸ ῥώμης τῶν πραγμάτων ἀναφερόμενος πρὸς τὸν πόλεμον.

20. ἐπαιρομένων . . . ἀντιλαμβάνεσθαι, c. 17, 1.

Αἰγύπτου πάλιν κτλ. Towards the end of the summer of 460 B.C. the Athenians sent out a great expedition to the support of Inaros, son of Psammetichus king of Libya, who had revolted against the Persians and been elected king of Egypt in the previous year (Thuc. i 104, Diod. xi 71, 3 ff.), but after a struggle with the Persians, which lasted six years, they sustained finally a crushing defeat (Thuc. i cc. 109, 110). Soon after the conclusion of the five years' truce, in the spring of B.C. 449, a fleet of 200 triremes was sent to Cyprus under the command of Cimon, who detached a squadron of sixty to Egypt at the request of Amyrtaeus, who still held out against the Persian monarch in the marshes of the Delta (Thuc. i 112, 2).

21. ἀντιλαμβάνεσθαι, c. 25, 3.   κινεῖν, *aggredi*.

22. βασιλέως, c. 3, 1 ; c. 10, 4.   ἀρχῆς, 'dominions,' part. gen. after τὰ πρὸς θαλάσσῃ, 'the maritime provinces.'

§ 3 l. 23. ὁ δύσερως . . . ἔρως, 'that inauspicious hankering,' a poetical expression like δυσφήμους φάμας Eur. *Hec.* 193, γάμους δυσγάμους *Phoen.* 1052, δύσνοστον νόστον *Troad.* 75.

ἤδη . . . εἶχε, 'already at that time possessed them.' Cp. c. 10, 2 ; *Them.* c. 9, 2 ὀργὴ τῆς προδοσίας εἶχε τοὺς Ἀθηναίους, c. 11, 4 ἔννοια καὶ δέος ἔσχε τὸν Εὐρυβιάδην, *Timol.* c. 22, 4 φρίκη καὶ μῖσος εἶχε πάντας, *Arist.* c. 15, 3 τὸν στρατὸν ἔχει δυσθυμία πολλὴ καὶ κατάπληξις, *Eum.* c. 10, 3 θαῦμα τοὺς παρόντας εἶχε. It appears also from Thuc. i 44, 2 that the Athenians had an eye upon Sicily in the time of Pericles.

24. ἐξέκαυσαν, c. 32, 3.

25. οἱ περὶ τὸν Ἀλκιβιάδην ῥήτορες, c. 14, 1. Cp. *Alcib.* c. 17, 1 Σικελίας δὲ καὶ Περικλέους ἔτι ζῶντος ἐπεθύμουν Ἀθηναῖοι . . . ὁ δὲ παντάπασι τὸν ἔρωτα τοῦτον ἀναφλέξας αὐτῶν . . . Ἀλκιβιάδης ἦν.

26. Τυρρηνία καὶ Καρχηδών: both were included in their later project, as appears from the speech of Alcibiades at Sparta, Thuc. vi 90, 1 ἐπλεύσαμεν πρῶτον μὲν Σικελιώτας καταστρεψόμενοι, μετὰ δ' ἐκείνους αὖθις καὶ Ἰταλιώτας, ἔπειτα καὶ τῆς Καρχηδονίων ἀρχῆς καὶ αὐτῶν ἀποπειρά-

σοντες, Nic. c. 12, 2, Alc. c. 17, 3 Ἀλκιβιάδης δὲ Καρχηδόνα καὶ Λιβύην ὀνειροπολῶν, ἐκ δὲ τούτων προσγενομένων Ἰταλίαν καὶ Πελοπόννησον ἤδη περιβαλλόμενος ὀλίγου δεῖν ἐφόδια τοῦ πολέμου Σικελίαν ἐποιεῖτο.

οὐκ ἀπ' ἐλπίδος, 'not away from hope,' 'not without a reasonable ground.'

Cp. Apoll. Rhod. *Argon.* II 863 μάλα πολλὸν ἀπ' ἐλπίδος ἔπλετο and the expressions οὐκ ἀπὸ τρόπου, *non absurde*, *Alc.* c. 16, 5, *Mar.* c. 11, 7, *Mor.* 4 A, 636 E, Plat. *Theaet.* 143 C, *Phileb.* 34 A, *Rep.* 470 B, οὐκ ἀπὸ σκοποῦ *Theaet.* 179 C, *Tim.* 25 E, ἀπὸ γνώμης Plut. *Alex.* c. 38, 4; c. 50, 1, Soph. *Trach.* 389.

27. **ὑποκειμένης**, 'actual,' 'existing.' Cp. *Sol.-Popl.* c. 4, 3 πρὸς τοὺς ὑποκειμένους καιροὺς τὰς πράξεις θεωρεῖν, *Cam.* c. 19, 2 τῇ ὑποκειμένῃ γραφῇ ἂν ἁρμόσειε, *Pelop.* c. 8, 3 τόλμης ὅσης ὅ τε καιρὸς ὀξὺς ὢν αἵ τε ὑποκείμεναι πράξεις ἀπῄτουν, *Cat. mi.* c. 59, 5, *Alex.* c. 47, 4 τοῖς ὑποκειμένοις πράγμασιν.

28. **εὔροιαν**, 'prosperous course,' 'full tide of success.'

The word is found in this sense only in this one passage of Plutarch, but is frequent in Polybius, generally with πραγμάτων, as II 44, 2 ἐγένετό τις εὔροια πραγμάτων, III 10, 6 τὴν εὔροιαν τῶν κατ' Ἰβηρίαν πραγμάτων Καρχηδονίοις, 15, 3 τὴν γενομένην εὔροιαν Καρχηδονίοις τῶν κατ' Ἰβηρίαν πραγμάτων, V 14, 8 τοῖς θεοῖς ἔθυε χαριστήρια τῆς γεγενημένης αὐτῷ περὶ τὴν ἐπιβολὴν εὐροίας, 71, 1, Diodor. XX c. 33 οὐ μὴν ἡ τύχη γε εἴασε τὴν εὔροιαν μένειν ἐπὶ τῆς αὐτῆς τάξεως.

CHAPTER XXI

§ 1 l. 1. **ἐκδρομήν**, 'impetuosity,' 'extravagant spirit of conquest,' literally 'sally.'

2. **περιέκοπτε**, 'was for clipping,' 'tried to curtail,' metaphor from pruning trees. Cp. *Cat. mi.* c. 2, 2 τὸν αὑτοῦ πάλιν οἶκον ἐφορῶν καὶ δίαιταν ἐπέτεινε τὴν αὐτουργίαν καὶ περιέκοπτε τὴν πολυτέλειαν, *Agis* c. 7, 4, *Amat.* c. 7. **πολυπραγμοσύνην** (c. 11, 5) 'meddlesomeness,' 'undue interference,' opp. to τὸ τὰ αὑτοῦ πράττειν. Cp. *Agis* c. 7, 3, *Pyrrh.* c. 29, 6.

4. **ἔτρεπεν**, 'was for diverting,' c. 12, 4. **βεβαιότητα**, 'security.'

5. **μέγα ἔργον** sc. εἶναι, 'that it was a hard enough task,' or 'a matter of great importance,' Thuc. III 3, 1 μέγα ἔργον ἡγοῦντο εἶναι Λέσβον προσπολεμώσασθαι, VI 8, 4.

6. **ἀνείργειν**, c. 12, 3.

8. **τοῖς περὶ τὸν ἱερὸν πραχθεῖσι πόλεμον**, 'the events of the Sacred War.'

In B.C. 448/7 = Ol. 83, 1, before the expiration of the five years' truce between Athens and Sparta, the Phocians, on the strength of their alliance with the former, took possession of the temple at Delphi, which they claimed as lying in their territory. The Delphians appealed to the Spartans, who sent troops and gave it back to them, and made them an autonomous community. In return for this timely aid, they received the right of consulting the oracle first (προμαντείαν), and their name was inscribed on the front of the great bronze wolf (Paus. x 14, 4 f.), near the chief altar. Soon after their departure, Pericles marched at the head of an Athenian force to Delphi, made himself master of the place and gave the temple back to the Phocians. He left the Lacedaemonian inscription undisturbed, but reasserted the προμαντεία for Athens by another on the right side of the same wolf (Thuc. I 112, 5). These events were distinguished by the name of the Sacred War (ἱερὸς πόλεμος) from its religious pretext. See Cl. A. IV 226, Busolt Gr. Gesch. II 545 f.

§ 2 l. 12. εὐθὺς ἐκείνων ἀπαλλαγέντων κτλ., 'directly they (sc. the Lacedaemonians) had taken themselves off, he reinstated the Phocians.' Cp. c. 39, 4 εὐθὺς ἐκ ποδῶν γενομένον.

14. ἔδωκαν, 'had given'; c. 17, 1; G. MT.² § 58. Others to whom the right of precedence (προμαντεία) for special services was accorded were Croesus (Herod. I 54) and Philip of Macedon (Dem. or. Phil. III § 32).

15. τοῦ χαλκοῦ λύκου, lupi aenei.

Pausan. x 14, 7 gives the legend thus :—λέγουσι τῶν τοῦ θεοῦ χρημάτων συλήσαντα ἄνθρωπον, τὸν μὲν ὁμοῦ τῷ χρυσίῳ κατακρύψαντα ἔχειν αὐτὸν ἔνθα τοῦ Παρνασοῦ μάλιστα ἦν συνεχὲς ὑπὸ ἀγρίων δένδρων, λύκον δὲ ἐπιθέσθαι οἱ καθεύδοντι, καὶ ἀποθανεῖν τε ὑπὸ τοῦ λύκου τὸν ἄνθρωπον, καὶ ὡς ἐς τὴν πόλιν ὁσημέραι φοιτῶν ὠρύετο ὁ λύκος· ἐπεὶ δὲ οὐκ ἄνευ θεοῦ παραγίνεσθαί σφισιν ὑπελάμβανον, οὕτως ἐπακολουθοῦσι τῷ θηρίῳ καὶ ἀνευρίσκουσί τε τὸ ἱερὸν χρυσίον καὶ ἀνέθεσαν λύκον τῷ θεῷ χαλκοῦν.

In the two next chapters Plutarch follows Thucydides closely as far as the return of the Athenian army from Euboea; he then avails himself of another source, which contains many pieces of information not found in Thuc., e.g. the bribery of Cleandridas, the expulsion of the Chalcidian Hippobotae etc. That source is most likely Ephorus, though others think that it was Theopompus or Stesichorus. See Busolt Gr. Gesch. II 548 Anm. 6.

CHAPTER XXII

§ 1 l. 1. ὀρθῶς . . . συνεῖχεν, 'that he did right to confine.' ἐν τῇ Ἑλλάδι, i.e. Hellas proper as opp. to Sicily etc.

2. ἐμαρτύρησεν αὐτῷ τὰ γενόμενα, 'actual events bore witness in his favour,' i.e. confirmed the correctness of his judgment. Cp. Timol. c. 8, 4.

4. **Εὐβοεῖς ἀπέστησαν**: this was in B.C. 446/5 = Ol. 83, 3, soon after the defeat at Coronea (c. 18, 3) (Thuc. I 114, 1, Diod. XII c. 7). Euboea had been a member of the Delian confederacy from the first, and remained the faithful ally of Athens for more than thirty years, and for two generations Athenian citizens had been settled as colonists in the island, but now the exiled oligarchs returned, following the example of the Boeotians. The defection of Euboea brought about an important reaction in the extent of the confederacy. W. W. Lloyd *The Age of Pericles* II pp. 83 ff.

5. **ἀπηγγέλλοντο ἐκπεπολεμωμένοι**, 'were reported to have become hostile.' For the construction, cp. c. 18, 3. As soon as Pericles had crossed over to Euboea with his army, the Megarians threw off their allegiance to Athens with the support of the Corinthians, Sicyonians and Epidaurians. Those of the Athenian garrison who were not cut down, took refuge in Nisaea.

7. **στρατιὰ Πελοποννησίων**: this was in B.C. 445/4 = Ol. 83, 4, when the five years' truce had expired. Pleistoanax, son of the regent Pausanias, became king B.C. 458/7 = Ol. 80, 3, under the guardianship of Nicomedes; his father died B.C. 469.

§ 2 l. 9. **πάλιν οὖν ὁ Περικλῆς κτλ.**: cp. Thuc. *l. c.* ὁ δὲ Περικλῆς πάλιν κατὰ τάχος ἐκόμιζε τὴν στρατιὰν ἐκ τῆς Εὐβοίας, καὶ μετὰ τοῦτο οἱ Πελοποννήσιοι τῆς Ἀττικῆς ἐς Ἐλευσῖνα καὶ Θριῶζε ἐσβαλόντες ἐδῄωσαν Πλειστοάνακτος τοῦ Παυσανίου βασιλέως Λακεδαιμονίων ἡγουμένου, καὶ τὸ πλέον οὐκέτι προελθόντες ἀπεχώρησαν ἐπ' οἴκου.

12. **συνάψαι εἰς χεῖρας**, *manus conserere*, 'to come to close quarters with.' Cp. *Philop.* c. 18, 6 καὶ συνάψαι εἰς χεῖρας οὐδεὶς ἐτόλμησεν αὐτῷ, πόρρωθεν δὲ βαλλόμενος ... χαλεπῶς μετεχειρίζετο, Polyb. I 76, 6 λύσαντες τὴν τάξιν ἐπέκειντο καὶ συνῆπτον εἰς τὰς χεῖρας ἐρρωμένως. More frequently συνάπτειν is used alone, as *conserere* in Latin.

13. **πολλοῖς καὶ ἀγαθοῖς ὁπλίταις**: c. 35, 1.

15. **νέον ὄντα κομιδῇ**: he was now about twenty years old.

16. **τῶι συμβούλων**, partitive gen., 'amongst his advisers.'

18. **ἐπειρᾶτο τούτου**, 'made proposals to,' 'opened negotiations with this functionary' sc. Cleandridas.

19. **χρήμασιν**, the sum of ten talents, according to c. 23, 1. When Pericles gave an account of the money which had passed through his hands as general, and put down ten or twenty talents as spent εἰς τὸ δέον 'for necessary service' (c. 23, 1), no questions were asked, the bribery of Pleistoanax and Cleandridas being an open secret.

§ 3 l. 22. **κατὰ πόλεις**, 'by states' i.e. to their several states.

24. **χρήμασιν ἐζημίωσαν**: we learn from Ephorus (ap. Schol. Arist. *Nub.* 859, Müller *FHG.* fr. 118) that the fine was fifteen talents. Being unable to discharge the full amount (ἐκτῖσαι), he incurred ἀτιμία and fled for his life to the temple of Zeus on Mount Lycaeum (Arcadia); where, for greater security, he lodged in a chamber communicating with the sacred buildings for nineteen years, until his return in B.C. 426/5 Ol. 88, 3. He was succeeded by his son Pausanias, during whose minority his uncle Cleomenes was regent.

The use of ἔχειν for δύνασθαι is common in the best authors, especially in the same connexion of paying, *Arist.* c. 26, 2 ἐκτῖσαι δ' οὐκ ἔχοντα τὴν καταδίκην, *Cat. ma.* c. 15, 2 ἣν (καταδίκην) οὐκ ἔχων ἀπολύσασθαι, Xen. *Oec.* c. 3, 6 οἳ οὐδ' εἰς τἀναγκαῖα ἔχουσι δαπανᾶν, Lucian *Cronos.* c. 15 οἵτινες ἂν καὶ τοῦτο (τὸ ἐνοίκιον) ὀφείλοντες καταβαλεῖν μὴ ἔχωσι, Matth. *Evang.* c. 18, 25 μὴ ἔχοντος αὐτοῦ ἀποδοῦναι.

25. **μετέστησεν ἑαυτόν**, 'he withdrew,' a milder expression than ἔφυγεν. Cp. *Lys.* c. 17, 1 and see my note to *Them.* c. 5, 4.

The transaction was carried through with such secrecy that he was punished on suspicion only, Thuc. II 21, 1 διὸ δὴ καὶ ἡ φυγὴ αὐτῷ ἐγένετο ἐκ Σπάρτης δόξαντι χρήμασι πεισθῆναι τὴν ἀναχώρησιν, V 16, 3 φεύγοντα αὐτὸν ἐς Λύκαιον διὰ τὴν ἐκ τῆς Ἀττικῆς ποτὲ μετὰ δώρων (δωροδοκήσεως) δοκοῦσαν ἀναχώρησιν, Ephorus *l. c.* ὑπολαβόντες δωροδοκήσαντας αὐτοὺς κτλ. Plutarch takes for granted the fact of bribery when he says that Pericles did not venture to accept the challenge of the many brave hoplites in the enemy's ranks. Cp. *Nic.* c. 18, 3 where (after Timaeus) he says of Cleandridas, father of Gylippus, δώρων ἁλοὺς ἔφυγε. There is a parallel in the case of another Spartan king, Leotychidas, who in B.C. 477/6 was charged with military remissness against the Thessalians because he allowed himself to be corrupted by those whom it was his business to chastise, and who, rather than abide the result of a trial, retired to Tegea, whence he was never recalled.

27. **φεύγοντος**, 'while he was living in exile' (c. 10, 1). He retired to Italy, where he fought as a general on the side of the people of Thurii (c. 11, 5) against those of Tarentum (Antiochus ap. Strabo *Geogr.* VI c. 1, 14, Diodor. XIII 106, 10), and also against the Lucanians (Polyaen. *Strat.* II 10, 1-5). Cp. Thuc. VI c. 93, 2; c. 104, 3.

28. **περὶ Σικελίαν**, 'in Sicily' B.C. 414.

30. **συγγενικὸν... νόσημα**, 'a congenital disease.' So *Nic.* c. 28, 3 Plut. calls it ἀρρώστημα πατρῷον. **αὐτῷ**, sc. τῷ Γυλίππῳ. **προστρίψασθαι**, 'to impart' prop. by rubbing something off oneself upon another. Cp. *Alex.* c. 8, 1 and see my note on Plutarch's use of this verb in *Agis-Cleom.-Gracch.* c. 5, 1, and Blaydes on Arist. *Eq.* 5, p. 175 ed. 1892.

32. **ἧς**, sc. φιλαργυρίας. **αἰσχρῶς** with ἐξέπεσε. **ἐπί**, *post*, c. 13, 8. Cp. *Lys.* c. 17, 1 ὁ μὲν οὖν Γύλιππος αἰσχρὸν

οὕτω καὶ ἄγεννες ἔργον ἐπὶ λαμπροῖς τοῖς ἔμπροσθεν καὶ μεγάλοις ἐργασάμενος μετέστησεν ἑαυτὸν ἐκ Λακεδαίμονος, Lysias or. 32, 17 ἐπὶ τοιούτοις ἔργοις οὐ τοὺς θεοὺς φοβεῖ.

33. ἁλούς, c. 37, 4.

34. ἐν τοῖς, 'in the memoir,' as *Cat. ma.* c. 12, 3. *Lysandr.* c. 16 ὁ δὲ Λύσανδρος τῶν χρημάτων τὰ περιόντα καὶ ὅσας δωρεὰς αὐτὸς ἢ στεφάνους ἐδέξατο, πολλῶν ὡς εἰκὸς διδόντων ἀνδρὶ δυνατωτάτῳ καὶ τρόπον τινὰ κυρίῳ τῆς Ἑλλάδος, ἀπέστειλεν εἰς Λακεδαίμονα διὰ Γυλίππου τοῦ στρατηγήσαντος περὶ Σικελίαν. ὁ δέ, ὥς λέγεται, τὰς ῥαφὰς τῶν ἀγγείων κάτωθεν ἀναλύσας καὶ ἀφελὼν συχνὸν ἀργύριον ἐξ ἑκάστου πάλιν συνέρραψεν, ἀγνοήσας ὅτι γραμματίδιον ἐνῆν ἑκάστῳ τὸν ἀριθμὸν σημαῖνον. ἐλθὼν δ' εἰς Σπάρτην ἃ μὲν ὑφῄρητο κατέκρυψεν ὑπὸ τὸν κέραμον τῆς οἰκίας, τὰ δ' ἀγγεῖα παρέδωκε τοῖς ἐφόροις καὶ τὰς σφραγῖδας ἐπέδειξεν. ἐπεὶ δ' ἀνοιξάντων καὶ ἀριθμούντων διεφώνει πρὸς τὰ γράμματα τὸ πλῆθος τοῦ ἀργυρίου καὶ παρεῖχε τοῖς ἐφόροις ἀπορίαν τὸ πρᾶγμα, φράζει θεράπων τοῦ Γυλίππου πρὸς αὐτοὺς αἰνιξάμενος ὑπὸ τῷ κεραμικῷ κοιτάζεσθαι πολλὰς γλαῦκας· ἦν γάρ, ὡς ἔοικε, τὸ χάραγμα τοῦ πλείστου τότε νομίσματος διὰ τοὺς Ἀθηναίους γλαῦκες. The story is told also more briefly in *Nic.* c. 28, 3.

CHAPTER XXIII

§ 1 l. 1. ἐν τῷ . . . ἀπολογισμῷ, 'in the detailed records which he gave of his generalship.' Cp. *Sull.* c. 34, 2 ἀπολογισμὸν τῶν πράξεων ποιούμενος, *Dem.* c. 8, 1 διεξῄει τάς τε πράξεις καὶ τοὺς ὑπὲρ αὐτῶν ἀπολογισμούς, *Mor.* 726 B τοῦ βίου διδοὺς ἀπολογισμῶν. This is usually taken to mean 'in the accounts which he kept,' as in Ps.-Lucian *Demosth. Enc.* c. 33 οὐδαμοῦ τοῖς ἀπολογισμοῖς ἐγγέγραπται τῶν ἐμῶν ἀναλωμάτων, but I do not find any such use of the word in Plutarch.

2. δέκα ταλάντων: Ephorus *fr.* 118 (ap. Schol. Arist. *l. c.*) mentions twenty talents as the amount.

4. εἰς τὸ δέον, 'for necessary public service.' Cp. Dem. *Ol.* 3, 28 ἀνηλώκαμεν εἰς οὐδὲν δέον, Aristot. Ἀθ. πολ. c. 30, 4 ὅπως ἂν (τὰ χρήματα) εἰς τὸ δέον ἀναλίσκηται. Hence the joke in Arist. *Nub.* 858-9 :—

Φ. τὰς δ' ἐμβάδας ποῖ τέτροφας, ὦ 'νόητε σύ ;
Σ. ὥσπερ Περικλέης, εἰς τὸ δέον ἀπώλεσα.

The phrase appears to have passed into a proverb. Suidas: ὅταν τις θέλῃ μὴ φανερῶς εἰπεῖν ὅπου τι πολλάκις ἀνάλωσε, λέγει "εἰς δέον." ἀπεδέξατο, *comprobavit.*

5. μὴ πολυπραγμονήσας, 'without meddling' *i.e.* without making enquiry. For the use of μή, see note to c. 3, 2 ; c. 29, 2.

6. ἱστορήκασιν, 'have recorded,' c. 9, 2, c. 28, 1. See also my n. to *Them.* c. 1, 3 ed. 3.

7. ὧν: partitive predicate gen., H.A. *Gr.* § 732 a.

8. **εἰς τὴν Σπάρτην**: if this statement of Theophrastus be true, that Pericles spent every year ten talents as secret service money, it was probably not reserved for Sparta only, but employed for general diplomatic purposes. See Holm *Gesch. Gr.* II p. 238 Anm. 7.   **ἐφοίτα**, as frequentative of ἔρχεσθαι, is used of things which recur periodically, as tribute, revenue ; *Cim.* c. 7, 2 Θρᾷκας ὅθεν αὐτοῖς ἐφοίτα σῖτος, Herod. V 17 τάλαντον ἀργυρίου Ἀλεξάνδρῳ ἡμέρης ἑκάστης ἐφοίτα, Thuc. VIII 18, 1 ἐκ τούτων τῶν πόλεων ὁπόσα Ἀθηναίοις ἐφοίτα χρήματα ἢ ἄλλο τι, Lys. *or.* 32, 15 ἀπέφηνε φοιτᾶν σῖτον αὐτοῖς ἐκ Χερρονήσου καθ' ἕκαστον ἐνιαυτόν.

According to Theophrastus and others, Pericles had ten talents placed yearly at his disposal for the purpose of bribing Spartan officers, and so procuring the continuance of peace and gaining time for efficient equipment. In the fourth century, there was a special fund called τὰ δέκα τάλαντα, which was under the management of the ταμίαι τῆς θεοῦ and therefore probably did not serve profane purposes. The Metoeci contributed to this fund. Whether it had anything to do with that of Pericles, must remain an open question. See Busolt *Gr. Gesch.* II 550 Anm. 1.

9. **τοὺς ἐν τέλει**, 'those who held supreme authority,' here therefore the king and Ephors.

10. **παρῃτεῖτο**, 'he sought to avert.' See Gr. Index s.v.   41

12. **ἐν ᾧ**, 'during which,' to be taken with παρασκευασάμενος καθ' ἡσυχίαν.

13. **ἔμελλε**, 'was like to,' in the natural course of things. **βέλτιον**, c. 8, 4.

§ 2 l. 13. **αὖθις**, in B.C. 445/4 = Ol. 83, 4.   **οὖν** here marks a return to the principal narrative after a digression.

16. **κατεστρέψατο**: Thuc. I 114, 2 καὶ Ἀθηναῖοι πάλιν εἰς Εὔβοιαν διαβάντες Περικλέους στρατηγοῦντος κατεστρέψαντο πᾶσαν. Cp. Arist. *Nub.* 211 ἡ δέ γ' Εὔβοι', ὡς ὁρᾷς, ἡδὶ παρατέταται ('lies stretched along') μακρὰ πόρρω πάνυ. B. οἶδ'· ὑπὸ γὰρ ἡμῶν παρετάθη ('was laid low') καὶ Περικλέους.

18. **τοὺς ἱπποβότας λεγομένους**, 'the so-called hippobotae,' *i.e.* knights or landowners. Herod. V 77, 11 οἱ δὲ ἱπποβόται ἐκαλέοντο οἱ παχέες ('rich') τῶν Χαλκιδέων. Fuhr thinks that this expulsion may perhaps have been confounded by Plut. with that of B.C. 507 mentioned by Herodotus *l. c.*; for there is nothing about it in Thucydides, nor in the convention (ὁμολογία Thuc. I 114, 3) sworn to between Athens and Chalcis, contained in an inscription which was discovered in 1876 on a slab in the exterior facing of the wall of the citadel, *CIA.* IV 27ᵃ, Dittenberger *Syll. Inscr. gr.* I 10, Hicks *Man. Gr. Inscr.* no. 28.

In this inscription the relations of the subjects to the sovereign city are set forth. The Chalcidians were compelled to swear that neither in word nor in deed would they revolt from the Demos of Athens; and, should any one revolt, they would not follow his example, but inform against him. They must engage to pay the phoros, as fixed by Athens, after hearing her proposals, to supply forces to the Athenian Demos against its enemies, and in general to be a loyal and hearty ally. On their part, the Athenians guaranteed to the Chalcidians the possession and integrity of their city. No Chalcidian was to be punished with forfeiture of his civic franchise, with banishment or imprisonment, or death or loss of property without a formal trial (οὐκ ἐξελῶ Χαλκιδέας ἐκ Χαλκίδος οὐδὲ τὴν πόλιν ἀνάστατον ποιήσω, οὐδὲ ἰδιώτην οὐδένα ἀτιμώσω οὐδὲ φυγῇ ζημιώσω οὐδὲ ξυλλήψομαι οὐδὲ ἀποκτενῶ οὐδὲ χρήματα ἀφαιρήσομαι ἀκ<ρ> ίτου οὐδὲ ἑνὸς ἄνευ τοῦ δήμου τοῦ Ἀθηναίων). In every action, whether private or public, the accused was to be formally summoned, and without such summons could not be proceeded against. The Prytaneis were to introduce the members of any deputation from Chalcis to the popular assembly within ten days of its arrival at Athens. These guarantees were to be contingent upon the continued allegiance of Chalcis to Athens (καὶ πρεσβείαν ἐλθοῦσαν προσάξω πρὸς βουλὴν καὶ δῆμον δέκα ἡμερῶν, ὅταν πρυτανεύω κατὰ τὸ δυνατόν· ταῦτα δὲ ἐμπ<ε>δώσω Χαλκιδεῦσιν πειθομένοις τῷ δή<μ>ῳ τῷ Ἀθηναίων).

19. **Ἑστιεῖς**, more accurately and usually Ἑστιαιεῖς, the inhabitants of Hestiaea, on the north coast of the island. The foundation of this colony gave Athens not only a new point of vantage in Euboea, but also a favourable position for commanding the Maliac and Pagasaean gulfs.

Cp. Thuc. I 114, 2 Ἑστιαιᾶς ἐξοικίσαντες αὐτοὶ τὴν γῆν ἔσχον, Diod. XII 7. The evicted inhabitants found a home in Macedonia. Cp. Strab. Geogr. X c. 1, 3 Θεόπομπος δέ φησι Περικλέους χειρουμένου Εὔβοιαν τοὺς Ἱστιαιεῖς καθ᾽ ὁμολογίας εἰς Μακεδονίαν μεταστῆναι, δισχιλίους δ᾽ ἐξ Ἀθηναίων ἐλθόντας τὸν Ὠρεὸν οἰκῆσαι, δῆμον ὄντα πρότερον τῶν Ἱστιαιέων. The official name of the colony continued to be Hestiaea (cp. e.g. CIA. I 28, 29, 30, Thuc. VII 57, 2), though the name Oreus prevailed in ordinary usage (cp. Thuc. VII 95, 7; Xen. Hell. V 4, 56; Diod. XV 30, 3, 4; Aristot. Pol. VIII 1303ᵃ, 18). Hierocles the seer who is mentioned in the Chalcidian decree appears to have received an assignment of land there because of a lucky prophecy of success in the Euboean expedition. Arist. Pax 1047 ὁ χρησμολόγος οὑξ Ὠρεοῦ, ib. 1125 ἤκουσας; ὁ κόραξ οἷος ἦλθ᾽ ἐξ Ὠρεοῦ. Eupolis in his Πόλεις (Mein. I p. 515, Kock I p. 316) calls him βέλτιστε χρησμῳδῶν ἄναξ. There was a decree for regulating the trade of the cleruchs in Hestiaea with Athens, and another for the administration of justice in the new settlement. See Busolt Gr. Gesch. II 552 f.

CHAPTER XXIV

§ 1 l. 1. **ἐκ τούτου**: soon after the subjugation of Euboea, the Athenians, because of the falling off of the tribute and for other reasons, were desirous of coming to terms with the Peloponnesians. So they sent ten plenipotentiaries, among them Callias, Chares and the grandfather of the orator Andocides, to Sparta, and a peace was concluded between the two states and the confederacies over which they presided at the end of the winter 445/4 = Ol. 83, 4 to last for thirty years. The terms of the treaty, a copy of which Pausanias (v 23, 3) saw at Olympia engraven on a bronze column, are not fully known. Thuc. I 115, 1 tells us that the Athenians restored or evacuated Nisaea, Pegae, Troezen and Achaia, in short all their acquisitions in Peloponnesus. Each party was to remain in possession of what belonged to it; the Athenians were not to admit Lacedaemonian cities, nor the Lacedaemonian Athenian into their symmachy without permission, nor were they to aid and abet deserters; but any city, independent of alliance with either, might join one or the other as she pleased (Thuc. ι c. 35, 1; cp. c. 66). The Aeginetans were to be autonomous (Thuc. ι 67, 2), but to pay their quota of the phoros. The Argives who, though not parties to this peace, were already on good terms with Lacedaemon were at liberty to conclude a separate peace with Athens (Pausanias *l. c.*). Any difference arising between the cities was to be settled by arbitration (Thuc. ι c. 140, 2, c. 145; vii 18, 2). Busolt *Gr. Gesch.* ιι 555 f.

3. **τόν**, anticipatory or assumptive or 'the well-known.' The operations against Samos began before July B.C. 440. Cp. Thuc. ι 115–117, Diod. xιι 27 f. For ψηφίζεται see c. 20, 2.

5. **κελευόμενοι διαλύσασθαι πόλεμον**, 'being requested to break off hostilities.' In Thuc. the Samians are treated at once as rebellious without any warning. For the origin of the war, see on c. 25, 1.

7. **Ἀσπασίᾳ χαριζόμενος**, 'to gratify Aspasia,' c. 7, 3; c. 10, 5. **δοκεῖ**, 'is commonly supposed.' The imputation of a petty personal motive originated no doubt with Duris of Samos (cp. *fr.* 58 ap. Müller *FHG.* ιι 482), who is taken to task by Plutarch in c. 28, 3 for another misstatement.

9. **διαπορῆσαι**, 'to enquire,' lit. 'to start a difficulty.' Cp. c. 36, 3; c. 38, 2, *Mor.* 413 A τοὐναντίον δ' ὑμῖν ἐγὼ προβάλλω διαπορῆσαι, πῶς οὐχὶ καὶ τότε ἀπείρηκεν, Polyb. 4, 20, 2 ἄξιον βραχὺ διαπορῆσαι περὶ τούτου πῶς etc. Aristot. *Pol.* ιιι 6, p. 1287ᵇ, 20 διαπορῆσαι καὶ ζητεῖν. **μάλιστα** goes with ἂν εἴη καιρός.

10. **τῆς ἀνθρώπου**, in a slightly contemptuous sense; cp. *Nic.* c. 13, 4. **τίνα τέχνην ... τοσαύτην ἔχουσα**, 'what sort of great art she possessed that' etc.

12. **ἐχειρώσατο**, c. 15, 3. **τοῖς φιλοσόφοις .. παρέσχε 42 λόγον**, 'gave philosophers occasion for no little or inconsiderable discussion about herself.' For ὑπέρ=περί, 'concerning,' see Gr. Ind. to *Life of Demosth.* p. 181.

§ 2 l. 16. **Θαργηλίαν**: Athenae. xιιι 89, p. 608 F ἐπὶ κάλλει δὲ διαβόητοι γεγόνασι γυναῖκες Θαργηλία ἡ Μιλησία, ἥτις καὶ τεσσαρσικαίδεκα ἀνδράσιν ἐγαμήθη, οὖσα καὶ τὸ εἶδος πάνυ καλὴ καὶ σοφή. The principal place of her triumph was Thessaly, where she won the favour of the prince Antiochus and exercised despotic sway for some thirty years.

17. **Ἰάδων**, 'Ionian women.' Athenae. v 62 p. 220 B Αἰσχίνης δ' ὁ Σωκρατικὸς ... ἐν τῇ Ἀσπασίᾳ τὰς ἐκ τῆς Ἰωνίας γυναῖκας συλλήβδην μοιχάδας καὶ κερδαλέας προσαγορεύει. **ζηλώσασαν**, 'in emulation of.' Cp. ζῆλος c. 1, 4. **ἐπιθέσθαι**, 'made a dead set upon,' 'captivated,' lit. as in c. 26, 2 'attacked.'

19. **χάριν μετὰ δεινότητος**, 'personal charms as well as cleverness,' cp. c. 18, 3 ; c. 31, 1. For the special meaning of δεινότης, see n. to c. 4, 1.

20. **συνῴκησεν**, 'was intimate with.'

21. **προσεποίησε βασιλεῖ**, 'won over to the Persian king's interest'; c. 3, 1 ; c. 10, 4.

22. **τοὺς πλησιάσαντας**, c. 13, 10.

§ 3 l. 25. **οἱ μέν** correlative to φαίνεται μέντοι § 5 l. 38.
ὡς σοφὴν τινα καὶ πολιτικήν, 'because of her superior sagacity and political insight.'

For this restrictive use of τις, like Lat. *quidam*, cp. c. 27, 4 and see my n. to *Them.* c. 22, 2. Cp. Lucian *Imagg.* § 17 τὴν δὲ ἐκ τῆς Μιλήτου ἐκείνην Ἀσπασίαν, ᾗ καὶ ὁ Ὀλύμπιος θαυμασιώτατος καὶ αὐτὸς συνῆν, οὐ φαῦλον συνέσεως παράδειγμα προθέμενοι, ὁπόσον ἐμπειρίας πραγμάτων καὶ ὀξύτητος ἐς τὰ πολιτικὰ καὶ ἀγχινοίας καὶ δριμύτητος ἐκείνη (sc. Aspasia) προσῆν κτλ.

26. **σπουδασθῆναι**, 'was courted and made much of.' Cp. *Artox.* c. 26, 2 ᾔτησεν Ἀσπασίαν ὁ Δαρεῖος τὴν μάλιστα σπουδασθεῖσαν ὑπὸ Κύρου, *Cim.* c. 4, 8, *Them.* c. 5, 2 with my note *ad l.*

27. **ἔστιν ὅτε**, c. 3, 2 ; c. 15, 3 ; c. 16, 6. **τῶν γνωρίμων**, 'his pupils,' not, as generally understood, 'his acquaintance.'

Cp. *Mor.* 63 Ε Λακύδης ὁ Ἀρκεσιλάου γνώριμος, 70 Ε Ἀμμώνιος ἐν δειλινῇ διατριβῇ τῶν γνωρίμων τινὰς αἰσθόμενος ἠριστηκότας οὐχ ἁπλοῦν ἄριστον, 71 C ἥκιστα δὲ πρέπει γαμετῆς ἀκονούσης ἄνδρα . . . ἢ γνωρίμων διδάσκαλον ἀποκαλύπτειν, 118 D Ἀναξαγόραν . . . διαλεγόμενον τοῖς γνωρίμοις, 220 D Ξενοκράτην ἐν Ἀκαδημείᾳ πρεσβύτερον ἤδη μετὰ τῶν γνωρίμων φιλοσοφοῦντα, 448 E ὥσπερ νέοι διδασκάλοις ἐπιτυχόντες ἀστείοις ὑπὸ χρείας τὸ πρῶτον ἕπονται . . . ὕστερον δὲ καὶ φιλοῦσιν ἀντὶ γνωρίμων καὶ μαθητῶν ἐρασταὶ ὄντες, 796 D Σωκράτης ὥραν διατριβῆς τοῖς γνωρίμοις τεταγμένην φυλάττων, [Plut.] 838 A ἀργύριον εἰσπράττων τοὺς γνωρίμους.

ἐφοίτα sc. ὡς αὐτήν. Cp. Xen. *Mem.* III 6, 36, *Oecon.* c. 3, 14 where Socrates offers to introduce Critobulus to Aspasia, adding that she will discourse to him on the subject of good wives ἐπιστημονέστερον than himself.

28. **οἱ συνήθεις** sc. αὐτοῦ, τοῦ Σωκράτους.

29. **προεστῶσαν ἐργασίας**, 'though she carried on a trade.' Cp. Her. II 135, 1 ἀφικομένη κατ᾽ ἐργασίην (de meretrice), Dem. *de cor.* § 129 ἀνέστησεν αὐτὴν ἀπὸ τῆς καλῆς ἐργασίας, [Dem.] c. *Neaer.* § 36 ὡς αὐτῇ ἡ ἀπὸ τοῦ σώματος ἐργασία οὐχ ἱκανὴν εὐπορίαν παρεῖχεν ὥστε διοικεῖν τὴν οἰκίαν, Theophr. *Char.* VI πορνοβοσκῆσαι καὶ μηδεμίαν αἰσχρὰν ἐργασίαν ἀποδοκιμάσαι : and for προΐστασθαι, Athenae. XIII 92 Σόλωνος οὐδ᾽ ἐπιτρέποντος ἀνδρὶ τοιαύτης προΐστασθαι τέχνης.

Athenaeus XIII 56 p. 589 D repeats some of the scandalous stories which were circulated about Pericles: ἦν δ᾽ οὗτος ὁ ἀνὴρ πρὸς ἀφροδίσια πάνυ καταφερής, ὅστις καὶ τῇ τοῦ υἱοῦ γυναικὶ συνῆν, adding ὡς Στησίμβροτος ὁ Θάσιος ἱστορεῖ κατὰ τοὺς αὐτοὺς χρόνους αὐτῷ γενόμενος καὶ ἑωρακὼς αὐτόν.

Well may Cobet exclaim with indignation 'Hi omnes testes nihili aut improbi aut stulti cum suis mendaciis facessant.'

30. σεμνῆς, *honestae*, 'respectable.'

Cp. Athenae. XIII 25 p. 569 F καὶ Ἀσπασία δὲ ἡ Σωκρατικὴ ἐνεπορεύετο πλήθη καλῶν γυναικῶν καὶ ἐπλήθυνεν ἀπὸ τῶν ταυτης ἑταιρίδων ἡ Ἑλλάς, ὡς καὶ ὁ χαρίεις Ἀριστοφάνης παρασημαίνεται, λέγων ὅτι Περικλῆς διὰ τὸν Ἀσπασίας ἔρωτα καὶ τὰς ἁρπασθείσας ἀπ' αὐτῆς θεραπαίνας ὑπὸ Μεγαρέων ἀνερρίπισεν τὸ δεινόν (*Ach.* 524). See c. 30, 4.

§ 4 l. 31. Aἰσχίνης ὁ Σωκρατικός, an Athenian rhetorician and sophist who lived about 400 B.C., in his dialogue *Aspasia*. See P. Natorp in *Philologus* Bd. 51 Heft 3 pp. 489-500.

Λυσικλέα: Lysicles, the sheep-dealer (προβατοπώλης) of Aristoph. *Eq.* 132, was for a short time after the death of Pericles (B.C. 429) political leader at Athens. He fell in an expedition to Caria, which he commanded, in the winter of B.C. 428 (Thuc. III 19, 2).

32. ἐξ ἀγεννοῦς: see note to c. 15, 1.

33. φύσιν: Gr. Ind. s. v. Ἀσπασία συνόντα, 'by his marriage with Aspasia.' Cic. (*de inv.* § 51) gives an example of her method of discussion from Aeschines.

Schol. Plat. *Menex.* p. 391 says of Aspasia:—ἐπεγήματο δὲ μετὰ τὸν Περικλέους θάνατον Λυσικλεῖ τῷ προβατοκαπήλῳ καὶ ἐξ αὐτοῦ ἔσχεν υἱὸν ὀνόματι Ποριστὴν καὶ τὸν Λυσικλέα ῥήτορα δεινότατον κατεσκευάσατο, καθάπερ καὶ Περικλέα δημηγορεῖν παρεσκεύασεν. The story is unworthy of belief. Plato's Menexenus contains a funeral oration over the Athenians who fell in the Corinthian war, which is put into the mouth of Socrates and ascribed by him in his introductory remarks (τὰ πρῶτα) to Aspasia ἥπερ καὶ ἄλλους πολλοὺς καὶ ἀγαθοὺς πεποίηκε ῥήτορας, ἕνα δὲ καὶ διαφέροντα τῶν Ἑλλήνων, Περικλέα τὸν Ξανθίππου. The joke (παιδιά) arises from the anachronism of the whole.

35. εἰ καί, 'although.'   μετὰ παιδιᾶς, c. 8, 3.

36. τοσοῦτόν γ' ἱστορίας ἔνεστιν, *tantum saltem inest historiae*.

37. δόξαν εἶχε = ἐδόκει, c. 33, 1 with note.   τὸ γύναιον, *muliercula*, in a slightly contemptuous sense; the diminutive would not be applied to a respectable matron any more than would ἡ ἄνθρωπος l. 6. Cp. *Them.* c. 26, 3. ἐπὶ ῥητορικῇ 'for instruction in the art of rhetoric.' Cp. Clem. Alex. *Strom.* IV c. 19 § 124 ed. Klotz Ἀσπασίας τῆς Μιλησίας, περὶ ἧς καὶ οἱ κωμικοὶ πολλὰ δὴ καταγράφουσιν, Σωκράτης μὲν ἀπέλαυσεν εἰς φιλοσοφίαν, Περικλῆς δὲ εἰς ῥητορικήν, Alciphron *Ep.* I 34, Athenae. V p. 219 B Ἀσπασία ἡ σοφὴ τοῦ Σωκράτους διδάσκαλος τῶν ῥητορικῶν λόγων.

38. ὁμιλεῖν is used of the relation between pupil and teacher, like πλησιάζειν, συνεῖναι. Cp. Xen. *Mem.* I ii 39 Κριτίας δὲ καὶ Ἀλκιβιάδης οὐκ ἀρέσκοντος αὐτοῖς Σωκράτους ὡμιλησάτην ὃν χρόνον ὡμιλείτην αὐτῷ.

§ 5 l. 38. μέντοι : see n. to l. 25.

39. ἐρωτική τις, 'of an amatory nature.'

41. γυνὴ προσήκουσα κατὰ γένος : this was probably Dinomache his cousin, mother of Alcibiades by her first husband Clinias. See the pedigree c. 3, 1, from which it will be seen that Alcibiades was stepson as well as cousin of Pericles. συνῳκηκυῖα, 'married to,' as in c. 36, 1 and very frequently in Plutarch. She must have been divorced from Hipponicus, because he outlived Pericles.

Blass thinks it more likely that Hipponicus was her second husband. Xanthippus was married at the time of his death in 429 B.C., and must therefore have been born before 450 B.C., whereas Callias figured in 371 B.C., as a legate at Sparta. He was one of the best known and richest persons in Athens, for he inherited a large fortune, which however he ended by squandering. Plutarch's statement is confirmed by Plato *Protag.* 314 E: συμπεριεπάτουν ἐκ μὲν τοῦ ἐπὶ θάτερα Καλλίας ὁ Ἱππονίκου καὶ ὁ ἀδελφὸς αὐτοῦ ὁ ὁμομήτριος Πάραλος ὁ Περικλέους ... ἐκ δὲ τοῦ ἐπὶ θάτερα ὁ ἕτερος τῶν Περικλέους Ξάνθιππος.

45. τῆς συμβιώσεως, a very expressive word, = κοινωνίας βίου (*Mor.* 138 B).

Cp. *Num.* c. 4, 2 ἠθικώτερον πρὸς συμβίωσιν, *Dion* c. 21, 1 ἦν λόγος ... ὡς οὐκ εἴη εὐάρμοστος ἡ πρὸς τὴν γυναῖκα συμβίωσις, *Arat.* c. 17, 1 ἐλπίδας ἐνδιδοὺς γάμων βασιλικῶν καὶ συμβιώσεως πρὸς οὐκ ἀηδὲς ἐντυχεῖν γυναικὶ πρεσβυτέρᾳ μειράκιον. The difference between συμβιοῦν and συνοικεῖν is well stated by Wyttenbach *Mor.* 142 F 'eorum, quibus concubitu tantummodo iunctum est coniugium, ratio eiusmodi esse dicitur ut συνοικεῖν ἄν τις ἀλλήλοις, οὐ συμβιοῦν νομίσειεν.' Cp. *Mor.* 139 A, 217 F, 769 F, 789 D τὸν πάλαι συνοικοῦντα καὶ συμβιοῦντα πολὺν χρόνον ἀμέμπτως, *Cim.* c. 4, 9, Themistius ap. Stob. *Flor.* 69, 22 αἱ δὲ ἄλλαι συνοικοῦσιν, οὐ συμβιοῦσιν, ὅταν λυπῶσι τοὺς ἄνδρας ἢ ζηλοτυπῶσιν ἢ διαφέρωνται περὶ χρημάτων ἢ κακῶς λέγωσιν ἢ φεύγωσι θρυπτόμεναι τὰς φιλοφροσύνας καὶ συνδιαιτήσεις, Musonius *ib.* 23 δεῖ δὲ ἐν γάμῳ πάντως συμβίωσίν τε εἶναι καὶ κηδεμονίαν ἀνδρὸς καὶ γυναικὸς περὶ ἀλλήλους.

46. βουλομένην, c. 15, 3 ; c. 29, 2.

47. συνεξέδωκεν *i.e.* together with her father or brother or, in default of these, her nearest male relative acting as guardian or trustee (κυρίῳ).

Athenaeus (XIII c. 45 p. 533 c) furnishes a specimen of contemporary misrepresentation :—Περικλέα δὲ τὸν 'Ολυμπιόν φησιν Ἡρακλείδης ὁ Ποντικὸς ἐν τῷ περὶ Ἡδονῆς ὡς ἀπήλλαξεν ἐκ τῆς οἰκίας τὴν γυναῖκα καὶ τὸν μεθ' ἡδονῆς βίον προείλετο ᾤκει τε μετ' Ἀσπασίας τῆς ἐκ Μεγάρων ἑταίρας καὶ τὸ πολὺ μέρος τῆς οὐσίας εἰς ταύτην κατανάλωσε.

§ 6 l. 49. ἀπ' ἀγορᾶς: on the omission of the article, see c. 5, 2 n. Plutarch's authority is a dialogue of Antisthenes, as appears from Athenaeus XIII c. 56 'Ἀντισθένης δ' ὁ Σωκρατικὸς ἐρασθέντα φησὶν αὐτὸν Ἀσπασίας δὶς τῆς ἡμέρας εἰσιόντα καὶ ἐξιόντα ἀπ' αὐτῆς ἀσπάζεσθαι τὴν ἄνθρωπον. Jacobs suggests that 'Ἀντισθένης is an error for Αἰσχίνης. ἠσπάζετο ... μετὰ τοῦ καταφιλεῖν: see § 2 l. 19 with note.

51. Ὀμφάλη νέα καὶ Δηιάνειρα : such are the names given

her by Eupolis in his Φίλοι, as the imperious mistress and wife respectively of the new Heracles. According to the Schol. on Plato's *Menexenus* she was also called by Eupolis in his Προσπάλτιοι the new Helen, as the originator of the Samian war.

56. "Ηραν ... Ἀσπασίαν, the Hera-Aspasia, as consort of the Zeus-Pericles (c. 3, 3; c. 13, 6). The lines are from the Χείρωνες, and are closely connected with those cited in c. 3, 3. By oἱ is meant Κρόνος the father of Hera.

57. Καταπυγοσύνη: the poet is very bitter in making *Impudicitia* the mother of Aspasia as 'a shameless concubine,' for in Attic law marriage with a foreigner was regarded as concubinage, and their children were illegitimate (νόθοι). See below c. 37, 2 note and *Them.* c. 1, 1 with my note *ad l.*

58. δοκεῖ *sc.* ὁ Περικλῆς, § 2 l. 7.   τὸν νόθον, Pericles the younger. He was born probably before B.C. 440: in B.C. 410 he was Hellenotamias and in B.C. 406 strategus. See c. 37, 5.

59. πεποίηκεν, c. 4, 2.   Δήμοις, c. 3, 4.

62. Μυρωνίδην, c. 16, 2.

63. καὶ πάλαι γ' ἄν, 'yes (he is alive) and, what's more, would have been a full-grown man (*i.e.* admitted to his full burgher rights) had he not been deterred by the shameful circumstances of his birth.'

§ 7 l. 66. τὸν πολεμήσαντα, in the war of which Xenophon wrote a history, B.C. 401 = Ol. 94, 3.

69. Μιλτώ: see *Artox.* c. 26, 3; Athenae. XIII c. 37 p. 576 D 44 Κῦρος δ' ὁ ἐπὶ τὸν ἀδελφὸν ἐπιστρατεύσας οὐχὶ ἑταίραν οὖσαν τὴν Φωκαΐδα τὴν σοφωτάτην <καὶ> καλλίστην εἶχε συστρατευομένην; ἣν Ζηνοφάνης φησὶ πρότερον Μιλτὼ καλουμένην Ἀσπασίαν μετονομασθῆναι. Her former name was given her because of her beautiful complexion; Aelian *VII.* 12, 1 ἐῴκει δὲ ἡ χροία ἡ κατὰ τοῦ προσώπου ῥόδοις· διὰ ταῦτά τοι οἱ Φωκαεῖς ἔτι παιδίον οὖσαν ἐκάλουν Μιλτώ.

71. τῇ μάχῃ, at Cunaxa.   ἀπαχθεῖσα, 'carried off as a prisoner,' c. 31, 5. Xenophon (*Anab.* I 10, 2) mentions her capture by the royal troops.

72. πλεῖστον ἴσχυσε, 'acquired very considerable influence.'

73. ἐπελθόντα τῇ μνήμῃ κατὰ τὴν γραφήν, 'occurring as they did to my memory in the course of my writing.'

74. παρελθεῖν, *praeterire*.   ἀπάνθρωπον ἦν, *inhumanum erat*, 'it would have been unnatural,' an affectation of austerity. See G. *MT.*² § 415 f. for the omission of ἄν.

CHAPTER XXV

§ 1 l. 2. αἰτιῶνται: a repetition of the statement made in c. 24, 1. μάλιστα, with διὰ Μιλησίους.

4. αἱ πόλεις, sc. Samos and Miletus. Miletus had joined the Delian confederacy not long after the battle of Mycale, B.C. 479.

5. τόν, c. 24 § 1 l. 3 note. περὶ Πριήνης, for the possession of Priene, a city of Caria, north of the Latmian Gulf, on the southern declivity of Mount Mycale.

The war commenced in the beginning of B.C. 440. Ten years before, troubles had broken out in Miletus, in which the Athenians had found it necessary to interfere: the constitution had been changed from an oligarchy into a democracy, and an Athenian garrison set up in the city. On the other side, the Samians had been at war in former days with Priene for the possession of certain places on the mainland. But, whatever the cause of strife, the two cities Miletus and Samos flew to arms and Miletus was defeated. The Milesians went with their complaint against the Samians to Athens: a party from Samos, who wished to overthrow the oligarchical government established there, joined in the appeal (Thuc. I 115, 2).

κρατοῦντες, ' being superior.'

7. δίκας λαβεῖν καὶ δοῦναι παρ' αὐτοῖς, lit. 'to give and accept arbitration before them,' *i.e.* to submit their differences to a peaceful settlement before them (the Athenians). Cp. Herod. V 83 δίκας ἐδίδοσάν τε καὶ ἐλάμβανον παρ' ἀλλήλων, Thuc. V 59, 5 ἑτοίμους εἶναι δίκας δοῦναι καὶ δέξασθαι ἴσας καὶ ὁμοίας.

8. πλεύσας, with forty ships, acc. to Thuc. *l. c.*

9. οὖσαν is not for ὑπάρχουσαν, but to be taken with ἐν Σάμῳ.

10. κατέλυσεν, c. 3, 1; c. 7, 5. τῶν πρώτων, *optimatium*, c. 25, 1; c. 28, 5. Cp. Thuc. I 115, 3 ὁμήρους ἔλαβον τῶν Σαμίων πεντήκοντα μὲν παῖδας, ἴσους δὲ ἄνδρας.

12. ἴσους, 'an equal number of.'

§ 2 l. 13. διδόναι, ' was ready to give,' ' offered,' the infinitive of the imperfect; G. *MT.*² §§ 25, 36. According to Diodorus (XII 27, 2), Pericles exacted eighty talents from the Samians.

16. Pissuthnes, son of Hystaspes, was satrap of Lydia and, as such, εἶχε Σάρδεις τότε (Thuc. I 115, 4).

17. χρυσοῦς (*sc.* στατῆρας) *i.q.* δαρεικούς, each of the value of twenty silver Attic drachmae; consequently the amount sent by the satrap was thirty-three and a half talents.

18. παραιτούμενος, 'begging the deliverance of,' 'interceding for'; cp. *Marc.* c. 20, 7 παρητεῖτο τοὺς πολίτας.

19. χρησάμενος ὥσπερ ἐγνώκει, 'treating them as he had made up his mind to do'; c. 23, 2.

21. ἀπέπλευσεν: Diodorus *l. c.* says that he returned to Athens ἐν ὀλίγαις ἡμέραις ἅπαντα συντετελεκώς.

§ 3 l. 22. ἐκκλέψαντος, 'removing by stealth,' c. 32, 3.

23. τἆλλα παρασκευάσαντος: ἐπικούρους ξυλλέξαντες ὡς ἑπτακοσίους Thuc. I 115, 5. Diod. XII 27, 3 attributes a sinister motive to him, ἐλπίζων τῆς Σάμου διὰ τούτου κυριεύσειν.

24. αὖθις, before July B.C. 440. Pericles was δέκατος αὐτός 45 (Thuc.) *i.e.* he was accompanied by the other nine στρατηγοί, one of whom was the poet Sophocles.

26. κατεπτηχότας from καταπτήσσειν.

27. καὶ πάνυ, c. 15, 3. ἐγνωκότας ἀντιλαμβάνεσθαι τῆς θαλάσσης, 'having made up their minds to contest the dominion of the sea.' In what a critical position their determined attitude placed Athens, appears from Thuc. VIII 76, 3 πόλιν σφίσιν ὑπάρχειν Σάμον οὐκ ἀσθενῆ, ἀλλ' ἢ παρ' ἐλάχιστον δὴ ἦλθε τὸ Ἀθηναίων κράτος τῆς θαλάσσης, ὅτε ἐπολέμησεν, ἀφελέσθαι, a passage referred to by Plut. himself c. 33, 1.

30. Τραγίας: the island which lay between Samos and Miletus at the entrance of the Latmian gulf. *Hyetussa* is the name given to the group to which it belongs. Strabo *Geogr.* XIV c. 1, 7 speaks of them as a group of islands: πρόκειται δὲ (τῆς Μιλήτου) ἡ Λάδη νῆσος πλησίον καὶ τὰ περὶ τὰς Τραγαίας νησία ὑφόρμους ἔχοντα λῃσταῖς, but Thuc. I 116, 1 has πρὸς Τραγίᾳ τῇ νήσῳ. See Pflugk-Harttung *Perikles als Feldherr* p. 124. λαμπρῶς, 'decisively.' For this meaning of λαμπρῶς, see *Pomp.* c. 58, 5 ὡς νενικηκὼς λαμπρῶς ὑπὸ χαρᾶς ἐξήλατο, *Sull.* c. 29, 5 and Thuc. VII 55, 1.

31. ἐνίκα, *victor erat*, 'remained conqueror,' νικᾶν being, like ἀδικεῖν, ἥκειν, a quasi-perfect.

33. στρατιώτιδες *i.q.* ὁπλιταγωγοί, 'troop-ships,' 'transports')(ταχεῖαι (τριήρεις), Thuc. VI 43, 1.

CHAPTER XXVI

§ 1 l. 1. τοῦ λιμένος κρατήσας, 'now that he had got possession of the harbour.' Diodorus also (XII 27, 4) gives the victory to the Athenians; Thucydides and Ephorus agree in taking the Athenian view of the struggle, while Aristotle (§ 3 l. 27) takes that of the Samians. The course and issue of the engagement was of such a nature that both sides could lay claim to have won.

3. **ἀμῶς γέ πως**)(οὐδαμῶς, 'in one way or other,' 'somehow at least' from obsolete ἀμός (= τις) a word of frequent occurrence in Plutarch.

5. **μείζων στόλος**, consisting of forty Athenian and twenty-five Chian and Lesbian triremes.

6. **παντελῶς κατεκλείσθησαν**: Thuc. I 116, 2 καὶ ἀποβάντες καὶ κρατοῦντες τῷ πεζῷ ἐπολιόρκουν ('Αθηναῖοι) τρισὶ τείχεσι τὴν πόλιν καὶ ἐκ θαλάσσης ἅμα.

7. **ἑξήκοντα τριήρεις**: the number blockading Samos was 109 (44+40+25), so that forty-nine were left behind.

8. **εἰς τὸν ἔξω πόντον**, into the open Mediterranean sea)(τὸν ἐντός, 'the Aegean'; otherwise the phrase is used to designate the Atlantic Ocean in opp. to the Mediterranean. *Alex.* c. 44, 2.

9. **οἱ πλεῖστοι**: these include Thucydides and Diodorus.

10. **ἐπικούρων** with τοῖς Σαμίοις. **προσφερομένων**, c. 8, 5. Stesagoras and others had been sent by the Samians with a small squadron in quest of the Phoenician ships (Thuc. *l. c.*). Nothing more is said about the latter.

11. **διαγωνίσασθαι** *sc.* αὐταῖς.

12. **πορρωτάτω**, as far as possible from Samos.

13. **Στησίμβροτος** *sc.* λέγει: it is not at all evident what motive Stesimbrotus had for making such a statement. Ad. Schmidt (*Perikl. Zeit.* II 35) supposes that he was misunderstood by Plutarch. For another solution, Busolt quotes Ulrich von Wilamowitz-Möllendorff *Hermes* XII 366. Possibly Stesimbrotus meant only in the direction of Cyprus, as Thuc. says ἐπὶ Καύνου καὶ Καρίας.

§ 2 l. 14. **δ' οὖν**, resumptive, 'be that as it may,' 'anyhow,' whether it be a likely story or not, c. 27, 1.

16. **Μέλισσος**: this was the philosopher who, like Zeno his fellow Eleatic, transferred the poetic philosophy of his great Pantheist predecessor Parmenides into Ionic prose, *Them.* c. 2, 3. Thucydides and Diodorus make no mention of him.
ἀνὴρ φιλόσοφος: see Gr. Ind. *s. v.* ἀνήρ.

21. **πολλοὺς μέν ... πολλὰς δέ**: c. 15, 1, 3.

23. **ἐχρῶντο**, 'had a free and unimpeded use of,' Thuc. I 117, 1 τῆς θαλάσσης τῆς καθ' ἑαυτοὺς ἐκράτησαν (οἱ Σάμιοι) ἡμέρας περὶ τέσσαρας καὶ δέκα.

24. **παρετίθεντο**, 'were busy providing themselves with,' properly said of meals. Thuc. *l. c.* ἐσεκομίσαντο καὶ ἐξεκομίσαντο ἃ ἐβούλοντο. (Plutarch here uses a Samian authority *i.e.* probably Duris. Cp. Aelian *VII.* VII 14.) The three preceding

aorist participles are complexive, i.e. they state summarily the events of the conflict.

§ 3 l. 27. **Ἀριστοτέλης**, probably ἐν τῇ τῶν Σαμίων πολιτείᾳ: the statement is unsupported.

29. **ἀνυβρίζοντες**, 'in retaliation for a similar affront.'

31. **γλαῦκας**, the common device on Athenian coins. Cp. *Nic.* c. 29, 1 στίζοντες ἵππον εἰς τὸ μέτωπον. The reverse process is more likely, that the Athenians branded the Samians, as their slaves, with an owl. Cp. Aelian *VH.* II 9 τούς γε μὴν ἁλισκομένους αἰχμαλώτους Σαμίων στίζειν κατὰ τοῦ προσώπου καὶ εἶναι τὸ στίγμα γλαῦκα. **ἐκείνους**, sc. τοὺς αἰχμαλώτους τῶν Σαμίων ἔστιζον σάμαιναν. For the construction, cp. Herod. VII 233 τοὺς δὲ πλεῦνας ... ἔστιζον στίγματα βασιλήϊα.

32. **ὑόπρῳρος**, 'with a beak turned up like a swine's snout.' This agrees with the description given by Didymus ap. Hesychium Σαμιακὸς τρόπος:—Δίδυμος δὲ τὰς Σαμίας ναῦς ἰδιαιτέραν παρὰ τὰς ἄλλας ναῦς τὴν κατασκευὴν ἔχειν· εὐρύτεραι μὲν γάρ εἰσι τὰς γαστέρας, τοὺς δὲ ἐμβόλους σεσίμωνται, ὡς δοκεῖν ῥύγχεσιν ὑῶν ὁμοίως κατεσκευάσθαι. The explanation is probably taken from the Scholiast on the verse from the *Babylonians* of Aristophanes (Mein. II 972, Kock I 408). Cp. Herod. III 59 τῶν νεῶν καπρίους ἐχουσέων τὰς πρῴρας ἠκρωτηρίασαν. Choerilus (fr. VI ed. Naeke 155 sqq.) speaks of νηῦς δέ τις ὠκυπόρος Σαμίη, ὑὸς εἶδος ἔχουσα.

33. **κοιλοτέρα** i.e. than an ordinary trireme.

34. **ποντοπορεῖν**, 'to sail in the high sea,' because of its broader keel, *Dion* c. 25, 1. **ταχυναυτεῖν**, because of the construction of its fore-part.

§ 4 l. 36. **Πολυκράτους**: the despotism of Polycrates began about B.C. 532 and he was killed in the year of Cambyses' death B.C. 522. Herod. III 125, Thuc. I 13, 6, Strab. *Geogr.* XIV c. 1, 16.

37. **πρὸς ταῦτα ... ᾐνίχθαι**, 'to have been indirectly aimed at these marks.' Cp. *Mor.* 727 D ὡς πρὸς τοὺς διαβόλους καὶ ψιθύρους τῶν συνήθων ᾐνιγμένον, Arist. *Av.* 970 ᾐνίξαθ' ὁ Βάκις τοῦτο πρὸς τὸν ἀέρα.

39. **πολγγράμματοc** primarily = στιγματίας. But evidently some *double entendre* is meant, perhaps in allusion to the use of the full alphabet of twenty-four letters having been first introduced by the Samians, or because of the enfranchisement on a large scale of (branded) slaves after the abolition of despotism. Possibly Plutarch may have attached too great importance to the explanation of some scholiast, and the reference does not really turn on the circumstance which he records.

CHAPTER XXVII

§ 1 l. 1. δ' οὖν, c. 26, 2.   ἐπὶ στρατοπέδου: cp. c. 10, 2, *Cat. mi.* c. 58, 3, *Timol.* c. 37, 6, *Cat. ma.* c. 10, 5 ἐπὶ στρατείας, Arist. *Vesp.* 354, 557, *Lys.* 100 ἐπὶ στρατιᾶς ἀπόντας.

2. ἐβοήθει: we are not told whether Pericles came across the Phoenician fleet. He went to Caunus and Caria, but his naval demonstration had no result. It is possible that it may have been merely a stratagem of the Samians, to draw off a part of the Athenian beleaguering force by false reports. κατὰ τάχος, c. 22, 2.

4. ἀντιταξαμένου: Plut. says nothing of the arrival of reinforcements under the command of Thucydides, Hagnon and Phormion, consisting of forty triremes, which were followed by twenty under Tlepolemus and Anticles, and thirty from Chios and Lesbos, so that the fleet now numbered 200 (cp. Isocr. *or.* XV 111), notwithstanding which the Samians ναυμαχίαν τινα βραχεῖαν ἐποιήσαντο. See Thuc. I 117, 2.

5. περιετείχιζε: this had been already done according to c. 26, 1, and Thuc. The latter says merely πάλιν ταῖς ναυσὶ κατεκλῄσθησαν (*i.e.* were locked up in their ports, as before), the blockade having been interrupted only ἐκ θαλάσσης.

7. τῶν πολιτῶν (*i.e.* the Athenians) depends on τραύμασι καὶ κινδύνοις.

8. συνελεῖν for ἑλεῖν: cp. *Lys.* c. 14, 1 ὡς ταχὺ συναιρήσων τὴν πόλιν.

§ 2 l. 11. ἔργον, 'a hard matter,' 'quite a business.' Cp. *Anton.* c. 40, 3, *Alc.* c. 15, 1 εἰ δ' ἐσφάλησαν, ἔργον ἦν τὴν Λακεδαίμονα περιγενέσθαι, *Num.* c. 4, 3 ἔ. ἤδη καὶ τοῦτο πεισθῆναι, *Thes.* c. 27, 2 ἔργον ἐστὶ πιστεῦσαι, Xen. *Cyr.* I i 5, III iii 27, VII v 51.   ὀκτὼ μέρη διελὼν τὸ πᾶν πλῆθος, 'dividing the whole number into eight parts,' the number of parts being placed in apposition to the whole, as being the sum thereof.

Kornës with others insert εἰς before ὀκτώ: but cp. *Lyc.* c. 8, 3 ἔνειμε τὴν ἄλλην τοῖς περιοίκοις Λακωνικὴν τρισμυρίους κλήρους, Xen. *Cyr.* VII v 13 τὸ στράτευμα διένειμε δώδεκα μέρη, Plat. *Politic.* 283 D διέλωμεν αὐτὴν δύο μέρη, *Crit.* 113 B κατενείμαντο γῆν πᾶσαν μείζους λήξεις καὶ ἐλάττους, Ε τὴν νῆσον . . . δέκα μέρη καταμείμας, Dem. *or.* XIV § 17 τούτων τῶν συμμοριῶν ἑκάστην διελεῖν κελεύω πέντε μέρη.

12. ἀπεκλήρου, 'proceeded to choose by lot,' as in *Thes.* c. 17, 2 ἀπεκλήρωσε τοὺς ἄλλους παῖδας.

13. τῷ λαβόντι s. μέρει.   τὸν λευκὸν κύαμον, 'the white bean' among the eight, the other seven being black.

14. σχολάζειν παρεῖχε, 'enabled them to take their ease.'

Cp. *Mor.* 126 ε φιλοσοφεῖν ἀρρωστίαι πολλοῖς παρέχουσι, *Cleom.* c. 24, 1 τοῖς φεύγουσιν . . . ἀσφαλῶς ἀπελθεῖν παρέσχον.

τῶν ἅ. τρυχομένων, 'while the other (seven) were distressing themselves' with work at the entrenchments. According to Diod. XII 27, 2, Pericles continued συνεχεῖς ποιούμενος προσβολάς.

15. **τοὺς ἐν εὐπαθείαις γινομένους**, 'those who have a day of enjoyment.' Cp. *Anton.* c. 56, 3 πλεύσαντες εἰς Σάμον ἐν εὐπαθείαις ἦσαν, *Demetr.-Anton.* c. 3, 1 ἐν εὐπαθείαις ὄντα πράξεων καιρὸς ἐξέφυγεν, Herod. I c. 22, c. 191.

16. **λευκὴν ἡμέραν ἐκείνην ... προσαγορεύειν**, 'called that a white day': ἐκείνην = ᾗ ἐν εὐπαθείαις ἐγένοντο. See Aesch. *Pers.* 305.

The following lines from the Κόλακες of Eupolis, bear on this siege:—

ἐκεῖνος ἦν φειδωλός, ὃς ἐπὶ τοῦ βίου
πρὸ τοῦ πολέμου μὲν τριχίδας ὠψώνησ᾽ ἅπαξ,
ὅτε τὰν Σάμῳ δ᾽ ἦν, ἡμιωβολίου κρέα.

ἀπό: cp. c. 8, 2, Thuc. I 46, 3 ἀφ᾽ οὗ καὶ τὴν ἐπωνυμίαν ἔχει.

§ 3 l. 17. **Ἔφορος** sc. φησί. See Müller *FHG.* I p. 265.

18. **μηχαναῖς**, 'military engines.' Cp. Diod. XII 28, 3 κατεσκεύασε δὲ καὶ μηχανὰς πρῶτος τῶν πρὸ αὐτοῦ τούς τε ὀνομαζομένους κριοὺς καὶ χελώνας Ἀρτέμωνος τοῦ Κλαζομενίου κατασκευάσαντος.

The Greeks had ordinarily no other means of reducing a town, but building a wall round it and starving out the inhabitants. This explains τὴν καινότητα, 'the novelty of the engines.' But Ephorus *fr.* 107 speaks also of Miltiades as τὰ κατὰ γῆν μηχανήματα ἄγων at the siege of Paros.

19. **Artemon**, the famous engineer of Clazomenae, according to Ephorus, bore the nickname ὁ Περιφόρητος, because he had to be carried about in a litter owing to his lameness. The epithet was given to the elder Artemon, a contemporary of Anacreon, for other reasons which are stated by Chamaeleon of Pontus (Athenae. XII c. 46) who says that he was so called διὰ τὸ τρυφερῶς βιοῦντα περιφέρεσθαι ἐπὶ κλίνης· καὶ γὰρ Ἀνακρέων αὐτὸν ἐκ πενίας εἰς τρυφὴν ὁρμῆσαί φησιν. There is an allusion to the elder Artemon in the epithet ὁ περιπόνηρος, Arist. *Ach.* 857.

20. **ὄντα ... προσκομιζόμενον**, causal participles.

21. **τὰ κατεπείγοντα τῶν ἔργων**, 'important works that required his immediate presence.' *Paroemiogr. Gr.* II 4, 41 χωλὸς δὲ ὢν περιεφέρετο ἐπὶ τῷ ὁρᾶν τὰς μηχανάς.

Cp. *Alex.* c. 72, 1 διώκησε τὰ κατεπείγοντα, *Brut.* c. 36, 1 ἐχρῆτο τῇ νυκτὶ πρὸς τὰ κατεπείγοντα τῶν πραγμάτων, *Pelop.* c. 27, 1 τοῖς θεοσσαλοῖς χρῆσθαι πρὸς τὸ κατεπεῖγον τῶν πραγμάτων ἀναγκαζόμενος. The expression is one of common occurrence in Polybius.

23. **τοῦτο ἐλέγχει**, 'disproves this,' viz. the fact of Artemon's

presence at the siege of Samos. **Ἡρακλείδης ὁ Ποντικός**: c. 35, 4. Heracleides probably borrowed this statement, as he did many others, from Chamaeleon, whom Athenaeus quotes as his authority. See the passage cited in note to l. 19.

26. **πολλαῖς ἔμπροσθεν ἡλικίαις κτλ.**, 'several ages before the Samian war' (c. 13, 1), viz. in the time of Polycrates. For ἡλικίαις, cp. c. 13, 1.

§ 4 l. 28. **φησί**, sc. Heracleides. **τρυφερόν τινα**: for this restrictive use of τις with adjectives to increase or weaken their notion, see n. to c. 24, 3. **τῷ βίῳ**, dat. of respect for acc., c. 3, 2 ; c. 29, 3.

29. **πρὸς τοὺς φόβους**, 'in the presence of terrors,' c. 15, 4. **μαλακόν**, 'unmanly.' Cp. Aristot. *Eth. Eud.* 1229 [b], 7 πρὸς τὸν θάνατον μαλακός. **καταπλῆγα**, 'timid,' 'apprehensive of danger.' *Mor.* 7 B ἄτολμον καὶ καταπλῆγα, 814 E καταπλῆγα καὶ περιδεῆ.

30. **τὰ πολλά**, *plerumque*, c. 7, 2. **καθέζεσθαι**, poetical form for καθῆσθαι, not used in Attic prose.

31. **δυεῖν**: this form does not appear in inscriptions until after B.C. 329. The Attic is δυοῖν: see n. to c. 6, 2.

32. **ὑπερεχόντων**: Hom. *Il.* IX 687, Arist. *Av.* 1508 μου τὸ σκιάδειον ὑπέρεχε, *Eq.* 1176 ἡμῶν ὑπερεῖχε τὴν χύτραν, Lucian *Tim.* c. 10 ὑπερέσχε γὰρ αὐτοῦ τὴν χεῖρα Περικλῆς. **τῶν ἄνωθεν** for τῶν ἄνω by attraction to ἐμπεσεῖν: see note to c. 3, 4 ; c. 34, 4.

33. **εἰ βιασθείη**, 'whenever he had been compelled': the opt. is used because the reference is to an indefinite number of acts in past time. **κλινιδίῳ κρεμαστῷ**, 'hammock.' Cp. *Coriol.* c. 24, 3 ἐν κλινιδίῳ φοράδην κομισθεὶς εἰς τὴν σύγκλητον.

34. **παρὰ τὴν γῆν αὐτήν**, 'close to the very ground.'

Cp. *Sull.* c. 15, 4 ὑπ᾽ αὐτὴν τὴν Τιθόραν, *Timol.* c. 31, 2 ἀπηλλάττετο παρ᾽ αὐτὴν τὴν Καλαυρίαν, *Them.* c. 27, 1 γενόμενος παρ᾽ αὐτὸ τὸ δεινόν, Xen. *Hell.* I v 12 παρ᾽ αὐτὰς τὰς πρῴρας τῶν Λυσάνδρου νεῶν παρέπλει, *Cyr.* V ii 29 παρ᾽ αὐτὴν τὴν Βαβυλῶνα παριέναι, iv 41 ἡ ὁδὸς παρ᾽ αὐτὸ τὸ τεῖχος φέρει.

CHAPTER XXVIII

§ 2 l. 1. **ἐνάτῳ μηνί**, i.e. reckoning from the commencement of the siege, § 5. The temporal dative is used of a particular day, month or year; an attributive therefore must, as a rule, accompany the substantive. **παραστάντων**, 'being brought to terms,' 'capitulating.'

Cp. Paus. x 33, 2 πολιορκηθέντες ὑπὸ Φιλίππου παρέστησαν κατὰ συνθήκας. Thucydides uses the aor. middle only, 'to reduce,' serving as causative to προσχωρεῖν, 'to submit' (I 117, 3), as I 29, 5 τοὺς τὴν Ἐπίδαμνον πολιορκοῦντας παραστήσασθαι ὁμολογίᾳ, c. 98, 2 πολιορκίᾳ παρεστήσαντο τοὺς Ναξίους, c. 124, 3 τὴν πόλιν παραστησώμεθα ἐπελθόντες, III 35 Ἔρεσον παρεστήσατο, IV 79, 2.

3. **χρήμασι**, as an indemnity for the expenses of the war (χρήματα τὰ ἀναλωθέντα), Thuc. I 117, 3.

The cost of the war, according to Isocrates (or. xv 111), who follows Ephorus as his authority, was 1000 talents, acc. to Nepos (*Timoth.* c. 5, 1) 1200. Diodorus (xII 28, 3) mentions 200 talents as the sum at which it was estimated by Pericles. But this is manifestly, as Thirlwall says, much too little, and one might almost suspect that the words καὶ χιλίων had slipped either out of his text or out of his head. We gather from the *C/A.* I 177 that 1276 talents were withdrawn from the treasury to meet the expenses; besides which, as Busolt suggests, the year's φόροι, amounting to 800 talents, would, as a matter of course, be appropriated to the same purpose. Moreover large and lucrative estates in the island must have been set apart for the Athenian cponymi and Athena Polias. See the authorities quoted by Busolt *Gr. Gesch.* II 600 note 3. The payment of the φόρος was not reimposed on the Samians, but they were still bound to furnish a contingent of land troops, like the other subject states (Thuc. II 9, 3); and we find (Thuc. VII 57, 4) that they did so in the Sicilian expedition. The island of Amorgos also was taken from them. As to the internal government, there is every reason to suppose, from the nature of the case and from the account given by Ephorus, that the Athenians re-established a democracy; see Diod. XII 28, 4 παρείλετο δὲ καὶ τὰς ναῦς αὐτῶν καὶ τὰ τείχη κατέσκαψε καὶ τὴν δημοκρατίαν καταστήσας ἐπανῆλθεν εἰς τὴν πατρίδα. Many of the nobles fled to Anaea on the opposite mainland. During the Peloponnesian war the island remained in a very unsettled state. In the summer of B.C. 412 there was a great revolution, when the oligarchs were deposed and dispossessed of their property, 200 slain, 400 exiled, and a democracy established (Thuc. VIII 21, 63, *C/A.* I 56). It must be supposed, therefore, that in the interval the oligarchs had gradually supplanted the democratic government and obtained the ascendancy.

5. **ταξάμενοι κατοίσειν**, 'covenanting to pay down.'

Thuc. uses τάττεσθαι in the sense of 'to get oneself rated,' either (*a*) with the accusative of the sum to be paid (I 108, 4) or (*b*) with a present or aorist infinitive (I 99, 3; I 117, 3) or (*c*) with both infin. and accus. (I 101, 3; III 50, 3). καταφέρειν in this sense is peculiar to post-classical writers, as Polybius 1, 62, 9; 33, 11, 6. Cp. καταβάλλειν *Them.* c. 24, 1, *Sull.* c. 24, 5, Thuc. I 27, 1, Plato *Legg.* V 742 B τῇ πόλει αὐτὸ (τὸ νόμισμα ξενικὸν) καταβαλλέτω, also κατατιθέναι Thuc. I 27, 2, Plat. *Protag.* 314 B.

6. On **Duris of Samos**, see *Introduction*.

7. **τούτοις ἐπιτραγῳδεῖ**, 'adds a pathetic story to this,' in exaggerated style. Cp. *Artax.* c. 18, 4 ταῦτα μὲν . . . ἐπιτραγῳδεῖται τῇ Κλεάρχου μνήμῃ, *Dem.* c. 21, 2, Heliodor. *Aethiop.* 2, 29 ἐπετραγῴδει τούτῳ τῷ δράματι καὶ ἕτερον πάθος ὁ δαίμων. Join κατηγορῶν πολλὴν ὠμότητα.

§ 2 l. 10. **ἱστόρηκεν**, c. 9, 2; c. 23, 1.

11. **ἀλλ' οὐδέ κτλ.**, 'nay, he does not even speak the

truth, as it appears.' Cp. e. 36, 4, *Alex.* e. 22, 3, Ar. *Nub.* 1396 τὸ δέρμα τῶν γεραιτέρων λάβοιμεν ἂν | ἀλλ' οὐδ' ἐρεβίνθου, Dem. ι *Aphob.* § 30 λῆμμα οὐδὲν ἐμοὶ γεγενημένον ἀποφαίνουσιν ἀλλ' οὐδὲ μικρόν, *Mid.* § 147 ἀλλ' οὐδ' ὁτιοῦν, *de f. l.* § 41 with Shilleto's note *ad l.*   ὡς ἄρα, 'to wit that,' but ἄρα conveys also the notion of something surprising.

12. τοὺς ἐπιβάτας = τοὺς ἀπὸ τοῦ καταστρώματος μαχομένους (*Them.* e. 14, 1) in opp. to the rowers and seamen.

14. σανίσι προσδήσας, 'fastening them to posts,' putting them in the stocks, as an ignominious punishment.
ἐφ' ἡμέρας δέκα, 'for (during) ten days,' e. 16, 2.

16. ἀνελεῖν, e. 10, 7. συγκόψαντας refers to the implied subject of this infinitive and of προβαλεῖν *i.e.* those whose business it was to execute Pericles' order.

17. προβαλεῖν, *Them.* e. 22, 2.

§ 3 l. 18. μὲν οὖν, 'so then,' in concluding the digression and going back to the former subject: the οὖν is resumptive, the μέν answers to the δέ of l. 22.   οὐδ(έ), 'not even.' πρόσεστιν, e. 7, 1; e. 8, 2.

19. ἴδιον πάθος, 'personal feeling,' 'self-interest.'
κρατεῖν τὴν διήγησιν ἐπὶ τῆς ἀληθείας, 'to keep his narrative within the bounds of truth.'

20. μᾶλλον ἐνταῦθα, 'in this case the rather,' because he had a personal interest, as a Samian by birth.

21. δεινῶσαι: Thuc. VIII 74, 3.   ἐπὶ διαβολῇ: c. 31, 5.

24. ταφὰς ... ἐποίησε: the ceremony took place in the outer Ceramicus. Cp. Plato *Menex.* 234 ταφὰς οἶσθ' ὅτι μέλλουσι ποιεῖν, but Thuc. II 34, 1 δημοσίᾳ ταφὰς ἐποιήσαντο τῶν ... ἀπογενομένων, Dem. *Lept.* § 141 μόνοι ἐπὶ τοῖς τελευτήσασι δημοσίᾳ ταφὰς ποιεῖσθε.

The custom was as old as the time of Solon, but the λόγος ἐπιτάφιος or 'funeral oration' was an after addition, dating from the times immediately after the Persian wars (Diod. XI 33, 3). This *ὅδε* is not to be confounded with the celebrated oration over those who fell in the beginning of the Peloponnesian war Ol. 87, 3 = B.C. 430, as given by Thuc. II cc. 35–46. Other specimens are (1) that contained in Plato's *Menexenus*, supposed to have been written by Aspasia, (2) the spurious ones bearing the name of Lysias (*or.* 2), and (3) Demosthenes (*or.* 60), and the genuine one by Hyperides, pronounced over the Athenian general Leosthenes who fell in the Lamian war. The quotation in c. 8, 5 and those in Aristot. *Rhet.* I 7 οἷον Περικλῆς τὸν ἐπιτάφιον λέγων τὴν νεότητα ἐκ τῆς πόλεως ἀνῃρῆσθαι ὥσπερ τὸ ἔαρ ἐκ τοῦ ἐνιαυτοῦ εἰ ἐξαιρεθείη and again III 10, 7 Περικλῆς ἔφη τὴν νεότητα τὴν ἀπολομένην ἐν τῷ πολέμῳ οὕτως ἠφανίσθαι ἐκ τῆς πόλεως ὥσπερ εἴ τις τὸ ἔαρ ἐκ τοῦ ἐνιαυτοῦ ἐξέλοι are taken from this speech. See the authorities quoted by Busolt *l. c.* II 602 note 2.

25. ἀποθανόντων, c. 8, 6 ; c. 30, 3.

28. ἐθαυμαστώθη, 'gained great applause,' 'was the object of great admiration,' the post-classical form stronger than ἐθαυμάσθη. It occurs again *Pomp.* c. 53, 1 ἐπὶ τούτοις θαυμασθωθεὶς καὶ ἀγαπηθεὶς. Cp. Aristot. *Hist. Anim.* IX c. 36 p. 633ᵃ, 8 ἡ φάττα ἐφθέγξατό ποτε χειμῶνος καὶ ἐθαυμαστώθη ὑπὸ τῶν ἐμπείρων.

§ 4 l. 30. ἐδεξιοῦντο, 'greeted.'

31. Ἐλπινίκη, c. 10, 5.

34. ὅς is used as if (ταῦτά) σου had preceded.   πολλοὺς καὶ ἀγαθούς, c. 22, 2.

37. συγγενῆ, as being an Ionian state and besides founded by Athens.

§ 5 l. 38. μειδιάσας ἀτρέμα : *Them.* c. 29, 1 ἀτρέμα στενάξας.

41. οὐκ ἄν ... Ηλείφεο: the conditional sentence is left to be supplied from Archilochus, εἰ ἐσωφρόνεις, or εἰ μὴ ᾖσθα μάχλος γυνή, G. *MT.*² § 410. Pericles' retort, unless it was a mere personal sarcasm, signified that Cimon's policy was now antiquated. Cp. the anecdote from Stesimbrotus in c. 10, 5. The same verse originally addressed to an old coquette is quoted by Athenaeus p. 688 e who tells us that Archilochus (c. 2, 1) was the first to use the word μύρον, which afterwards took the place of ἔλαιον.

42. θαυμαστόν τι ... φρονῆσαι, 'that he was elated to an extraordinary degree,' 'his vanity was something marvellous.' For τις, see n. to c. 27, 4.

43. ὁ Ἴων, c. 5, 3.

44. ὡς, 'under the idea that,' as c. 5, 1.   ἔτεσι δέκα, § 1 l. 1, c. 27, 3.

46. τοὺς πρώτους, 'the foremost men,' c. 25, 1.

§ 6 l. 47. ἑλόντος must be supplied in the first clause from the second.   ἀξίωσις, 'assumption,' 'pretension,' 'estimate of himself,' τὸ ἀξιοῦν ἑαυτὸν ὑπερβαίνειν τὸν Ἀγαμέμνονα. The expression is borrowed from Thuc. III 9, 2 καὶ οὐκ ἄδικος αὕτη ἡ ἀξίωσίς ἐστιν.

48. ἀδηλότητα, 'uncertainty' as to its issue, c. 18, 1.

50. Θουκυδίδης : VIII 76, 4.   παρ' ἐλάχιστον ἦλθε, 'came within a very little of.' The passage runs thus :— πόλιν τε γὰρ σφίσιν ὑπάρχειν Σάμον οὐκ ἀσθενῆ ἀλλ' ἢ παρ'

ἐλάχιστον δὴ ἦλθε τὸ 'Αθηναίων κράτος τῆς θαλάσσης, ὅτε ἐπολέμησεν, ἀφελέσθαι. For the phrase, cp. Isocr. or. 19, 22 παρὰ μικρὸν ἦλθεν ἀποθανεῖν and see my n. to Thuc. VII c. 2, 4. There is little doubt that the Samian war exercised an unfavourable influence for the Confederacy, for the number of the tributary Carian towns decreased from forty-three B.C. 440 to twenty-nine, and of these the greater number lay close to Ionia within reach of the Athenian power.

51. The double accusative after ἀφαιρεῖσθαι is normal; Plutarch has sometimes the genitive of the person, but the dative is mostly used.

CHAPTER XXIX

§ 1 l. 1. **μετὰ ταῦτα**: five years afterwards, Ol. 86, 4 = B.C. 133/2. **κυμαίνοντος**, a metaphor taken from a storm at sea, which is preceded by agitation and heaving of the waves.

2. **Κερκυραίοις**: see Thuc. I 24 ff. for details.

The local orthography was Κόρκυρα, Κορκυραῖοι, and such was that of Attic inscriptions of the fifth century, but after the year B.C. 375 we find Κέρκυρα, Κερκυραῖοι.

4. **προσλαβεῖν**, 'to take over,' 'fix in their interest.' Thuc. III c. 13, 7; VIII c. 2, 4.

5. **ναυτικῇ δυνάμει**: Thuc. I c. 25, 4 τριήρεις εἴκοσι καὶ ἑκατὸν ὑπῆρχον αὐτοῖς ὅτε ἤρχοντο πολεμεῖν.

6. **ὅσον οὐδέπω**, 'very little short of not yet,' 'as good as already.' So Alc. c. 14, 3 ὅσον οὐδέπω μεταμελομένους, Alex. c. 26, 2, Mor. 1103 D ὅσον οὐδέπω καταποθήσεσθαι τὴν ναῦν. The expression ὅσον οὔπω is very often found, generally with the infinitive or participle, as Cat. mi. c. 70, 3, Alc. c. 25, 3.

7. **ἐκπεπολεμωμένων**, c. 22, 1.

§ 2 l. 9. **δέκα ναῦς μόνας ἔχοντα**: cp. Thuc. I 45, 1, Diod. XII 33, 2 παραχρῆμα μὲν ἐξέπεμψαν τριήρεις κατηρτισμένας δέκα, μετὰ δὲ ταῦτα πλείους ἐπηγγείλαντο πέμψειν, ἐὰν ᾖ χρεία.

10. **οἷον ἐφυβρίζων**, 'as if he meant to humiliate him.' The statement is doubtless coloured by party feeling. Grote Hist. Gr. v c. 47 p. 325. Two other generals, Diotimus and Proteas, were associated with Lacedaemonius (Thuc. I c. 45, 1), whose names are found recorded in the inscription providing for the expenses of the expedition, CIA. I 179, Hicks no. 41.

13. **ὡς ἂν οὖν κτλ.**: here again we find a personal instead of a political motive imputed to Pericles, no doubt on the

authority of Stesimbrotus. For the use of ὡς ἄν with opt. in a purely final clause—which is peculiar to Xenophon among Attic writers—see G. *MT.*² *Appendix* pp. 400 ff.

It must be remembered, on the other hand, that the alliance between Athens and Corcyra was only a defensive one (ἐπιμαχία) and the ten ships had express orders μὴ ναυμαχεῖν Κορινθίοις, ἢν μὴ ἐπὶ Κέρκυραν πλέωσι καὶ μέλλωσιν ἀποβαίνειν ἢ ἐς τῶν ἐκείνων τι χωρίων· οὕτω δὲ κωλύειν κατὰ δύναμιν. The appointment of Lacedaemonius, who was not likely to precipitate a conflict, was dictated by the same motive, a desire to avoid a collision with the Peloponnesians which would endanger the peace.

15. **προσδιαβληθείη κτλ.**, 'his credit might be still more injured for his laconism,' as if he had intentionally not achieved any important exploit. Cp. *Cor.* c. 27, 3 τοὺς πατρικίους προσδιαβαλεῖν τῷ πλήθει. For **εἰς**, 'with reference to,' cp. c. 13, 10; *Cic.* c. 25, 4 διεβάλλετο δ' εἰς φιλαργυρίαν ὁ Κράσσος, Thuc. VIII 88 βουλόμενος αὐτὸν τοῖς Πελοποννησίοις ἐς τὴν ἑαυτοῦ καὶ Ἀθηναίων φιλίαν διαβάλλειν.

17. **μὴ βουλόμενον**: μή, according to Attic usage, is here abnormal, the participle not being conditional; cp. c. 3, 2, *Pelop.* c. 15, 2 μὴ βουλομένους αὐτοὺς πολεμεῖν διδάξας, *Agis* c. 2, 6.

§ 3 l. 17. **καὶ ὅλως διετέλει κολούων**, 'he persevered generally in abasing them' *i.e.* Cimon's sons, as implied in τῷ Κίμωνος οἴκῳ l. 12 or referring by anticipation to τῶν υἱῶν l. 19.

There is a constant confusion in the MSS. between κολούειν and κωλύειν. The former is a favourite word with Plutarch. Its primary meaning is 'to clip,' 'dock,' 'curtail,' hence figuratively 'to abase,' 'humble,' 'put down,' as *Rom.* c. 25, 1 ἐνίστασθαι τῇ αὐξήσει καὶ κολούειν τὸν Ῥωμύλον, *Poplic.* c. 10, 5 τὸν φθόνον καθαιρῶν καὶ κολούων, *Them.* c. 22, 2 τὸν ἐξοστρακισμὸν ἐποιήσαντο κατ' αὐτοῦ κολούοντες τὸ ἀξίωμα, *Alc.* c. 34, 4 κομιδῇ κολούσειν καὶ ταπεινώσειν τὸν Ἄγιν, *Arist.* c. 3, 1 κολούων τὴν ἐκείνου δύναμιν, *Lucull.* c. 1, 4 κολούσας τὸ φιλότιμον, *Pomp.* c. 47, 2 κολούουσα τὴν δόξαν αὐτοῦ, *T. Gr.* c. 15, 2; c. 16, 2 ἂν τὴν ἰσχὺν κολούσῃ, *Demetr.* c. 6, 1 τοῦ υἱοῦ τὸ φρόνημα καθελεῖν καὶ κολοῦσαι, *Oth.* c. 3, 2 ἐκολούειν τοὺς ἀξιολόγους, *Nic.* c. 6, 1 κολούοντα τὸ φρόνημα, *Fab.* c. 10, 1 ᾤοντο κεκολοῦσθαι καὶ γεγονέναι ταπεινὸν ἐκεῖνον, *Agesil.* c. 31, 4 ἑώρα τῆς πόλεως τὸ αὔχημα κεκολουμένον, *Artox.* c. 27, 5 τὸ κολούμενον οὐ ταπεινὸν ... ἀλλὰ τραχὺ ... ἔσχε. It is found in more than thirty passages in the *Moralia*. Herodotus uses it once only in this sense, VII 10, 5 φιλέει γὰρ ὁ θεὸς τὰ ὑπερέχοντα πάντα κολούειν, and so Thucydides VII 66, 3 ἐπειδὰν ᾧ ἀξιοῦσι προὔχειν κολουθῶσι, Plato several times *Apol.* 39 D, *Legg.* 731 A, *Prot.* 343 C, *Euthyd.* 305 D, *Rep.* 528 C ὑπὸ τῶν πολλῶν ἀτιμαζόμενα καὶ κολούμενα. It is probably to be restored to Euripides *Pleisth.* fr. 626, 6 κόλουε (κώλυε libri) δ' ἄνδρα παρὰ δίκην τιμώμενον.

18. **ὡς μηδὲ τοῖς ὀνόμασι γνησίους**, 'as not being even in their names genuine Athenians' but half-bloods (νόθους, *Them.* c. 1, 1).

The source of this statement is patent from *Cim.* c. 16, 1 ἦν μὲν οὖν (ὁ Κίμων) ἀπ' ἀρχῆς φιλολάκων· καὶ τῶν γε παίδων τῶν διδύμων τὸν ἕτερον Λακεδαιμόνιον ὠνόμασε, τὸν δ' ἕτερον Ἠλεῖον, ἐκ γυναικὸς αὐτῷ Κλειτορίας γενομένους, ὡς Στησίμβροτος ἱστορεῖ· διὸ πολλάκις τὸν Περικλέα τὸ μητρῷον αὐτοῖς γένος ὀνειδίζειν. Διόδωρος δ' ὁ περιηγητὴς καὶ τούτους φησὶ καὶ τὸν τρίτον τῶν Κίμωνος υἱῶν Θεσσαλὸν ἐξ Ἰσοδίκης γεγονέναι τῆς Εὐρυπτολέμου τοῦ Μεγακλέους. Cimon's reasons for the names which he gave his six sons are stated by the Scholiast on Aristides III p. 515 Dind. υἱοὺς δὲ ἔσχεν ἕξ, ὧν τοὺς μὲν τρεῖς ἀπὸ ἐθνῶν, ὧν προὐξένισεν, ὠνόμασε, Λακεδαιμόνιον, Ἠλεῖον, Θετταλόν, τοὺς δὲ τρεῖς ἀπὸ ὀνομάτων τῆς συγγενείας Μιλτιάδην, Κίμωνα καὶ Πεισιάνακτα.

19. ὅτι, 'because.'

21. ἐδόκουν, c. 30, 3.

51 22. Ἀρκαδικῆς : she was a native of Clitor (Arcadia), Strab. *Geogr.* VIII c. 8, 2.   κακῶς ἀκούων, c. 5, 2 ; c. 12, 1.

24. τοῖς δεηθεῖσι *sc.* βοηθείας.

25. τοῖς ἐγκαλοῦσι, to enemies complaining of the act of intervention.

26. ἑτέρας αὖθις πλείονας : he sent twenty triremes under the command of Glaucon and Dracontides, the appearance of which deterred the Corinthians from following up their victory at Sybota, an island lying to the east of Corcyra, off the coast (Thuc. I 50 f., Diod. Sic. XII 33, 4). Notice the un-Attic form πλείονας for πλείους.

§ 4 l. 29. κατηγοροῦσι κτλ. : Thuc. I 67, 1 (οἱ Κορίνθιοι) κατεβόων ἐλθόντες (ἐς τὴν Λακεδαίμονα) ὅτι σπονδάς τε λελυκότες εἶεν καὶ ἀδικοῖεν τὴν Πελοπόννησον.

31. πάσης ἀγορᾶς . . . εἴργεσθαι : τῆς Ἀττικῆς ἀγορᾶς, acc. to Thuc. I 67, 4 where the τὸ περὶ Μεγαρέων ψήφισμα—which was passed in the summer of B.C. 432—is first mentioned ; cp. c. 139, 1 ; c. 144, 1. See also Arist. *Ach.* 520 and *passim.*

34. παρὰ τὰ κοινὰ δίκαια, 'in violation of the common rights and privileges,' in virtue of which during the time of peace there was free interchange of communication for all Hellenic States.   τοὺς ὅρκους, 'the articles of peace sworn to,' the Thirty Years' truce of B.C. 445 (παρὰ τὰς σπονδάς Thuc. I 67, 4).

35. Αἰγινῆται : these did not belong to the allies but had been in dependence on Athens since B.C. 456. Cp. Thuc. I 67 2 Αἰγινῆταί τε φανερῶς μὲν οὐ πρεσβευόμενοι, δεδιότες τοὺς Ἀθηναίους, κρύφα δέ, οὐχ ἥκιστα μετ' αὐτῶν ἐνῆγον τὸν πόλεμον λέγοντες οὐκ εἶναι αὐτόνομοι κατὰ τὰς σπονδάς. From this it would appear that there was a general formula providing that the dependent states should revert to their independence.

> Müller *Proleg.* p. 411 refers this complaint of the Aeginetans to the ancient compact made before or immediately after the battle of Plataea. Yet, acc. to the report of the oath by Diodorus XI 29, 3, the parties were only restrained from utterly destroying any of the contracting cities— οὐδεμίαν τῶν ἀγωνισαμένων πόλεων ἀνάστατον ποιήσω.

36. ἐποτνιῶντο, 'appealed as suppliants,' 'complained bitterly,' a post-classical word, generally applied to women, as in *Caes.* c. 63, 6 ἡ Καλπουρνία ἔδοξε ποτνιᾶσθαι καὶ δακρύειν, *Cat. mi.* c. 27, 2 γυναῖκα καὶ ἀδελφὰς ποτνιωμένας καὶ δακρυούσας, *Ages.* c. 18, 1 τοιαῦτα ποτνιωμένη, *Artox.* c. 3, 3 ὀδυρομένη πολλὰ καὶ ποτνιωμένη, *Anton.* c. 35, 2 πολλὰ ποτνιωμένη καὶ πολλὰ δεομένη, *Mor.* 507 C ποτνιωμένης αὐτῆς ὡς πίστιν οὐκ ἐχούσης, but sometimes to men, as 62 D ὅλως ἐξαθυμῶν καὶ ποτνιώμενος, 408 A ἧκε δεύτερον ποτνιώμενος. See Ruhnken on Timaeus p. 221.

39. Ποτείδαια ... ἀποστᾶσα, 'the revolt of Potidaea,' Thuc. I cc. 56–66.

After the engagement of Sybota, the Athenians, suspicious of the designs of Corinth, the leading city of the Peloponnesus, and apprehensive of the revolt of their colony Potidaea, which occupied an important site on the isthmus of Pallene, called on the Potidaeans, as ἑαυτῶν ξυμμάχους φόρου ὑποτελεῖς, to give up the hostages and dismiss the magistrate (ἐπιδημιουργός) appointed yearly by Corinth; also to raze the wall of their town on the side of Pallene so that it might be accessible to them. The Potidaeans thereupon, encouraged by promises of support from Corinth and the assurance of the Lacedaemonians that they would march into Attica if the Athenians attacked them, determined upon secession from their alliance. The city, which was besieged by the Athenians in B.C. 432, surrendered to them in B.C. 430, when it was levelled to the ground and its inhabitants put to death.

§ 5 l. 42. οὐ μὴν ἀλλά is here used elliptically merely to mark the continuation of the narrative, 'however,' as in c. 8, 4. There is an example of the full construction in c. 34, 4.

43. πεμπομένων: embassies had been sent on three several occasions from Lacedaemon to Athens; the first was after the war which was concluded by the Thirty Years' truce.

44. Ἀρχιδάμου, c. 8, 4.

45. εἰς διαλύσεις ἄγοντος, 'trying to bring to a friendly settlement.' On διαλύσεις, see my n. to *C. Gracch.* c. 16, 2. The speech of Archidamus to the same effect is to be found in Thuc. I 80 ff.

47. πραΰνοντος, 'trying to pacify,' a poetical word of frequent occurrence in Plutarch.   οὐκ ἄν goes with συμπεσεῖν, =οὐκ ἄν συνέπεσε, *non accidisset*, of direct discourse. Such hyperbata are the rule with the verbs οἴεσθαι and δοκεῖν. συμπεσεῖν is followed by ὑπό, because of its quasi-passive meaning, c. 7, 5.

49. καθελεῖν, 'to rescind'; cp. c. 30 l. 3.

To obtain this object was the principal motive of the second embassy of the Lacedaemonians to Athens. Cp. Thuc. I 139, 1 μάλιστά γε πάντων καὶ ἐνδηλότατα προὔλεγον ('they solemnly assured them') τὸ περὶ Μεγαρέων ψήφισμα καθελοῦσι μὴ ἂν γενέσθαι πόλεμον. The greatest stress was laid on this point, probably because it was known to be that on which it was least likely that any concession would be made, and because this also furnished an occasion for malicious insinuation and popular clamour against Pericles, who maintained that the Spartan proposal relating to Megara had been held out merely to try the spirit and firmness of the Athenians.

52. μάλιστα with ἐναντιωθείς. By τοῦτο is meant the revocation of the decree.

55. ἔσχε τὴν αἰτίαν = ᾐτιάθη. Cp. c. 13, 10, *Cat. ma.* c. 12, 2 σάλον εἶχε = ἐσάλευε, c. 17, 6 οἶκτον ἔσχε, *Dem.* c. 7, 1 with my note *ad l.* So in Arist. *Pax* 605 f. Pericles is said to have kindled the war ἐμβαλὼν σπινθῆρα μικρὸν Μεγαρικοῦ ψηφίσματος.

CHAPTER XXX

§ 1 l. 1. **πρεσβείας**: the second of the three embassies, details of which are given by Thuc. I 139 who, however, does not mention Polyalces among the members of it. Construe: λέγουσι δὲ Πολυάλκη τῶν πρέσβεων τινὰ εἰπεῖν.

3. **προβαλλομένου**, 'using as a pretext.' On the various other meanings of this verb in Plutarch, see my note to *C. Gr.* c. 1, 1.

7. **σὺ δὲ μὴ καθέλῃς**, 'then don't take it down.' The δέ is in opp. to the objection of Pericles, 'I admit what you say, but...' As it cannot stand first by itself, the unemphatic σύ is added as a support, much as in Latin *ille* is used to support *quidem*.

8. **εἴσω**, 'inward' *i.e.* with its face to the wall, since the law says nothing about exposing any part of the psephism to public view.

9. **κομψοῦ**, 'neat,' 'smart,' *Cat. mi.* c. 5, 2 ὁ λόγος νεαρὸν οὐδὲν οὐδὲ κομψὸν εἶχεν.

10. **οὐδέν τι μᾶλλον**, 'never a whit the more' than if the proposal had not been made. Observe that the datives οὐδενί, τινί are never used with comparatives to denote the measure, whereas we have ὀλίγῳ and πολλῷ by the side of ὀλίγον and πολύ.

11. ἐνέδωκεν, c. 32, 3; c. 33, 2.

§ 2 l. 11. ὑπῆν is opp. to φανεράν, as ἰδία to κοινήν. ὡς ἔοικεν, *ut fertur.*

13. **κοινήν**, because every kind of profanation affected the public interests.

14. ἀποτέμνεσθαι τὴν ἱερὰν ὀργάδα, 'that they cut off and applied to their own use the holy field,' *i.e.* the portion of the ground (between Megara and Athens) consecrated to the Eleusinian deities, Demeter and Persephone. Cp. Thuc. I 139, 2 οἱ δ' Ἀθηναῖοι οὔτε τἆλλα ὑπήκουον οὔτε τὸ ψήφισμα καθῄρουν, ἐπικαλοῦντες ἐπεργασίαν Μεγαρεῦσι τῆς γῆς τῆς ἱερᾶς καὶ τῆς ἀορίστου.

Cobet remarks that it is easy to distinguish what is taken αὐτολέξει from the original decree, *e.g.* the expression τὴν ἱερὰν ὀργάδα is Plutarch's own; in the psephism he found τὴν ὀργάδα only, as in [Dem.] περὶ συντάξεως § 32 οἷον ἃ πρὸς τοὺς καταράτους Μεγαρέας ἐψηφίσασθε ἀποτεμνομένους τὴν ὀργάδα ἐξιέναι, κωλύειν, μὴ ἐπιτρέπειν. In later Greek the land came to be called τὴν γῆν (χώραν) τὴν ἱεράν.

16. κατηγοροῦντα, 'as accuser,' c. 11, 5.   G. $MT.^2$ § 840.

§ 3 l. 17. μὲν οὖν, c. 28, 3; c. 31, 1.   53

18. Περικλέους ἐστί, 'is the work of Pericles himself,' as opp. to that of Charinus.   εὐγνώμονος ... δικαιολογίας ἐχόμενον, 'combined as it is with a reasonable plea.'

Cp. *C. Gr.* c. 9, 1 νόμους ἔγραψεν οὔτε τῶν καλῶν τινος οὔτε τῶν λυσιτελῶν ἐχομένους where Reiske proposes to read ἐχόμενος, just as Holzapfel prefers ἐχομένου in the present passage. Cobet observes that Plutarch must have read through the whole psephism, on which he founds his judgment about its reasonableness, because there is no δικαιολογία in the quotation κήρυκα πεμφθῆναι ... τῶν Μεγαρέων. Cp. Plat. *Euthyd.* 306 D ἐχόμενον φρονήσεως πρᾶγμα, *de rep.* 496 A οὐδὲν φρονήσεως ἀληθινῆς ἐχόμενον, 568 A τοῦτο πυκνῆς διανοίας ἐχόμενον ἐφθέγξατο.

20. Thucydides speaks of an Athenian invasion of the Megarid twice every year (II 31, 1, IV 66, 1) without noticing the circumstance of the death of the Athenian herald, but incidental mention is made of it by Pausanias I 36, 3:—ἰοῦσι δὲ ἐπ' Ἐλευσῖνα ἐξ Ἀθηνῶν (*i.e.* by the Dipylon), ἥν Ἀθηναῖοι καλοῦσιν ὁδὸν ἱεράν, Ἀνθεμοκρίτου πεποίηται μνῆμα. ἐς τοῦτον Μεγαρεῦσίν ἐστιν ἀνοσιώτατον ἔργον, οἳ κήρυκα ἐλθόντα, ὡς μὴ τοῦ λοιποῦ τὴν χώραν <τὴν ἱερὰν> ἐπεργάζοιντο, κτείνουσιν Ἀνθεμόκριτον· καί σφισι ταῦτα δράσασι παραμένει καὶ ἐς τόδε μήνιμα ἐκ τοῖν θεοῖν. Cp. *Epist. Phil.* § 4 (ap. Demosth. p. 159) Μεγαρέων γοῦν Ἀνθεμόκριτον ἀνελόντων εἰς τοῦτο ἐλήλυθεν ὁ δῆμος ὥστε μυστηρίων μὲν εἴργειν αὐτούς, ὑπομνήματα δὲ τῆς ἀδικίας ἔστησαν ἀνδριάντα πρὸ τῶν πυλῶν. Plutarch must have often noticed the monument during his stay at Athens. 'The Megarians were so fully looked upon as the authors of the murder, that they were punished for it many ages afterwards; for upon that very account the Emperor Adrian denied them many favours and privileges which he granted to the other cities of Greece' (*Langhornes*).

21. ἀποθανεῖν, of a violent death, as c. 28, 3.   ἔδοξε, c. 27, 4. The ψήφισμα must have been proposed and carried by Charinus after a complete rupture with Sparta.

22. ἄσπονδον καὶ ἀκήρυκτον, 'without truce or herald,' 'irreconcileable and implacable,' excluding all possibility of a friendly settlement. Cobet thinks that Plutarch must have substituted ἔχθραν for πόλεμον, which he read in the original psephism. Cp. *Arist.* c. 1, 3 οὐ γάρ ἐστι τοῖς ἀγαθοῖς ἀκή-

ρυκτος καὶ ἄσπονδος πρὸς τὰς παρὰ τῶν φίλων δωρειὰς πόλεμος, *Mor*. 1095 Β τῷ καλῷ πολεμεῖν τὸν ἄσπονδον καὶ ἀκήρυκτον πόλεμον, Dem. *de cor*. § 262 ἦν γὰρ ἄσπονδος καὶ ἀκήρυκτος ὑμῖν πρὸς τοὺς θεατὰς πόλεμος, Plato *Legg*. 626 A πάσαις πρὸς πάσας τὰς πόλεις ἀεὶ πόλεμον ἀκήρυκτον κατὰ φύσιν εἶναι.

24. **ἐπιβῇ**, 'should set foot in'; Thuc. I 103, 1, III 106, 2. **Μεγαρέων**, partitive genitive, with ὅς.

26. **τὸν πάτριον ὅρκον**, 'the traditional oath.'

27. **ἐπομνύειν**, 'should take an oath besides,' an unusual meaning of the compound, which generally signifies no more than the simple ὀμνύειν. The καί indicates that these expeditions are to be independent of others which they may have to conduct.

The text of the decree was probably οἱ δὲ στρατηγοὶ ὅταν ὀμνύωσι τὸν πάτριον ὅρκον ἐπομνύντων ὅτι καὶ δὶς ἀνὰ πᾶν ἔτος εἰς τὴν Μεγαρικὴν ἐμβαλοῦσιν, where Cobet remarks on the archaic expression ἀνὰ πᾶν ἔτος and compares Thuc. IV 66, 1 Μεγαρῆς οἱ ἐν τῇ πόλει πιεζόμενοι ὑπ' Ἀθηναίων τῷ πολέμῳ ἀεὶ κατ' ἔτος ἕκαστον δὶς ἐσβαλλόντων πανστρατιᾷ ἐς τὴν χώραν.

29. **τὰς Θριασίας πύλας**: this, the old name of the Dipylon, as Plutarch explains, was in the original text. It was so called because it led to the Eleusinian deme Thria. Its other names were 'the Sacred (ἱερά) Gate' (*Sull.* c. 14, 3), and the Κεραμεικαὶ πύλαι, because it was between the Outer and Inner Ceramicus. The gate was in the N.W. city wall, between the Peiraic and Acharnian gates, *velut in ore urbis posita, maior aliquanto patentiorque quam ceterae*, as it is described by Livy XXXI c. 24. See also Baumeister *Denkmäler des kl. Alterth.* I 148 f., 160. An interesting account, with a view of its remains, is given in Miss Harrison's *Mythology and Monuments of Ancient Athens* pp. 7-9. It was here that Pausanias saw the grave (l. 28) of Anthemocritus.

§ 4 l. 32. **τὰς αἰτίας** sc. of their enmity to Athens. Cp. Isaeus 73, 37.

34. **δημώδεσι**, *pervulgatis*, 'hackneyed.' Cp. Aelian *V. H.* I c. 19 ὁ δημώδης λόγος καὶ ἐς πάντας ἐκφοιτήσας, III c. 3 ταῦτα δημώδη καὶ ἐς πολλοὺς ἐκπεφοίτηκε.

35. **τῶν Ἀχαρνέων**, 'the inhabitants of Acharnae' (Attica), c. 33, 3. Here the play of Aristophanes so called, vv. 524-527.

37. **μεθυσοκότταβοι**, 'in a drunken prank,' a comic word from μέθυσος, 'drunk with wine,' and κότταβος a game much in vogue at drinking parties. See Liddell-Scott *s. v.*

38. **πεφυσιγγωμένοι**, 'primed as with garlic,' like fighting-cocks, from φῦσιγξ, 'the outer skin of the garlic'; hence

'infuriated,' 'exasperated,' like ἐσκοροδισμένος *Ach.* 166, *Eq.* 494. Cp. Xen. *Sympos.* c. 4, 9 ἔνιοι τοὺς ἀλεκτρυόνας σκόροδα σιτίσαντες συμβάλλουσιν. There is also probably a side allusion to the growth of garlic in the Megarid.

39. ἀντεξέκλεψαν Ἀσπασίας, 'stole in reprisal from Aspasia,' c. 24, 3. For the construction, cp. *Eq.* 1149 ἀναγκάζω πάλιν ἐξεμεῖν ἄττ' ἂν κεκλόφωσί μου, *Vesp.* 1368 τὴν αὐλητρίδα τῶν ξυμποτῶν κλέψαντα, *Thesm.* 813 φορμὸν πυρῶν τἀνδρὸς κλέψασα.

CHAPTER XXXI

§ 1 l. 1. τὴν ἀρχήν *sc.* τοῦ ψηφίσματος, proleptic accusative. 54 For ὅπως ἔσχεν, cp. c. 10, 3.

2. λυθῆναι, c. 37, 2.

4. πλήν, *nisi quod*, 'only' his motive is disputed ; cp. c. 34, 1. οἱ μέν, as Thucydides ; see n. to c. 29, 3.

5. ἐκ φρονήματος μεγάλου is explained by τὴν συγχώρησιν ἐξομολόγησιν ἀσθενείας ἡγούμενον, and μετὰ γνώμης κατὰ τὸ βέλτιστον, 'combined with a wise calculation of the state's best interest,' by πεῖραν ἐνδόσεως τὸ πρόσταγμα ἡγούμενον.

6. ἀπισχυρίσασθαι *sc.* πρὸς τὸ λυθῆναι, 'made a firm stand against,' 'was violently opposed to (the suppression of the decree).' Cp. *Ayis* c. 4 πρὸς τὰς ἡδονὰς ἀπισχυρίσασθαι.

7. πεῖραν ἐνδόσεως, 'as a test of submission,' whether they would yield to their demand or not. Thuc. I 140, 5 τῆς μὲν γνώμης ἀεὶ τῆς αὐτῆς ἔχομαι, ὦ Ἀθηναῖοι, μὴ εἴκειν Πελοποννησίοις ... οἷς εἰ ξυγχωρήσετε, καὶ ἄλλο τι εὐθὺς ἐπιταχθήσεσθε ὡς φόβῳ καὶ τοῦτο ὑπακούσαντες.

8. ἐξομολόγησιν, 'a confession' (post-classical). Cp. *Alex.* c. 62, 3, *Mor.* 987 D ἐξομολόγησιν ἥττης, 1118 E αἰσχυνομένης ἀγνοίας ἐξομολόγησις, *Lucull.* c. 22, 5 ἐξομολόγησις δουλείας.

9. οἱ δέ *sc.* φασὶν αὐτόν.

11. πρὸς ἔνδειξιν, 'with a view to a display.'

§ 2 l. 12. χειρίστη, in moral sense.

13. πλείστους μάρτυρας: among others, Aristophanes *Pax* 605 ff., and Ephorus whose account was accepted by Diodorus XII cc. 38 f.

Cp. *Mor.* 855 F ἔτι τοίνυν ἐπὶ τῶν ὁμολογουμένων πεπρᾶχθαι, τὴν δ' αἰτίαν, ἀφ' ἧς πέπρακται, καὶ τὴν διάνοιαν ἐχόντων ἄδηλον, ὁ πρὸς τὸ χεῖρον εἰκάζων δυσμενής ἐστι καὶ κακοήθης· ὥσπερ οἱ κωμικοὶ τὸν πόλεμον ὑπὸ τοῦ Περικλέους ἐκκεκαῦσθαι δι᾽ Ἀσπασίαν ἢ διὰ Φειδίαν ἀποφαίνοντες, οὐ φιλοτιμίᾳ τινὶ καὶ φιλονικίᾳ μᾶλλον ἢ στορέσαι τὸ φρόνημα Πελοποννησίων καὶ μηδενὸς ὑφεῖσθαι Λακεδαιμονίων ἐθελήσαντος.

14. **πλάστης**, 'modeller,' c. 12, 6.

15. **ἐργολάβος**, 'contractor.' **τοῦ ἀγάλματος**, 'the statue' of Pallas Parthenos, which was 26 Greek cubits in height. See O. Müller *A. A.* §§ 114, 116. The most colossal statue, the brazen Promachos, which, standing between the Parthenon and the Propylaea and towering over both, was seen by mariners at a great distance, was not yet finished when Phidias died.

16. **ὥσπερ εἴρηται**, c. 13, 9.

19. **ἐχθρούς**, in apposition to τοὺς μέν. **οἱ δέ**, others who were not his personal enemies (δι᾽ αὐτὸν ἐχθροί) because of his position.

20. **ἐν ἐκείνῳ**, 'through him,' 'in his person' *sc.* Phidias. **ἔσοιτο**: G. *MT.*² § 128.

22. **ἐν ἀγορᾷ**: at the altar of the twelve gods.

23. **ἄδειαν**, 'protection,' 'indemnity' for the alleged embezzlement, in which he was himself concerned. μήνυσις was an information laid against a person by some one who had no right or inclination to appear as an accuser; it differed in this respect from εἰσαγγελία. Cp. *Timol.* c. 16, 4 ἄδειαν ᾐτεῖτο παρὰ τοῦ Τιμολέοντος ἐπὶ τῷ πάντα μηνῦσαι, *Cic.* c. 19, 2 ψηφισαμένης ἄδειαν ἐπὶ μηνύσει τῆς βουλῆς, *Alc.* c. 21, 2, Thuc. VIII 76, 2. See Schömann *de comitiis Athen.* p. 334. (See Addenda.) For ἐπί, cp. c. 17, 3 ; c. 24, 4.

§ 3 l. 24. **προσδεξαμένου**, 'receiving him favourably.' Cp. *Marc.* c. 2, 4 μὴ προσδεχομένων τὴν ἐπίκλησιν.

25. **ἐν ἐκκλησίᾳ**: c. 14, 1. It rested with the popular assembly to order a trial by jury. **διώξεως**: c. 10, 6 ; c. 32, 2.

26. **μέν**, 'although,' corresponds to δέ l. 31. The punishment for embezzlement (κλοπὴ δημοσίων χρημάτων) was payment of twice the amount embezzled.

27. **τῷ ἀγάλματι προσειργάσατο καὶ περιέθηκεν**, 'had superimposed it as an addition to (not, part and parcel of) the statue,' *Nic.-Crass.* c. 4, 1 προσεργάσασθαι τὴν Ἀσίαν οἷς Πομπήϊος ἐπῆλθε, Eur. *H. F.* 1012 ὡς μηδὲν προσεργάσαιτο τοῖς δεδραμένοις.

28. **γνώμῃ τοῦ Περικλέους**, 'by the advice of Pericles': cp. Thuc. II 13, 5 ἀπέφαινε δ᾽ (ὁ Περικλῆς) ἔχον τὸ ἄγαλμα τεσσαράκοντα τάλαντα σταθμὸν χρυσίου ἀπέφθου καὶ περιαιρετὸν εἶναι

ἄπαν, χρησαμένοις τε ἐπὶ σωτηρίᾳ ἔφη χρῆναι μὴ ἐλάσσω ἀντικαταστῆσαι πάλιν. Diodorus (XII 40, 3) gives fifty gold talents, and Philochorus (Sch. ad Arist. *Pax* 604) forty-four (= about £120,000) as the weight (τὸν σταθμόν) of the moveable drapery of the Parthenos ; yet its thickness did not much exceed a line. O. Müller *A. A.* § 113, 2.

29. **περιελοῦσιν** (sc. τὸ χρυσίον) depends on δυνατὸν εἶναι.

30. **δ... ποιεῖν** i.e. περιελόντας τὸ χρυσίον ἀποδεῖξαι τὸν σταθμόν. The καί implies that they were not to be satisfied with accusing him ; they ought to verify the fact for themselves.

§ 4 l. 33. **τὴν πρὸς Ἀμαζόνας μάχην ἐν τῇ ἀσπίδι ποιῶν**: the victory of the Athenians under the command of Theseus over the Amazons when they invaded Attica (*Thes.* c. 27, 3) was a very favourite subject of Attic art, as on one of the metopes of the north side of the Parthenon. Cp. Pliny *Nat. Hist.* XXXVI 4, 18 *sicuti eius in quo Amazonum proelium caelavit intumescente* ('convex') *ambitu parmae, eiusdem concava parte deorum et gigantum dimicationem*.

34. **ἐνετύπωσε**, 'cut in relief' or 'in intaglio.'

The shield which was brought from Athens by Viscount Strangford in 1864 and is now in the British Museum, professes to be a copy of the original shield, and it exhibits two figures which exactly tally with Plutarch's description—i.e. the bald old man, with both arms uplifted, about to slay an Amazon, and a fighting Greek close to him with the uplifted arm partly across his face. But Dr. A. S. Murray of the British Museum (*Encycl. Britann.* vol. XVIII p. 734) says with great probability : - 'These portraits answer so minutely to the description of Plutarch that there can hardly be a doubt of their having been produced subsequently to illustrate some current story on which that description was founded. The workmanship is several centuries later than Phidias, and it would be strange, if the portraits for which he had paid with his life had been left for so long a time on the shield, or had even been allowed at any moment to be perpetuated in a copy. In answer to this objection it was fabled that the portraits had been so fixed on the shield that they could not be removed without bringing down the whole work.' See Aristotle (*de mundo* c. 6) ὥστε ἐξ ἀνάγκης, εἰ τις βούλοιτο αὐτὸ περιαιρεῖν, τὸ σύμπαν ἄγαλμα λύειν τε καὶ συγχεῖν. Cp. Cic. *Tusc.* I 15, 34 *Phidias sui similem speciem inclusit in clypeo Minervae, cum inscribere non liceret*. (See Addenda.)

35. **πέτρον ἐπηρμένον**, 'poising a large stone which he has lifted.' Cp. *Pelop.-Marc.* c. 3, 1 διηρμένος κοπίδα καὶ παίειν μέλλων πολέμιον. In the Lenormant Statuette of Athena—a rude figure which was found in 1859 near the Mouseion at Athens, and of which there is a cast (97) in the South Kensington Museum—among the reliefs of the Amazonomachia the figure of the bald Phidias is clearly seen in the attitude here described. In the relief on the Strangford Shield he is represented as wielding an axe instead of poising a stone.

37. **ἐνέθηκε** sc. τῇ ἀσπίδι.

39. πρὸ τῆς ὄψεως, c. 35, 2.

40. οἷον ἐπικρύπτειν βούλεται κτλ., 'wishes so to say' (looks as if it wished) to conceal the likeness, though it is plainly visible on either side,' *i.e.* the face was only partly covered by the hand, and could be seen on either side of it.

§ 5 l. 42. μὲν οὖν : c. 28, 3.

43. ἀπαχθείς : c. 24, 7. νοσήσας, ingressive aorist participle (c. 7, 6 ; c. 9, 4), expressing the cause, and so answering to the dat. φαρμάκοις. The death of Phidias took place in Ol. 87, 1 = 432 B.C. This tradition of the cause rests on the authority of Ephorus. Philochorus makes him die in Elis. See HSauppe *die Qu. etc.* p. 32.

44. ἐπὶ διαβολῇ ... παρασκευασάντων, 'which his enemies contrived with a view to bringing discredit on Pericles,' as though it were he that had poisoned him in order to get rid of his evidence as an accessory, whose revelations might injure him. For ἐπὶ διαβολῇ cp. c. 28, 3.

46. γράψαντος Γλύκωνος, 'on the motion of Glycon,' c. 32, 2.

47. ἀτέλειαν, 'exemption from public burdens' (λῃτουργίαι) such as the choregia etc. Thus was an honour bestowed on deserving citizens and metoeci given him as μήνυτρα.

48. τοῦ ἀνθρώπου, c. 5, 2 ; c. 34, 1.

CHAPTER XXXII

§ 1 l. 2. δίκην ἔφευγεν : c. 10, 5. ἀσέβεια included all cases of breach of reverence due to the gods, which of course were of great variety. What the particular offence committed by Aspasia was, is unknown. 'Ερμίππου : c. 33, 7.

3. προσκατηγοροῦντος κτλ., 'accusing her besides' of προαγωγεία : cp. c. 24, 3.

4. Περικλεῖ ... εἰς τὸ αὐτὸ φοιτώσας, 'frequenting the same place as Pericles.' Cp. c. 13, 9. For εἰς τὸ αὐτό (*una, eundem in locum*, c. 11, 2) with dat., cp. *Num.* c. 4, 7 ἆρ' ἄξιόν ἐστιν ... ἀπιστεῖν εἰ Σαλεύκῳ καὶ Μίνῳ ... εἰς τὸ αὐτὸ ἐφοίτα τὸ δαιμόνιον ; *Alex.* c. 48, 5 ἐκέλευσε (τὸ γύναιον) φοιτᾶν εἰς ταὐτὸ τῷ Φιλώτᾳ, *Artax.* c. 19, 2 εἰς τὸ αὐτὸ φοιτᾶν καὶ συνδειπνεῖν ἀλλήλαις.

5. ὑποδέχοιτο, 'received into her house.' Cp. c. 13, 9.

6. ψήφισμα : Plutarch here refers to three psephisms. In the first, that of Diopeithes, Cobet traces archaic phrases of the original text in τὰ θεῖα for θεούς and περὶ τῶν μεταρσίων for π. τ.

μετεώρων. Diopeithes, like Lampon his brother-diviner (χρησμολόγος), was the butt of contemporary comic poets for his fanaticism and superstition. See my *Onomasticon Aristophan.* p. 808 a. He was opposed to the teaching of Anaxagoras, like most of the genuine old Athenians, *Nic.* c. 23, 3.

7. εἰσαγγέλλεσθαι: 'should be liable to the criminal process called εἰσαγγελία,' c. 31, 3. This was a criminal information before the Βουλή or Ἐκκλησία, designed to reach offences against the state which were not noticed or not described by law. But as this would have been applicable, without any decree, to such cases as are mentioned in the text, it would seem that the decree of Diopeithes must either have charged certain magistrates to enquire into such offences or have offered a reward to an informer (*Thirlwall*). τοὺς τὰ θεῖα μὴ νομίζοντας, 'all those who did not believe in gods,' the usual charge against philosophers, to which Socrates also was subjected. For τὰ θεῖα, cp. c. 6, 1.

8. λόγους, 'lessons,' c. 6, 1. τῶν μεταρσίων, c. 5, 1.

9. ἀπερειδόμενος . . . τὴν ὑπόνοιαν, 'directing his suspicion against Pericles.' Cp. *Mor.* 198 c τῶν εὐτυχημάτων τὴν νέμεσιν εἰς τὸν οἶκον ἀπερεισαμένης τῆς τύχης.

§ 2 l. 11. δεχομένου, c. 13, 10. προσιεμένου, 'being pleased with,' *Them.* c. 22, 1 τῶν πολιτῶν ἡδέως τὰς διαβολὰς προσιεμένων, *Marc.* c. 19, 2 τοῦτον οὐδὲ ὅλως προσήκατο τὸν λόγον, Herod. VI 123 οὐ προσίεμαι τὴν διαβολήν.

12. οὕτως ἤδη, when the people were in this mood, 'just then' was the opportunity for getting the decree passed. These adverbs joined to the principal verb of the sentence give greater emphasis to the temporal relation of the participle. Cp. c. 7, 2 and see G. *MT.*² § 855.

13. κυροῦται, 'is ratified.' The Dracontides here mentioned may be the same as the commander of the expedition to Corcyra, c. 29, 3. Another of the name appears in the *Wasps* of Aristophanes l. 157, where the Scholiast describes him as πονηρὸς καὶ πλείσταις καταδίκαις ἐνεχόμενος: the same name reappears under the Thirty Tyrants, and it would seem that he was the mover of the establishment of their authority.
ὅπως οἱ λόγοι . . . ἀποτεθεῖεν, 'to the effect that the accounts of the public moneys he had expended should be deposited with the Prytanes.' For the optative after ὅπως in an object clause after a verb of commanding etc., see G. *MT.*² § 355. It is not certain whether, in addition to his office of στρατηγός, Pericles was also ταμίας or ἐπιμελητὴς τῆς κοινῆς προσόδου—an appointment which was held for four years. The proper

officials for examining and passing such accounts were the λογισταί, and therefore we must assume that the proposal of Dracontides had reference to some extraordinary payments of Pericles. Cp. c. 23, 1. The extraordinary mode of voting also, which was intended to give the procedure greater solemnity, on which see *Them.* c. 17, 1, points to the same conclusion. The altar meant is that in the temple of Athena Polias.

17. ἐν τῇ πόλει, 'in the acropolis': cp. c. 37, 1, *Pelop.* c. 18, 1 τὰς γὰρ ἀκροπόλεις ἐπιεικῶς (*plerumque*) οἱ τότε πόλεις ὠνόμαζον. The town was properly called ἄστυ. Hagnon, probably the father of Theramenes one of the Thirty, was a leading democratic statesman, Xen. *Hell.* II iii 30, see *Nic.* c. 2, 1. Such amendments and supplementary clauses were added on the Tablet in the following form :—"Ἅγνων εἶπεν · τὰ μὲν ἄλλα καθάπερ Δρακοντίδης. By Hagnon's amendment the preliminaries of the legal process were more strictly defined. There were 1501 jurors also in the trial of Demosthenes in the affair of Harpalus, and in other extraordinary trials.

18. τοῦ ψηφίσματος with ἀφεῖλε (c. 30, 4), not, as partitive gen., with τοῦτο, which refers to the procedure of which mention is made.

19. κρίνεσθαι τὴν δίκην κτλ., 'that the cause should be tried (in the ordinary way but) before a body of 1500 jurors.' The same number of dicasts was empanelled to try Demosthenes on a charge of venality, Dinarch. *c. Dem.* § 107. Lysias *c. Agor.* § 35 speaks of 2000 in a case of high treason, and Dinarch. *c. Dem.* § 52 of 2500 in an εἰσαγγελία.

21. κλοπῆς sc. δίωξιν, 'a prosecution for embezzlement,' c. 31, 3. δώρων, 'bribery.' ἀδικίου, 'for wrong done to the interest or property of the state,' an archaic term. After verbs of accusing such genitive forms in -ιου are frequent, *e.g.* λειποταξίου, ἐνοικίου, ἀποστασίου, ἀγαμίου. Which of these names should be given to the offence for which Pericles was to be arraigned, depended in part upon the tribunal, in part on the accuser, to determine.

All three words are, as Cobet remarks, taken from the original text of Hagnon's psephism. He compares Arist. *Nub.* 591 :—

ἢν Κλέωνα τὸν λάρον δώρων ἑλόντες καὶ κλοπῆς
εἶτα φιμώσητε τούτου 'ν τῷ ξύλῳ τὸν αὐχένα,

Andoc. *de myst.* p. 10, 20 οὗτοι δ' αὖ ἦσαν ὁπόσοι κλοπῆς ἢ δώρων ὄφλοιεν· τούτους ἔδει καὶ αὐτοὺς καὶ τοὺς ἐκ τούτων ἀτίμους εἶναι.

§ 3 l. 23. ἐξῃτήσατο, 'begged off.' The aor. implies that his suit was successful. Cp. *Pyrrh.* c. 3, 3 ἐξαιτουμένων τῶν πολεμίων (the child Pyrrhus) οὐκ ἐξέδωκεν, *Cat. mi.* c. 16, 4, *Alex.* c. 11, 4, Xen. *Anab.* I i 3 συλλαμβάνει Κῦρον ὡς ἀποκτενῶν, ἡ δὲ μήτηρ ἐξαιτησαμένη αὐτὸν ἀποπέμπει, Luke XXII 31 ὁ Σατανᾶς ἐξητήσατο ὑμᾶς, 'hath procured you to be given up to him.'

24. παρὰ τὴν δίκην, not, as Stewart translates, 'contrary to justice' as if παρὰ δίκην, but 'during the trial.' Cp. *Pelop.* c. 25, 7 καὶ τὸν μὲν Χάρωνα παρὰ πᾶσαν τὴν δίκην ἐγκωμιάζων ἀφθόνως διετέλεσε, *Them.* c. 8, 1 with my note *ad l.* **Αἰσχίνης**, c. 24, 4. Athenaeus XIII 589 E quotes Antisthenes as the author of this story: Ἀντισθένης δ᾽ ὁ Σωκρατικὸς ἐρασθέντα φησὶν αὐτὸν (τὸν Περικλέα) Ἀσπασίας δὶς τῆς ἡμέρας εἰσιόντα καὶ ἐξιόντα ἀπ᾽ αὐτῆς ἀσπάζεσθαι τὴν ἄνθρωπον, καὶ φευγούσης ποτὲ αὐτῆς γραφὴν ἀσεβείας λέγων ὑπὲρ αὐτῆς πλείονα ἐδάκρυσεν ἢ ὅτε ὑπὲρ τοῦ βίου καὶ τῆς οὐσίας ἐκινδύνευε.

27. **ἐξέκλεψε**, 'got him out of the way,' c. 25, 3, *Them.* c. 24, 3. *Philop.* c. 5, 1 τοὺς πολίτας τῆς πόλεως ἐξέκλεψε προσμαχόμενος τοῖς ἐπιδιώκουσι, Dem. c. *Timocr.* § 80 ἐκκλέπτων (sc. iudicibus et poenae) τὸν ἠδικηκότα καὶ τὴν παράδοσιν αὐτοῦ τὴν τοῖς ἔνδεκα, Polyb. 4, 81, 7 ἐκκλαπεὶς διὰ φίλων, Xen. *Hell.* V 4, 12 ἦσαν δέ τινες οἳ ὑπὸ Ἀθηναίων ἐξεκλάπησαν καὶ διεσώθησαν. In *Nic.* c. 23, 2 Plut. says that Anaxagoras was thrown into prison, from which he was rescued by Pericles. After leaving Athens he went to Lampsacus, where he spent the remainder of his life. The lines 292–301 in the *Medea* of Euripides were probably written in view of the treatment of Anaxagoras.

29. **προσέπταισε**, 'fell foul of,' 'came into collision with,' though not directly. So *Cat. mi.* c. 30, 2 νομίζων οὐ μικρὰ προσπταίσειν τῷ Κάτωνι μὴ φίλῳ γενομένῳ. Cp. the allusion in Arist. *Pax* 605 ff. 57

31. **ὑποτυφόμενον**, *gliscentem*, 'beginning to burn secretly.' Cp. Diodor. XII 39, 3 ὁ δὲ Περικλῆς εἰδὼς τὸν δῆμον ἐν μὲν τοῖς πολεμικοῖς ἔργοις θαυμάζοντα τοὺς ἀγαθοὺς ἄνδρας διὰ τὰς κατεπειγούσας χρείας, κατὰ δὲ τὴν εἰρήνην τοὺς αὐτοὺς συκοφαντοῦντα διὰ τὴν σχολὴν καὶ φθόνον, ἔκρινε συμφέρειν αὐτῷ τὴν πόλιν ἐμβαλεῖν εἰς μέγαν πόλεμον, ὅπως χρείαν ἔχουσα τῆς Περικλέους ἀρετῆς καὶ στρατηγίας μὴ προσδέχηται τὰς κατ᾽ αὐτοῦ διαβολὰς μηδ᾽ ἔχῃ σχολὴν καὶ χρόνον ἐξετάζειν ἀκριβῶς τὸν περὶ τῶν χρημάτων λόγον.

διασκεδάσειν, un-Attic form for διασκεδᾶν.

35. **ἐκείνῳ** is substituted, as in c. 33, 2, for the reflexive pronoun, as if from the biographer's point of view, probably because of the reflexive ἑαυτήν which follows. **ἀξίωμα**, c. 37, 1.

36. **ἀναθείσης**, 'confiding,' 'entrusting.' Cp. *Mor.* 263 c τῇ γυναικὶ τὴν ἀρχὴν καὶ τὴν πόλιν ἀναθείς, 794 D, Thuc. VIII 82, 1 στρατηγὸν αὐτὸν εἵλοντο καὶ τὰ πράγματα πάντα ἀνετίθεσαν, Arist. *Nub.* 1154 ὑμῖν ἀναθεὶς ἅπαντα τἀμὰ πράγματα.

38. **ἐνδοῦναι**, c. 30, 1.

CHAPTER XXXIII

§ 1 l. 3. **καταλυθέντος**: c. 6, 2; c. 25, 1. **εἰς πάντα μαλακωτέροις χρήσονται**, 'will find them more easy to deal with in every respect,' more compliant towards any demand they may make.

Cp. *Brut.* c. 50, 4 χρώμενος (αὐτῷ) εἰς πάντα πιστῷ καὶ βεβαίῳ διετέλεσε, *Sertor.* c. 12, 1 ἐχρῆτο (αὐτοῖς) πρὸς ἅπαντα μετριωτέροις, *Cat. ma.* c. 13, 5 οἷς ἀεὶ πιστοῖς ἐχρῆτο καὶ προθύμοις, *Mar.* c. 5, 5 χαλεποῖς χρώμενος τοῖς δικασταῖς, *Lucull.* c. 30, 3 χαλεποῖς χρώμενοι καὶ δυσπειθέσι τοῖς στρατιώταις, *Sull.* c. 5, 3, *Timol.* c. 12, 4, *Alc.* c. 20, 4, Xen. *Oec.* c. 3, 11, c. 13, 10 πιθανωτέροις ἀνθρώποις χρῆσθαι, *Hier.* c. 5, 10. There is a similar use of the Latin *uti*, as Plaut. *Trin.* IV 1, 8 *placido te et clementi . . . usus sum in alto*, Cic. *Ep. ad fam.* IX 1 *cum placatis his utor*, Planc. *ad Cic.* x. 21 *scripsi tibi biduo ante confidere me bono Lepido esse usurum*.

5. **τὸ ἄγος ἐλαύνειν**, a formula meaning 'to get rid of the blood-guilty' (τὸ ἄγος = τοὺς ἐναγεῖς). The allusion is to some circumstances which had happened nearly two centuries before. Certain conspirators with Cylon at their head, who had taken refuge in the temple of Minerva, gave themselves up on condition of their lives being spared, and were then sacrilegiously murdered. The persons guilty of this offence against the deity (ἀλιτήριοι τῆς θεοῦ, Ar. *Eq.* 445) were expelled, together with Megacles who was archon at the time, but were recalled later. In B.C. 508 they were expelled again by Cleomenes, king of Sparta, but they soon afterwards returned to Athens—amongst them the Alcmaeonidae, the family to which Pericles' mother Agariste (c. 3, 1), the niece of Cleisthenes, belonged. See p. 81.

Thuc. 1 127 remarks upon the motives of the Spartans:—τοῦτο δὴ τὸ ἄγος οἱ Λακεδαιμόνιοι ἐλαύνειν ἐκέλευον δῆθεν τοῖς θεοῖς πρῶτον τιμωροῦντες, εἰδότες δὲ Περικλέα τὸν Ξανθίππου προσεχόμενον αὐτῷ κατὰ τὴν μητέρα καὶ νομίζοντες ἐκπεσόντος αὐτοῦ ῥᾷον σφίσι προχωρεῖν τὰ ἀπὸ τῶν Ἀθηναίων. οὐ μέντοι τοσοῦτον ἤλπιζον παθεῖν ἂν αὐτὸν τοῦτο ὅσον διαβολὴν οἴσειν αὐτῷ πρὸς τὴν πόλιν, ὡς καὶ διὰ τὴν ἐκείνου ξυμφορὰν τὸ μέρος ἔσται ὁ πόλεμος.

8. **περιέστη εἰς τοὐναντίον**, 'had the contrary effect' to what they intended. Cp. c. 6, 2.

11. **πίστιν ἔσχε**: see n. to c. 13, 10; c. 24, 4; c. 29, 5.

12. **ὡς**: l. 27, c. 5, 4; c. 14, 1; c. 16, 1.

§ 2 l. 15. **τὸν Ἀρχίδαμον**: c. 8, 4. **ἔχοντα**, 'with.'

18. **ἐκείνου**: c. 32, 3. **ξενίαν**, 'friendly relation.'

19. **διαβολῆς . . . ἐνδιδοὺς ἀφορμάς**, 'on purpose to give

his enemies a handle for traducing him,' *Them.* c. 23, 1. With the same object in view, Hannibal spared the property of his opponent Fabius Maximus, *Fab.* c. 7, 2, Liv. XXII 23, 4.

21. τὰς ἐπαύλεις, 'the homesteads' upon it. Cp. Thuc. II 13, 1 τοὺς ἀγροὺς τοὺς ἑαυτοῦ καὶ οἰκίας, ἦν ἄρα μὴ ὀψώσωσιν οἱ πολέμιοι ὥσπερ καὶ τὰ τῶν ἄλλων, ἀφίησιν αὐτὰ δημόσια εἶναι.

22. ἐπιδίδωσιν, 'offers as a free gift.'

§ 3 l. 22. ἐμβάλλουσιν: this was in 431 B.C.

23. στρατῷ μεγάλῳ, c. 10, 1.

26. Ἀχαρνάς, the largest of the demes or townships of Attica, about 7½ miles north of Athens, c. 30, 4.

Thucydides (II 20, 4) gives the reason why he took up a position there:— ἅμα γὰρ αὐτῷ ὁ χῶρος ἐπιτήδειος ἐφαίνετο ἐνστρατοπεδεῦσαι, ἅμα δὲ καὶ οἱ Ἀχαρνῆς μέγα μέρος ὄντες τῆς πόλεως (τρισχίλιοι γὰρ ὁπλῖται ἐγένοντο) οὐ περιόψεσθαι ἐδόκουν τὰ σφέτερα διαφθαρέντα ἀλλ᾿ ὁρμήσειν καὶ τοὺς πάντας ἐς μάχην.

28. ὑπ' ὀργῆς: cp. Arist. *Vesp.* 1083 ὑπ᾿ ὀργῆς τὴν χελώνην ἐσθίων, *Pax* 613 πίθος πληγεὶς ὑπ᾿ ὀργῆς ἀντελάκτισεν πίθῳ, *Ran.* 854 κεφαλαίῳ τὸν κρόταφόν σου ῥήματι θενὼν ὑπ᾿ ὀργῆς, *Lys.* 504 χαλεπὸν ὑπὸ τῆς ὀργῆς αὐτὰς (τὰς χεῖρας) ἴσχειν.

§ 4 l. 31. πρὸς τοὺς ἑξακισμυρίους Πελοποννησίων:

The same number is given also in *Mor.* 784 E, and by Aristides (after Plutarch) *de IV viris* p. 189 ed. Dind., where the Schol. remarks:— ἐπιτηδὲς αὔξει τοὺς Λάκωνας, δεικνὺς εὐλόγως οὐκ ἐπεξιόντα τὸν Περικλέα. The statement of 60,000 must be an exaggeration, though Androtion (fr. 45, Schol. to Soph. *Oed. C.* 697) puts the number still higher at 100,000. Thuc. gives no definite number; he merely says that a levy of two-thirds (τὰ δύο μέρη) was contributed by each state (II c. 10, 2), while he makes Archidamus say that it was the largest army ever raised by the Peloponnesians (c. 11, 1).

32. Βοιωτῶν: Thuc. II 12, 5 Βοιωτοὶ δὲ μέρος μὲν τὸ σφέτερον καὶ τοὺς ἱππέας παρείχοντο Πελοποννησίοις ξυστρατεύειν, τοῖς δὲ λειπομένοις ἐς Πλάταιαν ἐλθόντες τὴν γῆν ἐδῄουν.

33. ὑπὲρ αὐτῆς τῆς πόλεως κτλ., 'to risk no less than the existence of the city itself (with nothing between it and the enemy) in a single engagement.'

35. τοὺς ... δυσπαθοῦντας πρὸς τὰ γιγνόμενα, 'those who were impatient at the present proceedings,' *i.e.* the devastation of their lands. For πρός, see Gr. Ind. *s. v.*

37. δένδρα, 'fruit trees.' τμηθέντα καὶ κοπέντα, 'though hewed and hacked.'

§ 5 l. 39. τὸν δὲ δῆμον ... οὐ συνῆγε: Pericles was within his rights as στρατηγὸς αὐτοκράτωρ in preventing the regular meeting (κυρία ἐκκλησία) which was in ordinary times held in each prytany. Cp. Thuc. II 22, 1, Περικλῆς δὲ ὁρῶν μὲν αὐτοὺς πρὸς τὸ παρὸν χαλεπαίνοντας καὶ οὐ τὰ ἄριστα φρονοῦντας, πιστεύων δὲ ὀρθῶς γιγνώσκειν περὶ τοῦ μὴ ἐπεξιέναι, ἐκκλησίαν τε οὐκ ἐποίει αὐτῶν οὐδὲ ξύλλογον ('special meeting') οὐδένα, τοῦ μὴ ὀργῇ τι μᾶλλον ἢ γνώμῃ ξυνελθόντας ἐξαμαρτεῖν, τήν τε πόλιν ἐφύλασσε καὶ δι' ἡσυχίας μάλιστα ὅσον ἐδύνατο εἶχεν.

40. δεδιὼς βιασθῆναι: for the infinitive after a verb of fearing, see note to c. 7, 1. **παρὰ γνώμην**, 'against his inclination' (or 'judgment'). Cp. *Nic.* c. 11, 2 παρὰ γνώμην βιαζόμενος (αὐτοὺς) πρὸς τὸ συμφέρον, *Marc.* c. 25, 1 βιασθῆναι παρὰ γνώμην μὴ βουλόμενος, Thuc. IV 123, 2, VI 9, 2.

42. κατιόντος, 'sweeping down': cp. *Cam.* c. 34, 3 πνεύματος μεγάλου κατιόντος ἀπὸ τῶν ὀρῶν, *Lucull.* c. 10, 2 ἅμ' ἡμέρᾳ σάλον εἶχεν ἡ θάλασσα κατιόντος ἀκρίτου πνεύματος.

ἐν πελάγει, 'in the open sea.' For the omission of the article, see n. to c. 19, 3 and cp. *Them.* c. 11, 2.

43. κατατείνας τὰ ὅπλα, 'drawing the cordage and cables taut.' **χρῆται τῇ τέχνῃ**, 'acts according to his art.'

44. ἐπιβατῶν, 'passengers,' not as in c. 28, 1.

47. ἐχρῆτο τοῖς αὑτοῦ λογισμοῖς, 'exercised his own judgment'; cp. c. 26, 2, *Cat. mi.* c. 58, 4, c. 68, 4 ; *Dem.* c. 20, 1. The opposite is προέσθαι τοὺς αὑτοῦ λογισμούς, *Per.-Fab.* c. 1, 4. **βραχέα φροντίζων κτλ.**, 'little heeding them.' Cp. *Alex.* c. 15, 5 ἐλάχιστα φροντίζειν ἐκείνης ἔφη, *Cat. ma.* c. 19, 1, [Dem.] περὶ τῶν πρὸς Ἀλέξανδρον § 4 βραχὺ φροντίσας ὑμῶν.

§ 6 l. 49. δεόμενοι προσέκειντο, 'kept urging him with entreaties,' 'putting pressure upon him.' Cp. *Sol.* c. 14, 2 προσέκειντο τῷ Σόλωνι τυραννίδα προξενοῦντες, Thuc. VII c. 18, 1 ὁ Ἀλκιβιάδης προσκείμενος ἐδίδασκε, c. 78, 3, VIII 52, 2 ὁ Ἀλκ. προθύμως τὸν Τισσαφέρνη θεραπεύων προσέκειτο.

51. χόροι, 'the comic choruses.' See cr. n.

53. τὰ πράγματα, *rem publicam*, c. 39, 5.

§ 7 l. 54. ἐπεφύετο sc. αὐτῷ, 'made an attack upon him.' Illustrations of Plutarch's use of this verb are given in my n. to *Nic.* c. 10, 3. Cleon is the celebrated demagogue, who was the object of Aristophanes' ridicule in the *Knights*.

55. διὰ τῆς πρὸς ἐκεῖνον ὀργῆς ... τὴν δημαγωγίαν, 'making use of the general angry feeling against Pericles as a stepping-stone to the leadership of the people.'

57. ποιήσαντος, 'composed by'; so γράψαντος c. 32, 2. The anapaestic lines (τἀνάπαιστα) are taken from the play entitled Μοῖραι (Mein. II 395, Kock I 236–7), which was brought out Ol. 87, 2 soon after the first invasion of Attica.

58. βασιλεῦ σατύρων dicitur et propter libidines quibus deditus esse ferebatur et propter imbellem ignaviam. Cf. Eur. *Cycl.* 630–655. Satyros amicos Periclis—ad obsequium et adulationem pronos—interpretatur Meinekius (*Kock*).

61. ψυχὴ δὲ Τέλητος ὕπεστιν, 'but (beneath your fine talk) you have (only) the spirit of a Teles'; probably some notorious coward of the day. Kock raises a doubt as to the reading, objecting to the introduction of a paroemiac verse in the middle of an anapaestic system, whereas it is generally found at the close. His conjecture ψυχὴν δ' ἀτέλεστος ὑπεξίστης, *nihil eorum quae promisisti efficiens id unum curas quo modo animam periculis subtrahas*, has not a genuine ring and will not find many supporters.

62. κἀγχειριδίου δ' ἀκόνη κτλ.: the reading and meaning of these verses are alike obscure. Koraës paraphrases them thus: καὶ οὕτω δειλὸς εἶ ὥστε βρύχειν τοὺς ὀδόντας κἂν μόνον αἰσθῇ τὸν ψόφον ἐγχειριδίου κοπίδος (τούτεστι μικροτάτου ἐγχειριδίου) θηγομένης ἐν ἀκόνῃ σκληρᾷ. Blass retains the vulgate ἀκόνη σκληρὰ παραθηγομένη βρύκει κοπίδας and conjectures δηχθεῖσ' for δηχθείς, and extracts this far-fetched meaning:— 'even the whetstone of a poniard, so hard is it, eats into knives, when they are sharpened upon it, bitten by the flashing ('steel' he should have said, but he substitutes παρ' ὑπόνοιαν) Cleon,' with a direct reference to Pericles. So must Pericles also, were he not an arrant coward, be excited and embittered through the destructive iron (*i.e.* devastation) of the enemy and through Cleon's onslaught. Meineke extracts a somewhat different meaning from the last line:—'his verbis significat Cleonis pugnam identidem poscentis ferocia Periclem compelli ut ad arma capessenda se promptum esse confidat.'

64. αἴθωνι, as applied to Cleon, means 'violent,' 'impetuous.' It is a parody of the Homeric αἴθωνι σιδήρῳ (*Il.* 4, 485) and αἴθων λέων (10, 24). Cp. Thuc. III 36, 5, where Cleon is called βιαιότατος τῶν πολιτῶν, Diodor. XII 55, 8 ὠμὸς τὸν τρόπον καὶ βίαιος.

CHAPTER XXXIV

§ 1 l. 1. πλήν for πλὴν ἀλλά, *ceterum*, 'however,' in breaking off and passing to another subject (post-classical), c. 31, 1. **ὑπ' οὐδενὸς ἐκινήθη τῶν τοιούτων,** 'was not moved, stirred from his purpose, by any such things,' the importunity of his friends and the scoffs of his enemies. The article is used because the notion of a separate class is made prominent.

2. σιωπῇ, adverbial dative of manner, like ὀργῇ, βίᾳ, σπουδῇ, ἀνοίᾳ, κόσμῳ.

4. ἐπὶ τὴν Πελοπόννησον, 'against (i.e. to make descents on the coast of) the Peloponnese,' Thuc. II 23, 1.

6. οἰκουρῶν, § 4 l. 40, c. 11, 1.

7. διὰ χειρὸς ἔχων, 'keeping tight in hand' i.e. under control.

Cp. Cic. c. 16, 1 τὴν πόλιν εἶχε διὰ χειρός, Sert. c. 6, 5 διὰ χειρὸς εἶχε τὰς πόλεις, Demetr. c. 5, 4 τὰς πόλεις διὰ χειρὸς εἶχε, Num. c. 6, 3 τὰς ἡνίας διὰ χειρὸς ἔχειν, Mor. c. 10, 3 διὰ χειρὸς εἶχεν (Jugurtham regem), Eum. c. 4, 1 τὴν ὅμορον Ἀρμενίαν διὰ χειρὸς ἔξοντα, Thuc. II 13, 2 τὰ τῶν ξυμμάχων διὰ χειρὸς ἔχειν, Lucian Eun. c. 13 διὰ χειρὸς ἔχει τὸ πρᾶγμα, Arist. Vesp. 597 φυλάττει ἡμᾶς διὰ χειρὸς ἔχων. So διὰ στόματος ἔχειν τινα Plut. Nic. c. 9, 5, Xen. Cyr. I iv 25.

8. ἀπηλλάγησαν, c. 21, 1. θεραπεύων, 'making himself agreeable to,' *Agis* c. 13, 2; *Sert.* c. 6, 3; *Cleom.* c. 6, 1; *Phoc.* c. 21, 4.

9. ὅμως, notwithstanding the departure of the Peloponnesians. ἀσχάλλοντας is a poetical word, rare in good Attic prose; cp. Dem. *Mid.* § 125 ἐπὶ τῷ διδόναι δίκην ἀσχάλλειν. Plutarch uses it most often absolutely, but sometimes with a participle or the dative, as *Mor.* 26 B.

11. ἀνελάμβανε, c. 9, 2. κληρουχίας, c. 9, 1.

12. ἔγραφεν, c. 10, 3.

Αἰγινήτας: Thuc. II 27, 1 ἀνέστησαν δὲ καὶ Αἰγινήτας ἐν τῷ αὐτῷ θέρει τούτῳ ἐξ Αἰγίνης Ἀθηναῖοι αὐτούς τε καὶ παῖδας καὶ γυναῖκας, ἐπικαλέσαντες οὐχ ἥκιστα τοῦ πολέμου σφίσιν αἰτίους εἶναι (c. 29, 4)· καὶ τὴν Αἴγιναν ἀσφαλέστερον ἐφαίνετο, τῇ Πελοποννήσῳ ἐπικειμένην (c. 8, 5), αὐτῶν πέμψαντες ἐποίκους ἔχειν, Diod. XII 44, 2 Ἀθηναῖοι δ' ἐγκαλοῦντες Αἰγινήταις ὡς συνηργηκόσι Λακεδαιμονίοις ἀνέστησαν αὐτοὺς ἐκ τῆς πόλεως· ἐκ δὲ τῶν πολιτῶν οἰκήτορας ἐκπέμψαντες κατεκληρούχησαν τήν τε Αἴγιναν καὶ τὴν χώραν. Λακεδαιμόνιοι δὲ τοῖς ἐκπεπτωκόσιν Αἰγινήταις ἔδωκαν οἰκεῖν τὰς καλουμένας Θυρέας. This was as a set-off to the settlement of the Messenians at Ithome and from this point the exiles continued to molest the Athenians, until in B.C. 424 they were attacked and cut down to a man. They were re-established in their island by Lysander after the battle of Aegospotamos B.C. 405.

§ 2 l. 15. καὶ γάρ: this καί corresponds to that before κατὰ γῆν in next line; cp. c. 24, 6.

17. χώραν τε corresponds to κώμας τε to which καὶ πόλεις is coupled.

19. πᾶσαν: Thuc. II 31, 2 says δῃώσαντες τὰ πολλὰ τῆς γῆς (sc. τῆς Μεγαρίδος) ἀνεχώρησαν, Diod. XII 44, 3 πορθήσας

τὴν χώραν καὶ τὰς κτήσεις αὐτῶν λυμηνάμενος μετὰ πολλῆς ὠφελείας ('booty') ἐπανῆλθεν εἰς τὰς Ἀθήνας. ἢ καὶ δῆλον, 'whence (whereby) indeed it is plain' (because the Peloponnesians suffered so much).

20. δρῶντες sc. οἱ πολέμιοι.

23. (ἂν) ταχέως ἀπεῖπον, 'they would have soon called off,' 'given up,' c. 36, 4. See Greek Index s.v.

They did in fact give up the war and went back to Sparta; but Archidamus returned the next year, though Plutarch takes no notice of this circumstance; and it was during this, his second incursion, that the pestilence broke out (*Wrangham*).

25. See the speech of Pericles, Thuc. I 140. Note that προηγόρευσεν is an unclassical form for προεῖπεν, only the present and imperfect of ἀγορεύειν and its compounds being used in the best Attic prose.

§ 3 l. 28. νῦν δέ, 'as it was,' 'as the case stood,' is always in 61 this sense preceded by an unreal hypothesis, and is parallel to the protasis of the sentence which it contradicts.

πρῶτον μέν: there is no ἔπειτα or ἔπειτα δέ to correspond. Plut. had some other casualty in his mind, such as the death of Pericles, which however he omits. ἡ λοιμώδης φθορά (ἡ λοιμώδης νόσος Thuc. I 23, 3), the famous plague so vividly described in its origin, symptoms and effects by Thucydides (II cc. 47–54), who was himself a sufferer by it. ἐνέπεσε, 'attacked.' Cp. Thuc. II 49, 2 λύγξ τοῖς πλείοσιν ἐνέπεσε δεινή, Dem. de f. l. § 259 νόσημα δεινὸν ἐμπέπτωκεν εἰς τὴν Ἑλλάδα.

29. κατενεμήθη, 'ravaged,' properly of cattle 'pasturing bare.' Cp. *Artox.* c. 23, 3 ἀλφοῦ κατανεμηθέντος αὐτῆς τὸ σῶμα, *Mor.* 548 F ἡ χρόνοις ὕστερον πολλοῖς ἀψαμένη νόσος καὶ κατανεμηθεῖσα τοῦ σώματος, Thuc. II 54, 5 ἐπενείματο δὲ Ἀθήνας μὲν μάλιστα. So Virg. *Georg.* IV 458 *artus depascitur arida febris*. In the course of three years the Athenian loss was 4400 hoplites and 300 cavalry, that is, respectively a third and fourth of the whole number, Thuc. III 87, 2, cl. II 13.

30. δύναμιν, *robur*.

31. κακούμενοι, c. 29, 4.

32. ἠγριώθησαν, *efferati sunt*.

33. καθάπερ ἰατρὸν ἢ πατέρα, 'as (patients) do to a physician or (children) to a father.'

34. παραφρονήσαντες, ingressive aor., 'in a fit of delirium,' with τῇ νόσῳ.

37. συμφόρησις, 'crowding together.' So *Oth.* c. 11, 2 ἡ δ' ἐπὶ τοσοῦτο σωρεία καὶ συμφόρησις.

Cp. Nic. c. 6, 3 τοῦ δὲ λοιμοῦ τὴν πλείστην αἰτίαν ἔλαβε Περικλῆς διὰ τὸν πόλεμον εἰς τὸ ἄστυ κατακλείσας τὸν ἀπὸ τῆς χώρας ὄχλον ἐκ τῆς μεταβολῆς τῶν τόπων καὶ διαίτης ἀήθους γενομένου, Thuc. II 52, 1 οἰκιῶν γὰρ οὐχ ὑπαρχουσῶν ἀλλ᾽ ἐν καλύβαις πνιγηραῖς ὥρᾳ ἔτους διαιτωμένων ὁ φθόρος ἐγίγνετο οὐδενὶ κόσμῳ, ἀλλὰ καὶ νεκροὶ ἐπ᾽ ἀλλήλοις <καὶ> ἀποθνῄσκοντες ἔκειντο καὶ ἐν ταῖς ὁδοῖς ἐκαλινδοῦντο καὶ περὶ τὰς κρήνας ἁπάσας ἡμιθνῆτες τοῦ ὕδατος ἐπιθυμίᾳ.

38. ἀπεργάζεται, 'causes.'

§ 4 l. 39. πνιγηροῖς, 'stifling' from the great heat.

40. οἰκουρόν (c. 11, 2))(ἀναπεπταμένης, 'indoors')('in the open air.' Cp. Erot. c. 6 τῆς ἐν ἡλίῳ καθαρᾶς καὶ ἀναπεπταμένης διατριβῆς, Them. c. 8, 2 with my note ad l.

42. ὁ . . . καταχεάμενος, 'who caused to pour in.' τὸν ἀπὸ τῆς χώρας: for the attraction, cp. c. 3, 3 note, c. 27, 4.

45. ἀναπίμπλασθαι, impleri, 'to be infected.' Thuc. II 51, 2 ἕτερος ἀφ᾽ ἑτέρου θεραπείας ἀναπιμπλάμενοι ὥσπερ τὰ πρόβατα ἔθνῃσκον.

46. μηδεμίαν, unclassical for οὐδεμίαν: see note to c. 23, 1; c. 29, 2.

47. ἀναψυχήν, 'relief,' 'respite,' a poetical word.

CHAPTER XXXV

§ 1 l. 1. ταῦτα ἰᾶσθαι, sc. τὰ κακά. Cp. Alc. c. 25, 6 ἐπεχείρησαν ἰᾶσθαι μείζονι κακῷ τὸ κακόν, Alc.-Cor. c. 2, 5 πολλαῖς δεήσεσι μίαν ἰωμένων ὀργήν, Dem. c. 7, 2, Sol. c. 29, 3 εἴ τις αὐτοῦ τὴν ἐπιθυμίαν ἰάσαιτο τῆς τυραννίδος, Eur. Or. 651 ἁμαρτίαν τῆς σῆς γυναικὸς ἀδικίαν τ᾽ ἰώμενος, Thuc. v 65, 2 κακὸν κακῷ ἰᾶσθαι.

2. παραλυπεῖν, 'to inflict annoyance besides.' παρά might also imply stealthiness or suddenness, as in παρεισπίπτειν, Pelop. c. 11, 6; παρεισάγειν Lyc. c. 28, 4; παρεισρεῖν ib. c. 27, 3; παραδύεσθαι Erot. c. 5.

3. ἐπλήρου, 'manned.' Hence πλήρωμα, 'crew.' This was the second expedition, under the command of Pericles himself, who had been re-elected Strategus in Hecatombaeon 430 B.C.

Thuc. II 56, 1 ἔτι δ᾽ αὐτῶν (sc. τῶν Πελοποννησίων) ἐν τῷ πεδίῳ ὄντων (before they had moved on to the S.E. coast district of Attica), ἑκατὸν νεῶν ἐπίπλουν τῇ Πελοποννήσῳ παρεσκευάζετο καί, ἐπειδὴ ἑτοῖμα ἦν, ἀνήγετο· ἦγε δ᾽ ἐπὶ τῶν νεῶν ὁπλίτας Ἀθηναίων τετρακισχιλίους καὶ ἱππέας τριακοσίους ἐν ναυσὶν ἱππαγωγοῖς πρῶτον τότε ἐκ τῶν παλαιῶν νεῶν ποιηθείσαις. These are the transports which called forth the joke of Aristophanes (Eq. 599 ff.) for their novelty.

5. ἀναβιβασάμενος, 'causing to embark,' Thuc. VII 33, 1.   62

7. ἀπὸ τοσαύτης ἰσχύος: c. 39, 1.   Cp. *Philop.* c. 10, 1 ἀπὸ μεγάλης δυνάμεως ἐπιβουλεύοντα πᾶσι Πελοποννησίοις, *Pyrrh.* c. 11, 6, c. 18, 4, *Pel.* c. 17, 6.

11. τὸν ἥλιον ἐκλιπεῖν: Plutarch has confounded two expeditions. The solar eclipse (not total) happened not on this occasion but a year earlier, the 3rd of August 431 B.C. = Ol. 87, 2, when Pericles was not in command.   See Thuc. II 28.

The incident is recorded with many variations in later writers. Valerius Max. VIII 11 ext. 1 makes Pericles explain the phenomenon in the popular assembly:—*Pericles processit in medium et quae a praeceptore suo Anaxagora pertinentia ad solis et lunae cursum acceperat disseruit.* Cp. *Nic.* c. 23, Cic. *Rep.* I c. 16, 25.

13. σημεῖον, c. 6, 3.

§ 2 l. 14. περίφοβον sc. ὄντα.   G. *MT.*² §§ 902, 884.

15. διηπορημένον, 'puzzled what to do.'   τὴν χλαμύδα, 'his military cloak.'

17. παρακαλύψας sc. αὐτόν or τὰς ὄψεις αὑτοῦ.   So παρακαλύπτεσθαι is used by Plato *Rep.* 439 E for 'to cover one's face,' so as to avoid seeing a disagreeable object.

This use of μή = *num*, 'whether,' in an indirect question with the indicative, where the answer expected is negative, is common in late Greek. G. *MT.*² § 369 note 1.   Cp. *Cat. ma.* c. 24, 1 ἠρώτησε τὸν πατέρα μή τι μεμφόμενος . . . μητρυιὰν ἐπάγεται, *Demetr.* c. 9, 5 ἠρώτα μή τις εἴληφέ τι τῶν ἐκείνου.   So after πυνθάνεσθαι and its compounds *Sol.* c. 6, 2, *Arist.* c. 7, 6 etc., after ἐπερέσθαι *Alex.* c. 27, 3 and ἐπισκοπεῖν *ib.* c. 22, 5, after γράφειν *ib.* c. 41, 2 γράψον πῶς ἔχεις καὶ μή τινές σε τῶν συγκυνηγετούντων ἐγκατέλιπον, after ἀποπειρᾶσθαι *Cleom.* c. 37 ἀπεπειρᾶτο μή τις διαλανθάνει ζῶν, and εἰδέναι *Phoc.* c. 32, 4 οὐκ οἶδα μὴ μεῖζόν τι παραβαίνει.

18. οὐκ ἔφη sc. οἴεσθαι, *negavit se putare.*

22. σχολαῖς, *eruditorum disputationibus.*   Cp. *Mor.* 25 C ταῦτα ἐν ταῖς σχολαῖς ἀκούομεν, 790 D, 796 C, *Philop.* c. 2, 3, *Cleom.* c. 30, 2, *Arat.* c. 29, 6.

§ 3 l. 23. δ' οὖν, c. 26, 2; c. 27, 1.   οὔτε . . . τε: c. 18, 1.

25. τὴν ἱερὰν Ἐπίδαυρον: Epidaurus was an important town on the east coast of Argolis, famous for its temple of Asclepius and its theatre. The possession of this place would have been valuable, as it lay on the road to Argos. (Its colony Epidaurus Limera was situated on the east coast of Laconia, Thuc. VII 18, 3.)   Cp. Thuc. II 56, 4 ἀφικόμενοι δὲ εἰς Ἐπίδαυρον τῆς Πελοποννήσου ἔτεμον τῆς γῆς τὴν πολλὴν καὶ πρὸς τὴν πόλιν προσβαλόντες ἐς ἐλπίδα μὲν ἦλθον τοῦ ἑλεῖν, οὐ μέντοι προεχώρησέ γε.   There is nothing said here about a siege (πολιορκία).

For ἱεράν, cp. Pausan. 2, 26, 3 Ἀσκληπιοῦ ἱερὰν μάλιστα εἶναι τὴν γῆν συμβέβηκε, Strabo *Geogr.* VIII p. 374 καὶ αὕτη δ' οὐκ ἄσημος ἡ πόλις καὶ μάλιστα διὰ τὴν ἐπιφάνειαν τοῦ Ἀσκληπιοῦ θεραπεύειν νόσους παντοδάπας πεπιστευμένου καὶ τὸ ἱερὸν πλῆρες ἔχοντος ἀεὶ τῶν τε καμνόντων καὶ τῶν ἀνακειμένων πινάκων.

26. **διὰ τὴν νόσον**: cp. Thuc. II 57, 1 ἡ νόσος ἔν τε τῇ στρατιᾷ τοὺς Ἀθηναίους ἔφθειρε καὶ ἐν τῇ πόλει.

27. **τοὺς ὁπωσοῦν συμμίξαντας**, 'those who held any sort of communication with,' 'came into ever so little contact with them.'

29. **χαλεπῶς διακειμένους**, 'exasperated.' Thuc. II 59, 1 μετὰ δὲ τὴν δευτέραν εἰσβολὴν τῶν Πελ. οἱ Ἀθηναῖοι ... τὸν Περικλέα ἐν αἰτίᾳ εἶχον ὡς πείσαντα σφᾶς πολεμεῖν καὶ δι' ἐκεῖνον ταῖς ξυμφοραῖς περιπεπτωκότες.

30. **παρηγορεῖν**: Thuc. II 65, 1 ἐπειρᾶτο τοὺς Ἀθηναίους τῆς ἐς αὐτὸν ὀργῆς παραλύειν, ibid. 3 οὐ μέντοι πρότερόν γε οἱ ξύμπαντες ἐπαύσαντο ἐν ὀργῇ ἔχοντες αὐτὸν πρὶν ἐζημίωσαν χρήμασιν.

§ 4 l. 31. **παρέλυσε** (sc. αὐτούς), *liberavit cos.*

32. **πρότερον ἤ**, 'until,' only after past tenses. G. *MT.*² § 653.

33. **γενομένους κυρίους**, 'because they had become masters of his fate,' *i.e.* in their capacity of judges who could punish him according to will.

Cp. Diod. XII 45, 4 τὸν Περικλέα νομίζοντες αἴτιον αὐτοῖς γεγονέναι τοῦ πολέμου δι' ὀργῆς εἶχον. διόπερ ἀποστήσαντες αὐτὸν τῆς στρατηγίας καὶ μικράς τινας ἀφορμὰς ἐγκλημάτων λαβόντες ἐζημίωσαν αὐτὸν ὀγδοήκοντα ταλάντοις. Both Plutarch and Diodorus err in their statement that he was deprived of his command by the sentence which condemned him. An unfounded charge of embezzlement (κλοπῆς, Plat. *Gorg.* 516 A) was made against him as στρατηγός in a special ἐκκλησία on the vote of confidence (ἐπιχειροτονία) and he was brought to trial soon after he had entered on his new yearly office, so that his re-election could not take place until the next year B.C. 429.

35. **οἱ τὸν ἐλάχιστον** sc. γράφοντες.

36. **πεντήκοντα**: Diodorus gives still more, 80 talents.

39. **Ἰδομενεύς**: c. 10, 5. The technical term in such cases was συνήγορος, not κατήγορος which Plutarch uses again c. 10, 5.

40. Simmias is mentioned also in *Mor.* 805 C as an opponent and rival of Pericles.

41. **Ἡρακλείδης**: c. 27, 3.

CHAPTER XXXVI

§ 1 l. 1. **τὰ μὲν δημόσια παύσεσθαι κτλ.**, 'but although his public troubles were not like (c. 23, 1) to last long, now that the people had discharged their passion on him (or, if with Blass we read εἰς τοῦτο, 'in this trial') with the blow they inflicted, just as a bee leaves its sting behind it in the wound it inflicts, yet his domestic affairs . . .' Cp. Plat. *Phaed.* 190 γ ὥσπερ μέλιττα τὸ κέντρον ἐγκαταλιπὼν οἰχήσομαι.

3. ἀφεικότων, c. 8, 3.

5. κατά, 'at the time of,' 'during.'

6. στάσει, 'discord.'

7. πόρρωθεν, 'for a long time back.'

9. Ξάνθιππος: he was named after his paternal grandfather according to custom. His loose manner of life is mentioned by Antisthenes the Socratic, also ap. Athenae. v 220 D.

10. πολυτελεῖ, c. 9, 1.   συνοικῶν, c. 24, 2.

12. ἀκρίβειαν, c. 16, 5.

13. γλίσχρως καὶ κατὰ μικρὸν αὐτῷ χορηγοῦντος, 'making him a meagre allowance and in driblets.' Cp. *Alc.* c. 25, 1; c. 35, 4 γλίσχρως χορηγῶν, *Cleom.* c. 27, 2 γλίσχρως καὶ μόλις πορίζοντα, Plat. *Rep.* 553 c γλίσχρως καὶ κατὰ μικρὸν φειδόμενος. For χορηγεῖν, cp. c. 11, 2.

§ 2 l. 15. ἔλαβεν, 'he borrowed.'

16. ἀπαιτοῦντος sc. from Pericles.

17. καὶ δίκην αὐτῷ προσέλαχε, '(so far from paying him) he even brought an action against him to boot' for encouraging his son in extravagance. Cp. Dem. *or. c. Zenoth.* § 9 οὐκ ἐλήλυθε μόνον ἀλλὰ καὶ τοῦ σίτου τοῦ ἡμετέρου ἀμφισβητήσας ἡμῖν δίκην προσείληχεν.   Ξάνθιππος is in epexegetic apposition to τὸ μειράκιον: so Luc. c. 2, 5 τὸ μειράκιον ὁ Πτολεμαῖος.

18. ἐπὶ τούτῳ, *propter hoc*, with χαλεπῶς διατεθείς.

19. ἐκφέρων, *efferens*, 'disclosing,' 'divulging,' as *Pyrrh.* c. 5, 5, *Cleom.* c. 35, 3, Arist. *Eccl.* 412 τἀπόρρητ' ἐκφέρειν, Herod. IX 5.   ἐπὶ γέλωτι, 'to raise a laugh.' Cp. *Ran.* 404 ἐπὶ γέλωτι κἀπ' εὐτελείᾳ, *risus parsimoniaeque causa*.

20. διατριβάς, 'philosophical conversations.' See my note to *Them.* c. 2, 3.

21. σοφιστῶν, c. 4, 1.

§ 3 l. 21. πεντάθλου, 'one who contended in the πένταθλον' or *quinquertium*, which consisted of ἅλμα, ποδωκείην, δίσκον, ἄκοντα, πάλην (Simonides).

22. πατάξαντος, the proper active aorist, as πληγείς is the passive participle of τύπτειν, *ferire*. Cobet *V. L.* 335 ff.

24. ἀναλῶσαι infin. of ἀνήλωσα, not ἀνάλωσα which is only a dialectic form. Meisterhans *Gr.*² p. 137, note 1203 ᵈ.

διαπορούντα, c. 24, 1.   Protagoras of Abdera (480–411 B.C.), the first who called himself a sophist, and distinguished himself as such at Athens, where he accumulated a large fortune. The discussion of such questions served the sophists as an advertisement of their eristic skill.

25. τὸν βαλόντα μᾶλλον: μᾶλλον non ad βαλόντα sed ad ἤ pertinet. Dictum enim fuerit, si hanc lectionem sequamur, pro ἢ μᾶλλον τὸν βαλόντα (*Stephanus*).

26. τοὺς ἀγωνοθέτας, 'the judges of the games,' who were public officials, not to be identified, as is done in the *Dict. of Antiqq.* vol. I ed. 3, with the ἀθλοθέται (c. 13, 6).   κατὰ τὸν ὀρθότατον λόγον: there is here an allusion to Protagoras' characteristic use of the expressions ὀρθός and ὀρθότης in his discussions on language.

27. τοῦ πάθους: cp. Herod. II 133 μετὰ τὸ τῆς θυγατρὸς πάθος, *i.e. mortem*.   πρὸς δὲ τούτοις (c. 11, 4) answers to πρῶτον μέν.

28. περὶ τῆς γυναικός, *de sua ipsius uxore*; see c. 13, 11.

29. Στησίμβροτος: c. 26, 1.

30. τοὺς πολλούς, c. 7, 1.   καὶ ὅλως, c. 21, 1 ; c. 29, 3.

33. νοσήσας, c. 31, 5.

§ 4 l. 35. κηδεστῶν, c. 11, 1.

37. ἀπεῖπεν, c. 34, 2.

38. προὔδωκε τὸ φρόνημα, 'gave up his high spirit.' Cp. *Cleom.* c. 38, 1 καίπερ οὖσα γενναία γυνὴ προὔδωκε τὸ φρόνημα πρὸς τὸ τῆς συμφορᾶς μέγεθος.

39. ὑπό, *prae*; see Gr. Ind. s. v.   ἀλλ' οὐδὲ κλαίων οὔτε κηδεύων οὔτε πρὸς τάφῳ τινός, 'nay, he was not seen even weeping, either at the performance of funeral rites or later at the grave of any of his nearest relations.' Plut. prefers the use of the indef. pronoun τις after the neg. οὐδέ, cp. c. 39, 1, Stegmann p. 24. For ἀλλ' οὐδέ see note to c. 28, 2.

41. πρίν γε δή . . . ἀποβαλεῖν: there is a different story told by Protagoras, who was an eye-witness, in *Mor.* 118 D E, which is probably borrowed from the same source as that of Valerius Max. V 10 ext. 1:— τῶν γὰρ υἱέων νεηνιῶν ὄντων καὶ καλῶν, ἐν ὀκτὼ δὲ ταῖς πάσῃσιν ἡμέρῃσιν ἀποθανόντων, νηπενθέως ἀνέτλη.

§ 5 l. 44. καμφθείς, 'bowed down.'

45. ἐπιφέρων στέφανον, 'as he was placing the wreath on the dead body.'

46. ἡττήθη τοῦ πάθους πρός κτλ., 'he was overcome by his

emotion at the sight' of the lifeless body: Plutarch has a decided predilection for this use of πρός: cp. c. 33, 4; c. 35, 1.

47. **κλαυθμὸν ῥῆξαι**, 'burst into wailing.' Cp. Soph. *Trach.* 919 δακρύων ῥήξασα θερμὰ νάματα, Virg. *Aen.* IV 553 *tantos illa suo rumpebat pectore questus*, XI 377 *dat gemitum rumpitque has imo pectore voces*.

CHAPTER XXXVII

§ 1 l. 1. **τῶν ἄλλων** is to be taken with **ῥητόρων** ('politicians,' c. 7, 5), as well as **στρατηγῶν**.

2. **εἰς τὸν πόλεμον** with πειρωμένης.

3. **βάρος**, 'preponderance,' 'influence' (unclassical). **ἰσόρροπον**, 'of equal weight (as ἡγεμών) with' (the ἡγεμονία), hence 'adequate.'

4. **ἐχέγγυον πρός**, lit. 'giving security for,' hence 'sufficiently strong for,' 'competent for.' Cp. *Aem. Paul.* c. 8, 6 ἅμα τῇ βασιλείᾳ διεδέξατο τὴν πρὸς Ῥωμαίους ἔχθραν οὐκ ὢν ἐχέγγυος ἐνεγκεῖν διὰ μικρότητα καὶ μοχθηρίαν ἤθους. **ἡγεμονίαν**: c. 15, 1.

6. **καλούσης**, 'calling him,' as expressing the universal wish, not as inviting him officially. Cp. Aesch. *de f. l.* § 84 βοώντων ὑμῶν καὶ τοὺς προέδρους ἐπὶ τὸ βῆμα καλούντων. **τὸ στρατήγιον**, the official meeting-place or Board-room of the ten στρατηγοί at Athens; *Mor.* 813 E εὐσταλεστέραν δεῖ τὴν χλαμύδα ποιεῖν καὶ βλέπειν ἀπὸ τοῦ στρατηγίου πρὸς τὸ βῆμα, *Nic.* c. 5, 1; c. 15, 2, Aesch. *Ctes.* § 146, *de f. l.* § 85.

During the period of his administration the centre of gravity of public life all lay in this office. It was as Strategus that Pericles carried through the most important laws; as such he was the acting president of the Republic; and the helmet with which he caused himself to be represented by the sculptors served not to conceal the pointed form of his skull, as the comic poets mockingly averred (c. 3, 2), but to indicate the dictatorial power of the general-in-chief as the real foundation of his authority of government. The importance of the Strategy, as held by him, probably also explains the use of the word in Sophocles, e.g. *Antig.* 8. E. Curtius *Gr. Hist.* II 456-7, 599.

8. **Alcibiades was a near relative and ward of Pericles.** Cp. *Alc.* c. 1, 1 τοῦ δὲ Ἀλκιβιάδου Περικλῆς καὶ Ἀρίφρων οἱ Ξανθίππου, προσήκοντες κατὰ γένος, ἐπετρόπευον, Xen. *Mem.* I ii 40 λέγεται Ἀλκιβιάδην, πρὶν εἴκοσιν ἐτῶν εἶναι, Περικλεῖ ἐπιτρόπῳ μὲν ὄντι ἑαυτοῦ προστάτῃ δὲ τῆς πόλεως τοιάδε διαλεχθῆναι περὶ νόμων, Isocr. *or.* 16 § 28 Ἀλκιβιάδης κατελείφθη μὲν ὀρφανός, ὁ γὰρ πατὴρ αὐτοῦ μαχόμενος ἐν Κορωνείᾳ

τοῖς πολεμίοις ἀπέθανεν, ἐπετροπεύθη δ' ὑπὸ Περικλέους. The double relationship between them will be seen at a glance by referring to the family pedigree, c. 3, 1. Diodorus (XII 38) and Valerius Maximus (III 1) speak of Alcibiades as the nephew (ἀδελφιδοῦς) of Pericles.

9. **προελθεῖν,** 'to go out,' 'appear in public.' Cp. c. 27, 4, *Nic.* c. 13, 5, *Cat. mi.* c. 59, 1, *Brut.* c. 15, 1, *Dem.* c. 7, 3 ὑπὲρ τοῦ μηδὲ βουλομένῳ πάνυ προελθεῖν ἐνδέχεσθαι δι' αἰσχύνην.

§ 2 l. 10. **τὴν ἀγνωμοσύνην**: see note to c. 2, 4.

11. **ὑποδεξάμενος,** 'undertaking,' a post-classical meaning of the verb.

12. **τὰ πράγματα,** 'state affairs,' c. 33, 6 ; c. 39, 5. **στρατηγὸς αἱρεθείς** *sc.* αὐτοκράτωρ as before, but by an extraordinary additional election, as the representative of the entire civic community, perhaps because three strategi had fallen in Chalcidice. Cp. Thuc. II 65, 4 στρατηγὸν εἵλοντο καὶ πάντα τὰ πράγματα ἐπέτρεψαν. Diodorus (XII 45, 5) says ἠναγκάζοντο πάλιν τὸν Περικλέα στρατηγὸν αἱρεῖσθαι, when they found that the Spartans were not desirous καταλύσασθαι τὸν πόλεμον. As to the method of election of the strategi, see Aristot. Ἀθ. πολ. c. 43 χειροτονοῦσι δὲ καὶ τὰς πρὸς τὸν πόλεμον (ἀρχὰς) ἁπάσας.

13. **λυθῆναι,** 'should be broken,' *i.e.* an exception should be made to it in this one instance. Cp. *Arist.* c. 8, 1 λύσαντες τὸν νόμον ἐψηφίσαντο τοῖς μεθεστῶσι κάθοδον.

τὸν περὶ τῶν νόθων νόμον: see note to c. 24, 6. The statement of Plutarch on this subject, which was impugned by Duncker and Zimmermann (*De nothorum Athenis condicione*, Berlin 1886), is now confirmed by Aristot. Ἀθ. πολ. c. 26, 4 ἐπὶ Ἀντιδότου διὰ τὸ πλῆθος τῶν πολιτῶν Περικλέους εἰπόντος ἔγνωσαν μὴ μετέχειν τῆς πόλεως ὃς ἂν μὴ ἐξ ἀμφοῖν ἀστοῖν ᾖ γεγονώς, where, however, the motive for introducing such a measure can scarcely be correct, because he himself bears witness to the heavy losses incurred in the war. (Isocr. *de pac.* § 88 at a later date says :—ἔλαθον σφᾶς αὐτοὺς τοὺς μὲν τάφους τοὺς δημοσίους τῶν πολιτῶν ἐμπλήσαντες τὰς δὲ φρατρίας καὶ τὰ γραμματεῖα τὰ ληξιαρχικὰ τῶν οὐδὲν ἐν τῇ πόλει προσηκόντων.) The rights and material advantages attached in the time of Pericles to Athenian citizenship naturally made the possession of it more coveted on the one hand and caused greater exclusiveness on the other. The recent development of the city was the cause of a great increase of intercourse with foreigners, while it gave employ to the citizens in the confederate cities; hence the number of mixed marriages increased in an unusual degree, and the Athenian citizenship was combined with foreign elements in one or other of many ways. In the time of war especially, as later during the Peloponnesian war, irregular admissions into the phratriae and demi became frequent. In spite of the bill of Pericles, many persons succeeded in the next generation in obtaining the rights of citizens illegally.

15. **ἐρημίᾳ διαδοχῆς,** 'from default of succession.' Cp. *Agis* c. 11, 4 ὡς διαδοχῆς ἔρημον ἀνέλοιτο τὸ βασίλειον, Athenae.

593 Α Δημήτριος ὁ τῆς διαδοχῆς τελευταῖος, and [Dem.] *Macart.* § 73 ἐπιμέλειαν ἐποιησάμην τοῦ οἴκου τοῦ Ἁγνίου ὅπως μὴ ἐξερημωθήσεται. τὸν οἶκον ἐκλίποι, 'should fail the house.' Cp. Plat. *Legg.* 657 D τὸ παρ᾽ ἡμῖν ἡμᾶς ἐκλείπει νῦν, Lys. p. 113, 39 ἐκλελοίπασιν ὑμᾶς αἱ προφάσεις.

16. In the view of some historians the statute was only a revival of one of Solon's which had fallen into disuse in course of time, as is shown by the cases of Cleisthenes, Themistocles, Cimon and Hippocrates the grandfather of Pericles; all of whom were μητρόξενοι and yet in full possession of civic rights. It was also revived at a later period under Eucleides, Athenae. XIII 577 B; cp. Dem. *Eubul.* § 30 τοῖς χρόνοις οὕτω φαίνεται γεγονὼς ὥστε, εἰ καὶ κατὰ θάτερα ἀστὸς ἦν, εἶναι πολίτην προσήκειν αὐτόν, γέγονε γὰρ πρὸ Εὐκλείδου.

§ 3 l. 17. ἀκμάζων ἐν τῇ πολιτείᾳ : cp. c. 13, 1.

18. πρὸ πάνυ πολλῶν χρόνων : in B.C. 445.

19. ὥσπερ εἴρηται, c. 36, 1.

21. ἐκ δυεῖν Ἀθηναίων : the Attic expression would be ἐκ δυοῖν (c. 27, 4) ἀστοῖν.

22. τοῦ βασιλέως τῶν Αἰγυπτίων : this was Inarus, son of Psammetichus or, according to Philochorus ap. Schol. Arist. *Vesp.* 718, Psammetichus himself, an ally of the Athenians, in B.C. 445/444. Duncker quoted by Busolt thinks that the king was neither Inarus nor his father, but Amyrtaeus.

23. δωρειάν in apposition to μεδίμνους.

24. διανέμεσθαι, 'to divide amongst themselves,' reciprocal middle, cp. *Them.* c. 4, 1.

26. ἀνεφύοντο, 'kept springing up one after another.' Cp. *Thes.* c. 17, 1 αὖθις ἀνεφύοντο τῷ Αἰγεῖ διαβολαὶ πρὸς τοὺς πολίτας, *Arist.* c. 26, 1 φησὶ τὸν δῆμον ἀναφῦσαι πλῆθος συκοφαντῶν. ἐκ τοῦ γράμματος, 'as a consequence of that statute.' Cp. *Ti. Gr.* c. 8, 2 ἐγράφη νόμος . . . καὶ ἐπέσχε τὴν πλεονεξίαν τὸ γράμμα τοῦτο.

27. τέως, 'up to that time,' 'before.'

28. παρορωμένοις, 'overlooked.' *Luc.* c. 39, 5 οὐ τὰ παρορώμενα καὶ λανθάνοντα πλείονα τῶν φαινομένων ἐστί. συκοφαντήμασι περιέπιπτον, 'incurred vexatious informations,' and were declared νόθοι. *Cam.* c. 2, 2 πληγῇ περιπεσών, Lys. p. 108, 21 περιπίπτειν συκοφάνταις, Herod. I 96 περιπίπτοντες ἀδίκοισι γνώμῃσι, Aesch. *or.* c. *Tim.* § 165 λοιδορίαις περιπίπτων, Dem. *or. Phil.* II 31 τῇ ὑμῶν ὀργῇ περιπεσεῖν, *Ep.* II 15 τῇ πρὸς ἅπαντας τοὺς ἐν ταῖς αἰτίαις ὀργῇ περιπέπτωκα ἀδίκως.

§ 4 l. 29. ἐπράθησαν . . . ἀλόντες, 'were convicted and sold for slaves.' The severity of the punishment and the number of the victims has induced editors to substitute some other verb such as ἐφάνησαν (Koraes), ἐφωράθησαν (Orelli), ἀπηλάθησαν (Clinton, Cobet who remarks that the Athenians would have said ἀπεψηφίσθησαν), ἀπεκρίθησαν. But the matter is fully explained by Dionysius *judic. de Isaeo* v p. 617 ed. Reiske, who says : ἐγράφη γὰρ δή τις ὑπὸ τῶν Ἀθηναίων νόμος, ἐξέτασιν γίγνεσθαι τῶν πολιτῶν κατὰ δήμους· τὸν δὲ ἀποψηφισθέντα ὑπὸ τῶν δημοτῶν τῆς πολιτείας μὴ μετέχειν, τοῖς δὲ ἀδίκως ἀποψηφισθεῖσιν ἔφεσιν εἰς τὸ δικαστήριον εἶναι προσκαλεσαμένοις τοὺς δημότας· καὶ ἐὰν τὸ δεύτερον ἐξελεγχθῶσι, πεπρᾶσθαι αὐτοὺς καὶ τὰ χρήματα εἶναι δημόσια. There is a statement to the same effect given in the argument to the speech of Demosthenes against Eubulides.

31. According to Philochorus *l.c.*, the number retained on the burgher-roll was 14,240, and the number excluded as παρέγγραφοι not fewer than 4760, so that the list before revision contained exactly 19,000 : τῆς δὲ διανομῆς γενομένης τοῦ σίτου ξενηλασίαι ἐποίησαν Ἀθηναῖοι καὶ ἐν τῷ διακρίνειν τοὺς αὐθιγενεῖς εὗρον καὶ ἑτέρους τετρακισχιλίους ἑπτακοσίους ἑξήκοντα ξένους παρεγγεγραμμένους.

§ 5 l. 33. **ὄντος δεινοῦ τοῦ** . . . **λυθῆναι**, 'although it was a grave matter that the statute which had been enforced against so many people should be broken in the interest of the very person who had carried it.'

36. **περὶ τὸν οἶκον**: see n. to c. 2, 3 ; c. 8, 1.

37. **τῆς ὑπεροψίας**, c. 5, 3.

38. **ἐπέκλασε**, 'softened,' 'touched their hearts.' Cp. *Them.* c. 10, 5 with my note.   **δόξαντες**, *rati*.

39. **νεμεσητὰ παθεῖν**, 'that he had been punished by Nemesis.' See Greek Index *s.v.* νεμεσητός. Aelian *V.H.* VI 10 in speaking of the same law adds :—μετῆλθε δὲ ἄρα αὐτὸν ἡ ἐκ τοῦ νόμου νέμεσις, οἱ γὰρ δύο παῖδες οἵπερ ἤστην αὐτῷ κατὰ τὴν νόσον τοῦ λοιμοῦ ἀπέθανον, *ib.* XIII 24.   **ἀνθρωπίνων δεῖσθαι**, 'that his request was no more than was natural for a man to make and men to grant,' *i.e.* 'moderate.' See the exx. of this meaning given by Field in his *Otium Norv.* p. 108. AJacob explains it somewhat differently '"et qu'il avait besoin de mesures humaines," c'est-à-dire prises par les hommes, par opposition à celles (νεμεσητά) que les dieux semblaient avoir prises contre lui.'

40. **ἀπογράψασθαι**, 'should have the name of his νόθος registered in the family φρατρία,' so that he might be legitimated and admitted to civic rights. Such registration was usual in the first year after birth. Pericles the younger is designated as Χολαργεύς in *CIA.* I 188. Cobet points out that ἀπογράφεσθαι is not the Attic expression, but either εἰσάγειν εἰς τοὺς φρατέρας or ἐγγράφειν εἰς τὸ ληξιαρχικὸν γραμματεῖον. Cp. Ar. *Av.* 1669.

42. ὕστερον: in B.C. 406 = Ol. 93, 2 the Athenian fleet defeated the Peloponnesian under the command of Callicratidas off the islands Arginusae (coast of Aeolis). The Athenian ships were prevented by a storm from picking up the seamen off the wrecked vessels; in consequence all the generals were deposed except Conon, only six out of the ten returned to Athens—Pericles, Diomedon, Lysias, Aristocrates, Thrasyllus, and Crasinides—and these were condemned by an illegal process and executed. Diodor. XIII 98, 101, Xen. *Hell.* I 6, 28 ff.

CHAPTER XXXVIII

§ 1 l. 1. τότε: two and a half years after the beginning of the Peloponnesian war (Thuc. II 65, 6), therefore in the spring of B.C. 429 = Ol. 87, 4.

2. λαβέσθαι λαβήν: cp. *Mor.* 78 B εἰλημμένος ἦν προσήκει λαβὴν ὑπὸ φιλοσοφίας, 186 D ᾿Αλκιβιάδης ἔτι παῖς ὢν ἐλήφθη λαβὴν ἐν παλαίστρᾳ: λαβή is used for 'an attack of sickness' in medical writers. ὀξεῖαν—σύντονον, 'acute'—'violent.' Plutarch more frequently uses μή after ἔοικε.

4. βληχρᾷ, 'lingering.'

5. διαχρωμένην σχολαίως, 'using up slowly.'

6. ὑπερείπουσαν, 'gradually undermining' (unclassical).

Cp. *Mor.* 341 D διορύττουσα πανταχόθεν, ὑπερείπουσα, πᾶν μέρος ἀνοίγουσα τοῦ σώματος, 379 E δόξα δεινὴ τοὺς ἀσθενεῖς εἰς ἄκρατον ὑπερείπουσα τὴν δεισιδαιμονίαν, 446 A ταῖς ἡδοναῖς ὑπερειπόμενος, *Fab.* c. 19, 3 ὑφ' οὗ καὶ κατὰ μικρὸν ὑπαρρέοντος (ὡς ποταμοῦ) ... ὑπερειπόμενος ἐλάνθανε, *Pomp.* c. 74, 2 δεξαμένου ταῖς ἀγκάλαις αὑτὴν ὑπερείπουσαν, *Anton.* c. 82, 2 ἀπειλάς τινας καὶ φόβους οἷς ἐκείνη καθάπερ μηχανήμασιν ὑπηρείπετο, *Brut.* c. 7, 4 ἐκτέμνοντα τὴν ἀλκὴν καὶ τὸν θυμὸν ὑπερείποντα (Caesarem Bruti).

§ 2 l. 7. Θεόφραστος, not in his ἠθικοὶ χαρακτῆρες, but in his lost treatise on Moral Philosophy resembling the Ἠθικά of Aristotle. γοῦν, 'what is certain, is that': see note to c. 4, 2.

8. διαπορήσας εἰ, 'after raising the question whether,' c. 24, 1; c. 36, 3. πρὸς τὰς τύχας τρέπεται, 'vary according to outward circumstances.'

10. ἐξίσταται, 'degenerate from.' Cp. Plat. *Rep.* 380 D εἴπερ τι ἐξίσταιτο τῆς αὑτοῦ ἰδέας, Aristot. *Hist. Anim.* I 1, 14 γενναῖον δὲ (ἐστὶ) τὸ μὴ ἐξιστάμενον ἐκ τῆς αὑτοῦ φύσεως, *Rhet.* II, 15 ἐξίσταται τὰ στάσιμα ἤθη εἰς ἀβελτερίαν.

11. ἐπισκοπουμένῳ, 'when he came to visit him' in his

sickness. So Philemon Μύστις (Mein. IV 15, Kock II 490) πᾶσι τοῖς ἐπισκοπουμένοις δεῖ τὸν κακῶς ἔχοντα πῶς ἔχει λέγειν, Isocr. *Aegin.* c. 13 (where he is speaking of a man who had been ill for six months in Aegina) καὶ τούτων τῶν ταλαιπωριῶν οὐδεὶς τῶν συγγενῶν μετασχεῖν ἠξίωσεν, ἀλλ' οὐδ' ἐπισκεψόμενος ἀφίκετο, c. 15 ἡ μηδ' ἐπισκέψασθαι πώποτ' αὐτὸν ἀξιώσασα τοσοῦτον χρόνον ἀσθενήσαντα, Matth. *Ev.* c. XXV 36 ἠσθένησα καὶ ἐπεσκέψασθέ με. The act. is used in Xen. *Cyr.* V iv 10, VIII ii 25, *Oec.* c. 15, 9, *Mem.* III xi 10.

12. **περίαπτον**, 'an amulet.' Cp. *Mor.* 920 B οἱ ἐν νοσήμασι χρονίοις πρὸς τὰ κοινὰ βοηθήματα καὶ τὰς συνήθεις διαίτας ἀπειπόντες ἐπὶ καθαρμοὺς καὶ περίαπτα τρέπονται, Diog. Laert. IV 55 (Bion) ἐμπεσὼν εἰς νόσον περίαπτα λαβεῖν ἐπείσθη.

13. **ὡς σφόδρα κακῶς ἔχων**, 'as much as to say, he must have been very ill indeed,' c. 5, 4.   **ὁπότε**, *quoniam*.

14. **ὑπομένοι**, 'put up with.'

§ 3 l. 15. **πρὸς τῷ τελευτᾶν ὄντος**, 'when he was at the point of death.' Cp. Aesch. *or.* XI 5 πρὸς τῇ ἀνάγκῃ ταύτῃ γίγνεσθαι.

16. **οἱ βέλτιστοι**, *optimates*.   **οἱ περιόντες**, 'the survivors,' c. 36, 4.

17. **λόγον**, 'reckoning.'

18. **ὅσῃ γένοιτο**: for the agreement with only one of the two subjects, cp. c. 7, 1.   **ἀνεμετροῦντο**, *remetiebantur*, 'were summoning up remembrance of,' 'estimating.' Cp. Eur. *Or.* 14 τί τἄρρητ' ἀναμετρήσασθαί με δεῖ;

§ 4 l. 22. **καθῃρημένου τὴν αἴσθησιν**, 'having lost his consciousness.'

24. **εἰς μέσον**, 'aloud,' 'in the hearing of all.'

25. **ταῦτα . . . αὐτοῦ**, 'these acts of his.'

26. **πρὸς τύχην κοινά**, 'shared by him with fortune,' depending upon fortune as much as himself. There is a similar construction in Xen. *Hell.* VII i 40.

29. **τῶν ὄντων Ἀθηναίων**, 'of all the Athenians there are.' Cp. Dem. *de Pace* § 5 παθεῖν οἷα τῶν ὄντων ἀνθρώπων οὐδένες πώποτε πεπόνθασιν, *Chers.* § 58 ἀνοητότατος πάντων ἂν εἴη τῶν ὄντων ἀνθρώπων.   **δι' ἐμὲ μέλαν ἱμάτιον περιεβάλετο**, 'ever put on mourning because of me.' The Greeks, like the Romans, put on mourning not only for losses by death, but also in token of sorrow of any kind. For the sentiment, cp. Dem. *Lept.* § 82 πολλάκις ὑμῶν στρατηγήσαντος Χαβρίου οὐδενὸς πώποθ' υἱὸς ὀρφανὸς δι' ἐκεῖνον ἐγένετο.

CHAPTER XXXIX

§ 1 l. 1. **τῆς ἐπιεικείας**: the causal genitive after the verbal adjective implying emotion. HA. *Gr.* § 774, G. *Gr.* § 173, 1.

2. **ἥν** refers to one only of the two antecedents. Cp. c. 20, 3.

4. **φρονήματος**, 'lofty sentiment,' c. 4, 4 ; c. 36, 4.

5. **εἰ**, *siquidem*. **τῶν αὑτοῦ καλῶν**, 'of all his honourable achievements.'

6. **μήτε** is generally followed by the indefinite τις; Stegmann p. 24. For the succession μήτε—μήτε—μηδέ, cp. *Luc.* c. 36, 1 οὔτε γὰρ τιμῆς ὁ Λ. οὔτε τιμωρίας κύριος ὑπῆρχεν, οὐδ᾽ εἴα Πομπήϊος κτλ. = οὐδεμιᾶς οὔτε τιμῆς οὔτε τιμωρίας κύριος ὑπῆρχεν οὐδέ κτλ., *Cor.* c. 11, 4 ἐθίζοντες μήτε τυφλότητα μήτ᾽ ἄλλην τινὰ σωματικὴν ἀτυχίαν ὄνειδος ἡγεῖσθαι μηδὲ λοιδορίαν, *Phoc.* c. 4, 2 Φωκίωνα γὰρ οὔτε γελάσαντά τις οὔτε κλαύσαντα ῥᾳδίως εἶδεν οὐδ᾽ ἐν βαλανείῳ δημοσιεύοντι λουσάμενον, in all which passages the clauses containing οὔτε are to be looked upon as a whole in regard to that containing οὐδέ.

χαρίσασθαι, 'gratified,' 'indulged.' Cp. Athenae. 590 E ἐλέῳ χαρισαμένους. **ἀπό**, 'on the strength of,' 'availing himself of.'

7. **χρήσασθαι**: cp. c. 23, 2 ; c. 25, 2. **τινί**: see n. to c. 36, 4.

8. **ἀνηκέστῳ** = ἀκαταλλάκτῳ, 'incurable, past reconciliation,' c. 36, 3.

§ 2 l. 9. **μειρακιώδη**, (otherwise) 'childish,' 'unmeaning.' **σοβαράν**, 'arrogant.' **προσωνυμίαν**, c. 8, 2.

10. **ἓν τοῦτο**: instead of simply continuing: 'that it (*sc.* ἡ προσωνυμία) was given to so benevolent a character and a life so pure and unblemished,' the writer spoils his sentence by changing the construction to an appositive clause (τὸ) Ὀλύμπιον προσαγορεύεσθαι, in order to give point to his description of Olympus as the seat of the gods. The order is: ἓν τοῦτο, ἦθος οὕτως εὐμενὲς καὶ βίον ἐν ἐξουσίᾳ καθαρὸν καὶ ἀμίαντον προσαγορεύεσθαι Ὀλύμπιον, δοκεῖ μοι ποιεῖν τὴν ... προσωνυμίαν ἀνεπίφθονον καὶ πρέπουσαν. By ἐξουσία is meant power which encounters no opposition.

11. **βίον**: c. 27, 4, *Pyrrh.* c. 19, 4 τῶν βίων γενέσθαι θεατήν.

12. **ἀμίαντον**: *Nic.* c. 9, 5, *Mor.* 395 E καθαρὸν καὶ ἀμίαντον, 69 383 B καθαρὸν καὶ ἀβλαβὲς πάντῃ καὶ ἀμίαντον, Plat. *Legg.* 777 E.

13. **ἀξιοῦμεν**, 'we believe' in accordance with the dictates of reason and philosophy, in opposition to the 'ignorant fancies' (ἀμαθέσταται δόξαι) of the poets.

14. ἀναίτιον κακῶν πεφυκός, 'because they are naturally incapable of causing evil.' This sentiment is after Plato; see *Rep.* 379 c οὐδ' ἄρα ὁ θεός, ἐπειδὴ ἀγαθός, πάντων ἂν εἴη αἴτιος, ὡς οἱ πολλοὶ λέγουσιν, ἀλλ' ὀλίγων μὲν τοῖς ἀνθρώποις αἴτιος, πολλῶν δὲ ἀναίτιος. Cp. the Stoic Chrysippus (*Mor.* 1049 E) τῶν αἰσχρῶν τὸ θεῖον παραίτιον γίνεσθαι οὐκ εὐλογόν ἐστιν.

15. τῶν ὄντων, 'the universe.' οὐχ ὥσπερ οἱ ποιηταὶ ... ἁλίσκονται κτλ., 'not like the poets, who confuse us with mere ignorant fancies; and are themselves convicted by their own compositions of inconsistency in calling the place ... and yet at the same time representing the gods themselves as ...'

§ 3 l. 19. ἀσφαλὲς ἕδος: after Homer *Od.* VI 42 ff. :—

Οὔλυμπόνδ', ὅθι φασὶ θεῶν ἕδος ἀσφαλὲς αἰεὶ
ἔμμεναι· οὔτ' ἀνέμοισι τινάσσεται οὔτε ποτ' ὄμβρῳ
δεύεται οὔτε χιὼν ἐπιπίλναται ἀλλὰ μάλ' αἴθρη
πέπταται ἀνέφελος, λευκὴ δ' ἐπιδέδρομεν αἴγλη.

20. οὐ νέφεσι χρώμενον, 'free from clouds.' Cp. *Sertor.* c. 8, 2 ὄμβροις χρώμεναι μετρίοις σπανίως, τὰ δὲ πλεῖστα πνεύμασι μαλακοῖς καὶ δροσοβόλοις (of the Islands of the Blest). For the double οὐ instead of οὔτε—οὔτε, cp. *Cic.* c. 41, 2 and see note to c. 12, 3.

22. ὁμαλῶς with τὸν ἅπαντα: cp. c. 6, 3. ὡς, 'with the (proper) feeling that.'

23. διαγωγῆς, 'mode of existence.'

24. ταραχῆς is a synonym of ὀργῆς. Cp. *Cor.* c. 15, 4 ἀπῄει ταραχῆς μεστὸς ὢν καὶ πικρίας πρὸς τὸν δῆμον.

25. μεστούς sc. ὄντας. G. *MT.*[2] § 911.

26. ἀποφαίνοντες, 'representing.' οὐδέ, *ne—quidem*.

§ 4 l. 27. ἀλλὰ ταῦτα μέν κτλ., c. 6, 3.

30. ἐνειργάζετο, c. 6, 1.

31. οἱ βαρυνόμενοι, 'those who were dissatisfied with.' On this use of βαρύνεσθαι with an objective acc. generally of the thing, see my note to *Nic.* c. 21, 3 and cp. βαρυτέρας c. 16, 1. ζῶντος sc. αὐτοῦ.

32. εὐθὺς γενομένου, c. 21, 2.

33. ἐκ ποδῶν, 'out of the way.' Cp. *Alc.* c. 38, 4 ἐκ ποδῶν ποιήσασθαι τὸν Ἀλκιβιάδην. ῥητόρων, c. 7, 5.

34. δημαγωγῶν, such as Eucrates, Lysicles, Cleon.

Cp. Aristot. Ἀθ. πολ. c. 28 ἕως μὲν οὖν Περικλῆς προειστήκει τοῦ δήμου, βελτίω τὰ κατὰ τὴν πολιτείαν ἦν, τελευτήσαντος δὲ Περικλέους πολὺ χείρω.

πρῶτον γὰρ ὅτε προστάτην ἔλαβεν ὁ δῆμος οὐκ εὐδοκιμοῦντα παρὰ τοῖς
ἐπιεικέσιν· ἐν δὲ τοῖς πρότερον χρόνοις ἀεὶ διετέλουν οἱ ἐπιεικεῖς δημαγω-
γοῦντες . . . Περικλέους δὲ τελευτήσαντος . . . τοῦ δήμου προειστήκει
Κλέων ὁ Κλεαινέτου ὃς δοκεῖ μάλιστα διαφθεῖραι τὸν δῆμον ταῖς ὁρμαῖς.

ἀνωμολογοῦντο, 'were agreed,' 'were all of one and the same
opinion that there never was such a happy mixture of *gravitas*
and *clementia* in any character.' For μή after a verb of consenting, see G. *MT.*² § 685.

35. ἐν ὄγκῳ, as ἐν ἐξουσίᾳ l. 11. For the meaning of ὄγκος,
cp. c. 4, 4; c. 7, 4.

§ 5 l. 38. ἐφάνη τότε . . . γενομένη, 'showed itself then to 70
have been,' c. 24, 5.   ἔρυμα, c. 19, 1.   τῆς πολιτείας, 'the constitution.'

39. φθορά, 'moral corruption,' pernicious influence through
the unfettered κακία of the Demagogues.

40. ἐπέκειτο τοῖς πράγμασιν, 'weighed heavily upon, op-
pressed, the state (c. 33, 6).'

41. ἀπέκρυπτε, 'prevented from showing itself.'

42. ἐν ἐξουσίᾳ : see note to l. 10.

END OF EXPLANATORY NOTES

INDICES

I   INDEX AUCTORUM
II INDEX RERUM ET NOMINUM
III INDEX GRAMMATICUS
IV INDEX GRAECITATIS

INDEX I AUTHORITIES QUOTED OR REFERRED TO BY PLUTARCH

N.B. The References are by *Chapter* and *Section*

AESCHINES SOCRATICUS 24 4, 32 3
ANACREON 27 3
ARCHILOCHUS 28 5
ARISTOPHANES 26 4, 30 4
ARISTOTELES 4 1, 9 2, 10 7, 26 3, 28 1
COMIC POETS, the 4 2, 7 6, 8 3, 13 10, 16 1, 24 6
CRATINUS 3 3, 13 5 6, 24 6
CRITOLAUS 7 5
DURIS SAMIUS 28 1 3
EPHORUS 27 3, 28 1
EUPOLIS 3 4, 24 6
HERACLEIDES PONTICUS 27 3, 35 4
HERMIPPUS (COMICUS) 33 7
IDOMENEUS 10 6, 35 4
ION 5 3, 28 5
PLATO (COMICUS) 4 2
PLATO (PHILOSOPHUS) 7 6, 8 1, 15 4, 24 4
SOCRATES 13 5
STESIMBROTUS 8 6, 13 11, 26 1, 36 3
TELECLEIDES 3 4, 16 2
THEOPHRASTUS (PHILOSOPHUS) 23 1, 35 4, 38 2
THUCYDIDES 9 1, 15 5, 16 1, 28 1 6, 33 1

INDEX II MATTERS

A

Acamantis, one of the ten Attic phylae 3 1
Acarnania 17 2, 19 4
Achaea, friendly to Athens 19 4; A. Phthiotis 17 3
Acharnae, the Peloponnesian army at 33 3
Acharnians, the, a play of Aristophanes, quotation from 30 4
Achelous, the river 19 4
Aegina, saying of Pericles concerning 8 5; the inhabitants of, secretly complain to the Lacedaemonians of their treatment by Athens 29 4; they are expelled from the island by Pericles who sends cleruchs to occupy it 34 1
affection wasted on pet animals unnatural 1 1
Agamemnon 28 5
Agariste, mother of Pericles, niece of Cleisthenes, her dream 3 1
Agatharchus, the painter, and Zeuxis 13 2
Alcibiades, his ambitious schemes 20 3; urges Pericles to resume the administration of affairs 37 1

Alcmaeonidae 3 1 *n*
Alopeke, the Attic deme 11 1
Amazonomachia 31 4
Ambracia 17 2
Anacreon, the poet 2 1
Anaxagoras of Clazomenae (B.C. 500 – 428), the physicist, principal teacher of Pericles 4 4; his solution of a supposed portent 6 2, 8 1; how he mismanaged his estate and was rescued from abject poverty by Pericles 16 5 7; a saying of his *ib.* 32 1 3
Andros, cleruchs sent to 11 5
Annibal 2 4
Anthemocritus 30 3 4
Antisthenes, a saying of 1 5
Archidamus, king of Sparta, his attempts at conciliation 29 5; and Thucydides, son of Melesias 8 4; invades Attica 33 2 3
Archilochus, the poet 2 1; quoted by Pericles to Elpinice 28 5
archonship, election by lot to the 9 3
Areopagus 7 6; Pericles, why not a member of 9 3 *n*
Arginusae 37 5
Argos, statue of Hera at 2 1
Aristides 7 2

Aristodicus of Tanagra, murderer of Ephialtes 10 7
Artemon ὁ μηχανικός, nicknamed ὁ περιφόρητος 27 3 4
arts, manual and fine, do not supply such an incentive to imitation as do great actions, and heroic deeds 1 4, 2 2
Asia 17 1 2
Aspasia of Miletus, her history 24 2; said to have been the cause of the Samian war 25 1; and of the Peloponnesian war 30 4; satirical allusions to her by the comic poets of Athens 24 6; her great renown 24 7; her marriage with Lysicles after the death of Pericles 24 4; charged with ἀσέβεια and other enormities by Hermippus but acquitted 32 1 3
Aspasia, the younger 24 7
Ἀθηνᾶ Ὑγίεια, bronze statue of, on the acropolis 13 8
Athenians, their defeat at Tanagra 10 1; and victory at Oenophyta *ib. n;* the Thirty Years' truce between them and the Lacedaemonians 24 1; their naval supremacy jeopardized by the Samian war 28 6
Athens 26 1; completion of the fortifications of 13 5
Attic, the, comic poets 3 2, 4 2, 7 6, 8 3, 13 10, 16 1, 21 6; Plutarch's judgment on the 13 11
Attica 10 2, 22 1 2, 30 3, 33 2
Axiochus, father of Aspasia 24 2

B

Babylonians, the, a play of Aristophanes 26 4

Bisaltae (Thrace) 11 5
Boeotia, deputies sent to the cities of 17 2; invasion of, by Tolmides 17 3
Boeotian contingent in the invasion of Attica by Archidamus 33 4
[Brea, colony of 11 5 *n*]
Byzantium 17 2

C

Caesar, Augustus 1 1
Callias, 'the rich,' stepson of Pericles 24 5
Callicrates, contractor for the building of the Long Wall at Athens 13 5; joint architect with Ictinus of the Parthenon 13 4
Carthage (Καρχηδών), Athenian dreams of conquest of, discouraged by Pericles 20 3, 21 1
Chalcis (Euboea), the Hippobotae of, expelled by Pericles and the Athenians 23 2
Charinus, savage decree of, against the Megarians 30 3
Cheiron, name given by Plato, the comic poet, to Damon, Pericles' instructor 4 2
Cheirones, the, a play of Cratinus 3 3, 24 6
Chersonese, the Thracian, cleruchs sent to 11 5; expedition of Pericles to 19 1
Cholargus, the deme of Pericles 3 1, and of Xenocles 13 5
Cimon, son of Miltiades and Hegesipyle daughter of Olorus, King of Thrace, Ion's contrast between his affability and the haughtiness of Pericles 5 3; married

to an Arcadian lady 29 3 ;
his sister Elpinice 10 4, 28
4 ; his constant absence
from Athens on foreign
service 7 2 ; his great popularity with the aristocratic
class dictated to Pericles
his choice of party 7 3 ; his
Laconism 9 4 ; ostracised 9
4 ; he returns from exile to
serve in arms amongst his
tribesmen against the Lacedaemonians, that he might
wipe away the suspicion of
Laconism, but is driven back
by the party of Pericles
10 1 ; his absence much regretted by the Athenians
after their defeat at Tanagra
10 2 ; Pericles himself proposes the decree for his recall
10 3 ; his death when in
command at Cyprus 10 7 ; a
representative statesman 16
2 ; his three sons, the treatment of, by Pericles 29 3 ;
Plutarch's *Life of Cimon*
referred to 9 4

Cleandridas, father of Gylippus,
the chief adviser of Pleistoanax, condemned to death,
while living in exile, for
taking a bribe from Pericles
22 3

Cleisthenes, how related to
Pericles 3 1

Cleon attacks Pericles 33 7 ;
prosecutes him 35 4

cleruchies 11 5, 34 1

comic poets, Plutarch's judgment on the 13 11

contemporary history, how
liable it is to pervert the
truth 13 12

Corcyra and Corinth, beginning
of war between 29 1

Corinthians, their complaint
against the Athenians at
Sparta 29 4

Coroebus began the temple
(τελεστήριον) at Eleusis,
which was finished by
Metagenes 13 4

Coronea, battle of 18 2

Cratinus (B.C. 520-422) [of the
deme Oeneis, the creator of
political comedy : 21 pieces
are attributed to him, none
of which gained the prize]
quotation from his plays
Cheirones 3 3, 24 6 and
Nemesis 3 3 and *Thracian
Women* 13 6

Critolaus, a peripatetic philosopher of the 2nd cent. B.C.
He was one of the embassy
sent to Rome by Athens to
obtain a remission of the
fine of 500 talents, the other
two being Carneades and the
Stoic Diogenes 7 5. See
Cat. ma. c. 22, Pausanias
VII 11, 4, Aul. Gell. VI 14 8

Cylon, (τὸ Κυλώνειον ἄγος) 33 1

Cyprus 26 1 ; death of Cimon
at 10 7

Cyrus, the younger and Milto
24 7

D

Damon, Pericles' master in
music under which title he
dissembles his real talents 4
1 ; his ostracism 4 2 ; reference to him in the comic
poet Plato *ib.*

Damonides of the deme Oa,
adviser of Pericles 9 2

Deianeira, the new name
given to Aspasia by Eupolis
24 6

Delian league, the, becomes the Athenian empire 12 2 n
Delos, removal of the confederate treasure from the Apollonion of, to Athens 12 1
Delphi, restoration of the temple at, to the Delphians by the Lacedaemonians 21 2; recovered from them by Pericles for the Phocians ib.
Demi, the, a play of Eupolis 3 4, 24 6
dicasts, salary of the 9 3
Dinomache, the first wife of Pericles 3 1, p. 81, 24 5 n
Diopeithes, decree of, for the impeachment of atheist philosophers, aimed at Pericles indirectly 32 1
Dipylon, another name for the Thriasian gate at Athens 30 3
disfranchisement of a large number of the population of Athens in 444 B.C. 37 2
diviners (μάντεις), though regarded as interpreters of the divine will, were distinct from the priests; their science was a personal gift, an hereditary privilege or an acquired aptitude 6 2
Dorians, the Asiatic 17 2
Dracontides, psephism of, against Pericles 32 2
Duris of Samos, an untrustworthy authority 28 3
dynasts, alliance of Athenians with foreign 15 1

E

Eclipse, solar 35 1 2
Egypt, project for invasion of, discouraged by Pericles 21 2; gift of corn sent from a king of, to the Athenians 37 3
Elea 4 3
Eleios, son of Cimon 29 3
Eleusis, the τελεστήριον of, built by Coroebus and Metagenes 13 4
Elpinice, sister of Cimon, her influence over Pericles 10 5; said to have negotiated with Pericles the terms on which her brother should return to Athens 10 4; rebukes Pericles on his return from Samos 28 4 5
engines of war employed at the blockade of Samos 27 3
Ephialtes, son of Sophonides, a friend and ally of Pericles the people's advocate, a representative statesman 16 2; his attack on the Areopagus 7 6, 9 4; his secret assassination by Aristodicus, or an agent of the oligarchical party 10 7
Epidaurus, besieged by Pericles 35 3
Epilycus 36 1
Epitimos of Pharsalus 36 3
Euboea 7 6, 17 3; Athenian invasion of 22 1; conquest of 23 2
Eupolis, one of the masters of the ancient comedy, a contemporary of Aristophanes, his Δῆμοι 3 4, 24 6
Europe 17 1
Euryptolemus, son of Megacles, cousin of Pericles 7 4. See comm. p. 81
Evangelos, steward of Pericles 16 5

F

Fabius Maximus, the Roman general, opponent of Hannibal 2 4
'Few, the,' as opp. to the Demos 11 3
flute-players in disesteem at Athens 1 5
fortune, the goods of, contrasted with heroic and good deeds 2 3

G

Glycon, decree of, in favour of Meno 31 5
gods, immortality of the, how inferred 8 6; the abode of the gods as pictured by the poets in strange contrast with their own doings 39 3
Gylippus, son of Cleandridas, the Spartan commander against the Athenians in Sicily, his covetousness hereditary 22 3, his expulsion from Sparta therefor *ib.*

H

Hagnon, his amendment of the psephism of Dracontides 32 2
Hellas proper as opp. to Sicily etc. 22 1
Hellespont, deputies sent to the cities of the 17 2
Hera, statue of, at Argos 2 1; the new, name given by Eupolis to Aspasia 24 6
Hermippus, the comic poet, prosecutes Aspasia 32 1
Hermotimus 24 7
heroes who have fallen in battle, immortality of 8 6
Hestiaea (Euboea), population of, expelled, and an Athenian κληρουχία settled at 23 2
Hippobotae of Chalcis, treatment of the, by Pericles 23 2
Hipponicus, son of Callias, first husband of Pericles' wife 24 5: see p. 81
historical truth, difficulty of arriving at 13 12
Hygieia Athena, statue of, at Athens 13 8

I

Ictinus, joint-architect with Callicrates of the Parthenon 13 4
ignoble occupations 1 4
intellect and sense, contrasts between the objects of 1 2
Ion, the poet, misconstrues Pericles' manner as haughty and disdainful in contrast with Cimon's complaisance 5 3
Ionians, the Asiatic 17 2, the Samians the most powerful of the 28 5
Ionian woman ('Ιάς) 24 2
Islands, the, of the Delian-Attic confederacy 7 6
Ismenias, the flute-player 1 5
Italia 11 5
Ithagenes, father of the philosopher Melissus 26 2

K

Κρόνος 3 3

L

Labour spent on useless objects 2 1

Lacedaemon 22 3, 30 1
Lacedaemonians, opposition of, to the synod proposed by Pericles 17 3; his policy was to thwart them 21 1; their intrigues in Phocis upset by Pericles 22 1; Thirty Years' truce between them and the Athenians 24 1
Lacedaemonius, son of Cimon, sent to Corcyra in command of too small a squadron 29 2
Lacrateides, prosecutor of Pericles, according to one authority 35 4
Lamachus 20 1
Lampon ὁ μάντις and a supposed portent 6 2 3
learning and sight-seeing, love of, natural to man 1 1
Lemnos 25 1
Leocrates, a representative character 16 2
Lesbos 17 2
Locri 17 2
Lysander, Plutarch's *Life* of, referred to 22 3
Lysicles, the sheep-dealer, owed his rise to Aspasia, whom he married after the death of Pericles 24 4

M

Malian gulf, the 17 3
Medes, the 28 4
Megarians 30 2; revolt of the 22 1; join the Corinthians in their complaint against Athens 29 4; cause the death of Anthemocritus, the herald 30 3; make Pericles and Aspasia accountable for the Peloponnesian war 30 4; the Megarian decree upheld by Pericles 29 5, 30 3, 31 1
Megarid, the 30 3; invasion of, by Pericles 34 2
Melissus, the philosopher, persuades the Samians to attack the Athenians during the absence of Pericles 26 2 3, 27 1
Menexenus the so-called dialogue of Plato and Aspasia 24 4
Menippus, the wife of, and Pericles 13 10
Menon, one of Phidias' *collaborateurs* 31 2; informs against him and is rewarded with ἀτέλεια 31 5
Metagenes, of the deme Xupete, finished the temple at Eleusis, which was begun by Coroebus 13 4
metaphors from music 8 1, 15 2 4; from the management of horses 11 4, 15 3; from the wrestling school 1 1, 8 4; from metallurgy 11 3; from surgery 15 3; nautical 15 4, 23 5
Milesians, the 24 1, 25 1, 28 2
Miletus (Ionia), at war with Samos 24 1; birth-place of Aspasia 24 1
Milto, of Phocaea, daughter of Hermotimus and a concubine of Cyrus the younger, her name changed to Aspasia 24 6
Mnesicles, architect of the Propylaea 13 7
music, contests in, instituted by Pericles 13 6; metaphors borrowed from 8 1, 15 2
Mycale, victory of 3 1
Mycon 31 5
Myronides, a representative

statesman 16 2 ; a character in the Δῆμοι of Eupolis 24 6

N

Naxos, cleruchs sent to 11 5
Nemea 19 3
Nemesis, a play of Cratinus 3 3
Νοῦς, name given to Anaxagoras 4 4

O

Oa, a deme in the Pandionis phylē, to be distinguished from Oie in the Oeneis phylē 9 2
Odeum, the, built in imitation of the Royal Pavilion of the Persians 13 5
Oeniadae, the people of 19 4
Oenophyta, Athenian victory at 10 1 *n*
Oeta 17 3
Olympius, a nickname of Pericles 8 2, 39 1
Omphale, the new, name given to Aspasia by the comic poets 24 6
ostracism, purpose of 14 2 ; limitation of its duration to ten years 10 1 [Ostracism was a judgment pronounced by the people of Athens, by secret ballot of one name only, against any citizens whose influence and conduct appeared to menace the liberty or tranquillity of the state. Every year at the time of the general assembly of the sixth prytany, the people were consulted on the opportuneness of applying ostracism. If any one favoured it, on a day fixed for taking the votes, the ten tribes met in the agora, which was divided for that occasion into ten compartments. Each citizen wrote on a shell (ὄστρακον) the name of the person whom he wished to banish. At least 6000 suffrages were required to make the vote valid. He who had the largest number of votes against him was obliged to leave the country. Originally his banishment lasted ten years. It did not affect the honour of the person banished, nor his fortune, nor his civic rights. The law of ostracism was enforced for the first time in B.C. 488/7, in the person of Hipparchus son of Charmus (Plut. *Nic.* c. 11, 6, Aristot. Ἀθ. πολ. c. 22, 4). It was suppressed in the last part of the fifth century B.C.]

P

Panathenaea, musical festival at the, instituted by Pericles 13 6
Paralus, second son of Pericles 21 5 ; his death 36 4
Parmenides 4 3
Parthenon, architects of the 13 4
Pegae (Pagae), in the Megarid 19 2
Peloponnesian war 29 1 ; various accounts of the origin of 31 1
Peloponnesians, army of the 22 1, 33 4, 34 1

Peloponnesus, deputation from Athens to the cities of the 17 2 3, 19 2, 34 2

Pericles, 2 4; points of resemblance between him and Fabius Maximus 2 4; his deme and phylê 3 1; his lineage 3 1; dream of his mother Agariste before his birth 3 2; the peculiar conformation of his head turned into ridicule by the comic poets of the time 3 2 3; reference to him by Eupolis as a δημαγωγός 3 4; his teachers 4 1 3; his lofty tone and studied dignity of manner and carriage misrepresented by Ion as natural pride and haughtiness and contrasted with the affability of Cimon 5 3; more favourably judged by Zeno 5 4; Anaxagoras exercised the greatest influence in moulding his character 4 4; instance of his patience and imperturbability of temper under provocation 5 2 3; his exemption from superstitious fears due to Anaxagoras 6 1; his reason for abstaining from politics when young and preferring a military life 7 1; his choice of party, as a lever against Cimon, contrary to his natural bias 7 2 3; change in his mode of life and habits, when he entered upon public life 7 4; he reserved his appearance in public for exceptional occasions, relying on his friends for ordinary ones 7 5; influence of Anaxagoras on his style of speaking 8 1; why called 'Olympian' 8 2; the explanation given by the comic poets 8 3; jocular remark by Thucydides his rival on his art in speaking 8 4; he never spoke without the most careful preparation 8 4; he has left no writings, only psephisms, and only a few sayings of his are on record 8 5 6; the character and consequences of his administration variously judged 9 1; his rivalry with Cimon 9 2; by what arts he ingratiated himself with the people 9 3; his restriction of the jurisdiction of the Areopagus, through the agency of Ephialtes 9 4; by his powerful influence over the people he procures the ostracism of Cimon 9 4; but after the defeat at Tanagra repairs the wrong by himself proposing the decree for his recall 10 3; some ascribe his change of attitude to the mediation of Elpinice 10 4 5; at whose entreaty on a former occasion, when ordered to conduct an impeachment of Cimon, he had abstained from putting forth his power and his opponent was acquitted 10 5; charged by Idomeneus in his *Memoirs* with the treacherous murder of his friend and ally Ephialtes 10 6; means resorted to by Pericles for retaining his hold of popular favour, when Thucydides took Cimon's place as leader of the aristocratical party, to which he gives more cohesion

11 2 3 4; provides relief for the poorer citizens by cleruchies, which at the same time serve as a check on the neighbouring allies 11 5; his political opponents criticise the means he employed for making the city of Athens the most superb of capitals; they disapproved of the removal of the treasure from Delos to Athens, which they said belonged to the Confederacy and not to Athens alone 12 1 2; his arguments in reply 12 3 4; picture of activity and universal industry which prevailed in the city 12 5 6 7; marvellous rapidity of execution and exquisite finish of the masterly monuments of his age 13 1; they still retained their freshness five centuries afterwards, and seemed to wear the bloom of perpetual youth 13 3; Phidias director-general of his works 13 4 9; the Parthenon, the temple of Eleusis, the Odeion, the Propylaea 13 4 5 7; institutes a contest of music at the Panathenaea 13 6; the accident which led him to consecrate a statue to Athena as goddess of the healing art 13 8; calumnious misrepresentations of the relation between Pericles and Phidias, especially by the comic poets 13 9 10; attacked for his extravagant expenditure by the party of Thucydides, he offers to pay for the public works from his private fortune, if his name may be inscribed upon them, but the people could not think of sparing money at the cost of their artistical reputation and refused to allow him 14; effect of the ostracism of Thucydides upon his attitude and temper 15 1; his great personal ascendency 15 2; his vigour and energy of government 15 3; his tact in managing the people and their confidence in him 15 4; his disinterestedness and integrity 15 5; he died without adding a single drachm to his patrimony *ib.*; attacked for his abuse of power by the comic poets 16 1; long duration of his pre-eminence 16 2; he held the office of strategus for fifteen years without intermission after the death of Thucydides 16 3; his incorruptibility during that period, though he was not indifferent to making money and by his strict domestic economy he came to be regarded in his own family as close and too thrifty 16 4, 36 1; the careful management of his estate compared with the negligence of Anaxagoras who fell into extreme poverty 16 5; his charity 16 6; his decree, proposing a re-union of representatives from all the Greek towns of Europe and Asia at Athens for the discussion of a project for lasting peace and union, and for rebuilding the temples left in ruins by the Persian invasion and of

securing freedom of navigation in the Grecian seas 17 1; ambassadors for this purpose sent to the several city-states in Europe and Asia 17 2; his scheme frustrated in the Peloponnesus by Spartan intrigues 17 3; Pericles as a general 18 1; his opposition to the ill-timed expedition of Tolmides into Bœotia, which ended so disastrously at Coronea, brought him credit finally 18 2 3; his expedition to the Chersonese was more popular than any other, because it put a stop to the incursion of the neighbouring Thracians 19 1; his maritime campaign against the Peloponnese 19 2; his defeat of the Sicyonians 19 3; his raid on Acarnania 19 4; his demonstration in the Pontus 20 1; his intervention in favour of Sinope, to which a colony of 600 Athenians is sent 20 2; his discouragement of the ambitious schemes of foreign conquest, which were in favour at Athens 20 2 3, 21 1; he employs the forces of Athens to secure and consolidate their empire 21 1; his policy was henceforth to thwart the Spartans 21 1; he upsets their intrigues in Phocis and regains the right of προμαντεία in the temple at Delphi 21 2; the wisdom of his policy in confining the Athenian power within the limits of Greece proper proved by subsequent events; the revolt of Euboea, defection of Megara, and the invasion of Attica by the Peloponnesians under Pleistoanax, whose counsellor Cleandridas he bribes to withdraw the army 22; his employment of secret-service money to gain time for preparation 23 1; his re-conquest of Euboea, expulsion of the Hippobotae from Chalcis and of the entire population from Hestiaea 23 2; after the Thirty Years' truce he decrees war against Samos to please Aspasia 24 1, 25 1; his infatuation for Aspasia 24 5; he divorces his first wife by whom he had two sons Xanthippus and Paralus, in order to marry her 24 5; his half-blood son by Aspasia 24 6; overthrows the oligarchy at Samos and establishes a democracy 25 1; refuses the bribe of the Samian hostages, who were sent to Lemnos, as well as that of Pissuthnes satrap of Sardes *ib.*; the Samians revolt and Pericles returns from Athens and wins a decisive victory over them in a naval combat off Tragiae 25 3; he lays siege to Samos, which is defended by Melissus 26 1; sails southward to intercept, as some say, the Phoenician fleet which was expected to help the Samians 26 2; during his absence Melissus wins a victory and re-victuals the place *ib.*; branding of each other's captives 26 3; he defeats

Melissus and blockades Samos 27 1; he employs engines of war constructed by the engineer Artemon 27 3; Duris refuted for imputing barbarous acts to Pericles 28 1 2; his funeral oration, on his return to Athens, over those who had fallen in the Samian war 8 6, 28 3; justly proud of his subjugation of Samos, notwithstanding the ironical comparison of Elpinice and the sneers of Ion 28 4 5; the opinion of Thucydides on the crisis 28 6; Pericles sends Lacedaemonius, son of Cimon, in command of an insufficient force to help Corcyra against Corinth in order to compromise him 29 2; the re-inforcements sent by him afterwards arrive too late to be of use 29 3; complaints of the Corinthians and Megarians against Athens at Lacedaemon 29 4; the Aeginetans join in these secretly *ib.*; attempts at conciliation by Archidamus 29 5; but the decree against the Megarians, maintained at the instance of Pericles, whose feeling towards them amounted to a personal animosity (30 2), stands in the way; for which reason he is considered the sole cause of the war *ib.*; deputation from Lacedaemon on the subject of the decree; resistance of Pericles who accuses the Megarians of impiety 30 1 2; death of the herald whom he sent with remonstrances against them 30 3; savage decree of Charinus thereupon and definitive rupture *ib.*; the Megarians deny the murder of Anthemocritus and impute the blame to Aspasia and Pericles 30 4; whatever the motive may have been, Pericles was certainly the cause of the Megarian decree not being repealed 31 1; attack made upon him through Phidias as a test of the popular feeling for him 31 2; a bill of Diopeithes against atheism indirectly aimed at him through Anaxagoras 32 2; a bill of Dracontides, with the amendment of Hagnon, directed against his financial administration 32 2; his intercession in favour of Aspasia, who had been charged by Hermippus with impiety and other crimes (32 1), procures her acquittal 32 3; he is instrumental to the removal of Anaxagoras from Athens *ib.*; and kindles the war in order to make himself necessary *ib.*; the Lacedaemonian attempt to procure the expulsion of Pericles as an Alcmaeonid from Athens serves only to enhance his credit 33 1; his generous offer on occasion of the invasion of Attica by Archidamus 33 2; disregarding the importunity of his friends and the clamours of his adversaries, he keeps the people confined in the city and avoids engaging the enemy 33 3; he does what he can to soothe the general irritation at what was thought his cowardly policy 33 4; he abstains from summoning any public meeting at which the popular excitement might find expression 33 5; Cleon avails himself of the public indignation to attack him, as a stepping-stone to raise himself to power 33 7; Pericles, unmoved by complaints, sends a fleet of 100 vessels to ravage the shores of the Peloponnesus, but remains at home himself until the retirement of the enemy 34 1; he sends a body of cleruchs to Aegina after expelling the inhabitants *ib.*; the Megarid invaded and ravaged by him 34 2; the popular resentment against him increased by the outbreak of the plague 34 2 3 4; failure of the expedition undertaken by him to make reprisals for the damage done to Attica 35 1 3; his illustration of a solar eclipse 35 2; fails in an attack on Epidaurus because of the spread of the plague 35 3; becomes the object of an outbreak of popular odium, which leads to his deposition from the office of στρατηγός, and the imposition of a fine 35 4; his domestic misfortunes 36 1; misconduct of his eldest son with whom he is on bad terms 36 2 3; loses both of his sons and also his sister by the plague 36 4; his despair on the death of his younger son 36 5; is reinstated as strategus 37 1; the Athenians, moved by his domestic trials, pass a decree for making his son by Aspasia a citizen despite his own statute, and so saving his house from extinction 37 2 3 4 5; he is attacked by the plague, which in his case exhibits the symptoms of a lingering malady 38 1; scene at his death-bed 38 3; his last words to his friends 38 4; Plutarch's reflexions on his admirable qualities 39 1; his name 'Olympius' justified 39 2; his countrymen are soon made to feel their great loss 39 4; some sayings of Pericles 8 5 6, 18 2, 33 4

Pericles, the νόθος son of the former by Aspasia 24 6; made an Athenian citizen 37 5; is put to death after the battle of Arginusae *ib.*

Phidias, the sculptor of the statue of Olympian Zeus 2 1; and of the chryselephantine statue of Athena 13 9, 31 2; his close intimacy and influence with Pericles and his great reputation, and the fact of his having introduced into his *Amazonomachia* portraits of himself and Pericles brought him many enemies and created much jealousy 31 2 4, 32 3; he had the general superintendence of all the great works of Pericles 13 4 9; scandalous stories circulated about him 13 10; he is charged with theft and thrown into prison where he died 31 5

Philetas, the poet 2 1
Philip of Macedon, a saying of 1 5
Phleius (Argolis), Timon of 4 3
Phocaea, a woman of (Φωκαίς) 24 7
Phocians, the, and Delphi 21 2
Phocis, deputies sent to the cities of 17 2
Phoenicians 28 4; their fleet 26 1
Phthiotian Achaeans 17 3
physical science and oratory 8 1
Pisa (Olympia), statue of Zeus at, by Phidias 2 1
Pisistratidae 3 1; the new, name given to Pericles' friends 16 1
Pisistratus, the despot, resemblance between him and Pericles 7 1
Pissuthnes, a Persian, offers Pericles a bribe to spare Samos and being refused removes the Samian hostages from Lemnos 25 2
plague, outbreak of the 34 2
Plato, the comic poet, his play Σοφισταί 4 2
Plato, the philosopher, his dialogue Menexenus 24 4
Pleistoanax, the youthful king of Sparta, at the head of a Peloponnesian army, bribed by Pericles to recross the frontier of Attica 22 1 2; fined therefor, went into voluntary exile 22 3
poets, their inconsistent fancies about the abode of the gods 29 2 3
Polyalces, one of the second embassy from Sparta to Athens 30 1

Polycleitus, sculptor of the statue of Hera at Argos 2 1
Polycrates, despot of Samos 26 4
Pontus 20 1
portraits of Pericles and Phidias introduced in the *Amazonomachia* on the shield of Pallas 31 4
Potidaea, a subject city-state of Athens, and a colony of Corinth, revolt and siege of 29 4
Priene, war between Samos and Miletus for 25 1
Propylaea, the, took five years to build 13 7; Mnesicles architect of *ibid.*
Protagoras 36 3
psephisms, the only extant compositions of Pericles 8 5
public men, their daily life, interest of 7 5
Pyrilampes, ἑταῖρος of Pericles, scandal about 13 10 [He was wounded and taken prisoner at Delium; he probably took part in the mission of Callias to Susa, whence he introduced peacocks, hitherto unknown in Greece. His son Demos was famed for his personal beauty, and for his peacocks; Eupolis *fr.* 36 Kock, Arist. *Vesp.* 981, Plat. *Gorg.* 481 D, 513 B. Pyrilampes by his second wife Perictione, widow of Ariston, was the father of Plato's half-brother Ariston ; Plato *Parmen.* 126 E, Plut. *de frat. am.* c. 12]
Pythocleides, said by Aristotle to have been the instructor of Pericles in music 4 1

Q

Quoits, use of, for bells 6 4

R

Rhodes 17 2
riches, worthy employment of 16 6
Rome 1 1

S

Sacred war, the 21 1
Salaminian galley, the 7 5
salary of the dicasts 9 3
Samians, hostages of the, sent by Pericles to Lemnos 25 1; victory over, by Pericles 25 3; during the temporary absence of Pericles, they win a victory, which gives them the command of the sea 26 2; treatment of Athenian prisoners by the 26 3; cruelty said by Duris to have been practised on, by the Athenians 28 2; the most powerful of the Ionians 28 5
Samos, alleged cause of the war with 24 1, 27 3; supposed to have been brought about by Aspasia's partiality for her compatriots of Miletus 25 1; a democracy established by Pericles at 25 2; revolt of 25 3; siege of, by Pericles 26 1; blockade of, by Pericles 27 1; surrender of 28 1
[Shield, the Strangford 31 4 *n*]
Sicily, ambitious projects at Athens for invasion of, discouraged by Pericles 20 3
Sicyonians, defeat of the, by Pericles 19 3

Σιμαίθα 30 4
Simmias, prosecutor of Pericles according to some 35 4
Sinope 20 1; deposition of Timesilaus the tyrant of, and occupation of the city by Athenian colonists 20 2
Socrates, his frequent visits to Aspasia 24 3; his pupils and the wives of his friends attend her lectures *ib.*
Sophistae, a play of Plato's 4 2
Sophocles, a στρατηγός in the Samian war, the saying of Pericles about him 8 5
Sparta 23 1
Stesimbrotus quotes a sophistical enthymem from the Samian epitaphios of Pericles 8 6; memoir-like contemporary history of, unsatisfactory 13 11; his scurrilous story about Pericles and his son's wife *ibid.*
sun-dials 6 4
superstition, natural philosophy the enemy of 6 1
Sybaris re-founded 11 5

T

Tanagra (Boeotia), invasion of its territory by a Lacedaemonian army 10 1; Aristodicus of Tanagra, the murderer of Ephialtes 10 7
Teleclides [a poet of the ancient comedy, an opponent of Pericles and at a later period a friend of Nicias; there are fragments of five of his comedies extant] 3 4, 16 2
Teles 33 7
Thargelia, an Ionian beauty of Miletus 24 2

Themistocles, exile of 7 2
Thessalians 17 3
Thessalus, son of Cimon 29 3 [*Alc.* c. 19, 2; c. 22, 3]
Thirty Years' truce, the 24 1
Thrace, Athenian settlement in 11 5; deputies sent from Athens to 17 2
Thracians, bordering on the Chersonese 19 1
Thriasian gate, the 30 3
Thucydides, of the deme Alopeke, son of Melesias, the statesman 6 2 3; a jocular saying of his about the oratory of Pericles 8 4; appointed to succeed Cimon as political opponent of Pericles 11 1; how he organises and gives cohesion to his party 11 2; the rivalry of the two statesmen makes the cleavage deeper between the Demos and the Few and the conflict more bitter 11 3; a representative character 16 2; ostracism of 6 3, 14 2, 16 3
Thurii, colonisation of 11 5
time, the wisest counsellor 18 2
Timesilaus 20 1
Timon of Phleius, his lines on Zeno 4 3
Tisander, son of Epilycus, father-in-law of Xanthippus 36 2
Tolmides, son of Tolmaeus, a representative man 16 2, 18 2, 19 3; his death on the battle-field of Coronea 18 3
toreutic art, the 12 6
Tragiae (Tragia) an island off Samos 25 2

trial by dicasts, solemn method of special 32 2
Troy a βάρβαρος πόλις 28 5
Tyrrhenia 20 3

W

Wall, the Long, at Athens, built by Callicrates 13 5
white day, origin of the name 27 2
wolf, inscriptions on the brazen, at Delphi 21 2
work and workman 2 2

X

Xanthippus, father of Pericles, the victor of Mycale 3 1
Xanthippus, elder of the two legitimate sons of Pericles (named after his grandfather) 24 5; his extravagant wife 36 1; his ungrateful conduct to his father 36 2 3; falls a victim to the plague 36 4
Xenocles, of Cholargus, the architect who added the roof with a circular aperture (ὀπαῖον) to the Ἀνάκτορον at Eleusis 13 5
Xupete, a deme in the phylé Cecropis, birth-place of Metagenes 13 4

Z

Zenon, the Eleatic philosopher, one of the instructors of Pericles 4 3, 5 4
Zeus, statue of Olympian 2 1
Zeuxis the painter and Agatharchus 13 2

INDEX III GRAMMAR

abstract nouns, plural of, used distributively 2 4, 5 3, 13 12, 15 1

accusative of kindred formation 9 4, 11 3, 12 2, 16 7, 25 1, 34 4, 38 1; of kindred meaning 10 2 5, represented by neuter adjective 1 5; of contents 5 4; of point of view with verbs 11 2, 15 2, with adj. 3 2, 7 1, 24 1 2 4 7, 26 3, 34 3; after perfect pass. participle 32 4, 38 4; proleptic 31 1; double 34 2; after a verb of taking away 28 6; objective and cognate 9 4, 26 3; adverbial 7 2 5, 13 8, 15 2 3, 20 2, 27 4

adjective, assimilation of its gender to that of the dependent partitive gen. 19 3, 27 3; neuter, in collective sense 15 4; predicate 6 2, 8 5, 12 4, 13 8, 14 1, 16 5, 28 2

adverbs of intensity emphasised by καί, as πάνυ 25 3, μάλα 15 3

aorist, where we use pluperfect 15 5, 17 1, 21 2; gnomic 2 1

apposition, instances of 4 2

article, neuter, with participle or adjective for substantive 13 4, 15 4; anticipatory or assumptive 24 1; with τοιοῦτος to designate a definite class 1 5, 7 4; used for possessive pronoun 4 1, 6 2, 8 5, 10 1, 11 1, 12 7; omitted in enumeration 15 1; with designations of place as ἀπ' ἀγορᾶς 24 6, ἐν ἀγορᾷ 31 2, κατ' ἀγοράν 5 2, ἐπ' ἀγοράν 7 4, ἐξ ἀγροῦ 6 2, ἐν ἄστει 11 4, ἐν ἐκκλησίᾳ, 31 3, ἐν πελάγει 33 6, πόρρω θαλάττης 19 3

attraction 3 4, 27 4 (μηδὲν ἐμπεσεῖν τῶν ἄνωθεν), 34 4

chiasmus, instances of 7 2, 9 1

conditional sentences; imperfect in past unreal condition 1 5, 24 7, 28 5, 29 5, 34 2; ἄν omitted in apodosis 24 7; protasis with the opt. followed by a fut. with the indic. in apodosis 18 2

dative of specification 3 2, 13 1 3 5, 27 3, 29 3; (adverbial) of manner (σιωπῇ) 5 2, 34 1, (σπουδῇ) 8 3; of instrument or means 2 3, 9 2 3, 15 3

4, 18 3, 27 3; of cause 31
5, 31 3; of agency after
perfect 14 1; after aor. pass.
33 7; of degree of difference
15 5, 37 4; of time 13 1, 18
3, 27 3, 28 1 5; of interest
10 3, 13 4, 22 1, 36 1;
of accompaniment (*dativus
militaris*) 10 1, 19 2 3 4,
20 1, 23 2, 25 3, 33 3;
after verbs in composition as
ἐγκαρτερεῖν 36 5; ἐμμένειν 29
5; ἐμποιεῖ 14; ἐμφύεται 10
6; ἐνδιατρῖψαι 24; ἐνδιεσπάρθαι 11 2; ἐνεργάζεται 6 1;
ἐντίθησιν 13 2; ἐπιπροσθοῦντα
13 12; ἐπιτραγῳδεῖ 28 1;
ὑποχεόμενος 8 1; προπολε-
μοῦντες 12 3; προσεργάζεσθαι
31 3
ellipse of parts of εἶναι: ἐστίν
1 1, 2 1, 5 1, 18 1, 30 1, 33
2; ἦν 15 4, 16 5, 31 2; of
nouns (παραλίας sc. γῆς) 19
3; (Μεγαρικήν sc. γῆν) 34 2;
(γονεῖς) 3 1
epanaphora 3 4, 15 1 3, 16 4,
18 3, 26 2, 33 6, 37 3
genitive, predicate of origin,
possession etc. 3 1, 6 4, 8 4,
12 3, 23 1; of emotion after
verbal adj. 39 1; of separation 5 1; partitive 8 4, 12
1, 23 1, 24 4, 25 1, 30 3; of
a quality in 7 5, 38 4;
chorographic 19 2; demonymic 3 1; objective, equivalent to εἰς or ἐπί w. acc. 7 4,
15 5 (πίστις τοῦ ἀνδρός);
double, objective and sub-
jective 4 1
imperfect of attempted action
21 1, 23 1
infinitive after verb of fearing
7 1, 33 5; after ὡς 10 5, 12
7; telic with article 11 5

infinitive, articular, in the
nominative, as subject
8 5
,, in the genitive after
αἰτίαν 31 1, to denote
purpose 11 5, with
μετά 24 6, with ἐκ
18 1
,, in the dative to denote
means 1 3, cause 2 4,
with ἐν 5 1, 13 2, with
ἐπί 13 2, with πρός 8
1, 38 3, after ἀκολουθεῖν
1 4
,, in the accusative with
διά 9 3, 18 2, 26 4;
with πρός 1 4
ingressive aorist 7 2; participle
of the 7 6, 9 4, 31 5
middle, reciprocal 20 2, 37 3
optative of recurrence 8 3, 20
1; with ὅπως as an object
clause after a verb of commanding 32 2; future in
oblique clause 31 2; in dependent clause of an indirect
quotation 6 2
parataxis with μέν—δέ 28 5
participle, present, indicating
purpose 4 2, 7 3, 10 5, 11 5,
17 1, 24 1, 25 2; cause 31
5; future 11 1, 24 3, with
the article representing a
final relative clause 17 1; of
the imperfect 4 3, 5 3; as a
substitute for regular protasis 18 2; with article used
substantively 12 5, 29 3, 32
1; neuter, in collective sense
12 5, 15 4
pronoun, neuter, in collective
sense 15 4
transposition of correlative
particles 14 2, 20 1
verbal noun taking the construction of its verb 9 1

Words occurring in quotations from other authors are printed in small uncials

)(indicates 'as distinguished from,' 'opposed to'

The Numerals affixed to words denote respectively :—

- [1] Words or forms of words peculiar to Plutarch and late Greek, and not used in the best Attic
- [2] Words used by Plutarch in a sense other than classical
- [3] Poetical words
- [4] Words found only once in Plutarch
- [5] Ionic words

INDEX IV GREEK

A

ἀ-βελτερία : τὴν ἀ. 38 2
ἀ-βλαβής : ἡδονὰς ἀ. 15 3
ἀγαθός : 1. Of Persons, *fortis* 7 1; πολλοῖς καὶ ἀ. ὁπλίταις 22 2; πολλοὺς καὶ ἀ. ὁπλίτας 35 1; πολλοὺς καὶ ἀ. πολίτας 28 4, 18 3.—*probus*: ἀνὴρ ἀ. 7 1; τῶν ἀ. ἀνδρῶν 7 5; τῶν καλῶν καὶ ἀ. ἀνδρῶν 7 3, 8 4; τοὺς καλοὺς κἀγαθοὺς καλουμένους ἄνδρας 11 2.— 2. Of Things: of the feeling awakened by what is good, 'joyful,' μετ' ἐλπίδων ἀ. 6 1.—Neut. 'a blessing,' 'benefit': τὸ οἰκεῖον ἀ. 1 3; τῶν ἐκ τῆς τύχης ἀ. 2 3; αἴτιον ἀγαθῶν 39 2; τοῖς ἀ. ἃ παρέχουσιν 8 6
ἄγαλμα, 'the statue' of any god or deified hero: τὸ χαλκοῦν ἄ. 13 8; ἐργολάβος τοῦ ἀ. 31 2; τῷ ἀ. 31 3; περιαπτομένην ἀγάλματα 12 2
ἀγαπᾶν, 'to like,' 'to be fond of a thing': τὰς πράξεις ἀγαπῶμεν 2 3. PASS. ἠγαπήθη, *placuit* 19 1.—'to pet,' 'fondle': κυνῶν τέκνα ... ἀγαπῶντας 1 1.—PASS. *amari*, 'to be beloved': ὑπὸ τῶν καλῶν κἀγαθῶν ἀνδρῶν ἀγαπώ-

μενον 7 3; τὴν ἀγαπωμένην ὑπ' αὐτοῦ μάλιστα 21 7
ἀγάπησις [1] : ἐρωτική τις ἀ. 24 5
ἀγγεῖον cerebri 6 2
ἄγειν : τὰς γυναῖκας ἦγον ὡς αὐτήν 24 3; ὅ τι περ τῶν κάτωθεν ἤγαγες 3 4; τὰ ἐγκλήματα εἰς διαλύσεις ἄγοντος 29 5; βουλόμενον ἦγε τὸν δῆμον 15 3.—'to keep,' 'observe' Fr. *mener*: τὴν εἰρήνην ἄγωσι 17 1.—PASS. μουσικῆς ἀγῶνα ἄγεσθαι 13 6
ἀ-γεννής : ἐξ ἀ. καὶ ταπεινοῦ 24 4
ἀ-γήρως : ψυχὴν ἀγήρω 13 3
ἀ-γνοεῖν : τοῖς ἀγνοοῦσι τὰς αἰτίας 6 1
ἀ-γνωμοσύνη : τὴν ἀ. 37 2; ἀγνωμοσύνας = ἀγνωμόνως facta 2 4
ἀγορά : ἀπ' ἀ. 24 6; ἐξ ἀ. 16 4; ἐν ἀ. 31 2; ἐπ' ἀγοράν 7 4; εἰς τὴν Μιλησίων ἀ. 28 2; κατ' ἀγοράν 5 2; πάσης ἀ. 29 4
ἀγοραῖος, *forensis* 11 2
ἄγος, τό = οἱ ἐναγεῖς 33 1
ἀγριοῦσθαι : ἠγριώθησαν πρὸς τὸν Περικλέα 34 3
ἀγρός, *rus* : ἐξ ἀγροῦ 6 2
ἀγωγός, *adducens* : προθυμίαν ἀγωγὸν εἰς μίμησιν 1 4
ἀγών, *certamen* : μουσικῆς ἀγῶνα 13 6; τοῖς μουσικοὺς ἀ. 13

7 ; εἰς ἀ. περὶ τοῦ ὀστράκου καταστάς 14 2
ἀγωνίζεσθαι : ἀγωνιζομένων τὰ τοιαῦτα 1 5 ; τοὺς ἀγωνιζομένους 13 6 ; ἀγωνίσασθαι μάχην 10 2
ἀγωνο-θέτης : τοὺς ἀ. 36 3
ἀ-δεια, securitas: τὴν ἀ. 20 1.— maleficiorum impunitas 31 2
ᾄδειν 13 6 ; ᾖδον ᾄσματα 33 6
ἀ-δελφή : τῆς Κίμωνος ἀ. 10 4 ; τὴν ἀ. 36 4
ἀ-δελφός 28 4
ἀ-δεῶς 17 1
ἄ-δηλος : τὸ ἀληθὲς ἄδηλον 32 3
ἀ-δηλότης[1] : μάχης ἐχούσης πολλὴν ἀ. 18 1 ; πολλὴν ἀ. ἔσχεν ὁ πόλεμος 28 6
ᾅδης : ἐξ ᾅδου 3 4
ἀ-δικεῖν ἰατρόν 34 3 ; τῶν τὸν δῆμον ἀδικούντων 10 7
ἀ-δικίου[1] δίωξιν 32 2
ἄ-δικος ἀξίωσις 28 6
ἀ-δοξεῖν : ἀδοξεῖ 12 1
ἀ-δοξία : τὴν ἀ. 34 1
ἄ-δωρος : ἀδωροτάτου 15 5
ἀεί, 'at all times' : 7 5, 8 4, 11 4, 18 1 ; 'at any time' 1 3, 7 5
ἀει-θαλής[13] : ἀ. πνεῦμα 13 3
ἀ-θάνατος : τῷ μακαρίῳ καὶ ἀ. 39 3 ; μενοῦσιν ἀθάνατοι 18 1 ; ἀθανάτους γεγονέναι (εἶναι) 8 6
ἀ-θετεῖν[1], fidem derogare, 'to nullify' : τὰ τεχνητὰ τῶν συμβόλων ἀθετοῦντες 6 4
Ἀθήναζε 17 1, 29 5, 30 1
ἄ-θικτος : ἄθικτον ὑπὸ τοῦ χρόνου διατηροῦσα τὴν ὄψιν 13 3
ἀθλητής : ἀθλητῇ τῶν πολιτικῶν 4 2 ; ὥσπερ ἀ. νικηφόρον 28 4
ἀθλο-θέτης 13 6
ἀ-θόρυβος : πλάσμα φωνῆς ἀθόρυβον 5 1
ἀθρόος : καρποὺς ἀθρόους 16 4
ἄ-θρυπτος εἰς γέλωτα facies 5 1

ἀ-θυμεῖν : ἀθυμῶν 37 1 ; ἀθυμοῦντος 13 8
ἀΐδιος : δόξα ἀ. 12 2
αἴθρα[3] : αἴ. μαλακῇ 39 3
αἴθων : ΑΙΘΩΝΙ ΚΛΕΩΝΙ 33 7
αἰνίττεσθαι : ᾐνῖχθαι 26 4
αἱρεῖν, capere : ἑλόντος 28 5 ; ἑλόντες 26 2.—MID. eligere : τὰ τῶν πολλῶν ἑλόμενος 7 2.— PASS. creari : ἀθλοθέτης αἱρεθείς 13 6 ; στρατηγὸς αἱρεθείς 37 2
αἰσθάνεσθαι : αἰσθόμενος 10 3
αἴσθησις, 'perception by the senses' : τῇ αἰ.)(τῷ νῷ 1 2 ; καθῃρημένου τὴν αἰ. 38 4 ; 'perception by the intellect,' 'knowledge' : τοῦ Περικλέους ταχεῖαν αἴσθησιν ἐνειργάζετο τὰ πράγματα 39 4
αἰσχρῶς 22 3
αἰσχύνεσθαι : οὐκ αἰσχύνῃ καλῶς ψάλλων ; 1 5
αἰσχύνη, dedecus: πρὸς αἰσχύνην 33 6
αἰτεῖσθαι, 'to ask for oneself' : αἰτούμενον ἄδειαν 31 2 ; w. acc. and inf. ᾐτήσατο λυθῆναι τὸν νόμον 37 2
αἰτία, causa 15 5 ; ἡ αἰ. τῆς μεταβολῆς 9 1 ; αἰ. χειρίστη πασῶν 31 2 ; τῆς αἰ. τὴν εὕρεσιν 6 4 ; αἰτίᾳ τινι 6 4 ; τὴν αἰ.)(τὸ τέλος 6 3 ; ὑπὸ τῶν ἄλλων αἰ. 29 5 ; αἰ. αἰ. δι' ἅς 32 3 ; τὰς αἰ. 6 1, 30 4.—culpa, crimen: τὴν αἰτίαν ἐπιφέρουσι (τινί τινος) 31 1 ; αἰτίαν εἶχεν ὑφιέναι 13 10 ; ἔσχε τοῦ πολέμου τὴν αἰ. 29 5 ; κοινὴν ποιησάμενος αἰτίαν κατ' αὐτῶν 24 1, 30 2 ; αἰτίᾳ τῶν Μεγαρέων ἀποθανεῖν ἔδοξε 30 3
αἰτιᾶσθαι : αἰτιῶνται αὐτὸν ψηφίσασθαι 25 1 ; αἰτιώμενοι λιμένων εἴργεσθαι 29 4

αἴτιος, *auctor*: τούτου αἴ. 34 4;
αἴτιον ἀγαθῶν 39 2; αἰτίους
τοῦ πάθους 36 3
αἰχμ-άλωτος: τοὺς αἰ. 26 3.—de
navi, ναῦν αἰ. λαβόντες 23 2
ἀ-κήδευτος[14], *insepultus*: προβαλεῖν ἀκήδευτα τὰ σώματα
28 2
ἀ-κήρυκτος, 'implacable': ἀ.
ἔχθραν 30 3
ἀκμάζειν, *vigere*: ἀκμάζων ἐν τῇ
πολιτείᾳ 37 3; τὴν ἀκμάζουσαν
ἡλικίαν 34 3
ἀκμή[3], 'bloom': ἀ. ἀνθούσης ἐφ'
ὥραν πολιτείας 16 2; μιᾶς
ἀκμῇ πολιτείας 13 1.—*rigor*:
ἀκμῇ πρόσφατον 13 3
ἀ-κόλαστος: ἀκόλαστον)(σώφρονα 9 1; τῶν ἀ. 5 2
ἀκολουθεῖ 1 4
ἀκόνη σκληρᾷ 33 7
ἀκόντιον 36 3; ἀκοντίῳ πατάξαντος 36 3
ἀκούειν: ἀκοῦσαι 13 5; ἀκούσας
1 5; ἀκούσαντα 13 2; ἀ.
κακῶς ὑπό τινος 5 2, 12 1.
29 3
ἀκουσίως)(ἐκ προνοίας 36 3
ἄκουσμα: ἀκούσματα 1 2
ἄ-κρατος, *merus*: νοῦν καθαρὸν
καὶ ἄ. 4 4; ἄ. ἐλευθερίαν 7 6
(ex Platone)
ἀκρίβεια, 'perfection': κάλλους
ἀκρίβειαν 13 2.—'parsimony.'
'frugality': τὴν τοιαύτην ἀ.
16 5; τὴν τοῦ πατρὸς ἀ. 36 1
ἀκριβής in re familiari tuenda:
ἀκριβεστάτην οἰκονομίαν 16 3;
συνηγμένην εἰς τὸ ἀκριβέστατον
δαπάνην 16 4
ἀκροᾶσθαι ψαλλόντων 1 5;
ἀκροασομένας ἦγον 24 3
ἀκρό-πολις: τῆς ἀ. 13 7; ἐν ἀ.
13 8
ἄκρος, *summus*: ἄ. σοφιστής 4 1
ἄ-κων: ἄκοντος 8 4

ἀλαζών: ἀ. γυναῖκα 12 2
ἀλαπαδνός: ϹΘΕΝΟϹ ΟΥΚ ἈΛΑ-
ΠΑΔΝΌΝ 4 3
ἀλείπτης, *magister* 4 1
ἀλείφεσθαι, *oleo ungi*: ΗΛΕΊΦΕΟ
28 5
ἀλήθεια: κρατεῖν τὴν διήγησιν
ἐπὶ τῆς ἀ. 28 3; τὴν ἀ. 13 12
ἀληθεύειν 28 2
ἀληθής: τὸ ἀ. ἄδηλον 32 3;
τἀληθές 13 12
ἀληθινός[1]: τῆς ἀ. ἀρετῆς 7 5
ἁλίσκεσθαι, *capi*: ἁλωσομένην
(πόλιν) 35 3.—συνταράττοντες ἁλίσκονται 39 2; ἁλούς,
convictus 22 3; ἁλόντες 37 4
ἀλλ' οὐδὲ 28 2; 36 4
ἀλλήλων 34 4; ἈΛΛΉΛΟΙϹΙ
ΜΙΓΈΝΤΕ 3 3; διελέγοντο
πρὸς ἀλλήλους 38 4
ἄλλος: τῆς ἄ. δυνάμεως 18 2;
τὸν ἄ. χρόνον 13 7; ἄ. τι
ἄξιον 35 3; ἄ. πολλοί 9 1;
ἄ. πολλοῖς 21 1; πολλὰ ἄ. 25
2; τὰ ἄλλα 3 2; τἄλλα 20 2,
33 2; τῶν ἄ. 5 3, 27 2; τῶν
ἄ. ῥητόρων 37 1; ἄ. πολλοῖς
21 1; πᾶσι τοῖς ἄ. 4 4; τοῖς
ἄ. ἀνθρώποις 12 1; ἄ. μισθοφοραῖς 9 3; τοὺς ἄ. 19 3
ἀλουργής (ἀλουργός), *purpureus*.
τῶν ἀ. 1 4
ἅμα, Adv. 1 3, 2 2; ἅ. καταπραττόμενος 5 2, 11 4, 12
4.—Prep. ἅ. τοῖς θείοις 6 4;
ἅ. τῇ νίκῃ καὶ τῇ διώξει 26
1; ἅ. πληγῇ 36 1
ἀ-μαθής: ἀμαθεστάταις δόξαις
poetarum 39 2
ἁμαξο-πηγός: οἱ ὁ. 12 7
ἁμαρτάνειν, *errare*: οὐχ ἁμαρτήσεται 18 2; ἁμαρτεῖν 26 2
ἀμαυροῦν, *obscurare*: δύναμιν
ἀμαυροῦσαν αὐτούς 39 4.—
PASS. ἠμαυρωμένοις τὸ ἀξίωμα
11 2

ἀμβλύνειν, hebetare: τὴν δύναμιν (αὐτοῦ) ἀμβλύνοντα 11 1
ἀ-μελεῖσθαι: ἀμελούμενος (πλοῦτος) 16 3; ἀμελούμενον (ἄνδρα) 16 7
ἄ-μεμπτος, 'free from defect': τὴν ἰδέαν τοῦ σώματος ἄ. 3 2
ἀ-μίαντος in an ethical sense: βίον ἄ. 39 2
ἅμιλλα τῶν ἀνδρῶν 11 3
ἁμιλλᾶσθαι: ἁμιλλωμένων ὑπερβάλλεσθαι τὴν δημιουργίαν 13 1
ἀ-μίμητος: ἔργων μορφῇ ἄ. 13 1
ἄ-μοιρος, exsors: ὄχλον ἄμοιρον λημμάτων 12 5
ἄ-μουσος, inelegans: οὐκ ἄ. ἡδοναῖς 11 4
ἀμφι-εννύειν: τοὺς πρεσβυτέρους ἀμφιεννύων 9 2
ἀΜΦΟΤΕΡΟ-ΓΛΩCCΟΥ 4 3
ἀμφότερος: δι' ἄ. τῶν χειρῶν 31 4; κατ' ἀμφοτέρους (sc. γονεῖς) 3 1
ἀμῶς γέ πως, utcumque, aliquo modo)(οὐδαμῶς 26 1
ἄν i.q. ἐάν 1 5, 12 3, 33 2; ἄν τε—ἄν τε 1 2
ἄν: γένοιτ' ἄν 16 6; ἄν εἴη καιρός 24 1; in unreal suppositions with indic. imperf. 1 5, 34 2; ἄν ἦν 24 6; hyperbaton of, with δοκεῖν, οὐκ ἄν δοκεῖ συμπεσεῖν 29 5: omitted with conditional imperfect 24 7; ὡς ἄν w. opt. 29 2; in relative clauses: ὅς ἄν ἐπιβῇ 30 3
ἀνά in temporal distributive sense: ἀ. πᾶν ἔτος 30 3. Cp. ἀνὰ ἑκάστην ἡμέραν Polyb. 1 42, 10 etc.
ἀνα-βαίνειν ex inferis: τῶν ἀναβεβηκότων ἐξ ᾅδου δημαγωγῶν 3 4.—in navem: ἀναβεβηκότος ἐπὶ τὴν ἑαυτοῦ τριήρη 35 1.—ad magistratus honores:

ἀνέβαινον εἰς Ἄρειον πάγον 9 3.—ἀναβαινόντων² τῶν ἔργων, dum surgit opus aedificii 13 1
ἀνα-βιβάζεσθαι milites in naves: ἱππέας ἀναβιβασάμενος 35 1
ἀν-αγγέλλεσθαι: ἀνηγγέλθη τεθνεὼς 18 3
ἀν-άγεσθαι, solvere navem 35 1: ἀναχθεὶς 19 2
ἀναγκάζεσθαι: ἠναγκασμένων διαιτᾶσθαι 34 4
ἀναγκαῖος: 1. de re: οὐκ ἀναγκαῖον (sc. ἐστί) 2 2; τὰ ἀναγκαῖα 16 4 6; τῶν ἀ. πρὸς τὸν πόλεμον 26 2; τοῖς ἀ. 12 4.—2. de homine: τῶν ἀναγκαίων, necessariorum 36 4
ἀναγκαίως 12 2
ἀνάγκη (sc. ἐστίν) 1 1; οὐ τύχην οὐδ' ἀ. 4 4
[ἀνα-γράφεσθαι: ἐν τῇ στήλῃ ἀνα-γέγραπται (dub.) 13 9]
ἀνα-γραφή², libri commentalio: τῇ περὶ τοὺς βίους ἀ. 2 4
ἀνα-δεῖν, redimire: στεφάνοις ἀνέδουν 28 4
ἀνά-δοσις¹ 2 2
ἀνα-ζωπυρεῖν, 'to kindle up' (trop. 'to excite'), τὴν ὄψιν 1 3
ἀνα-θαρρύνειν¹, animos addere 35 3
ἀνά-θημα: ἡ τῶν ἀ. (templorum) κατασκευή 12 1; τῶν ἀ. τὴν ἐπιγραφήν 14 1
ἀν-αιρεῖν, tollere: τὴν πρόφασιν ἀνῄρηκε 12 2.—de medio tollere, interimere: κρυφαίως ἀνεῖλον 10 7; ἀνελεῖν 28 2.— MID. amovere: ἐκεῖθεν ἀνελέσθαι τὰ χρήματα 12 2
ἀν-αίρεσις: ἀναίρεσιν τοῦ σημείου 6 4
ἀν-αίτιος: ἀναίτιον κακῶν 39 2
ἀνα-κομίζεσθαι, reverti: ἀνεκομίζετο 22 2

ἀνα-κράζειν : ἀνέκραγον 14 2
ἀνάκτορον, Cereris aedes Eleusinia : ἐπὶ τοῦ ἀ. 13 5
ἀνα-λαμβάνειν, *milites secum ducere* : στρατιώτας ἀναλαβὼν εἰς τὰς τριήρεις 19 4. —*devincire*: ἀνελάμβανε τοὺς πένητας 9 2 ; ἀνελάμβανε τοὺς πολλοὺς 34 1. Cp. *Cleom.* c. 32, 2 ἀναλαμβάνων τιμαῖς καὶ φιλοφροσύναις τὸν Κλεομένη, *Sertor.* c. 6, 4 ἀνελάμβανεν ὁμιλίᾳ τε τοὺς δυνατοὺς καὶ φόρων ἀνέσει τοὺς πολλοὺς: *Philop.* c. 15, 3
ἀν-αλίσκειν pecuniam : ἐκ τῶν δημοσίων ἀ. 14 2.—PASS. δέκα ταλάντων ἀνηλωμένων εἰς τὸ δέον 23 1.—tempus: ἡμέραν ὅλην ἀναλῶσαι 36 3
ἀνα-λύειν : τὰc μὲν δεῖν τὰc δ' ἀναλγεῖν 16 2
ἀν-άλωμα ; δέκα ταλάντων ἀ. 23 1 ; παντὸς ἀ.)(λήμματος 16 4
ἀν-άλωτος, *inexpugnabilis* : ἀνάλωτον ὑπὸ χρημάτων 16 3
ἀνα-μένειν: σύμβουλον ἀναμείνας χρόνον 18 2
ἀνα-μετρεῖσθαι, *remetiri, recensere*: τὰς πράξεις (αὐτοῦ) ἀνεμετροῦντο 38 3
ἀνα-μιγνύναι : τῷ εἰς ἀνθρωπείας χρείας ἀναμιγνύντι τὴν ἀρετήν 16 6.—PASS. ἀναμεμῖχθαι ταῖς μεγαλαυχίαις 5 3 ; χώρα βαρβαρικαῖς ἀναμεμιγμένη γειτνιάσεσι 19 2
ἄν-ανδρος : στρατηγίαν ἄ. 33 6
ἀνά-παιστος : τἀνάπαιστα, 'anapaestic satirical verses' 33 7
ἀνα-πείθεσθαι, *aliud persuaderi, de sententia deduci*: ἀναπεισθέντες 34 3
ἀνα-πετάννυσθαι : ἀναπεπταμένης (διαίτης) 31 4

ἀνα-πίμπλασθαι, *impleri, inquinari* : ἀ. φθορᾶς ἀπ' ἀλλήλων 34 4
ἀν-άρμοστος, 'inapplicable' : ἀ. πρὸς τὴν χρείαν 8 4
ἀνα-τείνειν : ἀνατεινούσης δόρυ 31 4
ἀνα-τιθέναι, *committere* : τῆς πόλεως ἐκείνῳ ... ἀναθείσης ἑαυτήν 32 3
ἀνα-φύεσθαι, *pullulare* : trop. πολλαὶ ἀνεφύοντο δίκαι 37 3
ἀνα-ψυχή[3], *refrigerium*, 'relief,' 'respite' 34 4
ἀν-ἐγκλιτος [1], 'not changing for the worse' : ἀ. πολιτείᾳ 15 2. Cp. *Sull.* c. 1, 3 ; *Ag.* c. 3, 5 with Schömann's note *ad l.*
ἀν-είργειν, *coercere* 21 1 : τοὺς βαρβάρους ἀνείργοντες 12 3
ἀν-ελεύθερος : τοὺς βαφεῖς ἀνελευθέρους ἡγούμεθα 1 4
ἄνεμος : ἀνέμου κατιόντος 33 5
ἀν-επί-ληπτος, 'not open to censure ' : οὐκ ἀνεπιλήπτῳ 10 6
ἀν-επί-φθονος, 'without reproach ': προσωνυμίαν ἀ. 39 2
ἄνευ, *praeter*, ' without reckoning' 18 2
ἀν-ἔχειν, *attollere*: ἀνέσχε τὴν χλαμύδα 35 2.—MID. *pati*: οὐκ ἀνεξομένων 33 3
ἀνεψιός, *consobrinus* : τοῦ ἀ. 7 4
ἀν-ήκεστος : 1. de re *quod sarciri nequit* : ἀ. διαφοράν 36 3 ; ἀνήκεστον ἐν ἐξουσίᾳ κακίαν 39 5.- 2. de homine : ἀ. ἐχθρῷ 39 1
ἀνηρ 21 6 ; ἀ. ἀγαθός 7 1 : ἀ. φίλου 13 10 : τοῦ πρώτου ἀ. 9 1 ; ἀνδρὶ φρονίμῳ 18 3 ; ἄ. σώφρονα 11 1 ; ἄνδρες εἴκοσι 17 2 ; τῶν καλῶν κἀγαθῶν ἀ. 7 3 ; ἀνδρῶν διαφθαρέντων 33 4 ; τοῖς δυνατω-

τάτοις ά. 21 2 ; πολλούς αυτών ά. 26 2 ; τους ά. in navi 28 2. — ό ἀνήρ in repetitione subiecti 39 1 : τοῦ ἀνδρός 15 5 ; τὸν ά. 4 1, 10 3, 15 5, 16 7 ; τῷ ά. 8 2, 10 5, 15 5 ; τἀνδρί 10 6.—as appositive to a word expressing station or condition, ά. φιλόσοφος 26 2

ἀνθεῖν, *vigere*: trop. ἀνθούσης ἐφ' ὥραν πολιτείας 16 2. Cp. *Mor.* 801 E πολλοὶ πρὶν ἀνθῆσαι περὶ τὸ βῆμα κατεμαράνθησαν

ἀνθηρός, 'bright' : τὸ ά. (τῆς χρόας) 1 3.—'fresh,' 'new' : ά. ἀρμονίας 15 2

ἀνθ-ιστάναι, *opponere*: ἀντέστησαν ἐναντιωσόμενον 11 1

ἀνθρώπειος: εἰς ά. χρείας 16 6

ἀνθρώπινος: ἀνθρωπίνων (ἀνθρωπίνως v. *l.*) δεῖσθαι 37 5 ; τοῖς ά. λογισμοῖς 34 2

ἄνθρωπος : ά. μοχθηρός 1 5 ; ά. νοῦν ἔχουσι 39 3 ; ά. τοσούτοις 34 4 ; ά. σατυρικοὺς τοῖς βίοις 13 11 ; ἄνθρωποι)(θηρία 1 1. —for a personal pronoun, usually with a connotation of irony or pity : τοῦ ά. 5 2 3, 31 5 ; τὸν ά. 5 3, 13 8, 31 3 ; τῆς ά. 24 1

ἀνθ-υβρίζειν[3] : ἀνθυβρίζοντες 26 3

ἀν-ιέναι (ἀνίημι), *laxare*, *remittere* : τῷ δήμῳ τὰς ἡνίας ἀνείς 11 4.—PASS. τῆς ἀνειμένης δημαγωγίας 15 2.— *levare*: τὸ δύσθυμον αὐτῶν ἀνιείς 15 4.—*sinere*: τὴν χώραν ἀνῆκεν (v. *l.* ἀφῆκεν) ἀργήν 16 5

ἀν-ιστάναι, *erigere*: ἀνέστησεν ἄγαλμα138.—*sedibus pellere*: πάντας ἀναστήσας ἐκ τῆς χώρας 23 2.—ἀνίστασθαι, *surgere ad dicendum* : ἅπαξ ἀνέστη 10 5

ἀν-οικίζεσθαι[2], 'to be resettled' : ἀνοικιζομένης Συβάριος 11 5

ἀν-ομολογεῖσθαι[2], 'to acknowledge' : ἀνωμολογοῦντο 39 4

ἀν-όργανος[1] : ά. διάνοιαν 16 6

ἀντ-εκ-κλέπτειν : ἀντεξέκλεψαν 30 4

ἀντί, 'instead of' : 6 1, 7 2, 9 2, 33 1, 34 4.—of that for which anything is given or received : ἀνθ' οὗ 12 3

ἀντι-βολῶ 4 2

ἀντι-λαμβάνεσθαι, *appetere* : Αἰγύπτου ά. 20 2, 25 3.—*apprehendere* i.e. *percipere* : τῇ αἰσθήσει ἀντιλαμβανομένη τῶν προστυγχανόντων 1 2

ἀντι-λέγειν ὡς οὐ πέπτωκε 8 4

ἀντι-λογία, *disceptatio*, *contradictio* : δι' ἀντιλογίας 4 3

ἀντί-παλος : τὴν πολιτείαν εἰς ἀντίπαλον κατέστησε 11 2

ἀντι-πέρας, e *regione* : τὴν ά. ἤπειρον 19 4

ἀντι-πολιτεύεσθαι, *contrariae partis esse in republica* : ἀντεπολιτεύσατο τῷ Π. 8 4

ἀντι-τάσσεσθαι πρός τινα, *se opponere alicui* 9 2, 11 1 ; ἀντιταξαμένου 27 1 ; τὴν ἀντιτεταγμένην ἑταιρείαν 14 2

ἀντι-φιλοτιμεῖσθαι, 'to be moved by jealousy against' : πρὸς τὴν δόξαν ἀντιφιλοτιμούμενοι τῶν ἔργων 14 2

ἄνω : τοὺς ά. κίονας 13 4

ἄνωθεν, *desuper* : τῶν ά. 27 4

ἄξιος : τὰ μηδεμιᾶς ά. σπουδῆς 1 2 ; ά. σπουδῆς εἶναι τὸν εἰργασμένον 2 2 : ἄλλο τι τῆς παρασκευῆς ά. 35 3 ; ταῦτ' ἄξια στεφάνων 28 4

ἀξιοῦν, *dignum censere* : μεγά-

λων αὐτὸν ἀ. πραγμάτων 17
1.—*statuere*: 5 4, 39 2
ἀξίωμα, *dignitas*: τὸ ἀ. τοῦ
ἤθους 4 4; ἠμαυρωμένους τὸ
ἀ. 11 2; διὰ τὸ ἀ. καὶ τὴν
δύναμιν 32 3; οὐδεὶς βάρος
ἔχων οὐδ' ἀ. ἐχέγγυον 37 1
ἀξίωσις: οὐκ ἦν ἄδικος ἡ ἀ. 28 6
ἀπ-αγγέλλεσθαι: ἀπηγγέλλοντο ἐκπεπολεμωμένοι 22 1
ἀπ-άγειν, *abducere*: ἐκ τῆς
Ἀττικῆς ἀπαγαγεῖν τοὺς Πελ.
22 2.—PASS. εἰς τὸ δεσμωτήριον ἀπαχθείς 31 5; ἀπαχθεῖσα πρὸς βασιλέα ut captiva 24 7
ἀπ-ᾴδειν, c. gen. *ab aliqua re abhorrere, abludere*: ἀπᾴδοντα τῆς Ἀναξαγόρου σοφίας 16 5 [Cp. Ael. *V. H.* III 8, XII 1]
ἀπ-αίρειν: ἀπῆρεν ἐπ' οἴκου 19 4
ἀπ-αιτεῖν: ἀπαιτοῦντος (τὸ ἀργύριον) 36 2
ἀπ-αλλάττειν, *amovere*: ἣν (ἀπειρίαν) ἀπαλλάττων 6 1.
—PASS. *excedere*: ἀπηλλάγησαν 34 1; ἐκείνων ἀπαλλαγέντων 21 1
ἀπ-άνθρωπος)(φιλάνθρωπος: ἀπάνθρωπον ἦν 24 7
ἀπ-αντᾶν: ἀπαντῆσαι 26 1
ἅπαξ 10 4
ἀ-παρ-αίτητος: περὶ τὰς εὐθύνας ἀπαραίτητον 10 6
ἀ-παρ-αιτήτως χρησάμενος 23 2
ἀπ-αρνεῖσθαι: τὸν φόνον ἀπαρνούμενοι 30 4
ἅ-πας: τὸν ἅ. χρόνον 39 3; τὴν τοιαύτην ἅ. φιλοφροσύνην 7 4; αἱ εἰκόνες αὐτοῦ σχεδὸν ἅπασαι 3 2; τοὺς καρποὺς ἅπαντας 16 4, 34 1
ἀπειλεῖν: ἀπειλοῦντες 33 6
ἀπ-ειπεῖν, *renuntiare*, quod modo desperantis est, modo deficientis viribus aut voluntate ideoque desistentis: ἀπεῖπε 36 4; ταχέως ἂν ἀπεῖπον 34 2. Cp. Cleom. c. 30, 2; c. 34, 1, *Cam.* c. 18, 7 τῶν πολεμίων ἀπειπόντων πρὸς τὸν φόνον, *Luc.* c. 31, 8, *Cor.* c. 13, 3
ἀ-πειρία: τῆς ἀ. τῶν στρατηγῶν 26 2; δι' ἀπειρίαν αὐτῶν 6 1
ἀπ-ελαύνειν: ἀπήλασαν αὐτὸν ὡς φυγάδα 10 1.—PASS. 29 4
ἀπ-έοικεν [1] οὐδέν 8 2
ἀπ-εργάζεσθαι: τὴν νόσον ἀπεργάζεται 34 3
ἀπ-ερείδεσθαι, *reponere*: ἀπερειδόμενος εἰς Περικλέα τὴν ὑπόνοιαν 32 1
ἀπ-έχεσθαι, *abstinere*: ἀπέχηται τῶν ἐκείνου 33 2
ἀπ-έχθεια: ἰδίᾳ πρὸς τοὺς Μεγαρεῖς ἀ. 30 2; τὴν ἀ. 31 1; ἐν μεγάλαις ἀ. 39 1
ἀπ-έχθεσθαι: ἀπήχθοντο 10 3
ἀπ-ιέναι: ἀπῄει 5 2
ἀπ-ισχυρίζεσθαι[2], *omni ope resistere*: ἀπισχυρίσασθαι 31 1
ἀπό, *a, ab,* I. of Separation:
1. local, after a verb of motion: καταβαίνοντα ἀπὸ τοῦ βήματος 28 4, 32 2, 34 4, 19 3, 24 6.—
2. of a part from the whole: τὰς ἀπὸ τῶν κοινῶν εὐπορίας 12 5.—3. of any kind: ἀπ' ἐλπίδος, *procul a spe* 20 3
II. of Origin, local or causal:
1. ἀπὸ τύχης πρόσκρουσμα 19 4.—2. trop. of that *after* or *from* which a thing is called: ἀπὸ τῆς ἐν τῇ πολιτείᾳ δυνάμεως Ὀλύμπιον προσαγορευθῆναι 8 2; ἀπὸ τοῦ λευκοῦ κυάμου προσαγορεύεσθαι 27 2.—3. of the efficient cause from which anything proceeds, *per, cum*: τοῖς ἀπ' ἀρετῆς ἔργοις 1 4; τῶν ἀπ'

ἀρετῆς ἀγαθῶν 2 3; φθορᾶς ἀπ' ἀλλήλων 31 4; παρηγορία ἀφ' ὧν ἔπασχον οἱ πολέμιοι 34 1; ἀφ' ὧν ἀνελάμβανε τοὺς πένητας 9 2; ἀ. τοσαύτης ἰσχύος 35 1; ἀ. τηλικαύτης δυνάμεως 39 1; ἀ. τῶν δημοσίων ὠφελεῖσθαι 12 5

ἀπο-βάλλειν, *amittere, privari:* ἀπέβαλε 36 4; ἀποβαλεῖν 36 4; ἀποβαλόντι 36 1

ἀπο-γινώσκεσθαι[2], *deplorari, desperari:* ὑπὸ τῶν ἰατρῶν ἀπεγνωσμένος 13 8

ἀπο-γράφεσθαι, *nomen inscribendum curare:* ἀπο-γράψασθαι filium in τοὺς φράτερας 37 5

ἀπο-δεικνύναι: ἀποδεῖξαι τὸν σταθμόν 31 3

ἀπο-δέχεσθαι, *probare:* ἀπεδέξατο 23 1

ἀπο-διδόναι, 'to restore': τὸ ἱερὸν Δελφοῖς ἀπέδωκαν 21 2. — 'to repay with': τὴν ἰσχὺν ἀποδίδωσι 13 2

ἀπο-θνήσκειν: ἀποτεθνήκει 7 2; ἀπέθανεν ἐν τῷ λοιμῷ 36 4; ἀποθανόντος 13 4. — ἀποθανεῖν as pass. of ἀποκτείνειν: τῶν ἀποθανόντων κατὰ τὸν πόλεμον 28 3, 30 3; τοῖς ὑπὲρ τῆς πατρίδος ἀποθανοῦσι 8 6

ἀπο-θύειν: τὰς βλασφημίας ὥσπερ δαίμονι κακῷ τῷ φθόνῳ ἀποθύοντας 13 7

ἄπ-οικος: πόλις ἀ. Κορινθίων 29 4

ἀπο-καλεῖν: τὴν σεμνότητα δοξοκοπίαν ἀποκαλοῦντας 5 4

ἀπο-καρτερεῖν[1], *inedia mortem sibi consciscere:* ἀποκαρτεροῦντα 16 7

ἀπο-κληροῦν, *sorte deligere:* ἀπεκλήρου 27 2

ἀπο-κουφίζειν: ἀποκουφίζων ἀργοῦ ὄχλου τὴν πόλιν 11 5

ἀπο-κρίνειν, *secernere:* ἀποκρίνοντα 4 4. — MID. *respondere:* ἀποκρινόμενον 21 6

ἀπο-κρύπτειν, *obtercre, reprimere:* ἀπέκρυπτε τὴν κακίαν 39 5

ἀπο-κτείνειν: ἀπέκτεινεν 37 5; ἀπέκτειναν 23 2

ἀπο-λαύειν, *fructum capere:* ταῦτ' ἀπέλαυσε τῆς Ἀναξαγόρου συνουσίας 6 1

ἀπό-λαυσις: τὰς ἀ. τῶν ἀγαθῶν 2 3

ἀπο-λείπειν: ἀπέλιπε 20 1. - 'to leave behind one,' 'bequeath to posterity,' ἀπολέλοιπε 8 5: cp. *Cat. ma.* c. 21, 8. — PASS. 'to be inferior to,' 'fall short of': πλούτῳ μηδενὸς ἀπολειπόμενον 9 4

ἀπ-ολλύναι, *perdere:* τὰς προσόδους ἀπολλύντος 14 1.— *amittere:* εἰ τοιοῦτον ἀπολεῖ σύμβουλον 16 7; πολλοὺς ἀπώλεσας πολίτας 28 4

ἀπο-λογεῖσθαι: ἀπολογησαμένου τοῦ δήμου τὴν ἀγνωμοσύνην τὴν πρὸς αὐτόν 37 2

ἀπο-λογισμός[1], *ratio reddenda:* ἐν τῷ τῆς στρατηγίας ἀ. 23 1. Cp. *Sol.* c. 3, 3; *Sull.* c. 34, 2

ἀπο-λύεσθαι, *diluere, refellere:* δι' ἔργων ἀ. τὸν λακωνισμόν 10 1

ἀπο-μνημονεύεσθαι, *memorari,* ἀπομνημονεύεται ὀλίγα 8 5

ἀπ-ομνύναι: ἀπομόσαι μὴ τυραννήσειν 16 1

ἀπο-πλεῖν: ἀπέπλευσε 25 2

ἀ-πορεῖσθαι: ὑπὸ τῶν πραγμάτων ἠπορημένον 3 4

ἀ-πορία, *penuria:* ἐπανορθούμενος τὰς ἀ. 11 5.—*dialecticae effectus,* κατακλείουσαν εἰς ἀπορίαν ἕξιν 4 3

INDEX IV GREEK

ἀπό-ρρητος : τὸ ἀ., *arcanum* 23 1 ; ἀ. συνθήκας 10 4
ἀπο-σκιασμός [1, 4] : γνωμόνων ἀποσκιασμοῖς 6 4
ἀπο-στατεῖν [3], *deserere, abesse* : οὐκ ἀποστατοῦσαν (τοῦ ἔργου) 13 7
ἀπο-στέλλειν : ἀπέστειλε 25 1 2. 29 2 ; ἀποστεῖλαι βοήθειαν 29 1.—PASS. ἀπεστάλησαν 17 2
ἀπο-σφάλλεσθαι [1] : ἀποσφαλεὶς ἐξ ὕψους ἔπεσε 13 8
ἀπο-τεθνήκει (unclassical form for τεθνήκει) 7 2
ἀπο-τειχίζειν, 'to intercept by a wall' : ἀπετείχισε τὰς καταδρομάς 19 1
ἀπο-τέμνεσθαι : ἀ. τὴν ἱερὰν ὀργάδα 30 2
ἀπο-τιθέναι : ὅπως οἱ λόγοι τῶν χρημάτων εἰς τοὺς πρυτάνεις ἀποτεθεῖεν 32 2
ἀπο-τυγχάνειν sine objecto : ἀπέτυχε 35 3
ἀπο-φαίνειν : μεστοὺς ὀργῆς ὄντας ἀποφαίνοντες 39 3
ἀπο-χωρεῖν : ἀπεχώρησε 10 5, 22 3
ἀ-προσ-δεής [1] : ἀ. τῆς ἐκτὸς ὕλης διάνοιαν 16 6
ἅπτεσθαι : μάχης ἁπτόμενος 18 1
ἀπ-ωθεῖσθαι, *reicere* : ταῦτα ἀπώσασθαι 21 7
ἄρα : ὡς ἄ. 28 2 ; ἂν ἄρα 33 2
ἆρα, *nonne* 1 2
ἀργός, *ignavus*, 'unoccupied' : ἀ. ὄχλου 11 5 ; ὄχλον ἀ. 12 5 ; δίαιταν ἀργήν 34 4.— *incultus*, 'untilled' : τὴν χώραν ἀφῆκεν ἀργήν 16 5
ἀργύριον, 'a sum of money' 36 2
ἀργῶς ἔχων πρὸς χρηματισμόν 16 3
ἀρεστός [1], *placens, gratus* (of things) : τῆς συμβιώσεως οὐκ οὔσης αὐτοῖς ἀρεστῆς 24 5
ἀρετή, 'moral worth' : ἡ ἀ. 2 2 ; τῆς ἀληθινῆς ἀ. 7 5 ; τὴν ἀ. 5 4, 16 6 ; τοῖς ἀπ' ἀ. ἔργοις 1 4 ; λόγον ἐποιοῦντο τῆς ἀ. 38 2 ; εἰ τὰ ἤθη ἐξίσταται τῆς ἀ. 38 2 ; ἀναμιγνύντι τὴν ἀ. εἰς ἀνθρωπείας χρείας 16 6 ; τὴν ἀ. ἔχειν τι σατυρικὸν μέρος 5 4. —'any special moral excellence' : κατὰ τὰς ἄλλας ἀ. ὁμοίων 2 4
ἀριθμός : δι' ἀριθμοῦ καὶ μέτρου 16 4 ; ἀ. χρημάτων τὸν ἐλάχιστον 35 4
ἄριστα, *optime* 3 1
ἄριστος : τοὺς ἀ. 18 2
ἀριστο-κρατικός 7 3 ; ἀ. προαιρέσεως 11 3 ; ἀ. πολιτείαν 9 1, 15 2 ; οἱ ἀ. 11 1
ἀρκεῖν : ἀρκεῖ 1 5
ἁρμόζειν, *congruere* : τῷ μεγέθει τοῦ φρονήματος ἁρμόζοντα λόγον 8 1
ἁρμονία : ἀνθηρᾶς καὶ μαλακῆς ἁ. 15 2
ἀρχαῖος : κάλλει ἀρχαῖον (ἔργον) 13 3
ἄρχειν, *imperare* : ἄ. καὶ βασιλεύειν τῶν ὄντων 39 2.—MID. *incipere* : ἀρχομένων ἄχθεσθαι 17 1 ; ἤρξατο οἰκοδομεῖν 13 4
ἀρχή, *initium* : ἐξ ἀ. 11 3, 34 2 ; εὐθὺς ἐξ ἀ. 31 3, ἐν ἀ. 9 2 ; εἶχε τὴν ἀ. 6 2 ; διακοσμήσεως ἀρχήν 4 4 ; τὴν ἀ. ὅπως ἔσχεν γνῶναι 31 1 ; μηδισμοῦ ἀρχάς 21 2.—*imperium, principatus* : ὑπὸ τοῦ πρώτου ἀνδρὸς ἀρχήν 9 1 ; ἀ. καὶ δυναστείαν κτησάμενος 16 3.—*regnum* : τοσαύτην ἀ. 15 4 ; 20 2.—*honor, magistratus* : ἀ. κληρωταί 9 3

ἀρχι-τεκτονεῖν¹, 'to be the architect': ἀρχιτεκτονοῦντος 13 7
ἀρχι-τέκτων: μεγάλους ἀ. 13 4
ἄρχων 9 3
ἀ-cἀλεγτον³ ἕδος 39 3
ἀ-σέβεια: δίκην ἀσεβείας 32 1
ἀ-σέβημα: ἀ. μυθῶδες 13 11
ἀσέλγεια: πολλὴν ἀ. 13 10
ἀ-σθένεια: ἐξομολόγησιν ἀσθενείας 31 1
ἀ-σθενής: ἀσθενῆ (τὴν κακίαν) ποιῶν 39 5
ᾆσμα: ᾖδον ᾄσματα 33 6
ἀσπάζεσθαι, salutare in adventu et discessu: ἠσπάζετο αὐτὴν μετὰ τοῦ καταφιλεῖν 24 6
ἀσπίς: ἐν τῇ ἀ. 31 4; χαλκῆν ἀ. 27 4
ἄ-σπονδος, internecivus: ἀ. καὶ ἀκήρυκτον ἔχθραν 30 3
ἀcτpἀπτειν 8 3
ἄστυ: ἐν ἀ. 7 4, 10 4, 11 2 4; εἰς τὸ ἄ. 34 3; τὸ ἄ. 33 5
ἀ-σύμ-μετρος: ἀσυμμέτρου πρὸς δημοκρατίαν ὑπεροχῆς 16 1; ἀσύμμετρον τῇ κεφαλῇ 3 2
ἀ-σύν-τακτος, inconditus: ἀ. ὄχλον 12 5
ἀ-σφάλεια, 'safety': 7 3; τῆς ἀ. 31 5; πρὸς ἀσφάλειαν 33 5.—'cautiousness': διὰ τὴν ἀ. 18 1. Cp. Fab. c. 19, 3 τὴν Φαβίου βεβαιότητα καὶ ἀσφάλειαν, c. 25, 4 ἔοικε δ' ἀντιλέγειν ὑπὸ πολλῆς ἀσφαλείας καὶ προνοίας
ἀ-σφαλής, tutus: ἀcφaλἐc ἕδος 39 3.—certus, erroris expers: ἀ. εὐσέβειαν)(φλεγμαίνουσαν δεισιδαιμονίαν 6 1.—cautus 19 4
ἀσχάλλειν³: ἀσχάλλοντας ἐπὶ τῷ πολέμῳ 34 1
ἀ-σχολεῖσθαι¹, 'to be busily occupied': ἀσχολουμένου 16

7; ὡς ἀσχολουμένῳ πράγματα μὴ παρέχοι 16 3
ἀ-τέλεια: ἀτέλειαν ὁ δῆμος ἔδωκε 31 5
ἀ-τεχνῶς 15 3
ἀ-τρέμα: μειδιάσας ἀ. 28 5
αὔ 16 2
αὐθάδεια: αὐ. τινί 31 1
αὖθις 23 2, 25 3, 29 3, 33 4, 34 4, 37 2
αὐλεῖν 13 6
αὐλητής: σπουδαῖος αὐ. 1 5
αὔξησις, incrementum: τῇ αὐξήσει τῶν Ἀθηναίων 17 1
αὐτόθι = αὐτοῦ, ibi 19 1
αὐτός, ipse, 'self': 9 3, 10 3, 34 2; αὐ. τοῦ γράψαντος 37 5; τῆς προσποιήσεως αὐτῆς τῶν καλῶν 5 4; ὑπὲρ αὐ. τῆς πόλεως 33 4; τὸν Ἀναξαγόραν αὐ. 16 7; Περικλέα αὐ. 26 3; παρὰ τὴν γῆν αὐ. παραφερόμενον, 'close to the very ground' 27 4; διὰ τῶν πραγμάτων αὐ. 9 2; αὐ. τοὺς θεούς 39 3, 16 2.—to express opposition: ἐκείνην μὲν—αὐτὸς δέ 24 5.—with the addition of καί to indicate that a quality may be ascribed to one equally with another 5 4, 21 2; λαβὼν καὶ αὐτὸς προμαντείαν 21 2, 4 3 (v. l.)—added to personal pronouns: αὐτῶν τούτων τὰς αἰτίας 6 1; οὐδὲ γὰρ ἐκείνους αὐτοὺς ὁρῶμεν 8 6.—casus obliqui, eius, ei etc.: τὴν σύνεσιν αὐτοῦ 4 4; ἦν αὐτῷ γυνή 21 2, 24 5, 30 2; αὐτόν 28 5; γράφει ψήφισμα κατ' αὐτῶν 30 2; αὐτοῖς 21 2.—ὁ αὐτός, idem: οὐκέθ' ὁ αὐτὸς ἦν 15 2; οὐ ταὐτόν ἐστιν 16 6; τὸν αὐ. λύκον 21 2; συναγαγὼν εἰς ταὐτὸ (in eundem locum, una) τοὺς καλοὺς κά-

γαθούς 16 6 ; ταῦθ' ὑπάρχειν καὶ τοῖς ὑπὲρ τῆς πατρίδος ἀποθανοῦσιν 8 6.—w. dative : Περικλεῖ γυναῖκας εἰς τὸ αὐτὸ φοιτώσας 32 1
αὐτοῦ, -ῆς, -οῦ ί. *q.* ἑαυτοῦ reflexive : αὐτοῦ τινα μορφὴν 31 4 ; παρὰ τὴν αὐτοῦ φύσιν 7 2 ; ἐχρῆτο τοῖς αὐτοῦ λογισμοῖς 33 6 ; τὸν περίλοιπον αὐτοῦ τῶν γνησίων 36 4 ; πόλιν ἐξ αὐτῆς κοσμουμένην 12 4 ; ὑπὲρ αὐτῆς παρέσχε λόγον 24 1 ; μεγάλων αὐτὸν ἀξιοῦν πραγμάτων 17 1; τὰ χρήματα πρὸς αὐτὸν μεταγαγών 12 1 ; τὸ καλὸν ἐφ' αὑτὸ κινεῖ 2 3 ; ἁλίσκονται τοῖς αὐτῶν μυθεύμασιν 39 3
αὐτουργία [2]: ἡ αὐ. τῶν ταπεινῶν 2 1
αὐτουργός : τὸν δῆμον γενόμενον πολυτελῆ καὶ ἀκόλαστον ἀντὶ σώφρονος καὶ αὐ. 9 1
αὐχήν *i. q.* ἰσθμός : τὸν αὐχένα διαζώσας 19 1
ἀφ-αιρεῖν, *adimere* : τῶν χωρίων τοὺς φραγμοὺς ἀφαιρῶν 9 2 ; τοῦτο ἀφεῖλε τοῦ ψηφίσματος 32 2 ; ἀφελεῖν λήμην 8 5.— MED. ἀφελέσθαι (αὐτὸν) τὴν στρατηγίαν 35 4 ; ἀφελέσθαι τῆς θαλάττης τὸ κράτος τοὺς Ἀθ. 28 6.—PASS. ἀφαιρεθῆναι τὰς πλείστας κρίσεις 9 4
ἀ-φειδεῖν : ἀφειδήσας τοῦ σώματος 10 2
ἀφή [2], a musical term : μάλ' ἐμμελοῦς ἁ. 15 4
ἄ-φθονος : πράγμασιν ἁ. 16 4
ἀφ-ιέναι : τὴν χώραν ἀφῆκεν (*v. l.* ἀνῆκεν) ἀργήν 16 5.—*cedere*: πολλὰς ἀφεικότων φωνὰς εἰς αὐτόν 8 3 ; ἀφεὶς ὑπὲρ αὐτῆς δάκρυα 32 3.—*deponere*: καθ-

ἅπερ κέντρον τὸν θυμὸν ἀφεικότων 36 1
ἀφ-ικνεῖσθαι : ἐπὶ τέλος ἀφίξεσθαι 13 1 ; ἀφίκοντο 29 3 ; πρεσβείας ἀφιγμένης 30 1
ἀφ-ίστασθαι : ἀπέστησαν 22 1, 25 3 ; ἀποστᾶσα 29 4 ; τοὺς ἀφεστῶτας 23 2
ἀφ-ορμή, *occasio* : ἀφορμὰς διαβολῆς 33 2
ἀφ-οσιοῦσθαι : τὴν προβολὴν ἀφοσιούμενος 10 5
ἄχθεσθαι c. dat. rei 17 1
ἄ-χρηστος : rem ἄχρηστον)(χρήσιμον 1 3 ; τὸν ἐν τοῖς ἁ. πόνον 2 1
ἄχρι Λέσβου 17 2 : ἄχρι τῆς τελευτῆς 36 3 ; ἄχρι τῶν σπονδῶν 7 4

B

βαδίζειν, de personis : πρὸς τὸ βῆμα βαδίζων 8 4.—de rebus : ἀναλώματος δι' ἀριθμοῦ καὶ μέτρου βαδίζοντος 16 4
βαθύς : βαθυτάτην τομὴν 11 3
βάλλειν : τὸν βαλόντα 36 3
βάναυσος : τὸν β. ὄχλον 12 5 : ἀνελευθέρους καὶ β. 1 4. Cp. *Marc.* c. 17, 4
βαρβαρικός : β. γειτνιάσεσι 19 2
βάρβαρος : β. πόλιν 28 5 ; οἱ β. 17 1 ; β.)(Ἑλλήνων 15 1 ; βαρβάροις 9 4, 12 2 ; β. ἔθνεσι 20 1 ; τοὺς β. 9 4, 12 2 3, 17 1
βαρέως : β. φέροντες sine obiecto 22 3
βάρος, *soliditas, firmitas*: β. μόνιμον 13 2.—*gravitas*: βάρος ἔχων ἰσόρροπον ad res gerendas 37 1 (unclassical)
βαρύνεσθαι, *gravari* : οἱ ζῶντος βαρυνόμενοι τὴν δύναμιν 39 4
βαρύς, *molestus* : β. πόλεμον 10

R

2, 19 1.—*intolerabilis*, 'oppressive': βαρυτέρας ὑπεροχῆς 16 1
βασιλεύειν τῶν ὄντων 39 2
βασιλεύς 1 5; the king of the Persians 3 1, 10 4, 13 5, 20 2, 24 2 7; τοῦ β. τῶν Λακεδαιμονίων 29 5, 8 4; βασιλέως Λακεδαιμονίων 22 1; τοῦ β. τῶν Αἰγυπτίων 37 3; φιλίαις βασιλέων 15 1; πολλῶν β. 15 5; τοῖς β. (τῶν βαρβάρων ἐθνέων) 20 1; ΒΑϹΙΛΕϒ ϹΑΤϒΡⲰΝ (de Pericle) 33 7.—βασιλεύς archon 9 3
βασιλικός: β. πολιτείαν 15 2
βάσις: τὴν β. cerebri 6 2
βασκαίνειν, *invidere*: τοῦτο ἐβάσκαινον 12 1. Cp. *Cam.* c. 36, 1 τοὺς πάνυ βασκαίνοντας τῶν πολιτῶν καὶ πάντα βουλομένους εὐτυχίᾳ τινὶ μᾶλλον ἢ δι᾽ ἀρετὴν κατωρθῶσθαι, τότ᾽ ἠνάγκαζον αἱ πράξεις τῷ δραστηρίῳ τοῦ ἀνδρὸς ἀποδιδόναι τὴν δόξαν
ΒΑϹΤΑΖΕΙΝ ΔΟΡϒ 33 7
βαφεύς: βαφεῖς 12 6; τοὺς β. ἀνελευθέρους ἡγούμεθα 1 4
βαφή: βαφὴν ὑποχεόμενος 8 1
βδελυρός: τῶν β. 5 2
βεβαιότης: εἰς β. τῶν ὑπαρχόντων 21 1
βέλτιον: β. παλαίει 8 4; β. πολεμήσειν 23 1.—βέλτιστον τῶν αὐτοῦ καλῶν 39 1; πρὸς τὸ β. 15 2; κατὰ τὸ β. 31 1; διώκειν τὸ β. 1 3; τῶν πολιτῶν οἱ β. 38 3
βῆμα: ἀπὸ τοῦ β. 28 4; ἐπὶ τοῦ β. 8 6; ἐπὶ τὸ β. 37 1; περὶ τὸ β. 11 1; πρὸς τὸ β. 8 4
βιάζεσθαι, *cogi*: εἰ βιασθείη προελθεῖν 27 4; βιασθῆναι παρὰ γνώμην 33 5
βίαιος: βίαια πάσχειν 29 4

βιβλίον: τοῦτο τὸ β. 2 4
βίος, *vita*, 'period or course of life': ὁ καθ᾽ ἡμέραν β. 7 5; ἐν τῷ λοιπῷ β. 36 5.—'mode of life': διώκει τὸν β. 16 4; πολιτικοῦ βίος 16 6; τρυφερὸν τῷ β. 27 4; βίον ἐν ἐξουσίᾳ καθαρόν 39 2; τῇ περὶ τὸν β. κατασκευῇ 8 1; ἡ περὶ τὸν β. δόξα 15 5; σατιρικοὺς τοῖς β. 13 11.—'a biography' (unclassical) τὸν Περικλέους β. 2 4; τῇ περὶ τοὺς β. ἀναγραφῇ 2 4; ἡ τῶν βίων ἱστορία 13 12
βλασφημία: πάσῃ χρωμένου β. πρὸς αὐτόν 5 2; τοῦτο βλασφημίαν ἤνεγκεν (αὐτῷ) 13 9; τὰς κατὰ τῶν κρειττόνων β. ἀποθύοντας τῷ φθόνῳ τῶν πολλῶν 13 11
βληχρός[1 3 5]: β. τινὶ νόσῳ 38 1 ubi S ἀβληχρᾶ exhibet
βοᾶν: βοῶντες 12 1
βοήθεια, *suppetiae*: ἀποστεῖλαι βοήθειαν 29 1 2; παρεσχηκὼς μικρὰν β. 29 3
βοηθεῖν: βοηθοῦντι πολλοῖς τῶν πενήτων 16 6; ἐβοήθει κατὰ τάχος 27 1
βόσκημα: ὥσπερ βοσκήματα καθειργμένους 34 4
βούλεσθαι: βουλόμεθα 2 3; βουλόμενος 12 5, 27 1, 35 1; βουλόμενον ἦγε τὸν δῆμον 15 3; ἑτέρῳ βουλομένην συνεξέδωκε 24 5; μὴ βουλόμενον ἐξέπεμψε 29 2; βουλόμενοι 11 1; οἱ βουλόμενοι 9 2; τοὺς βουλομένους 33 4; εἴτε βούλοιτό τις 32 2; ᾗ βούλοιντο πλεόντων 20 1
βουλεύεσθαι: τοὺς βουλευσομένους 17 1
βούλευμα: μετέχειν τῶν β. 17 3
βουλευτήριον, τό 7 4
βουλή: τῆς ἐξ Ἀρείου πάγου β.

7 6, 9 3; κατεστασίασε τὴν
βουλὴν 9 4
βραδέως 13 5
βραχύνειν: βραχύνοντας τὴν
συλλαβήν 4 1
βραχύς: βραχέα (=ὀλίγα) φροντίζων 33 5. Cp. *Cat. int.*
c. 2, 4, c. 7, 2
ΒΡΟΝΤᾶΝ 8 3
βρύχειν: Βρύχεις 33 7
βωμολοχία: ὀχλικῆς β. 5 1
βωμός: τὴν ψῆφον ἀπὸ τοῦ β.
φέροντες 32 2

Γ

γαμεῖν: ἔγημε 3 1; γαμοῦντος
for γάμους ἑστιῶντος 7 4
γάρ introductory 3 1, 13 8.—
'else' 1 5
γαστροειδής[1]: γ. ναῖς 26 3
γε: τῶν γ' ἄλλων 1 4; ὑπό γε
τῶν ἄλλων αἰτιῶν 29 5; εἰ
μή γε 18 2; εἰ καὶ—γε 24 4;
ἀλλὰ—γε 2 2; καὶ—γε 24 6;
ἀμῶς γέ πως 26 1; πρίν γε δή
36 4
γειτνίασις[1], *vicinitas*: βαρβαρικαῖς γ. 19 2
γέλως: μετὰ γέλωτος)(σπουδῇ
8 3; ἐπὶ γέλωτι 36 2;
ἄθρυπτος εἰς γέλωτα 5 1
γέμειν[3]: χώρα γέμουσα λῃστηρίων 19 2
γένεσις operis 13 2
γενναίως 3 1
γένος, τό 37 2; τὸ μητρόθεν γ.
33 1; γ. λαμπροῦ 7 1; γ. τοῦ
πρώτου 3 1; πλούτῳ καὶ γένει
9 4; τὸ τῶν θεῶν γ. 39 2;
Μιλησία γένος 24 2; Φωκαῒς
τὸ γ. 24 7; γυνὴ προσήκουσα
κατὰ γένος 24 5
γέρων: οἱ σφόδρα γέροντες 7 1
γῆ: κατὰ γῆν 34 2; τεμὼν τὴν
γ. 19 4

γηραιός: ἤδη γηραιὼν 16 7
γίγνεσθαι 1.1. Of persons: *gigni,
nasci*: ἐκ γυναικὸς Ἀρκαδικῆς
γεγονέναι 29 3; οἱ ὕστερον
γεγονότες 13 12; τῶν ὑπὲρ
πεντήκοντα ἔτη γεγονότων 17
2; τοὺς ἐκ δυεῖν Ἀθηναίων
γεγονότας 37 3.—2. Of
things, 'to be produced': ἐκ
τινῶν . . . πρὸς τί γέγονε 6
3; γενέσθαι σκότος 35 1;
γενέσθαι δημοκρατίαν 25 2;
τῇ σωτηρίᾳ τοῦ γενομένου 13
2; γενομένων . . . γινομένων 12
4; ἐπὶ τῷ λόγῳ τὴν προσ-
ωνυμίαν γενέσθαι 8 3. — 3.
Of events: τὰ γιγνόμενα
33 4; συνθήκας γενέσθαι 10
4; γενομένης διώξεως 31 3;
γενομένης ναυμαχίας 25 3;
γενομένης μάχης 26 2; γενομένων σπονδῶν 24 1; τὰ
γενόμενα 22 1; εἰ μηδὲν
ἔργον μέγα γένοιτο 29 2; τὴν
ἐπίκλησιν γενέσθαι 8 2; ἃ
γέγονεν ἤδη πολλοῖς στρατηγοῖς 38 4; τοὺς γεγενημένους
ὅρκους 29 4
II. With a Predicate, *fieri*, 'to
come into a certain state,' 'to
be so and so' (in past tenses):
θεατὴς γιγνόμενος 1 5; φίλος
γενόμενος 31 2, 10 6; γενέσθαι
πάντων ἐπιφανέστατος 10 2;
γενόμενος δυνάμει πολλῶν
βασιλέων ὑπέρτερος 15 5;
σωτήριος γενομένη 19 1, 39
4; εἶδος εὐπρεπὴς γενομένη 21
2, 24 5; ἀδωροτάτου γενο-
μένου 15 5; ὁμαλῆς γενομένης
15 1; δύναμιν ἐμβριθῆ γενομένην 11 2; ὄργανον τῆς
ὑπηρεσίας γινόμενον 12 7;
ὠφελιμωτάτων ταῖς πατρίσι
γενομένων 2 4; χιλίοις γενομένους 18 2; γενομένους κυρί-

ους 35 4 ; μέγιστον γεγονότα 11 1 ; τοὺς ἐν εὐπαθείαις τισὶ γενομένους 27 2 ; ἐκ ποδῶν γενομένου 39 4
γινώσκειν, *cognoscere*: γιγνώσκοντες ὡς χρήσονται 33 1 ; τὴν ἀρχὴν ὅπως ἔσχε γνῶναι 31 1.—*statuere*: ὥσπερ ἐγνώκει 25 2 ; ἐγνωκότας ἀντιλαμβάνεσθαι τῆς θαλάττης 25 3
γλαῦξ : γλαῦκας 26 3
γλίσχρως, *parce*: γ. χορηγοῦντος in oeconomia 36 1
γλῶττα : τὴν γ. εὔτροχον 7 1 ; ΔΕΙΝΟΝ ΚΕΡΑΥΝΟΝ ΕΝ ΓΛΩCCΗ ΦΕΡΕΙΝ 8 3
γνήσιος : τῶν γ. υἱῶν 36 1 4 ; γνησίους)(ὀθνείους 29 3 ; παῖδας γ. 37 3
γνώμη, *prudentia* 31 1.—*consilium*: γνώμη τοῦ Περικλέους 31 3.—*voluntas, animi sententia*: βιασθῆναι παρὰ γνώμην 33 5 ; *sententia* (in senatu): εἰσηγουμένου γνώμην 13 5
γνώμων horologii : γνωμόνων ἀποσκιασμούς 6 4
γνώριμοι, οἱ, *discipuli* philosophorum 24 3
γνῶσις : τῇ γ. τῶν πραγμάτων 13 12
γοῦν, *exempli gratia* 4 2, 5 2, 38 2
γράμμα, *scriptum legis, plebiscitum*: τοῦ γ. ἐκείνου 37 3
γραῦς : γ. εἶ 10 5 ; ΓΡΑΥC ΕΟΥCΑ 28 5
γράφειν, *scribere*: γράφουσι 35 4 ; γράψαντος 23 1.—γράφει ψήφισμα 17 1, 30 2 3 ; κληρουχίας ἔγραφεν 31 1 ; ψήφισμα ἔγραψε 32 1 ; τὸ ψήφισμα γράψας 10 3 ; γράψαντος 31 5. 32 2, 37 5 ; νόμον ἔγραψε 37 3.—PASS. κρίνειν ἐκ τῶν γραφομένων 2 4 ; γέγραπται 9 4, 24 4 ; ἐν ᾧ γεγραμμένον ἐτύγχανεν 30 1 ; γραφῆναι τὴν κάθοδον 10 4
γραφή, *scriptio*: κατὰ τὴν γ. 24 7
γύναιον, τό, *muliercula* 24 4
γυνή, *femina*: γ. Ἀρκαδικῆς 29 3 ; ἀλαζόνα γ. 12 2 ; αἱ ἄλλαι γ. 28 4 ; τῶν γ. 38 2 ; ἐλευθέρας γυναῖκας 13 9 ; γ. ἐλευθέρας 32 1.—*uxor*: ἣν αὐτῷ γ. 24 5 ; γ. νέᾳ 36 1 : τὴν γ. 13 10 11 ; αἱ γ. 1 1 ; γυναιξὶ 16 4 ; τὰς γ. 24 5, 36 1 3

Δ

δαιμονᾶν³, *furore correptum esse*: τοῖς περὶ τὰ θεῖα δαιμονῶσι 6 1
δαιμόνιος : τι δ. 34 2
δαίμων : δ. κακῷ 13 11
δάκνειν : ΔΑΚΝΕΙΝ ΤΗΝ ΕΥΒΟΙΑΝ 7 6.—PASS. ΔΗΧΘΕΙC ΑΙΘΩΝΙ ΚΛΕΩΝΙ 33 7
δάκρυον : δάκρυα 32 3, 33 5 ; πλῆθος δακρύων 36 5
δαπανᾶσθαι (PASS.): πολλὰ δεδαπανῆσθαι 14 1 ; ἐμοὶ δεδαπανήσθω 14 1
δαπάνη : δ. καὶ χρόνῳ 27 1 ; τὴν ἐφήμερον δ. 16 4
δαπανηρὸς ὢν φύσει 36 1
δαψιλής⁵ de personis: δ. χορηγός 16 4
δέ : σὺ δέ in initio orationis 30 1 ; δὲ καί 7 4, 13 8, 20 3
δ' οὖν *resumptive* 26 2, 27 1, 35 3
δέησις : πᾶσαν δ. 16 7 ; δάκρυα καὶ δεήσεις 33 5
δείδω : δείσαντα τοὺς βαρβάρους 12 2 ; δείσαντας τὴν ἔφοδον 19 3 ; δεδιὼς βιασθῆναι 33 5 ; δεδιὼς ὑποψίᾳ περιπεσεῖν 7 2

δεικνύναι: έδειξε 15 4, 21 1; δείξειε 38 2
δεῖν, *oportere* 4 1; δεῖ 8 5, 12 3; ἔδει 37 3; τὸ δέον 23 1; τοῦ δέοντος 2 4
ΔΕῖΝ, *ligare*)(ἀΝΑΛΎΕΙΝ 16 2
δεινός: μετάνοια δ. 10 2; δεινὸν ἐφαίνετο 33 4; τι δ. ἢ δεινοῦ τινος σημεῖον 35 2; Δ. ΚΕΡΑΥΝΌΝ 8 3; ὄντος δεινοῦ, *cum res indigna esset* 37 5; δ. ὕβριν 12 2; δ. ἀσέβημα 13 11; ΔεΙΝΟΎς ΛΌΓΟΥς 33 7. —w. infin.: δειναὶ αἱ φιλοφροσύναι περιγενέσθαι 7 5
δεινότης oratoris: τὴν δ. 4 1, 8 4; χάριν ἔχουσα μετὰ δεινότητος 24 2
δεινοῦν: δεινῶσαι τὰς τῆς πατρίδος συμφοράς 28 3
δεῖπνον: ἐπὶ δεῖπνον ἐλθεῖν 7 4; δεῖπνον παρέχων 9 2; κλήσεις δείπνων 7 4
δεῖσθαι, *orare*: δ. πᾶσαν δέησιν 16 7; δεομένης 10 5; τῷ δεομένῳ 9 2; δεόμενοι προσέκειντο 33 6; δεηθεὶς τῶν δικαστῶν 32 3; δεηθείσης 25 1; τοῖς δεηθεῖσι 29 3. — *indigere*: ἐμμελοῦς ἀφῆς δεομένους 15 4; ὧν ἐδέοντο διεπράξατο 20 1; ἀνθρωπίνων δ. 37 5
δεισι-δαιμονία: δεισιδαιμονίας καθυπέρτερος 6 1; τῆς φοβερᾶς καὶ φλεγμαινούσης δεισιδαιμονίας 6 1
δεκα-ετία[1]: δεκαετίαν 10 1
δένδρον: δένδρα 33 4
δεξιός: τὴν δ. πλευράν 21 2
δεξιοῦσθαι: ἐδεξιοῦντο 28 4
δέον: *v. s.* δεῖ
δεσμωτήριον: εἰς τὸ δ. 31 5
δέχεσθαι calumniam: δεχομένου τὰς διαβολάς 32 2; δεξάμενοι τὸν λόγον 13 10

δηγμός medici: δηγμοὺς προσφέροντα 15 3
δῆλος: δῆλον (ἦν) ὅτι 34 2
δηλοῦν, 'to prove': δηλοῖ 33 7; δηλοῦσι 8 3.—'to make plain': δεδηλώκαμεν 22 3
δημ-αγωγία: φρόνημα δημαγωγίας ἐμβριθέστερον 4 4; τῆς ἀνειμένης δ. 15 2; τὴν δ. 33 7
δημ-αγωγός in good sense: τὸν δ. Ἐφιάλτην 10 6; δ. ἑτέρων 39 4; τῶν δ. 3 4; τῷ Περικλεῖ καὶ τοῖς ἄλλοις δ. 10 3
δημ-ηγορεῖν: ὅτε δημηγοροίη 8 3
δημι-ουργία: τὴν δ. 13 1
δημι-ουργός, *artifex* 13 9; τοῦ δ. 1 4; τῶν δ. 13 1
δημο-κρατία: λόγῳ οὖσαν δημοκρατίαν 9 1, 16 1, 25 2
δῆμος: 1. 'township': τῶν δήμων Χολαργεύς 3 1; ἐν τοῖς Δήμοις fabula 3 4.—2. *populus*, 'the commons,' 'free citizens': 12 1 3: ΣΑΜΊΩΝ ὁ ΔΉΜΟΣ 26 4; ὑπὸ τοῦ δ. 10 5; τὰς ἀπορίας τοῦ δ. 11 5; προσέπταισε τῷ δ. 32 3, 37 3; τὸν δ. 7 6, 9 1 2, 10 7, 14 1, 29 5, 32 3, 33 5; δήμων ἀγνωμοσύνας 2 4.—3. 'the democracy': τοῦ δ. ποιούμενος πεῖραν 31 2: τῷ δ. προσένειμεν ἑαυτόν 7 2; τῷ δήμῳ ἐπλησίαζε 7 5; τῷ δ. τὰς ἡνίας ἀνείς 11 4; χειροήθης τῷ δ. 15 2; τὸν δ.)(τοὺς καλοὺς κἀγαθούς 11 2; δῆμον)(ὀλίγους 11 3.— 4. *i.q.* ἡ ἐκκλησία 23 1, 29 2, 37 2 5; ὑπὸ τοῦ δήμου προβεβλημένος 10 5, 31 2, 32 2; ἐν τῷ δ. 9 4, 18 2; τὸν δ. εὐλαβεῖτο 7 1, 10 7; ἔπεισε τὸν δ. 29 1
δημόσιος: τὰ δ.)(τὰ οἰκεῖα 36 1; τῶν δ. 9 2, 12 5, 11 2

δημοτικός: δ. προαιρέσεως 11 3;
δ. φύσιν 7 2
δημώδης, *pervulgatus*: δ. στιχιδίοις 30 4
δηοῦν: δηῶν 33 2; δηοῦντες 33 3
διά: A c. Gen. (α) 'through': 1. of Place: διὰ Λοκρῶν 17 2; δι' Εὐβοίας 17 3; διὰ χειρὸς ἔχων τὴν πόλιν 34 1; ἐπηρμένου δι' ἀμφοτέρων τῶν χειρῶν 31 4.—2. of Time: ἐν τῷ διὰ μέσου 10 1.—3. tropically: διὰ τῆς πρὸς ἐκεῖνον ὀργῆς πορευόμενος ἐπὶ τὴν δημαγωγίαν 33 7; δι' ἀριθμοῦ καὶ μέτρου βαδίζοντος 16 4.—(b) Instrumental and modal: δι' Ἐφιάλτου 9 4; δι' ἐκείνων 24 2; δι' Ἀναξαγόρου 32 1; δ. Φειδίου 32 3; δι' Ἑλλήνων ἤκουσαν ἰσχύν 15 1; συνθήκας γενέσθαι δι' Ἐλπινίκης 10 4; δι' Ἀριστοδίκου κρυφαίως ἀνεῖλον (αὐτόν) 10 7; δι' αὐτῶν (τῶν ἀρχῶν) ἀνέβαινον εἰς Ἄρειον πάγον 9 3; θεωρείσθω διὰ τῶν πραγμάτων 9 1; εἴρηκε δ. τούτων 4 3; δι' ἔργων ἀπολύεσθαι τὸν λακωνισμόν 10 1. —B c. Acc. pers. 'because of': τὸν πόλεμον ψηφίσασθαι δ. Μιλησίους 25 1; οὐδεὶς δι' ἐμὲ μέλαν ἱμάτιον περιεβάλετο 38 4; δι' αὐτὸν ἔσχεν ἐχθροὺς φθονουμένος 31 2.—rei: αἱ αἰτίαι δι' ἃς 32 3; δι' ἀπειρίαν 6 1; εὐδοκίμει δ. τὴν ἀσφάλειαν 18 1; δ. τὰς εὐτυχίας 18 2, 20 3; δ. τὴν ἡλικίαν 22 2; δ. τὴν ξενίαν 33 2; δ. τὸ ἀξίωμα 32 3; δ. τὴν νόσον 35 3; κακῶς ἀκούων δ. τὰς δέκα τριήρεις 29 3; δ. τὸ πένθος 37 1; δ. ζηλοτυπίαν 10

6: δ. σχολήν 11 5; δ. φιλίαν Περικλέους 13 9; δ. τοῦτο 27 4; δ. τὸ μὴ λαχεῖν ἄρχων 9 3; διὰ τὸ πρῶτον ἐν Σάμῳ φανῆναι 26 4; δ. τὸ τιμᾶσθαι 18 2
δια-βαίνειν fretum: διέβη 22 1; διαβάς 23 2
δια-βάλλειν: τοῦτο μάλιστα διέβαλλον 12 1; εἰς τὴν Μενίππου γυναῖκα διαβάλλοντες (αὐτόν) 13 10
δια-βοᾶσθαι: διεβοήθη 19 2
δια-βολή: ἀντὶ ὑποψίας καὶ δ. 33 1; διαβολῆς ἀφορμάς 33 2; ἐπὶ διαβολῇ 28 3, 31 5; τὴν περὶ τῆς γυναικὸς δ. 36 3; προσιεμένου τὰς δ. 32 2
δι-αγωγή sc. βίου, *ratio vitae, vitae cultus*: τοιαύτης δ. 39 3
δι-αγωνίζεσθαι: διαγωνίσασθαι 26 1
δια-δοχή: ἐρημία διαδοχῆς 37 2; πολλαῖς δ. 13 1
διά-ζωμα[1], *corona*: τὸ δ. 13 4
δια-ζωννύναι, said of a line of fortifications reaching from one point to another: τὸν αὐχένα διαζώσας 19 1
διά-θεσις, 'plan of a building': τῇ ἐντὸς δ. 13 5
δι-αιρεῖν, *dividendo facere*: ὀκτὼ μέρη διελὼν τὸ πᾶν πλῆθος 27 2
δίαιτα, *vita, vivendi modus*: τὰ περὶ τὴν δ. 16 4; τοῖς περὶ τὴν δίαιταν 7 4; δ. οἰκουρὸν καὶ ἀργήν 34 4
διαιτᾶσθαι δίαιταν οἰκουρόν 34 4
δια-κεῖσθαι: διέκειτο μοχθηρῶς 13 8; κακῶς διακειμένους 28 2; χαλεπῶς διακειμένους πρὸς αὐτόν 35 3
δια-κινδυνεύειν: διακινδυνεύσας 14 2

διά-κόπτεσθαι, *diffindi*: τοῦ κρανίου διακοπέντος 6 2
διακόσιοι : ναῦς δ. 10 4
διά-κόσμησις²: διακοσμήσεως ἀρχήν 4 4
δι-ακούειν : διήκουσε Ζήνωνος 4 3
διά-κρίνειν : χωρὶς διακρίνας (αὐτούς) 11 2
δια-λανθάνειν, *delitescere* 37 3
δια-λέγεσθαι : γλῶτταν εὔτροχον ἐν τῷ δ. 7 1; δι-ελέγοντο πρὸς ἀλλήλους 38 4
διά-λειμμα: ἐκ διαλειμμάτων 7 5
δι-αλλάττεσθαι : διαλλαγῆναι πρὸς αὐτούς 29 5
δια-λύεσθαι, *dirimere*: διαλύσασθαι πόλεμον 24 1.—PASS. *dimitti*: ἡ στρατιὰ διελύθη κατὰ πόλεις 22 3
διά-λυσις : διαλύσεις, *conditiones pacis*: τὰ ἐγκλήματα εἰς δ. ἄγοντος 29 5
δια-μάχεσθαι 26 1 ; διαμαχουμένων 33 3
δια-μνημονεύεσθαι : διαμνημονεύεταί τις λόγος 8 4
δια-νέμειν : διένεμον . . . τὴν εὐπορίαν 12 7 ; διένειμε τὴν νῆσον 34 1.—MID. *inter se dividere* 37 3
διά-νοια *i.q.* νοῦς : τὴν δ. ἐπάγειν θεάμασιν 1 3 ; ὁ μὲν κινεῖ τὴν δ. 16 6
δια-νομή : τὴν τῶν δημοσίων δ. 9 2 ; διανομαῖς χρημάτων 34 1 ; μισθῶν διανομάς 9 1
δια-παιδαγωγεῖν¹, 'to entertain': διαπαιδαγωγῶν ἡδοναῖς τὴν πόλιν 11 4
δια-πολεμεῖν : τοῦ διαπολεμήσαντος πρὸς Ἀννίβαν 2 4
δια-πονεῖσθαι, *elaborare*: μουσικὴν διαπονηθῆναι 4 1 (an aorist of the middle verb,

passive in form ; not found elsewhere)
δι-απορεῖν, *disquirere* : διαποροῦντα πότερον χρή 36 3 ; διαπορῆσαι περὶ τῆς ἀνθρώπου τίνα τέχνην ἔχουσα ἐχειρώσατο 24 1 ; διαπορήσας εἰ τρέπεται 38 2.—MID. *consilii inopia laborare*: διηπορημένον 35 2
δια-πορθεῖν : διεπόρθησαν 34 2
δια-πράσσεσθαι πράγματα τηλικαῦτα 10 5 ; διαπράξασθαί τινί τι, *alicui aliquid apud alium efficere*: τοῖς Ἕλλησιν ὧν ἐδέοντο διεπράξατο 20 1
δια-σκεδαννύναι : διασκεδάσειν τὰ ἐγκλήματα 32 3
δια-σπείρειν : διέσπειρον τὴν εὐπορίαν εἰς πᾶσαν ἡλικίαν 12 7.—PASS. διασπαρῆναι (τὴν διαβολὴν) εἰς τοὺς πολλοὺς 36 3
δια-στρέφειν : ὅταν διαστρέφῃ τὴν ἀλήθειαν 13 12
δια-ταράσσεσθαι : στάσει διατεταραγμένα 36 1
δια-τάσσειν : διέταξεν καθότι χρή . . . αὐλεῖν 13 6
δια-τελεῖν c. participio : διετέλει κολούων 29 3
δια-τηρεῖν, *conservare*: ἄθικτον . . . διατηροῦσα τὴν ὄψιν 13 3 ; διετήρησε τὴν ἐπιείκειαν 39 1
δια-τιθέναι : οὕτω διατίθησιν ὥστε 2 2.—PASS. ἐπὶ τούτῳ χαλεπῶς διατεθείς 36 2.— MID. *testimonio constituere*: ὧν ἔνιοι καί τι τοῖς υἱέσι διέθεντο 15 5
δια-τριβή : παρέσχε διατριβήν, *materiem iocandi praebuit* 4 2.—'conversation': τὰς οἴκοι δ. 36 2.—'consumption of time': ἔργων διατριβὴν ἐχόντων 12 5 ; πράγματα καὶ διατριβὰς παρέχοι 16 3

διαφαίνεσθαι, *apparere*: τὴν σύνεσιν αὐτοῦ μεγάλην ... διαφανεῖσαν 4 4
διαφέρειν, *differre*: τί ἐκεῖνο τούτου διαφέρει; 35 2.— *praestare*: πλούτῳ διαφέροντας 23 2; πολὺ πάντων διήνεγκε 8 1
διαφερόντως τιμᾶσθαι 18 2: ἔστερξε δ. 24 5; δ. ἀγαπώμενον 7 3
διαφθείρειν, 'to destroy': ναῦς διαφθείραντες 26 2.—PASS. ἀνδρῶν διαφθαρέντων 33 4.— 'to corrupt': διαφθείρας χρήμασιν αὐτόν 22 2
διαφορά, *distractio*: διαφορὰν ὑποσημαίνουσα δημοτικῆς καὶ ἀριστοκρατικῆς προαιρέσεως 11 3.—*dissidium*: λυθείσης τῆς δ. 15 1; ἀνήκεστον δ. 36 3
διαφυλάττειν τὸ μεγαλόψυχον 36 5
διαχειρίζεσθαι: διαχειρίσασθαι ἕκαστα (τὰ πάθη) 15 4
διαχρῆσθαι, *conficere*: διαχρωμένην τὸ σῶμα 38 1
διδασκαλία: τραγικὴν δ. 5 4
διδάσκαλος τῶν πολιτικῶν 4 1; διδάσκαλον τῶν μουσικῶν 4 1; τῶν δ. = τῶν κωμῳδοδιδασκάλων 8 3
διδάσκειν: ἐδίδασκε τὸν δῆμον 12 3; διδάσκων τὸν δῆμον 15 3; λόγους διδάσκοντας 32 1
διδόναι 25 2; τῶν διδόντων)(τῶν λαμβανόντων 12 3; ὀλίγας ναῦς ἔδωκε 29 2; ἀτέλειαν ὁ δῆμος ἔδωκε 31 5; δίκας λαβεῖν καὶ δοῦναι 25 1; ὁμήρους ἔδωκαν 28 1; προμαντείαν ἣν ἔδωκαν 21 2.—δίκην τινὰ δεδωκότι τῆς ὑπεροψίας 37 5
διέπειν[3], *administrare*: πάντα διεῖπε 13 4. Cp. *Flam.* c. 18, 2 διέπων ἐπαρχίας

διηγεῖσθαι: τὴν δύναμιν αὐτοῦ σαφῶς διηγεῖται 16 1
διήγησις: τὴν δ. 28 3
διηνεκής[3]: δ. ἀρχὴν 16 3
δικαιολογία[1]: εὐγνώμονος δ. 30 3
δίκαιος: τὸν δ. πλοῦτον 16 3; παρὰ τὰ κοινὰ δ. 29 4
δικαιοσύνη: πρᾳότητα καὶ δ. 2 4
δικαστήριον, τό 32 3
δικαστής: οἱ δ. 32 2; τῶν δ. 32 3; ἐν δικασταῖς 32 2
δικαστικός: δ. λήμμασι 9 3
δίκη: τῇ δ. 35 4; τὴν θανατικὴν δ. ἔφευγε 10 5, 32 1; κρίνεσθαι τὴν δ. ἔγραψεν 32 2; δίκην αὐτῷ προσέλαχε 36 2; παρὰ τὴν δ. 32 3; πολλαὶ ἀνεφύοντο δ. 37 3.— δίκας λαβεῖν καὶ δοῦναι 25 1.— *poena*: δ. τινα δεδωκότι τῆς ὑπεροψίας 37 5
διό 1 5; διὸ καί 8 2, 9 4, 10 2, 11 4, 13 6, 27 2, 29 5, 33 2
διοικεῖν: διῴκει τὸν βίον 16 4
δίπλοη[1]: δ. τις ὕπουλος 11 3
Δίπυλον 30 3
δὶς ἀνὰ πᾶν ἔτος 30 3
δίσκος: ψόφους δίσκων 6 4
διώκειν (*sequi*) τὸ βέλτιστον 1 3. —*litem intendere*: δίκην ἔφευγεν Ἑρμίππου διώκοντος 32 1
δίωξις, 'pursuit': ἅμα τῇ δ. 26 1.—'prosecution': γενομένης ἐν ἐκκλησίᾳ δ. 31 3; κλοπῆς... ἀδικίου δίωξιν 32 2; τὰς δ. 10 7
δοκεῖν, *videri*: οὐ δοκεῖ πιθανὸν εἶναι 26 1; δόξει 39 4; δοκεῖ ὑβρίζεσθαι 12 2, 14 1.—*putare*: δόξαντες αὐτὸν νεμεσητὰ παθεῖν 37 5; κακοῦσθαι δοκοῦντες 29 4; in somniis ἔδοξε τεκεῖν λέοντα 3 2.—*vulgo existimari*: δοκεῖ 10 2, 24 1 6; ἐδόκει 7 1, 10 5; ἐδόκουν 29 3; ἀποθανεῖν ἔδοξε 30 3;

ἁμαρτεῖν ἔδοξε 26 2.—πρὸς τὸ δοκοῦν, *secundum mentis iudicium* 1 3.—Impers. *a.* ἔδοξεν ἡμῖν, 'it seemed good to me,' 'I determined' 2 4.— *b.* 'it seems to me,' 'I think': μοι δοκεῖ 39 1

δοκιμάζεσθαι: οἱ δοκιμασθέντες (ἄρχοντες) 9 3

δολο-φονεῖν: δολοφονήσαντος 10 6

δόξα, *opinio*: συνταράττοντες ἡμᾶς ἀμαθεστάταις δ. 39 2.— δόξαν εἶχεν (=ἐδόκει) ὁμιλεῖν 24 4.—*aestimatio, fama*: πρὸς τὴν Κίμωνος δ. 9 2; ἡ περὶ τὸν βίον δ. 15 5; δ. ἀίδιος 12 4; ἡ δ. τῶν ἔργων 31 4; τὴν δ. τῶν ἔργων 14 2; μεγάλην μετ' εὐνοίας δόξαν ἤνεγκεν 18 3; διὰ φθόνον τῆς δ. 10 6; πλούτῳ καὶ δ. διαφέροντας 23 2; συνδραμεῖν ἀπὸ πολλῶν τῷ ἀνδρὶ τὴν δ. 8 2

δοξο-κοπεῖν[1] 5 4

δοξο-κοπία[1]: τὴν σεμνότητα δοξοκοπίαν ἀποκαλοῦντας 5 4

δόρυ: ἀνατεινούσης δ. 31 4; ΔΟΡΥ ΒΑΣΤΑΖΕΙΝ 33 1

δρᾶν: πολλὰ δρῶντες κακὰ τοὺς Ἀ. 34 2; ἄλλο τι τῆς παρασκευῆς ἄξιον δρᾶσαι 35 3

δραστήριος, *strenuus, fortis*, 'a man of action' 19 4

δραχμή: μιᾷ δ. μείζονα τὴν οὐσίαν οὐκ ἐποίησεν 15 5

δύναμις, *robur*: τὴν ἀκμάζουσαν ἡλικίαν καὶ δ. 34 3.—*copiae*: ἄνευ τῆς ἄλλης δ. 18 2; τῆς δ. τὸ μέγεθος 20 1; τὴν δ. ἐν τῇ Ἑλλάδι συνεῖχεν 22 1; μετὰ δυνάμεως 22 1; ναυτικῇ δ. 29 1.—*potentia*: ἡ τοῦ λόγου δ. 15 5; τὰ πλεῖστα τῆς δ. 21 1; τῆς ἐν τῇ πολιτείᾳ καὶ ταῖς στρατηγίαις δ. 8 2, 38 3; ἀπὸ τηλικαύτης δ. 39 1; δυνάμει πολλῶν τυράννων ὑπέρτερος 15 5; συναγαγὼν εἰς ταὐτὸ τὴν πάντων δ. 11 2; τὴν λεγομένην δ. αὐτῆς (τῆς Ἑλλάδος) ἐκείνην 12 1; δύναμιν κατ' ἐκείνου παρασκευαζόμενος 7 3; τὴν ἐν ἄστει δ. 10 4; τίνα δ. ἔχουσα 24 1; τὴν δ. ἀμβλύνοντα 11 1, 16 1; τὸ ἀξίωμα καὶ τὴν δ. 32 3, 39 4; ΔΥΝΑΜΙΝ ΚΡΑΤΟΣ 16 2

δύνασθαι: τῷ δ. φέρειν 2 4; οἳ πλεῖστον ἠδύναντο 7 1; μέγιστον παρ' αὐτῷ δυνηθείς 31 2

δυναστεία: δυναστείαν κτησάμενος 16 3; δυεῖν δ. 6 2

δυναστής, *regulus*: συμμαχίαις δυναστῶν 15 1; τοῖς δ. 20 1

δυνατός, *potens*: δυνατωτάτων ὄντων 24 2; τοῖς δυνατωτάτοις ἀνδράσι 24 2; τοὺς δυνατωτάτους 28 5.—*possibilis* 31 3

δύο 30 4; δυεῖν[1] (this form is found in inscriptions for the first time in B.C. 329) 6 2, 27 4, 37 3

δύσ-ερως[2 3]: Σικελίας ὁ δ. ἔρως 20 3

δυσ-θήρατος: δυσθήρατον ἱστορία τἀληθές 13 12

δύσ-θυμος: τὸ δύσθυμον)(τὸ θρασυνόμενον 15 4

δυσ-μένεια: δυσμενείας μεστούς 39 3; δυσμενείαις 13 12

δυσ-παθεῖν[1]: τοὺς δυσπαθοῦντας πρὸς τὰ γιγνόμενα 33 4

δύσ-ποτμος[3]: ὁ δ. ἔρως 20 3

δυσ-τυχία: ἡ παροῦσα 37 5

δυσ-φύλακτος[2 3]: δυσφύλακτόν ἐστι 7 5

δυσ-χεραίνειν, *stomachari*: δυσχεραίνοντα κατατείνων 15 3; τῶν δυσχεραινόντων 33 5; δυσχεραίνοντας τῇ τριβῇ 27 2

δωρειά : δωρειάν 37 3
δῶρον : δώρων δίωξιν 32 2

E

ἰᾶν, sinere : ἐῶν (αὐτοὺς) ἀναπίμπλασθαι 34 4; ἐῶμεν (coni.) 5 4.—neglegere : δάκρυα καὶ δεήσεις ἐάσας 33 5. —οὐκ εἴασεν, velmit 11 2, 32 3
ἑαυτοῦ 25 2, 35 1; ἀσφάλειαν ἑαυτῷ παρασκευαζόμενος 7 3; ἑαυτόν 1 3, 7 2 5, 15 1; ὀλοφυρόμενον ἑαυτόν 16 7; μετέστησεν ἑαυτόν 22 3; ἀναθείσης ἑαυτὴν ἐκείνῳ 32 3
ἔβενος 12 6
ἔγ-γονος, nepIis 3 1
ἔγ-γραφος[1] : ἔγγραφον οὐδέν, nihil scripto consignatum 8 4
ἐγείρειν : πᾶσαν τέχνην ἐγείρουσαι (χρεῖαι) 12 4
ἐγ-καλεῖν : φανερῶς ἐ. 29 4; τοὺς ἐγκαλοῦντας 12 2; τοῖς ἐγκαλοῦσι 29 3
ἐγ-καρτερεῖν, perseverare, perstare : ἐ. τῷ ἤθει 36 5
ἐγ-κέφαλος, cerebrum : τὸν ἐ. 6 2
ἔγ-κλημα, crimen : τὰ ἐ. 32 3; τὰ πολλὰ τῶν ἐ. 29 5
ἐγ-κολάπτειν, insculpere : ἐγκολαψάντων 21 2
ἐγ-κωμιάζειν : ἐγκωμιάζων 8 6
ἐγ-χαράττειν : ἐνεχάραξεν 21 2
ἐγ-χειρίδιον : κἀΓΧΕΙΡΙΔΊΟΥ 33 7
ἔδαφος : ἐπ' ἐδάφους 13 4
ἕδος, sedes : ἀσφαλὲς ἕ. deorum 39 3.—i.q. ἄγαλμα, simulacrum in cella sedentis dei v. deae : τὸ χρυσοῦν ἕδος 13 9
ἐθέλεις 33 7
ἐθελοντής : ἐθελοντάς 20 2

ἐθελοντί[1][4] 18 2. Cp. Fab. c. 5, 2 ἀκοντὶ μὴ βιασθῆναι μάχεσθαι
ἐθίζεσθαι : κακῶς ἐθισθέντα 9 1
ἔθνος : ὑπηκόοις ἔθνεσι 15 1; βαρβάροις ἔ. 20 1
ἔθος : ὥσπερ ἔ. ἐστίν 28 3
εἰ, si : εἰ μὴ πείθοιτο 18 2; εἰ ἐπείσθησαν 29 5; εἰ μή τι ὑπηναντιώθη 34 2 etc.—quod 16 7, 39 1.—in oblique question 'whether' : εἰ ὀρθῶς στοχαζόμεθα . . . κρίνειν 2 4; ἠρώτησεν εἰ 14 1; ἠρώτησεν εἰ . . . οὔ 1 1.—εἴγε, siquidem 16 5.—εἰ καί 24 4
εἰδέναι : οὐκ οἶδ' ὁπόθεν (in parenthesi) 10 6
εἶδος, facies : τὸ εἰ. ἐμφερής 7 1; τὸ εἰ. εὐπρεπής 24 2
εἴδω : ἰδών 1 1
εἰκός : ὡς εἰκὸς (ἦν) 15 4
εἰκών, imago : εἰκόνα 13 5; εἰ. παγκάλην 31 4; αἱ εἰκόνες (τοῦ Περικλέους) 3 2
εἶναι : ἑτέρας ἐστὶ πραγματείας 6 4, 39 4; ἔστιν οὗ, alicubi, nonnumquam 16 6; ἔστιν ὅτε 3 2, 24 3; ἦν ὅτε 15 3; ἦσαν 25 3; ἔσοιτο 31 2; οὖσα 22 1; ἐοῦcα 28 5; οὔσης 16 1, 24 5; φωνὴν ἡδεῖαν οὖσαν 7 1, 7 2, 9 1, 25 1; τῶν ὄντων 39 2; τῶν ὅ. Ἀθηναίων 38 4; δυεῖν οὐσῶν 6 2
εἶπεν 10 5, 14 1; εἰπεῖν 13 2, 16 7, 28 5, 30 1; εἰπών 18 2, 28 3; εἰπόντος 14 2
εἴπερ, siquidem 28 6
εἴργεσθαι ἀγορᾶς . . . λιμένων 29 4
εἴρηκε 4 3, 10 7, 24 6, 35 4; εἰρήκαμεν 13 9; εἴρηται 9 2, 31 2, 37 3; εἰρημένος 8 4
εἰρήνη : ἐπ' εἰρήνῃ 17 3; εἰρήνην ἐποίησε ταῖς πόλεσι 10 3; εἰρήΝΗΝ 16 2 (ex Teleclide) ;

τὴν εἰ. ἄγωσιν 17 1; τὴν εἰ. ὠνούμενος 23 1
εἰς 6 5, 10 5, 16 5; ἐν τοῦτο 39 2; ἐκ μ. κορυφῆς 13 5; μιᾶς πολιτείας 13 1; τῆς πόλεως μ. γενομένης 15 1; μιᾷ δραχμῇ 15 5; ὧν ἕνα 7 6; ὁδὸν μίαν 7 4; μ. οὖσαν ἀρχὴν 16 3
εἰς I. of Place: ἔστειλεν εἰς Χερρόνησον κληρούχους 11 5; εἰς Βοιωτίαν ἐμβαλεῖν 18 2; εἰς τὰ τείχη συνέστειλε 19 3; κατέκλεισεν εἰς τὸ τεῖχος 19 4; στρατεύσαντες εἰς Δέλφους 21 1; εἰς τὴν Σπάρτην ἐφοίτα 23 1; ἔπλευσεν εἰς τὸν ἔξω πόντον 26 1; εἰς τὸν Πόντον εἰσπλεύσας 20 1, 26 1; πλεῖν εἰς Σινώπην 20 2; εἰς τὸν αὐτὸν λύκον ἐνεχάραξεν 21 2; διαβὰς εἰς Εὔβοιαν 23 2; ἀπέπλευσεν εἰς τὰς Ἀθήνας 25 2, 28 3, 30 3, 31 5, 32 1, 34 2; εἰς τοὺς πρυτάνεις οἱ λόγοι ἀποτεθεῖεν 32 2, 33 2 3; εἰς τοὺς πολλοὺς διασπαρῆναι 36 3; εἰς τὰ ἔργα φοιτώσας 13 9; περιήνεγκεν εἰς ἑαυτὸν τὰς Ἀθήνας 15 1.—of motion directed to the body or any of its parts; τὰς ψήφους λαβόντας εἰς τὰς χεῖρας 35 4; συνάψαι εἰς χεῖρας 22 2; ἔστιζον εἰς τὸ μέτωπον γλαῦκας 26 3.—before the neuter of the article with adjectives or pronouns: εἰς τὸ αὐτὸ φοιτώσας 32 1; συναγαγὼν εἰς ταὐτό 11 2; τὴν πολιτείαν εἰς ἀντίπαλον κατέστησε 11 2; ἡ πεῖρα περιέστη εἰς τοὐναντίον 33 1; φθεγξάμενος εἰς μέσον 38 4
II. of Time: (a) of the temporal limit for which anything is done: γενομένων σπονδῶν εἰς ἔτη τριάκοντα 24

1.—(b) of the time in which a thing is done: προσδοκῶντας βαρὺν εἰς ἔτους ὥραν πόλεμον 10 2
III. Metaphorically: 1. of motion to something: ἀγωγὸν εἰς μίμησιν 14.—2. of ethical direction or reference after verbs of saying: πολλὰς ἀφεικότων φωνὰς εἰς αὐτόν 8 3; λόγος εἰς τὴν δεινότητα τοῦ Περικλέους εἰρημένος 8 4; εἰς τὴν Μενίππου γυναῖκα διαβάλλοντες (αὐτόν) 13 10; δεινὸν ἀσέβημα ἐξενεγκεῖν εἰς τὴν γυναῖκα 13 11; προσδιαβληθείη εἰς τὸν λακωνισμόν 29 2.—3. of the end which one has in view: τῆς πόλεως πειρωμένης τῶν στρατηγῶν εἰς τὸν πόλεμον 37 1; ὁ εἰς τὴν γένεσιν προδανεισθεὶς χρόνος 13 2; εἰς ταῦτα τρέπειν τὴν εὐπορίαν αὐτῆς (τῆς πόλεως) 12 4; τὴν δύναμιν ἔτρεπεν εἰς φυλακὴν τῶν ὑπαρχόντων 21 1; εἰς πάντα μαλακωτέροις χρήσονται τοῖς Ἀθηναίοις 33 1.—4. of money spent on any object: τὸ φιλητικὸν ἐν ἡμῖν εἰς θηρία καταναλίσκοντας 11 1; ταλάντων ἀνηλωμένων εἰς τὸ δέον 23 1
εἰσ-αγγέλλεσθαι 32 1
εἰσ-άγειν: πάλιν εἰσήγαγε τοὺς Φωκέας 21 2
εἰσ-ηγεῖσθαι: εἰσηγουμένου γνώμην 13 5
εἰσ-ιέναι domum 5 3; εἰσιών 24 6
εἰσ-φέρειν conferre pecuniam: PASS. τοῖς εἰσφερομένοις ὑπ᾽ αὐτῆς ἀναγκαίως 12 2.—ferre ad populum: νόμον εἰσενηνόχει 37 2
εἴσω στρέψον τὸ πινάκιον 30 1

εἶτα 21 5, 28 2; πρῶτον μέν—
εἶτα 22 1; κᾆθ' 30 4
εἴτε—εἴτε 14, 11 2, 32 2
εἰωθώς 28 3
ἐκ I. 1. Of the Place from, out of, which : ἐκ ταύτης (sc. τῆς Πελοποννήσου) 17 2; ἐκ θαλάττης εἰς θάλατταν 19 1; ἐκ Πηγῶν τῆς Μεγαρικῆς 19 2; ἐκ τῆς Εὐβοίας ἀνεκομίζετο 22 2; ἐκ τῆς Ἀττικῆς ἀπαγαγεῖν 22 2, 30 1; καταντὲς ἐκ μιᾶς κορυφῆς πεποιημένον 13 5; ἐκ ποδῶν γενομένου 39 4.—2. of the direction whence: πολλὰ πάσχοντες ὑπ' ἐκείνων ἐκ θαλάττης 34 2.—3. of the Condition or state out of which one comes or is brought 15 2; τὴν πόλιν ἐκ μεγάλης μεγίστην ποιήσας 15 5; ἐξ ἀγεννοῦς καὶ ταπεινοῦ Ἀθηναίων γενέσθαι πρῶτον 24 4
II. Of the Origin, Source or Cause: (α) τιμᾶσθαι ἐκ τῶν πολεμικῶν 18 2; ἐκ τοῦ παραβαλέσθαι χρησαμένους τύχῃ λαμπρᾷ 18 1; πολλαὶ ἀνεφύοντο δίκαι ἐκ τοῦ γράμματος ἐκείνου 37 3.—(b) of the source of conduct: ἐκ φρονήματος μεγάλου ἀπισχυρίσασθαι 31 1. —(c) of that from which a rule of judging is derived: κρίνειν ἐκ τῶν γραφομένων 2 4. Cp. Pelop. c. 31, 3 ἤλπιζε τὴν οἰκίαν αὐτοῦ νοσοῦσαν ἤδη καὶ διεφθαρμένην εὑρήσειν ἐξ ὧν διείλεκτο τῇ Θήβῃ
III. Of the temporal point from which: ἐξ ἀρχῆς 11 3, 34 2; εὐθὺς ἐξ ἀρχῆς 31 3; ἐκ τούτου 21 1, 35 3; ἐκ παλαιοῦ 9 3

ἕκαστος : ἑ. τέχνη 12 7 ; καθ' ἕ. ἐνιαυτόν 11 4, 23 1; ὧν (ἔργων) ἕ. 13 1 3 ; ἕ. τῶν ὁμήρων 25 1 ; τῶν ἀναγκαίων ἕ. 16 4 ; ἕκαστα 15 4
ἑκαστότε 13 11
ἑκατέρωθεν 31 4
ἑκατόμ-πεδος : τὸν ἑ. Παρθενῶνα 13 4
ἐκ-βάλλειν : ἐξέβαλε 14 2, 23 2
ἐκ-δρομή²: κατεῖχε τὴν ἑ. ταύτην 21 1
ἐκεῖθεν 12 2, 39 5
ἐκεῖνος: τί ἐκεῖνο τούτου διαφέρει 35 2 ; τῆς μεγαλαυχίας ἑ. 37 5 ; ἡ ἐπίφθονος ἰσχὺς ἑ. 39 5 ; ἑ. τῶν ἀνδρῶν 11 3.— of remoteness in time : τὴν λεγομένην δύναμιν αὐτῆς ἑ. 12 1, 20 3 ; τῆς ἀνειμένης ἑ. δημαγωγίας 15 2 ; τῶν πραγμάτων ἑ. 27 3.—in place of reflexive pronoun 32 3.—the proper pronoun for emphatic reference to the speaker in opp. to some other person 15 5, 33 1
ἐκ-καίειν, inflammare: ἔρως ὃν ἐξέκαυσαν 20 3 ; τὸν πόλεμον ὑποτυφόμενον ἐξέκαυσεν 32 3
ἐκ-καλεῖν : ἃ τὴν διάνοιαν πρὸς τὸ οἰκεῖον ἀγαθὸν ἐκκαλεῖ 1 3
ἐκ-καλύπτεσθαι : ἐκκαλυψάμενον 16 7
ἐκ-κλείειν : πόλεμον βαρὺν ἐξέκλεισεν 19 2
ἐκ-κλέπτειν : Ἀναξαγόραν ἐξέκλεψεν iudicibus et poenae 32 3 ; ἐκκλέψαντος αὐτοῖς τοὺς ὁμήρους 25 3
ἐκ-κλησία : ἐν ἑ. 14 1, 31 3 ; εἰς ἑ. 33 5 ; ἐν ταῖς ἑ. 12 1
ἐκ-λαμβάνειν, nomen v. dictum accipere in aliquam sententiam : τοῦ τὴν αἰτίαν καλῶς ἐκλαμβάνοντος 6 3

ἐκ-λείπειν, *relinquere*: τὴν οἰκίαν ἐξέλιπε 16 5.—*deficere*, 'to fail': ὡς μὴ τὸν οἶκον ἐκλίποι τοὔνομα καὶ τὸ γένος 37 2.—*abrumpere*: ἐξέλιπε τὴν τοιαύτην ἅπασαν φιλοφροσύνην 7 3.—*deficere* (de sole); ἐκλιπεῖν 35 1
ἐκουσίως 18 1
ἐκ-πέμπειν: τριήρεις ἐκπέμπων 11 4; νεῶν στόλον ἐκπέμπων 34 1; μὴ βουλόμενον ἐξέπεμψε 29 2
ἐκ-πίπτειν, *eici civitate*: ἐξεπεπτώκει 7 2; ἐκπεσόντος 20 2; ἐξέπεσε τῆς Σπάρτης 22 3. —*excidere ex ore*: ῥῆμα μηδὲν ἐκπεσεῖν ἄκοντος αὐτοῦ 8 4
ἐκ-πλεῖν: ἐξέπλευσεν 8 5, 25 3; ἐκπλεῦσαι 10 4, 25 3; ἐκπλεύσας 35 3
ἐκ-πληξις: μεγίστην ἤνεγκε τοῖς ἄλλοις ἔκπληξιν 12 1
ἐκ-πλήττειν: πάντας θαυμαστῶς ἐξέπληττε 5 1.— PASS. τὴν φωνὴν ἐξεπλήττοντο πρὸς τὴν ὁμοιότητα 7 1; ἐκπλαγῆναι ὡς πρὸς μέγα σημεῖον 35 1; ἐκπλαγέντα 16 7
ἐκ-πολεμοῦσθαι, *hostis fieri*: ἐκπεπολεμωμένοι 22 1; ἐκπεπολεμωμένων πρὸς αὐτούς 29 1
ἐκ-πονεῖν, *exercere, tractare*: αἱ ταύτην (*sc*. τὴν ὕλην) ἐκπονοῦσαι τέχναι 12 6
ἐκ-πορίζειν: ἀναψυχὴν ἐκπορίζων 34 4
ἐκ-πρεπής[3]: ἔργον ἐ. 29 2
ἐκ-ταράττεσθαι[2], *perturbari*: πρὸς οὐδὲν ἐκταραττομένη πάθος 5 1
ἐκ-τίνειν: χρημάτων τὸ πλῆθος ἐκτῖσαι 22 3
ἐκτός: τῆς ἐ. ὕλης 16 6; τοῖς ἐ. 7 5; τοὺς ἐ. ἀνθρώπους 19 2
ἐκ-τρέφειν: ἐξέθρεψας 4 2
ἐκ-φέρειν, *pronuntiare* 4 1.— *divulgare*: ἐξενεγκεῖν ἀσέβημα 13 11; ἐκφέρων ἐπὶ γέλωτι τὰς οἴκοι διατριβάς 36 2
ἐκ-φεύγειν[2], *dilabi*: ὡς μὴ (ὁ πλοῦτος) ἐκφύγοι 16 3
ἐκ-χεῖν: πλῆθος ἐκχέαι δακρύων 36 5
ἔλαιον: ἔλαιον ἐπιχέουσιν 16 7
ἐλάττων: φόβον οὐκ ἐλάττονα 35 1; ἔλαττον 12 5; ἐλάττους, *pauciores* 37 4
ἐλαττοῦσθαι, *inferiorem esse*: ἐλαττούμενος πλούτῳ 9 2
ἐλαύνειν τὸ ἄγος 33 1
ἐλάχιστος: ἀριθμὸν τὸν ἐ. 35 4; παρ' ἐλάχιστον ἦλθε 28 6; ἐλάχιστα λυπήσας 10 5
ἐλεγκτικός: ἐ. τινα ἕξιν 4 3
ἐλέγχειν, *exculere*: ἐλέγξας τὸ ἀπόρρητον 23 1.—*confutare*: ἐλέγχει τοῦτο τοῖς Ἀνακρέοντος ποιήμασιν 27 3.—PASS. *convinci*: κλοπαὶ οὐκ ἠλέγχοντο 31 3.—*respui*: τῆς πείρας ἐλεγχθείσης 17 3
ἐλευθερία: ἄκρατον ἐ. 7 6
ἐλεύθερος: ἐ. γυναῖκας 13 9, 32 1
ἐλέφας, *ebur*: ἐλέφαντος 12 6
ἑλκύειν: ἑλκύσας 8 1
Ἕλλην: πάντας Ἕ. 17 1
Ἑλληνίς: ταῖς Ἑ. πόλεσι 20 1
ἐλπίζειν: ἐλπίζων διασκεδάσειν 32 3
ἐλπίς: οὐκ ἀπ' ἐλπίδος 20 3; ἐ. μεγάλην τοῖς πολίταις παρασχών 35 1; ἐλπίδα παρασχοῦσαν ὡς ἁλωσομένην 35 3; μετ' ἐ. ἀγαθῶν 6 1: ἐ. καὶ φόβοις 15 4
ἐμ-βάλλειν, *inicere*: μεγάλας ἐπιβολὰς ἐνέβαλε φέρων εἰς τὸν δῆμον 12 5.—*invadere*: ἐμβάλλουσιν εἰς τὴν Ἀττικήν

33 3; ἐμβαλοῦσι 30 3; εἰς
Βοιωτίαν ἐμβαλεῖν 18 2, 33 2;
ἐμβαλὼν εἰς τὴν Μεγαρικὴν 34
2; οἱ τὸ πρῶτον ἐμβαλόντες
33 4; ἐμβαλόντων εἰς τὴν
Ταναγρικὴν 10 1
ἐμ-βριθής, *gravis*: δύναμιν ἐ.
γενομένην 11 2; φρόνημα
δημαγωγίας ἐμβριθέστερον 4
4. See my n. to *Tib. Gr.*
c. 10, 1
ἐμ-μελής: τὸ Κίμωνος ἐ. 5 3;
μάλ' ἐμμελοῦς ἀφῆς 15 4
ἐμ-μελῶς: ἐ. ἕκαστα (τὰ πάθη)
διαχειρίσασθαι 15 4
ἐμ-μένειν, 'to persist in':
ἐμμεῖναι τῇ φιλονικίᾳ 29 5
ἔμ-μισθος, *mercede conductus*:
ποιοῦσιν ἔ. τὴν πόλιν 12 4;
ἔμμισθοι 11 4
ἔΜ-ΠΑΛΙΝ 16 1
ἐμ-πειρία: τὴν ναυτικὴν ἐ. 11 3
ἐμ-πιμπλάναι: ἐμπεπληκότα 9 4
ἐμ-πίπτειν, *subito incidere*:
ὥστε μηδὲν ἐμπεσεῖν 27 4;
ἡ λοιμώδης ἐνέπεσε φθορά 34 3
ἐμ-ποιεῖν: ἃ ζῆλον ἐμποιεῖ τοῖς
ἱστορήσασιν 1 4
ἔμ-πορος: ἔμποροι 12 6
ἔμπροσθεν, *ante*: πολλαῖς ἔ.
ἡλικίαις τοῦ πολέμου 27 3
ἐμ-φερής³⁵: Πεισιστράτῳ τὸ εἶδος
ἐ. 7 1
ἐμ-φύεσθαι: οἷς οὐδὲν ἐμφύεται
πάθος 10 6
ἐν I. Local: (*a*) of Place proper, within the limits of some space, 'in,' 'at': ἐν Μυκάλῃ
3 1; ἐν Ἀργινούσαις 37 5; ἐν
Ῥώμῃ 1 1; ἐν Ἐλευσῖνι 13 4;
ἐν Νεμέᾳ 19 3; ἐν Λακεδαίμονι
29 4; ἐν Πίσῃ 2 1; ἐν Ἄργει
2 1; ἐν Κύπρῳ 10 7; ἐν
ἐκκλησίᾳ 14 1, 31 3; ἐν ταῖς
ἐκκλησίαις 12 1; ἐν ἄστει 7 4,
10 4, 11 2; ἐν τῇ πόλει 3 4,
11 1; τὸ φιλητικὸν ἐν ἡμῖν 1
1; ἐν σιδήρῳ 11 3; ἐν οἰκίᾳ
μεγάλῃ 16 4; ἐν σκηνώμασι
πνιγηροῖς 34 4; ἐν τοῖς κόλποις
περιφέροντας 1 1; ΚΕΡΑΥΝΟΝ
ἐΝ ΓΛώccΗ ΦέΡΕΙΝ 8 3, 39
3; ἐν πελάγει 33 5; τὸ πινάκιον ἐν ᾧ τὸ ψήφισμα γεγραμμένον ἐτύγχανεν 30 1.—(*b*) of
the contents of a writing etc.:
ἐν τῷ Μενεξένῳ 24 4; ἐν ταῖς
κωμῳδίαις 24 6; ἐν τοῖς Ἠθικοῖς 38 2; ὡς ἐν τοῖς περὶ
ἐκείνου γέγραπται 9 4; ἐν
τοῖς περὶ Λυσάνδρου 22 3; ἐν
τῷ τῆς στρατηγίας ἀπολογισμῷ 23 1.—with neuter
adjective: φυλάττειν ἐν ὀχυρῷ
τὰ κοινά 12 2.—'with,'
'among,' 'in the presence
of': ἐν Ἐφιάλταις 16 2: ἐν
τῷ δήμῳ 9 4; ἐν ὄχλῳ 15 4;
κρίνεσθαι ἐν δικασταῖς 32 2.—
'in the case of': τοῦ δήμου
ποιούμενοι πεῖραν ἐν ἐκείνῳ 31
2; ἐν τῇ σωτηρίᾳ τοῦ γενομένου τὴν ἰσχὺν ἀποδίδωσιν
13 2

II. Of the State or Condition in which one exists,
acts or suffers: τοὺς ἐν
εὐπαθείαις τισὶ γενομένους 27
2; βίον ἐν ἐξουσίᾳ καθαρόν 39
2; σεμνότερον ἐν πραότητι
τρόπον 39 5; ἐν πράγμασι
πολλοῖς καὶ μεγάλαις ἀπεχθείαις 39 1; τοὺς ἐν τέλει 23
1; δυσφύλακτον ἐν συνηθείᾳ
7 5; ἐν πράγμασι μεγάλοις
καὶ κινδύνοις 32 3; ἡ ἐν τῷ
ποιεῖν εὐχέρεια 13 2; μῆκος
ἐχούσῃ ἐν ποικίλαις μεταβολαῖς 38 1

III. Of Time, denoting periods
and portions of time in
which anything occurs: ἐν

ἀρχῇ 9 2; ἐν τῷ διὰ μέσου 10 1; ἐν χρόνῳ ῥητῷ; ἐν ὀλίγῳ 13 3; ἐν τῷ λοίπῳ βίῳ 36 5; ἐν τῷ λοιμῷ 36 3; ἐν τούτῳ 29 4; ἐν οἷς χρόνοις 7 4; χρόνον ἐν ᾧ 23 1; ἐν πενταετίᾳ 13 7; ἔν τινι πότῳ 1 5; ἐν τῷ λέγειν 5 1

IV. In Composition, prefixed to verbs and general compounds followed by the dative, it denotes continuance in some place, state or condition, as ἐγ-καρτερεῖν 36 5; ἐμ-μένειν 29 5; ἐμ-ποιεῖν 1 4; ἐμ-φύεται 10 6; ἐν-διασπείρεσθαι 11 2; ἐν-διατρίβειν 2 4; ἐν-εργάζεσθαι 6 1, 39 4; ἐν-τιθέναι 2 3, 13 2, 31 4. — prefixed to adjectives, it denotes being in some place or condition, being possessed of something, or entering into, mingling in something, as ἔνοχος 33 1

ἐναντίος: τοὐναντίον by crasis for τὸ ἐναντίον 1 4

ἐναντιοῦσθαι: ἐναντιωσόμενον 11 1; πρὸς τοῦτο ἐναντιωθεὶς 29 5

ἔνατος: ἐ. μηνί 28 1

ἐν-δείκνυσθαι: ἐνδεικνύμενος αὑτοῦ τὸ φρόνημα 17 3

ἔν-δειξις: ἔνδειξιν ἰσχύος 31 1

ἐν-δεκά-κλινος: ἘΝΔΕΚΑΚΛΊΝΟΥ ΚΕΦΑΛΗ͂Σ 3 3

ἐν-δελεχής: πόλεμον ἐ. 19 1

ἐν-δια-σπείρεσθαι: ἐνδιεσπάρθαι 11 2

ἐν-δια-τρίβειν: ἐνδιατρῖψαι τῇ περὶ τοὺς βίους ἀναγραφῇ 2 4

ἐν-διδόναι: διαβολῆς τοῖς ἐχθροῖς ἐνδιδοὺς ἀφορμάς 33 2. — οὐδέν τι μᾶλλον ἐνέδωκε 30 1: ἐνδοῦναι Λακεδαιμονίοις 32 3

ἔν-δοξος: ταφὰς ἐ. 28 3

ἔν-δοσις[1]: πεῖραν ἐνδόσεως 31 1

ἐν-εῖναι, inesse: ἔνεστιν 24 4. — ἢ ἔνεστιν ('is possible') αὐτῷ πρόφασις 12 1

ἐν-εργάζεσθαι: ἐνεργάζεται 6 1; ἐνειργάζετο 39 4

ἔν-εργος: ὁ ἐνεργότατος τῶν τεχνιτῶν 13 8

ἐν-ήλικος[1], adultus: τοῖς ἐ. παισίν 16 4

ἐν-θουσιασμός: ὑπ' ἐνθουσιασμοῦ 16 5

ἐνιαύσιος: ἐ. στρατηγίαις 16 3

ἐνιαυτός: καθ' ἕκαστον ἐ. 11 4, 23 1

ἔνιοι 10 4, 15 5, 23 1, 31 5; ἔνια 15 2; ἐνίοις 20 3

ἔν-οχος: ἐ. ἄγει γένος 33 1

ἐνταῦθα 24 1, 28 3

ἐν-τείνεσθαι: βασιλικὴν ἐντειναμένος πολιτείαν 15 2

ἐν-τιθέναι: πρακτικὴν ὁρμὴν ἐντίθησιν 2 3; οὐκ ἐντίθησι βάρος ἔργῳ 13 2; εἰκόνα ἐνέθηκε (sc. τῇ ἀσπίδι) 31 4

ἐντός 13 5

ἐν-τυποῦν[1]: ἐν τῇ ἀσπίδι μορφὴν ἐνετύπωσε 31 4

ἐξ-αιτεῖσθαι: Ἀσπασίαν ἐξῃτήσατο 32 3

ἑξακισ-μύριοι: τοῖς ἐ. 33 4

ἘΞ-ΑΝΑ-ΤΈΛΛΕΙΝ ΘΌΡΥΒΟΝ ΠΟΛΎΝ 3 4

ἐξ-αν-ίστασθαι: ἐξανέστη 7 4

ἐξ-αρτᾶσθαι: τὰ τῶν Ἀθηναίων ἐξηρτημένα πράγματα 15 1

ἐξ-αρτύεσθαι: λόγον ἐξαρτυόμενος 8 1

ἐξ-ασκεῖν, educere: ἐλεγκτικὴν τινα ἐξασκήσαντος ἕξιν 4 3

ἘΞΈΘΡΕΨΑΣ (ἐκ-τρέφειν) 4 2

ἐξ-εῖναι: ἔξεστι κρίνειν 2 4

ἐξ-ελαύνειν: ἐξήλασε 3 1: ἐξελάσας 34 1

ἐξ-εργάζεσθαι[1], absolvi: τὰ Προπύλαια ἐξειργάσθη 13 7

ἐξ-ετάζεσθαι, censeri: ἐξητάσθησαν 13 4
ἐξ-ιέναι : καὶ ἐξιὼν καὶ εἰσιὼν ἀπ' ἀγορᾶς 24 6
ἕξις, *exercitatio et parata inde facilitas disputandi*: ἐλεγκτικήν τινα ἕ. 4 3
ἐξ-ίστασθαι τῆς ἀρετῆς 38 2
ἐξ-ομοίωσις[1]: τὴν ἑ. 2 2
ἐξ-ομολόγησις[1] : ἐξομολόγησιν ἀσθενείας 31 1
ἐξ-ονειδίζειν[3] 3 2
ἐξ-οστρακίζεσθαι : ἐξωστρακίσθη 4 2 ; ἐξοστρακισθῆναι 7 1, 9 4
ἐξ-οστρακισμός 10 1
ἐξ-ουσία, *licentia : ἐν ἑ.* 39 5.—*potentia* 39 2
ἐξ-υβρίζειν : ἐξυβρίσαντα 7 6
ἔξω: τὸν ἕ. πόντον (the Mediterranean) as opp. to τὸν ἐντός (the Aegean) 26 1; τῶν ἑ. στρατηγεῖν 10 4.—w. gen. : τῆς Ἑλλάδος ἔξω 7 2
ἔοικε 4 1, 13 12, 22 3, 28 1 2 3, 38 1 ; ὡς ἕ., *ut videtur* 3 2, 7 3 ; *ut perhibetur* 1 1, 5 1, 30 2
ἐοῦϲα Ionic form of οὖσα 28 5
ἐπ-άγειν τὴν διάνοιαν θεάμασι 1 3
ἐπ-αινεῖν : ἐπαινεῖ 5 3 ; ταῦτα ἐπαινοῦσιν αὐτοῦ 38 4 ; παῖδα καλὸν ἐπαινέσαντος 8 5
ἐπ-αίρειν : πέτρον ἐπηρμένου, *saxum sublatum tenentis* 31 4. — c. infin. ἐπαίρων τὸν δῆμον μέγα φρονεῖν 17 1.—pass. ἐπαιρομένων ἀντιλαμβάνεσθαι 20 2
ἐπ-ανθεῖν : ἐπανθεῖ καινότης τις 13 3
ἐπ-αν-ιέναι : ἐπανῆλθε 28 3
ἐπ-αν-ορθοῦσθαι: ἐπανορθούμενος τὰς ἀπορίας τοῦ δήμου 11 5
ἐπ-αυλις[2]: τὰς ἐπαύλεις 33 2
ἐπεί, *postquam* 7 2, 21 2, 26 1,

30 3, 37 3.—*quoniam* 1 4, 9 1, 24 1, 27 2, 30 3
ἐπείγειν : τὰ ἐπείγοντα negotia 5 2
ἐπειδή 13 6
ἐπ-εξ-ιέναι 26 1
ἐπ-έτειος : τοὺς ἑ. καρποὺς 16 4
ἐπί I. w. Gen. of Place: *super,* 'upon' : ἑ. τοῦ βήματος 8 6 ; τοὺς ἐπ' ἐδάφους κίονας 13 4 ; ἑ. τοῦ ἀνακτόρου 13 5 ; ἑ. τοῦ κρανίου 13 6 ; ἑ. τῶν σημάτων 28 3 ; ἑ. τῶν ὅρων 10 2 ; ἑ. ζυγοῦ 11 2.—ἑ. στρατοπέδου, *in exercitu* 27 1. — *versus,* 'in the direction of' : ἐπ' οἴκου 19 4. — of that on which anything rests, 'on the ground of' : κρατεῖν τὴν διήγησιν ἐπὶ τῆς ἀληθείας 28 3.—'in the case of': ἐπὶ τῶν μύρων 1 4
II. with Dat.—1. Of the place at or by which : στρατιὰ ἐπὶ τοῖς ὅροις οὖσα 22 1.—of the reason or motive underlying words or deeds, *propter,* 'for,' 'on account of' : ἐπὶ τῷ λόγῳ τὴν προσωνυμίαν γενέσθαι 8 3 ; ἀσχάλλοντας ἐπὶ τῷ πολέμῳ 3 4 ; ἑ. τούτῳ χαλεπῶς διατεθείς 36 2 ; 13 8 ; ἑ. τούτῳ καμφθείς 36 5 ; μέγα φρονοῦντος ἐπὶ τῷ ταχὺ τὰ ζῷα ποιεῖν 13 2. — 2. of the purpose and end, 'with a view to': μετέχειν τῶν βουλευμάτων ἐπ' εἰρήνῃ τῆς Ἑλλάδος 17 3 ; ἐπὶ ῥητορικῇ πολλοῖς Ἀθηναίων ὁμιλεῖν 24 4 ; ἐπὶ διαβολῇ τῶν Ἀθηναίων 28 3 ; ἐπὶ διαβολῇ τοῦ Π. παρασκευασάντων 31 5 ; αἰτούμενον ἄδειαν ἐπὶ μηνύσει τοῦ Φ. 31 2 ; ἐπὶ

γέλωτι 36 2 ; μέγα φρονοῦντος ἐπὶ τῷ ποιεῖν 13 2.—3. of the Occasion or Circumstances: οὐκ ἐπὶ παντὶ πράγματι λέγων 7 5, 16 2.— 4. 'in addition to': πέντε ἐπὶ τούτοις 17 2.—5. *penes*, 'in the power of': πάντα ἦν ἐπ' αὐτῷ 13 9 ; ὅσον ἐπ' αὐτῷ 18 1.— 6. 'after,' 'as a sequel to': αἰσχρῶς ἐ. καλοῖς ἔργοις ἁλούς 22 3
III. w. Acc. A. 1. Local: 'upon,' 'on to,' 'unto': τὴν ἐπ' ἀγορὰν ὁδόν 7 4 ; ἐπὶ δεῖπνον 7 4 (but here the final meaning is blended with the local); ἐπὶ τὴν πρόσοικον ἤπειρον 17 2 ; ἐπ' Οἰταίους 17 2 ; ἐπὶ τοὺς ἀφεστῶτας τραπόμενος 23 2, 35 1 ; θεῖν ἐπὶ τὸν ἄνδρα 16 7.—2. of direction towards a terminus: ἐ. τέλος ἀφιξέσθαι 13 1 ; ὁρμὴ ἐπὶ τὴν ἐξομοίωσιν 2 2 ; τὸ καλὸν ἐφ' αὑτὸ κινεῖ 2 3 ; ἐπὶ κληρουχίας προαχθῆναι 9 1 ; πορευόμενος ἐπὶ τὴν δημαγωγίαν 33 7.— 3. of the direction of the will and action: (*a*) of purpose and end: ἐπὶ ταῦτα ἐπέμφθησαν 17 2.—(*b*) of things done with hostility 'against' 20 1, 26 1, 35 4 ; Εὐβοεῖς ἐφ' οὓς διέβη μετὰ δυνάμεως 22 1 ; ὁρμησάντων ἐπ' αὐτούς 10 1 ; ἐξέπλευσεν ἐπ' αὐτούς 25 3, 34 1, 35 4
B. Of Time, 'for the space of': ἐφ' ἡμέρας δέκα 28 2 ; ἀνθούσης ἐφ' ὥραν πολιτείας 16 2
ἐπι-βαίνειν, *ingredi*: ὃς δ' ἂν ἐπιβῇ τῆς Ἀττικῆς 30 3
ἐπι-βάτης = ὁ ἀπὸ τοῦ καταστρώματος μαχόμενος : τοὺς ἐ. 28

2. — *rector*, 'a passenger': ἐπιβατῶν ναυτιώντων 33 5
ἐπι-βολή : μεγάλας κατασκευασμάτων ἐ. 12 5 (from ἐπιβάλλεσθαι, 'to design,' 'undertake')
ἐπι-βουλεύειν : ἐπιβουλεύσαντες ἀνεῖλον 10 7
ἐπι-γίγνεσθαι : ἐπιγενομένη (ἡ νόσος) 35 3
ἐπι-γράφεσθαι : ἐπεγράφη τῇ δίκῃ κατήγορος 35 4
ἐπι-γραφή : τῶν ἀναθημάτων τὴν ἐ. 14 1
ἐπι-δεικνύναι, *indicare*: ἐπιδεῖξαι τὸν ἐγκέφαλον οὐ πεπληρωκότα τὴν βάσιν 6 2.—MID. *ostentare*: ἐπεδείξατο τῆς δυνάμεως τὸ μέγεθος 20 1
ἐπι-διδόναι, *gratuito dare*: τῇ πόλει τὰς ἐπαύλεις ἐπιδίδωσι 33 2 ; ἑαυτὸν πρὸς τὰς μεγάλας χρείας ἐπιδιδούς 7 5
ἐπι-είκεια, *lenitas*: τῆς ἐ. 39 1
ἐπ-ιέναι, *obire*: τοὺς τόπους ἐπῄεσαν 17 2. — *subire*: ἐπελθόντα τῇ μνήμῃ 24 7
ἐπι-ζευγνύναι [4] : τοὺς κίονας τοῖς ἐπιστυλίοις ἐπέζευξεν 13 4
ἐπι-θυμεῖν : ἐπεθύμησεν 2 1
ἐπι-θυμία : ταῖς ἐ. 15 2
ἐπι-κεῖσθαι, *premere*, *aggredi*: τοσαύτη φθορὰ ἐπέκειτο τοῖς πράγμασιν 39 5
ἐπι-κλᾶν : ἐπέκλασε 37 5
ἐπί-κλησις : τὴν ἐ. 8 2
ἐπί-κουρος : ἐπικούρων τοῖς Σαμίοις 26 1
ἐπι-κρύπτειν, *tegere*, *celare* 31 4.—MID. πρὸς τοὺς πολλοὺς ἐπικρυπτόμενος τὴν δεινότητα 4 1
ἐπι-λήπτωρ : ΠΆΝΤΩΝ ἘΠΙΛΉΠΤΟΡΟϹ 4 3
ἐπι-μελεῖσθαι τῆς ἀσφαλείας τοῦ ἀνθρώπου 31 5

S

ἐπι-νοεῖν: οὐκ ἐπινοοῦσιν ἀθετοῦντες 6 4
ἐπι-πηδᾶν: ταῖς νήcοιc ἐπιπηδᾶν 7 6
ἐπι-προσθεῖν[1]: τὸν χρόνον ἔχωσιν ἐπιπροσθοῦντα τῇ γνώσει 13 12
ἐπισκοπεῖσθαι, aegrum invisere: ἐπισκοπουμένῳ 38 2
ἐπί-σκοπος: πάντων ἐ. 13 4
ἐπι-σκότησις[1]: τὴν ἐ. 35 2
ἐπι-στατεῖν: ἐπιστατοῦντος operi 13 5; ἐπεστάτει τοῖς τεχνίταις 13 9
ἐπι-στρατεύειν: ἐπιστρατεύσας 21 2
ἐπι-στύλιον: τοῖς ἐ. 13 4
ἐπι-ταχύνειν: ἐπετάχυνε τὸν πόλεμον 29 4
ἐπι-τερπῶς[1] 1 5
ἐπι-τήδειος, familiaris: οὐκ ὀλίγους τῶν ἐ. 36 1
ἐπι-τιθέναι: τοῖς περὶ τὴν δίαιταν ἑτέραν τάξιν ἐπέθηκεν 7 4.—MID. aggredi: ἐπιθέσθαι τοῖς 'Aθ. 26 2.—'to make up to': ἐπιθέσθαι τοῖς δυνατωτάτοις ἀνδράσι 24 2
ἐπι-τραγῳδεῖν[1]: τούτοις ἐπιτραγῳδεῖ 28 1
[ἐπί-τροπος: ἐπίτροπον διέθεντο v. l. 15 5]
ἐπι-τυγχάνειν, propositum assequi 6 3
ἐπι-φανής: πάντων ἐπιφανέστατος 10 2
ἐπι-φέρειν, afferre: ἐπιφέρων τῳ νεκρῷ στέφανον 36 5.—obicere: τὴν αἰτίαν (τούτου) ἐπιφέρουσι τῷ Περικλεῖ 31 1
ἐπί-φθονος: ἡ ἐ. ἰσχύς 39 5
ἐπι-φύεσθαι: ἐπεφύετο 33 7
ἐπι-χεῖν, infundere: ἐπιχέουσιν oleum lychno 16 7
ἐπι-χειρεῖν: ἐπεχείρησαν 34 3
ἔπ-οικος, colonus (in locum iam

antea habitatum missus): ἐ. χιλίους 19 1
ἐπ-ομνύειν[2] 30 3
ἔπος: ὡς ἔ. εἰπεῖν 12 7
ἐργάζεσθαι, fabricari, 'to make,' 'to build': τὸν ἑκατόμπεδον εἰργάζετο 13 4; εἰργάζετο τὸ ἔδος 13 9; τὸν εἰργασμένον . . . τοὺς εἰργασμένους 2 2.—'to cause to exist,' 'produce': τὴν νόσον ἐργάζεται (v. l. ἀπεργάζεται) 34 3
ἐργασία, quaesitus: οὐ κοσμίου ἐ. 24 3
ἐργο-λαβεῖν: ἠργολάβησε 13 5
ἐργολάβος: ἐ. τοῦ ἀγάλματος 31 2
ἔργον: 1. 'business': τὰ κατεπείγοντα τῶν ἔ. 27 10; συνεφαπτομένην τοῦ ἔ. 13 7.—2. 'the result of any work,' 'product of art, industry, mind': χαίροντες τῷ ἔ. τοῦ δημιουργοῦ καταφρονοῦμεν 1 4; εἰ τέρπει τὸ ἔ. ὡς χαρίεν 2 2; ἔργῳ 13 2; ἀναβαινόντων τῶν ἔ. 13 3; μεγάλους ἐχόντων τεχνίτας τῶν ἔ. 13 4; τὰ Περικλέους ἔ. 13 3 9; ἀειθαλὲς πνεῦμα τῶν ἔ. ἐχόντων 13 3; ἔ. διατριβὴν ἐχόντων 12 5; τὰ ἔ. καὶ τοὺς εἰργασμένους 2 2; ἡ δόξα τῶν ἔ. 2 2.—3. 'an act,' 'deed,' 'thing done': τοῖς ἀπ' ἀρετῆς ἔ. 1 4; μηδὲν ἔ. μέγα 29 2; τῇ ἱστορίᾳ τοῦ ἔ. 2 3; λόγῳ μὲν ἔ. δέ 9 1; αὐτὸ λόγοιcι προάγει—ἔργοιcι δ' οὐδὲ κινεῖ 13 5; δι' ἔργων ἀπολύεσθαι τὸν λακωνισμόν 10 1. —4. 'employment,' 'proper work': μέγιστον ἔ. αὐτῆς (τῆς ῥητορικῆς) 15 4.—c. inf. 'a hard task,' μέγα ἔ. 21 1; ἔργον ἦν κατασχεῖν 27 2

ἔρεψις¹, 'roofing,' 'roof': τῇ ἐρέψει 13 5
ἐρημία : ἐρημίᾳ διαδοχῆς 37 2
ἐρρωμένος, *robustus* (from ῥώννυσθαι*)*: *ἐ*. ναυτικῇ δυνάμει νῆσον 29 1 ; ἐρρωμενεστάτην μάχην 10 2.—Adv. ἐρρωμενέστατα 10 2
ἔρυμα 39 5 ; ἐρύμασι 19 1
ἔρχεσθαι, *venire*: ἦλθεν ἕτερος στόλος 26 1 ; ἐλθούσης πρὸς αὐτόν 10 5.—*redire*: ἐλθὼν ἐκ τῆς φυγῆς 10 1
ἔρως : Σικελίας ὁ δύσερως *ἔ*. 20 3
ἐρωτᾶν : οὕτως ἐρωτῶντα 24 5 ; ἠρώτησε μὴ οἴεται 35 2 ; ἠρώτησεν εἰ δοκεῖ 14 1 ; ἠρώτησεν εἰ οὐ τίκτουσιν 1 1
ἐρωτικός : *ἐ*. ἀγάπησις 21 4
ἑσπέρα : ἑσπέρας 5 2
ἑστίασις : ἑστίασιν 11 4
ἑταιρεία, 'a political club': τὴν ἀντιτεταγμένην *ἐ*. 14 2
ἑταιρεῖν, *quaestum corpore facere*: παιδίσκας ἑταιρούσας 24 3
ἑταῖρος 13 10 ; τῶν *ἑ*. 20 2 : τοὺς περὶ αὐτὸν *ἑ*. 16 1
ἕτερος : ὡς *ἕ*. οὐδείς 16 5 ; *ἕ*. στόλος 26 1 ; *ἑ*. πραγματείας 6 4, 39 4 ; *ἑ*. τάξιν 7 4 : ἑτέρων ἀγωνιζομένων 1 5 ; ἡμῖν παρ' ἑτέρων...ἑτέροις παρ' ἡμῶν ὑπάρχειν 2 3 ; τειρώμενοι ῥητόρων *ἑ*. 89 4 ; ἑτέρους καθιείς 7 5 ; *ἑ*. τριήρεις 29 3
ἔτι 26 1 ; ἔτι δέ 25 2 ; *ἔ*. μᾶλλον 17 1 ; *ἔ*. μείζονα πίστιν 33 1
ἕτοιμος : εὐπορία ἑτοίμη πάρεσται 12 4
ἔτος : εἰς ἔτους ὥραν 10 2 ; ἀνὰ πᾶν *ἔ*. 30 3 ; τεσσαράκοντα ἔτη 16 2 ; ἀρχὴν οὐκ ἐλάττω τῶν πεντεκαίδεκα *ἔ*. 16 3 ; ἔτεσι δέκα 28 5 ; ὑπὲρ πεντήκοντα ἔτη 17 2

εὖ : θέμενος εὖ πάντα in navi 33 5
εὐ-ανδρία : εὐανδρίᾳ 19 1
εὐ-γενής : φρόνημα εὐ. 10 6
εὐ-γνώμων : εὐ. δικαιολογίας 30 3
εὐ-δαιμονία : ΕϒΔΑΙΜΟΝίΑΝ 16 2
εὐ-δοκιμεῖν : εὐδοκίμει 18 1 ; εὐδοκίμησε 18 3
εὔθυνα : τὰς εὐ., 'audits' 10 7
εὐθύς 1 4, 2 3, 7 4, 13 3, 16 7, 22 1, 25 3, 27 1, 28 1 ; εὐ. ἐξ ἀρχῆς 31 3 ; εὐθὺς ἐκείνων ἀπαλλαγέντων 21 2 ; εὐθὺς ἐκ ποδῶν γενομένου 39 4
εὐ-λαβεῖσθαι : τὸν δῆμον εὐλαβεῖτο 7 1
εὐ-λαβής περὶ τὸν λόγον 8 4
εὐ-μενής : εὐμενὲς ἦθος 39 2
εὐ-μηχάνως 31 4
εὔ-νοιά τινι πρός τινα 29 2 ; μετ' εὐνοίας δόξαν 18 3 ; εὔ. ἔχων τινὰ πρὸς Σαμίους 25 2
εὐ-πάθεια : τοὺς ἐν εὐ. τισὶ γενομένους 27 2
εὐ-πορία¹ ⁴, *copiae, opes* 12 4 ; τὴν εὐ. αὐτῆς (sc. τῆς πόλεως) 12 4 ; διένεμον τὴν εὐ. 12 7 ; τὰς ἀπὸ τῶν κοινῶν εὐ. 12 5
εὐ-πρεπής, *decorus*: τὸ εἶδος εὐ. 24 2.—*speciosus*: εὐπρεπεστάτη τῶν προφάσεων 12 2
εὕρεσις : τῆς αἰτίας τὴν εὕ. 6 4
εὔ-ροια : τὴν εὔ. τῶν πραγμάτων 20 3
εὐ-σέβεια : τὴν ἀσφαλῆ εὐσέβειαν ἐνεργάζεται 6 1
εὔ-τροχος³ : τὴν γλῶτταν εὔ. 7 1
εὐ-τυχία : διὰ τὰς πρότερον εὐτυχίας 18 2
εὐ-φυής, 'endowed with a happy moral disposition' : εὐ. νέος 2 1 ; εϒφϒΗ̂C 8 1
εὐ-χέρεια artificum : ἡ ἐν τῷ ποιεῖν εὐ. 13 2

εὔχεσθαι: ηὔχετο τοῖς θεοῖς 8 4 (see n. to c. 7, 1); εὐξάμενοι τοῖς θεοῖς 17 1
εὐ-ωχεῖσθαι 27 2
ἐφ-ήμερος: τὴν ἐ. δαπάνην 16 4
ἐφ-ιστάναι, *addere, insuper ponere*: τοὺς ἄνω κίονας ἐπίστησε 13 4.—*praeficere*: τοῖς ὅλοις νοῦν ἐπέστησε 4 4
ἔφ-οδος, *adventus*: τὴν ἔ. 19 3
ἔφ-ορος: οἱ ἔ. 22 2
ἐφ-υβρίζειν: ἐφυβρίζων 29 2; ἐφυβρίζοντες 33 6
ἐχ-έγ-γυος, *idoneus*: ἀξίωμα ἐ. πρὸς τοσαύτην ἡγεμονίαν 37 1
ἔχειν: **A.** Trans. 1. 1. *habere*, 'to have': (*a*) αἰτία ἔχουσα πλείστους μάρτυρας 31 2, 5 4.—(*b*) 'to have (in itself or as a consequence),' 'involve': πολλὴν ἀδηλότητα καὶ κίνδυνον ἔσχεν ὁ πόλεμος 28 6; μάχης ἐχούσης πολλὴν ἀδηλότητα 18 1; ἔργων διατριβὴν ἐχόντων 12 5; νόσῳ μῆκος ἐχούσῃ 38 1.—(*c*) 'to have possession of the mind,' said of agitating emotions: μετάνοια καὶ πόθος ἔσχεν αὐτούς 10 2; ἔρως εἶχεν Σικελίας 20 3.—2. 'to have,' *i.e.* 'to own,' 'possess': (*a*) property: Φωκέων ἐχόντων τὸ ἱερόν 21 2; ὅσα μὴ πρότερον εἶχον 26 2; τοσαύτην ἀρχὴν ἔχοντι 15 4; τίνα τέχνην ἔχουσα 24 1.—(*b*) relatives: παῖδας ἔχων γνησίους 37 3.—(*c*) the present participle with verb = 'with': πρὶν ἐμβαλεῖν ἔχοντα τοὺς Πελ. 33 2; ἀπέστειλε δέκα ναῦς ἔχοντα τὸν Λακεδαιμόνιον 29 2.—(*d*) to have faculties, emotions, etc.: φρόνημα εὐγενὲς ἔχοντι 10 6; ἔχων τινὰ πρὸς Σαμίους εὔνοιαν 25 2.—(*e*) of age and time: τοῖς ἡλικίαν ἔχουσι καὶ ῥώμην 12 5.—(*f*) to have advantages, conveniences: ἔχουσι τιμάς 8 6; δόξαν εἶχε 24 4; μείζονα πίστιν ἔσχε καὶ τιμὴν 33 1; and the contrary: ὅταν τὸν χρόνον ἔχωσι ἐπιπροσθοῦντα τῇ γνώσει 13 12; αἰτίαν εἶχε 13 10; μόνος ἔσχε τοῦ πολέμου τὴν αἰτίαν 29 5; δι' αὐτὸν ἔσχεν ἐχθρούς 31 2.—(*g*) impersonal use: ἔχει λόγον, 'it stands to reason' 1 2
II. *tenere*, 'to hold': διὰ χειρὸς ἔχων τὴν πόλιν 34 1
III. *posse*, 'to have the means to': οὐκ ἔχων κτῖσαι 22 3
B. Intrans. with modal adverbs, 'to hold or find oneself so and so,' 'to be in such and such a condition': σφόδρα κακῶς ἔχων 38 2; τὰ οἰκεῖα μοχθηρῶς εἶχεν (αὐτῷ) 36 1; εἶχεν οὕτω τὰ περὶ τὸν νόμον 37 3; τὴν ἀρχὴν ὅπως ἔσχεν γνῶναι 31 1; with πρός and accus.: οἰκείως εἶχον πρὸς αὐτόν 10 3; ἀργῶς ἔχων πρὸς χρηματισμόν 16 3
C. Mid. c. gen. 'to hold on by,' 'to be connected with': ψήφισμα... εὐγνώμονος δικαιολογίας ἐχόμενον 30 3
ἔχθρα: ἄσπονδον καὶ ἀκήρυκτον ἔ. 30 3
ἐχθρός: ἐ. ἀνηκέστῳ 39 1; οἱ ἐ. 10 7; πολλοὶ τῶν ἐ. 33 6, 34 3; τοὺς μὲν δι' αὐτὸν ἔσχεν ἐ. 31 2
ἕως, conj. *donec*, *usque dum*: ἕως ἀπηλλάγησαν οἱ II. 34 1.—praepos. c. gen. (unclassical): ἕως 'Ακαρνανίας

17 2. Cp. Polyb. 1, 18, 2 ἕως ἀκροβολισμοῦ

Z

ζευγοτρόφος: οἱ ζ. 12 7
Ζεύς: τὸν Δία for τὸ τοῦ Διὸς ἄγαλμα 2 1; ὦ ΖΕῦ ΞΈΝΙΕ 3 4
ζῆλος: μιμητικὸς ζ. 2 2; ζ. τινὰ ἀγωγὸν εἰς μίμησιν 1 4; ὑποποιούσης τινὰ ζ. 5 4
ζηλοτυπία: διὰ ζηλοτυπίαν 10 6
ζηλοῦν, aemulari: ζηλῶν 18 1; ζηλώσασαν 21 2.—PASS. θαυμάζεσθαι καὶ ζηλοῦσθαι 2 2
ζημιοῦν: χρήμασιν ἐζημίωσαν 22 3, 28 1, 35 4.—PASS. θανάτῳ ζημιοῦσθαι 30 3
ζῆν: ΖΗ 24 6; ζῶντος 39 4
ζυγόν, 'a pair of scales': ὥσπερ ἐπὶ ζυγοῦ ῥοπὴν ἐποίησεν 11 2
ζωγράφος: τοῦ ζ. 13 2; ζωγράφοι 12 6
ζῷον: ποιεῖν τὰ ζῷα, figuras pictas vel intextas 13 1

H

ᾗ, qua 20 1.—ᾗ καί, quapropter 34 2
ἡγεῖσθαι, ducem esse: ἡγουμένου 22 2, 33 3.—existimare 36 3; ἡγούμεθα 1 4; ἡγούμενος 21 1; ἡγούμενον 31 1; ἡγεῖτο 39 1
ἡγεμονία militaris: πρὸς τοσαύτην ἐχέγγυον ἡ. 37 1.— regnum: τῆς ἡγ. τῶν Περσῶν 24 7; ἡγ. Atheniensium συμμαχίαις πεφραγμένην δυναστῶν 15 1; τὸ μέγεθος τῆς ἡγ. 20 3

ἡγεμονικῶς σφόδρα 1 1
ἥδεσθαι: τούτοις ἡδόμεθα 1 4; ἡσθεὶς τοῖς ποιήμασι 2 1
ἤδη, iam: 8 5, 16 7, 28 2, 33 7, 35 1, 38 3; ἤ. καὶ πρόσθεν 11 1; ἤ. γέγονε 38 4.—iam tum 20 3
ἡδονή: πλείστην ἡ. ἤνεγκε 12 1; οὐκ ἀμούσοις ἡ. 11 3; ἡ. ἀβλαβεῖς 15 3
ἡδύς, gratus 16 4; φωνὴν ἡ. 7 1
ἠθικός: ἐν τοῖς ἠ. 38 2
ἦθος εὐμενές 39 2; τὸ ἀξίωμα τοῦ ἤ. 4 4; τῷ ἤ. 36 5; τὰ ἤ. 38 2; τὰ ἤ. καὶ πάθη 15 4
ἠθο-ποιεῖν[1]: ἠθοποιοῦν 2 3
ἥκειν of things, redire: ἰσχὺν διὰ βαρβάρων ἥκουσαν 15 1
ἥκιστα 7 2
ἨΛΕΊΦΕΟ (ἀλείφεσθαι) 28 5
ἡλικία: πολλαῖς ἡ. ἔμπροσθεν 27 3, 13 1; πᾶσαν ἡ. 12 7; τῶν ἐν ἡ. 18 2; διὰ τὴν ἡ. 22 2; τὴν ἀκμάζουσαν ἡ. 34 3; τοῖς ἡλικίαν ἔχουσι 12 5
ἡλικιῶτις[1]: ἡ. ἱστορία 13 12
ἥλιος: τὸν ἥ. 35 1
ἡμέρα: ἡ. ὅλην 36 3; καθ' ἡμέραν, quotidie 7 2, 9 2, 24 6; ὀλίγαις ὕστερον ἡ. 18 3
ἥμισυς: κληρούχοις ἡμίσεις τούτων 11 5
ἡνία: τὰς ἡ. ἀνείς 11 4
ἡνίοχος: οἱ ἡ. 12 7
ἤπειρος: τὴν ἀντιπέρας ἠ. 19 4
Ἥρα: Ἥραν for τὸ τῆς Ἥρας ἄγαλμα 2 1
ἡσυχάζειν: ἡσυχάζοντας 25 3
ἡσυχία: καθ' ἡσυχίαν 23 1
ἡττᾶσθαι: ἡττημένοις 10 2; ἡττήθη τοῦ πάθους 36 5; ἡττηθῆναι 26 3; ἡττηθεὶς μάχῃ 18 3
ἧττον, minus 11 2; μηδὲν ἡ. 12 5

Θ

θάλαττα (θάλασσα): ἐκ θ. εἰς θ. 19 1; ἐκ θ. 34 2; τῆς θ. 17 1, 25 3; κατὰ θάλατταν 12 6; τῆς θ. τὸ κράτος 28 6; τὰ πρὸς θαλάσσῃ 20 2; ἐχρῶντο τῇ θ. 26 2; νήσους καὶ θάλασσαν 15 1; πᾶσαν τὴν θ. 20 1
θάμβος[3], τό 6 1
θανατικός: τὴν θ. δίκην 10 5
θάνατος: θανάτῳ ζημιοῦσθαι 30 3; θάνατον (αὐτοῦ) κατέγνωσαν 22 3
θάπτεσθαι: ταφῆναι 30 3
θαρρεῖν (θαρσεῖν): φανερῶς ἐγκαλεῖν οὐ θαρροῦντες 29 4; οὐκ ἐθάρσησε συνάψαι 22 2
θάρσος, τό 20 1
θαυμάζειν ὅτι 38 4; θαυμάσειε 13 11; τῷ θαυμάσαι 1 4; θαυμάσας 5 1; θαυμάσαντα 27 3; θαυμάσαντες 14 2.— PASS. θαυμάζεται 13 3; θαυμάζεσθαι 2 2; ἐθαυμάσθη 19 2; θαυμασθῆναι 6 3; θαυμασθέντας ὡς μεγάλους 18 1
θαυμάσιος: θαυμάσιον 7 5, 13 1
θαυμαστὸς τῆς ἐπιεικείας 39 1; τύχη θ. 13 7; θ. τι καὶ μέγα φρονῆσαι 28 5; ταῦτα θαυμαστὰ καὶ ἄξια στεφάνων 28 4; μηχαναῖς τὴν καινότητα θαυμασταῖς 27 3
θαυμαστοῦσθαι[1]: ἐθαυμαστώθη 28 3
θαυμαστῶς 5 1
θέα: τινὰ θ. πανηγυρικήν 11 4
θέαμα: τὰ θ. 1 2; θεάμασιν 1 3
θεᾶσθαι τοὺς μουσικοὺς ἀγῶνας 13 5; ἐθεῶντο 13 7; τοὺς θεωμένους 2 2; θεασάμενος 2 1

θεατής (ἀγώνων) γιγνόμενος 1 5; τὸν θ. (τῶν καλῶν) 2 3
θεῖν, currere 16 7
θεῖος: ὁ θ. Πλάτων 8 1; τὰ θ. 6 1, 32 1; τοῖς θ. (συμβόλοις) 6 4
θέλειν: τοὺς μὴ θέλοντας γενέσθαι δημοκρατίαν 25 2
θεός: ἡ θ. 13 8; τὴν θ. 13 7; θεοί 3 4; τὸ τῶν θ. γένος 39 2; τοῖς θ. 8 4; τοὺς θ. 39 3 4
θεραπεία: θεραπείᾳ χρῆσθαι 13 8; συνέταξε θεραπείαν 13 8
θεραπεύειν: τοὺς ἐν τέλει (χρήμασιν) θεραπεύων 23 1; θεραπεύων τοὺς πολλούς 34 1
θέρος: θέρους ὥρᾳ 34 4
θεσμοθέτης λαχεῖν 9 3
θεωρεῖν πᾶν τὸ φαινόμενον 1 2; ἵνα μὴ θεωρῇ μόνον ἀλλὰ καὶ τρέφηται τῷ θ. 1 3; θεωρῆσαι 6 3.—PASS. θεωρείσθω ἡ αἰτία 9 1
θεωρητικός: θ.)(πολιτικοῦ φιλοσόφου 16 6
θεωρικός: θεωρικά 9 1; θ. λήμμασι 9 3
θηρίον: θηρία (canes et simii))(ἄνθρωποι 1 1
θηριώδης: θ. πάθος 10 6
θητικός: τὸν θ. ὄχλον 12 7
θνήσκειν: τεθνεώς 18 3; τεθνεῶτες 18 3; τοὺς ἐν Σάμῳ τεθνηκότας 8 6
θόρυβος: ΘΟΡΥΒΟΝ ΠΟΛΥΝ ΕΞΑΝΑΤΕΛΛΕΙΝ 3 4
θρασύνεσθαι: τὸ θρασυνόμενον αὐτῶν 15 4. Cp. Fab. c. 26, 5 τὸ χαῖρον καὶ τεθαρρηκὸς τῶν πολιτῶν
θυγάτηρ 24 2; θυγατρί 36 1
θυμός: τὸν θ. ἀφεικότων εἰς τοῦτο 36 1; θυμῷ χαρίσασθαι 39 1
θυσία: τῶν θ. 17 1

I

Ἰάς : τῶν Ἰάδων 21 2
ἰᾶσθαι, *mederi*: ἰάσατο 13 8.—
fig. *damnum levare* 35 1
ἰατρός : ἰατρόν 15 3, 34 3 ; τῶν
l. 13 8
ἰδέα, *forma*, *species*: τὴν *l*. τοῦ
σώματος 3 2
ἴδιος: ὑπῆν τις *l*. ἀπέχθεια 30 2;
l. πάθος 28 3 ; ἰδίᾳ 37 5 ; *l*.
ἐμαυτοῦ ποιήσομαι τὴν ἐπιγραφήν 14 1
ἰδιώτης : τὸν *l*. ὄχλον 12 7
ἰέναι 17 3 ; ΙΟΝΤΕC Μέγαράδε 30 4
ἱερόν, *templum*: τὸ *i*. 21 2;
τῶν *l*. 17 1
ἱερός : τὸν *l*. πύλεμον 21 1 ; τὴν
l. Ἐπίδαυρον 35 3 ; τὴν *i*.
ὀργάδα 30 2
ἱκανῶς 12 4
ἱκέτης : ἱκέτην καθίζουσιν 31 2
ἱμάτιον : οὐδεὶς δι' ἐμὲ μέλαν *i*.
περιεβάλετο 38 4
ἵνα final with subj. 1 2, 12 5
ἱππεύς : ἱππέας 35 1
ἱπποβότης : τοὺς *i*. 23 2
ἵππος : ἵππον 7 6, 12 3
ἰσόρροπος, *oneri par*: *l*. βάρος
37 1. Cp. *Brut*. c. 46, 4
ἴσος : ἴσους (*totidem*) παῖδας 25 1
ἱστάναι : ἔστησε τρόπαιον 19 3
ἱστορεῖν, *cognoscere*: τοῖς ἱστορήσασι 1 4.—*memoriae prodere* (unclassical) : ἱστόρηκε
9 2, 28 1, 32 3, 33 1, 38 2 ;
ἱστορήκασιν 23 1
ἱστορία[2]: ἡ ἡλικιῶτις *i*. 13 12;
τοσοῦτον ἱστορίας 21 4 ; τῇ *l*.
τοῦ ἔργου 2 3 ; δυσθήρατον
ἱστορίᾳ 13 11
ἰσχύειν : πλεῖστον ἴσχυσε 24 7 ;
ἰσχύσας 9 4 ; νόμον ἰσχύσαντα
κατὰ τοσούτων 37 5
ἰσχυρός : *l*. καὶ στερεὸν κέρας 6 2

ἰσχύς, *potentia*: ἡ ἐπίφθονος *l*.
39 5 ; ἀπὸ τοσαύτης *l*. 35 1 ;
πρὸς ἔνδειξιν ἰσχύος 31 1 ;
τὴν *l*. ἀποδίδωσιν 13 2 ; *l*. καὶ
ἡγεμονίαν 15 1
ἴσως 1 2, 10 6, 24 7

K

ΚἀΓΧΕΙΡΙΔΙΟΥ by crasis for καὶ
ἐγχειριδίου 33 7
κᾷθ' by crasis for καὶ εἶτα 30 4
καθ-αιρεῖν, *demoliri*: τὰ τείχη
καθεῖλε 28 1.—*revellere*: καθελεῖν τὸ πινάκιον 30 1 ; μὴ
καθέλῃς τὸ πινάκιον 30 1.—
abrogare, 'to rescind': τὸ
ψήφισμα καθελεῖν 29 5. —
PASS. καθῃρημένου τὴν αἴσθησιν 38 4
καθ-άπερ 4 1, 8 6, 12 7, 34 3,
36 1, 39 2
καθαρός, 'clean,' 'pure': 1.
physically : κ. δίαιτας 34 4 ;
φωτὶ καθαρωτάτῳ 39 3 ; νοῦν
κ. καὶ ἄκρατον 4 4.—2. ethically : κ. βίος 39 2 ; κ. χεῖρας
... ὄψεις 8 5.—c. gen. λόγου
καθαροῦ βωμολοχίας 5 1
καθ-έζεσθαι[3] οἴκοι 27 4
καθ-είργεσθαι : ὥσπερ βοσκήματα καθειργμένοις 34 4
καθ-ῆσθαι 3 4
καθ-ιέναι : ἑτέροις καθιεὶς in
certamen 7 5
καθ-ίζειν : ἱκέτην ἐν ἀγορᾷ καθίζουσιν 31 2
καθ-ιστάναι : πολιτείαν κατέστησε 3 1 ; τὴν πολιτείαν εἰς
ἀντίπαλον κατέστησεν 11 2 ;
καταστῆσαί (τινα) πρὸς τὴν
οἰκίαν 5 2 ; καταστήσας δημοκρατίαν 25 2.—MID. πρὸς τὸν
Θουκυδίδην εἰς ἀγῶνα καταστὰς
περὶ τοῦ ὀστράκου 14 2
κάθ-οδος *exulis*: τὴν κ. 10 4

καθ-ορᾶν 8 5
καθ-ότι i.e. καθ' ὅτι, 'according to what,' 'after what fashion' 13 6
καθ-υπέρτερος δεισιδαιμονίας 6 1
καί, *ultro* 36 2
καὶ γάρ, *etenim* 7 1, 24 2 3, 26 3, 39 4.—where the καί means 'both,' being followed by another καί 24 6, 26 3, 34 1.
—καὶ . . . γε 24 6; καὶ μέντοι γε 16 7.—καὶ . . . δέ 33 7.—
καί intensive: καὶ μάλα 15 3; καὶ πάνυ 25 2; καὶ τί ἄν τις θαυμάσειε 13 11
καινότης[2], 'freshness': κ. τις 13 3.—'novelty': τὴν κ. (τῶν μηχανῶν) 27 3
καίπερ οὐ 24 3, 16 3
καιρός 16 2; ἄν εἴη κ. διαπορῆσαι 24 1; κατὰ καιρόν 15 3; σὺν οὐδενὶ κ. 18 2
καίτοι 8 2, 13 2, 16 1, 25 2, 33 6.—with participle, as καίπερ 13 2 (unclassical)
κἀκεῖνος by crasis for καὶ ἐκεῖνος 10 3
κακία, *pravitas*: πλῆθος κακίας 39 5
κακο-ήθως 16 1
κακόν: τὸ τῆc πόρνηc κακόν 24 6; ἀναίτιον κακῶν 39 2
κακός: δαίμονι κ. 13 11
κακοῦν, *infestare*: κακώσας τὴν γῆν 19 4.—PASS. κακοῦσθαι, *male affici* 29 4.—*frangi*, *debilitari*: τὰ σώματα καὶ τὰς ψυχὰς κακούμενοι 34 3
κακῶς: κ. ἀκούων 5 2, 29 3; κ. ἀκούει 12 1; κ. ἐθισθέντα 9 1; κ. διακειμένους 28 2; σφόδρα κ. ἔχων 38 2
καλεῖν, *nominare*: καλοῦσι 25 3; καλοῦντες 16 1, 39 3; ἐκάλουν 3 2; καλέογcιn 3 3.—

PASS. καλεῖσθαι 11 3; καλουμένην 24 7; κληθῆναι 27 4.
—*vocare*: ἐκάλει 10 3; καλούσης ἐκεῖνον ἐπὶ τὸ βῆμα 37 1
καλλι-τεχνία[1]: τῇ κ. 13 1
κάλλος: κάλλους ἀκρίβειαν 13 2; κάλλει ἀρχαῖον 13 3
καλλωπίζειν: τὴν πόλιν καλλωπίζοντας 12 2
καλόν: τὸ κ. 2 3; τῶν αὐτοῦ κ. βέλτιστον 39 1; τῶν κ.)(τῶν ἀναγκαίων 16 6; τῶν κ. καὶ ὠφελίμων παραμελοῦντας 1 2; τῆς προσποιήσεως τῶν κ. 5 4; ἐπὶ κ. ἔργοις 22 3; ἐπὶ τοῖς κ. 16 6; τῆς εἰς τὰ κ. ῥᾳθυμίας 2 1; τὸ κάλλιστον 38 4; τῆς ἀληθινῆς ἀρετῆς κάλλιστα 7 5; νίκας καλλίστας 9 4
καλός: παῖδα κ. 8 5; τῶν κ. κἀγαθῶν 7 3, 8 4; τοὺς κ. κἀγαθοὺς καλουμένους ἄνδρας 11 2
καλῶς ἔφη 1 5; κ. ψάλλων 1 5; κ. ἐκλαμβάνοντος 6 3
καλω-στρόφος: οἱ κ. 12 7
κάμπτεσθαι: ἐπὶ τούτῳ καμφθείς 36 5
καράνιος: ὦ Ζεῦ κapánie 3 3
καρη-βαρεῖν: καρhβαροῦντa 3 4
καρπός: τοὺς ἐπετείους κ. 16 4
καρτερός: κ. ναυμαχίας 25 3
κατά: A. c. Gen.: *contra*, 'against': μάρτυρα παρέχεται καθ' αὑτῆς 2 1; δύναμιν κατ' ἐκείνου παρασκευαζόμενος 7 3; τὰς κ. τῶν κρειττόνων βλασφημίας 13 11; ἐχρῆτο τῷ πλήθει κ. τῆς βουλῆς 9 3; αἰτίαν ποιησάμενος κατ' αὐτῶν 24 1; γράφει ψήφισμα κατ' αὐτῶν 30 3
B. c. Acc.: 1. of Place or

Region in which: κ. τὴν δεξιὰν πλευράν 21 2; κ. γῆν 12 7, 31 2; κ. θάλατταν 12 6; κατ' ἀγοράν 5 2; κ. τὸν τόπον 6 2.—2. of Time during which: κ. καιρόν 15 3; κ. τὸν πόλεμον 28 3; κ. τὸν λοιμόν 36 1; κ. τοὺς ὕπνους 3 2; κ. τὴν γραφήν 24 7.—3. of Reference, Relation, Proportion: (a) distributively: διελύθη κ. πόλεις 22 3; καθ' ἕκαστον ἐνιαυτόν 11 4, 23 1; ὁ καθ' ἡμέραν βίος 7 5, 9 2, 24 6; κατὰ μικρόν 36 1.— (b) 'so far as relates to': κ. γένος 24 5; κ. τὰς ἄλλας ἀρετὰς ὁμοίων 2 4; κατ' ἀμφοτέρους 3 1.—(c) 'according to a standard,' 'agreeably to': κ. τὸν ὀρθότατον λόγον 36 3.—(d) secundum, ut ait: κατὰ τὸν Πλάτωνα 7 6; κ. Πλάτωνα 15 4.—(e) of the mode in which a thing is done: καθ' ἡσυχίαν 23 1; κατὰ τὸ βέλτιστον 31 1; κατὰ κράτος 19 3; κατὰ τάχος 22 2, 27 1

κατα-βαίνειν: καταβαίνοντα ἀπὸ τοῦ βήματος 28 4

κατα-βάλλειν, prosternere: ὅταν καταβάλω (αὐτὸν) παλαίων 8 4.—diruere: κ. τείχη)(οἰκοδομεῖν: τὰ δὲ τἄμπαλιν αὖ καταβάλλειν 16 2

κατα-βοᾶν, obstrepere: καταβοώντων (without object) 33 5; κ. τοῦ Περικλέους 11 1

κατ-άγειν: εἰς ἀγορὰν αὐτοὺς καταγαγών 28 2

κατα-γιγνώσκειν: φεύγοντος θάνατον κατέγνωσαν 22 3

κατα-γράφεσθαι: καταγέγραπται v. l. 13 9

κατα-δημ-αγωγεῖσθαι[1]: καταδημαγωγούμενος τούτοις 9 2

κατα-δρομή, decursio: τὰς κ. τῶν Θρακῶν 19 1

κατα-δύεσθαι εἰς τὸ τῆς μουσικῆς ὄνομα 4 1

κατα-κλείειν: κατέκλεισεν Οἰνιάδας εἰς τὸ τεῖχος 19 4.—fig. δι' ἀντιλογίας κατακλείουσαν εἰς ἀπορίαν ἕξιν 1 3.—PASS. παντελῶς κατεκλείσθησαν 26 1

[κατα-κτείνειν: κατακτείναντος v. l. 36 3]

κατα-κωλύειν: κατεκώλυε (τὴν κακίαν) ἀνήκεστον γενέσθαι 39 5

κατα-λαμβάνειν: καταλαβὼν πάντα φυλακαῖς 33 5

κατα-λείπειν: τὴν οὐσίαν ἣν κατέλιπε 15 5

κατα-λύειν: κατέλυσε τὴν τυραννίδα 3 1; κατέλυσε τὸ κράτος τῆς βουλῆς 7 6; κατέλυσε τὴν ἀντιτεταγμένην ἑταιρείαν 11 2; τὴν ὀλιγαρχίαν κατέλυσεν 25 1.—PASS. of a single person: τοῦ Θουκυδίδου καταλυθέντος 6 3, 33 1

κατά-λυσις: μετὰ τὴν Θουκυδίδου κ. 16 3

κατα-μίγνυσθαι: ψυχὴν καταμεμιγμένην ἐχόντων 13 3

κατ-αν-αλίσκειν: τὸ φιλητικὸν εἰς θηρία καταναλίσκοντας 1 1

κατα-ναυμαχεῖν, navali proelio derincere: καταναυμαχήσας 25 3; καταναυμαχήσαντα 37 5

κατα-νέμεσθαι[2] de morbo: κατενεμήθη τὴν ἀκμάζουσαν ἡλικίαν 31 3

κατ-άντης: κάταντες de tecto Odei 13 5

κατα-πιμπράναι[1]: τῶν ἱερῶν ἃ κατέπρησαν 17 1

κατα-πλήξ : καταπλῆγα 27 4
κατα-πολεμεῖν, *debellare:* τοῦ
 Ἀθηναίους καταπολεμήσαντος
 22 3; καταπολεμήσαντα τοὺς
 Σαμίους 28 5
κατα-πράττεσθαι² : καταπραττό-
 μενός τι 5 2
κατα-πραΰνειν, *mitigare, pla-
 care:* κατεπράϋνε 33 4
κατα-πτήσσειν : κατεπτηχότας
 25 3. Cp. *Sull.* 7, 3
κατα-πγγοcγΝΗ 24 5
κατα-σκεδαννύναι : πολλὴν ἀσέλγειαν αὐτοῦ κατεσκέδασαν 13
 10
κατα-σκευάζειν : ναῦν κατασκευάσαντος 26 4.—PASS.
 τῆς πόλεως κατεσκευασμένης
 τοῖς ἀναγκαίοις 12 3; κατεσκευασμένος (*institutus*) πρὸς
 οἰκονομίαν 16 5
κατα-σκεύασμα, *aedificium:*
 κατασκευασμάτων ἐπιβολάς
 12 5
κατα-σκευή, *opificium:* ἡ τῶν
 ἀναθημάτων κ. 12 1. Cp.
 Lyc. c. 6, 3 οὔτε παστάδων
 οὐσῶν οὔτε ἄλλης τινὸς κατα-
 σκευῆς.—αἰτίᾳ τινὶ καὶ κ. 6
 4; τῇ περὶ τὸν βίον κ., *vitae
 rationi* 8 1
κατα-στασιάζειν¹ : κατεστασίασε
 τὴν βουλὴν 9 4
κατα-στολή¹ : κ. περιβολῆς 5 1
κατα-στρατοπεδεύειν : κατεστρατοπέδευσαν 33 3
κατα-στρέφεσθαι : καταστρεφόμενος 28 4 ; καταστρεφόμενον
 10 4 ; κατεστρέψατο 23 2 ;
 καταστρεψάμενος 28 3
κατα-τείνειν, *stringere habenas,
 intendere, cogere:* δυσχεραίνοντα κατατείνων 15 3 ; κατατείνας τὰ ὅπλα in navi 33 5
κατα-τρέχειν : Ἀκαρνανίαν κατέδραμε 19 4

κατα-φέρειν², *pendere, solvere:*
 κατοίσειν (τὰ χρήματα) 28 1
κατα-φιλεῖν 24 6
κατα-φρονεῖν : τοῦ δημιουργοῦ
 καταφρονοῦμεν 1 4 ; καταφρονήσας τῆς ὀλιγότητος τῶν
 νεῶν 26 2
κατα-χεῖσθαι² : ὁ καταχεάμενος
 hominum copiam in urbem
 34 4
κατα-χρῆσθαι, *abuti:* τοὺς καταχρωμένους τούτῳ (sc. τῷ φιλομαθεῖ) 1 2
κατα-χρυσοῦν : τὴν πόλιν καταχρυσοῦντας 12 2
κατ-επείγειν : τὰ κατεπείγοντα
 τῶν ἔργων 27 3
κατ-εργάζεσθαι : αἱ τὴν ὕλην
 κατεργαζόμεναι τέχναι 12 6
κατ-έχειν, *occupare:* χώραν ἣν
 κατεῖχον 20 2.—*cohibere, reprimere* 18 2 ; κατεῖχε τὴν
 ἐκδρομὴν ταύτην 21 1 ; κατασχεῖν 27 2. — *distringere:*
 Κίμωνα αἱ στρατεῖαι τῆς Ἑλλάδος ἔξω κατεῖχον 7 2
κατ-ηγορεῖν : πολλὴν ὠμότητα
 τῶν Ἀθηναίων κατηγορῶν 28
 1 ; κατηγοροῦντες 33 6 ; κατηγοροῦντι τοῦ Περικλέους 10 6 ;
 κατηγοροῦντα τῶν Μεγαρέων
 30 2 ; (τοῖς) κατηγοροῦσι τῶν
 Ἀθηναίων 29 4
κατ-ηγορία : ἐπὶ κατηγορίᾳ 31 2
κατ-ήγορος : ἐπεγράφη κ. 35 4 ;
 εἷς τῶν κ. 10 5 ; τῶν κ. ἐλάχιστα 10 5 ; τοὺς κ. 31 3
κατ-ιέναι de vento : ἀνέμου
 κατιόντος 33 5.— de exuli-
 bus : κατελθών 10 3
κατ-οικεῖν 39 3 ; τοῖς αὐτόθι
 κατοικοῦσι 19 1 ; τοὺς ὁπήποτε
 κατοικοῦντας 17 1
κατ-οικίζειν : Ἀθηναίους κατῴκισε
 23 2
κάτωθεν : τῶν κάτωθεν 3 4

κεῖσθαι : ἀμελούμενον κ. 16 7 ; κείμενος οἴκοι, a republica abstinens 37 1
κελεύειν : κελεύοντες 14 2, 15 1 ; κελευόντων 25 1 ; ἐκέλευον 33 1 ; ἐκέλευσε 31 4 ; τὸ κελεῦσαι 8 5 ; κελεύσαντος 36 2. —PASS. κελευόμενοι διαλύσασθαι πόλεμον 24 1
κέντρον 36 1
κεράννυσθαι : πολιτείαν ἄριστα κεκραμένην 3 1
κέρας : ἡ ῥίζα τοῦ κ. 6 2 ; τὸ κ. στερεὸν πεφυκός 6 2
κεραυνός : ΔΕΙΝΟΝ ΚΕΡΑΥΝΟΝ ΕΝ ΓΛΩCCΗ ΦΕΡΕΙΝ 8 3
ΚΕΦΑΛΑΙΟΝ 3 4
κεφαλή : ΚΕΦΑΛΗC ΕΝΔΕΚΑΚΛΙΝΟΥ 3 4 ; τῆς κ. ὑπερεχόντων 27 4 ; τῇ κ. 3 2 ; κριοῦ κεφαλήν 6 2 ; τὰς κ. 28 2
κεφαλ-ηγερέτης : ΚΕΦΑΛΗΓΕΡΕΤΑΝ 3 3
κηδεστής : κηδεστήν 11 1 : τῶν κ. 36 4
κηδεύειν : κηδεύων 36 4
κῆρυξ : ὁ πεμφθεὶς κ. 30 3 ; κήρυκα 30 2
κιθαρίζειν 13 6
κίνδυνος : ἐχούσης κίνδυνον 18 1 ; μέγαν ἔσχε κ. ὁ πόλεμος 28 6 ; κινδύνοις 27 1, 32 3
κινεῖν : κινοῦσα προθυμίαν 2 2 ; τὸ καλὸν ἐφ᾽ αὑτὸ κινεῖ 2 3 ; χρεῖαι πᾶσαν χεῖρα κινοῦσαι 12 4 : ἐπὶ τοῖς καλοῖς κινεῖ τὴν διάνοιαν 16 6 ; ἔΡΓΟΙCΙ Δ᾽ ΟΥΔΕ ΚΙΝΕΙ (τὸ ἔργον) 13 5.—PASS. ὑπ᾽ οὐδενὸς ἐκινήθη τῶν τοιούτων 34 1 ; (τὰ) ἤθη κινούμενα τοῖς τῶν σωμάτων πάθεσι 38 2.—appredi regionem : κ. τὰ πρὸς θαλάσσῃ 20 2
κίων : τοὺς ἐπ᾽ ἐδάφους κ. 13 4 : τοὺς ἄνω κ. ib.

κλαίειν : κλαίων 36 4
κλαυθμός [1 5] : κλαυθμὸν ῥῆξαι 36 5
κλεινός : κλεινὴν γενέσθαι 24 7
κλέπτειν : ΠΟΡΝΗΝ ΚΛΕΠΤΟΥCΙ 30 4
κληρουχία, a settlement of Athenian citizens in the city and lands of an expelled Greek population, as at Hestiaea and Chalcis (c. 23, 2), whereas an ἀποικία is a colony planted amongst barbarians on foreign soil, as at Brea : κληρουχίας 9 1, 34 1
κληροῦχος : χιλίους κ. 11 5
κληρωτός : κ. ἀρχαί 9 3
κλῆσις : κλήσεις δείπνων 7 4 [κλίνη, a unit of superficial measure, equal to 10 square cubits 3 3 note]
κλινίδιον, lectica : ἐν κ. κρεμαστῷ 27 4
κλοπή : κλοπῆς διώξις 32 2 ; κλοπαί 31 2
κοῖλος : ναῦς κοιλοτέρα 26 3
κοινο-πραγία [1] : ἐπὶ κοινοπραγίᾳ τῆς Ἑλλάδος 17 3
κοινός : κ. αἰτίαν 30 2 ; τὰ πρὸς τύχην κοινά 38 4 ; τὰ κ. τῶν Ἑλλήνων χρήματα 12 1 ; τὰ κ. 12 2 ; τὰς ἀπὸ τῶν κ. εὐπορίας 12 5 ; παρὰ τὰ κ. δίκαια 29 4
κοινωνός : κ. ὄντα τῆς προαιρέσεως 10 6
κολακεύειν : κολακεύουσα 13 12
κολοιέειν : κολοιῶν 29 3
κόλπος : ἐν τοῖς κ. περιφέροντας 1 1
κομιδῇ, plane, prorsus : κ. μοναρχίαν 11 1 ; νέον ὄντα κ. 22 2 ; μιᾶς γενομένης κ. 15 1
κομίζειν, vehere : κομίσας 19 1.—PASS. vehi 27 4 ; ἐκομίσθη

τῷ στόλῳ 19 3.—*afferri:* κομισθῆναι 6 2
κομιστήρ[1,3] : κομιστῆρες 12 6
κομψός : κ. λόγου 30 1
κοπίς : παραθηγομένης κοπίδος 33 7
κόπτεσθαι, *caedi:* δένδρα κοπέντα 33 4
κόρος[3], *satietas:* φεύγων τὸν κ. 7 5
κορυφή : ἐκ μιᾶς κ. 13 5
κορυφοῦν : τὸ ὀπαῖον ἐκορύφωσε 13 5
κοσμεῖν: οἷς ἐκόσμησε τὴν πόλιν 8 2.—PASS. πόλιν ἐξ αὐτῆς κοσμουμένην 12 4 ; στόλῳ κεκοσμημένῳ λαμπρῶς 20 1
κόσμιος : οὐ κ. ἐργασίας 24 3
κοσμίως 5 2
κόσμος : ὃ (πλεῖστον) κόσμον ἤνεγκε ταῖς Ἀθήναις 12 1
κράνιον : τοῦ κ. 6 2 ; ἐπὶ τοῦ κρανίου 13 6
κράνος, *galea:* κράνεσι 3 2
κρατεῖν, *superare:* κρατοῦντες, *victores facti* 25 1 ; τοῦ Μελίσσου κρατήσας 27 1 ; τοῦ λιμένος κρατήσας 26 1. — *obtinere:* c. gen. : πάντων λιμένων ὧν Ἀθ. κρατοῦσιν 29 4.—c. acc. rei : κ. τὴν διήγησιν ἐπὶ τῆς ἀληθείας 28 3
κράτος, τό, *imperium* 6 2 ; τῆς θαλάττης τὸ κ. 28 6 ; *potestas* 7 6, 9 4, 16 2 (ex Teleclide)
κρείττων : χρημάτων κρείττονος 15 5 ; τῶν κ.)(τῶν πολλῶν 13 11
κρεμαστός : ἐν κλινιδίῳ κ., 'a hammock' 27 4
κρίνειν ἐκ τῶν γραφομένων, *indicium facere* 2 4.—*cognitionem exercere:* ἐν τῇ πόλει κρίνοιεν 32 2.—PASS. κρίνεσθαι τὴν δίκην ἔγραψεν 32 2 ; οἱ κριθέντες Ἀθηναῖοι 37 4

κριός : κριοῦ 6 2
κρίσις : τὰς πλείστας κ. 9 4
κριτής 31 2
Κρόνος πρεσβυγενής 3 3
κροῦσις : ἐμμελοῦς κ. 15 4
κρύφα 22 2, 29 4
κρυφαίως 10 7
κτᾶσθαι : κέκτηται 1 2 ; κτησάμενος 16 3, 8 1 (ex Platone philosopho)
κτείνειν : κτείναντος (*v. l.*) 36 3
κτῆσις : τὰς κ. 2 3
κύαμος : τοῦ λευκοῦ κ. 27 2
κυβερνήτης : νεὼς κ. 33 5 ; τὸν κ. 35 2 ; κυβερνῆται 12 6
κυμαίνειν, *aestuare:* κυμαίνοντος τοῦ πολέμου 29 1
κυν-ῶπις : παλλακὴν κυνώπιδα 24 6
κυπάρισσος 12 6
κύριος : γενομένους κυρίους 35 4
κυροῦσθαι : ψήφισμα κυροῦται 32 2
κύων : κυνῶν τέκνα 1 1
κωλύειν : νόμον κωλύοντα καθελεῖν 30 1 ; ἐκώλυεν οὐδέν w. infin., *nihil obstabat quominus* 6 3
κώμη : κώμας τε καὶ πόλεις μικράς 34 2
κωμικός, late form of κωμῳδικός : οἱ κ. 'the comic poets' 13 10, 16 1 ; τῶν κ. 3 3 ; τοῖς κ. 4 2
κωμ-ῳδεῖν : κωμῳδεῖ τὸ ἔργον ὡς βραδέως περαινόμενον 13 5
κωμ-ῳδία : αἱ κ. 8 3 ; ἐν ταῖς κ. 24 6
κωμ-ῳδο-ποιός : τοῦ κ. 32 1 ; οἱ κ. 7 6

Λ

λαβή : τοῦ Περικλέους λαβέσθαι λαβὴν οὐκ ὀξεῖαν 38 1
λαγχάνειν, *sortiri:* τοῖς λαχού-

σιν 31 1.—*sorte eligi*: ἄρχων λαχεῖν 9 3
λάϊνος : λάϊΝΑ τείχη 10 2
λακωνισμός : τοῦ λ. 10 2 ; ἀπολύεσθαι τὸν λ. 10 1 ; προσδιαβληθείη εἰς τὸν λ. 29 2
λαμβάνειν 12 5 ; τῶν λαμβανόντων)(τῶν διδόντων 12 3 ; ἀνθ' οὗ λαμβάνουσι *ib.*; ἐλάμβανε τὴν συντέλειαν 13 1 ; ἔλαβεν ἀργύριον 36 2, 25 2 ; δίκας λαβεῖν καὶ δοῦναι 25 1 ; λαβὼν ὁμήρους 25 1 ; λαβὼν προμαντείαν 21 2 ; τὴν Ἀσπασίαν λαβών 24 5; τῷ λαβόντι τὸν λευκὸν κύαμον 27 2.— λαβών, 'with': λ. τριήρεις 26 1 ; φῶς λαβόντι 5 3 ; λαβόντα ναῦς 10 4 ; λαβόντας τὰς ψήφους εἰς τὰς χεῖρας 35 4.— MID. *corripere*: τοῦ Περικλέους λαβέσθαι λαβὴν οὐκ ὀξεῖαν 38 1
λαμπρός : γένους λ. 7 1 ; τύχῃ λ. 18 1
λαμπρῶς : στόλῳ κεκοσμημένῳ λ. 20 1.—λ. ἐνίκα 25 3
λανθάνειν : ἔλαθε χρώμενος 4 2
λάφυρα³: πολλῶν λ. 9 4
λέγειν : λέγουσι 4 1, 7 6, 8 2, 13 5, 16 7, 21 3, 30 1, 38 4, 39 3 ; ὡς λέγουσι 13 8, 26 1; ἐν τῷ λ. 5 1 ; λέγων ὡς 33 4 ; ἐπὶ παντὶ πράγματι λέγων 7 5 ; λέγων πρὸς τοὺς πολίτας ὡς 18 1 ; λεγούσης 28 5 ; λεγόντων 8 3 ; λέζον 4 2.— PASS. λέγεται 28 5, 31 2, 35 3 ; λέγονται 32 3 ; τὴν λεγομένην δύναμιν 12 1 ; τοὺς ἱπποβότας λεγομένους 23 2.— Impers. λέγεται 6 2 ; ὡς λέγεται 17 3
λεληθότως 5 4
λευκός : τὸν λ. κύαμον 27 2 ; λ. ἡμέραν 27 2

λέων : τεκεῖν λέοντα 3 2
λήμη : λήμην τοῦ Πειραιῶς 8 5
λῆμμα, *quaestus, emolumentum*: δικαστικοῖς λ. 9 3 ; ἄμοιρον λημμάτων 12 5.—*reditus*: παντὸς ἀναλώματος παντὸς δὲ λ. 16 4
λῃστήριον, *latrocinium*: λ. ὁμόρων 19 2. Cp. *Fab*. c. 17, 2 ὥσπερ λῃστηρίῳ μεγάλῳ τῷ στρατοπέδῳ πλανώμενον
λίθος 12 6 ; λ. πολυτελεῖς 12 2
λιθουργός : λιθουργοί 12 6
λιμήν : πάντων λ. 29 4 ; τοῦ λ. κρατήσας 26 1
λινουργός¹, *textor*: λινουργοί 12 7
λογισμός : ὁποτέρῳ τῶν λ. ἐχρήσατο 26 2 ; τοῖς ἀνθρωπίνοις λ. 34 2 ; ἐχρῆτο τοῖς αὑτοῦ λ. 33 5
λόγος : λόγῳ)(ἔργῳ 9 1 ; λόγοιcι)(ἔργοιcι 13 5 ; λόγους περὶ τοῦ πολέμου Δεινούς 33 5 ; ὑψηλὸν εἶχε τὸν λ. 5 1 ; τῷ μεγέθει τοῦ φρονήματος ἁρμόζοντα λόγον ἐξαρτυόμενος 8 1 ; ἐπὶ τῷ λ. τὴν προσωνυμίαν γενέσθαι 8 3 ; περὶ τὸν λ. εὐλαβὴς 8 4 ; τὸν λ. (*orationem funebrem*) εἰπὼν 28 3 ; λόγους περὶ τῶν μεταρσίων διδάσκοντας 32 1 ; λόγους ἐποιεῖτο μετὰ τῶν σοφιστῶν 36 2 ; τΗν τῶν λ. τέχΝΗΝ (ex Platone philosopho) 8 1 ; ἡ τοῦ λ. δύναμις 15 5 ; δεξάμενοι τὸν λόγον 13 10 ; κομψοῦ τοῦ λ. φανέντος 30 1.—*fama*, 'talk': ὑπὲρ αὑτῆς παρέσχε λόγον 24 1.—*ratio*: λόγον ἐποιοῦντο τῆς ἀρετῆς 38 3 ; ὁ φυσικὸς λ. 6 1 ; λόγον ἔχει 1 2 ; κατὰ τὸν ὀρθότατον λ. 36 3.— 'a saying': διαμνημονεύεταί τις λ.

8 3, 30 1.—'accounts': οἱ
λ. τῶν χρημάτων 32 2; χρημάτων οὐκ ὀφείλουσι λόγον
(αὐτοῖς) 12 3
λοιδορεῖν: ἐλοιδόρει 36 2.—PASS.
λοιδορούμενος 5 2
λοιμός, ὁ 38 1; ἐν τῷ λ. 36 3;
κατὰ τὸν λ. 36 1
λοιμώδης: ἡ λ. φθορά 34 3
λοιπός: ἐν τῷ λ. βίῳ 36 5; οἱ
λ. 17 3
λόχος: ἔθετο εἰς λόχον τὰ ὅπλα
10 1
λύεσθαι: τοῦ μὴ λυθῆναι τὸ
ψήφισμα 31 1; ᾐτήσατο
λυθῆναι τὸν νόμον 37 2 5;
λυθείσης τῆς διαφορᾶς 15 1
λύκος: τοῦ χαλκοῦ λ. 21 2; εἰς
τὸν αὐτὸν λ. *ibid.*
λυμαίνεσθαι: ὅταν ἡ ἱστορία
λυμαίνηται τὴν ἀλήθειαν 13
12
λυπεῖν: λυπήσας 10 5
λύρα: τῇ λ. 4 2
λύχνος: τοῦ λ. 16 7

M

μακάριος: τῷ μ. καὶ ἀθανάτῳ
39 3
μακρός: μ. νοσήματι 15 3; μ.
χρόνοις 7 4
μάλα: μάλ' ἐμμελοῦς ἁφῆς 15 4
μαλακός, *mollis*: μ. ἁρμονίας
15 2; αἴθρᾳ μ. 39 3.
—'effeminate': πρὸς τοὺς
φόβους μ. ὄντα 27 4.—*remissus*: μαλακωτέροις χρήσονται τοῖς Ἀθηναίοις 33 1
μαλακτήρ[1]: χρυσοῦ μαλακτῆρες
καὶ ἐλέφαντος 12 6
μάλιστα πρεπούσης 39 3; μ. μισούντων 33 1; μ. περιθεὶς 4 4;
τότε μ. 11 4; μ. ἐβάσκαινον
12 1; εὐδοκίμει μ. 18 1, 19
1: μ. θαυμάσιον 13 1, 15 4;

ἠγαπήθη μ. 19 1, 22 2, 24 1
7, 25 1, 29 5; ἄλλοις τε
πολλοῖς καὶ μ. 21 1; καὶ μ.
ὅτι 31 4
μᾶλλον 9 4, 13 3, 24 5, 28 3,
29 2 4 5, 31 2; μ. ἢ 27 1:
οὐδέν τι μᾶλλον 30 1; καὶ μ.
13 3; ἔτι μ. 16 7
μανθάνειν: μανθάνοντες τὴν
ναυτικὴν ἐμπειρίαν 11 4
μάντις: τὸν μ. 6 3
μαρτυρεῖν de rebus quae eventu
suo sententiam alicuius comprobant: ὁ τῇ Ἑλλάδι μαρτυρεῖ 12 1; ἐμαρτύρησεν αὐτῷ
τὰ γενόμενα 22 1
μάρτυς: μάρτυρα παρέχεται καθ'
αὑτῆς 2 1; αἰτία ἔχουσα
πλείστους μ. 31 2
μάχεσθαι 27 2, 33 4; ὅτε πρὸς
τοὺς βαρβάρους ἐμάχοντο 17
1; μαχομένου πρὸς Ἀμαζόνα
31 4
μάχη: μάχης ἐχούσης πολλὴν
ἀδηλότητα καὶ κίνδυνον 18 1;
γενομένης μάχης 26 2; ἐν τῇ
μάχῃ 24 7; ἡττηθεὶς μάχῃ
18 3; ἐρρωμενεστάτην μάχην
ἀγωνίσασθαι 10 2; μάχην
συνάψαι 33 4; συνάψαντας
μάχην 19 3; μετὰ τὴν μ. 29
3; τὴν πρὸς Ἀμαζόνας μ.
31 4
μεγαλ-αυχία: τῆς μ. 37 5; ταῖς
μ., 'grand airs' 5 3
μεγαλο-πράγμων 4 2
μεγαλο-φροσύνη: ὑπὸ μεγαλοφροσύνης 16 5; τὴν μ. 14 2,
17 3
μεγαλό-ψυχος: τὸ μ. 36 5
μέγας: μ. ἔργον 21 1; μ.
σημεῖον 35 1; ΜΕΓΑ ϹΘΕΝΟϹ
4 4; φρονήματος μ. 31 1;
τὴν πόλιν ἐκ μεγάλης μεγίστην
ποιήσας 15 1; στρατῷ μ. 10 1,
33 3; στόλῳ μ. 20 1; μ. κιν-

δννον 28 6; μ. πόλιν 17 1;
μ. δόξαν 18 3; μ. πρόφασιν
29 3; μ. ελπίδα 35 1; μ.
σύνεσιν 4 4; πράγμασι μ. 32
3; μ. απεχθείας 39 1; μ.
στρατηγούς 18 1; μ. επιβολάς
12 5; τὰς μ. χρείας 7 5.—
Adv. μέγα φρονεῖν 17 1;
μέγα φρονοῦντος 13 2; μέγα
φρονῆσαι 28 5
μέγεθος: τῆς δυνάμεως τὸ μ. 20
1; τὸ μ. τῆς ἡγεμονίας 20 3;
τοσαύτην τὸ μ. ἀρχὴν 15 4;
τὸ μ. τῆς ψυχῆς 36 4; ἔργων
ὑπερηφάνων μεγέθει 13 1; τῷ
μ. τοῦ φρονήματος 8 1
μέγιστος: Μ. ΤΥΡΑΝΝΟΝ 3 3;
μ. γεγονότα τῶν πολιτῶν 11
1; μ. ἔκπληξιν 12 1; μ.
ἔργον (τῆς ῥητορικῆς) 15 4;
δυνατωτάτων καὶ μεγίστων
ὄντων 24 2; τὸ κάλλιστον καὶ
μ. 38 4.—Adv. μέγιστον δυνηθεὶς 31 2
μέδιμνος: τετρακισχιλίους πυρῶν
μ. 37 3
μεθ-ιστάναι: μετέστησεν ἑαυτὸν
ἐκ Λακεδαίμονος 22 3
μέθ-οδος: τὴν περὶ τὰ ἤθη μ. 15
4
μεθυσο-κότταβος, *ebrius ex cotta-
bismo*: ΝΕΑΝΊΑΙ ΜΕΘΥϹΟ-
ΚΌΤΤΑΒΟΙ 30 4
μειδιᾶν: μειδιάσας 10 5, 28 5
μείζων: μ. στόλος 26 1; μεῖζόν
τι 35 2; μιᾷ δραχμῇ μείζονα
οὖσίαν 15 5; μ. πίστιν 33 1
μειράκιον, τὸ 36 2
μειρακιώδης: τὴν μ. προσωνυμίαν 39 2
μέλας: μ. ἱμάτιον 38 4
μελετᾶν: μελετῶντες 11 4
μέλλειν, *in eo esse ut*: ἔμελλεν
εἰσιέναι 5 3; ἔμελλεν ἀνάγεσθαι 35 1.—'to be like
to': ἔμελλε παύσεσθαι 36 1;

ἔμελλε πολεμήσειν βέλτιον 23
1.—*cunctari*: μέλλοντα τὸν
πόλεμον ἐξέκαυσεν 32 3
μέμφεσθαι: ἐμέμφοντο 16 4
μέν—δέ 4 3, 20 1.—μέν—μέντοι
24 3.—μέν οὖν 6 4, 10 1 7,
16 5, 18 3, 28 3, 30 3, 32 3,
35 3 4
μένειν: μενοῦσιν ἀθάνατοι 18 1;
ἔμεινεν οἰκουρῶν 34 1; οἱ
μείναντες ἐν τῇ πολιτείᾳ 37 4
μέντοι 8 1 3; καὶ μέντοι γε 16
7; μέν—μέντοι 24 3
μέρος: σατυρικὸν μ. 5 4
μέσος: ἐκ μ. τοῦ μετώπου 6 2;
ἐν τῷ διὰ μ. 10 1; φθεγξάμενος εἰς μέσον 38 4
μεστός: ὀργῆς ἄλλων τε μεστοὺς
παθῶν 39 3
μετά: A. c. Gen. 'concurrently,
jointly with': τοῦτον ἀπέκτεινεν ὁ δῆμος μ. τῶν συστρατηγῶν 37 5; τρισκαίδεκα ναῦς
ἀπέλιπε μ. Λαμάχου 20 1; ἐφ᾽
οὖς διέβη μ. δυνάμεως 22 1;
μ. τῶν γνωρίμων ἐφοίτα 24 3;
ἐμβάλλουσι μ. τῶν συμμάχων
33 3; συνέπλευσε μετ᾽ αὐτοῦ
8 5; μ. Πρωταγόρου δια-
ποροῦντα 36 3; λόγους ἐποιεῖτο μ. τῶν σοφιστῶν 36 2.—
*cum res alteri ita additur
ut partem obiecti efficiat*:
'with,' 'as well as': μετ᾽
εὐνοίας δόξαν 18 3; χάριν
ἔχουσα μ. δεινότητος 24 2;
ἐκ φρονήματος μεγάλου μ.
γνώμης 31 1; τὴν ἀσφαλῆ
μετ᾽ ἐλπίδων ἀγαθῶν εὐσέ-
βειαν 6 1; ἠσπάζετο αὐτὴν μ.
τοῦ καταφιλεῖν 24 6.—in-
dicat modum quo aliquid
fit, ut μετά c. nomine suo
adverbii partes sustineat:
μ. γέλωτος 8 2; μ. παιδιᾶς 8
3, 21 4

B. c. Acc. post : μ. ταῦτα 29 1 ; μεθ' ἡμέρας ὀλίγας 3 2 ; μ. τὴν Θουκυδίδου κατάλυσιν 16 3 ; μ. τὸν ὀστρακισμόν 16 3 ; μ. τὴν μάχην 29 3 ; μ. τὴν Περικλέους τελευτήν 24 4
μετα-βάλλειν ἑαυτόν 1 3
μετα-βολή : τῆς μ. 9 1 ; μηδεμίαν μ. 34 4 ; ποικίλαις μ. 38 1
μετ-άγειν : τὰ κοινὰ χρήματα πρὸς αὑτὸν μεταγαγών 12 1
μετα-λαμβάνειν 12 5
μεταλλεύς : μεταλλεῖς 12 7
μετά-νοια : μ. δεινὴ τοὺς Ἀθηναίους ἔσχε 10 2
μετα-πείθειν, *in aliam sententiam traducere*: μεταπείθει τοὺς ὁρῶντας 8 4 ; μετέπεισεν (αὐτούς) 35 4
μετ-αρσιο-λεσχία[2] : τῆς μ. 5 1
μετ-άρσιος : λόγους περὶ τῶν μ. διδάσκοντας 32 1
μετ-έχειν τῶν βουλευμάτων 17 3 ; μετεῖχε τῆς βουλῆς 9 3
μετ-εωρίζειν : μετεωρίσας 4 4
μετ-εωρο-λογία : τῆς λεγομένης μ. 5 1
μετ-έωρος : τὰ μ. 6 1
μέτριος : μετριώτερον ἐν ὄγκῳ τρόπον 39 4
μετρίως εὐδοκίμησε 18 3
μέτρον : ἀριθμοῦ καὶ μέτρου 16 4
μέτ-ωπον : ἐκ μέσου τοῦ μ. 6 2 ; ἔστιζον εἰς τὸ μ. γλαῦκας 26 3 ; τὸ μ. τοῦ χαλκοῦ λύκου 21 2
μέχρι, *usque*, of Time : μέχρι νῦν 13 3.—of Place : μέχρι Βυζαντίου 17 2
μή with participle for οὐ 3 2, 23 1, 29 2, 34 4 ; after a verb of consenting in indirect discourse 36 4, 12 1. —*num*, in indirect question after ἠρώτα 35 2

μηδέ, *ne—quidem* 8 4 ; for οὐδέ 29 3
μηδείς for οὐδείς 9 4, 14 2 ; τὰ μηδεμιᾶς ἄξια σπουδῆς 1 2 ; μ. ἔργον μέγα 29 2 ; μηδένα τῶν φίλων 7 4 ; μηδεμίαν 34 4. — μηδὲν ἧττον 12 5 ; μηδέν 28 3, 39 1.—after μήτε —μήτε 39 1 ; after μηδέ 8 4
μηδισμός : μηδισμοῦ ἀρχάς 24 2
μῆκος : μ. τοσοῦτον πολέμου 34 2 ; νόσῳ μῆκος ἐχούσῃ 38 1
μηλό-βοτος : μ. χώραν 16 5
μήν : μηνί 28 1 ; μησὶν ἐννέα 28 6 ; ὀκτὼ μ. 11 4
μήν : οὐ μήν 25 2, 35 4, 36 4 ; οὐ μὴν ἀλλά 29 5
μηνύειν : ἐμήνυσε τὴν θεὸν οὐκ ἀποστατοῦσαν 13 5
μήνυσις : ἐπὶ μηνύσει 31 2
μηνυτής : τῷ μ. 31 5
μήτε—μήτε μηδέν—μηδέ 39 1
μητρόθεν : τὸ μ. γένος 33 1
μηχανᾶσθαι : μηχανώμενος εἶναί τινα θέαν 11 4
μηχανή : μηχαναῖς bellicis χρήσασθαι 27 3
μηχανικός : τοῦ μ. 27 3
μίγνυσθαι : μεμιγμένοις)(ἀκράτοις 4 4.—ἀλλΉλοιcι μιΓέΝΤε (de concubitu) 3 2
μικρός : μ. πόλιν 17 1 ; μ. βοήθειαν 29 3 ; κατὰ μικρόν 36 1 ; πόλεις μ. 34 2 ; οἰκήμασι μ. 34 4
μιμεῖσθαι : μιμούμενος 15 3, 18 1
μίμημα, *simulacrum* 13 5
μίμησις : τῇ μ. 2 3 ; προθυμίαν ἀγωγὸν εἰς μίμησιν 1 4
μιμητικὸς ζῆλος 2 2
μισεῖν : μισούντων 33 1
μισθός : μισθῶν διανομάς 9 1
μισθο-φορά : ἄλλαις μ. 9 3
μισό-δημος : μισόδημον 9 4
μνήμη : ταῦτα ἐπελθόντα τῇ μ. 24 7

INDEX IV GREEK

μνημονεύειν: μνημονεύουσι 38 4.
—PASS. τὸ μνημονευόμενον, tritum dictum 18 2
μοθωνικός [1,4], protervus: μ. ὁμιλίαν 5 3
μολεῖν: Μόλ' ὦ Ζεῦ 3 3
μόλις 13 1
μον-αρχία 39 5; κομιδῇ μοναρχίαν 11 1
μόνιμος: βάρος μ. 13 2
μονό-κερως [1]: κριοῦ μ. 6 2
μόνος 15 4, 29 5; μόνῳ 32 3; μόνον 12 1; μόνοις 23 2; μόνους 37 3; μόνας 29 2; Μόνον (solum) 3 2.—Adv. 12 3; οὐ (μὴ) μόνον—ἀλλὰ καί 1 3, 5 1, 6 1, 8 5, 19 1 3, 35 3
μορφή: μορφῇ ἀμιμήτων ἔργων 13 1.—effigies: αὐτοῦ τινα μ. 31 4
Μοῦσα: ταῖς Μ. 1 5
μουσικός: τῆς μ. (sc. τέχνης) 4 2; μουσικῆς ἀγῶνα 13 6; μουσικὴν διαπονηθῆναι 4 1; διδάσκαλον τῶν μ. 4 1; τοὺς μ. ἀγῶνας 13 7
μουσοῦσθαι: τὸ μεμουσωμένον Cimonis 5 3
μοχθηρός: ἄνθρωπος μ. 1 4
μοχθηρῶς: διέκειτο μ. 13 8; μ. εἶχεν 36 1
μύθευμα [1]: τοῖς αὐτῶν μ. 39 3
μυθώδης: ἀσέβημα μ. 13 11
μυρ-εψός, unguentarius: τοὺς μ. 1 4
μύριοι: μυρίους χρυσοῦς 25 2
μύρον: ἐπὶ τῶν μ. 1 4; Μύροισι 28 5

Ν

ναός: ν. χιλιοταλάντους 12 2
ναυμαχεῖν: ναυμαχοῦντα 26 3
ναυμαχία: καρτερᾶς ν. 25 3
ναῦς γαστροειδής 26 3; νεώς 33 5; ναῦν 12 3; ν. Ἀττικήν 23 2; νεῶν 19 3, 26 1 2, 34 1, 35 1; ναυσίν 23 2, 25 3; πολλὰς ναῦς 26 2; τὰς ν. παρέλαβε 28 1; ὀλίγας ν. 29 2; ναῦς ἐπλήρου 35 1, 20 1
νούτης: ναῦται 12 6
ναυτιᾶν: ναυτιώντων 33 5
ναυτικός: ν. δυνάμει 29 1; τὴν ν. ἐμπειρίαν 11 4
νεανίας: Νεανίαι Μεθυσοκότταβοι 30 4
νεανίσκος: τῷ ν. 36 3
νέμειν, tribuere: πολὺ νέμει ταῖς Μούσαις 1 5.—MID. inter se partiri, incolere: νειμαμένους οἰκίας 20 2
νεμεσητός: νεμεσητὰ παθεῖν, nemesin expertum esse 37 5
νέος, novus, alter 16 1; Ὀμφάλη νέα 24 6.—iuvenis 2 1, 7 1; ν. ὄντα κομιδῇ 22 2; γυναικὶ ν. 36 1; νέους 16 1
νεουργός, recens factus: ἀκμῇ πρόσφατον καὶ νεουργόν 13 3
νέφος: τύπον οὐ νέφεσι χρώμενον 39 3
νεωτερίζειν τι 11 5
νησιώτης: τοὺς ν. 17 2, 22 2
νῆσος: τὴν νῆσον 29 1, 34 1; νήσους 15 1; ταῖς νήσοις ἐπιπηδᾶν 7 6
νικᾶν: νικᾷ 8 4; νικῶν 38 3; λαμπρῶς ἐνίκα 25 3; ὁ νικήσας τοὺς στρατηγούς 3 1; νικήσαντες 26 2; νίκας καλλίστας νενικηκότα τοὺς βαρβάρους 9 4
νίκη: ἅμα τῇ ν. 26 1; ν. καλλίστας 9 4
νικη-φόρος: ἀθλητὴν ν. 28 4
νόθος: ὁ νόθος δέ μοι Ζῆ 24 6; τὸν ν. 24 6; ἀπογράψασθαι τὸν ν. 37 5; νόθων)(γνησίων 37 2; τοῖς ν. 37 3

νομίζειν : τοὺς τὰ θεῖα μὴ νομίζοντας 32 1
νόμος 30 1 ; τὸν περὶ τῶν νόθων
ν. 37 2 ; τὰ περὶ τὸν ν. 37 3 ;
νόμον ἔγραψε 37 3 ; ν. τινα
προβαλλομένου 30 1 ; νόμους
ἔθετο 3 1
νοσεῖν : νοσῶν 38 2 ; νοσήσας
31 5. 36 3
νόσημα : ν. συγγενικόν 22 3 ;
ποικίλῳ ν. 15 3
νόσος : τῇ ν. παραφρονήσαντες
34 3 ; βληχρᾷ τινι ν. 38 1 ;
διὰ τὴν ν. 35 3
νου-θετεῖν : νουθετήσας 1 1
νοῦς)(αἴσθησις 1 2 ; τῷ ν.
χρῆσθαι 1 3 ; νοῦν)(τύχην
and ἀνάγκην 4 4 ; πᾶσι τὸν
νοῦν προσεσχηκώς 38 4 ; ἀνθρώποις νοῦν ἔχουσι 39 3.—
Νοῦς Anaxagoras dictus 4 4
νῦν δέ, 'as it was' 34 3

Ξ

ξενία : διὰ τὴν ξ. 33 2
ξένιος : ὦ Ζεῦ ξένιε 3 3
ξένος : ξ. πλουσίους 1 1 ; ὀθ.
νείους καὶ ξ. 29 3
ξύλον, *fustis* : ξύλοις τὰς κεφαλὰς συγκόψαντας 28 2

Ο

ὁ, ἡ, τό for demonstrative pronoun : ἀπὸ τῶν οἷς ἐκόσμησε
8 2 ; τὸ μέν—τὸ δέ 11 3 ; οἱ
μέν—οἱ δέ 31 1 ; τῳ μέν—τῷ
δέ 6 3, 13 9, 29 3 ; τοὺς μέν
—οἱ δέ 31 1 ; τὰς μέν—τὰς
δέ 16 2 ; τὰ μέν—τὰ δέ 2 3,
13 12 ; οἱ μέν—Αἰσχίνης δέ
24 3
ὄγκος : ὁ περιθεὶς ὄγκον αὐτῷ
4 4 ; παντὸς ὄ. περιγενέσθαι
7 5 ; μετριώτερον ἐν ὄ. 39

4. Cp. *Alc.* c. 31, ὁ ἀξίωμα
δ' οὐ προσῆν οὐδ' ὄγκος αὐτῷ
(τῷ Λαμάχῳ) διὰ πενίαν
ὁδο-ποιός : ὁδοποιοί 12 7
ὁδός : ὁ. μίαν 7 4
ὀδύνη : ὀΔΥΝΑΙC ΠΕΦΥCΙΓ-
ΓωΜΕΝΟΙ 30 4
ὅθεν : τὸν τόπον ἐκεῖνον ὅ., *unde*
6 2.—in initio periodi, *quare*
2 2, 3 2, 13 3, 16 4, 33 2
ὀθνεῖος, *alienigena* : ὀθνείους)(
γνησίους 29 3
οἴαξ : οἴακι 15 4
οἴεσθαι : οἴεται 35 2 ; οἴονται 8
2 ; ᾤετο 16 3 : ᾤοντο 13 1 ;
οἶμαι in parenthesi 6 3, 16
6
οἴκαδε 5 2
οἰκεῖος : τὸ οἰ. ἀγαθόν 1 3 ; τὰ οἰ.
)(τὰ δημόσια 36 1
οἰκείως εἶχον πρὸς αὐτόν 10 2
οἰκέτης 16 5 ; τῶν οἰ. 5 3 ; δυεῖν
οἰκετῶν 27 4
οἴκημα : ἐν οἰ. μικροῖς 34 4
οἰκία : οἰ. μεγάλῃ 16 4 ; τὴν οἰ.
5 3, 16 5 ; νειμαμένους οἰκίας
20 2
οἰκο-δομεῖν 13 4 ; ΤΑ ΜΕΝ ΟΙΚΟ-
ΔΟΜΕΙΝ ΤΑ ΔΕ ΚΑΤΑΒΑΛΛΕΙΝ
16 2
οἰκο-δομία : τὴν οἰ. 13 7
οἴκοι 27 4, 36 2, 37 1
οἰκο-νομία : εὖ πεφυκὼς πρὸς οἰκονομίαν 16 5 ; τὸν πλοῦτον
συνέταξεν εἰς οἰ. ἀκριβεστάτην
16 3
οἶκος : οἴκου καὶ γένους τοῦ πρώτου 3 1 ; τῷ Κίμωνος οἴκῳ
29 2 ; δυστυχία περὶ τὸν οἶ.
37 5 ; τὸν οἶ. ἐκλίποι 37 2
οἰκ-ουρεῖν : οἰκουρῶν 11 2, 34 1 ;
τὸ οἰκουροῦν 12 5
οἰκ-ουρός : δίαιταν οἰ. 34 4
οἰνο-χοεῖν : οἰνοχοῶν libertatem
meram 7 6 (ex Platone philosopho)

οἷον, *ut fit* 16 4; *ut*, 'as for example' 8 5; *tamquam*, 'as it were' 7 5, 8 1, 15 1, 29 2, 31 4
ὀκνεῖν: οὐκ ὤκνησε χαρίσασθαι 10 3
ὀκτὼ μῆνας 11 4
ὄλβος: τὸν παλαιὸν ὄ. 12 1
ὀλιγ-αρχία: τὴν οὖσαν ὀ. 25 1
ὀλιγ-αρχικός: τοῖς ὀ. 10 7
ὀλίγος: ἐν ὀ. (sc. χρόνῳ) 13 3; ὀλίγῳ ὕστερον 6 2; ὀλίγῳ ἐλάττους 37 4; ὀ. ὕστερον ἡμέραις 18 2; οὐκ ὀλίγοις τῶν ἐπιτηδείων 36 1; ὀ. ἡμέρας 3 2; ὀ. ναῦς 29 2.—τῶν ὀ.)(τῶν πολλῶν 7 2; τοὺς ὀ.)(τὸν δῆμον 11 3; ὀλίγα, '(only) a few' 8 5
ὀλιγότης: τῆς ὀ. τῶν νεῶν 26 2
ὅλος: ὅ. ἡμέραν 5 2; ἡμέραν ὅ. 36 3; τοῖς ὅ. = τῷ κόσμῳ 4 4
ὀλοφύρεσθαι: ὀλοφυρόμενον ἑαυτόν 16 7
Ὀλύμπιος: Ὀλύμπιον προσαγορευθῆναι 8 2
ὅλως τε 4 4; καὶ ὅ. 21 1, 29 3, 36 3
ὁμαλός: τῆς πόλεως ὁ. γενομένης 15 1
ὁμαλῶς, *pariter*: ὁ. ἁπάντων 6 2; πάντες ὁ. 10 2; τὸν ἅπαντα χρόνον ὁ. 39 3
ὅμηρος: ἕκαστον τῶν ὁ. 25 2; λαβὼν ὁμήρους 25 1; ὁμήρους ἔδωκαν 28 1; ἐκκλέψαντος τοὺς ὁ. 25 3
ὁμιλεῖν ut discipulo magister 24 4
ὁμιλία, *consuetudo privata* 5 3
ὀμνύναι: ὅταν ὀμνύωσι τὸν πάτριον ὅρκον 30 3
ὁμοιο-μέρεια: τὰς ὁ. 1 4
ὅμοιος: ἀνδρῶν κατὰ τὰς ἄλλας ἀρετὰς ὁ. 2 4
ὑμοιότης: τὴν ὁ. 7 1, 31 4
ὁμοίως 15 2

ὁμο-λογεῖσθαι: ὁμολογεῖται, *in confesso est* 21 2
ὁμό-νοια: πρὸς ὁμόνοιαν 3 1
ὄμ-ορος: ὁμόρων 19 2
ὁμοῦ, *simul* 34 4
ὅμως 11 1; ὅμως ἀσχάλλοντας 34 1
ὄναρ 13 8
ὄνειρος 20 3. Cp. *Thes.* c. 6, 7 οὕτως τῷ Θησεῖ τοῦ Ἡρακλέους θαυμάζοντι τὴν ἀρετὴν νύκτωρ ὄνειρος ἦσαν αἱ πράξεις: *Marc.* c. 28, 3 τοῦτο νύκτωρ ὄνειρον ἦν αὐτῷ καὶ ἓν βούλευμα καὶ μία πρὸς θεοὺς φωνή, παρατατττόμενον Ἀννίβαν λαβεῖν
ὄνομα 4 1, 29 3, 37 2; ὄνομα θέμενον τὸ αὐτοῦ 37 5; τοῖς ὀ. 29 3
ὀνομάζειν 32 2; ὀνομάζουσιν 3 2; ὀνομάσαι 24 7; ὀνομάζεται 27 3; ὀνομάζονται 30 3; ὠνομάσθη 3 4, 26 4; ὀνομασθῆναι 27 3
ὀνομαστός: ὀνομαστὴν γενέσθαι 24 7
ὄντως 28 6
ὀξύς: ὀξὺν ὥσπερ ᾠόν 6 2; λαβὴν οὐκ ὀξεῖαν 38 1
ὀπαῖον, τό 13 5
ὁπήποτε Εὐρώπης 17 1
ὁπλίτης: ὁπλίτην 12 3; τοῖς ἀπὸ τῶν νεῶν ὁ. 19 3, 23 2; ἀγαθοὺς ὁ. 35 1; πρὸς τοὺς Βοιωτῶν ὁ. 33 4
ὅπλον: τὰ ὅ. (*rudentes*) κατατείνας 33 5; ἔθετο εἰς λόχον τὰ ὅ. (*arma*) 10 1
ὁπόθεν: οὐκ οἶδ' ὁ. (in parenthesi) 10 6
ὁπότε, causal, *quando, quoniam* 38 2
ὁπότερος: ὁποτέρῳ τῶν λογισμῶν 26 2
ὅποι, *ubi* 28 3.— *quandoquidem* 12 6, 13 11

ὀπωρίζειν : ὀπωρίζωσι 9 2
ὅπως, final : ὅ. πλέωσι 17 1 ; ὅ. ὀπωρίζωσι 9 2 ; ὅπως οἱ λόγοι ἀποτεθεῖεν 32 2
ὀπωσ-οῦν, tantillum 35 3
ὀρᾶν : ὁρῶμεν 8 6 ; ὁρῶν ... παρασκευαζόμενον 18 1 ; ὁρῶν νέον ὄντα 22 2 ; ὁρῶσα 12 2 ; ὁρῶντες ... μέγιστον γεγονότα 11 1 ; ὁρῶν περίφοβον τὸν κυβερνήτην 35 2 ; τοὺς ὁρῶντας 8 4.—PASS. ἑωρᾶτο πορευόμενος 7 4 ; οὐ κλαίων ὤφθη 36 4
ὄργανον, 'an implement' : ὅ. τῆς ὑπηρεσίας 12 7 ; 'a musical instrument' 8 1
ὀργάς : τὴν ἱερὰν ὅ. 30 2
ὀργή : τῆς πρὸς ἐκεῖνον ὀ. 33 7, 35 4 ; ὑπ' ὀργῆς 33 3 ; ὀργῆς μεστούς 39 3
ὀρθός : ὀ. καὶ ἀνεγκλίτῳ πολιτείᾳ 15 2 ; κατὰ τὸν ὀρθότατον λόγον 36 3
ὀρθῶς 2 4, 22 1
ὁρίζεσθαι : ὡρισμένην νόμῳ 10 1
ὅρκος : τὸν πάτριον ὅ. 30 3 ; παρὰ τοὺς ὅ. 29 4
ὁρμᾶν : ὁρμησάντων ἐπ' αὐτούς 10 1
ὁρμή, 'impulse' : ὁ. πρὸς τὸ πρᾶξαι 1 4 ; κινοῦσα προθυμίαν καὶ ὁ. ἐπὶ τὴν ἐξομοίωσιν 2 2 ; ταῖς ὁ. τῶν πολιτῶν 20 2
ὀρνιθο-τροφία [14] : τὰς ὀ. 13 10
ὅρος : τῶν ὅ. 10 2 ; τοῖς ὅ. 22 1
ὅς 7 6 ; ὑφ' ἧς 7 6 ; ᾗ βούλοιντο 20 1, 34 2 ; ὧν ἕνα 7 6
ὅσος : ὅσῃ 38 3 ; ὅσον ἐπ' αὐτῷ, quatenus facere ipse possit 18 1 ; ὅσην 6 1 ; καὶ ὅσα τοιαῦτα (sc. ἐστι) 5 1 ; ὅσα μὴ πρότερον εἶχον 26 2 ; ὅσον οὐ, 'almost' only of time : ὅσον οὐδέπω, iamiam 29 1
ὅσπερ : ὅπερ 26 1

ὅστισπερ : ὅ τι περ κεφάλαιον 3 4.—Cp. Cor. c. 15, 5 οἱ δ' ἐν ἡλικίᾳ τῶν πατρικίων, ὅτι περ ἦν ἐν τῇ πόλει μάλιστα γαυρούμενον εὐγενείᾳ καὶ ἀνθοῦν
ὀστρακισμός : τὸν ὀ. 16 3
ὄστρακον : τοῦϲτρακον παροίχεται 13 4 ; ἀγῶνα περὶ τοῦ ὀ. 14 2
ὅταν, quandocumque 8 4, 30 3 ; quandoquidem 13 12
ὅτε 10 5, 17 1 ; c. opt. 8 3 ; ἔστιν ὅτε = ἐνίοτε 3 2, 24 3 ; ἦν ὅτε 15 3
ὅτι, quia 4 4, 23 3, 29 3.—quod 6 2 ; φησὶν ὅτι 8 6 ; ἐδίδασκε τὸν δῆμον ὅτι 12 3, 22 1, 23 1, 24 1 2 4, 30 3, 33 2, 34 2, 38 2, 4
οὐχ—οὐ—οὐχ 12 3 ; οὐ—οὐ 39 3.—οὐ redundant with ὡς after a verb of disputing or denial ἀντιλέγων ὡς οὐ πέπτωκε 8 4 ; transposed 10 5
οὐ μὴν 4 2, 35 4, 36 4.—οὐ μὴν —οὐδέν 25 2.—οὐ μὴν ἀλλά 8 4, 10 5, 29 5
οὐδέ in a clause after οὔτε— οὔτε 39 1 ; οὐδέ, ne—quidem 2 2, 13 5, 19 4, 28 2 ; οὐδέ γάρ, neque enim 8 6
οὐδείς 38 4 ; οὐ. πάθος 10 6 ; οὐ. πρόσκρουσμα 19 4 ; οὐδενὸς (neut.) τῶν τοιούτων 34 1, 16 4 ; σὺν οὐ. καιρῷ 18 2 ; οὐδέν 7 5 ; πρὸς οὐδέν χρώμενος 34 4 ; οὐδέν τοιοῦτον 37 5.—οὐδέν (adv.) ἀπέοικεν 8 2 ; οὐδέν τι μᾶλλον, nihilo magis 30 1
οὐδέποτε 36 5
οὐδέπω 29 1
οὐκέτι 7 6, 15 2, 38 4
οὑμός crasis for ὁ ἐμός 28 4
οὖν vi consecutiva post primum vocabulum 2 4, 4 2, 9

1, 23 2, 25 3; τί οὖν 35 2;
post alterum: πῶς ἂν οὖν 10
5; ὡς ἂν οὖν 29 2; ὑπῆν μὲν
οὖν 30 2
οὐσία: τὴν οὐ. 15 5
οὔτε—οὔτε—οὐδέ 39 1; οὔτε—
οὔτε—τε 18 1; οὔτε—τε 35 3
οὗτος: αὗται αἱ αἰτίαι λέγονται
32 3; αὗται αἱ ἀρχαί 9 3; τοῖς
δημώδεσι τούτοις στιχιδίοις 30 4
οὕτω δή, sic, tum demum 7 2;
οὕτως ἤδη 32 2; πυνθανόμενον
οὕτω 4 2; οὕτως ἐρωτῶντα 24
6; οὕτω πως 31 2.—οὕτως
(tam) εὐμενὲς ἦθος 39 1;
καλῶς οὕτω ψάλλων 1 5.—
οὕτως—ὥστε 2 2, 8 4, 24 7,
31 3; οὕτω—ὡς 7 5.—usque
adeo 13 3 12
ὀφείλειν: τῶν θυσιῶν ἃς ὀφείλουσιν 17 1; χρημάτων οὐκ
ὀφείλουσι τοῖς συμμάχοις λόγον
12 3.—PASS. τὸ φύσει φιλητικὸν εἰς θηρία καταναλίσκοντας
ἀνθρώποις ὀφειλόμενον 1 1
ὀφθαλμός: ὀφθαλμῷ 1 3
ὀχλικός, multitudini gratus:
ὀ. βωμολοχίας 5 1
ὄχλος: ἀργοῦ ὀ. 11 5; ἐν ὀ. 15
4; τὸν ἀπὸ τῆς χώρας ὀ. 34
4; τὸν βάναυσον ὀ. 12 5;
τὸν θητικὸν ὀ. καὶ ἰδιώτην 12
7
ὀχυρός: φυλάττειν ἐν ὀ. 12 1
ὄψις, species: ἄθικτον ὑπὸ τοῦ
χρόνου διατηροῦσα τὴν ὀ. 13
2.—spectaculum: ἡττήθη τοῦ
πάθους πρὸς τὴν ὄψιν 36 5.—
sensus videndi, πρὸ τῆς ὀ. 31
4; παρακαλύψας τὴν ὀ. 35 2;
ἀναζωπυρεῖ τὴν ὀ. 1 3; ἀνέσχε
τὴν χλαμύδα πρὸ τῶν ὀ. αὐτοῦ
35 2; καθαρὰς ἔχειν τὰς ὀ. 8
5.—This is a poetical use of
the word: see Soph. Ant.
52 διπλᾶς ὄψεις ἀράξας αὐτός,

Oed. T. 1328 πῶς ἔτλης σὰς
ὄψεις μαρᾶναι; Plutarch has
it not infrequently: as
Pyrrh. c. 34, 2; Num. c.
7, 2 πανταχόσε τὰς ὀ. περι-
φέρων, Popl. c. 6, 3 τὰς ὀ.
ἀπαγαγεῖν ἀλλαχόσε, Sert.
c. 17, 6 ἀπεσκοτοῦντο τὰς ὀ.,
Alex. c. 3, 1 ἀποβαλεῖν τῶν
ὀ. τὴν ἑτέραν, Arat. c. 10, 3,
Mor. 481 E

II

πάγ-καλος: εἰκόνα π. 31 4
πάγος: τῆς ἐξ Ἀρείου π. βουλῆς
7 6, 9 3; ἀνέβαινον εἰς
Ἄρειον π. 9 3
πάθος, fucinus, calamitas: αἰτίους τοῦ π. (mortis) 36 3;
ἡττήθη τοῦ π. 36 5; πρὸς οὐδὲν
ἐκταραττομένη πάθος 5 1.—
affectus: π. ὠμόν 10 6; ἴδιον
π. 28 3; παντοδαπῶν π. 15 4;
ὀργῆς ἄλλων τε π. 39 3; τοῖς
τῶν σωμάτων π. 38 2; τὴν
περὶ τὰ ἤθη καὶ π. μέθοδον 15
4.—in sensu rerum exter-
narum: κατὰ πάθος <τὸ>
τῆς πληγῆς 1 2
παιδιά: μετὰ παιδιᾶς 8 3, 24 4
παιδίον: παιδία 1 1
παιδίσκη: παιδίσκας ἑταιρούσας
24 3
παίζειν: παίζει πρὸς αὐτόν 13 6
παῖς: π. καλόν 8 5; ἐνηλίκοις π.
16 4; π. γνησίους 37 3; π.
ἴσους 25 1
πάλαι 13 6
παλαίειν: παλαίει βέλτιον 8 4;
ὅταν καταβάλω παλαίων 8 4
παλαιός: ἐκ π. 9 3; τὸν π. ὄλβον
12 1; τῶν π. Ἰάδων 24 2
πάλιν, contra 37 5.—rursus:
3 4, 13 6, 21 2, 22 2, 24 6
παλλακή: ΠΑΛΛΑΚΗΝ 24 6

παλλακίs, *pellex:* τῶν π. 24 7
πάμ-πολυs : πάμπολλα 14 1
παν-ηγυρικόs : θέαν π. 11 4
παν-οῦργοs : π. βωμολοχίαs 5 1
παντά-πασιν : ὀλίγα π. 8 5; π.
 λυθείσηs 15 1 ; π. ἠγριώθησαν
 33 3 ; π. ἐκλίποι 37 2 ; οὐ π.
 ἀργῶs ἔχων 16 3
παν-τελῶs[3] κατεκλείσθησαν 26 1
πάντῃ 8 1 (ex Platone ph.),
 10 6, 13 12
παντο-δαπόs : π. ἐργασίαs 12 4;
 π. παθῶν 15 4
πάντωs 5 4
πάνυ : πολλὰ π. 32 3 ; π.
 πολλῶν 37 3 ; καὶ π. προ-
 θύμωs 25 3
παρά : **A.** w. Gen. of person,
 from whom anything pro-
 ceeds : ἐφοίτα δέκα τάλαντα
 παρὰ τοῦ Περικλέουs 23 1 ;
 τὰ μὲν ἡμῖν παρ' ἑτέρων
 ὑπάρχειν βουλόμεθα 2 3.—
 B. w. Dat. indicates that
 something is done in the
 immediate vicinity of some
 one, or in his mind, *apud:*
 παρ' αὐτοῖs 1 1 ; ἔτεκε π. τῷ
 Περικλεῖ Ξάνθιππον 24 5;
 παρ' ᾧ γένοιτο τὸ σημεῖον 6
 2 ; μέγιστον παρ' αὐτῷ δυνη-
 θείs 31 2 ; μείζονα τιμὴν ἔσχε
 π. τοῖs πολίταιs 33 1 ; δίκαs
 λαβεῖν καὶ δοῦναι παρ' αὐτοῖs
 25 1 ; π. Πυθοκλείδῃ μουσικὴν διαπονηθῆναι 4 1.—**C.**
 w. Acc. **I.** Local: **1.** 'near,'
 'beside,' 'at' : π. τὰs Θρια-
 σίαs πύλαs 30 3 ; παρὰ τὴν γῆν
 αὐτὴν παραφερόμενον 27 4 ;
 π. τὸν βωμόν 13 8.—παρ'
 ἐλάχιστον ἦλθε . . . ἀφελέσθαι
 28 6.—**2.** *praeter, contra,*
 'beyond,' 'contrary to' : π.
 τὴν αὐτοῦ φύσιν 7 2 ; π. τὰ
 κοινὰ δίκαια καὶ τοὺs ὅρκουs

29 4 ; βιασθῆναι π. γνώμην
 33 5.—II. Temporal : 'during' : π. τὴν δίκην 32 3. Cp.
 Alex. c. 52, 5 παρὰ δεῖπνον
 λόγων ὄντων, *Cat. mi.* c.
 37, 4 πλέον μηθὲν φιλοφρο-
 νήσασθαι παρὰ τὸ δεῖπνον,
 Lucian *Dial. mort.* 22, 3 οἷα
 δὲ καὶ ἐλάλει παρὰ τὸν πλοῦν
παρα-βάλλεσθαι, *temere pug-
 nare:* ἐκ τοῦ παραβαλέσθαι
 18 1
παρα-γίγνεσθαι : παραγενόμενοs
 (δείπνῳ) 7 4
παρα-διδόναι : παραΔεΔωκέναι 16 2
παρα-θήγεσθαι : παραθηγο-
 μένηc κοπίΔοc 33 7
παρ-αιτεῖσθαι, *deprecari*, 'to
 avert': παρῃτεῖτο τὸν πόλεμον
 23 1.—'to beg off,' 'inter-
 cede for' : παραιτούμενοs τὴν
 πόλιν 25 2. Cp. *Artox.* c.
 3, 5 μέλλοντα δ' ἤδη ἀποθνῄ-
 σκειν ἡ μήτηρ παρῃτήσατο
παρα-καθῆσθαι : παρακαθήμενοι
 38 3
παρα-καλεῖν 17 1, 18 2 ;
 παρεκάλει 5 4 ; παρεκάλουν
 17 2
παρα-κάλυμμα, *praetextus, ob-
 tentus:* τῇ λύρᾳ παρακαλύμματι χρώμενοs 4 2
παρα-καλύπτειν[2] : παρακαλύψαs
 τὴν ὄψιν 35 2
παρα-κατ-οικίζειν[2]: παρακατοικίζων τοῖs συμμάχοιs 11 5
παρ-ακολουθεῖν : παρακολουθοῦν-
 τοs 5 2
παρα-λαμβάνειν, 'to take over':
 τὰs ναῦs παρέλαβε 28 1
παρ-άλιοs : τῆs π. 19 3
παρα-λύειν : οὐ μὴν παρέλυσεν
 (αὐτοὺs) τῆs ὀργῆs 35 4
παρα-λυπεῖν : τι π. τοὺs πολε-
 μίουs 35 1

παρ-α-μελεῖν : τῶν καλῶν παραμελοῦντας 1 2
παρα-μένειν, *permanere*: παραμεῖναι 36 3
παρα-μυθεῖσθαι[2] in affectibus, *lenire, mitigare*: τὸ δύσθυμον παραμυθούμενος 15 4. Cp. *Alc.* c. 13, 4 παραμυθούμενοι τὸν φθόνον μᾶλλον ἢ τὸν φόβον
παρα-πέμπειν : παραπέμψαι 5 3
παρα-πλεῖν, *praeterlegere*: παραπλεύσας τὸν Ἀχελῷον 19 4
παρα-σκευάζειν : τἆλλα παρασκευάσαντος πρὸς τὸν πόλεμον 25 3 ; τῶν ἐχθρῶν παρασκευασάντων (φάρμακα) 31 5.
—MID. δύναμιν κατ' ἐκείνου παρασκευαζόμενος 7 3 ; παρασκευαζόμενον ἐμβαλεῖν 18 2 ; παρασκευασάμενος 18 3, 23 1
παρα-σκευή : τι τῆς π. ἄξιον 35 3
παρα-τίθεσθαι[2], *apponere*: παρετίθεντο τὰ ἀναγκαῖα πρὸς τὸν πόλεμον 26 2.—*afferre, memorare* (unclassical) : τοῦτο παρεθέμην 17 3
παρα-φαίνεσθαι : παραφαινομένην 31 4
παρα-φέρεσθαι : παραφερόμενον 27 4
παρα-φρονεῖν : παραφρονήσαντες 34 3
πάρ-εδρος : φύλακα καὶ π. 22 2
παρ-εῖναι : πάρεσται 12 4 ; ἡ παροῦσα δυστυχία 37 5 ; παρόντος 27 3 ; τῶν παρόντων 6 3
παρ-εμ-φαίνειν[1], *innuere, significare*: παρεμφαίνουσιν 16 1
παρ-εν-τείνειν[1]: παρενέτεινε 8 1
παρ-έρχεσθαι, *praeterire, transire*: ταῦτα παρελθεῖν 21 7
παρ-έχειν, *praebere*: δεῖπνον παρέχων 9 2 ; τοῖς ἀγαθοῖς ἃ παρέχουσι 8 6 : παρεῖχον 12 5 ; ἂν παρέχωσιν ἀνθ' οὗ λαμβάνουσι 12 3 ; παρέσχε τοῖς κωμικοῖς διατριβὴν 4 2 ; ἐλπίδα τοῖς πολίταις παρασχὼν καὶ φόβον τοῖς πολεμίοις 35 1 ; ἐλπίδα παρασχοῦσαν ὡς ἁλωσομένην 35 3 ; ὡς μὴ πολλὰ πράγματα παρέχοι 16 3 ; βοήθειαν . . . πρόφασιν παρεσχηκὼς 29 3 ; τοῖς φιλοσόφοις οὐ φαῦλον ὑπὲρ αὐτῆς παρέσχε λόγον 24 1.—*permittere, copiam facere*: τῷ λαβόντι τὸν λευκὸν κύαμον σχολάζειν παρεῖχε 27 2. [Cp. *Philop.* c. 18, 1 τοῦ βίου τὸ λοιπὸν αὐτῷ μεθ' ἡσυχίας καταβιῶναι τὰ πράγματα παρέξειν, *Pelop.* c. 1, 4 Λακεδαιμονίοις καὶ ζῆν ἡδέως καὶ θνήσκειν ἀμφότερα ἀρετὴ παρεῖχεν, *Cleom.* c. 24, 1 τοῖς φεύγουσι τῶν πολιτῶν ἀσφαλῶς ἀπελθεῖν παρεῖχον, *Pyrrh.* c. 13, 1 προεμένῳ τὴν Μακεδονίαν ἢ τύχῃ παρεῖχε ζῆν ἐν εἰρήνῃ, *Num.* c. 4, 5 τελευτήσαντι τυχεῖν ταφῆς ἄλλος θεὸς παρέσχε, *Aem. Paul.* c. 13, 1, *Marc.* c. 13, 5, *Lucull.* c. 3, 7 Μιθριδάτῃ μὲν ἐκπλεῦσαι παρέσχε, c. 15, 2.]—*reddere, efficere* with obj. and pred. acc. : τὸν Περικλέα πρᾳότερον παρασχεῖν 10 5.—MID. τὴν προαίρεσιν παρεχόμενον 2 3 ; μάρτυρα τὸν πόνον παρέχεται καθ' αὑτῆς 2 1 ; τί ποτε περὶ τογ πολέμογ λόγογς δεινογ̇ς παρέχη 33 7
παρ-ηγορεῖν 35 4
παρ-ηγορία 34 1
παρ-ιέναι : παριὼν εἰς τὸ πλῆθος 7 5
παρ-ίστασθαι, *deditionem facere*: παραστάντων 28 1

παρ - οίχεσθαι: τοΥcτpακον παροίχεται 13 6
παρ-οξύνειν: παροξύνας τὸν δῆμον ἐμμεῖναι 29 5
παρ-ορᾶσθαι: παρορωμένοις 37 3
πᾶς: π. ἀναλώματος... λήμματος 16 4; π. ἀγορᾶς 29 4; π. πράγματι 7 5; π. βλασφημίᾳ 5 2; π. τὸν χρόνον 18 1; π. τέχνην, π. χεῖρα 12 4; π. ἀκρίβειαν 16 5; π. δέησιν 16 7; π. ἡλικίαν καὶ φύσιν 12 7; ἀνὰ πᾶν ἔτος 30 3, 31 3; πάντες ὁμαλῶς 10 2; πάντες ὡσαύτως 31 1; πάντων 8 1, 11 2; π. λιμένων 29 4; πᾶσι (masc.) τοῖς τεχνίταις 13 9, 38 4; πᾶσι (neut.) τοῖς ἄλλοις 4 4; π. Ἕλληνας 17 1; τοὺς ἐν τέλει π. 2 3; καταλαβὼν πάντα φυλακαῖς 33 5.—c. art. ἐκ τοῦ π. ἀγγείου 6 2

πάσχειν: βίαια π. 29 4; πολλὰ πάσχοντες (κακὰ) ὑπ' ἐκείνων 34 2; ἀφ' ὧν ἔπασχον 34 1; νεμεσητὰ παθεῖν 37 5

πατάσσειν, ferire: ἀκοντίῳ πατάξαντος 36 3

πατήρ, ὁ 15 5, 22 3; τοῦ πατρὸς 36 1; πατέρα 34 3; τὸν π. 36 3

πάτριος: τὸν π. ὅρκον 30 3

πατρίς: τῆς π. 8 6, 28 3; ταῖς π. 2 4

πατρῷος: τὸν π. πλοῦτον 16 3

παύεσθαι: παύσεσθαι 36 1; παύσασθαι 25 1

πειθαρχεῖν 7 6

πείθειν: πείθων 15 3; ἔπεισε 22 2, 26 2, 29 1; πείσαντες 31 2; πεπεικότα 18 2.—MID. οὐκ ἐπείθοντο 25 1; εἰ μὴ πείθοιτο 18 2.—PASS. ἐπείσθη 37 1; εἰ... ἐπείσθησαν 29 5

πεῖρα: ἡ π. περιέστη εἰς τοὐναντίον 33 1; τῆς π. ἐλεγ-

χθείσης 17 3; πεῖραν ἐνδόσεως 31 1; τοῦ δήμου ποιούμενοι πεῖραν ἐν ἐκείνῳ 31 2

πειρᾶσθαι c. infin., conari: κατέχειν ἐπειρᾶτο 18 2; ἐπειρᾶτο παρηγορεῖν 35 3; ἐπειρᾶτο ἐγκαρτερεῖν 36 5.— c. gen. pers. 'to make trial of': τῆς πόλεως πειρωμένης τῶν ἄλλων στρατηγῶν καὶ ῥητόρων 37 1; πειρώμενοι ῥητόρων ἑτέρων 39 4; ἐπειρᾶτο τούτων κρύφα 22 2

πέλαγος, altum mare: ἐν π. 33 5

πέμπειν εἰς σύλλογον 17 1; πέμψας 36 2; πέμψαντος 37 3; τοῖς πέμψασιν 33 1.—PASS. πρεσβειῶν πεμπομένων 29 5; ἐπέμφθησαν 17 2; πεμφθῆναι 30 2

πένης: τῶν π.)(τῶν πλουσίων 7 2; πολλοῖς τῶν π. 16 6; τοὺς π. 9 2

πένθος: διὰ τὸ π. 37 1

πεντα-ετία[1]: ἐν π. 13 7

πέντ-αθλος: π. τινός 36 3

πεντακισ-χιλίων 37 4, 23 2

πεντα-κόσιοι: χιλίοις καὶ π. 32 2

πεντήκοντα ἔτη 17 2

περαίνεσθαι: περαινόμενον 13 5

περί: A. w. Gen. 'about,' 'concerning': περὶ οὗ ἀκοῦσαί φησιν 13 5; περὶ οὗ πεποίηκεν ἐρωτῶντα 25 6; πυνθανόμενος π. ἑκάστου 3 4; ὡς ἐν τοῖς π. ἐκείνου γέγραπται 9 4, 22 3; εἰς ἀγῶνα π. τοῦ ὀστράκου καταστάς 14 2; βουλευσομένους π. τῶν Ἑλληνικῶν ἱερῶν 17 1, 24 1 7, 30 1, 36 3.— B. w. Acc. I. Local: circa, juxta, 'at,' 'near': π. τὸ βῆμα 11 2; π. Χερρόνησον 19 1; π. Κορώνειαν 18 3; π. νῆσον 25 3; τοῦ π. Σάμον

πολέμου 27 3; τῶν π. Θουκυδίδην ῥητόρων 14 1.—II. Temporal: π. τοῦτον τὸν χρόνον 32 1; π. τὴν οἰκοδομίαν 13 7. —III. as a periphrasis for the simple genitive: ἡ π. τὸν βίον δόξα 15 5; ἡ π. τοὺς βίους ἀναγραφή 2 3; τῇ π. τὸν βίον κατασκευῇ 8 1; τοὺς π. αὐτὸν ἑταίρους 16 1; βαρυτέρας π. αὐτὸν ὑπεροχῆς 16 1; ἡ π. τὸν οἶκον δυστυχία 37 5; τὰ π. τὴν δίαιταν 7 4, 16 4. Cp. Schäfer ad Dion. Hal. p. 23, D'Orville ad Char. p. 552.—π. τὰς διώξεις ἀπαραίτητον 10 7; τοῖς π. τὰ θεῖα δαιμονῶσι 6 1; π. τὸν λόγον εὐλαβής 8 4, 13 7; πραγματευομένου π. φύσιν 4 3; συνέβη π. τοὺς στρατευομένους 19 4
περι-αιρεῖν, 'to strip off,' 'to take away that which envelops a thing': πᾶν (τὸ χρυσίον) περιελοῦσι 31 3
περι-άπτεσθαι: περιαπτομένην λίθους πολυτελεῖς 12 2
περί-απτον, τό 38 2
περι-αρτᾶσθαι: περίαπτον τῷ τραχήλῳ περιηρτημένον 38 2
περι-βάλλεσθαι, induere: μέλαν ἱμάτιον περιεβάλετο 38 4
περι-βόητος: τοῖς π. στιχιδίοις 30 4
περι-βολή: καταστολὴ περιβολῆς 5 1
περι-γίγνεσθαι e. gen.: περιγενέσθαι 27 1; παντὸς ὄγκου περιγενέσθαι 7 5
περι-εῖναι, superesse: οἱ περιόντες 38 3
περι-έχειν: βιβλίον τὸν Περικλέους βίον περιέχον 2 4.— PASS. cingi: αἱ εἰκόνες αὐτοῦ κράνεσι περιέχονται[2] 3 2

περι-ίστασθαι: εἰς ἕνα περιστήσεται τὸ κράτος 6 2; ἡ πεῖρα περιέστη εἰς τοὐναντίον 33 1
περι-καθ-ῆσθαι: περικαθήμενοι (v. l.) 38 3
περι-κλινής[1]: τῇ ἐρέψει περικλινές 13 5
περι-κόπτειν[2], 'to curtail': περιέκοπτε τὴν πολυπραγμοσύνην 21 1
περι-λάμπεσθαι: φωτὶ καθαρῷ περιλαμπόμενον 39 3
περί-λοιπος, superstes: τὸν π. τῶν γνησίων 36 4
περι-οικεῖν: τοῖς περιοικοῦσι βαρβάροις ἔθνεσι 20 1
περι-πίπτειν: ὑποψίᾳ περιπεσεῖν τυραννίδος 7 3; πολλοὶ συκοφαντήμασι περιέπιπτον 37 3
περι-πλεῖν: οἱ περιπλέοντες τὴν Πελοπόννησον 34 2; περιπλεύσας Πελοπόννησον 19 2
περι-ρρεῖν: οὐδενὸς περιρρέοντος 16 4
περι-τειχίζειν: περιετείχιζε 27 1
περι-τιθέναι: τὸ χρυσίον τῷ ἀγάλματι περιέθηκε 31 3; ὁ περιθεὶς ὄγκον αὐτῷ 4 4
περιττός opponitur vulgari: π. σύνεσιν 4 4. Cp. Cat. ma. c. 25, 1 ἐν παντὶ φιλοτιμούμενος περιττὸς εἶναι καὶ ἴδιος
περι-φανῶς 12 2, 15 5
περι-φέρειν: ἐν τοῖς κόλποις περιφέροντας 1 1; περιήνεγκεν εἰς ἑαυτὸν τὰς Ἀθήνας 15 1.— PASS. circumferri: ἐν κλινιδίῳ περιφερόμενον
περί-φοβος: περίφοβον 35 2
Περι-φόρнтос 27 3
περι-φρονεῖν: περιφρονῆσαι Λακεδαιμονίων 31 1
περι-φρόνησις[1]: πολλὴν π. τῶν ἄλλων 5 3
περι-χεῖσθαι: τῶν περικεχυμένων τῇ Χερρονήσῳ 19 1

πέτρος, *suum*: πέτρον 31 4
ΠΕΦΥCΙΓΓѠΜΕΝΟΙ ΟΔΥΝΑΙC 30 4
πιέζειν: ἐπίεζε φθόνῳ τὸν Φειδίαν 31 4
πιθανός: πιθανόν, *verisimile* 26 1
πίθηκος: τέκνα πιθήκων 1 1
πινάκιον, τό 30 1
πιπράσκειν: τοὺς καρποὺς ἐπίπρασκε 16 4.—PASS. ἐπράθησαν ἁλόντες 37 4
πίπτειν: πέπτωκε 8 4; ἔπεσε 13 8; ἔπεσον 10 2; ἐν τῇ μάχῃ πεσόντος 24 7
πιστεύειν: πιστεύσειε 10 6
πίστις τοῦ ἀνδρός 15 5; ἔτι μείζονα πίστιν ἔσχε καὶ τιμήν 33 1
πλάσμα[2] φωνῆς 5 1. Cp. *Brut.* c. 34, 4 μετὰ πλάσματος φωνῆς ἔπη περαίνων οἷς τὸν Νέστορα χρώμενον Ὅμηρος πεποίηκε
πλάστης: ὁ π. 31 2; πλάσται 12 6
πλεῖν 20 2; ἔπλεον 11 4; τῶν πλεόντων 12 5, 20 1; πλέωσι 17 1; ἔπλευσεν 26 1; πλεύσας 25 1, 26 1; πλεύσαντος 26 2
πλεῖστον (adv.), *plurimum*: π. ἠδύναντο 7 1; π. ἴσχυσε 24 7; ὁ πλεῖστα συγγενόμενος 4 4
πλεῖστος: π. χρόνον 8 4; π. ἡδονήν 12 1; τὸν π. ἀριθμόν 35 4; οἱ π. 4 1, 26 1; πλ. ἀνδράσι 24 2; τῶν κηδεστῶν τοὺς π. 36 4; π. μάρτυρας 31 2; τὰς π. κρίσεις 9 4; τὰ π. τῆς δυνάμεως 21 1
πλείων: πλείονας (τριήρεις) 29 3
πλευρά: τὴν δεξιὰν π. 21 2
πληγή, *ictus*: ἅμα πληγῇ 36 1. —*sensus a visis externis*: κατὰ πάθος <τὸ> τῆς π. 1 2

πλῆθος, 'a great number of people': ὑπὸ πλήθους ἡμαυρωμένους 11 2; τοῦ χωριτικοῦ π. 'the country population' 34 3; τὸ πᾶν π. 27 2.—τὸ πλῆθος = δῆμος, *plebs*: συνδεκάσας τὸ π. 9 3; παριὼν εἰς τὸ π. 7 5.—'number in the abstract': μύριοι τὸ π. 37 4. —'quantity,' 'amount': π. δακρύων 36 5; π. κακίας 39 5; τῶν τροπαίων τὸ π. 38 3; τὸ π. χρημάτων 22 3
πλήν: 1. as Prep. w. gen. 8 5. —2. as Adv. at beginning of sentence, *ceterum* 31 1, 34 1; for πλὴν ὅτι 7 4; πλὴν ὅτι 35 2
πληροῦν: οὐ πεπληρωκότα τὴν βάσιν 6 2; ναῦς ἐπλήρου 35 1.— PASS. πεπληρωμένων τῶν νεῶν 35 1
πλησιάζειν: τῷ δήμῳ ἐπλησίαζε 7 5.—*rem habere cum muliere*: γυναιξὶν αἷς ὁ Π. ἐπλησίαζε 13 10; τοὺς πλησιάσαντας αὐτῇ 24 2
πλησίον 28 4
πλοῦς: τὸν εἰς Σάμον π. 24 1
πλούσιος: τὸν π. 24 5; τῶν π.)(τῶν πενήτων 7 2; ξένους π. 1 1; πόλιν πλουσιωτάτην 15 5
πλοῦτος 16 6; π. καὶ γένους προσόντος αὐτῷ 7 1; π. καὶ χρήμασι 9 2; π. καὶ γένει 9 4; π. καὶ δόξῃ διαφέροντας 23 2; τὸν πατρῷον καὶ δίκαιον π. 16 3; ΠΛΟΥ͂ΤΟΝ Τ' ΕΥ͂ΔΑΙΜΟΝΙΑΝ ΤΕ 16 2
πνεῦμα, *aura*: οὐ πνεύμασι χρώμενον 39 3.—*spiritus*: ἀειθαλὲς π. 13 3
πνιγηρός: σκηνώμασι π. 34 4
πνοή, *ventus*: πνοαῖς, 'gusts of passion' 15 2

ποθεῖν: τῆς πόλεως ποθούσης ἐκεῖνον 37 1
πόθος 10 2; σαφῆ π. 39 4
ποιεῖν: I. *efficere*, 'to make': 1. (a) ῥᾳδίως τὰ ζῷα ποιεῖν 13 2. —PASS. τὸ σχῆμα πεποιημένον εὐμηχάνως 31 4; κατ' ἀντὲς πεποιημένον 13 5.—(b) 'to be the author or instrument of,' 'to cause': τοῦ πεποιηκότος τὴν ἐπισκότησιν 35 2; εἰρήνην ἐποίησε ταῖς πόλεσι 10 3; ῥοπὴν ἐποίησεν 11 2.—with acc. and inf. τὸ μὲν δῆμον ἐποίησε καλεῖσθαι 11 3.— PASS. σημεῖον εἶναί τινος πεποίηται 6 4.—(c) 'to compose': τἀναπαιστὰ ποιήσαντος 33 7.—'to represent' in portraiture: τὴν πρὸς Ἀμαζόνας μάχην ἐν τῇ ἀσπίδι ποιῶν 31 4; in poetry: πυνθανόμενον αὐτοῦ τινα πεποίηκεν 4 2; πεποίηκεν αὐτὸν οὕτως ἐρωτῶντα 21 6.— 2. ποιεῖν τινα with an accusative of the predicate: ἀσθενῆ ποιῶν τὴν κακίαν 39 5; ποιοῦσιν ἔμμισθον τὴν πόλιν 12 4; τὴν πόλιν ἐκ μεγάλης μεγίστην ποιήσας 15 5; μείζονα τὴν οὐσίαν οὐκ ἐποίησεν 15 5; τὴν προσωνυμίαν ποιεῖν ἀνεπίφθονον 39 2.—MID. ἰδίαν ἐμαυτοῦ ποιήσομαι τὴν ἐπιγραφήν 11 1; πᾶσαν ὑφ' αὐτοῖς πεποιημένων τὴν θάλασσαν 20 1.—With acc. of abstract nouns forms a periphrasis for the verb cognate to the subst. τοῦ δήμου ποιούμενοι πεῖραν = πειρώμενοι 31 2; λόγον ἐποιοῦντο τῆς ἀρετῆς αὐτοῦ 38 3; αἰτίαν ποιησάμενος κατ' αὐτῶν = αἰτιασάμενος 21 1, 30 2; ἐποιεῖτο λόγους μετὰ τῶν σοφιστῶν 36 2

II. *agere*, 'to do': οὐδέποτε τοιοῦτον οὐδὲν πεποιηκώς 36 5; used vicariously ἀποδεῖξαι τὸν σταθμόν, ὃ ποιεῖν ἐκέλευσεν (αὐτούς) 31 3
ποίημα: τοῖς Ἀνακρέοντος π. 27 3, 2 1; τοῖς αὐτῶν π. (*v. l.*) 39 3
ποιητής: ὁ π. Ἴων 5 3; οἱ π. 39 2; οἱ Ἀττικοὶ π. 3 2
ποικίλος: π. νοσήματι 15 3; π. χρειῶν 12 4; π. μεταβολαῖς 38 1
ποικιλτής: ποικιλταί 12 6
ποῖός τις 31 2
πολέμ-αρχος 9 3
πολεμεῖν: ἐπολέμουν τὸν περὶ Πριήνης πόλεμον 25 1; οὐ Φοίνιξι πολεμῶν 28 4; πολεμήσειν βέλτιον 23 1; τὸν πολεμήσαντα βασιλεῖ 24 7.— PASS. *bello vexari*: πολεμουμένοις ὑπὸ Κορινθίων 29 1
πολεμικός, *bellicae rei peritus*)(πολιτικός 11 2.—τῶν π., *rerum bello gestarum* 18 2
πολέμιος: οἱ π. 34 1; τῶν π. 33 1; τοῖς π. 33 6, 35 1; τοὺς π. 27 1, 35 1
πόλεμος, ὁ 29 5; μῆκος πολέμου 34 2; τοῦ Πελοποννησιακοῦ π. 29 1; μόνος ἔσχε τοῦ π. τὴν αἰτίαν 29 5; λόγογς περὶ τογ πολέμογ Δεινογς 33 7; τῷ π. 34 1 4; τὸν ἱερὸν π. 21 1; ἐπετάχυνε τὸν π. 29 4; κατὰ τὸν π. 28 3; τὸν ἐν τῇ Ἀττικῇ π. 22 2; τὸν πρὸς Σαμίους π. 25 1, 27 3; παρῃτεῖτο τὸν π. 23 1; τοῖς ἀναγκαίοις πρὸς τὸν π. 12 4; τὸν π. ἐπολέμουν 25 1; τὸν π. καθορᾶν προσφερόμενον 8 5; π. ἐνδελεχῆ καὶ βαρὺν ἐξέκλεισεν 19 2; διαλύσασθαι πόλεμον 21 1; τὸν π. ἐξέκαυσε 32 3

πολι-ορκεῖν: ἐπολιόρκει 26 1;
πολιορκήσας 35 3. — Pass.
πόλις πολιουρκουμένη 29 4
πόλις: π. ὑπήκοος Ἀθηναίων 29
4; τῆς π. τὸ μὲν—τὸ δέ 11 3;
τῆς π. κατεσκευασμένης τοῖς
ἀναγκαίοις 12 3: τῆς π. πειρωμένης τῶν ἄλλων 37 1; ὑπὲρ
αὐτῆς τῆς π. 33 4; ἐκ τῆς π.
32 3; τῇ π. 33 2; σύμμαχον
καὶ συγγενῆ π. 28 4; διὰ
χειρὸς ἔχων τὴν π. 34 1, 9 4,
11 4 5, 12 4, 27 1; τῇ π. τὴν
χώραν ἐπιδίδωσι 33 2; τὴν π.
ἐκ μεγάλης μεγίστην ποιήσας
15 5; π. μικρὰν καὶ μεγά-
λην 17 1; αἱ π. 17 3; ταῖς
π. 10 3, 24 2; π. μικράς 34 2;
ἔρρωσε τὰς π. 19 1; κατεστρέψατο τὰς π. 23 2; ΠΟΛΕΩΝ
ΤΕ ΦΟΡΟΥΣ ΑΥΤΑΣ ΤΕ
ΠΟΛΕΙΣ 16 2; ταῖς Ἑλληνίσι
π. 20 1, 24 2; διελύθη κατὰ
πόλεις 22 3.—for ἀκρόπολις:
ἐν τῇ π. 3 4, 32 2, 37
1; τὴν π. 12 2; ἐκόσμησε
τὴν π. 8 2.—civitas: ἐν τῇ
π. 11 1, 25 2; τῆς π. ὁμαλῆς
γενομένης 15 1; τῆς π. ἀναθείσης ἑαυτὴν ἐκείνῳ 32 3
πολιτεία: 1. civitas: οἱ μείναντες
ἐν τῇ π. 37 4. — civitatis
forma et ordo: π. ἄριστα
κεκραμένην κατέστησεν 3 1.—
2. administratio publica:
σωτήριον ἔρυμα τῆς π. 39 5;
μιᾶς ἀκμῇ π. 13 1; ἀνθούσης
ἐφ' ὥραν π. 16 2; τῆς π.
σύμβουλον 16 7; τῆς ἐν τῇ
π. καὶ ταῖς στρατηγίαις δυνάμεως 8 2; τῆς ἐν τῇ π.
προαιρέσεως 10 6; ἀκμάζων
ἐν τῇ π. 37 3; τὴν π. εἰς
ἀντίπαλον κατέστησεν 11 2;
τοὺς χρησιμωτάτους πρὸς τὴν
π. 36 4.—3. = πολιτείας εἶδος:

βασιλικὴν π. 15 2; ἀριστοκρατικὴν π. 9 1, 15 2
πολιτεύεσθαι: ἐν οἷς ἐπολιτεύσατο χρόνοις 7 4; ἐπολιτεύετο πρὸς χάριν 11 4
πολίτευμα: τῶν π. 12 1
πολίτης: τῶν π. 11 1, 18 3, 33
7, 38 3; συγκινδυνεύσας τοῖς
π. 10 1, 19 4; παρὰ τοῖς π. 33
1, 35 1; τοὺς π. 26 2, 28 4, 37 3
πολιτικός)(πολεμικός 11 2.—
'a practical statesman': π.
)(θεωρητικοῦ φιλοσόφου 16
6; σοφήν τινα καὶ π. 24 3;
τῶν π. τοὺς πρωτεύοντας 24
1.—neut. τῶν π. οὐδὲν ἔπραττεν 7 1; τῶν π. ἀλείπτης καὶ
διδάσκαλος 4 1
πολλάκις 1 4
πολλαχοῦ 8 1
ΠΟΛΥ-ΓΡΑΜΜΑΤΟΣ i. q. στιγματίας 26 4
πολύ-εδρος[1]: πολύεδρον (de
Odeo) 13 5
πολυ-πραγμονεῖν, investigare:
μὴ πολυπραγμονήσας 23 1
πολυ-πραγμοσύνη: τὴν π. 21 1
πολυ-πράγμων: π. ὄχλου 11 5
πολύς: π. χρόνῳ 13 2; π. χρόνον
13 3, 15 2; τῆς παραλίας
πολλήν 19 3; π. ἰσχύν 15 1;
χώραν π. 34 2; π. ὑπεροψίαν
5 3; π. ἐλευθερίαν 7 6; π.
ὠμότητα 28 1; π. ἀδηλότητα
28 6; πολλοὶ τῶν φίλων
ἐχθρῶν 33 6; ἄλλοι π. 9 1;
πολλοὶ τῶν πολιτῶν 11 4; π.
κἀγαθοὶ τῶν πολιτῶν 18 3;
πολλῶν ὁμοῦ 34 4; πολλαὶ
πάνυ δίκαι 37 3; πρὸ πάνυ
π. χρόνων 37 3; π. (neut.)
προσόντων τῷ ἀνδρὶ 8 2; π.
λαφύρων 9 4; ἄλλοις π. 21
1; π. καὶ ἀγαθοῖς ὁπλίταις 22
2; χρήμασι π. 28 1; πολλοῖς
τῶν πενήτων 16 6, 24 4; π.

INDEX IV GREEK

διαδοχαῖς καὶ ἡλικίαις 13 1:
π. αὐτῶν ἄνδρας πολλὰς δὲ
ναῦς 26 2; π. καὶ ἀγαθοὺς
πολίτας 28 4; π. καὶ ἀγαθοὺς
ὁπλίτας 35 1; π. φωνάς 8 3;
π. ἄλλα (τάλαντα) 25 2; π.
πάνυ δάκρυα 32 3.—οἱ πολλοί,
plebs: τῶν π. 7 2, 13 11, 15
2, 36 1; τοῖς π. 10 3, 19 4;
τοὺς π. 4 1, 7 3, 34 1, 36 3;
τὰ π. τῶν ἐγκλημάτων 29 5.
—πολύ adv. 8 1.—τὰ πολλά,
plerumque 7 2, 15 3, 27 4
πολύ-στυλος: πολύστυλον (de
Odeo) 13 5
πολυ-τελής: 1. de persona:
γενόμενον πολυτελῆ)(αὐτουρ-
γόν 9 1; γυναικὶ π. 36 1.—
2. de re: λίθους π. 12 2
πολύ-τεχνος: π. ὑποθέσεις ἔργων
12 5
πομπή: τινὰ π. 11 4
πομπός: πομποί 12 6
πόνος: τὸν ἐν τοῖς ἀχρήστοις
π. 2 1; ὁ τῷ π. προδανεισθεὶς
χρόνος 13 2
ποντοπορεῖν [3] 26 3
πόντος: τὸν ἔξω π. 26 1
πορεία, incessus: πραοτης
πορείας 5 1
πορεύεσθαι: πορευόμενος ἐπὶ τὴν
δημαγωγίαν 33 6; ὁδὸν μίαν
πορευόμενος 7 4; ἐπ᾿ Οἰταίους
ἐπορεύοντο 17 3
πορθεῖν: ἐπόρθησε 19 3
πόρνη: τὸ τῆς πόρνης
κακόν 21 6; πόρνην ...
πόρνα 30 4
πόρρω θαλάττης 19 3; πορ-
ρωτάτω 26 1
πόρρωθεν, iampridem 36 1
ποτέ, aliquando 5 2, 6 2, 8 5,
13 2: ποτὲ μὲν—ποτὲ
δέ 3 4
πότερον—ἤ 8 4; π. ἤ—ἤ 36 3
ποινιᾶσθαι [1] = μετ᾿ οἰμωγῆς

ἱκετεύειν (Hesychius): ἐπoτ-
νιῶντο πρὸς τοὺς Λακεδαι-
μονίους 29 4
πότος, ὁ, potatio: ἔν τινι π. 1 5
πούς: ἐκ ποδῶν (e conspectu)
γενομένου 39 4. Cp. Pyrrh.
c. 27, 5 ἐκ ποδῶν οὖσα καθ᾿
ἑαυτήν
πρᾶγμα: προσπεσόντος τοῦ π.
16 7; ἐπὶ παντὶ π. 7 5; τὰ
π. 39 4; π. τηλικαῦτα 10 5,
15 1; τῶν τοῦ δήμου π. 6 3;
τὴν εὔροιαν τῶν π. 20 3; τῇ
γνώσει τῶν π. 13 12; τῶν π.
αὐτῶν 9 1; τῶν π. ἐκείνων 27
3; μεγάλων π. 17 1; ἐν π.
μεγάλοις 32 3.—fortuna: ἐν
οἰκίᾳ μεγάλῃ καὶ π. ἀφθόνοις
16 4.—respublica 33 6, 37 2,
39 4; τοῖς π. 39 5.—negotia:
ἐν π. πολλοῖς 39 1.—molestia:
ὡς μὴ πολλὰ πράγματα ἀσχολουμένῳ παρέχοι 16 3; ὑπὸ
τῶν π. ἠπορημένον 3 4
πραγματεία [1]: ἑτέρας ἐστὶ π. 6
4, 39 4
πραγματεύεσθαι, quaestionem
aliquam via ac ratione
instituere: πραγματευομένου
περὶ φύσιν 4 3
πρακτικός: π. ὁρμήν 2 3
πρακτικῶς 2 3
πρᾶξις: τῶν π. 13 12; ταῖς π.
2 2; τὰς π. 2 3, 38 3
πρᾶος, tranquillus, sedatus:
πραΰτερον 10 5
πραότης, lenitas: π. πορείας 5 1.
Cp. Fab. c. 17, 5 ἐφοίτα διὰ
τῆς πόλεως πρᾴῳ βαδίσματι.
—mansuetudo morum: τῆς
π. 39 1; ἐν π. 39 4; π. καὶ
δικαιοσύνῃ 2 4
πράττειν: τῶν πολιτικῶν οὐδὲν
ἔπραττεν 7 1; τἆλλα ἔπραττεν
7 5; ταῦτ᾿ ἔπραττεν 11 5;
ὁρμὴ πρὸς τὸ πρᾶξαι 1 4;

πρᾶξαι τὰ πρὸς Σαμίους 24 1.
—PASS. ἐπράχθη οὐδέν 17 3;
τὸ πραχθέν 1 4; τοῖς πραχθεῖσι 21 1
πραΰνειν³, *mitigare*: τοὺς συμμάχους πραΰνοντος 29 5
πράως καὶ σιωπῇ 34 1
πρέπειν: προσωνυμίαν πρέπουσαν 39 2; τοιαύτης τῷ μακαρίῳ διαγωγῆς μάλιστα πρεπούσης 39 3
πρεσβεία: πρεσβείας ἀφιγμένης 30 1; πρεσβειῶν πεμπομένων 29 5
πρεσβευτής, *legatus*: τῶν πρέσβεων τινά 30 1
πρεϲβγενής Κρόνος 3 3
πρεσβύτερος 36 1; τοὺς π. 9 2
πρεσβύτης, *senex*: π. φαλακροῦ 31 4
πρὶν ἐμβαλεῖν 33 2; πρίν γε δὴ ἀποβαλεῖν 36 4
πρό Local: π. τοῦ τείχους 26 1; π. τῆς ὄψεως 31 4, 35 2.—
Temporal: π. πάνυ πολλῶν χρόνων 37 3
προ-άγειν: λόγοιϲι προάγει (ἔργον) 13 5.—PASS. ὑπ' ἐκείνου ἐπὶ κληρουχίας προαχθῆναι 9 1
προ-αγορεύειν: προηγόρευσεν (post-classical form) 34 2; προεῖπε 33 2
προ-αίρεσις (= βουλευτικὴ ὄρεξις τῶν ἐφ' ἡμῖν Aristot.): τὴν π. παρεχόμενον 2 3.—'a deliberate course of action,' 'policy': τῆς ἐν τῇ πολιτείᾳ π. 10 6; δημοτικῆς καὶ ἀριστοκρατικῆς π. 11 3
προ-βαίνειν: οὐκ ἂν εἰς μῆκος τοσοῦτον πολέμου προὔβησαν 34 2
προ-βάλλειν, *proicere*: προβαλεῖν ἀκήδευτα τὰ σώματα 28 2.—MID. νόμον τινὰ προβαλλομένου 30 1.—PASS. *publice creari*: ὑπὸ τοῦ δήμου προβεβλημένος 10 5
προβατο-κάπηλος: τὸν π. 24 4
πρό-βλημα: ἐρύμασι καὶ π. 19 1
προ-βολή: τὴν π. 10 5
προ-δανείζεσθαι: ὁ τῷ πόνῳ προδανεισθεὶς χρόνος 13 2
προ-διδόναι, *proicere*: οὐδὲ προὔδωκε τὸ φρόνημα 36 4
προ-ειπεῖν 6 3; προεῖπε 33 2
προ-θυμεῖσθαι: μάχεσθαι προθυμουμένους 27 2
προ-θυμία: ἀνάδοσις κινοῦσα προθυμίαν καὶ ὁρμὴν ἐπὶ τὴν ἐξομοίωσιν 2 2; ἃ ζῆλόν τινα καὶ π. ἐμποιεῖ 1 4
πρόθυμος: προθυμότατος 13 8
προ-θύμως 25 3
προ-ιέναι (πρόειμι) *progredi*: προῆλθον 33 3; πόρρω θαλάττης προελθών 19 3.—*e domo exire, prodire in publicum*: προελθεῖν 27 4, 37 1
προ-ιέναι (προίημι).—MID. *in potestatem tradere, arbitrio alienius permittere*: στρατηγίαν προϊεμένην τὰ πράγματα τοῖς πολεμίοις 33 6
προ-ίστασθαι: οὐ κοσμίου προεστῶσαν ἐργασίας 24 3
προ-καλεῖσθαι: προκαλουμένοις 22 2
προ-κεῖσθαι: τὴν προκειμένην χρείαν 8 4
προ-μαντεία: τὴν π. 21 2
προ-μήκης: προμήκη τῇ κεφαλῇ 3 2
προ-πέμπειν, *comitari, deducere*: Ἀναξαγόραν προὔπεμψεν ἐκ τῆς πόλεως 32 3
προ-πολεμεῖν: προπολεμοῦντες αὐτῶν 12 3
προ-πύλαιος: τὰ Π. 13 7
πρός: A. w. Dat.: 1. 'at,' 'near,'

'hard by,' denoting close local proximity, always of things not men : τὰ π. θαλάσσῃ 20 2 ; π. τάφῳ 36 4 ; π. τῷ τελευτᾶν ὄντος 38 3.—2. to express union or addition : π. τούτοις (*insuper*) 11 5, 36 3 ; π. τῷ εὐφυῆς εἶναι 8 1 (ex Platone philosopho)

B. w. Acc. 1. to express motion or direction towards an object or person, *ad*: π. τὰ ἔργα προσκομιζόμενον 27 3 ; κήρυκα πεμφθῆναι π. αὐτούς 30 2 ; καταστῆσαι αὐτὸν π. τὴν οἰκίαν 5 3 ; π. μηδένα τῶν φίλων ἐλθεῖν 7 4 ; τὰ χρήματα μεταγαγὼν π. αὐτόν 12 1 ; ἐλθούσης π. αὐτόν 10 5 ; πέμψας π. τινα τῶν φίλων 36 2 ; ὁρμὴ π. τὸ πρᾶξαι 1 4.—2. of hostile motion, *adversus, contra*, 'against' 5 2, 29 5, 33 3 ; τῆς π. ἐκεῖνον ὀργῆς 33 6 ; ἐκπεπολεμωμένων π. αὐτούς 29 1 ; τὸν π. Μιλησίους πόλεμον 24 1 ; τὰ π. Σαμίους 24 1 ; τὸν π. Σαμίους πόλεμον 25 1 ; ἰδίᾳ π. τοὺς Μεγαρεῖς ἀπέχθεια 30 2 ; τὴν π. Ἀμαζόνας μάχην 31 4 ; π. τὸν Θουκυδίδην εἰς ἀγῶνα καταστάς 14 2 ; π. αὐτὸν ἀντιταξαμένου 27 1 ; πρὸς τοῦτο ἐναντιωθείς 29 5.—3. without any hostile sense, esp. with verbs of speaking : λέγων π. τοὺς πολίτας 18 1 ; π. τοὺς πολλοὺς ἐπικρυπτόμενος (= οὐ λέγων) 4 2 ; διελέγοντο π. ἀλλήλοις 38 4 ; εἰπεῖν π. αὐτόν 16 7 ; διεβοήθη π. τοὺς ἐκτός 19 2 ; π. τὸν υἱὸν εἶπεν 1 5 ; τὸ τοῦ Ἀρχιλόχου π. αὐτὴν εἰπεῖν 28 5 ; ἐποτνιῶντο π. τοὺς Λακεδαιμονίους 29 4.— Hence generally of all sorts of personal intercourse, *erga, in, cum*: διαλλαγῆναι π. αὐτούς 29 5 ; ἐρωτική τις ἀγάπησις π. Ἀσπασίαν 24 5 ; πολλὴ ἦν εὔνοια τῷ Κίμωνος οἴκῳ π. Λακεδαιμονίους 29 2 ; ἀνήκεστον π. τὸν πατέρα διαφοράν 36 3.—4. Of relation between two things, 'in respect of,' 'in regard to': π. ἃ μιμητικὸς οὐ γίγνεται ζῆλος 2 2 ; ἀργῶς ἔχων π. χρηματισμόν 16 3 ; π. ταῦτα τὰ στίγματα λέγουσι τὸ Ἀριστοφάνειον ᾐνίχθαι 26 4 ; παίζει π. αὐτόν 13 6 ; εὖ πεφυκὼς π. οἰκονομίαν 16 5 ; τὸ π. φόβους μαλακόν 27 4 ; ἃ π. τύχην ἐστὶ κοινά 38 4.—5. Of an intended end or purpose : π. τὸν λόγον ἅπαξ ἀνέστη 10 5 ; τοῖς εἰσφερομένοις π. τὸν πόλεμον 12 2 ; τοῖς ἀναγκαίοις π. τὸν πόλεμον 12 4, 25 3 ; ἀνεκομίζετο π. τὸν ἐν τῇ Ἀττικῇ πόλεμον 22 2 ; πολιτείαν ἄριστα κεκραμένην π. ὁμόνοιαν 3 1 ; καταλαβὼν πάντα φυλακαῖς π. ἀσφάλειαν 33 5 ; π. οὐδὲν ἀνθρώποις τοσούτοις χρώμενος 34 4 ; τοῖς καταχρωμένοις τούτῳ (τῷ φιλομαθεῖ) π. τὰ μηδεμιᾶς ἄξια σπουδῆς 1 2 ; π. τοσαύτην ἐχέγγυον ἡγεμονίαν 37 1 ; χρησιμωτάτοις π. τὴν πολιτείαν 36 4 ; τὸ π. δόξαν σεμνόν 7 5 ; ἐπολιτεύετο π. χάριν 11 4 ; χρώμενος αὐτῇ (τῇ δημαγωγίᾳ) π. τὸ βέλτιστον ὀρθῇ 15 2 ; π. τί γέγονε τὸ σημεῖον 6 3 ; ἑαυτὸν π. τὰς μεγάλας χρείας ἐπιδιδούς

7 5; ᾖδον ᾄσματα καὶ σκώμματα π. αἰσχύνην 33 6.— *propter*, 'in presence of,' 'because of': π. οὐδὲν ἐκταραττομένῃ πάθος 5 1; τὸ π. τὰ μετέωρα θάμβος 6 1; ἐξεπλήττοντο π. τὴν ὁμοιότητα 7 1; δυσπαθοῦντας π. τὰ γιγνόμενα 33 4; ἐκπλαγῆναι ὡς π. μέγα σημεῖον 35 1; ἡττήθη τοῦ πάθους π. τὴν ὄψιν 36 4.— *secundum, ad alienius normam*, 'according to': εἰ πρὸς τὰς τύχας τρέπεται τὰ ἤθη 38 2

προσ-αγορεύειν: λευκὴν ἡμέραν ἐκείνην π. 27 2; ὃν Νοῦν προσηγόρευον 4 4; προσηγόρευσαν (un-Attic form) 11 5. —P.188. προσαγορεύεται 24 6; προσαγορεύεσθαι 39 2; προσαγορευθῆναι 8 2

προσ-βάλλειν: ταῦτα ὥσπερ χολὴν τἀνδρὶ προσβέβληκε 10 6

προσ-βιβάζειν, *adducere, suadere*: προσβιβάζων τῷ συμφέροντι 15 3

προσ-γίγνεσθαι, *accedere, adiungi*: χαλεπαίνουσι προσεγένοντο 29 4

προσ-δεῖν: σανίσι προσδήσας 28 2

προσ-δέχεσθαι, *accipere, probare*; προσδεξαμένου τὸν ἄνθρωπον 31 3

προσ-διαβάλλεσθαι: προσδιαβληθείη 29 2

προσ-διαφθείρειν: προσδιέφθειρεν 35 3

προσ-δοκᾶν: προσδοκῶντας 10 2

προσ-εἶναι *i.q.* ὑπάρχειν: ὅπου μηδὲν αὐτῷ πρόσεστιν ἴδιον πάθος 28 3; πολλῶν προσόντων τῷ ἀνδρὶ 8 2; γένους προσόντος αὐτῷ λαμπροῦ 7 1

προσ-εργάζεσθαι, *operi aliquid addere*: προσειργάσατο 31 3

προσ-έρχεσθαι: προcέρχεται 13 6; προσελθοῦσα πλησίον 28 4

προσ-έχειν: τὸν νοῦν προσεσχηκώς 38 4

προσ-ήκειν: προσήκουσα κατὰ γένος, *propinqua* 24 5.—*consentaneus*: οὐκ ἀνθρώποις νοῦν ἔχουσι προσηκόντων 39 3

προσ-ίεσθαι: προσιεμένου τὰς διαβολάς 32 2

πρόσθεν 11 1

προσ-κατηγορεῖν: προσκατηγοροῦντος 32 1

προσ-κεῖσθαι, *instare*: δεόμενοι προσέκειντο 33 6

προσ-κομίζεσθαι: προσκομιζόμενον 27 3

πρόσ-κρουσμα², *offensio, damnum*: οὐδὲν π. 19 4

προσ-λαγχάνειν: δίκην αὐτῷ προσέλαχε 36 2

προσ-λαμβάνειν, *adsciscere* (*socium*): προσλαβεῖν τὴν νῆσον 29 1

προσ-νέμειν: τῷ δήμῳ προσένειμεν ἑαυτόν (post-classical) 7 2

πρόσ-οδος: τὰς π. 14 1

πρόσ-οικος: τὴν π. ἤπειρον 17 2

προσ-πίπτειν, *accidere ad aures*: προσπεσόντος τοῦ πράγματος τῷ Περικλεῖ 16 7

προσ-ποιεῖν, *conciliare*: πάντας προσεποίησε βασιλεῖ 24 2

προσ-ποίησις: τῆς π. τῶν καλῶν 5 4

προσ-πταίειν: προσέπταισε τῷ δήμῳ 32 3

προσ-στέλλειν, *adstringere*: φόβοις προσστέλλων τὸ θρασυνόμενον αὐτῶν 15 4

πρόσ-ταγμα: τὸ π. 31 1

προσ-τάττειν: προσέταξέ τινι

παραπέμψαι 5 3; προσέταξεν ἀνελεῖν 28 2; προσέταξε τοῖς στρατηγοῖς ἐπιμελεῖσθαι 31 5
προσ-τρίβεσθαι, *afficere*: προστρίψασθαι νόσημα αὐτῷ 22 3
προσ-τυγχάνειν : τῶν προστυγχανόντων 1 2
πρόσ-φατος: μέχρι νῦν πρόσφατόν ἐστι 13 2
προσ-φέρειν, *adhibere*: φάρμακα προσφέροντα σωτήρια 15 3.—
PASS. *accedere*: τὸν πόλεμον καθορᾶν προσφερόμενον 8 5; νεῶν ἐπικούρων προσφερομένων 26 1.—MID. *se gerere*: ταῖς πόλεσι προσηνέχθη φιλανθρώπως 20 1. Cp. *Fab. Max.* c. 20, 3 σκληρότερον προσφέρεσθαι καὶ βιαιότερον ἤπερ οἱ γεωργοῦντες ἐρινεοῖς καὶ ἀχράσι καὶ κοτίνοις προσφέρονται: c. 24, 1 τῷ Φαβίῳ προσεφέροντο λαμπρῶς
πρόσ-φορος : ὀφθαλμῷ χρόα π. 1 3; τὸ πρόϲφορον 8 1
προσ-ωνυμία : τὴν π. 8 3, 39 2
πρόσ-ωπον : προσώπου σύστασις 5 1
πρότερον (adv.) 11 2, 13 8; τὰς π. εὐτυχίας 18 2, 19 3, 20 2, 24 5 7, 26 2 3, 34 4, 37 2, 39 5; πρ. ἢ ἀφελέσθαι 35 4; οὐ π. ἢ . . . γενέσθαι 10 4
πρότερος : τὴν π. συλλαβὴν 4 1; ναυμαχοῦντα πρότερον 26 3
πρό-φασις, 'pretext': εὐπρεπεστάτη τῶν π. 12 2; μεγάλην π. τοῖς ἐγκαλοῦσι παρεσχηκὼς 29 3. — 'real ground': ἵνα ἔχῃ πρόφασιν ὠφελεῖσθαι 12 5
πρύτανις : τοὺς π. 32 2
πρωτεύειν : πρωτεύων 16 2; τοὺς πρωτεύοντας 24 1
πρῶτον (adv.) 9 1, 13 6, 26 4; πρῶτον μὲν πρὸς δὲ τούτοις 36 3; πρῶτον μὲν—εἶτα 22 1; π.

μέν without ἔπειτα following 4 2, 34 3; τὸ π. 17 3, 33 4
πρῶτος, *primus*: τὰ π. 24 4 : *princeps* 4 4; γένους τοῦ π. 3 1; τοῦ π. ἀνδρός 9 1; Ἀθηναίων πρῶτον 24 4 : τῶν π. 25 1; τοὺς π. 28 5
πύλη : παρὰ τὰς Θριασίας π. 30 3
πυνθάνεσθαι, *percontari*: πυνθανόμενος περὶ ἑκάστου 3 4 : πυνθανόμενον αὐτοῦ τινα οὕτω 4 2; πυνθανομένου πότερον 8 4.—*comperire*: πυθόμενος τὴν συμφοράν 27 1
πυρός, *triticum*: πυρῶν μεδίμνους 37 3
πυρσός, *i.q.*: φῶτα πυρσῶν 6 4
πως : οὕτω πως 31 2
πῶς πέφυκε 6 3

Ρ

ῥᾴδιος : ῥ. ὑπείκειν 15 2; οὐ ῥᾴδιόν ἐστι 33 4; οὐ ῥᾴδιον 31 1; ῥᾴστην οἰκονομίαν 16 3
ῥᾳδίως : ταχὺ καὶ ῥ. 13 2 8: ῥᾷστα 1 3
ῥᾳθυμία : τῆς εἰς τὰ καλὰ ῥ. 2 1
ῥηγνύναι : κλαυθμὸν ῥῆξαι 36 5
ῥῆμα 8 4
ῥητορική : τῇ ῥ. 8 1; ἐπὶ ῥητορικῇ ὁμιλεῖν 24 4; τὴν ῥ. 15 4
ῥητός : ἐν χρόνῳ ῥ. 28 1
ῥήτωρ : οἱ ῥ. 20 3; ῥητόρων 11 1, 37 1, 39 4; ῥ. ἑτέρους 7 5
ῥίζα : ἡ ῥ. τοῦ κέρατος 6 2.— Cp. *Fab. Max.* c. 6, 6 πυρούμενον τὸ κέρας ἄχρι ῥίζης διέδωκε τῇ σαρκὶ τὴν αἴσθησιν
ῥοπή, *inclinatio*, *momentum*: ὥσπερ ἐπὶ ζυγοῦ ῥοπὴν ἐποίησεν 11 2
ῥώμη : ὑπὸ ῥ. καὶ τύχης ἐπαιρομένων 20 2; τοῖς ἔχουσι ῥώμην 12 5

ῥωννύναι¹, *confirmare*: ἔρρωσεν εὐανδρίᾳ τὰς πόλεις 19 1.— PASS. ἐρρωμένην ναυτικῇ δυνάμει νῆσον 29 1

Σ

σάμαινα², navigii genus Samii: σάμαιναν 26 3
σανίς: σανίσι προσδήσας 28 2
σατυρικός¹, 'low,' 'vulgar': σ. μέρος 5 4.—'lewd': ἀνθρώπους σ. τοῖς βίοις 13 11. Cp. *Cat. ma.* c. 7, 1 σατυρικὸν καὶ ὑβριστὴν τοῖς ἐντυγχάνουσι φαινόμενον
σάτυρος: ΒΑϹΙΛΕῦ ϹΑΤΎΡΩΝ 33 7
σαφής: σ. πόθον 39 4
σαφῶς, *diserte* 16 1
σεμνός: οὐ σ. ἐργασίας 24 3; τὸ πρὸς δόξαν σ. 7 5; σεμνότερον ἐν πραότητι τρόπον 39 4
σεμνότης: τὴν σ. 5 4
σῆμα, *sepulcrum*: ἐπὶ τῶν σ. 28 3
σημαίνειν, *portendere*: τί σημαίνει 6 3
σημεῖον, *signum*: σ. τινός 6 4. —*prodigium, ostentum* 6 2; ἀναίρεσιν τοῦ σ. 6 4; μέγα σ. 35 1; δεινοῦ τινος σημεῖον 35 2
σθένος: ΜΈΓΑ ϹΘΈΝΟϹ 4 3
σίδηρος: ἐν σ. διπλόη 11 3
σίμωμα: ναῦς ὑόπρωρος τὸ σ. 26 3
σιωπή: σιωπῇ, *tacite* 5 2, 34 1
σκηνή: τῆς βασιλέως σ. 13 5
σκήνωμα: ἐν σ. πνιγηροῖς 34 4
σκίλλα, 'sea-onion,' a plant of the liliaceae family: τὴν σ. σχῖνον ὀνομάζουσι 3 2
σκληρός: ἀΚΌΝΗ ϹΚΛΗΡᾷ 33 7
σκότος, τὸ 35 1; σκότους ὄντος 5 3

σκυτο-τόμος: σκυτοτόμοι 12 7
σκῶμμα: σκώμματα 33 6
σοβαρός: τὴν σ. προσωνυμίαν 39 2.—bono sensu: τὸ φρόνημα σ. εἶχε 5 1
σοφία: τῆς Ἀναξαγόρου σ. 16 5
σοφιστής: ἄκρος σ. 4 1; μετὰ τῶν σ. 36 2. The name was applied in the 5th cent. B.C. generally to a wise man, and more particularly to one who practises wisdom as a profession, and goes from place to place to offer instruction to those who require it, and are disposed to pay for it
σοφός: σ. τινὰ καὶ πολιτικὴν 24 3; τὸν σοφώτατον σύμβουλον 18 2
σπαθᾶν, *prodigere*: σπαθῶντος τὰ χρήματα 14 1
σπονδή: ἄχρι τῶν σπονδῶν 7 4. —*induciae*: γενομένων σ. 24 1; ϹΠΟΝΔΆϹ 16 2
σπουδάζεσθαι, *coli, magni aestimari*: ὑπὸ τοῦ Περικλέους σπουδασθῆναι 24 3
σπουδαῖος: σ. αὐλητής 1 5
σπουδή: τὰ μηδεμιᾶς ἄξια σπουδῆς ἀκούσματα 1 2; ἄξιον σπουδῆς εἶναι τὸν εἰργασμένον 2 2.—σπουδῇ, *serio*)(μετὰ γέλωτος 8 3
σταθμός, *pondus*: ἀποδείξαι τὸν σ. 31 3
στάσις: στάσει διατεταραγμένα 36 1.—personified: ϹΤΆϹΙϹ ΚΑῚ ΠΡΕϹΒΥΓΕΝῊϹ ΚΡΌΝΟϹ 3 3
στέλλειν: ἔστειλεν 11 5, 29 3.— PASS. ἐπὶ Κύπρον στελλόμενος 26 1
στέργειν uxorem: τὴν Ἀσπασίαν ἔστερξε διαφερόντως 24 5
στερεός: τὸ κέρας σ. πεφυκός 6 2

στέφανος: ἐπιφέρων τῷ νεκρῷ στέφανον 36 5; ἄξια στεφάνων 28 4; στεφάνοις ἀνέδουν 28 4
στήλη: ἐν τῇ σ. 13 9
στίγμα: πρὸς ταῦτα τὰ σ. ἠνίχθαι 26 4
στίζειν: ἔστιζον τοὺς Ἀθηναίους εἰς τὸ μέτωπον γλαῦκας 26 3
στιχίδιον: τοῖς περιβοήτοις σ. 30 4
στόλος, exercitus missus 26 1; τῷ σ. 19 4, 20 1; νεῶν στόλον 34 1
στοχάζεσθαι: ὀρθῶς στοχαζύμεθα τοῦ δέοντος 2 4
στρατεία: αἱ σ. 7 2, 12 5; ἐν ταῖς σ.)(τοῖς πολιτικοῖς 7 1
στρατεύειν: στρατεύσαντες 21 2.
—MID. ἐθελοντὶ στρατεύεσθαι 18 2; τῶν στρατενομένων 12 5; τοὺς σ. 19 4
στράτευμα: ἴδιον σ. 12 7; στρατεύματα 15 1
στρατηγεῖν 38 3; τῶν ἔξω σ. 10 4; στρατηγῶν 10 7; στρατηγῶν τῆς Σάμου 26 2, 38 3
στρατηγία: τῷ τῆς σ. ἀπολογισμῷ 23 1; ἐν τῇ σ. 29 2; τὴν σ. 33 6, 35 4; τῶν σ. 19 1; ἐν ταῖς σ. 8 2, 16 3, 18 1
στρατήγιον: ἐπὶ τὸ σ. 37 1
στρατηγός 12 7; τοὺς σ. decem 30 3; τοῖς σ. 31 5; σ. αἱρεθείς 37 2; τὸν σ. 8 5; τῶν σ. 26 2, 37 1; πολλοῖς σ. 38 4; τοὺς βασιλέως σ. 3 1; τοὺς θαυμασθέντας σ. 18 1
στρατιά 22 1 3; τῇ σ. 35 3
στρατιώτης: στρατιώτας 19 4, 20 1
στρατιῶτις: στρατιώτιδες (νῆες) 25 3
στρατόπεδον: ἐπὶ στρατοπέδου 27 1
στρατός: σ. μεγάλῳ 10 1, 33 3

στρέφειν: στρέψον εἴσω τὸ πινάκιον 30 1
συγ-γενής: σ. πόλιν 28 4
συγ-γενικός: σ. νόσημα 22 3
συγ-γίγνεσθαι: ὁ πλεῖστα Περικλεῖ συγγενόμενος magister discipulo 4 4
συγ-καλύπτεσθαι: συγκεκαλυμμένον 16 7
συγ-κατ-οικεῖν Σινωπεῦσι 20 2
συγ-κινδυνεύειν: συγκινδυνεύσας τοῖς πολίταις 10 1
συγ-κλείειν: τὸ ἄστυ συγκλείσας 33 5
συγ-κόπτειν, concidere: ξύλοις τὰς κεφαλὰς συγκόψαντας 28 2
συγ-χωρεῖν, obsecundare: οὐ συνεχώρει ταῖς ὁρμαῖς τῶν πολιτῶν 20 2.--veniam dare: συνεχώρησαν ἀπογράψασθαι τὸν νόθον 37 5
συγ-χώρησις: τὴν σ. 31 1
συκο-φάντημα: συκοφαντήμασι περιέπιπτον 37 3
συλ-λαβή: τὴν προτέραν σ. 4 1
σύλ-λογος, conventus: εἰς σ. πέμπειν 17 1
συμ-βαίνειν: συνέβη 19 4, 35 1; συμβᾶσα 13 7
συμ-βίωσις[1]: τῆς σ. 21 5
σύμ-βολον: τὰ τεχνητὰ τῶν σ. 6 4
συμ-βουλεύειν: συμβουλεύσαντος 9 2
σύμ-βουλος: τοιοῦτον τῆς πολιτείας σ. 16 7; τὸν σοφώτατον σ. 18 2; τῶν συμβούλων 22 2
συμ-μαχία: συμμαχίαις δυναστῶν 15 1
σύμ-μαχος: σ. πόλιν 28 4; μετὰ τῶν σ. 33 3; τοῖς σ. 11 5, 12 3; τοὺς συμμάχοις 29 5
συμ-μιγνύναι: τοὺς τῇ στρατιᾷ συμμίξαντας 35 3.—PASS. συμμεμῖχθαι πρὸς τὸν δῆμον 11 2

συμ-πείθειν: συμπείθοντες ἰέναι 17 3
συμ-πέμπειν: πάρεδρον αὐτῷ συνέπεμψαν 22 2
συμ-περι-φορά: ἐν ταῖς σ. 5 3
συμ-πίπτειν, accidere: οὐκ ἂν δοκεῖ συμπεσεῖν ὁ πόλεμος αὐτοῖς 29 5
συμ-πλέκεσθαι: περὶ τὸ βῆμα τῷ Περικλεῖ συμπλεκόμενος 11 2
συμ-φέρειν: τῷ συμφέροντι 15 3
συμ-φορά: τὴν σ. 27 1; τῶν σ. 36 4; τὰς σ. 28 3
συμ-φόρησις[1]: ἡ τοῦ πλήθους εἰς τὸ ἄστυ σ. 34 3
σὺν οὐδενὶ καιρῷ 18 2
συν-άγειν, cogere: συναγαγὼν εἰς ταὐτὸ τὴν πάντων δύναμιν 11 2; τὸν δῆμον εἰς ἐκκλησίαν οὐ συνῆγε 33 5; ταῦτ' οὐκ οἶδ' ὁπόθεν συναγαγών 10 6.—PASS. in angustius contrahi spatium: συνηγμένην[2] εἰς τὸ ἀκριβέστατον δαπάνην 16 4
συν-αιρεῖν[2], capere: συνελεῖν τὴν πόλιν 27 1
συν-άπτειν: συνάψαντας μάχην 19 3; μάχην συνάψαι 33 4; συνάψαι εἰς χεῖρας πολλοῖς ὁπλίταις προκαλουμένοις 22 2
συν-άρχειν: συναρχόντων ἀγνωμοσύνας 2 4
συν-δεκάζειν[4]: συνδεκάσας τὸ πλῆθος 9 3
συν-εῖναι: τῷ Περικλεῖ συνῆν magister discipulo 4 1; Ἀσπασίᾳ συνόντα (γυναικί) 24 4; τοῖς συνοῦσι)(τοῖς ἐκτός 7 5
συν-εκ-διδόναι: συνεξέδωκε 24 5
συν-εκ-πίπτειν[2]: οὐ συνεξέπιπτεν ταῖς ὁρμαῖς 20 2.—Cleom. c. 37, 3 τῇ πρώτῃ συνεξέπεσεν ὁρμῇ προθύμως
συν-εκ-πλεῖν: οὐ συνεξέπλευσεν (τῷ στόλῳ) 34 1

συν-εν-διδόναι ταῖς ἐπιθυμίαις τῶν πολλῶν 15 2
συν-εξ-αίρειν[1]: ὁ συνεξάρας τὸ ἀξίωμα τοῦ ἤθους 4 4
συν-επ-αιτιᾶσθαι: οὓς συνεπῃτιᾶτο τοῦ λακωνισμοῦ 10 2
συν-επι-τελεῖν[2]: συνεπιτελοῦσαν (τὸ ἔργον) 13 7
σύν-εργος: τῶν Φειδίου σ. 31 2
συν-έρχεσθαι: συνῆλθον 17 3
σύν-εσις: σ. μεγάλην 4 4
συν-εφ-άπτεσθαι: συνεφαπτομένην τοῦ ἔργου 13 7
συν-έχειν, administrare oeconomiam: ὁ πᾶσαν συνέχων τὴν ἀκρίβειαν 16 5.—continere: ἐν τῇ Ἑλλάδι τὴν δύναμιν συνεῖχεν 22 1.—PASS. premi, urgeri: πόλεμον ᾧ συνείχετο ἡ χώρα 19 2
συν-εχής: τὸ σ., continuitas 7 5
συν-ήθεια, convictus: ἐν σ. 7 5; ζῆλον καὶ σ. 5 4; φιλοφροσύνην καὶ σ. ἐξέλιπεν 7 4
συν-ήθης: οἱ σ., familiares 24 3
συν-θήκη: σ. ἀπορρήτους 10 4
συν-ιέναι: οὐκέτι συνιέντος 38 4
συν-ίστασθαι, 'to cabal': συστάντες 10 1
συν-οικεῖν: Βισάλταις συνοικήσοντας 11 5.—πλείστοις συνῴκησεν ἀνδράσι 21 2; γυναικὶ πολυτελεῖ συνοικῶν 36 1: συνῳκηκυῖα, nupta 24 5
σύν-οικος: λῃστηρίων σ. 19 2
συν-ολισθάνειν: συνωλισθηκότα 6 2
συν-ουσία philosophi: τῆς Ἀναξαγόρου σ. 6 1
συν-ταράττειν: συνταράττοντες ἡμᾶς ἀμαθεστάταις δόξαις 39 2
συν-τάττειν, dispensare: τὸν πλοῦτον συνέταξεν εἰς οἰκονομίαν 16 3.—conscribere (unclassical): τοῦτο τὸ βιβλίον

INDEX IV GREEK

συντετάχαμεν 2 4. —'to prescribe': συνέταξε θεραπείαν 13 8.—pass. *ordinari*: ὄχλον συντεταγμένον 12 7
συν-τέλεια, *finis*: ἐλάμβανε τὴν σ. 13 1
σύν-τονος: σ. λαβὴν 38 1
συν-τρέχειν: συνδραμεῖν 8 2
σύ-στασις, *stabilitas*: προσώπου σ. 5 1
συ-στέλλειν: τοὺς ἄλλους εἰς τὰ τείχη συνέστειλε 19 3
συ-στρατηγεῖν: συστρατηγῶν 8 5
συ-στρατηγός: μετὰ τῶν σ. 37 5
σφόδρα εὐλαβεῖτο 7 1; σ. κακῶς ἔχων 38 2; ἡγεμονικῶς σ. 1 1; οἱ σ. γέροντες 7 1
σχεδὸν ὅλην 12 4; σ. ἅπασαι 3 2; πάντα σ. 13 9
σχῆμα: τὸ σ. τῆς χειρός 31 4
cχινοκέφαλος 3 2, 13 6
σχῖνος *i.q.* σκίλλα *q.v.*: σχῖνον ὀνομάζουσι 3 2
σχολάζειν, *feriari* 27 2; ἀργὸν καὶ σχολάζοντα 12 5.—c. inf. ἂν σχολάζῃ ἀκροᾶσθαι] 5
σχολαίως, *sensim* 38 1
σχολή: ἐν ταῖς σ. τῶν φιλοσόφων 35 2
σῶμα, *corpus* 3 2; τὰ σ. 28 2, 34 3; τοῖς τῶν σ. πάθεσιν 38 2; ὄργανον καὶ σ. τῆς ὑπηρεσίας 12 7. [Cp. *Marc.* c. 17, 2 πάντες οἱ λοιποὶ Συρακούσιοι σῶμα τῆς Ἀρχιμήδους παρασκευῆς ἦσαν, ἡ δὲ κινοῦσα πάντα καὶ στρέφουσα ψυχὴ μία: *Arist.* c. 1, 4 τὸν λόγον, ὥσπερ δεύτερον σῶμα καὶ τῶν καλῶν ὄργανον, ἐξηρτύετο.]—*rita*: ἀφειδήσας τοῦ σ. 10 2
σωτηρία operis: τῇ σ. τοῦ γενομένου 13 2; σωτηρίαν reip. 3 1

σωτήριος, *salutaris* 19 4; σωτήριος γενομένη (αὐτοῖς) 19 1; σ. ἔρυμα τῆς πολιτείας 39 5; σ. φάρμακα 15 3
σώ-φρων: ἀκόλαστον ἀντὶ σ. 9 1; ἄνδρα σ. 11 1

T

ταινία: στεφάνοις ἀνέδουν καὶ τ. 28 4
τάλαντον 25 2; δέκα τάλαντα 23 1; ταλάντων 23 1
τἀληθές crasis for τὸ ἀληθές 13 12
τἄλλα for τὰ ἄλλα 7 5, 20 2, 33 2
τἄμπαλιν for τὰ ἔμπαλιν 16 2
τἀναπαιστά for τὰ ἀ. 33 7
τάξις: τοῖς περὶ τὴν δίαιταν ἑτέραν τ. ἐπέθηκεν 7 4
ταπεινός: 1. de re: ἡ αὐτουργία τῶν τ. 2 1; τὴν κακίαν ἀσθενῆ καὶ τ. ποιῶν 39 5.— 2. de homine: ἀγεννοῦς καὶ τ. τὴν φύσιν 24 4
ταπεινοῦν: ταπεινώσειν τὸν φθόνον 32 3
ταράττεσθαι: τοῖς περὶ τὰ θεῖα ταραττομένοις δι' ἀπειρίαν 6 1
ταραχή[2], *perturbatio*: ταραχῆς καὶ ὀργῆς μεστούς 39 3
τάττεσθαι, *sibi imponere*: ταξάμενοι κατοίσειν (τὰ χρήματα) 28 1
ταφή: τ. ἐνδόξους ἐποίησε 28 3
τάφος: πρὸς τάφῳ τινός 36 4
ταχέως 34 2, 36 1
τάχος, τό 13 1; κατὰ τάχος 22 2, 27 1
ταχυ-ναυτεῖν 26 3
ταχύς: τ. αἴσθησιν 39 4; γλῶτταν τ. 7 1.—ταχύ (adv.) 9 3, 11 2, 13 2 8, 22 2
ταχύτης: ἡ ἐν τῷ ποιεῖν τ. 13 2
ταῶς, *pavo*: ταῶνας 13 10
τε—μάλιστα δέ 2 3
τεῖχος: τὸ μακρὸν τ. 13 4; τὸ

τ. 19 4 ; πρὸ τοῦ τ. 26 1 ;
λάϊνα τείχη 16 2 ; τὰ τ. 19
3, 28 1, 34 4
τεκμαίρεσθαι : τεκμαιρόμεθα 8 6
τέκνον : κινῶν τέκνα 1 1
τεκνοῦν, *gignere* : τὸν νόθον ἐκ
ταύτης τεκνῶσαι 24 6
τέκτων : τέκτονες 12 6
τελεῖν, 'to contribute' : χρήματα τελούντων 12 3
τελεσιουργός : ΠΆΝΤΗ ΤΕΛΕΣΙΟΥΡΓΌΝ (ex Platone philosopho) 8 1
τελεστήριον, τό 13 4
τελευταῖος 3 4
τελευτᾶν, *vitam finire* : πρὸς τῷ τ. ὄντος αὑτοῦ 38 3 ;
ἐτελεύτησε 10 7, 31 5
τελευτή : μετὰ τὴν Περικλέους τ. 24 4
τέλος, *finis* 13 1.—*propositum* 6 3.—τοὺς ἐν τέλει, *principes, magistratus* 23 1. — Adv.
tandem 14 2
τέμνειν, *scindere* : βαθυτάτην τομὴν τεμοῦσα 11 3.—*vastare* : τεμὼν τὴν γῆν 19 4.—
PASS. *caedi, succidi* : δένδρα τμηθέντα 33 4
τέρπειν : τέρπει τὸ ἔργον 2 2
τερπνός : τὸ τ. coloris 1 3
τετρακισμύριοι : τ. πυρῶν μεδίμνους 37 3
τετρακισχίλιοι 37 4
τέχνη ἑκάστη 12 7 ; χρῆται τῇ τ. κυβερνήτης 33 5 ; πᾶσαν τ. 12 4 ; τ. ἢ δύναμιν 24 1 :
ΤῊΝ ΤῶΝ ΛΌΓΩΝ ΤΈΧΝΗΝ 8 1.—αἱ ταύτην (sc. τὴν ὕλην) ἐκπονοῦσαι τέχναι 12 6
τεχνητός [4] : τὰ τ. τῶν συμβόλων)(τὰ θεῖα 6 4
τεχνικῶς ψήλαντα 1 5
τεχνίτης : τῶν τ. 3 2, 13 8 ;
πᾶσι τοῖς τ. 13 9 ; μεγάλους τ. 13 4

τέως, *hactenus* 37 3
τηλικοῦτος : τ. δυνάμεως 39 1 ;
πράγματα τ. 10 5
τιθέναι : ἔθηκεν 13 4. — MID.
ἔθετο εἰς λόχον τὰ ὅπλα, *stationem locumque cepit* 10 1 ; θέμενος εὖ πάντα in navi 33 5 ; νόμους ἔθετο 3 1 ;
ὄνομα θέμενον τὸ αὐτοῦ 37 5
τίκτειν : Ἥραν οἱ Ἀσπασίαν
ΤΊΚΤΕΙ ΚΑΤΑΠΥΓΟΣΎΝΗ 24 6 ; ΜΈΓΙΣΤΟΝ ΤΊΚΤΕΤΟΝ
ΤΎΡΑΝΝΟΝ 3 3 ; εἰ παιδία οὐ τίκτουσιν αἱ γυναῖκες 1 1 ; ἐξ οὗ Καλλίαν ἔτεκε 24 5 ; τεκεῖν λέοντα 3 2
τιμᾶσθαι διαφερόντως 18 2
τιμή : μείζονα τ. εἶχε 33 1 ;
ταῖς τ. ἃς ἔχουσι 8 6
τις indef. 24 2 ; after οὔτε 35 3 ; w. adj. 27 4, 28 5 ; ποιός τις 31 2 ; ἦν τις παρηγορία 34 1 ; πεντάθλου τινός 36 3 :
τινὸς τῶν ἀναγκαίων 36 4 :
τινὶ τῶν φίλων 38 2, 36 1, 39 1 ; ἔν τινι πότῳ 1 5 ; βληχρᾷ τινι νόσῳ 38 3 ; τινὰ τὸν ἀντιτασσόμενον 11 1 : δίκην τ. 37 5 ; σοφήν τινα 24 3 ;
νόμον τινά 30 1 ; τῶν πρέσβεων τινά 30 1 ; τινὰ τῶν συνέργων 31 2 ; τι παραλυπεῖν 35 1 ; τι δεινόν 35 2 : τινὲς οἴονται 8 2
τίς interr. : ΤΊ ΠΟΤ' ΟΥ̓Κ
ἘΘΈΛΕΙΣ 33 7 ; τίνα τέχνην ἔχουσα 24 1 ; πρὸς τί γέγονε 6 3
τοίνυν 14 1
τοιοῦτος : τ. σύμβουλον 16 7 ;
τι τοιοῦτο 5 4 ; τ. οὐδὲν πεποιηκώς 36 5 ; τ. τινὸς διαγωγῆς 39 3.—with article :
τὴν τ. φιλοφροσύνην 7 4 ; τὴν τ. ἀκρίβειαν 16 5 : οὐδενὸς τῶν τ. 34 1 ; τὰ τ. 1 5, 2 2

τολμᾶν : τολμῶντας ἐπεξιέναι 26 1 ; τολμᾶν πειθαρχεῖν 7 6 ; ἐτόλμησεν 13 11
τομή, 'cleavage' : τ. βαθυτάτην τεμοῦσα 11 3. Cp. Cor. c. 16, 4 τῆς πόλεως οὐκέτι μιᾶς οὔσης ἀλλὰ δεδεγμένης τομήν
τόνος : τινὰς τ. ψυχῆς 15 4
τόπος : τὸν τ. 6 2, 39 3 ; τοὺς ἐν Ἑλλησπόντῳ τ. 17 2
τορευτής, caelator : τορευταί 12 6
τοσοῦτος : τ. φθορά 39 5 ; τοσοῦτον ἱστορίας 24 4 ; τ. ἦν τὸ κράτος 9 4 ; τ. τύχης 20 2 ; τ. ἰσχύος 35 1 ; τ. τὸ μέγεθος ἀρχὴν 15 4 ; δύναμιν τ. 24 1 ; τ. ἡγεμονίαν 37 1 ; εἰς μῆκος τ. 31 2.—τοσοῦτοι, tot 33 4 ; κατὰ τοσούτων 37 5 ; ἀνθρώποις τ. 34 4
τότε 36 4, 38 1 ; τότε μὲν— ὀλίγῳ δ' ὕστερον 6 3, 18 3 ; τ. μάλιστα 11 4 ; καὶ τ. καὶ τὸν ἄλλον χρόνον 13 7 ; εὐθὺς τ. 13 3 ; τ. πρῶτον 13 6 ; οἱ τότ' ἄνθρωποι 4 4 ; τῶν τ. διδασκάλων 8 3 ; τῶν τ. πολιτευμάτων 9 1.—for ποτέ 13 1
τοὐναντίον crasis for τὸ ἐναντίον 1 4, 33 1
τοὔνομα crasis for τὸ ὄνομα 4 1, 37 2
τοὔστρακον crasis for τὸ ὄστρακον 13 6
τραγικός : τ. διδασκαλίαν 5 4
τραῦμα : τραύμασι 27 1
τράχηλος : τῷ τ. 38 2
τρέπειν : τὰς αἰτίας (τοῦ φόνου) εἰς Περικλέα τρέπουσι 30 4 ; τρέπειν ἑαυτὸν πρὸς τὸ δοκοῦν 1 3 ; τὰ πλεῖστα τῆς δυνάμεως ἔτρεπεν εἰς φυλακήν 21 1 ; εἰς ταῦτα τὴν εὐπορίαν τ. αὐτῆς 12 4.—MID. fugare :

κατὰ κράτος τρεψάμενος 19 3. 27 1.—convertere se : τρέπεται πρὸς τὴν διανομήν 9 2 ; ἐπὶ τοὺς ἀφεστῶτας τραπόμενος 23 2.—PASS. mutari : εἰ πρὸς τὰς τύχας τρέπεται τὰ ἤθη 38 2
τρέφειν : τρέφει τὴν ὄψιν 1 3 ; παιδίσκας τρέφουσαν 24 3.— PASS. ἵνα τρέφηται τῷ θεωρεῖν 1 3 ; πόλιν ἐξ αὐτῆς τρεφομένην 12 4
τριβή, mora : τῇ τ. 27 2
τρι-ήραρχος : τοὺς τ. 28 2
τρι-ήρης : τὴν ἑαυτοῦ τ. 35 1 : τὴν Σαλαμινίαν τ. 7 5 ; τὰς τ. 15 1, 19 4, 29 3 ; ἑξήκοντα τριήρεις 11 4, 26 1 ; ἑκατὸν τριήρεσιν 19 2
τρόπαιον : ἔστησε τρόπαιον 19 3 ; τῶν τ. τὸ πλῆθος 38 3 ; ἐννέα τ. ἔστησεν 38 3
τρόπος, 'character,' 'temper' : σεμνότερον τ. 39 4
τρυφερός : τ. τινα τῷ βίῳ 27 4
τρύχεσθαι [3] : τρυχομένων 27 2
τυγχάνειν : ἐν ᾧ τὸ ψήφισμα γεγραμμένον ἐτύγχανεν 30 1 : ἐτύγχανε τὸν νοῦν προσεσχηκώς 38 4.—nancisci : ἀνδρῶν τυχεῖν 33 4
τυραννεῖν : μὴ τυραννήσειν 16 1. —PASS. τυραννεῖσθαι 12 2
τυραννίς 39 5 ; ὑποψίᾳ τυραννίδος 7 3 ; κατέλυσε τὴν τ. 3 1
τύραννος : Πολυκράτους τοῦ τ. 26 4 ; Πεισιστράτῳ τῷ τ. 7 1 ; μέγιστον τύραννον 3 3 ; Τιμησίλεων τύραννον 20 1 ; οἱ τ. 20 2 ; πολλῶν τ. 15 5
τῦφος, fastus : δοξοκοπίαν τε καὶ τ. ἀποκαλοῦντας 5 4
τύχη θαυμαστὴ συμβᾶσα 13 7 ; ἀπὸ τ. 19 4 ; τῶν ἐκ τῆς τ. ἀγαθῶν 2 3 ; οὐ τύχην οὐδ'

ἀνάγκην 4 4; χρησαμένους τ. λαμπρᾷ 18 1; πρὸς τύχην κοινά 38 4
τῳδεῖον crasis for τὸ ὠδεῖον 13 6

Υ

ὑβρίζεσθαι δεινὴν ὕβριν 12 2
ὕβρις: δεινὴν ὕ. 12 2
ὑγρός, *facilis*: τὸ Κίμωνος ὕ. 5 3
υἱός: τοῦ υἱοῦ 13 11; τὸν υἱόν 1 5; τῶν υἱῶν 29 3; τῶν γνησίων υἱῶν 36 1 4; τοῖς υἱέσι 15 5
ὕλη, *materies* 12 6; τῆς ἐκτὸς ὕ. 16 6
ὑό-πρῳρος[4] ναῦς 26 3
ὑπ-ακούειν: κελευόμενοι οὐχ ὑπήκουον 24 1
ὑπ-άρχειν 2 3, 8 6, 10 4; τῶν ὑπαρχόντων 21 1
ὑπ-είκειν: ῥάδιος ὕ. 15 2
ὑπ-εῖναι: ὑπῆν 30 2; ψυχη δὲ τέλητος ὕπεστιν 33 7
ὑπ-εναντιοῦσθαι: ὑπεναντιούμενος ἐκείνοις 21 1; ὑπηναντιώθη τοῖς λογισμοῖς 34 2; ὑπεναντιωθέντων 17 3
ὑπέρ: I. w. Gen. *pro*, 'for' *i.e.* for one's safety or advantage, with verbs of doing or saying: τοῖς ὕ. τῆς πατρίδος ἀποθανοῦσιν 8 6; διδόναι τάλαντον ὕ. ἑαυτοῦ 25 2; ἀφεὶς ὕ. αὐτῆς δάκρυα 32 3; ὕ. αὐτῆς τῆς πόλεως μάχην σινάψαι 33 4; τρόπαια ἔστησεν ὕ. τῆς πόλεως 38 3.—*loco v. nomine* alicuius: ὕ. τῆς Ἑλλάδος 17 1. — for περί, 'concerning': οὐκ ὀλίγον ὕ. αὐτῆς παρέσχε λόγον 24 1
II. w. Acc. *i. q.* πέρα, *supra*, 'beyond,' 'more than':

τῶν ὕ. πεντήκοντα ἔτη γεγονότων 17 2
ὑπερ-βάλλεσθαι, *superare, praecellere* 13 1
ὑπ-ερείπειν[1], *subruere, fundamenta subducere*: (νόσον) ὑπερείπουσαν τὸ φρόνημα 38 1
ὑπερ-έχειν: ἀσπίδα τῆς κεφαλῆς ὑπερεχόντων 27 4
ὑπερ-ήφανος: ἔργων ὕ. μεγέθει 13 1
ὑπερ-οχή: ἀσυμμέτρου πρὸς δημοκρατίαν ὕ. 16 1
ὑπερ-οψία: πολλὴν ὕ. 5 3; δίκην δεδωκότι τῆς ὕ. 37 5
ὑπέρτερος: δυνάμει πολλῶν τυράννων ὕ. 15 5
ὑπερ-φυῶς θαυμάσας 5 1
ὑπ-έρχεσθαι 'to truckle to': ὑπῆλθε τοὺς πολλούς 7 3
ὑπ-ήκοος: πόλις ὕ. Ἀθηναίων 29 4; ὕ. ἔθνεσι 15 1
ὑπ-ηρεσία: τὸ σῶμα τῆς ὕ. γιγνόμενον 12 7
ὕπνος: κατὰ τοὺς ὕ. 3 2
ὑπό: A. w. Gen. denotes 1. the efficient cause, 1. after passive verbs (*a*) with the gen. of the person: λοιδορούμενος ὕ. τινος 5 2; θαυμασθῆναι ὕ. τῶν παρόντων 6 2; ὑπ' ἐκείνου προαχθῆναι 9 1; γραφῆναι ὕ. τοῦ Περικλέους 10 4 5; ὕ. πλήθους ἡμαυρωμένους τὸ ἀξίωμα 11 2; τοῖς εἰσφερομένοις ὑπ' αὐτῆς 12 2; ὕ. τῶν ἰατρῶν ἀπεγνωσμένος 13 8; κατεσκευασμένος ὕ. τοῦ Περικλέους 16 5, 24 3; τὴν ἀγαπωμένην ὑπ' αὐτοῦ 24 7; ὕ. τοῦ Μελίσσου ἡττηθῆναι 26 3; πολεμουμένος ὕ. Κορινθίων 29 1; ὅπως ὕ. Περικλέους ἀποτεθεῖεν οἱ λόγοι 32 2, 34 3; ὕ. τοῦ Ξανθίππου διασπαρῆναι 36 3, 37 1; τὸν

νόμον ὑπ' αὐτοῦ λυθῆναι 37 5; ὑ. τῶν γυναικῶν περιηρτημένον 38 2.—(b) with the gen. of the thing: ὑ. ῥώμης καὶ τύχης ἐπαιρομένων 20 2; ὑπ' οὐδενὸς ἐκινήθη τῶν τοιούτων 34 1; ὑφ' ἧς (φθορᾶς) τὰ σώματα κακούμενοι 34 3; ἄθικτον ὑ. τοῦ χρόνου 13 3; ἐφύλαξεν ἑαυτὸν ἀνάλωτον ὑ. χρημάτων 16 3.—2. after neuter and active verbs which carry a passive meaning: (a) of persons: πολλὰ πάσχοντες κακὰ ὑπ' ἐκείνων 34 2; κακῶς ἀκούων ὑ. τινος 5 2.—(b) of things: οὐκ ἂν δοκεῖ συμπεσεῖν ὑπό γε τῶν ἄλλων αἰτιῶν ὁ πόλεμος 29 5; γενόμενον ἀκόλαστον ὑ. τῶν τότε πολιτευμάτων 9 1; ὑφ' ἧς (sc. φιλαργυρίας) αἰσχρῶς ἐξέπεσε 22 3.—3. after verbal substantives: ὑ. τοῦ πρώτου ἀνδρὸς ἀρχὴν 9 1
II. the proximate cause, or the agency of feelings, passions etc., prae, propter: ὑ. τῶν πραγμάτων ἠπορημένον 3 4; ὑφ' ἧς (ἐλευθερίας) ἐξυβρίσαντα 7 6; ὑπ' ὀργῆς καὶ φρονήματος διαμαχουμένων 33 3; τὴν χώραν ἀφῆκεν ἀργὴν ὑπ' ἐνθουσιασμοῦ 16 5; οὐ προύδωκε τὸ φρόνημα ὑ. τῶν συμφορῶν 36 4.
B. w. Dat. sub: ὑφ' αὑτοῖς πεποιημένων τὴν θάλασσαν 20 1; τῶν πραγμάτων ὑ. τῷ Περικλεῖ γενομένων 6 3
ὑπο-γράφειν, delineare: ὑπογράφει πολιτείαν 9 1
ὑπο-δέχεσθαι, excipere, 'to entertain': γυναῖκας ὑποδεχομένου 13 9; γυναῖκας

ὑποδέχοιτο 32 1.—suscipere quid agendum, 'to undertake': ὑποδεξάμενος τὰ πράγματα 37 2
ὑπό-θεσις, 'plan,' 'design': πολυτέχνοις ὑ. ἔργων 12 5
ὑπο-θρύπτεσθαι[14]: ὑποθρυπτομένης ἔνια δημαγωγίας 15 2
ὑπο-κεῖσθαι, propositum esse: ὑπέκειτο τῷ μὲν θεωρῆσαι 6 3; τῆς ὑποκειμένης (quae aderat) ἡγεμονίας 20 3
ὑπο-μένειν, remanere: ὑπέμεινε κατ' ἀγοράν 5 2.—tolerare: ταύτην ὑπομένοι τὴν ἀβελτερίαν 38 2; λοιδορούμενος ὑπέμεινε 5 2
ὑπό-νοια, suspitio: τὴν ὑ. 32 1
ὑπο-πίμπλασθαι: μεταρσιολεσχίας ὑποπιμπλάμενος 5 1
ὑπο-ποιεῖν[1]: ὑποποιούσης τίνα ζῆλον 5 4.—MID. clam, sensim sibi conciliare: ὑπεποιεῖτο τὸν δῆμον 9 2
ὑπ-ορρωδεῖν: ὙΠωΡΡΏΔΕΙ 24 6
ὑπο-σημαίνειν, latenter significare: διαφορὰν ὑποσημαίνουσα 11 3
ὑπο-σπείρειν: ὑπέσπειρεν ἀρχὰς μηδισμοῦ ταῖς πόλεσι 21 2
ὑπο-στρατηγεῖν: ὑποστρατηγοῦντος 13 10
ὑπο-τύφεσθαι, gliscere: τὸν πόλεμον ὑποτυφόμενον ἐξέκαυσεν 32 3
ὑπό-τυφος[12]: ὁμιλίαν ὑ. 5 3
ὕπ-ουλος: διπλόη τις ὕ. 11 3
ὑπο-χεῖσθαι: βαφὴν τῇ ῥητορικῇ ὑποχεόμενος 8 1
ὑπ-οψία: ἀντὶ ὑποψίας 33 1; ὑποψίᾳ περιπεσεῖν τυραννίδος 7 3
ὕστερον, postea 6 3, 13 12, 18 3, 36 2, 37 5
ὑφ-ιέναι 13 10

ὑφ-ίστασθαι: πράως τὴν ἀδοξίαν ὑφιστάμενος 34 1.—abs. ὑποστάντας 19 3
ὑψηλό-νους: τὸ ὑ. (ex Platone philosopho) 8 1
ὑψηλός: τὸν λόγον ὑ. εἶχε 5 1
ὕψος: ἐξ ὕψους ἔπεσε 13 8

Φ

φαίνεσθαι: φαίνεται ἡ ἀγάπησις γενομένη 24 5; ἐφάνη γενομένη 39 5; κομψοῦ τοῦ λόγου φανέντος 30 1; οὐδεὶς βάρος ἔχων ἐφαίνετο 37 1; τῷ II. δεινὸν ἐφαίνετο 33 4; πᾶν τὸ φαινόμενον 1 2; τὰ μάλιστα φαινόμενα 7 5; πρῶτον ἐν Σάμῳ φανῆναι 26 4; φοβερὸς φανεὶς τοῖς πολεμίοις 19 4; ὄναρ φανεῖσα 13 8; φανείσης 12 4
φαλακρός, calvus: πρεσβύτου φ. 31 4
φάναι: τὸ φ. 8 5; φησί 3 4, 4 1; ἀκοῦσαί φησιν αὐτός 13 5, 16 2, 24 3, 28 5, 36 3; ὥς φησι 8 1, 15 5; φησὶν ὅτι 8 6; φησὶ Κριτόλαος in parenthesi 7 5; φασί 4 1, 7 6, 9 1, 10 4, 13 2, 24 2, 25 2, 27 2, 31 1 5; ὧc φACI 4 2; ὥς φασιν ἔνιοι 31 5; ἔφη 38 4; οὐκ ἔφη, negavit 35 2; φησάντων 14 1
φανερός: φ. αἰτίαν 30 2
φανερῶς 29 4
φάος (φῶς): φῶτα (= φάεα) 6 4
φάρμακον: φ. σωτήρια 15 3; ἐτελεύτησε νοσήσας φαρμάκοις 31 5
φαῦλος: οὐ φ. παρέσχε λόγον 24 1
φείδεσθαι: μηδενὸς φειδόμενον 14 2
φέρειν, ferre: τὴν ψῆφον ἀπὸ τοῦ βωμοῦ φέροντες 32 2; ΚΕΡΑΥΝΟΝ ΕΝ ΓΛΩCCΗ ΦΕΡΕΙΝ 8 3.—afferre: τῷ μὲν φθόνον τῷ δὲ βλασφημίαν ἤνεγκεν 13 9; μεγάλην δόξαν ἤνεγκεν 18 3; ἡδονὴν ... κόσμον ... ἔκπληξιν ἤνεγκε 12 1.—solvere: ἤνεγκαν χρήματα 28 1.—tolerare: φ. δήμων ἀγνωμοσύνας 2 4; βαρέως φέροντες 22 3; χαλεπῶς ἔφερε τὴν τοῦ πατρὸς ἀκρίβειαν 36 1. —φέρων, 'hastily,' 'eagerly' 7 2, 12 5
φεύγειν, ritare: φεύγων τὸν κόρον 7 5.—exulare: φεύγοντος 22 3; τοῖς φεύγουσι 10 1.—reum esse: δίκην ἔφειγεν 10 5, 32 1
φθέγγεσθαι[3]: φθεγξάμενος εἰς μέσον 38 4
φθείρειν: τὴν Μεγαρικὴν ἔφθειρε πᾶσαν 34 2
φθόγγος: τινας φ. ψυχῆς 15 4
φθονεῖσθαι: φθονούμενος 31 2
φθόνος: διὰ φθόνον 10 6; ἐπίεζε φθόνῳ 31 4; φθόνῳ χαρίσασθαι 39 1; τῷ φ. τῶν πολλῶν ἀποθύοντας 13 11; τοῦτο φθόνον ἤνεγκεν (αὐτῷ) 13 9; ταπεινώσειν τὸν φ. 32 3; φθόνοις καὶ δυσμενείαις 13 12
φθορά: ἡ λοιμώδης φ. 34 3; ἀναπίμπλασθαι φθορᾶς ἀπ' ἀλλήλων 34 4.—'moral corruption' 39 5
φιλ-άνθρωπος: φ. δικαιολογίας 30 3
φιλ-ανθρώπως προσηνέχθη ταῖς πόλεσι 20 1
φιλ-αργυρία: τὴν φ. 22 3
φιλητικός[1]: τὸ φ. ἐν ἡμῖν 1 1
φιλία 29 2; φιλίαις βασιλέων 15 1
φιλο-θεάμων: φιλοθεάμον τι 1 2
φιλο-κίνδυνος: ἀνὴρ ἀγαθὸς καὶ φ. 7 1

φιλο-λάκων : φιλο-λάκωνα 9 3
φιλο-μαθής : φ. τι 1 2
φιλο-νικία : τῇ πρὸς Μεγαρεῖς φ. 29 5 ; φ. τινι πρὸς ἔνδειξιν ἰσχύος 31 1
φιλο-πολίτης[1] for φιλόπολις : ἀνδρὶ φ. 18 3
φίλος : ἀνδρὸς φ. 13 10.—for φίλιος : ἐξ Ἀχαίας φ. οὔσης (unclassical) 19 4.—subst. φίλος γενόμενος 31 2 ; οἱ φ. 10 1 2 ; φίλον γενόμενον 10 6 ; μηδένα τῶν φ. 7 4, 33 6, 36 2, 38 2 ; φίλους 7 5
φιλό-σοφος, ὁ 23 1 ; ἀνὴρ φ. 26 2 ; τῶν φ. 35 3 ; τοῖς φ. 24 1
φιλό-στοργος : τὸ φ. 1 1 de amore parentum erga liberos
φιλο-τιμεῖσθαι : φιλοτιμούμενος 13 6
φιλο-τιμία : ἡ φ. 11 3
φιλό-τιμος : ψυχὴν φ. ἔχοντι 10 6 ; τοὺς φιλοτιμοτάτους 18 2
φιλο-τύραννος 4 2
φιλο-φροσύνη : τὴν τοιαύτην φ. 4 2 ; αἱ φ. 7 5
φλεγμαίνειν : φλεγμαινούσης δεισιδαιμονίας 6 1
φοβεῖσθαι : φοβούμενος ἐξοστρακισθῆναι 7 1 ; φοβουμένων ἐκεῖνον 33 1 5 ; φοβηθεὶς τὸ δικαστήριον 32 3
φοβερός, timidus : τῆς φ. δεισιδαιμονίας 6 1.—terribilis : φοβερὸν ὄντα τοῖς ὀλιγαρχικοῖς 10 7 ; φοβερὸς φανεὶς τοῖς πολεμίοις 19 4
φόβος : φόβον παρασχών 35 1 : φόβον παρακατοικίζων τοῖς συμμάχοις 11 5.—Pl. terrores : ἐλπίσι καὶ φ. 15 4 ; πρὸς τοὺς φ. μαλακόν 27 4
φοιτᾶν de persona : εἰς τὰ ἔργα φοιτώσας 13 9 ; εἰς τὸ αὑτὸ φοιτώσας 32 1 ; μετὰ τῶν γνωρίμων ἐφοίτα 24 3.—

de re : comportari, redire : εἰς τὴν Σπάρτην ἐφοίτα δέκα τάλαντα 23 1
φόνος : τὸν φ. 30 4
φορεῖον : φορείῳ προσκομιζόμενον 27 3
φόρος, vectigal : φόρους 15 1 : πόλεων φόρογc 16 2
φραγμός : τοὺς φ. 9 2
φράτηρ : ἀπογράψασθαι εἰς τοὺς φράτερας 37 5
φράττεσθαι : ἡγεμονίαν συμμαχίαις πεφραγμένην 15 1
φρονεῖν : μέγα φ. 17 1 ; μέγα φρονοῦντος ἐπὶ τῷ ποιεῖν 13 2 ; θαυμαστόν τι καὶ μέγα φρονῆσαι 28 5
φρόνημα, τό 17 3 ; τὸ φ. σοβαρὸν εἶχε 5 1 ; φ. εὐγενές 10 6 ; φ. δημαγωγίας ἐμβριθέστερον 14 ; τὸ φ. 17 3 ; τῷ μεγέθει τοῦ φ. 8 1 ; ἐκ φ. μεγάλου 31 1 ; ὑπ' ὀργῆς καὶ φ. 33 3 ; θαυμαστὸς τοῦ φ. 39 1 ; οὐ προῦδωκε τὸ φ. 36 4 : νόσῳ τὸ φ. τῆς ψυχῆς ὑπερείπουσαν 38 1
φρόνιμος : ἀνδρὶ φ. 18 3
φροντίζειν : βραχέα φροντίζων τῶν καταβοώντων 33 5
φρουρά : φρουρὰν τοῦ μὴ νεωτερίζειν παρακατοικίζων τοῖς συμμάχοις 11 5
φρουρεῖν : τῶν φρουρούντων 12 5
φυγάς : φυγάδα 10 1
φυγή, exilium : ἐλθὼν ἐκ τῆς φ. 10 1. Cp. Cat. mi. c. 40, 1 ἐκ τῆς φυγῆς ἣν ἔφυγεν ὑπὸ Κλωδίου κατελθών
φύεσθαι : δένδρα φύεται ταχέως 33 4 ; παθῶν φυομένων 15 4 ; φῦναι 39 4 ; πῶς πέφυκε 6 3 : εὖ πεφυκὼς πρὸς οἰκονομίαν 16 5 ; τὸ κέρας στερεὸν πεφυκός 6 2.—c. infin. τρέπειν ἑαυτὸν πέφυκεν 1 3 ; ἕκαστα

διαχειρίσασθαι πεφυκώς 15 4;
πεφυκὸς ἄρχειν 39 2
φυλακή, *custodia*: εἰς φ. τῶν
ὑπαρχόντων 21 1; καταλαβὼν
πάντα φυλακαῖς (*praesidiis*)
33 5
φύλαξ: φύλακα καὶ πάρεδρον 22 2
φυλάττειν ἐν ὀχυρῷ τὰ κοινά 12
2; ἐφύλαξεν ἑαυτὸν ἀνάλωτον
ὑπὸ χρημάτων 16 3
φυλέτης: μετὰ τῶν φ. 10 1
φυλή: τῶν φ. 3 1
φυσιγγοῦσθαι: ΟΔΥΝΑΙΣ ΠΕ-
ΦΥΣΙΓΓΩΜΕΝΟΙ 30 4
φυσικός: ὁ φ. λόγος 6 1; τὸν φ.
(ἄνδρα) 6 3
φυσιολογία[1]: ἐκ φ. 8 1; τὴν φ.
8 1, 4 4
φύσις, ἡ 22 3; τὸ φύσει φκλη-
τικόν 1 1; φύσει δαπανηρός
36 1; πᾶσαν φ. 12 7; πραγματευομένου περὶ φύσιν 4 3;
παρὰ τὴν αὐτοῦ φ. 7 2; ταπεινοῦ τὴν φ. 24 4
φωνή: πλάσμα φωνῆς 5 1; φ.
ἡδεῖαν 7 1; πολλὰς ἀφεικότων
φ. 8 3
φῶς: φωτὶ καθαρωτάτῳ περιλαμπόμενον 39 3; φῶς λαβόντι
5 3.—Fl. φῶτα πυρσῶν 6 4

X

χαίρειν: τῷ χ. 1 3; χαίροντες
τῷ ἔργῳ 1 4
χαλεπαίνειν: (τοῖς) χαλεπαί-
νουσιν 29 4
χαλεπός: χαλεπόν 13 12
χαλεπῶς: χ. ἔφερε 36 1; χ.
διακειμένους πρὸς αὐτόν 35 4;
χ. ἐπὶ τούτῳ διατεθείς 36 2
χαλκός 12 6
χαλκο-τύπος: χαλκοτύποι 12 6
χαλκοῦς: τὸ χ. ἄγαλμα 13 8;
τοῦ χ. λύκου 21 2; χ. ἀσπίδα
27 4

χαρίεις: χ. ἔργον 2 2
χαρίζεσθαι (*a*) w. dat. of person:
Ἀσπασίᾳ χαριζόμενος 24 1;
χαρίσασθαι τοῖς πολλοῖς 10 3.
—(*b*) w. dat. of thing, 'to
humour a passion': χαρί-
σασθαι φθόνῳ ... θυμῷ 39 1.
—abs. χαριζομένη 13 12
χάρις: ἔργων μορφῇ ἀμιμήτων
καὶ χ. 13 1; χάρις ἀνθούσης
ἐφ' ὥραν πολιτείας 16 2;
χάριν ἔχουσα μετὰ δεινότητος
24 2; ἐπολιτεύετο πρὸς χάριν
11 4
χείρ: τῆς χ. 31 4; διὰ χειρὸς
('control') ἔχων τὴν πόλιν 34
1; πᾶσαν χ. κινοῦσαι 12 4;
δι' ἀμφοτέρων τῶν χ. 31 4;
λαβόντας εἰς τὰς χ. 35 4; τὰς
χ. καθαρὰς ἔχειν 8 5; συνάψαι
εἰς χεῖρας πολλοῖς ὁπλίταις
22 2
χείριστος: χ. αἰτία 31 2
χειρο-ήθης τῷ δήμῳ 15 2
χειροῦσθαι: ἐχειροῦτο 15 3;
ἐχειρώσατο 24 1
χίλιοι: χ. δικασταῖς 32 2; χ.
γενομένους 18 2, 12 2; χ.
κληρούχους 11 5; ἐποίκους χ.
19 1
χιλιο-τάλαντος: ναοὺς χ. 12 2
χλαμύς: τῆς χ. 35 2; τὴν χ.
35 2
χολή, *fel*: ταῦτα ὥσπερ χολὴν
τἀνδρὶ προσβέβληκε 10 6
χορηγεῖν[2], *suppeditare* 14 2;
γλίσχρως χορηγοῦντος 36 1
χορηγία[12]: ἄλλαις μισθοφοραῖς
καὶ χορηγίαις 9 3
χορηγός, *qui sumptus praebet*:
δαψιλὴς χ. 16 4
χορός: χόροι 33 6
χρεία, *negotium*: πρὸς τὴν
προκειμένην χ. ἀνάρμοστον 8
4.—*usus, ministerium*: αἱ
χ. 12 7; ποικίλων χ. 12 4;

τὰς μεγάλας χ. 7 5; ἀνθρωπείας χ. 16 6.—*opus*: οἱ τοῦ λύχνου χρείαν ἔχοντες 16 7
χρή 13 6, 36 3
χρῆμα: τὰ κοινὰ χ. 12 3; τὰ χ. 14 1; διανομαῖς χρημάτων 34 1, 12 3; οἱ λόγοι τῶν χ. 32 2; χρημάτων κρείττονος 15 5; χρήμασιν ἐζημίωσαν 22 3, 28 1, 35 4; ἐλαττούμενος χρήμασιν 9 2; διαφθείρας χρήμασιν 22 2
χρηματισμός: χρηματισμόν 16 3
χρῆσθαι: χρῆται τῇ τέχνῃ 33 5; ἐχρῆτο (τῷ πλήθει) κατὰ τῆς ἐξ Ἀρείου πάγου βουλῆς 9 3; χρῆσθαι τῷ νῷ 1 3; πρὸς οὐδὲν ἀνθρώποις τοσούτοις χρώμενος 34 4; ᾗ χρώμενος (θεραπείᾳ) 13 8; πάσῃ χρωμένους βλασφημίᾳ πρὸς αὐτόν 5 2; τόπον οὐ πνεύμασι, οὐ νέφεσι χρώμενον 39 3; χρώμενοι στιχιδίοις 30 4; ἐχρῆτο τοῖς αὐτοῦ λογισμοῖς 33 5; ὁποτέρῳ ἐχρήσατο τῶν λογισμῶν 26 2; ἐχρῶντο τῇ θαλάσσῃ 26 2; μηχαναῖς bellicis χρήσασθαι 27 3.—c. dupl. dat.: τῇ λύρᾳ παρακαλύμματι χρώμενος 4 2; χρώμενον Κλεανδρίδῃ (συμβούλῳ) 22 2; χρήσασθαι ἐχθρῷ ὡς ἀνηκέστῳ 39 1; ἐχρῆτο (τῷ πλήθει) χρώμενος αὐτῇ (sc. τῇ πολιτείᾳ) ὀρθῇ 15 2.—with modal adverb: 'to treat so and so': μόνοις τούτοις ἀπαραιτήτως χρησάμενος 23 2; χρησάμενος ὥσπερ ἐγνώκει τοῖς Σαμίοις 25 2.—*experiri*: χρησαμένους τύχῃ λαμπρᾷ 18 1; μαλακωτέροις χρήσονται τοῖς Ἀθηναίοις 33 1
χρήσιμος: χρήσιμον)(ἄχρηστον 1 2; τοὺς χρησιμωτάτους πρὸς τὴν πολιτείαν 36 4

χρόα, *color* 1 3
χρόνος 13 2; πολλῷ χρόνῳ 13 2; δαπάνῃ καὶ χ. 27 1; ἐν χ. ῥητῷ 28 1; τὸν σοφώτατον σύμβουλον χ. 18 2; πρὸς πολὺν χ. 13 3; τὸν ἄλλον χ. 13 7; τὸν χ. ἐπιπροσθοῦντα τῇ γνώσει 13 12; πάντα τὸν χ. 18 1, 19 2; τὸν χ. ὠνούμενος 23 1; τὸν ἄπαντα χ. ὁμαλῶς 39 3; πλεῖστον χ. 8 4; περὶ τοῦτον τὸν χ. 32 1; πρὸ πολλῶν χ. 37 3
χρυσίον: τὸ χ. 31 3
χρυσός 12 6; χρυσοῦ μαλακτῆρες 12 6
χρυσοῦς, *aureus*: τὸ χ. εἶδος 13 9.—sc. στατήρ = δαρεικός: μυρίους χ. 25 2
χύδην, 'promiscuously' 34 4
χωλός: χωλὸν ὄντα 27 3
χώρα, *regio*: ἡ χ. 19 2; ἐκ τῆς χ. 23 2; νειμαμένοις χώραν 20 2; τὴν βασιλέως χ. 10 4; δῃοῦντες τὴν χ. 33 3; χ. πολλὴν διεπόρθησαν 34 2.—*ager*, 'a landed estate': τὴν χ. καὶ τὰς ἐπαύλεις 33 2; τῶν χ. τοὺς φραγμοὺς ἀφαιρῶν 8 2.—*rus*: τὸν ἀπὸ τῆς χ. ὄχλον 34 4
χωρίον: τῶν χ. 9 2
χωρίς, adv. 11 2
χωριτικός[4], *rusticus*: τοῦ χ. πλήθους 34 3

ψ

ψάλλειν: ψάλλων 1 5; ψαλλόντων 1 5; ψήλαντα 1 5
ψέγειν 1 2
ψεύδεσθαι (PASS.): μὴ ψεύδεσθαι τὴν δύναμιν 12 1
ψηφίζεσθαι, *ferre plebiscitum, auctorem esse et suasorem* ψηφίσματος: ψηφίζεται τὸν

πλοῖν 24 1; ἐψηφίσατο μουσικῆς ἀγῶνα ἄγεσθαι 13 6; ἐψηφίσατο πλεῖν εἰς Σινώπην ἐθελοντάς 20 2; τὸν πόλεμον ψηφίσασθαι 25 1; ψηφισαμένου τὴν βοήθειαν 29 2
ψήφισμα: τὸ ψ. 30 3; τὸ πινάκιον ἐν ᾧ τὸ ψ. γεγραμμένον ἐτύγχανεν 30 1; ψ. κυροῦται 32 2; τοῦτο ἀφεῖλε τοῦ ψ. 32 2; γράφει ψήφισμα 17 1, 30 2; ψ. ἔγραψεν 32 1; τὸ ψ. γράψας 10 3; τὸ ψ. καθελεῖν τὸ Μεγαρικόν 29 5; τοῦ μὴ λυθῆναι τὸ ψ. 31 1; ἔγγραφον οὐδὲν πλὴν τῶν ψ. 8 5
ψῆφος: τὴν ψ. ἀπὸ τοῦ βωμοῦ φέροντες 32 2; τὰς ψ. λαβόντες εἰς τὰς χεῖρας 35 4
ψιλῶς[2], tantummodo 15 5
ψόφος: ψόφους δίσκων 6 4
ψυχαγωγία; ψυχαγωγίαν 15 4
ψυχή, ἡ 1 1; ΨΥΧΗ ΤΈΛΗΤΟΣ ΫΠΕϹΤΙΝ 33 7; τὸ μέγεθος τῆς ψ. 36 4; τὸ φρόνημα τῆς ψ. 38 1; ψ. φιλότιμον 10 6; ψ. ἀγήρω (de templis) 13 3; τὰ σώματα καὶ τὰς ψ. κακούμενοι 34 3

Ω

Ὠιδεῖον: ἐν Ὠιδείῳ 13 7
ὠμός: πάθος ὠ. 10 6
ὠμότης: πολλὴν ὠ. 28 1
ὠνεῖσθαι, emere: ἐξ ἀγορᾶς ὠνούμενος 16 4. — redimere: οὐ τὴν εἰρήνην ὠνούμενος ἀλλὰ τὸν χρόνον 23 1
ᾤν 6 2
ὥρα: θέρους ὥρᾳ 34 4; εἰς ἔτους ὥραν 10 2; ἀνθούσης ἐφ' ὥραν πολιτείας 16 2
ὡρισμένην (ὁρίζεσθαι) νόμῳ 10 1

ὡς, relative adverb of manner, sicut, 'as': 1 4, 15 5; ὡς ἕτερος οὐδείς 16 5; ὡς τἀναπαιστὰ ταῦτα δηλοῖ 33 7; ὡς ἔδειξε 21 1; ὡς λέγει 35 4; ὡς λέγεται 17 3; ὥς φασι 4 2, 31 5; ὡς λέγουσιν 13 8, 26 1; ὡς—οὕτω 1 3; οὕτω—ὡς 7 5; ὥς που εἴρηκε 4 3, 10 7; ὡς εἰρήκαμεν 13 9; ὡς ἱστόρηκε 9 2, 33 1; ὡς γέγραπται 9 4; ὡς πρότερον 11 2. — 'that': γιγνώσκοντες ὡς χρήσονται 33 1, 18 2, 32 1; βοῶντες ὡς ὁ δῆμος ἀδοξεῖ 12 1, 34 4.—with nom. partcp. referring to the subject of the sentence: δείξειεν ὡς σφόδρα κακῶς ἔχων 38 2; ἀκούων κακῶς ὡς μικρὰν βοήθειαν παρεσχηκώς 29 3.—with absol. infin.: ὡς ἔπος εἰπεῖν 12 7; γραῦς εἶ ὡς διαπράσσεσθαι 10 5.—with acc. participle: ἐλπίδα παρασχοῦσαν ὡς ἁλωσομένην 35 3. — w. participle in the gen. abs. referring to the subject or object of the sentence: ὡς τῆς προσποιήσεως ὑποποιούσης 5 4; κατεστρατοπέδευσαν ὡς τῶν Ἀθηναίων οὐκ ἀνεξομένων 33 3, 28 5; ἔλαβεν ἀργύριον ὡς τοῦ Περικλέους κελεύσαντος 36 2; ταῦτα ὡς οὐκέτι συνιέντος διελέγοντο 38 4, 13 9, 33 1, 39 3.—in reference to a quality, real or supposed, belonging to the person or thing: εἰ τέρπει τὸ ἔργον ὡς χαρίεν 2 2; ὡς λήμην τοῦ Πειραιῶς 8 5; ἐκπλαγῆναι ὡς πρὸς μέγα σημεῖον 35 1; ὡς φιλοτύραννος ἐξωστρακίσθη 4 2, 9 4; ἀπήλασαν αὐτὸν ὡς φυγάδα 10 1, 13 5: θαυμα-

σθέντας ὡς μεγάλοις 18 1 3,
29 3, 33 6, 37 5.—as a
temporal particle, 'when,'
with aor. as usual 3 4, 15
1, 18 3; ὡς προσέπταισε 32
3; ὡς δ' οὐκ ἔφη 35 2; ὡς δ'
ἀπεχώρησε 22 3; ὡς ἐπανῆλθε
28 3; with imperf. 5 3, 37 1.
—final, 'in order that':
ὡς μήτ' ἀμελούμενος ἐκφύγοι
16 3; ὡς μὴ ἐκλίποι τὸ γένος
37 2; ὡς ἂν προσδιαβληθείη
29 2. —as a consecutive
particle with infin. 'so that'
for ὥστε 7 4.—in exclama-
tions 'how!' 26 4
ὡς = πρός: τὰς γυναῖκας ἦγον ὡς
αὑτήν 21 3
ὡσ-αὐτως, itidem: πάντες ὠ. 31 1
ὥσπερ, quemadmodum, 'just
as,' 'even as' (a) in a protasis with finite verb, followed by οὕτως in the apodosis: ὥσπερ νεὼς κυβερνήτης
χρῆται, οὕτως ἐχρῆτο 33 5.
(b) in close relation to what
precedes: ἑαυτὸν ὥσπερ τὴν
Σαλαμινίαν τριήρη πρὸς τὰς
μεγάλας χρείας ἐπιδιδούς 7 5;
ὥσπερ ἵππον ἐξυβρίσαντα 7
6, 10 3; ὠ. προηγόρευσεν
31 2; ὠ. ἀλαζόνα γυναῖκα 12
2: ὠ. οἴαξι 15 4, 16 6;

λαβὴν ἐξεῖαν ὠ. ἄλλων 38
1; ὀξὺν ὥσπερ ᾠὸν 6 2; ὠ.
ὄργανον 8 1, 11 3, 15 2 4,
28 4; ἀξιοῖμεν... οὐχ ὥσπερ
οἱ ποιηταὶ ἁλίσκονται for οὐχ
ὠ. οἱ ποιηταὶ ἀξιοῦσι οἳ ἁλίσκονται 39 2: ὠ. εἴρηται 9 2,
31 2, 37 3; ὠ. ἔθος ἐστιν 28 3.
—in relation to what follows
5 4.—tamquam, 'as it were,'
to limit or modify an assertion: ταῦτα ὠ. χολὴν προσβέβληκε 10 6; ὠ. πνοαῖς 15 2;
ὠ. ἀειθαλὲς πνεῦμα ἐχόντων
13 3; ὠ. συγγενικὸν προστρίψασθαι νόσημα 22 3
ὥστε, ita ut, 'so as to': ὠ. μὴ
μοναρχίαν εἶναι 11 1, 27 4;
ἡττήθη τοῦ πάθους ὠ. κλαυθμὸν ῥῆξαι 36 5; οὕτω διατίθησιν ὠ. θαυμάζεσθαι τὰ ἔργα 2
2, 8 4, 9 4, 24 7, 26 3, 31 3.—
'on condition that,' 'to the
effect that.' συνθήκας ὥστε
ἐκπλεῦσαι 10 4.—quocirca,
itaque: ὠ. χρὴ διώκειν 1 3
ὠφελεῖν: οὐδ' ὠφελεῖ τὰ τοιαῦτα
τοὺς θεωμένους 2 2.—PASS.
ἀπὸ τῶν δημοσίων ὠφελεῖσθαι
12 5
ὠφέλιμος: τῶν καλῶν καὶ ὠ. 1
2; ὠφελιμωτάτων ταῖς πατρίσι
γενομένων 2 4

www.ingramcontent.com/pod-product-compliance
Lightning Source LLC
Chambersburg PA
CBHW020232240426
43672CB00006B/503